Music in American Life

*Volumes in the series Music in American Life
are listed at the end of this book.*

Bluegrass

Bluegrass

A HISTORY

NEIL V. ROSENBERG

University of Illinois Press

Urbana and Chicago

Illini Books edition, 1993

© 1985 by the Board of Trustees of the University of Illinois
Manufactured in the United States of America
4   5   C   P   5   4   3   2   1

Portions of this book appeared initially in "From Sound to Style: The
Emergence of Bluegrass," *Journal of American Folklore* (not for further
reprint); "Into Bluegrass: The History of a Word," *Muleskinner News;*
and "Image and Stereotype: Bluegrass Soundtracks," *American Music.*

This book is printed on acid-free paper.

Library of Congress Cataloging-in-Publication Data
Rosenberg, Neil V.
  Bluegrass: a history.
  (Music in American life)
  Bibliography: p.
  Discography: p.
  Includes index.
  1. Bluegrass music—United States—History and
criticism.   I. Title.   II. Series.
ML3520.R67 1985   784.5'2'00973   84–15747
ISBN 0-252-00265-2 (cl : alk. paper)
ISBN 0-252-06304-X (pb : alk. paper)

*To the memory of Marvin Hedrick, Birch Monroe,
and Shorty Sheehan*

Contents

Acknowledgments

It has been more than a decade since I began working on this book. During that time my labors have been lightened by the help of many individuals and a number of institutions.

Scholars and students responded to my queries; shared with me their research findings, ideas, and theories; and, knowing I was working on this topic, sent me materials unsolicited. I am indebted to Thomas A. Adler, Cheryl Brauner, Robert Cogswell, Carl Fleischhauer, Christopher J. Goertzen, Kenneth S. Goldstein, Antony Hale, Scott Hambly, Herbert Halpert, Loyal Jones, William E. Lightfoot, Toru Mitsui, Beatrice McLain, Peter Narváez, Ralph Rinzler, Ivan Tribe, Herb Troutman, D. K. Wilgus, Otto Willwood, David Whisnant, and Charles Wolfe.

I value highly the interest and cooperation of musicians, broadcasters, writers, fans, private collectors, promoters, and others involved with the bluegrass music business. This work would not have been possible without the help of individuals like Fred Bartenstein, Pat Chappelle, John Cohen, Charles and Pleasance Crawford, J. D. Crowe, Jim Dickson, John Duffey, Alice Gerrard, Frank Godbey, David Grisman, John Hartford, Gary Henderson, Don Hoos, Fred Isenor, Jan Jerrould, Michael Kolonel, Pete Kuykendall, Jesse McReynolds, Jim McReynolds, Wade Mainer, Don Miller, Vic Mullen, Bob Osborne, Sonny Osborne, Herb Pedersen, Charlie Pennell, Erdie. Phillips, Ray Phillips, Don Pierce, Gary Reid, Sandy Rothman, Mike Seeger, Earl and Louise Scruggs, Pete Seeger, Scott Swindon, Roger Sprung, Donna Stoneman, Rusty York, and Phil Zimmerman.

Several institutions gave valuable assistance by providing me with obscure recordings and ephemeral publications, essential to my research and otherwise unavailable, from their collections. My thanks to Norm Cohen and the John Edwards Memorial Forum (formerly Foundation) at UCLA; Joe Hickerson at the Archive of Folk Culture in the Library of Congress; and the staff of the Country Music Foundation in Nashville, including Doug Green, Danny Hatcher, Bill Ivey, Bob Pinson, Ronnie Pugh, John Rumble, and Charlie Seemann.

Appropriate photographs and illustrations are never easily obtained so I am particularly grateful to a number of individuals for their help in this regard: Doug Benson, Byron Berline, John Cohen, Carl Fleischhauer, Scott Hambly, Pete Kuykendall, Don Pierce, Jon Sievert, Eddie Stubbs, and Charles Wolfe. Charlie Seemann at the Country Music Foundation and Rob Sinclair at the Mariposa Folk Foundation also aided me in gathering illustrations. Along the way, Bill Wheeler of University Relations' Photographic Services Lab at Memorial University of Newfoundland gave valuable assistance in copying and printing many of the photos.

The manuscript of this book benefited from the attention and comments of readers at several stages. Memorial University of Newfoundland Folklore Department graduate student David Taylor read a first draft. His useful comments shaped the draft which was read and commented upon by Carl Fleischhauer, Pete Kuykendall, Sandy Rothman, Mayne Smith and Charles Wolfe, all of whom drew from their own considerable experience in matters editorial and musical to provide valuable recommendations for a subsequent revision. The final manuscript profited from comments and suggestions made by the editorial staff at the University of Illinois Press, including Judith McCulloh, Cynthia Mitchell, and Richard Wentworth. For the production of readable draft manuscripts the labor of typists Sharon Cochrane and Dallas Strange is gratefully acknowledged. I am grateful also to Teya Rosenberg for taking time during a busy semester to assist in proofreading and indexing.

Memorial University of Newfoundland provided many necessary services and facilities without which I would not have been able to carry on my work. With the exception of my fieldwork in Canada's maritime provinces, one year of which was generously supported by the Canada Council, my research on bluegrass has been, like the music itself, generally unsubsidized by grants or stipends from public funds. Hence my thanks to those individuals and institutions named above is strongly felt, for without their support I would not have been able to complete this work. If I have left out some names I hope that those overlooked will accept my apologies for a lapse of memory; no slight is intended. And while their contributions have shaped and informed this work, I am responsible for its final form and for any errors or oversights.

Finally, I want to express appreciation and thanks to my family for their support and interest in this endeavor.

Bluegrass

A H I S T O R Y

Bluegrass

Introduction

Bluegrass is part of country music; it originated with Bill Monroe and his band, the Blue Grass Boys, during the 1940s. During the fifties it was named and recognized as a unique form—a music in which singers accompany themselves with acoustic rather than electric instruments, using the fiddle, mandolin, guitar, five-string banjo, Dobro, and bass. Its performance demands mastery of virtuoso instrumental techniques (such as Earl Scruggs's banjo style), often executed at rapid tempos. This emphasis on individual virtuosic self-expression led some to call bluegrass the jazz of country music. Bluegrass singing is high-pitched, lonesome sounding; it often involves tightly arranged harmonies. The form and content of its songs and its vocal styles, reminiscent of mountain folksinging traditions, have prompted some observers to define it as modern folk music. As important as any defining characteristics of this contemporary hillbilly music is the way it has spread far from the original culture and class in which it emerged. Bluegrass bands and their followers exist all over North America, in Japan, Australia, New Zealand, and in Europe. Like jazz and blues, bluegrass is an American cultural export.

I first heard and read the word *bluegrass* in 1957 when I started college in Ohio. A native of the far West, I had little direct contact with the southeastern United States (where bluegrass began), but I had grown up listening to country and western music on the radio, at movies, and on records. As a teenager I became enamored of what was innocently and enthusiastically called "folk music." This is the context in which, as a college student, I learned about bluegrass. By the time I moved to Bloomington, Indiana, to begin graduate study in folklore, I was involved in it as a musician. From 1961 to 1968, during my spare time, I immersed myself in this music, spending many Sundays at Bill Monroe's Brown County Jamboree in nearby Bean Blossom, Indiana. I played in the house band, hung out backstage to listen to and pick in jam sessions, entered banjo contests, shared meals with musicians, taped shows, managed the Jamboree during the 1963 season, and helped run the band contests at Monroe's first two Bean Blossom bluegrass festivals in 1967 and 1968. I got to know a great many musicians and fans.

It was clear to me from this intense immersion that I was in the midst of a vital process not previously documented. It was a cultural scene that brought together amateur and professional musicians, and mixed urban and rural, working class and middle class, young and old, and a variety of musical genres.

During this period I was also completing my graduate work at Indiana University. Perhaps this would have been the right time and place for me to study what was happening at Bean Blossom, a scene of ferment during those years because of the revival of interest in Bill Monroe and his music then taking place. But I was hesitant about studying something in which I was so deeply involved, and my teachers and most of my fellow students gave me little encouragement in this direction. Virtually no one in the folklore department seemed to know much about Bean Blossom or the Jamboree. I recall coming early to a class one Monday morning in 1961 and breathlessly telling several fellow students that I'd played banjo with Bill Monroe and his Blue Grass Boys the day before. They didn't recognize the name, and there wasn't time to explain before the professor arrived.

Moreover, Indiana University was a school that took pride in international scholarship, and there was relatively little interest in local traditions in the folklore department at that time. The department had tried a team fieldwork project in Brown County during 1960. It had not been a great success, and project leader Richard M. Dorson had come to believe that the county, a rural backwater which had become a tourist haven, presented poor pickings for folklorists.

Though Indiana University was well situated for the study of hillbilly music (as many people still called it then), the folklorists interested in this topic were elsewhere. The serious study of such music seemed to engender strong feelings in a region immersed in it. Folklore department head Dorson had built his reputation by opposing what he termed "fakelore"—the inauthentic and commercial material palmed off in popular culture as the real folklore, for big bucks. He reacted viscerally against projects which had any sort of connection with the folk music boom or revival, then at its height and obviously permeated with fakelore. Bluegrass was fashionable in the folk revival, had clear popular-culture connections, and was associated with the southern Appalachians, a region Dorson considered stereotyped as the folklorists' preserve and thus overstudied. It was not something that seemed appropriate to study under these circumstances.

Yet surprisingly the first scholarly work on bluegrass did take place at Indiana, when Mayne Smith undertook a master's thesis in folklore on bluegrass in 1963–64. He was able to do this primarily because he had the support and guidance of anthropologist and pioneer ethnomusicologist Alan P. Merriam, who was newly arrived on campus and still on good terms with the folklorists. Without Merriam's support, the thesis topic would not have been approved, and the finished work would probably have been rejected. Even then, it was a close thing. I recall helping Mayne with last-minute disco-graphical research on traditional songs done by bluegrass musicians in order to "prove" to the satisfaction of his examiners that bluegrass had some rela-tionship to folk music.

It is unfortunate that the thesis prompted this sort of response, for it obscured other serious, even political, questions raised in studying bluegrass. First, there is the vexing question of how and where one draws the line between folk and popular culture. Bluegrass, like many other cultural phe-nomena, is now coming to be recognized by scholars as existing in both realms; distinctions between the two are important, but in real life it is rarely possible or desirable to draw a bold dividing line between them. I believe that bluegrass admirably demonstrates the many ways in which folk and popular art commingle in contemporary society.

The second question central to this work is, How can we be sure there really is such a thing as bluegrass music? An experienced student of the genre, William Henry Koon, stated his "contention . . . that no such thing as pure bluegrass exists," and while such a statement is perhaps extreme, it does attack the basic problem, for the word *bluegrass* has been used much more by fans and scholars than by musicians.[1] Indeed, it is tempting to conclude that the word was foisted on the musicians by overzealous individuals who felt a need to catalog a mutation or sketch a kaleidoscope image. It is possible that those of us who have studied and written about the music have been its chief perpetuators. But it is important to know that almost all of the individuals who have contributed significantly to research and writing about bluegrass have also performed the music. As we shall see, the distinction between bluegrass fan and musician usually resolves itself into one of professional and amateur (in the sense of doing something out of love): this is often called a musician's music. And there is here, as with the folk-popular distinction, no clear dividing line between amateur and professional. My own perceptions of bluegrass changed considerably as my experiences as a semiprofessional mu-sician exposed me to new ways of perceiving musical categories and the realities of the marketplace. But from beginning to present my point of view has been, like most of the writing about this genre, an interior one: we all believe there is such a thing as bluegrass.

I will return to these and related questions. But, leaving them for the moment, let us ask what is meant by the word *bluegrass*. Smith's 1964 thesis, "Bluegrass Music and Musicians," and the article he distilled from it in 1965, "An Introduction to Bluegrass," remain the starting point for definitions and descriptions of bluegrass music. Like Mike Seeger, whose 1959 brochure notes to the Folkways album *Mountain Music Bluegrass Style* constitute the first full description of the genre, Smith accepted the testimony of fans and musicians that bluegrass began with the 1945–48 band of Bill Monroe and his Blue Grass Boys. Using a large body of recordings, a small number of published documents, interviews with musicians, and personal experience as a citybilly bluegrass musician, he synthesized a body of defining characteristics for blue-grass. Readers of this book are strongly urged to read Smith's "Introduction." I offer my own definitions and description.

Bluegrass—What Is It?

Bluegrass, which takes its name from Grand Ole Opry star Bill Monroe's band, the Blue Grass Boys, is a type of "hillbilly"/"country and western"/"country" music initially most popular in the rural upland South, particularly the Appalachians, in the decade following the Second World War. Audiences for the music in its formative years were blue-collar workers, farm families, and other working-class people of rural origin. Subsequently the music found additional audiences among middle-class urbanites, a fact which helps to account for its survival and growth as a distinct musical genre.

Although bluegrass has traditional antecedents and has gradually created its own traditions, it has been a professional and commercial music from its beginning. Occasionally used for dancing, it is most frequently performed in concert-like settings, and sound media—radio, records, television—have been important means of dissemination for the music. Bluegrass depends upon the microphone, and this fact has shaped its sound.

Most definitions, however, rarely linger on or even mention this point and instead dwell upon another and contrasting fact: bluegrass is performed on acoustic—nonelectric—string instruments. That this is usually the first char-acteristic which bluegrass followers mention in defining the genre can be seen from a joke told by Ricky Skaggs, a young Grand Ole Opry county star whose early training was in bluegrass: "How many bluegrass musicians does it take to change a light bulb? One, and three to complain because it's elec-tric!"[2] Many of the men who first played bluegrass grew up without electricity in their homes, so they learned music on acoustic instruments. Electric instruments were frowned upon by conservative country-music people like Grand Ole Opry founder George D. Hay. Until the mid-fifties the acoustic aspect of bluegrass was not unique within country music, and in that sense the use of acoustic instruments in bluegrass is a historical accident. But because it was performed on such instruments, particularly the antique five-string banjo, it was virtually the only form of contemporary country music acceptable to the folk boom of the late fifties and early sixties, where electric instruments were considered inauthentic and symbols of the alienation of mass culture. Through the folk boom bluegrass gained new audiences and recognition as a distinctive musical form. Today the insistence upon acoustic instruments has become a philosophical position. Bluegrass festivals advertise that they prohibit dogs, drugs, alcohol, motorcycles, loud portable stereos—and electric instruments.

Bluegrass musicians and fans alike devote much attention to the instruments used in the genre. Of these, two—guitar and string bass—have mainly rhythmic roles, while the others—fiddle, five-string banjo, mandolin, lead guitar, and Dobro ("steel" or Hawaiian guitar)—play melody ("lead") and provide rhythmic and melodic background ("backup") for vocalists. Certain individuals have initiated basic bluegrass instrumental techniques—notably Bill Monroe for the mandolin and Earl Scruggs the banjo. Considerable value is placed upon the ownership and use of the proper instruments. The most successful bluegrass performers are virtuoso instrumentalists as well as singers, taking solo breaks between verses of songs and providing harmonic and rhythmic background behind other singers, often in antiphonal relationship to the vocal. Instrumental pieces feature alternating solos, as in jazz—a clear stylistic departure from the old-time southeastern string band music from which bluegrass developed.

These acoustic instruments are used in bands of from four to seven individuals who sing and accompany themselves. The band members are almost always men; in fact, in its formative years bluegrass was virtually a male music. Vocal delivery tends to be relatively impersonal and rather stylized, as is typical in Anglo-American folk singing and most country music. In contrast with other forms of country music, bluegrass is characterized by very high-pitched singing. This preferred vocal tone, often described as "clear" or "cutting" or, sometimes, "piercing," is the direct legacy of Bill Monroe's singing style, which during the sixties came to be called "the high lonesome sound." There are some important exceptions to this—lead singers who have rather more relaxed and mellow-sounding voices. But usually they have been paired with tenor singers who do have the high lonesome sound.

Harmony—in duets, trios, and quartets—is an important dimension of bluegrass singing. In duets, the second part ('tenor') is sung above the melody; trios usually add a part below the melody ('baritone'), and in religious quartets a bass part is added. Basically these are harmony parts, but there is a tendency—particularly in duets—toward vocal polyphony. In trios, the tenor and baritone parts are sometimes rearranged so that the melody is the lowest or highest part. In the former, the baritone part is sung an octave higher than is normal; in the latter the tenor part is sung an octave lower than is normal. One band, Flatt and Scruggs, generated a five-part harmony by adding the octave-high baritone part to a quartet. Unison singing is rare; either there is a solo voice or multiple voices, each with a different part.

Just as bluegrass singing tends to be at a generally higher pitch than that of most country music, so its average tempo is faster. Most bluegrass is in duple meter—that is, it uses 2/4 or 4/4 time or other combinations of meter divisible by two. Fans and musicians call performances which they find musically exciting "driving" and praise "punch" in the music. These and similar terms refer in a general way to a number of tendencies in bluegrass peformance which create tensions. There is, first of all, a rhythmic tension between the bass and guitar (both of which stress the first and third beat), on the one hand, and, on the other hand, between the mandolin and other lead instruments (which, when they are playing rhythm, stress the second and fourth beat). Often this latter element is perceived as a stress on the offbeat. A similar tension exists between the rhythm instruments and the single lead instrument, which often pushes its tempo ahead of that maintained by the rhythm instruments, creating a kind of surge in tempo during instrumental breaks, particularly by the banjo. Although the musicians insist on keeping what they consider good solid time, this surge can be detected with a metronome.

The classic bluegrass repertoire resembles that of older (1925–55) country music. A significant number of traditional folksongs and tunes can be identified within this repertoire, but recent and newly composed music predominates. Secular songs deal with such topics as memories of the old home and family, love affairs, and (to a lesser extent) the problems of modern urban and suburban life. The sacred repertoire comes from a wide range of sources, from old spirituals to newly composed gospel songs; religious songs are performed by virtually every bluegrass band, usually in vocal quartets. Instrumentals form an important component of the repertoire, demonstrating the virtuosity expected of musicians and also symbolizing the music's ties with the fiddle-dominated dance music of the past.

Country music historian Norm Cohen contrasts the bluegrass repertoire with that of contemporary country music and suggests that until recently "bluegrass songs have largely avoided the favorite themes of country music—adultery, divorce and alcohol." He concludes that "it would seem bluegrass has been considerably slower than country music in reflecting the social concerns of what D. K. Wilgus has called the 'urban hillbilly'—the generation of southern expatriates who have moved to the major cities fringing the southeast."[3] While I agree with Cohen's assessment of themes, I would argue, as have Atelia Clarkson and W. Lynwood Montell, that the bluegrass repertoire does reflect the social concerns of urban hillbillies by dwelling upon "down home." In *Early Downhome Blues* Jeff Titon defines "down home" as "a *sense* of place evoked in singer and listener by a style of music."[4] Instead of dealing directly with the problems of urban life, bluegrass responds to them by offering contrasting themes and tunes from down home, this happier, simpler existence. In this way it maintains a stance that has been part of American popular culture for over a century. Because the content of the bluegrass repertoire is so often clearly symbolic (rather than directly oriented toward current concerns), it is more accessible to people from very different cultural milieux who relate to the music as an art form, enjoying it as many enjoy opera sung in languages they do not comprehend.

Virtuoso performance on acoustic instruments; high-pitched, fast-paced harmony singing; and predictable lyrics are combined in a music which is notable for its attention to execution and form. Those who come to bluegrass from outside its original cultural context frequently compare it to baroque classical music or jazz. Most bluegrass songs are so conventionalized, with music following consistent patterns of rhythm and chord structure, that it is easy for casual acquaintances to play it together extemporaneously in jazz-like jam sessions. For the same reasons, a new band member can find the approximate vocal and instrumental parts with relative ease after only a few run-throughs. Often only the lead singer knows the full lyrics to more than a few songs; other band members know only the words to the choruses for which harmony parts are required.

Indeed, its formal aspects have attracted more attention than its affective dimensions. Today many of the most popular bluegrass performers, particularly those in the "progressive" school, juxtapose the classic repertoire with newly composed songs from folk, rock, folk-rock, and modern Nashville writers. They have moved away from the older lyrics in order to reach wider audiences. But as long as they maintain the proper formal characteristics, their music is still considered bluegrass by most fans.

The importance of these formal aspects was noted by folklorist Howard Wight Marshall: "It seems to me that there is no folk musical form that is more restrictive and bound by an established tradition than. is bluegrass."[5] In light of the relative youth of this "established tradition" when compared with the other folk musical traditions with which it co-exists, such as fiddling, Marshall's statement bears examination. Unlike most of the other musical forms found in the rural upland South, where it had its first and most lasting popularity, bluegrass is an ensemble form with performance conventions which demand a high degree of integration. Appalachian (and adjacent upland South) culture is often said to place high value on individuality. In contrast, bluegrass performance conventions are indeed restrictive and binding; they limit musical individuality. Bluegrass seems symbolic of responses to outside pressure for social change through group solidarity. This helps to explain its popularity with Appalachian migrants in northern urban areas, since these people are frequently subjected to such pressure. It is ironic that those aspects of bluegrass which are restrictive and bound by tradition are, culturally speaking, the most innovative part of the music, since they place the group ahead of the individual.

While the integration called for in bluegrass performance practice suggests group solidarity, the high rate of turnover in band personnel within established groups and the short life of most new bands suggests that beneath the veneer of these performance conventions the individualism typical of the culture remains a strong factor. This general instability in the makeup of the bands is usually explained in terms of economic marginality of the music, but perhaps the marginality is a product of the instability. From this perspective it is certainly significant that a high proportion of the successful bands have had as their nucleus some kind of family relationship. As we will see in chapter 5, when the two Osborne Brothers rearranged their vocal trio parts so that they took the two highest and most important voices, they were freed from having to advertise the name of a non-family member in their band, easing considerably the problems caused by turnover in personnel. This is but one example of the connections between musical structure and social structure found in bluegrass.

Innovation viewed as tradition and performance integration belying band cohesiveness—these are the seeming paradoxes which a student of bluegrass music faces. I have come to believe that they are best resolved through a careful examination of the music's history.

How Bluegrass Got Started—A Debate

That Mayne Smith's thesis which discussed the formal, behavioral, and cultural aspects of the music, created problems for his folklore mentors is an indication of the preoccupation of folklorists in the sixties with the study of historically verifiable texts. At the same time, the enthusiastic acceptance of his article by bluegrass fans—it was reprinted serially in four early issues of *Bluegrass Unlimited* during 1966–67—reflected their belief that bluegrass is a unique genre worthy of serious study. As historian John Rumble later noted, "While Smith's work was the product of the growing acceptance of all hillbilly music styles, including Country-Western, as fit subjects for scholarship, it nevertheless imbued bluegrass with a peculiar respectability and dignity."[6] But at the time most interesting to me was Bill Monroe's response. Smith's statement that the music began with Monroe's post-war band and his inclusion of Earl Scruggs-style banjo as one of the defining characteristics of the music were, Monroe told Smith angrily, "damn lies" as far as he was concerned.[7]

Monroe's angry response to Smith's reporting of two basic assumptions about the nature of bluegrass confirmed my own growing feeling that the beginnings of bluegrass needed further study. At the time the most important question seemed one of origins: did bluegrass date from 1939 when Bill Monroe organized and brought his Blue Grass Boys to the Grand Ole Opry, or from 1945–48 when his most famous band, the one which included Lester Flatt and Earl Scruggs, was active?

My years of hanging out backstage at Bean Blossom had alerted me to the fact that animosity existed between Monroe and Flatt and Scruggs; Monroe himself had expressed to me privately his chagrin at the way in which Flatt and Scruggs labeled their music bluegrass: "They're not playing it right," he said, shaking his head. And yet I knew from talking with his banjo players that he instructed each one to play certain tunes and breaks the way Earl Scruggs did them. I had also heard stories of conflict between Monroe and the Stanley Brothers, vague rumours of a fight concerning "Molly and Tenbrooks." Also current were legends of fights between Bill and his brother Charlie Monroe. And I learned firsthand of other feuds—misunderstandings about common repertoire like that which occurred in 1965 between Jim and Jesse and Flatt and Scruggs over "Memphis." Bluegrass musicians quarreled and backbit about "stolen" repertoire as if it were buried treasure. While the fans saw the unifying characteristics which, for them, defined the music, the musicians were (understandably) more concerned with developing unique identities while at the same time claiming credit for their contributions.

I knew that inteviewing musicians was an important way in which to learn about bluegrass; this technique was used by Mayne Smith and by Ralph Rinzler, who in 1962–65 brought Monroe out of his withdrawn silence and helped revive his career. But I felt it was not the only way. Because of my training in history I was aware of the importance of circumstantial evidence and primary documents. To that end I had been compiling discographical information since 1961, attempting to date influential bluegrass recordings in order to understand developments in technique and repertoire and the roles played in this by various bands and individuals. We are indeed fortunate to have a musical style as well documented on record as is bluegrass. But what other primary documents existed?

A fellow folklorist, Joe Hickerson, pointed me toward *Billboard*, the show business weekly. During the summer of 1964, while studying for graduate comprehensive exams, I began browsing through back issues of *Billboard* from the late forties and found, in the lists of record releases and the country music news columns, primary documents which helped me make sense out of the personal testimony I'd heard at Bean Blossom and read in the work of Smith and Rinzler. In particular, the November 1949 item which told of Monroe's move from Columbia to Decca because he objected to Columbia signing the Stanley Brothers was a key find which confirmed the stories of conflict I had heard. From this grew my first scholarly work on bluegrass, "From Sound to Style: The Emergence of Bluegrass," which I read at the 1966 meeting of the American Folklore Society and which was published in the *Journal of American Folklore* in 1967. Chapter 3 of the present work is derived from that study, which argued that bluegrass became a "style" (I now prefer the term *genre*) in 1947–48 when bands like the Stanley Brothers began copying Monroe's sound.

A key figure in helping me edit and develop the "Sound to Style" paper was Archie Green, who prompted me to document the genesis of the word *bluegrass*. I discovered that when I encountered the word in print in 1957 in Ralph Rinzler's notes to *American Banjo Scruggs Style*, a Folkways record album, I was reading its very first printing. I also learned that the word was first used by fans and followers of the music and that musicians have always used it with hesitation because it is potentially limiting, not just artistically but more importantly in a commercial and professional sense.

Yet in spite of this ambivalence, by the time I did the "Sound to Style" research a bluegrass revival had begun. It was heralded by Carlton Haney's Roanoke Bluegrass Festivals, the first of their kind in 1965 and 1966; the

new magazine *Bluegrass Unlimited,* which began publishing in July 1966 in
Washington, D.C.; and the growth of New York-based County Sales, with
its regular newsletters to bluegrass and old-time music record buyers. These
events (covered in chapter 7) were not as clearly significant to me then as
they are now, and I did not discuss them in the paper. This is typical of the
historian's dilemma: it is always hard to see the forest for the trees when
dealing with the present and the near past. The consumer and festival movements, which began in the mid-sixties, led to the great growth of the music's
audiences during the early seventies. I was involved in this process myself in
several ways: I began writing for *Bluegrass Unlimited* in 1967 and in 1969
compiled one of the first historical bluegrass reissue albums for RCA's Vintage
Series. In 1967 and 1968 I assisted Bill Monroe in the operation of his first
festivals at Bean Blossom, and in 1971 began a long association with the first
Canadian bluegrass festival, held annually in Nova Scotia.

In the years following my move to Canada in 1968 I acquired new perspectives about bluegrass. Through interviews with and observation of musicians
in the rural areas of the maritime provinces, particularly New Brunswick, I
developed a theoretical model to help understand better the relationships
between country and folk musics. Through it I realized that there exists
between local musicians and internationally known professionals not so
much a wide gulf as a system of status (apprentice, journeyman, craftsman,
etc.) and market levels (local, regional, national, etc.). Individual musicians
move through these levels, often accepting a lower status in a higher market,
in order to advance their careers. The same model also describes the hierarchy which emerges whenever musicians from different levels come into
contact with one another.

This model has been most helpful to me in understanding the history of
bluegrass music, for that history is replete with examples of interaction (particularly in the copying of styles and repertoires) between musicians of different statuses on the local, regional, and national market levels. Such
interaction has had important results for the music. In the present work I do
not refer to such structural matters directly, but I have used my findings based
on the model to address what now seems to me to be the crucial question:
How and why has this musical form continued to exist and grow in spite of
the ambivalence which its name seems to engender among the very musicians
who have been most instrumental (pun intended) in advancing it? For two
reasons this seems the most important question.

First, there is ample evidence that the term *bluegrass* is one with which
musicians have not always been comfortable. Yet because of fans and followers it persists. My studies of exchanges between folk and country music lead
me to believe that such persistance is uncommon. Fans recall and preserve
favorite songs and tunes, and separately preserve or copy the performance
styles of individual stars. But that fans should preserve and name a musical
genre—a combination of repertoire and styles—in spite of the hesitancy of

the performers runs counter to the eclectic and individualistic tendencies in both country music and folk music.

Second is the interesting fact that while much has been written about bluegrass, making it a familiar musical descriptive term today, it is and always has been perpetuated by a relatively small number of people. Primary documents (trade and fan magazines of the late forties and early fifties) show that the period many writers now describe as the golden years of bluegrass (which without doubt they were in the sense of being formative years) were years in which the music was (1) rarely identified as a distinctive form and (2) generally considered to be marginal within country music —called "backwoods," "rural," "for the old folks," etc., by trade papers. No one wrote about bluegrass per se before 1956.

Bluegrass is well known today because it was discovered in the fifties by people who perceived it as a vital new musical form coming from America's handiest folk pocket, Appalachia. The spiritual and cultural descendants of the Yankees who made that region a symbol into which they could pour their zeal and guilt saw in bluegrass the latest authentic expression of poor, rural, working-class, pioneer America. As an exciting new form it became, for young intellectuals, a rock-and-roll surrogate and the vanguard of a rapprochement between country and folk music during the late sixties.

It is important to understand that the idea of Appalachia as a cohesive unit has a large element of mythology to it. When studied closely Appalachia turns out to have many histories, to be as much a patchwork of ethnic settlements, geographical facts, and local traditions as any other so-called homogeneous region in North America. This is as true for the music of the region as for any other aspect of its culture. Jean Ritchie, Chet Atkins, Loretta Lynn, Little Jimmy Dickens, Dolly Parton, and many other non-bluegrass performers are just as representative of Appalachia (and unique in themselves) as are the Stanley Brothers, Red Smiley, Doyle Lawson, or Jimmy Martin. While elements of bluegrass repertoire, style, and instrumentation do come from that region and many important bluegrass musicians are natives or second-generation descendants of mountaineers, it is by no means the only indigenous musical form in the region. And any list of important bluegrass musicians would include many who do not come from Appalachia proper: Bill Monroe, Lester Flatt, Chubby Wise, Earl Scruggs, John Duffey, Rodney and Douglas Dillard, Bill Keith, Clarence White, Jerry Douglas— the list could go much further. Bluegrass found a home in the mountains, but it is not co-terminous with Appalachia.

So it is mythology that seems in the final analysis to be important, and that is what I have sought to penetrate in this study—not the mythology of Appalachia, which a number of scholars have dealt with, but the mythology of bluegrass. This mythology, which Robert Cantwell has described as "believing in bluegrass," started in the mid-sixties with the festival and consumer movements and during the seventies created a separate business structure for bluegrass. This successful revival or revitalization movement has built a blue-grass establishment, a steady state as it were, in which musicians and fans seem to have come to terms with each other, solving, or reaching a truce concerning, conflicts between innovation, commercialism, tradition, and art.

So these are my concerns in writing *Bluegrass: A History.* Hence its readers will not find extensive musical or textual analysis, nor will they find every important or influential bluegrass musician mentioned. This is *a* history, not *the* history. I have agonized about not finding room to tell about Art Stamper, the Church Brothers, the Gray Sky Boys, the Lost and Found, Dick Tyner, and many other bluegrass notables. I wish I had the kind of space for the wealth of detail I have enjoyed presenting in my column "Thirty Years Ago This Month" in *Bluegrass Unlimited.* But this is not a genealogy; it is a history showing the development of the *idea* that bluegrass exists and must be pre-served and promoted. This idea made the music and its name into a symbol that led to the present reality of the bluegrass business with its clubs, maga-zines, record companies, instrument builders, festival circuits, and other manifestations.

There is now much in print concerning country music in its early years, thanks to the efforts of scholars such as Bill C. Malone, Archie Green, Norm Cohen, and Charles Wolfe. And as for bluegrass's larger debt to the many forms of vernacular music that precede it, from Elizabethan balladry to min-strel shows, that too has been dealt with, in Bob Cantwell's *Bluegrass Break-down.* I turn at once to the immediate origins of bluegrass, hillbilly music in the thirties, and carry this discussion down to the present. Following each chapter are brief biographical and discographical sections designed to point the reader toward further sources. At the end of the book is a full bibliography and discography, with commentary on the nature of those sources and the general challenge of working in a field that has only recently developed its own traditions of scholarship.

Notes

Full citations for items given in the notes may be found in the Bibliography.
1. William Henry Koon, "Newgrass, Oldgrass, and Bluegrass."
2. Pamela J. Barker, "Nashville Fan Fair."
3. N[orman] C[ohen], "Record Reviews."
4. Jeff Titon, *Early Downhome Blues,* p. xiii.
5. Howard Wight Marshall, " 'Keep on the Sunny Side of Life,' " p. 14.
6. John Woodruff Rumble, "Traditionalism and Commercialism in Amer-ican Bluegrass Music," p. 20.
7. Mayne Smith, "Notes and Interviews from the First Annual Bluegrass Festival at Roanoke, Virginia—1965," p. 1.

Bibliographical Notes

Full citations for the items discussed in these notes and those which follow each subsequent chapter are given in the Bibliography. These notes are intended to refer readers to my source materials and, at the same time, to indicate directions of further inquiry relating to events and issues discussed in each chapter.

Most of the fieldwork from the Indiana University Folklore Program's Brown County Project was published in *Midwest Folklore*. Donald M. Winkelman's "The Brown County Project" described the work, and Richard M. Dorson proposed to carry it on in "A Southern Indiana Field Station." Both were much more optimistic about the project than Dorson later came to be in describing it to his students at Indiana. Dorson's coinage was first published in 1950: "Folklore and Fake Lore." In 1969 he surveyed the impact of the term in an article entitled "Fakelore."

Alan P. Merriam was writing his seminal *The Anthropology of Music* during the year he was acting as Mayne Smith's thesis advisor; Merriam's concepts are reflected in Smith's work. Smith's thesis had considerable impact because he duplicated and sold some twenty-five copies to interested scholars and enthusiasts. An early version of his research was published as "Bluegrass as a Musical Style." His "An Introduction to Bluegrass" appeared in D. K. Wilgus's "Hillbilly Issue" of the *Journal of American Folklore*, hereafter *JAF*. Subsequently it was reprinted with additions and corrections, in *Bluegrass Unlimited*, hereafter *BU*. The *John Edwards Memorial Foundation* (JEMF) included it in their reprint series, and it also appeared (with mixed-up paging) in Linnell Gentry's *A History and Encyclopedia of Country, Western, and Gospel Music*.

Mike Seeger's brochure notes to the Folkways album *Mountain Music Bluegrass Style* are discussed in chapter 5. These notes were reprinted separately—unfortunately without the photos and appendices—under the same title in *Sing Out!* magazine. My own definitions and descriptions of bluegrass have appeared, with more detail than I give here, in (1) the liner notes to *Hills and Home: Thirty Years of Bluegrass*, (2) "Bluegrass Music" in *The New Grove Dictionary of Music and Musicians*, and (3) in the forthcoming *Encyclopedia of Southern Culture* presently being edited by William Ferris and Charles R. Wilson at the Center for the Study of Southern Culture at the University of Mississippi. A discussion of the various books which published definitions and descriptions of bluegrass music appears in chapter 12, and early formulations are described in chapters 4 and 5. I follow Seeger and Smith in using the single word *bluegrass* rather than the two words as in Monroe's band name. But where my sources have used the two-word form, I have kept that usage when quoting them.

D. K. Wilgus, whose record reviews in *JAF* between 1959 and 1969 form a virtual primer for the serious student of issues concerning folk music vis-à-vis country music, has written extensively on the topic. His "Country Western Music and the Urban Hillbilly" deals with mainstream country music in urban contexts. By contrast, Atelia Clarkson and W. Lynwood Montell illustrate the down-home stance of bluegrass and old-time country music fans in similar contexts in their "Letters to a Bluegrass D.J."

The question of personality and culture, always a difficult and complex one, is particularly thorny with respect to Appalachia, a region that has served as a laboratory for all manner of scholarly research and social action. Stephen L. Fisher et al's "A Guide to Appalachian Studies" is a good start-ing point for those interested in following my suggestions concerning individuality and solidarity within bluegrass music. The problems in maintaining a band are rarely brought out into the open; one useful study of such problems was done by folklorist William E. Lightfoot: "Playing Out-side: Spectrum."

The conflicts between Monroe, his brother Charlie, Flatt and Scruggs, and the Stanley Brothers are discussed in various chapters of this book. I have outlined the "Memphis" flap in my brochure notes to *Country and Western Classics*, p. 24. I find stories about such conflicts similar to treasure legends because of the points suggested by anthropologist George M. Foster in his "Treasure Tales, and the Image of the Static Economy in a Mexican Peasant Community." I would suggest that to the extent bluegrass musicians perceive their market as a limited one (and there is, in our progress-oriented culture, much ambivalence about such a perception), they tend to explain lack of personal success and/or the success of others in terms of luck, de-viousness, or greed rather than ability. In any case, bluegrass feud stories (which are legion) definitely reflect fierce competition.

Ralph Rinzler initiated the canonization process for Bill Monroe with "Bill Monroe—'The Daddy of Blue Grass Music' " in 1963. Like Smith's "Introduction," my "From Sound to Style" article was subsequently issued in the JEMF reprint series, reprinted by Gentry, and published with revisions in *BU*. My preliminary research on the genesis of *bluegrass* the word ap-peared as "Into Bluegrass: The History of a Word." Of my writing in *BU*, the two most cited articles are "Bluegrass and Serendipity" (which in a sense remains my definitive statement of personal involvement with the music) and "A Brief Survey of Bluegrass Haberdashery." Since August 1980 I have written a monthly column, "Thirty Years Ago This Month," for *BU*. The RCA album was *Early Blue Grass*. Now out of print, it introduced one error into the traditions of bluegrass history which I hereby repudiate: Carter Stanley did *not* work with Roy Hall; when I wrote those notes I confused Hall with Roy Sykes, with whom Stanley did work. My model based on research in the maritimes (which also owes much to interviews with the Osborne Brothers) is outlined in "Big Fish, Small Pond: Country Musicians and their Markets," an article that is, as this is written, about to be pub-lished in *Media Sense: Folklore and Popular Culture*, a volume of essays edited by Martin Laba and Peter Narváez for the Bowling Green Popular Culture Press.

I have already touched on sources for Appalachian studies; I found Henry Shapiro's *Appalachia on Our Mind* a provocative starting point for the reader interested in exploring this extensive topic. My own perceptions were set forth in "Regional Stereotype and Folklore— Appalachia and Atlantic Canada." Robert Cantwell's "Believing in Bluegrass" is discussed in chapter 10. Most of the people and groups I mention have been written about. See Marty Godbey, "The Lost Fiddler: Art Stamper"; Walter V. Saunders and the Rounder Folks, liner notes to *The Church Brothers*; Linda Stanley, "The Lost and Found"; and, on Dick Tyner, Burney Garelick and Don Ridgway, "The Sun Also Rises on California Bluegrass." The Gray Sky Boys, active in the late fifties and early sixties, were the first of several New Haven, Connecticut, bluegrass bands and consisted of Yale students.

Bill C. Malone's *Country Music U.S.A.* remains the standard history of country music. His southern perspective is outlined in *Southern Music American Music*. Archie Green's "Hillbilly Music: Source and Symbol" introduced his careful approach to the study of the early years of country music, and his *Only a Miner,* a study of recorded coal mining songs, is a superb introduction to the cultural dynamics of early country music. Similarly, Norm Cohen's *Long Steel Rail,* a study of recorded railroad songs, parallels and complements the work of Green and Wilgus in exploring folk-country relationships through case studies. Charles K. Wolfe's surveys of country music in Tennessee and Kentucky—*Tennessee Strings* and *Kentucky Country*—likewise touch upon questions of folk vis-à-vis popular culture. I will cite other works by these scholars in later bibliographical notes.

Chapter 1

Hillbilly Music and the Monroe Brothers

During the 1950s and 1960s, when country music became an industry centered in Nashville, it began developing an interest in its own history and
mythology. The Country Music Association created a Hall of Fame, and
there, in 1970, Bill Monroe was enshrined as the Father of Bluegrass Music.
Like all myths, those of country music are based on truth but not necessarily
the whole or literal truth. Bill Monroe was and is the central figure in
bluegrass, but he and his music were molded by culture and circumstance.
Monroe began his career in the early 1930s and, with his brother Charlie,
became a "hillbilly" (a word he detests) star in the Piedmont and Appalachian regions of the Carolinas during 1935–39. To learn how bluegrass began,
we must first look at the hillbilly (or "old-time," for that is the word preferred
by many of the musicians) music scene of the thirties—particularly in this
region—and the spectacular rise to popularity of the Monroe Brothers.

Hillbilly/Old-Time Music in the 1930s

Most of the people involved with this musical form during the 1930s were
white Protestants of rural origin. Performers were predominately young men.
A large proportion of them were in the process of moving from the farm to
some less rural setting, often to join the industrial work force. This move,
similar to those taking place in many parts of the world since the beginning
of the century (and some places much earlier), followed predictable lines:
young rural people (more men than women) joined older family members or
former neighbors, settling in certain urban and suburban neighborhoods and
there mixing with immigrants from their own community or region.

Among such migrants were, inevitably, some who enjoyed music. Mechan-
ically reproduced music from records or radio was still a novelty for many who
did not have this luxury on the farm. If they enjoyed music they made it
themselves or sought out neighbors who did. This was not difficult, as music

was a pastime shared with family or neighbors. Country music biographies usually begin with allusions to fathers, uncles, and grandfathers who fiddled, and mothers and sisters who played the piano or organ. Everyone sang. In the early 1930s most young rural people had some exposure to radio and records, though these new media were not as pervasive as they were to become later. A smaller number of these youths had actually seen the musicians who played on the radio or were on records. So when they came to seek musical models they usually found them in the neighborhood or family first and only later began learning from records and radio.

This homemade music is best characterized as the vernacular tradition—a mixture of religious, dance, popular, and folk musics. Then as now the vernacular music of rural North America was not homogeneous; there were regional variations. What people called "old-time" in upper New York state or Nova Scotia was not quite the same as "old-time" in East Texas or in the Piedmont. Repertoires, vocal and instrumental performance styles, and instrument preferences all differed. Even so there were many similarities, enough so that individuals raised on the old-time music of one region could appreciate and recognize at least some parts of the old-time music of another region.

During the twenties radio and records gave rural people for the first time the awareness of regional differences and similarities in vernacular music. Although records had been around since before the turn of the century it was not until the twenties that the record companies became interested in recording the vernacular musics of rural and ethnic America. At this time record companies, seeking new markets, found them in the rural, immigrant, and working classes, whose popular performers were heretofore active only on a local or, at best, regional basis. By the end of the decade records had helped bring these performers, many of whom were already professionals, further into the orbit of national show business, including radio, movies, and the theater. With the help of these new media, greater audiences became available. This made the profession attractive, more individuals began to enter it, and it became more competitive.

In 1927, the first big southeastern-born country music stars, Jimmie Rodgers and the Carter Family, made their legendary first recordings at Bristol, straddling the Tennessee-Virginia border in the heart of Appalachia. By this time the word *hillbilly* was taking hold as a description of this patchwork quilt of professionalized rural vernacular musics. It was applied to performers as different as the Carters, a family-based group from the mountains of southwest Virginia who sang sentimental and religious songs, and blue yodeller Rodgers, a self-styled railroad drifter from eastern Mississippi who mixed a generous proportion of rambunctious blues with his sentimental songs. Even when performers came from the same region there were contrasts. Folklorists have remarked upon Fiddlin' John Carson's archaic style and repertoire (the Georgia politicians who patronized him found it amusing); Clayton

McMichen's fiddle style and repertoire were militantly modern (young musicians all over the southeast emulated him). Both were from North Georgia and active in the Atlanta music scene during the twenties. Similar contrasts could be found in every region.

In retrospect the emergent old-time (or hillbilly) music of the twenties seems as multifaceted as today's country music. In part this is due to the cultural plurality upon which it was based, but the variability was also a result of the new professional standards (created in part by records) which stressed uniqueness for commercial identity. Those who copied established artists did not advance as rapidly or as far as those who created their own brand of music. But such advances did not entail radical innovation, for musicians and audiences alike preferred certain kinds of musical execution and thematic content. Variations significant enough to be regarded as unique by performers and their regular audiences seem in retrospect quite small. We can liken most such differences to personal or local idiosyncracies of vocabulary, syntax, or pronunciation within a regional dialect.

One such region, the Piedmont, lies on a plateau to the east of the Appalachians and includes portions of the states of Virginia, North Carolina, and South Carolina. This region was one of the centers of migration for the largely rural counties of the adjacent Appalachian region. Many of the musicians associated with bluegrass music in its beginnings came from or formed their musical careers in Appalachia or the highland South regions adjacent to it, particularly the Piedmont.

In the early 1930s the Depression began to cut down the amount and distance of migration from rural to urban centers. In Appalachia fewer people left farms than at any other time in the century. Yet some did migrate, and these young men were the ones who made the hillbilly music in the region. Most of them followed a pattern I have already described: they left the family farm, often overcrowded because of a large family, and set out to seek their fortune. Such mobility was expected of them, for it would ease the burden on the family and bring in extra cash. Generally these men headed toward the small and medium-sized towns which had factories, particularly the textile mills. And usually they arrived with brothers or cousins and lived near or with older married relatives or neighbors from back home.

They not only worked, they played. Running through the narratives of the musicians from this milieu who helped create bluegrass is a thread of allusions to baseball. Like the music, it was a team activity requiring practiced coordination and a series of standard roles, each with special skills. It too was performed before an audience; the diamond was a kind of stage. The bats and gloves were, like musical instruments, tools of the trade in which young men invested and traded. And it had a strong element of competition, which, according to Bill Monroe (a lover of baseball), was also part of the music: "All the way through, bluegrass is competition with each man trying to play the best he can, be on his toes. You'll find it in every group. You'll find it in one group and another group following him. It works that way. They'll still be friends, but they'll work hard to be better than the other."[1] Like music, baseball was a manly art which held some promise of fame and fortune for the very best and most persistent. And it was good recreation for young farm boys getting used to factory work and urban life.

Just as those who played baseball joined local sandlot or company teams, those who played music quickly found others who shared their interest. When new musicians arrived in town, news of their presence was quickly relayed by word of mouth to others in the community of old-time musicians. During these lean years men had to move frequently to find work. The Depression made regular jobs harder to get; hence musical jobs became more attractive than they had been in better times. Musicians seldom worked alone, and frequent changes in band personnel as men sought better jobs kept groups unstable and new musicians in demand. Fledgling musicians preferred to make their career debuts in company, either with more experienced men or with their equally inexperienced friends. There was safety in numbers.

In the early thirties hillbilly bands were looser in structure and sound than those that followed in the forties and fifties when bluegrass music emerged. Most performers had solo specialties—comedy, instrumental skills, or songs—within the band. Particularly popular was duet singing by men who were often brothers or cousins. Such combinations were called "brother duets" because they were so common. Brothers were thought to be able to sing together closely, having acquired the same accents and intonations through kinship and rearing.

Occasionally a religious quartet was formed. This type of singing was being popularized by traveling quartets sponsored by religious music publishers, as well as by black quartets newly popular in the Carolinas, like the Golden Gate Quartet.

The hillbilly singing of the region was accompanied by string instruments. Most prominent was the fiddle; everyone had a relative or neighbor who played the fiddle, and many people could play a little—much as many teenagers today can play a little guitar. The guitar, on the other hand, was relatively new; it was the instrument young fellows chose, even though their older relatives or neighbors seldom played it. The banjo—in its five-string form, introduced in the nineteenth century by blacks and minstrel show performers—was played by men of all ages, but fewer younger than older men. Young men were taking up instruments introduced through urban middle-class fads several decades earlier; these were new to the region and gaining popularity—the mandolin and the Hawaiian guitar. The string bass was rare.

While most of these men had grown up performing and listening to unaccompanied singing at home and in church, there was almost no unaccompanied singing in their music, and they almost always accompanied themselves. But singing was the focus of the music. Jimmie Rodgers had popularized yodeling, and yodels were tacked onto all manner of song—slow and fast, serious and comic. Also in fashion were duet harmonies, in the already-mentioned brother duets popularized by the Delmore Brothers and a host of others.

The content of the music varied from band to band according to personal taste. But a high proportion of religious song was heard; as much as 50 percent of the song repertoire of some groups was religious. Such songs could be newly composed or taken from popular gospel music, spiritual traditions, or standard church hymnbooks. The secular songs, which might be newly composed, borrowed from urban popular musics, or taken from oral traditions, dealt in sentimental terms with love, home and the family, and notable events. Pathos, tragedy, and disappointment loomed large; singers spoke of the popularity of "sad songs."

The instrumental music consisted of familiar pieces from the dance repertoire which functioned like songs about home and family to reify aspects of the rural life of the singers and their audiences and newly composed tunes which functioned as did the songs about notable events, by focusing on contemporary novelties: train imitations and blues were especially popular. Because of radio and records, new popular songs from Tin Pan Alley reached rural audiences sooner than ever before, and some of these were included in the repertoires of the more adventurous groups. All were sung in a manner which contrasted with popular and classical musics by its impersonality of delivery. The dynamics of the story were not carried over into the dynamics of singing; a humorous novelty item was performed in basically the same way as a serious sad song. This impersonality is a chief characteristic of the Anglo-American folksong performance styles in which most hillbilly musicians were nurtured, a sign of the close links with older traditions exhibited by so many facets of their music.

This predominantly serious and sad music constituted only part of the stock in trade of hillbilly performance. Balancing it was comedy. Then as now performers occasionally told jokes between songs. But more typical was the comedian in blackface who dressed in outlandish costume (sometimes "cross-dressing" as an old maid) and did a "routine." Frequently the routines were brief skits done by several musicians in costume and makeup. Just as the songs were sharply drawn in their sentimentalism, the comedy segments were boldly executed in terms of physical action (slapstick) and social content (stereotype). This reflected the influence of vaudeville, the popular entertainment medium of the era.

Hillbilly music was a form of theater, and just as comedians dressed in costume, the musicians dressed for their role. A wide variety of costume can be seen in the photographs performers of the thirties hawked over the air and at personal appearances. Very often men playing together wore matching outfits, which (like baseball uniforms) reinforced team identity for both performers and audience. Some were wearing cowboy duds, but this was not as common as it was to become in the forties. Frequently the dress was "fancy"—satin shirts with contrasting borders on collar and sleeves, pants with panels of contrasting colors. A number of performers wore jodhpurs, riding boots, and campaign hats; small-brimmed Stetsons of the kind worn by state troopers were also popular. Occasionally exaggerated rural clothing was worn—straw hats, spotless new overalls, gingham shirts, and neckerchiefs tied as carefully as a cravat. Some dressed like bankers in expensive suits, ties, shoes, and hats.

While these men were not bankers, they were businessmen, and part of hillbilly music consisted of direct retailing. Between the songs, tunes, and comedy came sales pitches. Performers frequently had sponsors and often sold their sponsor's tonics or laxatives from the stage and over the air. In addition the performers sold pictures of themselves and songbooks illustrated with such photos and containing the words to their most popular songs.

The most enterprising and popular musicians hired or worked in partnership with other men who were not musicians but constituted part of the business: announcers, who, given the elegant title of "master of ceremonies" (m.c., emcee) were important figures. Managers, often from the same regional and cultural network as the performers themselves, were employed by a few.

From what elements of the regional culture did these theatrical expressions spring? Some parts constituted home entertainment—the songs, the dance music. But only when young men sought to perform outside the home did they consider themselves to be embarking upon a musical career. Small local events put on to raise money within the community—pie suppers, dances, special church events—would sometimes feature aspiring young professionals. These events were just a step away from performing at home, but often this step led to a professional career.

Frequently the beginnings of a professional career came with access to the latest new medium, radio. During the thirties radio stations were being opened in regional centers, and it was sometimes possible for musicians to obtain fifteen-minute programs on these new stations. Rarely did the station pay salaries to such performers. They were allowed to promote their public appearances on the air in exchange for a percentage of their profit to the station. Whenever possible, sponsors were obtained; they would pay the radio station for the time used for advertising. The performers usually only got the free air time from their sponsors, though a few were paid salaries. Most hillbilly musicians worked not on salary but on a performance-to-performance piecework basis: the advantage of radio work lay in its advertising value.

By the mid-thirties the bigger radio stations—ones reaching a larger number of listeners owing to a stronger signal—generally had sponsors for all shows and frequently had Saturday night (or afternoon) "barn dance" shows at which all of the hillbilly performers broadcasting during the week on fifteen-minute shows would appear. Competition for programs on these stations was intense, reflecting the fact that radio vied with movies as the most powerful medium. Radio audiences came out to personal appearances where they bought pictures, songbooks, and, occasionally, the sponsors' products. At the same time, the men who owned and operated radio stations often were not particularly enamored of this music. Most were middle-class, urban, educated people who looked down on the music and the men who made it. Their condescending attitude and idiosyncratic treatment of the musicians was one of the hazards of the professional hillbilly musician's life. Bill Bolick, who with his brother Earl constituted the Blue Sky Boys, one of the most popular brother duets in the southeast during the late thirties, recalled vividly this aspect of radio work:

> Most radio stations, especially, believe it or not, in the South, where this music was more popular, were very much opposed to our type of music, and it was pretty hard to get a spot on the air. . . . I suppose it was what they considered a necessary evil; they knew it was popular with most of their listeners and yet they frowned on it very much, and, I think, really tried to hold the country musician down as much as they possibly could. I think that most of them felt that this type of music was strictly beneath their dignity.[2]

Typically a group, containing two to four men, would establish itself at a station and through mail response determine likely sites for personal appearances. The mail might come unsolicited, but more often than not performers stimulated it through calls for requests and dedications, and through mail offers for pictures or songbooks. Good response to radio broadcasts impressed the often cynical station owners and ensured tenure at the station for a few months. Most importantly, it enabled musicians to arrange for the personal appearances at which they made most of their money.

A very frequent site for personal appearances during the thirties was the rural school. This was often the only place available to house large audiences who were from farms and small towns. Arrangements would be made with the school board or principal to split the money collected at the door, with part going to the musicians and the other to the school. Prices charged at the door were rarely higher than those charged at movies—between ten cents and a quarter. The school officials, like the radio station owners, were often hostile and condescending to the performers, whom they considered ignorant and uncultured. Bill Bolick recalls: "A lot of the teachers, and especially the principals and the higher ups in the schools, felt that this music wasn't conducive to a good way of life and they were pretty much opposed to it. Mainly our sponsors at these places weren't schools, but perhaps religious organizations or outside organizations that got permission to use these schools."[3] Alton Delmore, of another popular brother duet in the region during this period, spoke of "having to beg the egotistical high school principals for a place to put on a show."[4]

Another location was the movie theater. Cinema during this period was, like radio, expanding into smaller cities. Although the talkies had made movie pianists, organists, and pit orchestras obsolete, many theaters still had stages and presented live performances between pictures. Some theater owners booked hillbilly acts. The musicians would appear as often as five times a day between showings. It was grueling but lucrative. Such bookings were not easy to obtain, for movie people were no more in touch with the music than those at schools and radio stations: "Theater managers don't listen to the radio and they don't give a damn, or didn't used to, if they had not heard of you and most of them didn't know or ever had heard of The Delmore Brothers."[5]

Other performance venues were considerably older than movies or radio. A few medicine shows provided seasonal employment. At these, traveling pitchmen sold herbal tonics from a portable stage and offered entertainment which combined features of the carnival, the circus, and the theater. Singers and instrumentalists appeared in the medicine shows, but the most popular entertainer was the comedian. Few hillbilly musicians stayed with a medicine show more than one season.

One of the most ancient of all venues was that of the open-air performance on the street corner, the town square, or similar public location. Singing and playing in this way for the money of passersby was often done by blind musicians, a few of whom became early hillbilly recording artists, notably George Reneau, Charlie Oaks, Blind Alfred Reed, Richard Burnett, and J. W. Day ("Jilson Setters"). Others like Tom Ashley and Tommy Jackson, who were not blind, also worked in this way, but most have neglected to report it to historians and fans, as it was not a prestigious way of making a living as a musician—too much like begging.

Another kind of performance popular at this time, also based on earlier forms, was the fiddlers' convention. Reports of such events go as far back in the history of the region as colonial times. During the late 1800s and early 1900s the conventions became a popular form. These were essentially small local festivals, most frequently promoted and organized by civic groups for fund-raising purposes, at which a fiddling contest was held. They attracted every grade of fiddler, from novice to pro. During the thirties some of the more enterprising hillbilly professionals refashioned the fiddlers' convention to suit their own needs. They would advertise a fiddlers' convention at which two or more well-known fiddlers would be present. Often hyperbolic claims of superiority would be bandied about on the radio before the convention as the competing fiddlers built audience interest in the manner of professional wrestlers or boxers. Large crowds attended, as much to see the fiddling as to find out who won; frequently the winners were determined prior to the contest.

An important medium for performance was the phonograph record. Though many record companies had issued hillbilly music during the twenties, the Depression caused a precipitous drop in sales, with the low point coming in 1933. A number of companies went bankrupt; inventories of unissued recordings changed hands; and many of the performers from the earlier period ceased to record.

In the wake of this attrition, record companies regrouped and set out to recapture their markets. In 1934 the new American Decca label began selling records for thirty-five cents instead of the previous industry standard of seventy-five cents. They were followed by ARC (the American Record Company), which owned a group of labels sold by dime store chains and through Sears' mail-order catalogs: Melotone, Perfect, Oriole, etc. RCA Victor responded with its own low-priced label, Bluebird, from which they leased recordings to Montgomery Ward for mail-order sales. All three—Decca, ARC, and RCA Victor—included hillbilly performers in their catalog. Decca and ARC concentrated on the southwest, signing up new cowboy and western swing band acts. RCA Victor, on the other hand, focused their efforts in the southeast, and during the thirties their Bluebird record line became the label on which many of the popular hillbilly recording artists from this region appeared. Most of these "artists" were radio performers. By the mid-thirties record companies were taking advantage of the network of performers active in other media. Successful radio and personal appearances were seen as a key to successful records, and performers were contacted after they had proven themselves. For the performer, records might provide an added source of income. But hillbilly record artists only occasionally had royalty arrangements with their company—most were paid a flat fee by the session for each song—and royalties were not substantial in any case. Often the companies would avoid royalty payments altogether by issuing records under pseudonymns on subsidiary labels. Few performers owned the publishing rights to the songs they recorded and therefore rarely benefitted from that potent source of income. Performers did not carry copies of their own recordings with them to sell at personal appearances because the 78s were too heavy and bulky. While Sears and Montgomery Ward marketed hillbilly records by mail, there were no specialized mail-order retailers advertising these records over the radio or in magazines. Only in a few places were there shops specializing in records. Instead most record sales were made in the furniture stores which sold phonographs. So more important for the recording artist than the income derived was the publicity generated. Like radio, records were a potent form of advertising.

Records, radio, personal appearances—all brought hillbilly music to the public in the southern Appalachians and adjacent highlands during the thirties. Who was the public? Primarily people of rural residence or background. Farmers, miners, factory workers with their spouses and children—the show was for the whole family. For these people the music was a form of popular music with regional, local, class, and family connections. The songs, tunes, and comedy routines expressed values and wove fantasies which appealed to them. One of the biggest regional hits during the thirties was "Maple on the Hill," an old pop song recast by J. E. Mainer's Mountaineers. Wade Mainer (J. E.'s brother) and Zeke Morris sang this duet at the band's first recording session for Victor's Bluebird label at Charlotte, North Carolina, in August 1935. It is a monologue by a man speaking to his true love, recalling their courtship and vows of love from the vantage point of old age and the certainty of separation by death; even the strongest emotion, true love, will soon be severed tragically by death: "Don't forget me, little darling." Another big hit was the Monroe Brothers' duet "What Would You Give in Exchange for Your Soul," a reminder that worldly values should not overshadow the more primary and lasting spiritual ones. These were hard times, and the stories told by the songs were sad but true.

For audiences hillbilly music was a popular form of entertainment wherein young men from the same milieu as the audience presented familiar and acceptable values; for the performers it was a special kind of job. It was a means to a number of ends. A way of seeing the world and sowing wild oats, it presented an opportunity to get off the farm, to leave the crowded family. For those already away from the farm, it was an alternative to hard, dangerous, and boring work in shops, factories, mills, and mines. It could be a source of supplementary income and eventually might become lucrative enough to provide a comfortable income for a full-time professional. It was also a way of expressing artistic impulses—one of the few available to these young men at this time. It was a way of validating one's identity, expressing one's inner sense of values, and asserting personal power in order to fulfull psychological and social needs. It led to prestige and status in the community, similar to that which came with the glamorous railroad or professional baseball jobs.

During the thirties much Appalachian migration was from county to county. Often it was from farm or mine work to mill or factory work in the few urban centers within the region—Chattanooga, Knoxville, Asheville, Roanoke, Huntington, Charleston. Others moved farther, to the fringes of Appalachia—central Tennessee, north Georgia, the Piedmont, Ohio, Pennsylvania, Maryland, and Washington, D.C. Many migrants headed for more heavily industrialized areas, with those from the western counties going to Ohio, Indiana, and Michigan while those from the eastern slopes went to the Piedmont or Maryland-Washington, D.C.

While many of the musicians who helped create bluegrass were part of such patterns, Bill Monroe and his brother Charlie were not, for they came from outside Appalachia, from western Kentucky. Yet a corollary of migration theory holds that "each migration current is accompanied by a countercurrent,"[6] and the Monroe Brothers' move into the Piedmont represents one such movement. Moreover it underscores the fact that hillbilly musicians were more adventurous and were forced to travel further from home in search of work than many of their peers.

Bill Monroe and the Monroe Brothers

Born on September 13, 1911, near Rosine, Ohio County, in western Kentucky, William Smith Monroe was the youngest child in a family of six. His father made a living from the six-hundred-and-fifty-five-acre property on which the family lived, mining its coal, cutting its timber, and farming. Bill and his brothers and sisters all helped the family work the farm.

Folk traditions of home entertainment were part of the family life. Bill's father was a fine dancer, and his mother sang old-time songs and ballads, and played the harmonica, button accordion, and fiddle. Her brother, Pen Vandiver, who lived nearby, was a fiddler and frequently played at dances in the community. Most of Bill's brothers and sisters played instruments, but the four younger children were most involved in music. Birch took up the fiddle, Charlie and Bertha the guitar. When Bill was eight or nine, be began trying the guitar and mandolin. He would have liked to specialize in the fiddle or the guitar, but as the youngest and smallest he was overruled by his older brothers and assigned the mandolin in the family orchestra. He still likes to tell how his brother would only let him use four (instead of the usual eight) strings on the mandolin, so that he wouldn't make too much noise. Such setbacks strengthened his resolve to become a musician. Bill's resolve came naturally. Not only was he the youngest by eight years, he had very poor vision. His handicap made him shy, and he felt left out and lonely. As a youth he could not even play baseball. Music was an important, overriding outlet, a way of channeling the frustrations he grew up with.

Bill's musical schooling did not take place exclusively in the home. In the Baptist and Methodist churches of Rosine visiting teachers conducted "singing schools" regularly. Here, along with the rest of his brothers and sisters, he learned how to sing from the old "shape note" hymnals, though his poor vision forced him to learn as much by ear as by reading the notes.

When Bill was ten years old, his mother died. Several years after this Bill began playing in public, providing guitar accompaniment for his Uncle Pen at dances. Years later he would describe his uncle as "the fellow that I learned how to play from," write one of his most popular songs about "Uncle Pen," and record an album of his uncle's fiddle tunes.

There were other teachers as well. At one dance he met Arnold Schultz, a local black man who worked in the coal mines by day and played guitar and fiddle at country dances at night. Bill played guitar behind him at dances and, like a number of other country musicians in the region, was impressed and influenced by the unique ideas of this virtuoso.

The black musical traditions of western Kentucky spanned a variety of forms, from religious to dance music. Monroe absorbed much from the frequent contact he had, not just with Schultz, but with other black people around Rosine. He recalled, for example, hearing laborers "whistling the blues," a musical form which was the dominant popular black music of this decade. Later in his career Bill continued to listen carefully to black musicians. A gospel quartet he recorded in the fifties, "Walking in Jerusalem," was learned from black singers he met while touring in Norwood, North Carolina. And when, around 1960, Ray Charles recorded his "Blue Moon of Kentucky," he spoke of it with pride.

The family music at home, church-sponsored singing schools, apprenticeship to older dance musicians, and contacts with black musicians—all were typical musical experiences for a rural southern white youth of the time. Added to these influences were new media, particularly records. Older brother Charlie, who'd moved away from home to work, was buying records by the new hillbilly singers like Charlie Poole, Jimmie Rodgers, and the Carter Family. Monroe carefully preserved in his memory these musical influences from his youth; many of the folk and popular songs, dance tunes, and religious pieces he learned in western Kentucky were later to appear in his recorded and performed repertoire.

When Bill was sixteen, his father died. Most of his older siblings had moved away from home by this time, and for several years he "batched it" with Uncle Pen, who became a role model for Bill. His uncle was not only a fine fiddler but, by all accounts, a wonderful person who, according to Birch Monroe, "never did get in a hurry over anything."[7]

During the late twenties, while Bill was still a teenager, his brothers Birch and Charlie, like so many other young men of their generation, had left the farm for the burgeoning factories associated with the auto industry. They worked for a while in Detroit and then moved into the East Chicago area, first to Hammond and then to Whiting. Here they took jobs in oil refineries. Around 1929, Bill, barely eighteen, came north to join them. Because of his prowess on the company baseball team, Charlie was able to help Bill get a job working in the barrel house at the Sinclair refinery, a job which he kept for nearly five years. It was hard work but it could be exhilarating. He describes how they would unload a freight car full of barrels in forty-five minutes: "There would be two inside the car and two or three of us outside and they would spin those barrels down on you and you would have to catch them—just like playing ball."[8] Arriving at the beginning of the Depression, Bill was lucky to find and keep that job throughout the early thirties. Often his brothers were out of work—Charlie was fired by his foreman at Sinclair when he got into a fight—and for long periods Bill supported his brothers and a sister who lived in the area. Later he recalled, "I never could put any money away it seems. They [his family] hung right on . . . I worked every day for five years and all I got out of it was I spent forty dollars for a mandolin and I got a couple suits of clothes [but] . . . it wouldn't be right not to support your people."[9]

It is difficult to piece together the exact chronology of the Monroe Brothers' musical career in the East Chicago area, for Birch, Bill, and Charlie each give slightly different accounts. They played for dances and performed for four or five months on WAE in Hammond before moving to a weekly show on WJKS in Gary. In 1932 the three brothers and a friend named Larry Moore were "discovered" at a square dance in Hammond by Tom Owen, who had a set of exhibition dancers on the "National Barn Dance," a Saturday night radio show on Chicago station WLS. The National Barn Dance was the oldest and, at the time, the most substantial program of its kind. WLS, founded in the early twenties by Sears (World's Largest Store), was powerful (50,000 watts, the legal limit) and had a "clear channel": no other station could use its frequency, which permitted it to broadcast its signal in all directions. WLS was heard all over eastern North America, bringing the National Barn Dance into millions of homes. The show had become so popular that in March 1932 WLS began broadcasting it from the Eighth Street Theater in downtown Chicago to paying customers. It was the first such show to play regularly before theater audiences. And Tom Owen's dancers were part of the show. Bill says Owen had one set of dancers at the theater and that they were hired as a second set to dance on the road; Birch recalls dancing at the Eighth Street Theater; Charlie speaks of playing with other National Barn Dance Acts at the Palace, a local vaudeville theater.

It is significant that Charlie recalled playing music as well as dancing, for during these formative years of the Monroe Brothers he was clearly their leader. As guitarist he did the lead singing and found and taught his brothers much of the repertoire of the band. Affable, outgoing, jolly, Charlie had a personality which made him their natural spokesman.

While Bill was shy and laconic, he was not hesitant about his mandolin playing. One of the first country professionals to recognize his talent was Karl Davis, of the WLS brother duet Karl and Harty. Playing on tour in Hammond at the Paramount Theater, they were visited regularly backstage by Bill and Charlie. Years later Davis told an interviewer of the first time Bill Monroe played mandolin for him: "He took this mandolin and I've never heard anybody play as fast in my life, and I went across the stage and got (WLS cast members) Red Foley and Linda Parker and Harty and I said, 'come over here and listen to this man play this mandolin.' "[10] As WLS employees, Bill and Charlie were working as dancers, but Charlie's singing and Bill's mandolin playing were developing, leading both toward a singing career.

Whether or not they actually appeared on the shows which were broadcast over WLS, between 1932 and 1934 the three brothers and their dancing partners, along with Moore and his wife, toured extensively in the upper midwest with WLS road shows, each earning the (then) magnificent sum of $22.55 a week, traveling in a Packard automobile. Not only did they have a chance to practice their music on the side, the brothers also had the opportunity of meeting and hearing the big stars of the Barn Dance—people like the members of the Prairie Ramblers, a hot string band from Kentucky, and fiddler Clayton McMichen and his Georgia Wildcats.

Bill Monroe, still dissatisfied with the conventional mandolin role, was determined to develop his own style. Because the mandolin was tuned the same as the fiddle, it was natural for him to choose fiddlers to emulate: "Years ago people played a little on the mandolin just to fill in or to be playing. But to have heard really good fiddle players back in the early days—Clayton McMichen and people like that—and to really get on a mandolin and play the old-time notes that's in a fiddle number has really helped to create an original style of music on the mandolin."[11]

During their years with WLS Birch and Charlie were in and out of refinery jobs; Bill remained at Sinclair fulltime but as his activity with the tours increased he had to take time off more and more frequently. Finally in 1934 the opportunity to become a full-time professional musician presented itself. At this time much of the then-called hillbilly music was sponsored on radio by patent medicines. Texas Crystals, a cathartic product similar to the better known Crazy Water Crystals, sponsored several programs in the prairie states, and they approached Charlie about working as a solo performer on their program at KFNF in Shenandoah, Iowa. Charlie didn't want to go by himself, so he arranged for Bill to come along. Birch had gotten a job at a refinery and preferred to stay and work, especially since he was supporting his sisters. So at this time Bill and Charlie became the Monroe Brothers.

After ninety days in Shenandoah, Bill and Charlie were transferred to Texas Crystals' larger outlet WAAW, in Omaha. Here they met an announcer, Byron Parker, who became part of their act and played an important role in their success. Parker, a native of Hastings, Iowa, was the same age as Bill. He had sung gospel songs on KFNF before Bill and Charlie were there, and when they arrived at WAAW he had just begun as an announcer, but he excelled as a radio salesman. An old friend recalled, "Byron Parker could have sold struck matches!"[12] and Charlie Monroe said of him: "That man could sell water. Put it in a bottle, he could sell it! And get cash for it. But he just had a voice you could understand and he talked nice and he wasn't excited, and he could just talk you right out of it!"[13] Parker, who called himself the Old Hired Hand, was liked by the Monroes and, it appears, by everyone who knew him or heard him over the air. He helped the boys musically by singing bass on their hymns. The Monroe Brothers and Byron Parker were on WAAW for about six months. Then in 1935, still working for Texas Crystals, they were shifted to Columbia, South Carolina, where they began broadcasting on WIS. The rest of their career together was spent in the Carolinas and Georgia, playing out of radio stations to the south and east of the southern Appalachians.

From WIS they moved to WBT in Charlotte, North Carolina, where Texas Crystals sponsored them on their Tennesse Barn Dance. At this station Texas Crystals had to contend with a sponsor with a similar product, Crazy Crystals. According to Charlie Monroe, "competition struck. And [Texas Crystals] pulled [the] program and left us hanging. So we went over with Crazy Crystals, the 'Crazy Crystals Barn Dance.' "[14]

The "Crazy Water Crystals Barn Dance" was the brainchild of J. W. Fincher, who had come to Charlotte in 1933 as general manager of the company's operations in the two Carolinas and Georgia. Beginning with a fifteen-minute show on WBT in August 1933, Fincher extended his Crazy-Water-Crystals-sponsored shows to fourteen stations in the three states and, with the Barn Dance, which began in March 1934, had a hillbilly radio show network which drew into its orbit during the remaining years of the decade virtually all of the best known performers in the region. Among the thirty or more acts which appeared on their programs were the Blue Sky Boys, Mainer's Mountaineers, and Fisher Hendley.

Included among these acts were a number of string bands which would influence Bill Monroe's thinking when he later formed his own band. Even though Bill and Charlie (like Karl and Harty, the Delmore Brothers and the Blue Sky Boys) represented the newer brother duet form that was, to some extent, replacing the old fiddle-based string band that had dominated early southeastern hillbilly music in the twenties, some such bands remained active. Bill had been impressed with the hot sound of the Prairie Ramblers at WLS. But the Carolina bands included a different sound, that of the five-string banjo played in a three-finger picking style that was new to Monroe. In the twenties a sound like this had been popularized by the colorful Charlie Poole and his North Carolina Ramblers. Bill had heard this band through Poole's Columbia records, several of which his brother Charlie owned. Now he heard in person groups like Jenkins' String Band, with Dewitt ("Snuffy") Jenkins on banjo, and Homer Sherrill's East Hickory String Band, with Lute Isenhower on banjo. These bands kept this mountain-region banjo and fiddle music popular in the Carolinas through their broadcasts for the "Crazy Water Crystals Barn Dance" programs.

Not only did Crazy Water Crystals sponsor live broadcasts, they distributed transcribed (pre-recorded on disc) programs, which enabled performers to be heard from several stations at the same time; they also sponsored "remote" broadcasts from the sites of personal appearances. The Monroe Brothers were heard on at least four different stations: WBT in Charlotte, WGST in Atlanta, WFBC in Greenville, and WPTF in Raleigh. Lester Woodie, who fiddled with the Stanley Brothers in the late forties, recalled listening to them on WPTF in 1937: "I had been listening to Bill and Charlie Monroe over the radio since I was in the first grade of school. They were on a noontime show on WPTF in Raleigh, North Carolina. I used to listen to them while I came home from school to each lunch. There was a lot of good music on that station."[15]

Although Fincher did not pay a salary to his musicians, he covered their travel expenses and helped them promote personal appearances. Like the radio, the car was becoming a common family possession during this period. With it came newly paved roads. The Monroe Brothers and their contemporaries belonged to the first generation of professional entertainers who used the automobile as a tool of the trade, traveling to concerts within the driving distance and broadcast coverage of their stations.

Fincher's son Hubert, who was assistant manager, told inteviewer Pat Ahrens "the musicians could not fulfill all the requested engagements . . . and the shows were always sell-outs."[16] Charlie Moore, a popular bluegrass singer who came from Piedmont, a town of about 2500 people ten miles south of Greenville, South Carolina, recalled: "When a show came to town the admission would be about 15 or 20 cents. I remember the first show I ever saw in my life. It was Charlie and Bill Monroe and the Old Hired Hand, Byron Parker. I can remember that show and they had about 1000 or 1500 people in the town hall in Piedmont."[17]

The Monroe Brothers were broadcasting in both Greenville and Charlotte early in 1936 when Eli Oberstein, Victor Records' A&R man ("artists and repertoire"—a combination of talent scout and producer) for the region attempted to contact them to record for his Bluebird label. Unconvinced of the commercial benefits and saddled with the busy schedule which Byron Parker, who worked not only as announcer and bass singer but also as manager, had arranged, they had paid little attention to the overture. Oberstein, who was in Charlotte recording other hillbilly and race performers for Bluebird, had only a few days left before he would have to return to New York. Desperate, he sent a telegram. It must have impressed the brothers, since both repeated it verbatim decades later in separate interviews: WE MUST HAVE THE MONROE BROTHERS ON RECORD STOP WE WON'T TAKE NO FOR AN ANSWER STOP ANSWER REQUESTED.[18] Oberstein followed up with an urgent and convincing phone call to Charlie at the Greenville station, and arrangements were made for them to drive to Charlotte and make their first recordings. Because of their tight schedule, Oberstein interrupted a recording session by fiddler Arthur Smith and the Delmore Brothers to fit the Monroes in, and on February 17, 1936, they recorded ten songs between 3:30 and 6:00 in the afternoon. Many years later Bill Monroe recalled the setting: "It was a warehouse, where they handled their records in Charlotte. Victor Record Company. And it was just right back, they had two mikes set up in this place where they kept the records. Looked just like a warehouse, wasn't nothing fancy. So we went back and sung right in the middle of this warehouse and recorded there."[19]

The major record companies did not maintain permanent recording studios in the South at this time, so performers from the region either went to the company studios—mostly in New York, Chicago, or Los Angeles—or the record companies sent teams of engineers and A&R men along with portable equipment to record at hotels, warehouses, or other makeshift studios in southern cities. Portable recording operations had been common in the twenties, but during the depression only Victor and ARC were doing this frequently in the southeast. In order to keep the cost of producing records down so they could be sold for thirty-five cents, the company arranged its recording sessions so that only one master take of each song was done, instead of the two generally made in the twenties. Trips such as those of Oberstein to Charlotte generally produced twenty-five or more masters per day instead of the eight common in the twenties.[20] During the period when the Monroe Brothers were making records, the sessions in Charlotte were Bluebird's only southeastern recording sessions outside of a few trips to New Orleans. Recorded during these same Charlotte sessions, which usually occupied a period of a week to ten days twice a year, were "race" artists like the Heavenly Gospel Singers, the Golden Gate Quartet, and the Cedar Creek Sheik (Philip McCutchen, a bluesman); popular dance bands from the region; and a considerable number of hillbilly groups.

Apparently the Monroes had arrived in the region following Oberstein's earlier Charlotte visit in August 1935, at which Mainer's Mountaineers had made their first recordings. Oberstein seems to have learned of the newcomers only after he arrived in February 1936 to begin recording the other Bluebird regulars like the Mainers, the Delmore Brothers, and Fiddling Arthur Smith, all established Bluebird artists who had been summoned to the sessions in advance.

For the next two years every five or six months the Monroe Brothers were included in the regular Charlotte sessions. At each they recorded ten songs. At the end of their last session in January 1938 they had recorded sixty songs. All but six were issued not only on Bluebird but also on the even cheaper Montgomery Ward label, which made them available through mail-order catalog sales. Generally their records sold well, but their biggest hit appears to have been their very first record, Bluebird B–6309, with "What Would You Give in Exchange" and "This World Is Not My Home," which RCA advertised in April 1936 as a "Great Hill Country Hit."[21]

The impact of the Monroe Brothers on the music scene in the Carolinas cannot be overstated. There were many brother duets like theirs, most of them featuring similar harmonies and the instrumentation of guitar and mandolin. A number of factors made the Monroes different. They sang higher and played faster than the others. Charlie's bass runs on the guitar were snappy and attracted attention; Bill's mandolin playing, with its speed and dexterity, was unique. He showed how versatile and potent it could be as a lead instrument. Bill Bolick, then just beginning his career with his brother Earl as the Blue Sky Boys on WWNC in Asheville, recalled: "People kept writing in and wanted me to play the mandolin more, so in a very short time, I discarded the guitar entirely and we did practically all the numbers with the mandolin and guitar. This I attribute to the popularity of Bill Monroe's mandolin . . . Bill Monroe was making the mandolin a popular instrument."[22]

Bill and Charlie were broadcasting on the area's most powerful stations and making frequent personal appearances to packed houses. When the Delmore Brothers left Nashville in September 1938 and moved into the Carolinas, they found that "the Monroe Brothers . . . had done so well over there and had taken so much money out of schools that the schools had raised their percentage and we just couldn't make it."[23]

The Monroe Brothers' 78-rpm records were in circulation long after Bill and Charlie split, and they reached listeners beyond the range of their broadcasts and personal appearances. Their repertoire became accessible to many younger men who emulated their music. Few of the songs were new or original compositions by the brothers. Their songs—half of which were religious—came instead from earlier records, songbooks, and other singers. Nevertheless the Monroe Brothers' recordings of such songs as "My Long Journey Home," "Roll in My Sweet Baby's Arms," "All the Good Times Are Passed and Gone," "Nine Pound Hammer Is Too Heavy," "New River Train," "He Will Set Your Fields on Fire," and many others were more or less responsible for the popularity of such songs in the repertoires of singers all over the southeast and particularly in the upland South.

In April 1937 Byron Parker, the Old Hired Hand, left the Monroe Brothers to begin managing his own program and band, Byron Parker and His Mountaineers, on WIS in Columbia, South Carolina, a position he was to remain at until his untimely death at the age of 37 in 1948. Bill and Charlie continued as equal partners under their own management until early in 1938 when they had a falling-out and parted company. The many facets of their breakup are the subject of legends endemic to the country music business. Perhaps a candid statement by garrulous brother Charlie gives the best insight: "We were hot-headed and mean as snakes."[24] Birch liked to tell of a fight between members of another Crazy Water Crystals band who shared the same station as the Monroes in which, during a disagreement over which song to play, a knife was pulled. Such stories were told by others about the Monroe Brothers. These were, after all, young men from the rural South; serious fighting was as much a part of their life as music and baseball. Their falling-out might have been about money, wives (both were newly married), or a song; perhaps all played a part in the dispute. Bill put it this way: "If we'd had a manager, you know, no telling how far we could have gone. But so many times brothers can't get along good . . . one wants to be the boss and the other one's mad because he does and so it was just better that we split up."[25]

Both Monroes were ambitious and hard working; each felt he could succeed on his own, and they were to remain rivals for the rest of their lives. Bill had spent most of his musical career so far in subordinate roles, playing guitar for fiddlers, singing tenor to his brother's lead vocal parts, and providing mandolin backup and breaks during songs. As of 1938, at the age of 27, he had never recorded an instrumentai or a vocal solo. He was ready to try his own ideas.

Notes

1. James Rooney, *Bossmen*, p. 61.
2. Bill Bolick, " 'I Always Liked the Type of Music That I Play,' "
pp. 4–5.
3. Ibid., p. 5.
4. Alton Delmore, *Truth Is Stranger than Publicity*, p. 133.
5. Ibid., p. 132.
6. James S. Brown and George A. Hillery, Jr., "The Great Migration, 1940–1960," p. 63.
7. Neil V. Rosenberg, "A Front Porch Visit with Birch Monroe," p. 59.
8. Rooney, *Bossmen*, p. 26.
9. Ibid.
10. Charles K. Wolfe, "What Ever Happened to Karl and Harty?" p. 29.
11. Rooney, *Bossmen*, p. 28.
12. Pat J. Ahrens, *A History of the Musical Careers of "Snuffy" Jenkins and "Pappy" Sherrill*, p. 14.
13. Doug Green, "The Charlie Monroe Story, Part II," p. 10.
14. Ibid.
15. Wayne Erbsen, "Lester Woodie," p. 43.
16. Pat J. Ahrens, "The Role of the Crazy Water Crystals Company," p. 108.
17. Tom Henderson, "Charlie Moore," p. 10.
18. Green, "The Charlie Monroe Story, Part II," p. 11; Ralph Rinzler, "Bill Monroe—'The Daddy of Blue Grass Music,' " p. 17.
19. Charles K. Wolfe, "Bluegrass Touches: An Interview with Bill Monroe," p. 8.
20. These statistics come from Robert Dixon and John Godrich, *Recording the Blues*, p. 86.
21. This ad was reprinted on the back cover of *Muleskinner News* 4 (Feb. 1973).
22. Bolick, " 'I Always Liked the Type of Music That I Play,' " p. 4.
23. Delmore, *Truth Is Stranger than Publicity*, p. 132.
24. Green, "The Charlie Monroe Story, Part II," p. 11.
25. Rooney, *Bossmen*, p. 32.

Bibliographical Notes

The studies of Malone, Green, Cohen, and Wolfe, listed in the bibliographical notes to the Introduction, are sources for the study of old-time/hillbilly

music of the thirties. I have drawn upon the biographies of the first generation of bluegrass musicians, who started their careers in the thirties in some
cases or were youths listening to this music in other cases. These biographies appear in such bluegrass publications as *Bluegrass Unlimited, Muleskinner News, Pickin',* and *Frets.* In addition to these, the older, more
established performers of this era have been chronicled in the many studies,
discographies, biographies, and the like published by the JEMF since 1965
and *Old Time Music* since 1971. A useful brief overview is Bob Coltman,
"Across the Chasm: How the Depression Changed Country Music." Another important perspective is provided in Anne and Norm Cohen, "Folk
and Hillbilly Music: Further Thoughts on Their Relation."

Nolan Porterfield's *Jimmie Rodgers* is a brilliant biography of the most
influential figure in early country music. John Atkins edited *The Carter
Family,* the definitive work on that important group. John A. Burrison's
"Fiddlers in the Alley" is a good introduction to the Atlanta scene in which
Fiddlin' John Carson and Clayton McMichen coexisted, and includes a bib-
liography for Carson. McMichen recorded a long interview with Fred
Hoeptner and Bob Pinson, which was published in the first four issues of
Old Time Music. Later Charles Wolfe synthesized from this and other sources
to create "From the Fiddling Archives: McMichen in Kentucky." Part of my
knowledge of this powerful individual comes from the personal experience
of meeting and playing with him at the Brown County Jamboree in Bean
Blossom, Indiana, in July 1966.

The Blue Sky Boys' story is told well in the brochure edited by Paul F.
Wells to *Presenting the Blue Sky Boys.* This includes a discography, Bolick's
autobiographical piece quoted in this chapter, and David E. Whisnant's
insightful analysis of their career and repertoire.

Two studies of blind buskers who became early country music performers
are Charles K. Wolfe, "Man of Constant Sorrow: Richard Burnett's Story,"
and the Rounder Collective's brochure notes to their Blind Alfred Reed
album, *How Can a Poor Man Stand Such Times and Live?* J. W. Day was
romanticized by Jean Thomas into Jilson Setters, *The Singin' Fiddler of Lost
Hope Hollow.* A brief review of his career, along with a discography, is given
by Stephen F. Davis in "Jilson Setters." Wolfe discusses two other blind
street singers, Charlie Oaks and George Reneau, in *Tennessee Strings.*
Though not blind, both Tommy Jackson and Clarence Ashley worked as
street musicians: see Wolfe, "From the Fiddling Archives (No. 32 in a Series)," and Ambrose N. Manning and Minnie M. Miller, "Tom Ashley."

The commercialized fiddle contests of the thirties are discussed in Bob
Sayers, "Leslie Keith"; Wayne Erbsen, "Jim Shumate"; and Ivan Tribe,
"Curly Fox."

The best single piece on the tangled histories of the Mainer Brothers and
their various bands is Ivan M. Tribe and John W. Morris, "J. E. and Wade
Mainer." A useful chronology for the two is given in "J. E. and Wade Mai-

ner—Bluegrass Roots," and a discography is provided by Brad McCuen—
"Mainer's Discography."

For the narrative of the Monroe Brothers I have utilized the same sources
upon which I based a chapter on this subject in my *Bill Monroe and His Blue
Grass Boys*, pp. 11–19, footnote 7, pp. 113–14. See as well Ralph Rinzler's
"Bill Monroe." An interesting figure from Monroe's home territory, black
guitarist and fiddler Arnold Schultz, is profiled in Keith Lawrence's "Arnold
Schultz." Schultz and other local influences on and parallels to Monroe's
music are discussed in the chapter titled "Bluegrass Picking" in Charles
Wolfe's *Kentucky Country*, pp. 98–129.

For WLS and its National Barn Dance, see James F. Evans, *Prairie Farmer
and WLS*, pp. 213–31. Wolfe gives a brief history of the Prairie Ramblers (as
well as other Kentucky-born members of the WLS cast) in *Kentucky Country*. For a discography of this important group, see Bob Healy, "The Prairie
Ramblers."

The history, discography, and recorded repertoire of Charlie Poole is presented by Kinney Rorrer in *Rambling Blues*. Most of my information on
Byron Parker comes from Pat J. Ahrens's two works, cited in the notes to
this chapter. The Monroe Brothers' discography is given in Brad McCuen's
"Monroe Brothers on Records."

Discographical Notes

Full citations for the items presented in these notes and those which follow
each subsequent chapter are given in the Discography, along with a discussion of the special problems of discography. In general, two types of reference are included in these notes. Where I have discussed a specific
recording, its original issue is cited and, when this is out of print, in-print
recordings of it are also cited. Where I have discussed the recorded sound or
repertoire of an individual or group, I cite available albums, usually reissues.

Bill Monroe's 1950 recording of "Uncle Pen" has been reissued several
times, most recently on *The Best of Bill Monroe*. His uncle's fiddle tunes are
presented on *Bill Monroe's Uncle Pen*. "Walking in Jerusalem" was reissued
on *A Voice from on High*.

A considerable number of recordings from the early decades of country
music have been reissued on albums. A comprehensive listing of these reissues is Willie Smyth's *Country Music Recorded Prior to 1943*. The recordings
of Jimmie Rodgers and the Carter Family are listed in full in the books by
Porterfield and Atkins, cited in the bibliographical notes to this chapter.
For an album with the archaic sound of Fiddlin' John Carson, see *"The Old
Hen Cackled and the Rooster's Going to Crow."* Clayton McMichen is under-
represented on reissues, but a sampling of his work can be heard on *The
Skillet Lickers*, vols. 1 and 2—this was the band he recorded with in Atlanta

in the twenties—and on his own recordings from the thirties: *McMichen: The Traditional Years*. A reissue sampling from the Prairie Ramblers' extensive repertoire is *Tex's Dance*.

A selection of the Delmore Brothers' early work is on *Brown's Ferry Blues*. Mainer's Mountaineers' "Maple on the Hill" has been reissued on the *Smithsonian Collection of Classic Country Music*. For examples of thirties recordings by this influential band, see *Mainer's Crazy Mountaineers*, vols. 1 and 2. The Monroe Brothers' "What Would You Give in Exchange?" is also included in the *Smithsonian Collection*; a two-record set of their most influential recordings is *Feast Here Tonight*. Charlie Poole, whose band was contemporaneous with the Skillet Lickers, has had most of his recordings reissued by County: *Charlie Poole and the North Carolina Ramblers*, vols. 1–4. County has also documented the music of Arthur Smith (including some recordings from the session interrupted by the Monroe Brothers, as well as several from a later session at which he was accompanied by Bill Monroe's Blue Grass Boys) on *Fiddlin' Arthur Smith*, vols. 1 and 2. The Blue Sky Boys' early recordings are sampled on *"The Sunny Side of Life,"* an album titled after one of their most popular songs. The sound of Byron Parker's Mountaineers, the Columbia, South Carolina, band which included fiddler "Pappy" Sherrill and three-finger banjoist Snuffy Jenkins, can be heard on reissues of three recordings made in 1940: "Married Life Blues" on *The Early Days of Bluegrass*, vol. 1; "Peanut Special" on *The Railroad in Folksong*; and "Up Jumped The Devil" on *Early Rural String Bands*.

Chapter 2

No One Was Calling It Bluegrass: Bill Monroe, 1938–45

After they split up, Bill Monroe was at a disadvantage in comparison with his brother. Charlie had done all of the lead singing and could carry on with their old repertoire. In fact he did just that, hiring Zeke Morris, a veteran of Mainer's Mountaineers and the Morris Brothers, to sing tenor and a mandolin player to fill Bill's instrumental spot. Charlie kept the Victor contract, appearing at the very next Bluebird recording sessions which were in Rock Hill, South Carolina (instead of Charlotte, North Carolina), in September 1938. Here he recorded a series of duets which are so close in sound to the final Monroe Brothers recordings that Victor included three of them on a Monroe Brothers reissue album in 1962. As tenor singer and mandolinist, Bill was faced with the practical problem of finding a new partner. His first venture, a band called the Kentuckians which he formed in Little Rock, Arkansas, lasted from the split in early 1938 to the end of that summer but, in Bill's words, "it played out there . . . "[1] so he moved to Atlanta, Georgia, where in August 1938 he placed an ad in the newspaper for a guitarist and singer.

Among the men who answered his ad in the Atlanta *Journal* was a nineteen-year-old lad from northwest Georgia named Cleo Davis. The former farm hand had recently come to Atlanta, moved in with a cousin, and found a lucrative dollar-a-day job working on an ice truck. He had never been a professional musician but had grown up singing and playing the guitar. A friend brought Monroe's ad to his attention, and, with the urging of the friend and his cousin, Davis decided to audition. He purchased a guitar for $2.40 in a pawn shop. He and his cousin went together to the address listed in the ad, which was a trailer sitting next to a service station.

Davis, nervous in the presence of a professional, didn't catch the name of the man who was auditioning him. He used as his audition tunes two songs from his favorite record, the Monroe Brothers' "This World Is Not My Home" and "What Would You Give in Exchange for Your Soul." When they began singing, it dawned on Davis that "this had to be one of the Monroe Brothers. I got so scared that I lost my voice and had to quit playing." Eventually he got through a song. Davis recalls that Bill Monroe asked his wife Carolyn what she thought: "She said that I sounded more like Charlie than any man she ever heard not to be Charlie Monroe. I seen a grin come over Bill's face and he said 'Let's try that number again.' "[2]

The next day, Monroe took Davis downtown and bought him a good guitar and then took him to a men's clothing store where Bill fitted them both out, "from the floor up," shoes to Stetson, in matching suits. Davis recalled, "When I got through dressing, James Cagney or George Raft had nothing on me, so long as I kept that Stetson pulled down over my eyes."[3] Later in this chapter I will discuss the image Monroe's choice of costume conveyed to Grand Ole Opry audiences. Bill was carrying on a style of sharp dressing he and Charlie had followed. They wore matching Stetsons, white shirts, and ties, either with suits or with riding boots, jodhpurs, and sports coats. Movie stars Cagney and Raft were well-known and among the most highly paid for their roles as well-dressed gangsters. Shady, tough, self-made, lady-killers, they commanded respect.

Even though they were ready to dress for the part, Monroe and Davis did not immediately begin performing in public. Instead, for the next two months, the two men practiced two and a half hours every afternoon. Bill taught Cleo all the songs he knew and showed him what he could about the guitar: "Since Bill knew all the guitar chords and runs that his brother Charlie had played, it wasn't very long until Bill had me sounding just like Charlie Monroe. I truly think that at that moment what Bill was looking for was not a group, but the Monroe Brothers' sound. I'm not even sure Bill realized this fact."[4]

After Christmas 1938 Monroe and Davis auditioned at two Atlanta stations. WSB, which had a popular show called the "Crossroad Follies," told them they were only hiring groups, not duets. WGST already had the Blue Sky Boys and was not interested in adding another duet. With trailer in tow, they headed north toward the mountains. Stopping at WFBC in Greenville, South Carolina, they found no vacancies. Another duet, the Delmore Brothers, had just started at that station. They had been on the Grand Ole Opry, the big show in Nashville, and were popular recording artists. Monroe and Davis continued on to Asheville, North Carolina, where they auditioned at WWNC. They were hired to do a daily fifteen-minute program, "Mountain Music Time," every afternoon at 1:30.

According to Davis, the WWNC announcer billed them as "Bill Monroe and Cleo Davis," but they received letters from listeners addressed to the Monroe Brothers. Monroe, Davis recalls, "was back in the area where the Monroe Brothers had once worked so he was trying to stay with that sound to regain his popularity over the airwaves as he was building his own group."[5]

Gradually they expanded their repertoire to include songs other than those done by the Monroe Brothers. At the same time, Monroe advertised for other musicians.

First hired was a fiddler from Marion, North Carolina—Art Wooten. Wooten had, in addition to his fiddle, a one-man band contraption—part organ, banjo, and guitar. Playing this was part of his act with Monroe. Also hired at this time was a local musician named Tommy Millard who played spoons, bones, and jug and did blackface comedy.[6] With this expanded group, Monroe began using the name Bill Monroe and his Blue Grass Boys, a title he had chosen because he was from Kentucky, the Blue Grass State. Monroe and his new band did personal appearances most frequently in rural schoolhouses, charging fifteen and thirty-five cents for admission and playing to crowds of fifty to seventy people. In addition to the music a comedy routine, usually a skit involving the entire band, was part of each show.

After three months on WWNC, Monroe learned that the Delmore Brothers had left Greenville and made arrangements to move there to begin playing on WFBC. When they moved Millard stayed in Asheville. Bass player and singer-comedian Amos Garen took his place. The string bass was not a common instrument in hillbilly bands during the thirties, though it was being used by some groups, like those of Clayton McMichen and Roy Acuff. It gave a much firmer rhythmic foundation to Bill's sound, making it different from that of the Monroe Brothers, which had been characterized by Charlie's tendency to constantly increase the tempo.

In Greenville Monroe was again living in his trailer next to a service station. He made arrangements with the station owner for the band to clean up an unused grease house at the back of the station to use as a rehearsal hall. Here began the development of the band's sound and repertoire later to become familiar through recordings and live performances. He worked on his own solos, on new duets, on the development of the fiddle style he wanted, and on the organization of a vocal quartet to sing gospel songs.

During this period, Monroe was gaining his competence as a lead singer and vocal soloist. According to Davis, Bill used the guitar for accompaniment when he sang solos. Like much of the Monroe Brothers' repertoire, Bill's solos came from oral tradition and from earlier country performances. "Mule Skinner Blues" was one of Jimmie Rodger's blue yodels; "Footprints in the Snow" was an old song which he had first heard at WLS, rewritten to suit his own style.

At the same time, he was quick to recognize and adapt for himself promising material introduced by his band members. When Cleo Davis slowed down "No Letter in the Mail," a Carlisle Brothers' song arranged as a duet with Art Wooten, it soon became a duet between Davis and Monroe.

In addition to developing repertoire, Monroe worked diligently on technique. Just as he had shown Davis what he wanted in the way of guitar runs, so he took Art Wooten aside and began showing him what he wanted in the way of fiddling. Because Bill's mandolin was tuned the same as the fiddle, it was relatively easy for him to tutor his fiddlers. He would play the notes he wanted and explain how he wanted them bowed.

From the very beginning Monroe had in mind a certain type of fiddler, one with a high degree of technical ability and the willingness to learn certain ways of playing from him. His favorite fiddler, one who was quite influential throughout the South in the thirties, was Clayton McMichen. Bill admired and emulated him, particularly for his technical competence and rhythmic savvy. Monroe had heard McMichen often at WLS; his records were widely available and his radio broadcasts from various stations in Pittsburgh, Cincinnati, and Louisville were popular at this time. He was well-known, too, for having played on some of Jimmie Rodgers's recordings. Other fiddlers who inspired younger musicians like Monroe and Wooten were Arthur Smith, the Tennesseean whose 1936 recording session Eli Oberstein had halted in order to make room for the Monroe Brothers, and Curly Fox, another Tennessee fiddler, then best known for his appearances at fiddle contests of the type described in the previous chapter.

Quartet singing also required rehearsal and training. Monroe's childhood schooling in church singing was shared by most of the men who worked with him. But just as he had been exposed at an early age to secular music from outside the traditions of the community, he was influenced by new popular styles of religious harmony singing. These were performed by male quartets which, during the twenties and thirties, were organized and sponsored by gospel music publishers such as Vaughn and Stamps-Baxter. When touring they often appeared at "singing schools" and other church functions. Today's white gospel music industry began with these performers. In 1937, the Chuck Wagon Gang began their career as recording artists; according to Harlan Daniel, they were the first full-time white professional singers of gospel songs without a connection with a publisher, school, or evangelist. The independence of such singing groups reflected their growing popularity. This popularity could be seen also in the country music of the thirties. Just as earlier forms like Hawaiian music had been absorbed into country music, so gospel quartets took their place in the music at this time. By the early forties they had become quite popular; in 1941 one of the quartets sponsored by publisher Vaughn, Claude Sharpe's Old Hickory Singers, left the fold to join the Grand Ole Opry.

Not only were such quartets popular among whites, but similar quartets were very popular with blacks. Between 1934 and 1938 the number of black gospel quartets on recordings grew from eight to fifty.[7] Among the most popular and influential was the Golden Gate Jubilee Quartet (later to drop the "Jubilee" from their name), a Virginia tidewater group that began their professional career in the Carolinas. Between 1935 and 1938 they appeared regularly on WBT in Charlotte and WIS in Columbia, South Carolina, stations at which the Monroe Brothers also were performing. They too recorded in Charlotte for Bluebird, beginning in 1937. This group and the many others like it popular in the Carolinas influenced the style of and shared repertoire with white quartets. By the early forties, black gospel groups like the Four Knights (founded by one of the original Golden Gate Quartet members and also known as the Southern Sons) and the Sons of the South were playing on radio shows and at personal appearances out of Charlotte with local hillbilly acts.

Often there was little stylistic difference between the black and white quartets, and both shared audiences. One of the first professional white quartets, the Swanee River Boys, formed during the late thirties in Chattanooga, was thought by many of its listeners—including the Golden Gate Quartet—to be a black group. Another white group active in the forties, the Browns Ferry Four, supplemented their repertoire from black quartet recordings.

Monroe's quartets partook of the same influences. Although he and Charlie had frequently done religious songs, the Blue Grass Quartet was clearly a new departure for him. In 1979 he recalled that while he was influenced in some ways by the Methodist and Baptist church singing of his youth, "that was way before baritone singing came around . . . I don't believe I ever heard a quartet there in church."[8] With this as with other aspects of his music, there was a synthesis based upon several models. The repertoire was eclectic, including his own compositions, songs learned as a youth in church, and some material from the contemporary popular professional black and white gospel quartets. Like these groups, most of which sang a cappella or with subdued instrumental backing, Monroe placed emphasis on the vocal; only guitar and mandolin were used for instrumental background. In this sparser instrumentation Monroe's quartet remained closer to the Monroe Brothers' sound but at the same time brought to the gospel quartet form a new dimension—hot mandolin breaks between verses.

Amos Garen did the lead singing in the first quartet, with Monroe singing tenor, Wooten baritone, and Davis bass. Later quartets would vary the part assignments, particularly those quartet arrangements in which Monroe did the lead singing. From the very beginning he would shift parts, some times doing lead solo on verses and switching to tenor on the choruses, something he also did on secular songs. This was the vocal equivalent of his trading off mandolin for guitar on vocal solos. He was playing the roles of both Monroe Brothers, but in the context of the expanded band his role switching had a different meaning. As with a switch-hitting batter or a utility outfielder, a man who could play at more than one position strengthened the team. In this sense the band Monroe organized and rehearsed in Greenville was less like the Monroe Brothers and other acts then active in the Carolinas because it was conceived of as a cohesive unit, much as were the big dance bands of the era. Descriptions of the band's cohesive, team-like aura are reminiscent of descriptions of the Calloway, Ellington, Lunceford, and Goodman jazz dance bands from the same period, or for that matter, some of the contemporary southwestern country bands like Bob Wills' Texas Playboys.

However, his was not a dance band; their performances were shows which depended not just on the music but also on the comedy routines. And unlike the dance bands, Monroe was playing on a relatively small station and before small crowds. Cleo Davis says: "We were not making much money. Sometimes, we'd take in $25 or $30 a night in the little shows and we'd play most every night. Bill paid me $15 a week, when we were working. When we weren't working, he couldn't pay me anything, though he did pay for my haircuts and my laundry."[9] By the fall of 1939 Monroe needed to move on and felt ready to try the Grand Ole Opry in Nashville.

The Grand Ole Opry

In 1925 the National Life and Accident Insurance Company of Nashville went into the broadcasting business. Their new radio station was WSM, call letters which echoed their motto, "We Shield Millions." By the end of the year they had hired an award-winning announcer from Chicago's WLS, George D. Hay. Hay was a former newspaper reporter whose humorous column, "Howdy, Judge," in the Memphis *Commercial Appeal* led to a permanent title, Judge Hay. At WLS he had acted as announcer for the National Barn Dance and taken note of its popularity. Like WLS and many other stations at the time, WSM had discovered that their listeners liked hearing old-time music, and by the end of 1925 Hay had instituted a Saturday-night program patterned after the Barn Dance. By 1927 it had taken on the title "Grand Ole Opry." Hay gradually shaped the image of the program, making it consciously and theatrically down-home. The name was one aspect of this—a rural burlesque of formal and classical music. He invented colorful names for the string bands (the Binkley Brothers became the Binkley Brothers Dixie Clodhoppers), gave the performers fanciful nicknames (Uncle Dave Macon was the Dixie Dewdrop), and changed the visual appearance of the show by dressing the performers in rural costume.[10] When Hay began, the Opry cast consisted mostly of talented amateurs from the Nashville area. Photos of these early performers show them all dressed in their Sunday best. At that time the Opry was primarily a radio broadcast, with a very small studio audience present. By the late thirties Hay had developed it into a stage show held before large audiences, staffed mainly by full-time professionals (many with theater experience) for whom rural or western costume was part of the show. In October 1939, when Bill Monroe and his band auditioned, the Opry's most popular performer was Roy Acuff, who had been in the cast since February 1938. Acuff is often described as the first popular vocalist on a show that had previously highlighted fiddles and string bands, but that view ignores the popularity of the Delmore Brothers, the Vagabonds (a smooth vocal trio),

Asher Sizemore and Little Jimmy (a father and son team that specialized in sentimental songs), and several other popular singers active on the station during the thirties. Even Fiddling Arthur Smith, who like Clayton McMichen was an idol of young fiddlers during this period, was as much a singer as a fiddler during his years in the mid-thirties on the Opry. Still, old-time string band music was more important on the Opry than it was on many other barn dance shows of the period.

During the late thirties, the movie industry had made singing cowboys popular, and the rise of urban swing bands was echoed in the music of western swing outfits like those of the Light Crust Doughboys, Bob Wills, and Bill Boyd. The impact of jazz on American popular music was indelibly reflected in country music by the time Monroe started his band. The popular country acts of the time were, then as now, closer to the popular music of their era than to the folk music, yet more conservative, sentimental, and religious. Although radio crooners and swing bands had their country counterparts, Judge Hay was pitching the Opry as "authentic hill-country music" and urging his musicians to "keep it close to the ground." He fought for years during the forties to keep drums from the stage of the Opry and discouraged early attempts to use electric instruments. Hay could be annoyingly paternalistic and strong-willed in his insistence on such "authenticity." But he clearly believed in the dignity of the music and the musicians—he refused to use the word *hillbilly*, for example—and this gained him the respect and loyalty of his performers, particularly Bill Monroe.

The Blue Grass Boys Come to the Opry

" 'Mule Skinner Blues' and 'John Henry' were the numbers we tried out with," Bill Monroe once told Jim Rooney.[11] Cleo Davis's memory of the same event is somewhat different: "They put us in one of the studios and we really put on the dog. We started out with 'Foggy Mountain Top,' then Bill and I did a duet tune with a duet yodel, fast as white lightning. We came back with the 'Mule Skinner Blues' and 'Fire on the Mountain,' and I think that really sewed it up."[12] The Opry representatives, Judge Hay and David Stone, liked what they heard and told Monroe "if you ever leave the Opry, it'll be because you've fired yourself."[13]

"Mule Skinner Blues," the one song Monroe and Davis agree was played at the audition, became one of the central pieces in Monroe's repertoire and, hence, in bluegrass music. Not only has Monroe recorded the song four times (1940, 1950, 1971, 1973) but he has emphasized its importance to his musical thinking: "Charlie and I had a country beat I suppose, but the beat in my music—bluegrass music—started when I ran across 'Mule Skinner Blues' and started playing that. We don't do it the way Jimmie Rodgers sung it. It's speeded up, and we moved it up to fit the fiddle and we have that straight time to it, driving time. And then we went on and that same kind of time would work with 'John Henry.' And we put it on that."[14]

Monroe had found a way to fuse the popular hillbilly songs of the time with the older string band music. No one had ever conceived of singing a newfangled Jimmie Rodgers blue yodel to the same beat as an old folksong like "John Henry" so that it could incorporate driving country fiddle. Monroe had done to Rodgers's song what Elvis Presley would later do to his "Blue Moon of Kentucky" in 1954: he rhythmically reshaped it to fit a new genre. With this synthesis Monroe was perfect for the Grand Ole Opry, in 1939 the most self-consciously down-home of the big country radio shows: he was professionally up-to-date but preserved some of the old-time feeling in his new music.

His "Mule Skinner Blues" was, according to Monroe, the first song he ever played on the Opry and the first song to receive an encore there. Cleo Davis recalls the impact of their music: "Such performers as Roy Acuff, Pee Wee King, Uncle Dave Macon, and Sam and Kirk McGee who were standing in the wings watching the Blue Grass Boys when they pulled the curtain on us, could not believe when we took off so fast and furious. Those people couldn't even think as fast as we played, I believe. In fact, there was absolutely nobody living who had ever played with the speed that we had."[15]

It would be nice to have a contemporary report of the impact of the new group to compare with Davis's somewhat hyperbolic account, but I have yet to find one.[16] Nevertheless Monroe and Davis agree that a number of aspects of their band were perceived as new, unique, striking by their contemporaries.

As Davis indicated, and many others have noted since, the Blue Grass Boys played everything faster than usual, even the slow- and medium-paced tunes. This emphasized the skill required to execute the tunes properly: both instrumental dexterity and vocal precision were needed if the fast-paced performances were to be coordinated not to sound sloppy. And it demanded the solid rhythmic support of the string bass, stressing that dimension of the band's sound to an extent not found in other Opry bands.

In addition to the speed with which they played, their musical innovations included the use of unconventional keys. According to Monroe: "We was the first outfit to ever play in B-flat or B-natural and E. Before that it was all C, D, and G. Fiddle men had a fit and they wouldn't hardly tackle it and they'd swear that they wanted to play straight stuff and they figured that that's where I should sing."[17] Monroe was developing his voice as a lead singer and finding it most comfortable to sing in higher keys. Jimmie Rodgers recorded "Mule Skinner Blues" in D; Monroe moved it up to G. C, D, and G (as well as A) were the keys typically used by country musicians at this time because they were the traditional keys for old-time fiddle tunes and therefore were familiar to most musicians. It is relatively easy to play string band instruments, espe-cially the fiddle, in these keys. The left hand makes simple chords when playing rhythm and open strings are used frequently for melody. As Monroe moved songs and tunes up from G or A to B-flat or B and from C or D to E, he went beyond the competence of many fiddlers and guitarists. Such keys required more rigorous left-hand work. In insisting that his musicians, partic-ularly fiddlers, play in whatever key he wished to sing in, Monroe was setting high professional standards.

He also expected his musicians to play the older fiddle tunes and tradi-tional songs properly, even if that meant, because of quicker tempo and/or higher key, relearning the piece. Like Clayton McMichen, he perceived such music as part of a creative, rather than a fixed, legacy.

Also musically demanding and similarly novel at the Opry was the gospel quartet form. Both Monroe and Davis state that the Blue Grass Quartet was the first of its kind on the Opry, pre-dating by two years the arrival of the Old Hickory Quartet. These elements of musical skill—speed, command of odd keys, mastery of the quartet form—were aspects of the band with which Monroe built his identity at the Opry. Aurally it was a coordinated, inte-grated unit.

The identity had a visual dimension, too. Unlike the other cast members, Monroe and his Blue Grass Boys were wearing shirts and ties, once common at the Opry but by 1939 rather unusual. Costumes then common conveyed stereotypes Bill's band didn't agree with: they were not cowboys, and they did not want to look like or be called hillbillies. Just as they took their music seriously, so they took the image seriously. They wanted to look respectable even if they were, in Davis's words, "wild and rough and ready."[18]

Monroe and his contemporaries were, essentially, independent business-men looking out for their own interests in a rough and tumble business. Most of the non-performers with whom they did business—radio station owners, high school principals, theater owners, even record company representa-tives—had a low opinion of them and their music. Few performers had managers, and those that did were usually managed by radio station owners or sponsors, businessmen who tended to treat them as if they were disposable commodities. Byron Parker, The Old Hired Hand, was unusual in that he was a talented manager as well as a performer, an individual who was to the Monroes and the others who worked with him, "one of us." Bill and Charlie lasted together less than a year after Parker left them. Charlie had been doing the managing, and so Bill was adrift during his first few months alone in 1938, even though his wife helped with the business.

Monroe ran his business as a building contractor would. He advertised publicly for his band members, using the newspaper and the radio; he paid his workers a fixed salary. He bore the risk of maintaining the business and took the profits. It was not an easy task; he found early on that duets were not in demand in Atlanta, for example, and that there were pressures on contractors like him to expand the outfit into a full show instead of just a duet. In doing so he had come into competition with a number of similar contractors in the region, men like Roy Hall.

Hall, like Bill, had started in the mid-thirties as one half of a brother duet and then branched out on his own as an independent contractor. In the fall of 1938 Roy and his string band, the Blue Ridge Entertainers, had a radio show sponsored by Dr. Pepper, the soft drink manufacturer, in Winston-Salem. By the following year they had moved to WDJB in Roanoke, Virginia, under the same auspices. There "The Blue Ridge Jamboree," a Saturday night show in which they hosted such Hollywood cowboy stars as Tex Ritter, Roy Rogers, and Gabby Hayes as well as the best known regional acts, was a great success. So popular was Hall's band that he had to form two units of the Blue Ridge Entertainers to meet the demand for personal appearances. Hall worked with Dr. Pepper to organize other bands in the region under their sponsorship. An enterprising contractor like Hall could quickly build a strong business within a region.

Bill's brother Charlie followed a similar model as an independent contractor. During the early forties he made his own transcribed half-hour radio shows on which he advertised Man-O-Ree, a laxative he'd concocted. He sold the shows to radio stations. The shows generated great demand for Man-O-Ree, so much that Charlie eventually leased that part of his business to a jobber so he could concentrate on his music. The radio shows also generated great demand for Charlie and his band. Wherever they toured, they would draw customers who had heard the radio shows and thought that they were from the local station.

But this kind of hustling took time, and Bill Monroe instead chose at the beginning to devote his time to developing his music. During the fall of 1938, while Roy Hall was landing his Dr. Pepper contract, making records, and building a radio audience, Bill Monroe was practicing every afternoon in a secluded room with Cleo Davis. During 1939, when Roy Hall was hosting Hollywood cowboys and maintaining two bands to handle the business he was creating, Monroe was playing schoolhouses and a fifteen-minute daily show on small stations while he rehearsed the band in the back of a garage. Part of this contrast can be attributed to Monroe's caution in setting out on his own for the first time, for in the beginning he seemed to have little idea of going beyond the style of the Monroe Brothers. But there is more to it than that: then as now Bill Monroe placed music before business. A man of few words, to outsiders he often seemed distant and unapproachable. But the musicians who worked with him found him easy-going, patient—like a teacher or, in Davis's eyes, an older brother. Bill treated the younger men with whom he worked the way that he wished his older brothers had treated him.

At the give-and-take of business Monroe was less adept. He didn't like to haggle or discuss, and organizational details bored him. He would not have succeeded if he had not been on the Grand Ole Opry, a large, corporation-owned operation, with its musical activities overseen by a sympathetic and understanding individual, the paternalistic Judge Hay. The assurance that he could expect job security as long as he behaved himself appealed to Monroe's sense of loyalty; he repeated it whenever he told the story of his successful audition. It paralleled his story of working at Sinclair, where he kept his job through the depths of the depression while Charlie, his loquacious and aggressive brother, lost jobs because he quarrelled with foremen and got into fights. At the Opry, Hay's strong concept of the program made for continuity. And the conservative insurance company's management practices strengthened the continuity by developing mechanisms for promoting their talent.

Like the National Barn Dance in the early thirties, the Opry developed during the mid- and late thirties from a radio program with a small studio audience to a stage show (still on the air today) with a large live audience. In July 1939 they had moved into downtown Nashville's War Memorial Auditorium. For the first time they began charging admission (twenty-five cents) in an unsuccessful attempt to cut down the crowds now coming to the 2200-seat theater for the two shows each Saturday night.[19] WSM, already broadcasting at 50,000 watts clear channel, reached most of eastern and central North America. In October 1939 a half-hour portion of the Opry, sponsored by R. J. Reynolds' Prince Albert Tobacco, was placed on the NBC Red Network, a national linkup which initially included twenty-six stations, and within a year the Opry was being aired coast to coast on network radio.[20] The local and national radio exposure and the 4400 live studio-audience members each Saturday night combined to give extensive exposure to the cast members and to create a demand for personal appearances.

The structure was already in place to cope with this demand. In 1934 WSM had created its Artists' Service Department "to handle all personal appearances of WSM artists regardless of the type of work they did.[21] In 1939 this in-house booking agency was dealing mainly with Opry acts and was managed by David P. Stone, brother of WSM manager Harry Stone and the man who was with Hay when Monroe auditioned. The Artists' Service Department helped Opry performers promote their careers effectively by booking newcomers like Monroe in traveling tent shows. These were packages which included established stars with bands, single acts, comedians—all members of the Opry cast. Like the rural theater companies popular in earlier decades, they utilized large tents to solve the problem of where to put audiences that rural schoolhouses and small town halls could not hold. When combined with the radio coverage and the large Saturday-night audiences, this service made a position on the Opry attractive for performers like Monroe, even though the actual broadcast salary was (and remains) minimal.

1940–41

Monroe came to WSM with a well-rehearsed band of young men who had little or no previous experience as professionals. They were well received, and by the beginning of 1940 he was starting to get requests to do personal appearances. The first bookings were not very different from those he'd had while playing in Asheville and Greenville—fairly small places close to the station. But now he was being heard all over the southeast and beyond. Soon the Blue Grass Boys were playing in Alabama, Kentucky, West Virginia, and the Carolinas. When Cleo Davis left the band at the end of the summer of 1940 to go on his own with a radio station in Florida, Bill replaced him not with another raw recruit but with a seasoned veteran, Clyde Moody.

Born in Cherokee, North Carolina, of Indian and Scots-Irish parents, Moody had grown up in Art Wooten's home town of Marion. He became a professional musician at about the same time as Monroe, following several years' work as a baseball player in Asheville. He and Roy Hall's brother Jay Hugh Hall, calling themselves the Happy-Go-Lucky Boys, were sponsored by a chain of liquor stores in the Carolinas. In 1937 they joined Wade Mainer's Sons of the Mountaineers (Mainer and his brother J. E. had just split). For the next three years they played radio stations in the Carolinas and recorded for Bluebird. Moody and Hall continued to bill themselves as the Happy-Go-Lucky Boys while working with Mainer and even had one recording session in 1940 under this rubric. A few months later Moody and Hall parted company with Wade Mainer and went to work with brother J. E., who had kept the name of Mainer's Mountaineers and was also recording for Bluebird. After a few months with him at an Alabama radio station, Moody had a falling out with Hall and J. E. and returned to North Carolina, where he received an offer to join Bill Monroe's band.

Clyde Moody played guitar in a bluesy style, using a thumb pick and a finger pick on the index finger, as did Charlie Monroe. His most popular song, one he had already recorded (it was never issued), was "Six White Horses," a blues he'd arranged to a driving guitar riff backing. His mellow voice contrasted well with Monroe's higher tenor in duets. On the night of September 6, 1940, Moody joined the Blue Grass Boys in Bluefield, West Virginia. Amos Garen and Art Wooten had left; their replacements were, like Moody, also veterans. On the fiddle was Tommy Magness, a highly regarded fiddler who had been working with Roy Hall and his Blue Ridge Entertainers since 1938.

The showpiece in Magness's repertoire was a tune called "Orange Blossom Special," a very significant piece composed during the mid thirties in Jacksonville, Florida, by two young fiddlers, Robert R. ("Chubby") Wise and Ervin Rouse; later Rouse and his brother Jack wrote several verses for it. In a practice typical of the time, Wise gave his interest in the song to the Rouses,

who copyrighted it. Just how Magness learned the tune is not known. Cleo
Davis says that Magness got it from a record by the Rouses. But the Rouses
did not make this recording until June 1939, some seven months after Magness had recorded it with Roy Hall. Hall's recording was never issued because
the Rouses threatened the record company with legal action, wishing to have
first rights at recording the tune. Their 1939 recording was not widely distributed and, according to Rouse, was withdrawn from the market soon after it
was issued. But Magness continued to perform the song on radio and in
personal appearances. Art Wooten had learned it from Magness, so "Orange
Blossom Special" was already in the Blue Grass Boys' repertoire when Magness
joined them.

Also with Monroe when Moody joined was a bass player and comedian
named Willie Egbert Wesbrooks, who was known by the stage name of Cousin Wilbur. He'd been with Monroe for a little over a month. Son of share-
croppers from Gibson County, Tennessee, he had worked during the thirties
on medicine shows and carnivals as well as on a number of different radio
stations. In July 1940 he hit Nashville, approached Judge Hay about a job,
and was told Monroe was looking for a comedian. He was hired within the
week. Wilbur had a number of routines and featured comic singing, including
trick yodels. Like most comedians in country music he dressed for the part,
in a costume which featured ragged pants which ended just below the knees
and were held up by ancient suspenders and together by a giant safety pin.
He wore a little boy's cap, lensless glasses, and blacked-out teeth.

With this band—Moody, Magness, and Wesbrooks—Monroe made his first
records for Victor at the October 1940 Bluebird sessions in Atlanta. Brother
Charlie had recorded for Victor in 1939 but was not present at these sessions.
No doubt Bill's position on the Opry brought his band to the attention of
Victor. When he travelled to Atlanta he took Fiddling Arthur Smith with
him. Monroe recorded eight numbers, and his band backed Smith on eight
more, including one fiddle duet by Smith and Magness.

The session opened with Bill's version of "Mule Skinner Blues"; he played
guitar on this as he had on most of his vocal solos in the early months of the
Blue Grass Boys. They went on to record two duets, a gospel quartet, Moody's
"Six White Horses," and another Monroe solo on "Dog House Blues." The
session ended with two instrumentals, Monroe's "Tennessee Blues" and Magness's version of "Katy Hill." As "Mule Skinner Blues" was the prototypical
bluegrass vocal, so "Katy Hill" was the archetypal bluegrass fiddle piece.
Magness played this traditional dance tune at a pace few dancers could
follow. It was meant for show, in the same way the Monroe Brothers' WLS
dance sets were for the appreciation of connoisseurs of the form. This was
Monroe's first recorded statement, as it were, on playing the old-time tunes
the "right way," as he himself acknowledged: " 'Katy Hill' had more in it
when we recorded it than it ever had before. Those old-time fiddlers didn't
have nobody to shove them along. Now Tommy Magness had been playing

with Roy Hall and they were trying to play off of bluegrass. He'd heard the way we played when Art Wooten was with me so it was right down his alley to get somebody behind him with that, because that kind of little bow that he worked he could move you right along."[22]

How is Monroe's claim that Roy Hall was "trying to play off of bluegrass" to be interpreted? The term *bluegrass* was not in use at this time, so what he means is that Hall was copying or borrowing from his musical style. Although Hall's string band resembled Monroe's in instrumentation, it placed more emphasis upon the steel guitar (never used in Monroe's band) than on the fiddle. About the closest Hall came to Monroe was in a song recorded at Hall's October 1940 session in Atlanta—two days after the Monroe session— entitled "Loving You Too Well." It was an uptempo duet in waltz time which had the same melody as "No Letter in the Mail," one of the two duets Bill and Clyde Moody had just recorded. But Hall's big hit, recorded at the same session, was a slower song called "Don't Let Your Sweet Love Die." Records, of course, cannot be taken as the deciding evidence in questions such as this; perhaps it is sufficient to note that Monroe's "Orange Blossom Special" came via Hall and that there was an interchange of material in both directions. But Monroe's statement indicates his view towards such interchanges: whether copying, borrowing, or stealing, he viewed them with suspicion.

When Monroe made his first records in 1940, only a few Opry acts—most notably Roy Acuff—were appearing regularly on records. That a city like Nashville, with the Opry, was not itself a recording center showed how relatively unimportant records were to the country musicians of the time. But this was beginning to change. Once a month *Billboard,* the entertainment industry trade paper, published a list of "Hillbilly Record Hits"—four or five titles. In July 1940 George C. Biggar, then director of the WLW Cincinnati radio barn dance, "The Boone County Jamboree," and formerly with WLS, penned an apologia for the music, "The Case for Hillbillies," which appeared in *Billboard.*[23] Hillbilly radio shows like those of WLW, WLS, and WSM (regarded as the big three in the early forties) and personal appearances were big business; Biggar was telling the entertainment industry about the ins and outs of this new music boom. Records were not selling as they would in the post-war years, but they were useful for promotion. When the very first Blue Grass Boys single was released by Bluebird, "Mule Skinner Blues" was paired with Clyde Moody's "Six White Horses." Within a few months Clyde Moody had left Monroe, moving to radio station WBBB in Burlington, North Carolina, where he reactivated the Happy-Go-Lucky Boys, hiring Lester Flatt, a young mill worker who had been performing in the Roanoke region.

Monroe replaced Moody with a twenty-year-old lad from Mississippi who had also recorded for Bluebird in Atlanta the previous October, Pete Pyle. Pyle had been hired at the Opry on the strength of his recording contract, and soon he was part of Monroe's band. Pyle's position was unique, as he was also a solo member of the Opry cast: "I kept my solo spots on the Opry even though I worked with Bill on the road. Bill didn't sing too much at that time; he'd come in with "Mule Skinner Blues" every now and then and knock the house down."[24]

That summer Tommy Magness left the Blue Grass Boys, returning to Roy Hall. Art Wooten returned as fiddler and was with Cousin Wilbur, Pyle, and Monroe when Victor held their final pre-war southeastern recording sessions at Atlanta in October 1941. Pyle recorded again on his own as well as with Monroe. Because he was under exclusive contract as a singer with Victor, he was told by the company not to sing on Monroe's recordings.[25] The effect of this ruling shows the extent to which Bill relied upon the band to shape his repertoire. Two duets that he and Pyle had been working on could not be recorded as planned, and Cousin Wilbur had to take Pyle's place on a third, "In the Pines," the only duet recorded that day. The eight songs they recorded included several second choices in place of the two cancelled duets; there were two instrumentals and two quartets as well as pieces which featured Monroe, Cousin Wilbur, and Wooten.

Monroe sang "Blue Yodel Number 7," in an attempt to follow up his hit of the previous session with another Jimmie Rodgers song. Cousin Wilbur recorded his comedy showpiece, "The Coupon Song." Wooten fiddled "Orange Blossom Special," doing the talking parts while Monroe and Pyle sang the single verse in the middle. Also included on this recording was a dialogue between Wooten and the other band members:

WOOTEN: Coming right on down the line now, pulling up a heavy grade. Hey, Bill, where you gonna get off this train at?
MONROE: Down about Atlanta, Georgia, boy, where's you gwine?
WOOTEN: I'm going up about Nashville, Tennessee. Where you going, Cousin Wilbur?
WILBUR: I'm going down to Birmingham, Alabama.
WOOTEN: What for?
WILBUR: Ain't no ham like Birmingham!
WOOTEN: Pete, where you gonna get off?
PYLE: Well I'm Memphis bound believe.[26]

It is now difficult not to think of "Orange Blossom Special" as an overplayed tour de force banned at most high-toned fiddle contests, but in 1941 it was known only to the few that had purchased the Rouse Brothers record and to those who had heard it performed live by Rouse, Wise, Magness, or Wooten. As recorded by Monroe, it was a band showpiece. At the center was the fiddle, fast, accurate, and hot. In the middle was a verse of brother-style duet; and the dialogue, with its touch of comedy, alluded to the shows Monroe was putting on while at the same time introducing the Blue Grass Boys to the listener.

This session represents the first documented instance of a musical practice which the Blue Grass Boys were to follow for the next decade and a half—

tuning their instruments a half step above standard pitch. By stretching the strings tighter they achieved more volume, and a brighter sound, which seemed to better suit their vocals.

1942–45

By the time the first of Monroe's recordings from his second session had been released, the United States was at war. Military service interrupted or ended the careers of some of the most popular country performers, as well as many just getting started. The draft threatened to make it difficult for Monroe to maintain his band. First to go was Pete Pyle; he was replaced by Clyde Moody, returning to remain with Monroe for the next three years, senior member of the band—what George Hay called the "first lieutenant."

Bill had a new fiddler, too, a west Tennesseean named Howdy Forrester. Forrester was another veteran of the business, having started his professional career at WSM with the band of Herald Goodman. Formerly a member of the Vagabonds, Goodman had returned to the Opry in 1938 with a band which included twin harmony fiddles by Forrester and Georgia Slim Rutland—the first such combination heard on WSM, according to Forrester. By 1939 they had moved to Texas, and at the time of Pearl Harbor, Forrester was working on his own in San Antonio. In anticipation of being drafted he returned to Tennessee with his wife Wilene, a singer and accordionist. Early in 1942, he joined Monroe. Forrester, though from Tennessee, had by this point been schooled in Texas-style fiddling. When he arrived there in 1939, "we played a certain style and played right on the tune, the style that Georgia Slim and I played, but when we went into Texas and Oklahoma, those fellows actually scared the dickens out of me because they were reaching up into the second position and getting notes I'd never seen before. I looked at Slim and he looked at me and we said we'd better go to work here and do something— and we did. If you're in somebody's backyard, you'd better get a hoe just like he's got."[27]

This was the kind of fiddling Monroe most appreciated; Forrester, like Clayton McMichen (some of whose tunes he played), could do popular songs as well as the older fiddle tunes; also he was used to playing in non-standard keys. And he could approach the old traditional tunes from the Texas perspective of fiddlers like Benny Thomasson, an approach which placed high value on the ability to introduce substantial melodic variations into them. Although with Monroe for a comparatively short time, Forrester had quite an impact, setting a standard by which all subsequent bluegrass fiddlers would be measured.

By May 1942 Monroe's last Bluebird record was released. Wartime shortages of shellac and a dispute between the musician's union and the record companies which kept the major labels idle until 1945 were factors leading to Monroe's absence from the recording studio during the next two-and-a-half years. But his career was by no means quiescent. He was laying plans that summer to tour with an Opry tent show featuring one of the last minstrel acts in the business, a popular blackface duo named Jamup and Honey.

For this 1942 season Monroe added a fifth musician to his band, a tall lanky Kentuckian named David Akeman and known by the stage name of "String Beans" (later "Stringbean"). He played the five-string banjo in the old "clawhammer" (or "frailing") style and had been a professional singer and comedian since 1935. Cousin Wilbur, who had met Stringbean in 1939, says the banjoist came to Nashville looking for a job on the Opry and was hired by Monroe on his advice. Monroe says he wrote asking for a job and was hired: "Stringbean was the first banjo player with me. What I wanted was the sound of the banjo, because I'd heard it back in Kentucky, and I wanted it in with the fiddle and the rest of the instruments. So Stringbean gave us a touch of the banjo and he was a good comedian."[28] In August 1942 *Billboard* reported on Monroe's new comedy team: "Two of Bill Monroe's . . . Boys are striking out on their own to form a new act called String Beans and Cousin Wilbur. They'll be used with the Monroe crew on the Grand Old Opry program."[29] Cousin Wilbur says "he (Stringbean) would play the dead pan part and I would play the kind of smart alecky part. . . . We worked together for two years."[30] Though given separate billing on the Opry, they remained members of the Blue Grass Boys.

At the end of the 1942 season, as Bill was arranging for his own tent show the following summer, Howdy Forrester entered the Navy. Joining the band for the first time at this point was the co-composer of "Orange Blossom Special," Robert Russell (later "Chubby") Wise. He had been in Gainesville, Florida, playing with a radio dance band whose repertoire required him to play old traditional tunes, western swing, and pop songs. By mid-1942 his group had broken up:

> I was listening to the Grand Ole Opry one Saturday night . . . I heard
> Big Howdy Forrester with Bill Monroe and heard Bill announce Howdy
> had to go in the Navy and that would be his last night with them. That
> told me somethin'. I said "Bill's going to need a fiddle player." The next
> Monday I took the train to Nashville. I just sat around until the week-
> end. On Saturday night, I just threw my fiddle under my arm, went back
> stage—I told the man at the door, "My name's Wise, I'm from Florida,
> I've come to see Bill Monroe. I want to have a job. Now he's got to have
> a fiddle player and I'm a fiddler." . . . so he said, "Alright, he's in the
> dressing room."[31]

He played "Katy Hill" and "Footprints in the Snow" for Monroe and was hired on a trial basis, as "some doubt existed as to whether or not Chubby would adapt his western swing influenced fiddle to the Monroe sound."[32] During this period (1942–44) Monroe was occasionally carrying two fiddlers with the band so that he could break in the less experienced man on the job with a veteran. Among them, in addition to Wise, were Floyd Ethridge and Carl Story.

During the summer of 1943 Monroe organized his own tent show: "I went out with a fellow named Bill Whalley [Wehle] from Miami, Florida. He furnished the tent and I furnished the music." And in 1944 he purchased his own tent, having gained the experience and capital to run his own road show, which usually included not just the Blue Grass Boys but other performers as well. It was like an old-time minstrel show, or a circus or a carnival, and it hit town that way: "We had seven trucks and twenty-eight men working at first. We carried tent, bleachers, chairs, electric light and power, and a cook house. Later we cut it down to seven men. They could set it up in two and a half hours. And it didn't cost you a lot to put on a show in a town those days. Sixty-five dollars tops would cover newspaper ads, window cards, the license, everything."[33]

Notice that with his tent Monroe was not giving a concert but putting on a "show." What is meant by this term? The Monroe Brothers began their career on radio and in personal appearances as part of a show. As dancers for the National Barn Dance they shared the stage with male and female vocalists, comedians, quartets, fiddlers, and other specialized entertainers. The concept of the show had its roots in entertainment forms which were common in rural areas prior to the growth of radio- and record-oriented hillbilly music. Medicine shows, chautauquas, minstrel shows, traveling repertory theater, fiddlers' conventions—all involved a sequence of acts, with emphasis upon the variety of different performances. As country musicians became full-time professionals, they adopted the trappings of show business, fusing these forms into the "show," a kind of bucolic vaudeville. This form really came into its own during the mid-thirties, just as radio and the talkies were driving the traveling repertory theater tent shows and the urban-based vaudeville circuits out of business. As had happened with the minstrel show, an older form persisted in the hinterlands long after it had died out at the center.

The country show as it developed in the thirties did not "evolve" directly from any single earlier form. The show is best thought of as the dramatic equivalent of an idealized family "get-together." The total ensemble was symbolic of a small community or an extended family; to this day shows like "Hee Haw," the WWVA "World's Jamboree," and the Opry allow and even encourage performers to appear casually onstage; most shows of the thirties featured everyone on stage whether they were actively performing or not. They constituted an audience within an audience, a kind of framing device which suggested that the audience was viewing an old-time corn-shucking or evening of parlor entertainment. This emphasized the communal aspects of the show, projecting a feeling of onstage group solidarity. Another aspect of this practice of keeping the entire troupe onstage was that, dramatic considerations aside, there was often no backstage area to which they could retire.

Within this communal or extended-family aggregation were smaller identifiable units. There was the brother duet, symbolizing in its very form the
children of the nuclear family unit. The religious quartet reflected the close
ties between church, family, and community in most of the towns where the
show appeared, as well as the affirmation of coordinated small-group activities (like sports) by men. Solo singing by both male and female vocalists
highlighted the personalities found in any such aggregation. Fiddle tunes—
often in conjunction with a show square dance set or a step dancer—reflected
the role of the local fiddler, still well known as the communal provider of
music for dances. Finally there was the comedian, who acted out roles familiar not only on stage but also in real life—the foolish, blackfaced, stereotyped
"niggers" (who often played an instrument associated with Afro-American
music, the banjo), the eccentric uncle, silly cousin, old-fashioned grandpa,
or the "village idiot."

While the center of the show was the performance of the latest favorite
songs by the solo singers and duos, all of the other elements were considered
necessary to the success of the show. The Opry's "Tours" were tent shows
initiated in the mid-thirties. When Roy Acuff came to WSM in 1938, he
was popular enough to subsume most of the entire show cast in his own band;
he could afford to hire a band large enough to do most of the "show" itself.

Monroe's Blue Grass Boys followed the "show as band" and "band as show"
example of Acuff's Smoky Mountain Boys. Although the Blue Grass Boys
(particularly guitarists and fiddlers) reflected Monroe's special emphasis upon
musical style, the band's makeup—and musical sound—varied considerably
in the years between 1938 and 1945, including at different times a jug player,
a harmonica player, a tenor banjoist, and so on. It is probably not pure
coincidence that Stringbean, the comedian banjoist who joined Monroe in
1942, had a role similar to Rachel, the comedienne banjoist who had been
with Acuff since 1938 or that Monroe and Acuff both added accordion
players to their band during the war years when this instrument was popular
in country groups and featured by Pee Wee King, one of the Opry's most
successful bandleaders.[34] Monroe never used the Dobro steel guitar heard in
Acuff's band. But the important difference between the two groups was that
Acuff laid aside his fiddle to concentrate on the roles of star vocalist and
master of ceremonies, while Monroe placed less emphasis upon his solo
vocalizing and continued to work as a bandleader and instrumentalist, actively shaping and participating in the musical sound of the band.

Jim McReynolds was a teenager in the mountain town of Coeburn, Virginia, when he saw Bill Monroe and his Blue Grass Boys for the first time:

> Back in the early days at the Grand Ole Opry you never did hear too
> much about the different styles of music. It was all just Grand Ole Opry
> or hillbilly music. And at that time Bill Monroe, I guess, was one of the
> biggest draws on the Opry. And he worked more personal appearances,

that's for sure. They'd set up just a big tent. I don't know how many people it would seat. It was quite a large tent. And a usual thing that you couldn't even get people in. I know this Curley Bradshaw, he played harmonica. . . . Curley traveled with Bill for about two or three years, I think that Bradley Kincaid was on tour with him some time. And, but it was just more or less Bill's, you know. *Bill and all his Blue Grass Boys, what really drew the crowd.* And think Curley was telling one time that they stayed in Pikeville, Kentucky for two or three days, I think, but he said his last night they worked there that they just rolled up the sides of the tents and turned them in the ball park. Couldn't even get 'em into tents.[35]

Like baseball games, these tent shows were essentially outdoor events. Their flavor would be evoked by the bluegrass festivals that began in 1965 and became a national phenomenon in the seventies. But during the war years, gasoline rationing and restrictions on the use of automobiles for pleasure trips cut down on attendance at shows. Nevertheless Monroe, working tent shows in the rural southeast, was still able to attract large crowds. Some devised ingenious ways of getting around the travel restrictions, as this 1943 report indicates: "Playing Danville, Va., recently with a WSM Grand Ole Opry tent show, Bill Monroe and his Blue Grass Boys were surprised to see a farmer and his large family come rolling up to the tent in an old-fashioned farm wagon towed by a tractor. 'Gas rationing for pleasure cars has got us,' explained the Opry fan, 'but we can get plenty tractor gas, so we take an occasional holiday trip in our old wagon.' "[36]

By the following year, when Monroe was operating his own tent show, an Opry spokesman told a reporter that "there are no names with more drawing power than Roy Acuff, Bill Monroe, Jamup and Honey, Zeke Clements and Uncle Dave Macon, the headliners of the Grand Ole Opry."[37]

At about this time Monroe added a new dimension to his show, taking advantage of his love of baseball to reconstitute the band as a baseball team. While the crew setting up the tent show finished their job (they traveled in advance of the band), Monroe or one of the band members would issue a challenge to the local ball club. Fiddler Jim Shumate, with Monroe in 1944–45, recalls that "we had good crowds just for a ball game. We had a lot of fun. We played for keeps and had a good team. We had uniforms and everything. I played shortstop."[38] Former pro-ball player Clyde Moody pitched and Monroe, who would, but for his poor sight, "have liked to be a baseball player," recalled "I could hit good and could've been a fair player."[39] Other members of the band and the crew that worked on the tent also helped out on the baseball team. Not only was it an outlet for the band and crew, it was good show biz, for it attracted its own audience, including people who might not otherwise come to the show, thus creating additional revenue.

Although this aspect of Monroe's shows seems to have been unique in the country music of the time, there were other contemporary musical outfits doing the same thing. According to Cab Calloway's former band member Benny Payne, Calloway's was "the first of the big bands to have its own baseball . . . teams." As with Monroe, they played local semi-pro teams, and the idea was such a success that "a few years after we put a team together, Tommy Dorsey got one of his own, then some of the other bands, and it became a common thing. This was in the forties." Echoing Shumate's comment about the fun they had playing baseball, Payne adds that "having the team was good for our spirit; it helped to build morale in the band. Those road trips were sometimes as long as six months, . . . and it could get pretty wearing."[40]

Playing with the Blue Grass Boys was not a particularly high-paying job, but it was a good way of acquiring musical skills. All musicians who have worked for Monroe have commented on this aspect of the job. Bill had a way of working with his men like a coach to bring out the best in them. He always kept one or two veterans in the band if he could, but he seemed to enjoy having at least one "rookie" on the team. Within the Blue Grass Boys there was a hierarchy reflecting length of tenure, previous experience, and personal relationship with the bandleader. When Judge Hay called Clyde Moody Bill Monroe's "first lieutenant," he was alluding to Moody's position near the top of this hierarchy.

Being a Blue Grass Boy also made for good publicity. Monroe was now headlining shows with Bradley Kincaid, Uncle David Macon, DeFord Bailey, and others who had been well-known radio and record performers when Bill was still a dancer on WLS. With his popular show it was not difficult to keep a band together, because young musicians saw it as an opportunity for personal exposure. And every Saturday night when they were at WSM, Judge Hay ran the Opry in a way which ensured that members of the band could display their solo talents and be recognized for them. Stringbeans and Cousin Wilbur, Clyde Moody, and Pete Pyle all, at one time or another, had solo spots on the Opry while at the same time appearing with the Blue Grass Boys. And all of them eventually became cast members and left Monroe's group. Other members of the band were regularly identified by name on the Opry, by either Hay or Monroe.

Many performers passed through the ranks of Monroe's band during this period. Often there was more than one fiddler. Some musicians traveled with him on a trial basis. Others, living in Nashville, worked on a free-lance basis, available when needed. The vagaries of the music business, exaggerated by wartime uncertainty, created a high rate of turnover in personnel. Often seven days a week were spent on narrow roads in cramped auto seats, and men eventually tired of the rigorous life on the road. A call might come from a friend who had a position on a radio station where there was a chance for a good job with less travel. If Monroe was like a building contractor, his employees were in many ways like the construction workers. Their skills ranged from those of the apprentice to the master journeyman; accustomed to seasonal work patterns and individual career decisions, they came and went.

At the beginning Bill advertised in the paper and on the radio. By 1944 he had more efficient ways of acquiring new band members. One source was other band members; the veteran musicians like Clyde Moody and Cousin Wilbur knew others whom they would recommend or introduce to Bill. Another method was a sort of audition by radio; when traveling in the band vehicle, the "Blue Grass Special" (a converted airport limousine) his radio was frequently tuned to country music shows in the regions he was passing through. In this way, for example, he first heard Jimmy Shumate, the fiddler who joined his band in 1944. Frequently musicians would arrive unannounced at the Opry or at a show and ask for an audition, as with Chubby Wise. Monroe, covering thousands of miles a week, barely had time to stop and listen; gone were the long days of rehearsals. It was not just that he was too busy; he had more confidence in his own music, and he could count on musicians being familiar with it through his shows, broadcasts, and records.

Back to the Recording Studio

During the war years hillbilly music blossomed. On the West Coast Bob Wills was breaking the ballroom attendance records previously held by big-name swing bands. And cowboy singers like Tex Ritter and Gene Autry were also drawing SRO (Standing Room Only) crowds with their theater tours. Recordings like Al Dexter's "Pistol Packing Mama" were popular on juke boxes not just in rural areas of the South but also in the northern and urban markets which had previously been dominated by popular music.

A number of factors were involved. There were massive migrations of rural dwellers to urban centers for wartime jobs. These people brought their tastes with them and now had income which allowed them to indulge these tastes by consuming their favorite music on juke boxes, at shows, and on records. A large number of the men and women who went into the services either already liked this kind of music or were exposed to it and came to like it. The entertainment industry quickly perceived and responded to its popularity. As early as 1942 *Billboard* was running an occasional news column about this music. In July 1943 this became a weekly feature: "American Folk Tunes and Tunesters: Cowboy Songs, Hillbilly Tunes, Spirituals, etc." In January 1944 the first popularity chart, "Most Played Juke Box Folk Records," was instituted, as were reviews of new "folk" records.

Hillbilly ("folk") records, new or old, were selling well, particularly on juke boxes. Victor had reissued some of the most popular earlier hillbilly records, like Roy Hall's "Don't Let Your Sweet Love Die," which by early 1945 had sold over 100,000 copies, even though Hall was not around to promote it, having been killed in an auto accident in 1943. When the musicians' union recording ban ended late in 1944, the record companies eagerly sought new acts. In February 1945 Columbia's Art Satherly reported from Nashville that he had signed six Grand Ole Opry acts, including Bill Monroe and his Blue Grass Boys.[41] Monroe moved to Columbia because he wanted to be on a different label than his brother Charlie, who was to continue with Victor in the postwar years.

The band Monroe used at his February 1945 Columbia session included three veterans who had been with him during the past few years—String-bean, Chubby Wise, accordionist "Sally Ann" (Wilene Forrester). Clyde Moody and Cousin Wilbur had just left the band; their places were taken by Tex Willis and a bassist-comedian named Howard Watts, who used the stage name "Cedric Rainwater." Curley Bradshaw played second guitar. The banjo, accordion, and second guitar gave the band a fuller sound than that of the 1940–41 recordings.

Monroe performed four solos, including his own composition, "Kentucky Waltz," "Rocky Road Blues," and "Footprints in the Snow." Monroe had written the tune for "Kentucky Waltz" while he was still with Charlie and added words in 1939. During the early forties Clyde Moody, whose specialty was waltzes, had used it as a featured solo with the Blue Grass Boys. In Moody's absence Monroe performed "Kentucky Waltz" himself in a relatively low-pitched vocal with sedate fiddle and accordion backing. "Rocky Road Blues" had been given by Stringbean to Bill, who copyrighted it in his own name. Monroe frequently copyrighted songs composed or brought to the group by band members; this was a standard practice at the time. "Footprints in the Snow," was an old song Bill had reworked into his own and had been singing regularly since 1939. He sang one duet, "True Life Blues," with Willis. Written by Pete Pyle but copyrighted in Monroe's name, it included a banjo break by Stringbean, the first such usage on a Blue Grass Boys record.

In addition to two trios (Sally Ann sang tenor, Willis baritone, Monroe lead) which remained unissued until the late seventies, the session included an instrumental blues in the key of A, "Blue Grass Special," to which every-one in the band contributed a solo break, in the manner of contemporary jazz presentation. It lent the performance (which Monroe was later to char-acterize as a good dance piece) some of the same functions as "Orange Blossom Special" in showcasing the band members, stressing a balance of individual personalities with the togetherness of the band.

In 1945, not long after this recording session, Judge Hay wrote a short biography of Monroe for the souvenir book which was sold to Opry patrons, *A Story of the Grand Ole Opry.* "Bill Monroe and his Blue Grass Boys," said Hay, "are true representatives of our show."[42] Describing Monroe's 1939 audition, he set it in the context of the Opry's musical traditions, calling the show "one of the largest national centers for American folk music and homespun entertainment," and detailing the immense numbers of performers

who wrote or showed up for auditions, usually unsuccessful. Monroe, however, had given "a sample of folk music 'as she should be sung and played.' "

> There is that authentic wail in his high pitched voice that one hears in
> the country when Mother Nature sighs and retires for the night. His
> handling of "blues" numbers is stellar and his biggest hit to date is "The
> Mule Skinner Blues," during the rendition of which he hits the top of the
> barn. For several years his first lieutenant was Clyde Moody, from North
> Carolina, who is now doing a single act on the Opry . . . Bill's other boys
> have come and gone, but he maintains a good act, capable of filling any
> theater or auditorium you might mention this side of Madison Square
> Garden in New York and he could do well there with some help.[43]

In calling Monroe and his band an "act," Hay not only betrayed his show-
biz orientation (albeit "folk" and "homespun") but indicated the area in which
Monroe was considered an asset to the Opry; he was a good drawer of crowds.
As Jim McReynolds testified, people came to hear the music of the band, so
we know that Monroe's attention to the hiring of veteran journeymen and
the training of young apprentices had paid off. His repertoire, however, was
still in its formative stages. "Mule Skinner Blues," his first record, was his
only big hit to date.

Well known in the southeast, particularly in the highland areas, Monroe
received far less national publicity than other Opry stars of the time like
Ernest Tubb and Roy Acuff, who were by this time making movies in Hollywood. Part of this lack of acclaim can be attributed to regional rather than
national popularity, but it is also a result of the fact that he was not a featured
vocalist ("star") in the same way Acuff and Tubb were. Of the twenty-four
songs he recorded in 1940, 1941, and 1945, only seven were vocal solos. On
the remainder he was submerged in duets, trios, or quartets or represented by
his mandolin on instrumentals. But instrumentally the fiddle dominated the
sound of the band. Because he was not a featured vocalist (nor yet a prolific
songwriter), he didn't fit the media image of the popular musical star of the
time, hence he didn't receive much publicity.

It was not until the early fifties, when Decca tried to fit Monroe to the
nascent Nashville studio sound, that people in the country music business
began to see Monroe as a bandleader. Again the preconceptions of the people
who reported about this music are reflected; Bob Wills's band, with his horn
and fiddle sections, written arrangements, and dance orientation, was clearly
a country/western version of the popular music of the time, the big swing
band. Monroe, with four and five musicians playing string instruments and
playing in a concert rather than a dance context, had no clear parallel in the
popular music of the time and so received less attention. Moreover, because
he did not use the new electric instruments that were now becoming popular
in country music, his band did not seem particularly innovative to most
contemporary observers who were not following his music closely.

While the band's music was recognized by its audiences as exciting and new, the contents of the songs were for the most part conservative and old-fashioned. The love songs dealt with lost love, expressing despair. Marriage was described in terms of conflict, both humorous and serious. The blues expressed a sassy male viewpoint of hostility and independence; indeed in "Mule Skinner Blues" when Monroe sings "I'm going to town," Clyde Moody cries out, "Bring the ambulance, boys." There is toughness and fatalism about relationships with true love. The fiddle instrumentals are fast, furious—too fast for dancers. In contrast with some of the popular country songs of the period, such as "Pistol Packing Mama," these songs appealed mainly to rural listeners and dealt with older values. Thus within the spectrum of country music, Monroe's band was not viewed as being particularly different (even if the quality of music was high) and the songs were not unique. It was a good act, consistent; it drew the crowds. No one was calling it bluegrass.

Notes

1. James Rooney, *Bossmen*, p. 32.
2. Wayne Erbsen, "Cleo Davis," p. 30.
3. Erbsen, "Davis—Conclusion," p. 59.
4. Ibid.
5. Ibid., p. 60.
6. Monroe says he was "John Miller, from Asheville" (Rooney, p. 32). Davis identifies him as Tommy Millard from Canton, a small town a few miles from Asheville. This is the same Tom Millard, nicknamed "Snowball," who in 1944 had a group called the Blue Ridge Hillbillies on WWNC (Dick Spottswood, "Carl Sauceman," p. 13); his partner in 1944, Carl Sauceman, says Millard played on the Opry with Bill Monroe.
7. Robert Dixon and John Godrich, *Recording the Blues*, p. 85.
8. Dix Bruce, "An Interview with Bill Monroe," p. 21.
9. Erbsen, "Davis—Conclusion," p. 62.
10. Charles K. Wolfe, *The Grand Ole Opry*, pp. 17–19.
11. Ibid., p. 33.
12. Erbsen, "Davis—Conclusion," p. 63.
13. Ralph Rinzler, "Bill Monroe—'The Daddy of Blue Grass Music,'" p. 7.
14. Rooney, *Bossmen*, p. 33.
15. Erbsen, "Davis—Conclusion," p. 63.
16. Monroe's name first appears in the radio schedule of the Nashville *Tennesseean* for Saturday, Oct. 28, when he was listed for two fifteen-minute Opry segments beginning at 8:45 and 10:45. He was still playing those two segments six years later, as noted in Douglas B. Green, "The Grand Ole Opry, 1944–45," pp. 92-122.

17. Rooney, *Bossmen*, p. 34. However, this practice must have developed gradually, for none of Monroe's Victor Bluebird recordings of 1940 and 1941 were in unconventional keys: "No Letter in the Mail" is in F, but this key was a favorite in the Monroe Brothers repertoire.

18. Erbsen, "Davis—Conclusion," p. 63.

19. George D. Hay, *A Story of the Grand Ole Opry*, p. 27.

20. William R. McDaniel and Harold Seligman, *Grand Ole Opry*, p. 30.

21. Hay, *Story*, p. 23.

22. Rooney, *Bossmen*, pp. 35–36. Bluegrass fiddlers have used both short and long bow styles; frequently both approaches are used. A transcription of Magness's "Katy Hill" appears in Stacy Phillips and Kenny Kosek, *Bluegrass Fiddle Styles*, and the authors report of it: "At this tempo, Magness' bowing is impossible to decipher completely and it seems that, at times, he is barely keeping up" (p. 10).

23. *Billboard*, Apr. 13, 1940, pp. 12, 64.

24. Douglas B. Green, "Pete Pyle," p. 22.

25. While Pyle did not perform as a featured vocalist, in fact he did sing bass on the two quartets recorded and lead on one verse of "Orange Blossom Special."

26. Bill Monroe, "Orange Blossom Special."

27. Tex Logan, "Big Howdy! Howdy Forrester, Fiddler," p. 15.

28. Charles K. Wolfe, "String," p. 49. Doc Roberts recalled that Monroe had come to Lexington to hire Stringbean because of his talents as a baseball pitcher. Charles K. Wolfe, *Kentucky Country*, pp. 126–27.

29. *Billboard*, Aug. 29, 1942, p. 73.

30. Cousin Wilbur (Wesbrooks) with Barbara M. McLean and Sandra S. Grafton, *Everybody's Cousin*, p. 178.

31. Mike Carpenter and Don Kissil, "Chubby Wise . . . Sweet Fiddler from Florida," p. 10.

32. Ivan M. Tribe, "Chubby Wise," p. 11.

33. Rooney, *Bossmen*, p. 36.

34. But Monroe attributed his hiring of Wilene "Sally Ann" Forrester (after husband Howdy went into the Navy) to the memory of his mother's accordion playing, while Acuff hired his accordionist, Jimmy Riddle, while making a movie in Hollywood (*Billboard*, Oct. 9, 1943, p. 63).

35. Jim McReynolds, interview with author and Scott Hambly, Chicago, Ill. Feb. 5, 1966.

36. *Billboard*, Sept. 4, 1943, p. 64.

37. *Billboard*, Oct. 28, 1944, p. 345.

38. Wayne Erbsen, "Jim Shumate," p. 19.

39. Rooney, *Bossmen*, p. 56. See also Ivan M. Tribe and John W. Morris, "Clyde Moody," pp. 28, 31.

40. Cab Calloway and Bryant Rollins, *Of Minnie the Moocher and Me*, pp. 156, 158.

41. *Billboard*, July 24, 1943, p. 68; Jan. 8, 1944, p. 59; Feb. 2, 1945, p. 67; Feb. 24, 1945, p. 73.

42. Hay, *Story*, p. 5.

43. Ibid., p. 37.

Bibliographical Notes

The extent and nature of black-white exchanges and connections in the field of quartet singing are difficult to determine. Among the evidence is Merle Travis's testimony that the Brown's Ferry Four, a quartet he sang with in Cincinnati during the war years, turned to black quartet records by the Golden Gate Quartet and similar groups for their repertoire. See Mark Humphrey, "Interview: Merle Travis," p. 22. Tony Heilbut, in his history of black gospel music, *The Gospel Sound*, p. 40, stresses the popularity of quartets in the Carolinas. The Swanee River Boys, a white group from Chattanooga, tell of being mistaken for a black quartet by the Golden Gate Quartet (who'd listened to their broadcasts). See Wayne W. Daniel, " 'We Had to be Different to Survive,' " p. 62. For a history of the Golden Gate Quartet, see Peter A. Grendysa's liner notes to *The Golden Gate Quartet*. Information about black groups like the Four Knights and the Sons of the South, who performed on white country-music radio shows in the late thirties and early forties in the Carolinas, came to me through the courtesy of John Rumble of the Country Music Foundation, who uncovered this information through his oral history research. Finally, the story of Monroe's learning of "Walking in Jerusalem," mentioned in the previous chapter, is told by Ralph Rinzler and Alice Foster in the liner notes to *A Voice from on High*.

Arthur Smith's story is told by Charles Wolfe in "Fiddler's Dream." For information on Roy Hall, see Ivan Tribe, brochure to *Roy Hall and His Blue Ridge Entertainers*. Charlie Monroe's laxative and radio transcription businesses are detailed by David Freeman in his liner notes to *Charlie Monroe on the Noonday Jamboree* and Bill Vernon in the liner notes to *The Songs of Charlie Monroe*.

Recently Wayne Ledford, a North Carolina singer, told an interviewer that "Bill (Monroe) got that 'Muleskinner Blues' like I play it from me." See Frank Weston and Silvia Pitcher, " 'We Got a Few Old Songs That We Do,' " p. 7. The interview context in which these remarks are made is ambiguous, however, as is the reported date of learning—one year after Monroe recorded the song.

For additional information on Howdy Forrester, see Perry Harris and Howard Roberts, "Howard 'Big Howdy' Forrester," and Howdy Forrester, "Howdy Forrester Recalls." For information on Benny Thomasson, see chapter 8.

Carl Story's tenure with Monroe is reported by Ivan Tribe in "Carl Story," pp. 9–10. Don Rhodes also alludes to this part of Story's career in his "Carl Story," p. 8.

Roy Acuff's story is told by Elizabeth Schlappi in "Roy Acuff." Charles R. Townsend's *San Antonio Rose* is a biography of Bob Wills, a central figure in western swing. A useful survey of the genesis of this form is given by Bill C. Malone in *Country Music, U.S.A.*, pp. 171–83. A number of articles relating to this music have appeared in *Old Time Music* and the *JEMF Quarterly*.

The rural theater to which I refer at several points in this chapter has been described by Clifford Ashby in "Folk Theater in a Tent," and by Ashby and Suzanne DePauw May in *Trouping through Texas*. Often called "opera" to avoid the word *theater* (offensive to some fundamentalists), it came to be called "rag op'ry," a term which may have influenced George Hay's naming of the WSM show, though Hay does not mention this in his story. Several aspects of this genre—the frequent use of comedy, the holding of baseball games between members of the troupe and local players, and the use of tents—were carried over into the traveling country music shows of the thirties and forties.

Discographical Notes

The recordings made by Charlie Monroe in 1938 and 1939 are available on *Charlie Monroe's Boys*.

Bill Monroe's four recordings of "Mule Skinner Blues" include the Victor Bluebird recording from 1940, a 1950 "New Mule Skinner Blues" reissued on *Bill Monroe's Greatest Hits*, a 1970 version on *Bill Monroe's Country Music Hall of Fame*, and a live performance from 1973 on *Bean Blossom*.

Of the 1940–41 Monroe recordings mentioned in this chapter ("Mule Skinner Blues," "Six White Horses," "Dog House Blues," "Tennessee Blues," "Katy Hill," "No Letter in the Mail," "In the Pines," "Blue Yodel Number 7," "The Coupon Song," and "Orange Blossom Special"), all but "The Coupon Song" were reissued on *The Father of Bluegrass Music*.

The two Roy Hall songs, "Loving You Too Well" and "Don't Let Your Sweet Love Die," were reissued on *Roy Hall and His Blue Ridge Entertainers*. The Rouse Brothers' rare "Orange Blossom Special" was reissued on *The Railroad in Folksong*.

Of the songs from Monroe's in 1945 Columbia session, "Rocky Road Blues" was reissued on *Sixteen All-Time Greatest Hits*; "Kentucky Waltz," "True Life Blues" and "Blue Grass Special" are on *The Classic Bluegrass Recordings*, vol. 1; "Footprints in the Snow" is on *The Classic Bluegrass Recordings*, vol. 2.

Al Dexter's "Pistol Packin' Mama" was reissued on *The Smithsonian Collection of Classic Country Music*.

Chapter 3

From Sound to Genre:
1946–49

Bill Monroe and his Blue Grass Boys flourished during the postwar years. In personal appearances, he set attendance records, touring more frequently and farther from home. He played as far west as Oklahoma, as far north as Ontario, Canada, and he developed a strong following in the upper South and adjacent midwestern and mid-Atlantic states. His tours were enlivened by the baseball team which by 1949 had become so popular that he created a second club and was hiring professional players. His records were played frequently on juke boxes and sold well at record stores. His most popular songs were "covered" or copied by a host of other performers, including popular contemporaries like Pee Wee King and his Golden West Cowboys and venerable old-timers like Bradley Kincaid. He began these years with a band still remembered as his best, one which brought his musical ideals closer to realization than any previous band. Indeed the sound of this particular team of Blue Grass Boys was so popular and familiar that by 1948 other groups were copying it even when they were not playing Bills' songs.

The Blue Grass Boys, 1946–48

A key figure in Monroe's best-known band was guitarist, singer, and song-writer Lester Flatt, a native of Sparta, Tennessee. One year Bill's junior, Flatt had worked in textile mills in Tennessee and Virginia during the twenties and thirties. His radio career began at the end of the thirties and had included a brief partnership with Clyde Moody on a Burlington, North Carolina, station in 1941 when Clyde had left Monroe for a few months. Lester had also worked with Charlie Monroe in 1943 and 1944, playing mandolin and singing tenor. Exactly when he joined the Blue Grass Boys is uncertain. The date is often given as 1944 (Clyde Moody had left the band, remaining on the

Opry cast, in December), but Flatt was not present at Monroe's Columbia session in February 1945. He was definitely playing with the band by April 1945.

Flatt's guitar style was similar to that of Clyde Moody and Charlie Monroe in that he wore a thumb pick and a finger pick on the index finger to create a brushing effect alternating with the bass notes and downstrokes on the higher strings. Flatt's guitar work was smoother, more syncopated than Charlie's; he used more open-string chords and bass runs than Moody. The very fast tempo of many of Monroe's songs forced Flatt to use these runs as a means of catching up at the end of phrases. One such run, heard at the close of virtually every verse which Flatt and Monroe sang, was used so often it became known among bluegrass enthusiasts as "the Lester Flatt G run." In fact this ascending phrase which ended on the tonic was a variation of a commonplace phrase in much of American popular music. It had been used by a number of country guitarists—including Charlie Monroe. Bill Monroe had played it on his recording of "Mule Skinner Blues."

Flatt sang solo lead on more Monroe recordings than any other guitarist before or after him. After Flatt left the band, Monroe took to singing lead on the verse and shifting to tenor on the chorus, so that the lead singer-guitarist's voice was rarely heard in solo. Flatt has the distinction of being the *only* lead singer (other than Monroe's son James) ever listed on the labels of Monroe's singles. The vocal blend which Monroe and Flatt achieved in their duets was striking. Lester's mellow lead complemented Bill's sharp, clear tenor. Monroe's tenor harmony arrangements moved from paralleling the melody toward a separate melody line, with unexpected intervals and leaps which gave the music added excitement.

Howard Watts, the bass player and comedian who used the stage name Cedric Rainwater, joined Monroe in 1944 after Cousin Wilbur left. Rainwater did comedy routines with Stringbean during the 1945 season. He apparently came and left the band several times during the following years. He participated in the seminal recording sessions of 1946 and 1947, contributing at least one song to the band's repertoire. He was later to play with Hank Williams's band and became one of the most-recorded Nashville studio musicians during the early fifties. He sometimes sang bass or baritone parts but is today remembered chiefly for his fine string bass playing. His frequent use of the four-beats-to-the-measure walking-bass technique (which was common in the hillbilly and popular music of the period) helped to underpin the rhythm of the band, particularly on the slow- and medium-tempo numbers. This approach influenced several of the most respected later bluegrass bassists, particularly George Shuffler and Tom Gray.

Because he appeared on all of the records which this influential band made, Chubby Wise gained the reputation of establishing high standards for bluegrass fiddling. It is more accurate to say that he maintained those established by Art Wooten, Tommy Magness, and Howdy Forrester, although he also contributed a distinctive style of melodic interpretation. And Wise himself acknowledges Monroe's strong role in developing his driving bluegrass fiddle work. Along with this came a smoothness and richness of tone (he used more vibrato than most fiddlers, a legacy from playing pop music with his early Florida band) unequaled by any of the others. He could also provide the jazzy hot fiddle breaks that were now the style in country music, as well as the older tunes like "Katy Hill" and "Boil Them Cabbage Down."

In September 1945 Stringbean had left Monroe, teaming up with Lew Childre in a comedy act. Monroe did not immediately replace Stringbean, but later in the year he found a new banjo player, a young man who was not a comedian. Twenty-one-year-old Earl Scruggs from Cleveland County in the North Carolina Piedmont had played with local groups in the late thirties and while still a teenager had worked for a few months with the Morris Brothers, a popular band in the region. During the war years he had worked at a textile mill, supporting his widowed mother. After draft restrictions were lifted he had gone back to music, traveling with a local band to audition at WNOX in Knoxville; the band had not been hired, but one of the other bandleaders on the station, Lost John Miller, heard Scruggs and hired him. Miller and his band, the Allied Kentuckians, played not only in Knoxville; they also had a weekly radio show on WSM in Nashville. During their visits to Nashville Scruggs ran into Bill Monroe's fiddler, Jim Shumate, a North Carolinian who knew him from back home and thought highly of his banjo picking. Shumate enthusiastically urged Scruggs to audition with Monroe.

Scruggs was reluctant. This was his best job to date and he didn't want to gain a reputation as a drifter, someone who would jump from one outfit to another at the drop of a hat. Besides, he was helping to support his mother and didn't want to take any risks with something that might not pan out. But a few months later when Lost John Miller decided to stop working on the road and Scruggs was in need of a job, he called Shumate and an audition with Monroe was arranged.

Lester Flatt's reaction to this was not very positive. He had liked Stringbean as in individual and a showman, but he felt the lanky comedian could not keep up with the Blue Grass Boys' fast tempos. He hoped Bill wouldn't hire another banjoist. Scruggs remembers playing two tunes: "One was 'Sally Gooden' [sic] which was an oldtime tune that I knew he [Monroe] could relate to because I'd heard him play it with fiddle players. Then I thought I would go to the extreme with something that he possibly never heard tell of before on the banjo. And that was 'Dear Old Dixie.' "[1] Lester Flatt, who had been skeptical about hiring another banjo picker, was "just dumb-founded. I had never heard anybody pick a banjo like he did. He could go all over the neck and do things you just couldn't hardly believe. Bill said, 'What do you think?' and I said if you can hire him, get him whatever it costs."[2] Monroe asked Scruggs to play with him on his next Opry broadcast, and after that arrangements were made for him to join the band the following week. According to Scruggs, "He never did say 'You can have the job' "; it was understood that he was hired.[3]

Monroe liked the sound of the five-string banjo but had definite ideas about how he wanted it to fit in his band. He had worked with Stringbean to alter his style from the old minstrel brushing style (known variously as drop-thumb, frailing, framming, clawhammer, etc.) to the two-finger, Wade Mainer–type picking style heard on Monroe's 1945 recordings. Bill saw how Scruggs could fit into the band in a similar way. However, in the hands of the young North Carolinian the five-string banjo was not just an occasional lead instrument but a versatile country music lead instrument like the fiddle. Scruggs took breaks on a wide variety of songs—slow waltzes, blues, medium tempo duets, fast breakdowns.

Scruggs had developed his three-finger (thumb, index, middle) picking style from a technique indigenous to western North Carolina (though found occasionally in other regions as well). Dewitt "Snuffy" Jenkins, a banjo picker and comedian who had worked for Byron Parker's Hillbillies on WIS in Charlotte since 1937, used this technique to play lead breaks on fiddle tunes and breakdowns as well as on slower songs. During the same period Wade Mainer was also playing lead in a two-finger style which sounded similar. In addition there were a number of other lesser-known three-finger banjo pickers active in the region during the late thirties and early forties, and in recent years these musicians—men like Hoke Jenkins, Johnny Whisnant, Wiley Birchfield, and others—have been singled out as prototypical bluegrass banjoists. Don Reno, who like Scruggs had listened to Snuffy Jenkins and worked with the Morris Brothers, tells of being taken to Bill Monroe for an audition in 1943 by Clyde Moody; offered a job by Monroe, he declined because of impending Army duty (he followed Scruggs in Monroe's band). This and similar narratives by other banjo pickers reflect their envy of the impact which Scruggs had at this time. His banjo solos on the Opry in 1945–48 made him a star country music instrumentalist virtually overnight. Scruggs did for the banjo what Clayton McMichen, Arthur Smith, and Curly Fox had done for the fiddle, creating a technique and a repertoire. And he made his style of banjo a permanent part of Monroe's sound.

With the band at the time of Scruggs's audition were Flatt, Shumate, Sally Ann Forrester, tenor banjoist-comedian Jim Andrews, and Monroe. By the following week Monroe had a different fiddler: Howdy Forrester had returned from the Navy and, in accordance with draft regulations, had been given his old job back. So Shumate, who had played an important role in bringing Scruggs to Monroe, did not work with Earl in the Blue Grass Boys. Forrester stayed with the band until the end of the year, and then he and his wife left for Texas. Andrews too did not remain long in the band. By the beginning of the 1946 season Chubby Wise and Cedric Rainwater were back.

1946

On September 7, 1946, *Billboard* magazine published the following report: "Bill Monroe and His Blue Grass Boys are on a successful tour thru Ohio, West Virginia and Pennsylvania. Bill's show is composed of Cubby [sic] Wise, fiddle; Lester Flat [sic], singer and guitarist; Earl Scruggs, mandolin [sic], and Cedric Rainwater, comedian, who also plays bass and dances."[4] They had just finished a summer of non-stop touring and the following week would be in Chicago to record twelve songs, Monroe's biggest recording session to date.

During the summer of 1946 Bill was exploiting the success of his first Columbia record. "Kentucky Waltz" had been released in January. In March it appeared on *Billboard*'s "Most-Played Juke Box Folk Records" chart in the number six position and was on this chart five more times in the next two months, reaching number three. At the end of the year *Billboard* ranked it number twenty-three overall in this category. "Kentucky Waltz," the first song Monroe had composed, was thus also his first "hit" in terms of publicly documented sales, though "Mule Skinner Blues" seems also to have been a best-seller. When "Mule Skinner" had appeared in 1940, *Billboard* was not tabulating juke box plays and sales for such music. Now, as this music was consolidating the gains made during the war years, statistics were being kept. Hillbilly records were big business.

With the war's end had come new record companies. These independents, as they were called, were located in virtually every large urban center in the country, and almost all of them established hillbilly series, attracted to the music because of the popularity of "folk" recordings on the juke boxes. Because Monroe was recording for Columbia, a "major" label, he had the benefit of greater exposure and better distribution. But the independents were quick to cash in on the popularity of his "Kentucky Waltz" with their versions ("covers") of the song. The first was Cincinnati's King Records, whose cover by Cowboy Copas appeared in January 1947. In the next fourteen months covers of the song appeared on labels such as Majestic (Eddie Dean), Continental (Jimmy Hinchee) and Flint (J. Day) as well as on another of the major labels in the form of Pee Wee King's Victor recording. And the song set a fashion for waltzes: Clyde Moody, who had featured "Kentucky Waltz" when he was with Bill, now wrote and recorded the "Shenandoah Waltz," and Pee Wee King (with Redd Stewart) wrote and recorded his "Tennessee Waltz." Though the "Kentucky Waltz" was not a giant hit, it was a respectable one which did much to establish Monroe's stature as a composer and performer in the burgeoning post-war "folk" music marketplace. It would have further commercial life when revived by Eddy Arnold in 1951 (seven covers were recorded then, including one by Monroe) and stands as Monroe's biggest record success.

The practice of making covers of hit songs was well established in the popular music field, where it was standard music-publishing practice to place a song with several performers. Publishers encouraged this because they believed that various performers having different styles would sell to different audiences, leading to greater sales. The pop recording industry assumed that the song was more important than the performer and that it was beneficial for the company to have their artists recording the proven sellers. With the growth of BMI (Broadcast Music Incorporated) as the clearing house for country music publishing royalties during the forties, covers became fashionable with country music performers. BMI promoted Monroe's composition, which is why it was covered by other singers. Monroe encouraged others to record his song as well.

His next Columbia record was "Footprints in the Snow," released in October 1946. It was on the the same *Billboard* juke box chart during December and January, when it appeared four times in the number five slot. It did not have as many covers as "Kentucky Waltz" but probably inspired WLS pioneer Bradley Kincaid, who was on the Opry at the time and had been working shows with Monroe, to record his own more traditional version of the song for Majestic Records, a New York independent.[5]

"Kentucky Waltz" and "Footprints in the Snow," along with "Mule Skinner Blues" (which Victor re-released in October 1948 with "reissued by popular request" on the label) established Monroe as a singer of "folk" (previously "hillbilly," soon to be "country and western") hit tunes. All three were vocal solos by Monroe in which the fiddle alternated with the vocalist. In these performances Monroe's sound was typical of the period. The band was subordinated to the singer; accordion was heard on two of the three; a banjo was audible in one; the mandolin was heard on two; and a string bass and guitar were present throughout. This was not a particularly special sound. The musicians who had played on these recordings were (with the exception of Wise and Rainwater) no longer with the Blue Grass Boys when the records were issued.

During 1946 Monroe was working with members of his band on new material. Earl Scruggs's banjo playing was novel; he could play the melody on the banjo in a way never before heard. And he had the speed that Monroe required. On the road, Earl recalls, Monroe began trying new tunes with him: "Bill had a four-seat, stretched-out 1941 Chevrolet limousine, and he and I would sit in the back seat while traveling and go over some of the old songs Bill knew but didn't use in his show, like "Molly and Tenbrooks" and "Little Joe" and some of those songs. We'd ride a lot of nights after a show, going to another gig, and sit back there and pick. He was writing some new songs, Lester was writing some new songs, and I was helping."[6] Recordings made from Opry broadcasts during this period give a good picture of what was happening. On March 23, 1946, Monroe sang "Little Maggie," a traditional

mountain lyric associated with North Carolina fiddler Steve Ledford. He
sang it fast, and between every verse Earl picked a solo. Behind one of these
Bill can be heard shouting, "That's right!" The sound was infectious; their
Opry performances of "Little Joe," "My Dixie Home," "Careless Love" and
"Molly and Tenbrooks" followed the same pattern of breakneck pace and
alternation of vocal and banjo. Judge Hay took to introducing them with
"Here's Earl and Bill . . . " or just "Earl Scruggs and his fancy banjo . . . "
And more often than not Earl's solos brought down the house. Although
there were other banjo pickers who had a style similar to Earl's, most people
had never heard the five-string played this way. Scruggs recalls that "when I
started here no one had heard the three-finger style before. People would
gather around me like I was a freak almost."[7] And certainly no one had heard
the style played with such virtuosity. The impact of Scruggs in Monroe's band
cannot be overstated; but he was not the only factor in the popularity of the
group at this time.

As Earl says, Lester and Bill were writing songs; in September 1946 two of
the twelve songs they recorded bore Lester's name as co-author with Bill's:
"Why Did You Wander" and "Will You Be Loving Another Man." In fact they
were Lester's compositions in which Bill shared the copyright, common practice with band leaders at that time. Monroe says of a third, "Mother's Only
Sleeping": "Lester Flatt brought this one to me. He put it in both our names,
but it was the first time I'd ever heard it. We used to share some songs that
way; when he first came to work with me he thought it was the most wonderful thing in the world that I could get advance money for him from BMI."[8]
Bill and Lester and Earl were rehearsing such songs and playing them on the
radio and at shows before recording them.

This may explain why two other performers recorded "Mother's Only
Sleeping" in 1946. One might call these recordings "covers" except that,
unlike "Kentucky Waltz" and "Footprints," Monroe's version was not the first
one released but the last. And while the three versions are musically similar,
featuring duet singing with prominent guitar and and mandolin backing,
there is almost no commonality between their verses. Textually they share
only the chorus (even here there is some variation). The first release, by
J. E. Mainer's Mountaineers, was issued by King in July 1946. Bill and Lester
did their version for Columbia in mid-September; two weeks later Bill's
brother Charlie, singing with Curly Seckler, recorded it for Victor. Charlie's
recording was issued (as "Mother's Not Dead, She's Only Sleeping") in December, and Bill's the following March.

Late in 1947 a fourth recording was issued on the Majestic label. Sung by
Mel and Stan Hankinson, the Kentucky Twins, who had been touring with
Bill Monroe, it most resembled Mainer's version but added a unique third
verse. That every recording of the song differed from the others suggests that
all—including Flatt's—derived from some earlier version. But I have been

unable to find any evidence for this save a recent comment by Earl Scruggs that he recalled Lester saying that the song was performed by a duet who had worked with Charlie Monroe while he was in the Carolinas in the early forties.

"Mother's Only Sleeping" is an early example of a process that was just beginning in 1946—the copying of Monroe's material more on a stylistic basis than as a simple cover of the song. With covers the text and tune of the song were shaped to the style or sound of each performer making the record- ing. Here we have the Monroe "sound"—a duet with prominent guitar and mandolin—even though the text is not closely copied. Monroe's response to these recordings at the time is not documented.

Flatt and Scruggs recorded twenty-eight songs with Monroe in 1946 and 1947. Only six, including "Mother's Only Sleeping" and "Blue Moon of Kentucky," a new waltz meant to exploit the success of "Kentucky Waltz," were issued while they were still with the band. But the available documents (home recordings, a songbook) show that a large proportion of the material which the Blue Grass Boys were marketing in person and on the air was not recorded or, if recorded, was not yet released. What is the explanation for this?

During the war years Monroe had not recorded, and he, like most profes- sional musicians of the period, was obliged to include material not on record in his broadcasts and personal appearances. Monroe had always paid rela- tively little attention to recordings. For him a career had not seemed to depend upon them. Now country record sales were burgeoning. Disc jockeys were becoming important. Emphasis was gradually shifting from the live show by the local radio station's staff musicians to the *record* "hits" as sung by the "stars." The growth of this hit-star system in country music put pressure on local radio stations; there were not enough stars to go around, and the live daily shows and weekend jamborees were beginning to lose listeners to the d.j. shows. Only a few stations were able to overcome this trend, most notably WSM, whose Opry enjoyed the benefits of national network broad- casts. Understanding the importance of the hit-star concept, WSM began hiring singers with hit records and regularly booked touring stars with hits for guest appearances. Prior station policy had been simply to hire enough per- sonnel to afford a well-balanced show. Now more attention was being paid to the drawing power of individual singers. This policy and the appearance of independent record companies like Bullet in Nashville presaged the growth of that city as a country music center. Monroe was well situated to take advantage of these changes.

But ever the conservative, Bill paid much more attention to his shows than to his recordings, and the live performance repertoire of his band was meant to put across the show. On shows and broadcasts Lester Flatt not only sang solo lead on duets, he did solos on songs he'd composed as well as popular hits of other country singers. And he did much of the emcee work, too. Earl Scruggs contributed banjo solos and his up-tempo accompaniments to Bill's songs, Chubby Wise played fiddle showpieces and driving or jazzy breaks in songs, and Cedric Rainwater had comic songs and routines. Each individual band member was given an opportunity to step into the spotlight, while the gospel quartet singing underscored the solidarity of the group, as did their musical interplay on the many songs where each instrument took its turn. Nevertheless, the popularity of "Kentucky Waltz," "Mule Skinner Blues," and "Footprints in the Snow" gave Monroe hits and secured his reputation as a star.

While his hits undoubtedly drew people to his show, which was indeed popular, many were listening quite closely to the band as a whole, tuning into the integrated sound of a group of musicians who had become, through force of habit and long days on the road together, not just a troupe but a tight unit. Those who had been listening regularly to Monroe noticed a difference. Curly Seckler, a singer and mandolinist who would eventually work with many bluegrass groups (most notably that of Flatt and Scruggs), remembers how people in his North Carolina home commented: "in China Grove, everybody was saying, 'What has happened to Bill Monroe's music? It don't sound like it used to.' "[9] And young musicians who had never paid much attention to Monroe were listening carefully.

1947

In March 1947 *Billboard* reported that Bill Monroe had just returned from a tour of Ohio with Jamup and Honey, Grandpa Jones, and the York Brothers: "At Dayton more than 4000 saw them in two performances, for what local residents said was the biggest crowd in history. At Akron, the SRO sign was out again, as for the first time since the building of the Armory, a folk music act packed in more than 3,000 a show with still others left outside the door."[10] Among those in the crowd at Dayton was fifteen-year-old Bobby Osborne. Born in Hyden, Kentucky, he had come with his family to Dayton during the war when his father took a job at the National Cash Register plant. Bobby's father played the old-time, five-string banjo and sang some Jimmie Rodgers songs around the house; his mother's brother played guitar in the style of Merle Travis with a local hillbilly band.

> At that time, Ernest Tubb . . . was my favorite. I tried to sing like him but when I was about sixteen my voice changed and I had to take to something else. And that something else was old man Monroe. I used to listen to Bill back on the Opry. The first time I ever paid any attention to him was about in 1945 or 46. I didn't even know what Bill played. I never had any idea he played the mandolin. I didn't even know what it

[mandolin] was. But I was under the impression Monroe played the fiddle until I saw him in person in 1947 . . . . About '47 I really got to listening to Bill and . . . I got to singing Bill's songs and playing the guitar and I had me a thumb pick and a finger pick—I seen Flatt play with one of them so I got me a thumb pick.[11]

Bobby Osborne's "conversion" is typical of that of many young men of his background and age who were attracted to Bill Monroe and the Blue Grass Boys.

In April 1947 the Opry reported that Monroe was gearing up his tent show for the summer season, and by June he was again working in the midwest with Jamup and Honey, Grandpa Jones, and the York Brothers, this time with shows in Detroit, neighboring communities in Michigan, and southern Ontario. By August he was touring the Carolinas and then "moving into Tennessee, West Virginia and Virginia."[12] At the end of October, with news of another recording boycott set to begin in 1948, the Blue Grass Boys were back in Chicago for another recording session. This time they cut sixteen tunes, including the banjo-oriented instrumental "Blue Grass Breakdown," "Molly and Tenbrooks," five quartets, six Flatt-Monroe duets, one trio, and two other Monroe solos.

Not long after this session Peer International published *Bill Monroe's Grand Ole Opry WSM Song Folio No. 2* which, in an introduction by Monroe's agent at that time, Gene Dudley, described the band as it was near the end of 1947:

Bill Monroe came to the Grand Ole Opry eight years ago . . . . He has fast risen to be one of the top stars on WSM. He is heard over the Grand Ole Opry every Saturday night, besides his early morning programs. He has a band known as the Blue Grass Boys on the air and on personal appearances, which is backing him. They consist of Lester Flatt from way up in the Cumberland Mountains, who has his own style of singing solos. Lester plays a guitar and also sings duets with Bill. Next we have Chubby Wise, the Swanee River Fiddle Player, who hails from Lake City, Florida and plays top fiddle. Also Earl Scruggs, the boy from North Carolina, who makes the banjo talk. And last, but not least, comes Chick Stripling, who we think is one of the finest comedians in the country. Besides the Blue Grass Boys, there is the famous Blue Grass Quartet, which consists of Bill, Lester, and Earl, and last but not least, Bill's brother, Birch, who sings bass.[13]

This was the last time a Monroe band would be described in such detail for over a decade and a half. Notice that Rainwater was not with the band at the time, though he had recorded only a short time before; his place was taken by veteran Georgia fiddler and comic Stripling, who was with the band only a few months.

1948

At the beginning of 1948 Monroe was working in Virginia and West Virginia. On January 25th disc jockey Al Rogers of WSAZ in Huntington booked a Hillbilly Hay Ride at the City Auditorium which was broadcast over WSAZ and featured, in addition to Rogers's own group, "Bill Monroe and his Blue Grass Boys, Bradley Kincaid, the Blue Grass Quartet." *Billboard* called it "the biggest folk show ever to hit that city."[14] This was one of the last shows Lester, Earl, Cedric, and Chubby were to play with Monroe.

The first to leave was Chubby Wise. He had gotten a job, along with Clyde Moody, working for Washington, D.C., area entrepreneur Connie B. Gay at Gay's radio station WARL in Arlington, Virginia. They began their broadcasting on the first of February. Benny Martin, a nineteen-year-old from Sparta, Tennessee, who had been working at WLAC, another Nashville station, took Chubby's place as fiddler with the Blue Grass Boys. Martin worked only a few weeks with the other veteran members of the band, for they, like Wise, had given their notice to Monroe that they were leaving.

There are no contemporary written reports concerning the events which led up to Flatt and Scruggs leaving the Blue Grass Boys. In retrospect it was one of the most significant events in the history of bluegrass music, but only in recent years has the testimony of the participants become public. As is so often the case with oral history relating to sensitive events, what is unsaid is as important as what is said. Monroe himself has consistently downplayed the event by placing the departure of his two star band members in the context of regular band turnover: they had their good points, he says, but then others came along who had *their* good points, and so forth. Yet by his actions at the time and in the years following Monroe made it clear that he was angered by their leaving.

Scruggs was the first to come forth in print about leaving Monroe, in his 1968 book, *Earl Scruggs and the Five-String Banjo* (New York: Peer International). He said that he had decided to quit because after years of grueling travel, he was tired. And he wanted to return home, find a job, and look after his aging mother. That the "job" might be musical was a possibility he did not rule out. Scruggs says the day he left Monroe, Flatt gave his two weeks notice.

Flatt's story, told in a 1971 interview, resembles Scruggs's but adds some new details:

Bill might have always had the feeling that we had planned it, but actually we hadn't. . . . I had made up in my mind to quit I hadn't said

anything about it. Earl was going to go home just to get off the road.
. . . After Earl turned his notice in to Bill . . . I told him I was going to
quit, too. We decided we might go to Knoxville and work as a team or go
to work with Carl Story or some group that might need us. I turned in my
notice then and before my notice was up, fellows like Cedric Rainwater
said, "Let me join in with you and we'll form a band."[15]

Recently, a somewhat different account of Flatt and Scruggs's final days
with Monroe was given by Jake Lambert, Flatt's long-time friend and biographer. It is an explanation which makes sense and helps explain Monroe's
attitude about the event.

> Flatt and Scruggs, as well as the rest of the boys, were making about sixty
> dollars a week, and that wasn't bad money, with the exception of the
> long hours. Lester Flatt did the MC work on all the shows, while Earl
> took care of the money. Earl was the only one in the group that had a
> high school education. Earl told me that on many Saturdays, when the
> Blue Grass Boys rolled into Nashville, he would be carrying from five to
> seven thousand dollars. So, both Flatt and Scruggs could see where the
> money was. They knew it would never be made as "side men" but as the
> "star," or leader. Monroe was making all the money, yet he was doing less
> work than the side men.[16]

According to Lambert, Flatt and Scruggs met together during a few days that
Monroe had given them off from the band at Christmas. It was at this time
that they decided to go out on their own: "Flatt had saved a little money and
he would put this up to get them started." Cedric Rainwater sat in on their
planning meetings and decided to go with them. "The last of January, Lester,
Earl, and Howard Watts all gave Monroe their notice. They would be leaving
in a couple of weeks. Monroe was furious, but the boys had made their minds
up. In a few weeks they departed Nashville and headed East. . . ."[17] Monroe
had previously had the experience of band members leaving him to strike out
on their own. But he had never had most of the band leave and go into direct
competition with him. It was particularly galling to have so much of the
show—a "first lieutenant" like Flatt, a hot instrumentalist like Scruggs, and
a comedian like Rainwater—move en bloc to another group. As we will see,
he did not like it, and as Flatt noted in 1971, he assumed (correctly, it seems)
they had planned the whole thing.

Monroe responded to the impact of Flatt and Scruggs's departure in several
ways. At the time, Bill's touring and Opry obligations remained, and he was
left with only his fiddler, Benny Martin. The first response, then, was to
assemble a new band quickly. Scruggs's place was taken by Don Reno, Flatt's
by Jackie Phelps, and Rainwater's by Joel Price. The new version of the Blue
Grass Boys had been together at least a month before Flatt, Scruggs, and
Rainwater began playing with Jim Eanes on a station in Danville, Virginia.

Fiddler Jim Shumate soon joined them. Within a week Eanes was hired by Monroe, and Flatt, Scruggs, Rainwater, and Shumate moved to Shumate's home town of Hickory, North Carolina. They spent a month playing on the station there. Then in May they moved to WCYB in Bristol, on the Tennessee-Virginia border, where a fifth band member was added, guitarist-tenor singer Mac Wiseman. Wiseman had worked with his own band on WCYB in 1947 and was already becoming known for his high, clear singing style. Their new band was called Lester Flatt, Earl Scruggs, and the Foggy Mountain Boys; four of the five band members were former Blue Grass Boys.

Mountain Radio and the Stanley Brothers

Just as many new record companies appeared in the immediate post-war years, there were many new radio stations. WCYB had opened its doors in December 1946. Though it was only a 5000-watt station, it had a clear broadcasting channel which gave it excellent coverage: it reached listeners in the mountain regions of Tennessee, North Carolina, Virginia, West Virginia, and Kentucky. Prior to going on the air the station auditioned some thirty-five different "rustic string bands" before hiring Curly King and the Tennessee Hilltoppers, and the Stanley Brothers and the Clinch Mountain Boys.[18]

The Stanley Brothers, from Dickenson County, Virginia, were guitarist and lead singer Carter and banjoist and tenor vocalist Ralph, both young war veterans who were embarking on a country music career. A key figure in this group of mountain boys, which had begun its career on Norton, Virginia, radio station WNVA, was Darrell ("Pee Wee") Lambert, a native of Mingo County, West Virginia. Since the early forties (with an interruption for army service) Lambert and Carter Stanley had been playing with the band of Roy Sykes in Norton. Sykes recalled in 1979: "He was a duplicate to Monroe. There's some that can play the mandolin . . . and some that have the high voice . . . but Pee Wee could do both."[19] Lambert, the Stanley brothers, and fiddler Bobby Sumner won their audition on WCYB and moved to the station early in 1947. Sumner, however, was uncertain about taking the risk of a musical career and decided to leave the band. Carter Stanley and his father Lee got in touch with an older fiddler well known in the region, Leslie Keith.

Keith had put together a fiddle tune which he called "Black Mountain Blues," based on an old Alabama tune, "The Lost Child." He had played it over the radio and at fiddle contests during the thirties, and it was picked up in that way by Tommy Magness and Curly Fox, both of whom were playing it during the war years on the Opry under the title of "Black Mountain Rag." Fox's King recording of the tune was to become one of the best-selling fiddle records of all time. Keith was well known as the composer of the tune, and when he was hired by the Stanley Brothers, it was significant enough to make the pages of *Billboard* in March 1947. Years later he recalled the band as he found it: "Pee Wee played the mandolin and Ralph he played the banjo, just forefinger and thumb, and Carter he was learning Lester Flatt strokes. They was getting pretty good at it 'cause they practiced, they didn't fool around. At the time we started out, Pee Wee did the tenor singing and Ralph did the baritone. Carter did the leading." Working with bassist-comedian Ray ("Pickles") Lambert (no relation to Pee Wee), they appeared daily on a mid-day show, "Farm and Fun Time." And from this base they began booking personal appearances. Keith recalled: "We'd travel 25, 50, 100 miles and play six nights a week and sometimes seven. . . . We never went anywhere but what we had a packed house. Our share when we played a schoolhouse was 70 percent after two or three shows. Sometimes I'd make, 50, 75, 100 dollars a night."[20]

In 1947 Jesse McReynolds was eighteen and just beginning a career as a country musician with his brother Jim on WNVA in Norton. He watched the new band's swift rise in popularity with interest.

The Stanley Brothers had a great thing going there, far as playing show dates and everything. On the whole, fact was, they started the thing off wrong, the Stanley Brothers and a couple more went in there and started giving stations . . . 10 or 15 percent . . . of their show dates [receipts] to be on the station. They started paying off that way and the station actually got rich off it. . . . And for a while there it was as hard to get on that station as it would have been Grand Ole Opry. You just couldn't get on, you know, because it was the hottest thing going. . . . That's where the Stanley Brothers done their biggest, they used to clean up there, everywhere they'd go. They'd play ball parks and things, and fill 'em up.[21]

Their popularity attracted the attention of a new local independent record company owner, James Hobart Stanton, variously known as Jim or Hobe. In his late twenties, Stanton was from Johnson City, Tennessee, not far from Bristol, where he had been working since his teens with a juke box operator. He felt that he could produce records as good as those from major labels he was placing in juke boxes. Selling out his interest in the juke box operation, he founded Rich-R-Tone records and, using the studios of WOPI in Bristol, made his first records in the fall of 1946. Peddling the discs from the trunk of his car in pressings of a thousand at a time, Stanton quickly found buyers and began to operate through more conventional sales channels—distributors and mail-order ads on the radio. There was no other independent record label operating in Appalachia at that time, and Stanton did well with his new product. He paid particular attention to popular groups on local radio and soon heard about the Stanley Brothers: "The Stanley Brothers had a song called 'Little Glass of Wine' and they impressed me with the fact that they actually got a big U.S. Mail sack of letters every day requesting them to sing it and so naturally we hopped into a session on that."[22]

The Stanley's first Rich-R-Tone record had come, however, some months before. In September 1947 they had recorded four songs—two duets ("The Girl behind the Bar" and "Mother No Longer Awaits Me at Home") and two quartets ("Death Is Only a Dream" and "I Can Tell You the Time")—at WOPI, and the duets were released on their first record that December. Their second record had "Little Glass of Wine," a duet by Carter and Pee Wee. With "Little Maggie" (a solo by Ralph featuring his vocal and two-finger-style banjo work) on the other side it was released at the end of March 1948. "Little Glass of Wine" was the Stanley Brothers' first "hit."

At the time a twenty-six year old musician from Greenville, South Carolina, Carl Sauceman, was working part-time as a distributor for Mercury and Rich-R-Tone: "Every time I walked into a record store and they found out I was selling Rich-R-Tone, they'd holler for me to bring them a load of Stanley Brothers records. . . . if I hadn't been to a place for a week . . . they'd be out of Stanley Brothers, so I'd take a carload with me, deliver them and bring the money back to [Stanton]."[23] In this region they were outselling even Eddy Arnold, who at that time was topping the "folk" charts and crossing over onto the pop sales as well. But theirs was only a regional popularity, as Stanton recalls:

> We could sell like 5000 Stanley Brothers in Kentucky and absolutely not give one away in Georgia . . . I've gone into department stores, like in Atlanta, Georgia, and to a salesgirl I knew well, and if I put a bluegrass sound on her turntable, it would embarrass her to the point that she would look around to see who was listening and in turn it would reflect back on me, I would be embarrassed for doing it. . . . People tied a banjo and fiddle with Kentucky, with coal mining, with rural hillbillies and, socially, people that were more educated, maybe more socially prominent, they turned their nose down at it.[24]

Billboard record reviews of the period verify this: Monroe's recordings were described as "backwoods style," "rural," or "for the old folks at home,"[25] and while a trade paper could not overlook popularity, the music was given little serious attention at the time, except by its followers, rural working-class people in this region.

For these people it was quite an event when, in May 1948, Lester Flatt and Earl Scruggs and their Foggy Mountain Boys arrived at WCYB. Jim McReynolds describes the impact of Flatt and Scruggs's arrival:

> The Stanleys, they'd always copy Bill, and Flatt and Scruggs, they came in with the, more or less original sound, 'cause they'd been with Bill and recorded, on everything [sic] that he had out. And so when Flatt and Scruggs came to Bristol why they just snowed 'em under as far as the real sound of bluegrass, 'cause, well Earl, he was the top banjo man, and they'd gotten a lot of publicity off the Opry. And everything [the Stanley Brothers] done, Flatt and Scruggs come in on the same program, just

about, with the original thing. . . . As far as the really bluegrass sound, I think Flatt and Scruggs had more of the sound *then* than what they had done with Bill, 'cause they had Jim Shumate, and he was at that time, a knocked out fiddler—he could cut it! And of course, Mac Wiseman, he was with 'em singing tenor.[26]

It was a hot band, and they attracted attention at once. One of their first acts was to prepare a songbook to be sold over the air and at personal appearances for fifty cents. Flatt said that "they would only let us advertise it on the station for four weeks . . . I don't remember just how many we sold on our personal appearances, but we mailed out ten thousand books."[27] Soon a second book was printed. The introduction reflected their growing success:

Early last spring we decided to organize an outfit of our own. It was like going into a dark room to find a light. But we tried and tried hard. We can truthfully say that we found we had far more friends than ever expected. And we want you all to know that we deeply appreciate everything you have done to help us along. Your cards, letters and seeing our show when it was in your community, and, too, your purchase of this songbook. We sincerely hope you are pleased with our book, and we hope to have even a far better one next time.[28]

Not only did their music have an impact upon the people listening to WCYB and attending their shows, it also affected the Stanley Brothers.

As McReynolds observed, the Stanley Brothers and the Clinch Mountain Boys were already sounding like Bill Monroe—particularly Pee Wee. Ralph Stanley describes Lambert's style: "When Pee Wee was with us we had a sound (that) resembled Bill Monroe a little bit. Pee Wee sung a lot like Bill did. His idol was Bill Monroe and he played a lot like Bill with the exception (that) he played it, I think, a little bit straighter than Bill at times. He got a lot of things from Bill but he developed it more or less into a style of his own."[29] According to Leslie Keith, the group was not satisfied with its sound, particularly after they began hearing Flatt and Scruggs: "On . . . the early records, we wasn't too bluegrassy at that time. It was kinda bluegrass and old-time mixed, on the fiddling end of it and also on the singing end of it. . . . Monroe's type of stuff was coming up real fast, and they wondered if I'd consider letting them get a faster fiddler . . . "[30] Keith recalls that Shumate was the fiddler they hired, but according to other sources it was Art Wooten who joined the Stanleys during the summer of 1948 when Keith moved to Curly King's band. In Wooten they had a former Blue Grass Boy and grew even closer to the Monroe sound.

The presence of Flatt and Scruggs at Bristol drew the sound of the Stanley Brothers toward that of the Blue Grass Boys. The final step which brought them firmly into this orbit was a change in Ralph Stanley's banjo style. Carter was already introducing him to WCYB listeners as Ralph "and his fancy banjo," the very words used to describe Scruggs to Opry audiences. Now in the (approximately) six-month period between the time "Little Maggie" was recorded and the next Stanley Brothers recording session, Ralph Stanley abandoned his two-finger style and began playing in a three-finger style similar to Scruggs's. There is some uncertainty about the way in which Stanley learned the style. Some assert that he learned from Scruggs during their joint tenure at WCYB. Ralph Stanley, however, claims that he learned from the playing of Snuffy Jenkins, the North Carolina banjoist who had some influence on Scruggs.

In September 1948, Rich-R-Tone released the Stanleys' recording of "Molly and Tenbrooks," sung by Pee Wee Lambert. This song came to them through Bill Monroe. It did not, however, come from Monroe's Columbia recording, for that, though recorded in October 1947, was not released until September 1949. And Lambert's words differed from those on Monroe's record, for Bill knew many verses to this old traditional blues ballad and combined different ones each time he sang it. Pee Wee Lambert had assembled his version from Monroe's live performances.

This was not the only one of Monroe's live performances that was the source of a Rich-R-Tone recording. In 1947 Wilma Lee and Stoney Cooper, then working at WWVA in Wheeling, West Virginia, heard the Blue Grass Quartet singing "Wicked Path of Sin." Monroe had recorded the song, which he composed, in 1946, but it was not released until October 1948. Thinking the song was already on record, Wilma Lee copied it, using shorthand, from one of Monroe's Opry broadcasts. They recorded it for Rich-R-Tone and it was released at the same time as the Stanley Brothers' "Molly and Tenbrooks." They had not realized the song was a Monroe composition; as Wilma Lee said, "they'd sing songs they didn't write." Stoney Cooper vividly remembered Monroe's reaction: "I was there at the Opry one Saturday night, and I said, 'Bill, sure do like that "Wicked Path of Sin." ' I said, 'you know, we recorded it.' 'Yeah, I know,' he said, 'Don't it seem to you a little when you sing other people's songs, after a while you sort of get yourself patterned like them?' That really hurt me, you know."[31]

Monroe's comment to Stoney Cooper was harsh because at the time he was also being copied by the Stanley Brothers. Their performance of "Molly and Tenbrooks" was unmistakably "patterned like" that of the Monroe band. As in Monroe's version, the banjo and fiddle, but not the mandolin, took instrumental breaks. Ralph Stanley's banjo playing closely resembled that of Scruggs. Still another aspect of resemblance between the two performances lay in the fact that in both the song was sung by the mandolinist. If anything the Stanley Brothers' version was more Monroe-esque than Monroe's: it was faster and pitched a half-step higher.

Mac Wiseman, who was working with Flatt and Scruggs at WCYB when the Stanley Brothers' "Molly and Tenbrooks" was released in 1948 and who went on to work and record with Monroe in 1949, speaks of Monroe's reaction:

> The Bill Monroe that I've know through the years, it used to be both an art form and a style with both he and Charlie and people like that, and they'd just as soon you didn't do 'em at all. In fact, this is so accurate and known by enough people that I don't even hesitate to say it. When the Stanley Brothers first started, whatever Bill did Saturday night on the Opry, they did the next week on the Bristol program that we were on. And if Bill didn't do it, that was out. Well, Bill used to see red. He used to hate the word Stanley Brothers. Now Ralph, I'm sure, will confirm this—they're good friends today and was before Carter passed away [1966]—but they were such close imitators that it irritated Bill so much that they would take his stuff and copy it so closely. It wasn't that they were out to steal corn out of his corn crib, it was just that they worshipped him so much. They had a mandolin player that could pick just like him. Pee Wee Lambert was his name.[32]

The Stanley Brothers' record of "Molly and Tenbrooks" is the first direct evidence that the total "sound" of Monroe's 1946–48 band was being imitated by other bands. It marks the transition from the sound of Monroe's band to the musical genre known as bluegrass, as Monroe himself eventually acknowledged in 1965 at the first bluegrass festival, in Roanoke. At that time Monroe was able to view the Stanley Brothers' copying in a magnanimous way. He and Carter Stanley had just sung a duet in a portion of the show called "The Story of Bluegrass," an illustrated history of the music which reunited Monroe with former Blue Grass Boys. Monroe told the narrator, Carlton Haney: "You might not know this, and a lot of these folks here might not know this, but the Stanley Brothers was the first group I ever heard that was following in my footsteps on the Grand Ole Opry with the banjo, guitar, mandolin, the bass fiddle and the little fiddle. They're the first group that I ever knowed that had a bluegrass string band. . . . I heard 'em at Bristol, and they was really picking and singing mighty good."[33]

The Stanley Brothers and Flatt and Scruggs were by no means the only groups copying Monroe's sound in 1948. In December 1947 the Bailey Brothers, who had been on the Opry, moved to Knoxville. There they added the five-string banjo of Wiley Birchfield to their band, which already had a string bass, fiddle, guitar, and mandolin. During 1948 they recorded six songs for Rich-R-Tone, including three which reflected Monroe's influence: "Rattlesnake Daddy Blues," a fast blues in the mold of "Mule Skinner Blues"; "Happy Valley Special," an instrumental which is in the same key as and follows an arrangement similar to that of "Blue Grass Special" (and got its name similarly—the Baileys' band was the Happy Valley Boys); and "John Henry," in an arrangement which resembles the one used by Monroe and Flatt on their

Opry performances of 1946 and 1947. On these three cuts, the banjo of
Birchfield—whom Charlie Bailey says listened to Snuffy Jenkins and was an
enthusiastic fan of Earl Scruggs—is heard doing both background and lead
parts.

Carl Sauceman, the young musician who was helping distribute records for
Mercury and Rich-R-Tone, was also playing at WGRV in Greenville, South
Carolina, in 1948. In his band was Thomas Martin, a banjo picker who
played in the two-finger style; he played on at least two of the six recordings
by Sauceman which were issued by Mercury in the summer of 1948. This
band, with guitar, fiddle, and Tiny Day's prominent string bass in the style of
Cedric Rainwater, had a sound somewhere between that of Monroe and the
early Stanley Brothers.

And over in Charlotte, North Carolina, on WBT, a group known as the
Briarhoppers, featuring Whitey (Roy Grant) and (Arval) Hogan, recorded
their locally popular version of "Jesse James" with the help of a three-finger-
style banjoist named Shannon Grayson. It was released in December 1948
by a small Pennsylvania independent, Cowboy Records.

Playing every afternoon on WLTC in Gastonia, North Carolina, were the
Blue River Boys, a group which included the Murphy brothers Dewey (mandolin), Fred (guitar), and John (bass) along with the Davis brothers, fiddler
Pee Wee and banjoist Hubert. The Davises were from Earl Scruggs's home
territory, Cleveland County, North Carolina, and Pee Wee had been with
the local band that Scruggs had auditioned with in Knoxville when he was
hired by Lost John in 1945. Pee Wee recalls that he and Hubert had met the
Murphys at a fiddlers' convention Thanksgiving 1947 or 1948: "We joined up
with them. That's when bluegrass music got in my heart. The Murphys were
bluegrass all the way and that was for us."[34]

These and other groups (most of which did not make records) at radio
stations large and small in the upland South were copying Monroe's sound by
adding five-string banjoists and hot fiddlers; by borrowing from or modeling
on his repertoire; and by incorporating his ideas about tempo, rhythm, and
keys. But in 1948 only the Stanley Brothers and Flatt and Scruggs had
combined and recorded all the elements that made them closely parallel to
the sound of the Blue Grass Boys. Hence it was they who drew Monroe's ire.

Angered at Flatt and Scruggs because he suspected they had connived to
leave him and start a new band in his style, he did not speak to them until
after they split up in 1969. In the early fifties, he used his influence at WSM
to keep them off the cast of the Grand Ole Opry for several years. After 1948
Monroe would take precautions to prevent the kind of publicity that Flatt
and Scruggs had received being given to his band members. Never again, for
example, would his lead singer's name be identified on his record labels. He
would avoid hiring close friends or more than one member of a band. Monroe
would also endeavor to keep teams from developing in the band.

This maneuvering by Monroe reflects the nature of competition in the music business, where the performer is both product and salesman and yet has no way of fully protecting the most important part of his product, the intangibles of style. Others had left the Blue Grass Boys to establish their own careers—Clyde Moody, Cousin Wilbur, Pete Pyle, Stringbean—but none of them had taken so much of the Monroe sound with them. And it is well to remember Jim McReynolds's comment that they had "recorded . . . on everything that he had out." By 1948 the recordings that the band had made in 1946 and 1947 were being issued by Columbia every two months. In December 1948 and January 1949 "Little Community Church," a Blue Grass Quartet recording, made both the "Juke Box" and the new "Best-Selling Retail" charts, and later in 1949 two others from these sessions also made the charts, both duets by Flatt and Monroe in which Flatt sang solo lead on the verses: "Toy Heart" and "When You Are Lonely." At the end of July 1949 *Billboard* published a list of "Top Selling Folk Artists over Retail Counters" during the first half of the year. Monroe was ranked seventeenth, with his six most recent Columbia records—all from the Flatt and Scruggs sessions— listed as selling well. These records were not making the charts but were selling consistently enough to give Monroe a high rating not on the basis of a single record but on the basis of a repertoire. While these records were thus helping Bill Monroe, they were also helping Flatt and Scruggs, since it was widely known that they were singing and playing on them and Flatt's name appeared on their labels. Flatt and Scruggs's first recordings for Mercury— four singles, eight songs—appeared in 1949 as well. Since so many of Monroe's recordings featured Flatt's lead singing, the effect of all of this was to reinforce the reputation of the new band. This accounts at least in part for Monroe's antagonism toward them.

Another element of the Blue Grass Boys which Flatt and Scruggs took with them was visual rather than musical. Although Monroe and Cleo Davis emphasized the fact that they wore white shirts and ties when they first appeared on the Opry, these were worn most of the time along with riding pants (jodphurs) and high-topped riding boots. This costume, which had been used by the Monroe Brothers, was said (in liner notes written in 1958) to reflect Monroe's Kentucky heritage: "Unlike many other country groups, the Blue Grass Boys don't strut in hillbilly garb, but wear the traditional dress of Kentucky planters."[35] Flatt and Scruggs continued to wear these outfits after they left Monroe, thus maintaining the look of the earlier band—a minor detail, perhaps, but another indication of the extent to which touches of the Blue Grass image lingered with the Foggy Mountain Boys for at least a while. At the same time, Flatt and Scruggs were attempting to distance themselves from Monroe by writing new songs and by adding new touches to their music, like Earl's lead guitar on gospel quartets.

In March 1949 the Stanley Brothers switched from the obscure Rich-R-Tone to Columbia Records. On Columbia they mostly featured a "high baritone" vocal trio form in which both Pee Wee Lambert and Ralph Stanley

sang above Carter Stanley's lead. It had been suggested to them by Art
Wooten, and although Monroe, Flatt, and Rainwater had recorded a similar
trio for one song on Columbia in 1947, "I Hear a Sweet Voice Calling," the
high baritone trio became identified with the Stanley Brothers. But their
second Columbia single, released in June, included "Let Me Be Your Friend"
a Carter Stanley–Pee Wee Lambert duet which closely resembled in all aspects except lyrics the Monroe–Flatt duet "It's Mighty Dark to Travel," released by Columbia just six months earlier.

In November 1949 Bill Monroe signed a recording contract with Decca
records; his main reason for leaving Columbia was "their inking of the Stanley Brothers, a combo which he felt sounded too much like his own work."[36]
In this negative way he acknowledged the fact that his sound had spawned a
musical genre.

In literary and art criticism the word *genre*, borrowed from French (but
ultimately from the Latin *genus*), is used to describe classes of material (paint-
ings, novels, etc.) which share certain definable formal characteristics. The
word is best translated into English as *type*. As we will see in the next chapter,
one of the first appearances of the word *bluegrass* in print wedded it with *type*:
"bluegrass type music." The formal characteristics to which Monroe objected
in the Stanley Brothers were encompassed by the word *sound*. They are in
fact the formal characteristics which were identified by the scholars and
enthusiasts who first described and defined bluegrass in print a decade after
Monroe made his negative acknowledgment—a combination of instruments,
instrumental techniques, vocal styles, tempo, pitch, repertoire. As Mac
Wiseman pointed out, Monroe considered his music an individual art form,
and while he encouraged covers of his compositions, he plainly did not like
copying.

Monroe's feelings in this matter were bound to be negative, for bands such
as Flatt and Scruggs and the Stanley Brothers were economic threats. Imita-
tion could not be seen as flattery when record sales and bookings were at
stake. Not until the early sixties, when Monroe began to accept the bluegrass
fans' idea that he had created a historically significant genre, was the emula-
tion he had deplored seen as a compliment.

Rivalry between professional musicians, engendered by the competitive
nature of show business, was an important factor in the process through
which bluegrass developed. The Stanley Brothers recalled years later that
they had problems not only with Bill Monroe but with his brother Charlie,
who complained to WCYB about their doing "his" songs "Roll in My Sweet
Baby's Arms" and "Mother's Only Sleeping." Similarly, Flatt and Scruggs
complained to WCYB about the Stanleys doing "Cumberland Gap" and "Roll
in My Sweet Baby's Arms." All three were songs of obscure folk origin which
Charlie Monroe and Flatt and Scruggs were regularly featuring as part of their
own repertoires. While these songs raised difficult legal questions concerning
ownership, the performers felt strongly enough about the matter to lay claim

to them. Like Flatt and Scruggs, busily writing new songs at that time so as to get away from the Monroe image, the Stanley Brothers eventually resolved problems of this sort by writing new material for their own use.

Nevertheless, the Stanleys' recording of a song from Monroe's repertoire before Monroe's disc appeared started a pattern that has been repeated with variations by many bands since that time. Occasionally one band will refuse to appear at the same show with another because of bad feelings about the "stealing" of material. But more than rivalry and competition is involved, for the constant turnover in band personnel leads to recombinations of musicians in a limited number of bands. With this exchange of personnel comes an exchange of repertoire and musical techniques which constitutes an oral tradition within the profession. Artistic motives—the enjoyment of and need for exchange with other musicians—conflict with commercial motives—the need to have original material and sound to enhance commercial and professional product identity. This conflict creates an ambivalence which tempers relations between musicians and among bands.

In another way, the events from this period of bluegrass history have been continually repeated as band members decide, like Flatt and Scruggs, to start their own groups. Even today many bluegrass bands have one or more members who have worked with Monroe. The example of Flatt and Scruggs drew to the Blue Grass Boys many ambitious young musicians who hoped to follow in Lester and Earl's path, especially during the late forties and fifties.

This made it relatively easy for Monroe to carry on his sound. During the late forties and early fifties talented singer-guitarists like Mac Wiseman, Jimmy Martin, and Edd Mayfield followed Flatt in the Blue Grass Boys. Similarly, banjoists like Rudy Lyle, a young Virginian who'd been raised on the music of Snuffy Jenkins before hearing Scruggs, and fiddlers like Charlie Cline, tutored by Arthur Smith, who boarded at his parents' home in the early forties, maintained the sound that Monroe had developed with the band of 1946–48. But never again would Monroe's combination of sound and repertoire have quite so great an impact. As we will see later, Monroe's Columbia repertoire influenced everyone from Elvis Presley to the Lewis Family and remains at the core of the bluegrass repertoire today, heard on superstar albums and at festival jam session. While he developed an interesting new repertoire and added nuances to his sound on his Decca recordings, Monroe now had to market it to people who could compare it with the similar music of other groups, particularly Flatt and Scruggs.

It is possible today to view the spread of the bluegrass sound from Monroe's band, which took place following 1948, as the growth of a musical genre. Were people calling it bluegrass in the late forties? A recently discovered radio broadcast transcription made by the Stanley Brothers at WCYB in the spring of 1949 carries the words of Carter Stanley as he introduced Bobby Sumner as a "bluegrass fiddler from way down in old Kentucky." The usage is ambiguous, for *bluegrass* in this context can be taken to mean a simple association with Sumner's home state. But even if Stanley meant to imply a connection with the music of Bill Monroe in his statement, it is essential to remember that what is now called bluegrass was, at this time, still considered by most people to be just country music. The musicians who emulated Monroe, Flatt and Scruggs, and the Stanley Brothers did not at first think of themselves as performing within the artistic genre of "bluegrass." That idea emerged only gradually during the fifties.

Notes

1. Neil V. Rosenberg, brochure notes to *Country and Western Classics*, p. 21.
   2. Jake Lambert, *A Biography of Lester Flatt*, p. 113.
   3. Roger H. Siminoff, "Earl Scruggs," p. 26.
   4. *Billboard*, Sept. 7, 1946, p. 120.
   5. Loyal Jones to Rosenberg, Sept. 10, 1982.
   6. Siminoff, "Earl Scruggs," p. 30.
   7. Rosenberg, *Country and Western Classics*, p. 18.
   8. Douglas B. Green, liner notes to *The Classic Bluegrass Recordings*, vol. 1. Monroe is in error when he says it was put in both names. It was (and remains) copyrighted in Bill's name only.
   9. Lambert, *Biography of Lester Flatt*, p. 113.
   10. *Billboard*, Mar. 15, 1947, p. 108.
   11. Bob Osborne, interview with author, Bean Blossom, Ind., Sept. 26, 1965.
   12. *Billboard*, Aug. 30, 1947, p. 109.
   13. Gene Dudley, *Introduction to Bill Monroe's Grand Ole Opry WSM Song Folio No. 2*, p. 4.
   14. *Billboard*, Jan. 31, 1948, p. 117, Jan. 17, 1948, p. 96.
   15. Pete Kuykendall, "Lester Flatt and the Nashville Grass," p. 5.
   16. Lambert, *Biography of Lester Flatt*, p. 7.
   17. Ibid., pp. 7–8.
   18. *Billboard*, Oct. 4, 1947, p. 118. Pioneer hillbilly musician Clarence Ashley, who later worked as a comedian with the Stanleys, claimed that he "worked to help to get the Stanley Brothers in their first beginning at Bristol"; he does not explain how. See David Kahn, "I Play Because This Is My Life."
   19. Frank Godbey, "Pee Wee Lambert," p. 13.
   20. Bob Sayers, "Leslie Keith," pp. 16–17.
   21. Jesse McReynolds, interview with author and Scott Hambly, Chicago, Ill., Feb. 5, 1966.
   22. Rounder Collective, brochure notes to *The Rich-R-Tone Story*, p. 4.
   23. Richard Spottswood, "Carl Sauceman," p. 15.
   24. Rounder Collective, *Rich-R-Tone Story*, p. 4.

25. *Billboard*, Nov. 23, 1946, p. 30.

26. Jim McReynolds, interview, Feb. 5, 1965.

27. Lambert, *Biography of Lester Flatt*, p. 114.

28. *Foggy Mountain Boys Number Two Edition of Radio Favorites*, p. 1.

29. Godbey, "Pee Wee Lambert," p. 15.

30. Sayers, "Leslie Keith," p. 17.

31. Robert Cogswell, " 'We Made Our Name in the Days of Radio,' " p. 74.

32. Tom Henderson, "Mac Wiseman," p. 11.

33. Bill Monroe, recorded onstage, First Annual Roanoke Bluegrass Festival, Fincastle, Va., Sept. 5, 1965.

34. Clarence H. Greene, "Pee Wee Davis," p. 13.

35. Charles Lamb, liner notes to *Knee Deep in Blue Grass*.

36. *Billboard*, Nov. 12, 1949, p. 35.

Bibliographical Notes

To the sources noted in the first half of this chapter, which constitute the major writings on Monroe's so-called "original" bluegrass band, a number of other books and articles add information. Lester Flatt's story has been told in Olan Bassham, *Lester Flatt Baron of Bluegrass*, and in Bill Vernon's "A Conversation with Lester Flatt." There is, to my knowledge, nothing in print on Cedric Rainwater (Howard Watts). For more on Chubby Wise (in addition to references given in chapter 2), see Tex Logan, "A Conversation with Chubby Wise." The starting point for information on Earl Scruggs is in his *Earl Scruggs and the Five-String Banjo*, pp. 147–56. Occasional historical information appears in Scruggs's column in *Frets*.

The thorny question of the extent to which Scruggs's banjo style was based on regional traditions is complicated by the lack of aural evidence prior to Scruggs's recordings with Monroe in 1946–47. Biographies of two banjoists, Johnny Whisnant and Don Reno, who were playing the three-finger style prior to Scruggs's rise to prominence, shed some light on the situation. See Walter V. Saunders, "Johnny Whisnant Musical History"; Pete Kuykendall, "Don Reno, Red Smiley, Bill Harrell and the Tennessee Cutups, Part 2"; Bill Vernon, "The Don Reno Story Part 1"; Bill Vernon, "The Don Reno Story, Part 2"; and Don Reno, *Musical History of Don Reno*, pp. 4–9. In recent years Scruggs has stated that the Morris Brothers were essentially playing bluegrass music when he was with them in the early forties. For more on the Morris Brothers, with whom first Reno and then Scruggs worked, see Wayne Erbsen, "Wiley and Zeke—The Morris Brothers." Scruggs, who followed Reno in the Morris' band in about 1940, told one interviewer that Reno was playing two-finger rather than three-finger banjo at that time.

Bob Osborne's early days in Dayton are recounted in Bill Emerson, "The Osborne Brothers: Getting Started" and my "The Osborne Brothers, Part One."

The perspective of a WCYB listener is given in Joe Wilson, "Bristol's WCYB: Early Bluegrass Turf."

For more on Leslie Keith and "Black Mountain Rag," see Charles K. Wolfe, "The Mystery of 'The Black Mountain Rag.' "

Jim and Jesse McReynolds were working on a radio station in Norton, Virginia, not far from Bristol, when the Stanleys formed their band. See Nelson Sears, *Jim and Jesse.* For an evaluation of this source and further bibliographical references on this group, see Scott Hambly, *"Jim and Jesse, A Review Essay on Fan Historiography."*

The Stanley Brothers' early recording career was documented in Pete Kuykendall, "The Stanley Brothers." Gary Reid has revised, corrected, updated, and added to this work in recent years and hopes to publish soon the definitive Stanley Brothers discography. I am indebted to him for helping me with details on this subject. Some questions about personnel turnover remain obscure; for example, Jim Shumate seems to indicate that he replaced Leslie Keith, albeit briefly, in the Stanley Brothers band. See Wayne Erbsen, "Jim Shumate," p. 22. But this appears to have occurred at a later date, 1949, after Shumate had left Flatt and Scruggs. Art Wooten took Shumate's place in the Flatt and Scruggs band in 1949.

"Molly and Tenbrooks," the song from Bill Monroe's repertoire which the Stanley Brothers recorded in 1948, was one of the few traditional pieces he recorded for Columbia—most were newly-composed. For more on this song, including a discussion of the Monroe and Stanley recordings, see D. K. Wilgus, " 'Ten Broeck and Mollie': A Race and a Ballad."

Articles on some of the bands which began incorporating aspects of the Monroe sound in their music during 1947–48 include Gary A. Henderson and Walter V. Saunders, "The Bailey Brothers," and Curtis Douglas, "The Murphy Brothers." See also Wayne Daniel, "From Barn Dance Emcee to Recording Company Executive," for the story of Cotton Carrier, a Georgia singer who, during the late forties, included bluegrass instrumentation in his band. Carrier states that he thought of it not as bluegrass but as "hillbilly music" (p. 235), an attitude typical of the period.

Discographical Notes

Only a few of the three-finger banjo players who were contemporaries of Scruggs recorded before Earl was heard on radio and record with Monroe. Hence it is difficult to know for certain how much of his style was personal and how much of it common coin among younger, three-finger-type, North Carolina banjoists. One of these contemporaries, Johnny Whisnant, can be heard on *Carl Story and the Original Rambling Mountaineers, 1939.*

Bill Monroe's "Kentucky Waltz" was issued in January 1946. Cowboy Copas's cover of it came out in February 1947, Pee Wee King's in May 1947. In September another cover was done by Jimmy Hinchee and the Mississippi River Valley Boys, and in March 1948 J. Day's version was issued.

Monroe's "Footprints in the Snow" was released in October 1946. Bradley Kincaid's version—textually and musically quite different from Monroe's—appeared on Majestic in March 1947. When Majestic went out of business, its catalog was taken over by Mercury, and Kincaid's "Footprints" appeared again in February 1949 on that label.

Clyde Moody's "Shenandoah Waltz" was issued in June 1947, Pee Wee King's "Tennessee Waltz" appeared in February 1948. The latter was reissued on the *Smithsonian Collection of Classic Country Music*.

Monroe's "Mule Skinner Blues" was reissued, along with "Blue Yodel No. 7," in October 1948. Two months later RCA Victor also reissued his "Katy Hill" and "Back Up and Push."

An album containing copies of disc recordings made at the Grand Ole Opry preserves nineteen live performances by Monroe's legendary band as broadcast over WSM: *Bluegrass Classics: Radio Shows 1946–1948*.

Although recorded in 1946, Monroe's "Why Did You Wander?" remained unissued until released by New World Records on *Hills and Home*. It subsequently appeared on Bill Monroe, *The Classic Bluegrass Recordings*, vol. 2. "Will You Be Loving Another Man?" was issued in July 1947.

"Mother's Only Sleeping" was first released by J. E. Mainer's Mountaineers in July 1946. Charlie Monroe's version came in December 1946, Bill Monroe's in March 1947, and Mel and Stan's in November 1947.

Monroe's "Blue Moon of Kentucky" appeared in September 1947, "Blue Grass Breakdown" in March 1949, and "Molly and Tenbrooks" in September 1949. These and most of the other Columbia recordings which feature the Flatt-Scruggs-Wise-Rainwater band have been reissued on several Bill Monroe albums: *Sixteen All-Time Greatest Hits; The Classic Bluegrass Recordings*, vols. 1 and 2; and *Bill Monroe with Lester Flatt and Earl Scruggs, "The Original Bluegrass Band."*

Curley Fox's "Black Mountain Rag" was released in June 1948. Of the Stanley Brothers' Rich-R-Tone singles, "The Girl behind the Bar"/"Mother No Longer Awaits Me at Home" appeared in December 1947; "Death Is Only a Dream"/"I Can Tell You the Time" was issued in February 1950, and "The Little Glass of Wine"/"Little Maggie" in April 1948. All of these, along with the rest of their Rich-R-Tone recordings, were reissued on *The Stanley Brothers, Their Original Recordings*. Their "Molly and Tenbrooks" is on this album and is also on *The Rich-R-Tone Story*, as is Wilma Lee and Stoney Cooper's "Wicked Path of Sin."

The three Bailey Brothers songs, "Rattlesnake Daddy Blues," "Happy Valley Special," and "John Henry," were reissued on their *Have You Forgotten?* Two of the 1948 Mercury recordings of the Sauceman Brothers were reissued on *The Sauceman Brothers*: "Your Trouble Ways Keep Us Apart," and "Please Don't Make Me Cry." Whitey and Hogan's "Jesse James" was reissued on *The Early Days of Bluegrass*, vol. 1.

Monroe's "Little Community Church" was issued in October 1948, "Toy Heart" in March 1949, and "When You Are Lonely" in December 1948.

Flatt and Scruggs's first four Mercury singles were issued as follows: "God Loves His Children"/"I'm Going To Make Heaven My Home," January 1949; "My Cabin In Caroline"/"We'll Met Again Sweetheart," April 1949; "Baby Blue Eyes"/"Bouquet in Heaven," July 1949; and "Down the Road"/ "Why Don't You Tell Me So" in October 1949. All were reissued (along with the twenty Flatt and Scruggs Mercury recordings made in 1950) on three Mercury albums: *Country Music, Flatt and Scruggs,* and *Original Sound.* A new reissue of these twenty-eight cuts, in a two album set, is in production by Rounder Records as this is written.

Monroe's "I Hear a Sweet Voice Calling" was released in July 1948. The Stanley Brothers' Columbia recording, "Let Me Be Your Friend" was issued in June 1949. It was reissued on the Stanley Brothers, *The Columbia Sessions, 1949–50.* Monroe's "It's Mighty Dark To Travel" came out in December 1948. Jim Eanes's "A Sweeter Love than Yours I'll Never Know," which also used the "It's Mighty Dark To Travel" tune and arrangement, was released by Eanes in December 1952; it was also recorded by the Church Brothers. Both were reissued on, respectively, *Jim Eanes and the Shenandoah Valley Boys* and *The Church Brothers.*

Chapter 4

Naming the Genre:
1950–57

In 1948 bluegrass emerged as a genre within the burgeoning post-war country music industry. Many new groups playing it appeared during the first half of the fifties. This period is frequently characterized today as "the golden era" or wellspring of "traditional bluegrass." But at the time it was rarely called bluegrass. It was considered in the industry to be a rustic, down-home, hillbilly, old-fashioned part of country music, relatively unimportant. Yet when, in the mid-fifties, country music was suddenly threatened by rock and roll, the demand for bluegrass as a genre appears to have increased. And at this time the word *bluegrass* was first used in print to describe the music. This public naming set bluegrass on the road toward its present situation as a distinctive genre which owes its continued existence to rock and roll and the folk revival as well as to country music and the perseverance of Bill Monroe.

Country music had become big business during the post-war years as economic prosperity gave the predominantly working-class followers of the music the wherewithal to purchase record players and records and to buy cars which enabled them to attend shows. The widespread rural electrification programs of this era also stimulated the sales of radios and record players. The lure of profit drew promoters and other show business entrepreneurs toward the music, which had previously not paid enough to warrant investment.

Until the early fifties, all but the most successful country music performers acted as their own promoters. The small local radio stations which proliferated in the post-war years provided such performers with an excellent means of promotion. Appearances on live broadcasts—early morning and noontime shows during the week and "barn dances" on Saturday nights—offered little or no pay but allowed the artist an opportunity to sell his products, publicize himself, and gain the bookings which were the bread and butter of his existence. These bookings were personal appearance engagements, generally in small rural communities. Though the income from such concerts was limited, overhead was low, and a performer could make a living within a limited area playing such small engagements almost continually for many months or even a few years. Typically acts moved on frequently, going from one small rural station to another seeking fresh audiences, in a sense rotating the crop.

This pattern, developed in the thirties, still existed in the early fifties, but big business, which had begun to affect country music in the post-war years, would soon make the old pattern obsolete. The hit-star system created a demand for certain nationally or regionally popular stars, at the expense of the careers of journeyman entertainers who were not stars. Record sales became increasingly important. Because even star performers still charged only a few hundred dollars for a single evening's performance, it was possible for promoters to organize "package shows" on a one-night basis. In these a number of "stars" with "hits"—often from the Grand Ole Opry—would appear together. Such combined bookings eventually led to package tours, but these were not common in the early fifties.

More common at this time was another kind of live appearance which took place on weekends (usually Sundays) at country music "parks." These parks, picnic grounds which had an outdoor stage or a large barn containing a stage, were located in rural settings within easy driving distance of metropolitan areas throughout the U.S., but especially in the South, Midwest, and lower Northeast. They were in existence during the thirties, but their period of greatest growth seems to have been the early fifties, and they flourished throughout this decade. Such parks had a local "house band," an emcee, and one or two "stars" on hand each Sunday to perform two or three shows. Contests were frequently held for amateur singers and instrumentalists. Food was sold, and there was "plenty of room for the entire family." The parks, like the package shows, depended upon "stars" to draw their audience, and again the relatively low cost of even the biggest "star" made such operations profitable.

The Rise of the Deejay

The old patterns of artists' self-promotion obviously did not work in these new situations in which stars traveled long distances to appear in package shows or at parks. Because of this the country music disc jockey (= d.j. = deejay) became the key person in promotion. By 1951 the country record show had begun to take the place of the live broadcast as the most common form of country music radio. According to *Billboard* there were 1400 hillbilly record programs in the U.S. at that time, playing an average of eleven hours per week of records.[1] Although there were a few stations with full-time country programming, most stations broadcast many kinds of music.

This varied format meant that the "rustic platter pilots" had a good deal of control over what they played. Country music disc jockeys of the early fifties chose their own music and did so on the basis of their personal tastes and those of their audiences. In 1953—by which time the average number of hours per week had risen to seventeen—a *Billboard* survey showed that 92.9 percent of the country deejays selected the records they played. Criteria for selection were multiple, but most important were listener requests (71.1 percent), then personal opinion (62.3 percent), and, quite a bit below that, the data presented in trade publications (35.1 percent).[2]

The deejays certainly had a good idea of who was popular and what was selling. First-hand knowledge of the local market, combined with the inherent promotional power of a regular radio program, put country deejays in a very special position during the early fifties. They became performers in their own right, taking on colorful personae such as "Uncle" so-and-so or "Cowboy" somebody. Many became involved with the local show parks in their regions, usually as emcees, and they often performed the same services for package shows in their territories. Frequently such involvement went beyond the personal-appearance level: the deejay invested in the park or the package and helped to finance its promotion. Some also ventured into record sales, purchasing record shops or promoting mail-order sales over their programs.

Not only were country disc jockeys influential in promoting and financing local shows utilizing stars, they were also important promoters of local talent, including themselves. Like comedians and dancers, country disc jockeys were performers in their own right; during this period many were also singers or musicians. They were in a good position to promote their music-performing careers since they had access to promotional channels, goodwill connections with local parks and other show outlets, and contacts with record company representatives. The disc jockeys who sent letters to *Billboard's* country music column regularly reported not only on the popularity of certain stars' records but also on their own forthcoming or recent performances. Beyond this, though, the local deejay was in a good position to recognize and promote local talent in his region. For example, Elvis Presley's first manager was a Memphis deejay; when Presley's initial Sun recording was released in mid-August 1954 it appeared first in the country music "Territorial Best Seller Charts" for Memphis.

When *Billboard* introduced country "Territorial Best Seller Charts" in 1952, it was an indication that in spite of the growth of the nationalized hit/star system there were important differences in regional country music tastes at this time. Disc jockeys were aware of this and sought to share their knowledge in various ways. They were an important part of a system which communicated consumer preferences to the people who produced and marketed country music. And although country songs like those of Hank Williams were being recorded by pop singers, country deejays generally played only country recordings to an audience which had rather clear-cut preferences.

During these years record service seems to have been very spotty, for the growth of country radio record shows outstripped the record companies' awareness of such shows, so when deejays wrote to *Billboard*'s country music editor, they asked through the publication for more records to be sent to them. They also reported recent concerts and, often, conveyed the preferences of their listeners: "Al Morris, WONE, Dayton, O., conducted a popularity poll of his listeners with Eddy Arnold, Hank Snow, Bill Monroe, Hank Williams and Carl Smith finishing in that order."[3] While such reports varied widely, they had a common purpose of attempting to communicate tastes within the listening area of the station. Very often they commented not only upon who was most popular but also told of audience dislikes: "Homer M. Quaun, WSVA, Harrisonburg, Va., reports his listeners don't enjoy the pop-styled country discs, featuring choir, organ and other instruments not strictly h.b. (hillbilly)."[4] And of successful shows in the area: "Cliff Rogers, WHKK, Akron, reports that a Grand Ole Opry troupe featuring Bill Monroe, Grandpa Jones and Randy Hughes did capacity in two shows December 7 in the local auditorium."[5]

Calling It Bluegrass

As we will see, disc jockeys played an important role in the popularization of bluegrass music during the middle fifties. But they probably did not, as is sometimes hypothesized, invent the word. When Bill and Charlie Monroe split in 1938, each chose a name for his group that referred to his home state, Charlie calling his group the Kentucky Partners and Bill (after briefly using the name the Kentuckians) calling his band the Blue Grass Boys. Monroe was not the first country performer to name his group after his home state, nor was he the first country musician to use the words *Blue Grass*. As early as 1925 the Bluegrass Trio, three Kentuckians, was playing in Texas. As late as 1954–55, there was a Blue Grass record label and a Blue Grass Publishing Company active in country music, neither dealing with the genre known as "bluegrass."

During the forties "Blue Grass" was like a corporate image or trademark for Monroe. Between 1945 and 1950 he recorded four instrumentals using the words *Blue Grass* in their title. He called his band's limousine the Blue Grass Special, and the professional baseball team that travelled with his show was the Blue Grass Club. His 1950 songbook had the title *Bill Monroe's Blue Grass Country Songs* (New York: Hill and Range Songs).

There is, however, no evidence that he or any of his musicians were, in 1950, calling the music they played bluegrass. The earliest documented instance of Monroe describing the music in this way does not come until May 1956 when, at New River Ranch in Rising Sun, Maryland, he praised the operator of that country music park as "a wonderful booster of the bluegrass type of music.[6] By then *bluegrass* was being used to describe the other bands which, as we have seen, Monroe had not approved of because of their copying of him. Indeed because he felt one such band, the Stanley Brothers, sounded too much like him, he had moved from Columbia to Decca in 1950.

During his first sixteen months with Decca, his sound remained similar to that of his Columbia recordings. But he was recording in Nashville now instead of in Chicago. With the Opry's rise to prominence Nashville had become a recording center. New studios were opened and the major labels like Decca, Columbia, and Victor moved their A&R men there to supervise recording sessions. Under these circumstances what would come in the sixties to be called the Nashville Sound began developing.

This came about as the result of the adoption of a practice that had been standard in recording centers like New York and Los Angeles—the use of a pool of skilled studio musicians for recording sessions. Many singers didn't have their own bands. For those who did, the theory behind this practice was that using studio musicians would enable the companies to control and improve the quality of their products. The often rapid turnover in band personnel meant that even the biggest stars might have in their group musicians unfamiliar with their arrangements. And some of the musicians who performed well on radio and at live appearances were liable to "freeze" in the recording studio. Experienced studio musicians lowered recording costs by reducing the time taken to work out arrangements and by diminishing the number of "takes" needed to produce an acceptable recording. Nashville studio musicians, unlike those in New York and Los Angeles, did not have to be able to read music, for country songwriters rarely wrote musical scores. But they did have to be able to quickly learn melodies, chord progressions, and rhythms of new songs and to arrange suitable settings for them. The first musicians to perform this role came from Opry star Red Foley's band—rhythm guitarist Louie Innis, lead guitarist Zeke Turner, fiddler Tommy Jackson, and steel guitarist Jerry Byrd. They and a handful of others who had what it took—men like bassist Ernie Newton and guitarist Grady Martin—were heard on thousands of country recordings during the fifties. The system they and the producers who employed them developed became a successful commercial production formula.

Of the companies which used Nashville studio musicians, none entered the field with more enthusiasm than Decca. In the spring of 1951, under the direction of Decca A&R man Paul Cohen, Bill Monroe did ten songs in two sessions using Nashville studio musicians. The main reason for this was that Eddy Arnold's version of "Kentucky Waltz" was a hit, and Cohen wanted Monroe's cover of it to reach as broad a market as possible. He felt the use of studio musicians would produce a more marketable sound.

Owen Bradley, who played piano and organ, was one of the studio musicians at the first session. A pioneer in the Nashville studio recording work, he would later produce most of Monroe's sessions from the mid-fifties into the early sixties. In reminiscing about these two 1951 sessions, he said that even though the material was strong, the attempt to fit Monroe's style to the studio formula was a failure. Monroe did not like the setup, and most of the performances were not of marketable quality. At this point, Bradley recalled, Decca realized that Monroe's band "sound" was an important part of his success as a recording artist. To Bradley, the job of the producer at a Monroe session was similar to that of an A&R man working with one of the popular dance bands of the thirties and forties like Guy Lombardo, in which the sound was essentially produced by the bandleader, and the A&R man's task was just to see that it was properly recorded. The producer might make suggestions, but the bandleader made all the decisions. Bradley tells of asking a newly arrived associate to take over production of a Monroe session; some time after the session had started, he received a call from the substitute producer who complained that he'd been in the studio for an hour and a half with Monroe and had only done one song: "I can't understand a word he says!" Bradley told him not to worry about that and just let Monroe do what he wanted; when he was satisfied with a take, go on to the next song.[7] Monroe was fortunate that Decca came to view his music in this way; a lesser star as stubborn as he would not have had the same clout with the company and probably would have been forced to leave Decca or to conform to the new fashion of using studio musicians.

While Monroe had been able to retain his own sound in the face of pressure from Decca to adopt the new studio sound, he had also established a cordial relationship with one of the bands whose copying he had earlier resented. In July 1951, following the unsuccessful Nashville studio-musician sessions, Monroe returned to record for Decca in Nashville with his own band, which now included Carter Stanley. Although there had been "words" between the two men when they first met following Monroe's angry departure from Columbia, their differences had been settled, for the Stanleys now understood the importance of having their own distinctive repertoire and sound, and Monroe no longer was threatened by or isolated from these competitors. In the winter of 1950–51 business had been slow for the Stanleys, and Ralph was not certain he wanted to follow a career in music. The brothers disbanded, and Monroe then offered Carter a job as a Blue Grass Boy. Carter's willingness to step down from the position of bandleader to that of band member was the final move in the resolution of the tensions that had existed between him and Monroe. They became fast friends.

At the end of 1951 the Stanleys regrouped (without Pee Wee Lambert, who was replaced briefly by young Bobby Osborne) and by the fall of 1953 were recording for Mercury and broadcasting at WCYB. Bill Monroe helped them in various ways: he gave them songs he'd written but not recorded; he co-authored several songs with Carter and even helped to direct one session (to be discussed later in this chapter). During the mid-fifties the Stanley Brothers became Monroe's proteges, and his bad feelings of the past were forgotten.

But tensions still remained between Monroe and Flatt and Scruggs. When they formed the Foggy Mountain Boys, they took with them much of the sound that had characterized the Blue Grass Boys up to that point. They did strive to differentiate their sound from Monroe's: Scruggs played finger-style guitar on their gospel quartets, for example, and they used the mandolin sparingly, mainly for rhythm. But even though they developed their own repertoire, they still performed a number of songs they'd been doing with Monroe—Earl's banjo solos, some quartets, and Lester's solos and duets. Some of these they recorded, like "Pike County Breakdown," which Monroe had composed, and "Why Did You Wander," a Monroe-Flatt composition. Monroe was not pleased about such recordings (in 1952 he quickly recorded his version of "Pike Country Breakdown" when the Flatt and Scruggs recording was issued), but what seems to have caused most of his resentment was their success.

Unlike the Stanley Brothers, Flatt and Scruggs did not disband, and their career was marked by one success after another. Following their stint at Bristol, they had worked at medium-to-large stations in the southeast— Knoxville, Lexington, Tampa, Roanoke, and Raleigh. Meanwhile their records were being released frequently and doing well. They had recorded for Mercury from 1948 to 1950, and when they were signed by Columbia at the end of 1950 they cut twelve songs for Mercury in order to fulfill their contractual obligations. Consequently their recordings were appearing on both Mercury and Columbia during 1951–52 at a rate of eight or nine a year. The situation resembled that which had occurred when Flatt and Scruggs left Monroe and Columbia had continued to issue his recordings with them as sidemen.

By 1953, Lester and Earl's records were regularly advertised by Columbia as "best sellers." They were working out of Knoxville in May 1953 when they acquired the sponsorship of Martha White Flour, an arrangement that would last for the remainder of their career together and provide a solid foundation for their success. Company salesman Efford Burke had attended one of their shows and reported back enthusiastically to company president Cohen Williams. Martha White already sponsored a daily, fifteen-minute, early-morning show on WSM. But the band they were using played western swing music, and Burke, who was in charge of sales in the eastern part of middle Tennessee, was certain that Flatt and Scruggs could sell more flour with their music. Williams agreed and approached them about taking over the WSM show. They jumped at the opportunity. The Opry management, however, was lukewarm about the arrangement, leery of offending Monroe, whose displeasure with Flatt and Scruggs was no secret. And WSM would not allow Williams to place them on Martha White's half-hour portion of the Opry. Monroe was using his influence with Opry manager Jim Denny to keep his former band members out.

While Flatt and Scruggs did not wish to be associated with Monroe (though they did not share his intense resentment), fans who had followed them since their days as Blue Grass Boys could scarcely avoid making the connection between them and Monroe. It is in this context that the use of the word *bluegrass* to describe the musical genre seems to have arisen. Everett Lilly, who played mandolin and sang tenor with Flatt and Scruggs from November 1950 to August 1952, recalled:

> I remember when I went to Lester and Earl the first time in 1950—around nineteen and fifty, somewhere there. When we would come out on the stage and open our show up, Lester would m.c. the first half, I would m.c. the last half of it, usually. Lester would say "Howdy, friends, we got a little clean country sober show here we hope you'll enjoy." We'd do our show. They didn't call it bluegrass.
>
> But I do recall people saying this to us, they would ask Lester and Earl to do a Bill Monroe tune. Lester and Earl didn't want to hear that name, or I don't believe they did, and I believe the public could feel that. The public began to say, "Boys would you please do us one of them old Blue Grass tunes like you used to do?" They knew me and Lester could sing them duets like him and Bill. They'd say "would you please do an old bluegrass tune?" . . . the public named bluegrass music . . . through the fear to speak Bill's name to 'em.[8]

Lilly now calls *bluegrass* a "feud word" and prefers to describe his music as "American folk and country music."[9]

Country music fans—Lilly's "the public"—addressed their requests not only to disc jockeys and performers, but also to country music park operators. In 1951 Bill Monroe purchased a country music park, the Brown County Jamboree, in Bean Blossom, Indiana. Marvin Hedrick, native of the county, musician, fan, and regular patron, repeatedly asked Monroe's brother Birch, who was managing the Jamboree, to book his favorites—groups such as the Stanley Brothers, the Lonesome Pine Fiddlers, and Mac Wiseman. "Bluegrass or old-time, what I was interested in," he said. Asked when he'd heard the term *bluegrass* used, he replied: "You know, I guess, bluegrass, the first guy I remember [using] that was Harold Lowry [another local musician]. It was in 1953, and Harold says, 'Why don't we come out some night and we'll pick a little bluegrass?' That's the first time I ever heard the term used. I think the term come into being right about that time."[10] Hedrick did not remember hearing Monroe or his musicians use the term; it came from persons like himself, fans of the music who also played informally or semi-professionally. Requests at shows and interest in the music on the part of country music amateurs can be translated as consumer interest, and there is evidence that this consumer interest was soon recognized by the merchants who were most in touch with bluegrass fans.

In 1951 country singer Jimmie Skinner opened his Music Center in Cincinnati, Ohio. This was reported in *Billboard*: "Lou Epstein and Jimmie Skinner are working a one-hour d.j. show over WNOP, Covington, Ky., from their disc shop in Cincinnati. They are seeking guests for the shows. Chuck Seitz, who works the shop, is managing Joe (Cannonball) Lewis, the new MGM singer."[11]

Seitz managed Lewis (some of whose records had bluegrass-type instrumentation) until July 1952. During the same period he had become associated with Carl Burkhardt in forming a record company in Cincinnati which issued recordings on the Gateway and Kentucky labels.

In the fall of 1952 Burkhardt and Seitz contacted a teenager named Sonny Osborne who had spent the past summer as banjoist with Bill Monroe. At fourteen he was the youngest person ever to record with Bill, playing banjo on Monroe's version of "Pike County Breakdown." Sonny was the younger brother of Bobby Osborne, the mandolinist from Hyden, Kentucky, by way of Dayton who had played briefly with the Stanley Brothers and was at this point with the Marine Corps in Korea. Seitz and Burkhardt asked Sonny to make some recordings for them. Of the twenty-six songs cut by Osborne and his band in two sessions at the end of 1952, over half were from the recorded repertoire of Bill Monroe and Flatt and Scruggs.[12]

Like the Stanley Brothers' "Molly and Tenbrooks" these were not so much covers as copies. In virtually every one Osborne's five-string banjo was prominent, closely following the sound of Earl Scruggs. Thus by 1952 the fledgling musicians (Sonny had been playing less than two years) were beginning to catch up with the leading performers, and the repertoire of Monroe and Flatt and Scruggs was becoming very well known indeed.

Burkhardt and Seitz issued the original material on the Gateway label and the copies on Kentucky. The making of such copy covers had been going on in country music since at least the early thirties, when Gene Autry's first discs hewed closely to the sound of Jimmie Rodgers. And Kentucky had issued mainstream country music sound-alikes before they began recording Sonny Osborne. But these recordings were unique because they represented the first time this company had found someone who could recreate the bluegrass sound.

These recordings, appearing eventually on many other labels, were in print for years. Since they were sold almost exclusively through the Jimmie Skinner Music Center's radio and magazine mail-order offers, they were not listed in *Billboard* charts, nor were they the object of interest on the part of disc jockeys other than those pitching the Skinner offers. The first ad for a Sonny Osborne recording, in a May 1953 issue of *Billboard*, tells us how the music was being marketed: Gateway 3005, with "A Brother in Korea" and "Sunny Mountain Chimes," was advertised as "featuring the five-string Banjo."[13] The record combined two of the handful of original tunes recorded by Osborne, which probably accounts for this ad. One wonders why the Korean war motif was not plugged in the ad: this song, written by Osborne's sister Louise, told a true story about their brother Bobby. But Gateway knew their market, for while "A Brother in Korea" was little sung and remains an obscure piece,

"Sunny Mountain Chimes" became a popular bluegrass instrumental. Five-string banjo music sold records!

The five-string banjo has never been confined solely to bluegrass music, but within the country music scene of the early fifties the most popular five-string banjo style was that of Earl Scruggs. Everett Lilly mentioned the popularity of the vocal duets done by Lester Flatt and Bill Monroe as a cause for the use of the word, but Earl's banjo was the thing which caught many listeners' attention. Its importance in popularizing Flatt and Scruggs can be seen in the fact that when Columbia introduced their "Hall of Fame" reissue series in the fall of 1954, Flatt and Scruggs were represented by four of Earl's instrumentals. In three of them, "Earl's Breakdown," "Flint Hill Special," and "Foggy Mountain Chimes," Earl used his new "tuners" (later called "Scruggs pegs"), devices which allowed him to produce striking effects by accurately retuning two strings of his banjo while playing. Even today it is Earl's style of banjo which seems to first attract many neophytes to bluegrass, and often the label *bluegrass* is affixed to groups whose only affinity to the genre's instrumentation, style, or repertoire is the use of Scruggs-style five-string banjo. In the early and mid-fifties the word *bluegrass* was used only by those people already immersed in the genre, an in-group of committed fans. The phrase "featuring 5-string banjo" was an attempt to reach these consumers.[14]

Popular interest in bluegrass as a genre had been growing in the early fifties. By 1955 this interest, which was focused more on the instrumental sound of the music than on the vocal repertoire of particular stars like Monroe, was emerging as a commercial factor. Notice of this interest came first from country deejays on the eastern seaboard around the Mason-Dixon line: "Wild Bill Price, operator of WCOJ's C&W turntable in Coatesville, Pa., is readying a new hillbilly jamboree with live talent. Show will air every Saturday, 2–4 p.m. Price advises that folks in his area are going for fast banjo material by such well-knowns as Flatt and Scruggs, Reno and Smiley and the Lonesome Pine Fiddlers." The following month Price reported "many requests lately for old-time tunes by such well-knowns as Reno and Smiley, Monroe and Scruggs and Flatt." He asked "fellow deejays" to send him extra copies of records by these artists.[15]

The phrase "old-time tunes" was also a kind of code for the musical genre known to its devotees as bluegrass, although it also referred to other, though similar, styles within the country field. Back in the twenties "old-time" had been used by some record companies to describe what eventually came to be called "hillbilly." So by using this term Price was reporting a surge of interest in bluegrass and other kinds of older country music. At this time Elvis Presley, Carl Perkins, and Johnny Cash, all recording for Sun Records of Memphis, were doing one-nighters in the country field, playing with package shows and at parks. Their music was creating pandemonium in the country music business, and record companies were rushing to get on the bandwagon. In the context of this move toward rhythm-and-blues-influenced, teen-oriented, rockabilly music, the interest in old-time and five-string banjo music may be seen as both a reaction to nascent rock and roll and a parallel involvement in a vital new form.

While the rockabillies were beginning to dominate the country music charts, the surge of interest in five-string banjo music was strong enough to be reflected in *Billboard*'s country charts, albeit at a regional rather than a national level. In April 1955 Colonial Records, a small company in North Carolina whose previous recording stars were comedian Andy Griffith ("What It Was, Was Football") and sportscaster Dizzy Dean ("Wabash Cannon Ball"), released a recording of "Home Sweet Home" by Hack Johnson and his Tennesseeans. The central feature of this recording was Scruggs-style banjo by North Carolinian Allen Shelton, who used his "tuners" (Scruggs pegs) to play most of the melody. The recording was favorably reviewed in *Billboard* and was listed as a best-seller in the Richmond, Virginia, region during May and June 1955. Although there was singing on the record, its popularity was due largely to Shelton's innovative banjo arrangement. This was evident when "covers" of the hit appeared, all using similar banjo solos.

The most successful cover of "Home Sweet Home"—it sold more than Johnson's recording and was in print for years—was issued under the name of a group that had been recording for King Records since 1952, Don Reno, Red Smiley, and the Tennessee Cutups. Reno, the five-string banjoist who had auditioned with Monroe back in 1943, joined the Blue Grass Boys after Scruggs left in 1948. Leaving Monroe the following year, he met singer-guitarist Red Smiley, and they worked together in the bands of Tommy Magness and Toby Stroud. In 1951 they formed their own band, and at the start of 1952 recorded sixteen songs for King. Their first record, a gospel quartet written by Reno entitled "I'm Using My Bible for a Roadmap," sold well, and for the next twelve years King would issue five or six singles a year by the band. But in 1952 Reno and Smiley were unable to maintain a full-time band. They took other jobs and came together solely as a recording band.

Between January 1952 and November 1954 they recorded sixty sides for King. Half were gospel and the remainder just about evenly split between instrumentals and secular songs. There is no better testimony to the importance of records in the spread of bluegrass than these discs, which established Reno and Smiley as one of the leading groups in the genre. Smiley was a strong lead singer with a distinctive vocal style, like Flatt's in that it was relatively full sounding, in contrast to Reno's high, clear tenor. His solid rhythm guitar work underpinned the sound of the band. But the effusive and flamboyant Reno dominated the group in many ways. His banjo playing was clearly identifiable and gave the band much of its distinctive sound. Originally it had been similar to Scruggs's, but by the early fifties he had made it purposely different. When he picked phrases which paralleled Scruggs's, Reno articulated them differently. Unlike other three-finger banjoists, he constructed solos out of two- and three-note chords, sometimes accompanied slow songs in double-time, and used the thumb and one finger of his right hand alternating on single strings to execute guitar-like runs. Reno was also an accomplished guitarist, the first to play lead guitar with a flat pick on bluegrass recordings. On top of all this, he was a prolific composer. All but a handful of the sixty numbers recorded by the group in 1952–54 bore his name as composer or co-composer. Reno also looked after the arrangements for the band's recording sessions, two of which he produced at WBT in Charlotte. He hired the musicians and kept abreast of new recording techniques, like overdubbing parts on tape.

When Hack Johnson's record of "Home Sweet Home" "broke," King Records president Sydney Nathan wanted a cover in a hurry. Reno recalls: "Syd called me and told me he wanted the record in by the next day. I couldn't find any musicians so I went to the studio in Charlotte and cut it by myself. I dubbed in three vocal parts, and banjo, fiddle, guitar and bass."[16] The record was released within a few weeks of Johnson's.

This was in April, 1955, just as the country music parks were opening for their summer season: "Mac Wiseman and Pete Pike will headline a show at the opening of Sunset Park, West Grove, Pa., April 24. Wild Bill Price, who twirls 'em from WCOJ, Coatesville, Pa., is also emcee and advertising manager for the spot. He wonders if anyone knows how he may contact Don Reno and Red Smiley."[17] By May Reno and Smiley had organized a band, and by that summer they were playing on a Saturday night barn dance at WRVA in Richmond, Virginia, on a television program on WXEX in Petersburg, Virginia, and touring the parks. "Home Sweet Home" was their latest release at the time they organized a full-time band. With Reno acting as emcee and masterminding elaborate comedy routines in which the entire band dressed in costume, Don Reno, Red Smiley, and the Tennessee Cutups became one of the most successful bluegrass units in the late fifties and early sixties.

For at least this one group, the demand for banjo music was the key to launching a successful country music career at a time when the main trend was away from the older basic country music.

Reno and Smiley were not alone though; 1955 was a banner year for Flatt and Scruggs too. In January, Cohen Williams's Martha White Flour began sponsoring a thirty-minute show on WSM-TV for them. They had been working out of Crewe, Virginia, since late in 1953, sending their early morning radio shows to WSM on tape. Now they moved back to Nashville. Their new TV shows, aired at 6:00 P.M. Saturdays, was immediately successful, receiving lots of mail. Flatt's biographer Jake Lambert tells what happened next:

Williams, knowing that WSM always paid attention to the amount of mail a group could pull, collected a huge mail bag full and took it to

WSM. There he dumped it out on the office floor of (WSM general manager) Jack DeWitt. Not only did he take the mail with him, he had decided it was time for him to make his move. Either they put Flatt and Scruggs on his half hour of the Opry or he would pull his company's advertising off the station. So they allowed the boys to work the Martha White show, but they still were not considered members of the Opry.[18]

Flatt was not allowed to emcee the band's Opry broadcasts. However, the following year, 1956, Jim Denny, who had sided with Monroe in opposition to Flatt and Scruggs, was succeeded as Opry manager by Walter D. "Dee" Kilpatrick. Kilpatrick had known Flatt and Scruggs from the late forties, when they were all with Mercury records, and he made them regular members of the Opry, much to Monroe's chagrin.

By this time their sound and Monroe's were diverging. In 1954 Monroe had begun recording with three fiddles; in 1955 Flatt and Scruggs added to their band the acoustic steel guitar sound of Uncle Josh Graves's Dobro. Graves picked in the style of Scruggs on the faster tunes. On slower songs he used blues phrasing or the sweet-sounding slides associated with the Hawaiian-style steel guitar accompaniment that had been popular in country music since the thirties. He could play the kind of lead that the mandolin or fiddle might take, which was advantageous, for as Flatt recalled, "Back then you couldn't give a fiddle away. No one liked a fiddle."[19] Dislike of the fiddle was particularly strong in Nashville during the mid-fifties. To the A&R men there it symbolized the older style country music which rock and roll was outselling. Fiddles were said to "squawk" or sound "sour"; but the important point was that teenagers didn't buy records on which the fiddle was heard.

Though country music seemed under seige, Flatt and Scruggs were doing fine. Martha White was now sponsoring them on television in six different cities. This was before the days of videotape, so they had to do the shows live in Nashville and Jackson, Tennessee; Florence, South Carolina; Atlanta and Columbus, Georgia; and in Huntington, West Virginia. Traveling 2500 miles a week in their bus they found time to prerecord their early morning radio shows, play personal appearances, and perform every week on the Opry. Maintaining this grueling pace through the southeastern states, Flatt and Scruggs showed that their kind of music was definitely popular with a substantial segment of country music fans.

In December 1955 a new country music monthly from the publishers of the jazz magazine *Down Beat*, *Country and Western Jamboree*, printed the results of their first readers' poll. Mainstream country dominated the poll— Hank Williams was the "all time favorite," Faron Young and Kitty Wells were the most popular male and female singers—but the impact of newer music could be seen in some of the results. Elvis Presley was voted "Best New Male Singer," and this was considered an "upset" by the compilers of the data. Receiving less comment was the domination of the "Instrumentalist" sections of the poll by groups with five-string banjo: winners in the "Best Instrumentalist Group" listing were Flatt and Scruggs; Reno and Smiley placed fourth, and the McCormick Brothers, a Tennessee group that had started recording bluegrass instrumentals for Hickory Records in 1954, came fifth. In the "Best New Instrumentalist Group" section first place was taken by the Stanley Brothers, and the McCormick Brothers appeared again, this time in second place.[20]

The interest which was noted first by disc jockeys like Price, then in record sales as reported by *Billboard*, and next by the reader poll in *Country and Western Jamboree* did not take long to reach those involved in marketing such music. In the very next issue of *Country and Western Jamboree*, dated January 1956, a full-page ad for the Jimmie Skinner Music Center appeared. The ad was for the complete catalog of Sonny Osborne's Gateway and Kentucky recordings "featuring 5-String Banjo."[21] A similar full-page ad with a special offer on "Sonny Osborne (Featuring 5-String Banjo)" appeared at about the same time in the February issue of Charlton Publications' *Country Song Roundup*.[22] In the March issue of *Country and Western Jamboree* the full-page Skinner ad featured "5-String Banjo Instrumentals" and listed recordings by Flatt and Scruggs, Reno and Smiley, the McCormick Brothers, Jim Eanes (who had recorded a cover of "Home Sweet Home"), the Stanley Brothers, and Hack Johnson.[23] The same ad appeared in the April issue of *Country Song Roundup*. Such ads with "specials" on either the Osborne mail-order offer or five-string instrumentals continued to appear regularly in these monthlies and fanzines during the next few years.

Charlton Publications, publishers of *Country Song Roundup* and *Cowboy Songs*, maintained their predominance in the field of country music magazines from their inception in the late forties through the seventies because they carried the words to the latest hit songs. Along with these were feature articles on stars, vignettes on up-and-coming young performers or deejays, and various kinds of country music gossip columns. The ads by the Jimmie Skinner Music Center fit well in this format, for his mail-order service catered to a wide range of tastes. Skinner was by no means specializing in instrumentals "featuring the 5-string banjo" or in bluegrass. He regularly advertised the latest releases by everyone from radical Elvis Presley to arch-conservative Doc Williams. He also enticed customers with specials on Hank Williams, Johnny Cash, and other current or recent favorites. But he specialized in mail-order offers on country music recordings which were difficult to find in regular record stores. For example, he frequently advertised gospel and sacred "offers."

Like Skinner, disc jockeys like Wild Bill Price were not committed to a single country music sound. Price merely strove to determine the tastes of his listeners and to provide them with the music they wanted. This was relatively easy for a country deejay to do in this period (if he could obtain records) because as we have seen, few stations told them what to play by maintaining a "playlist" or following the country charts closely as is done today. The deejays couldn't afford to play just the songs on the charts because at this time only fifteen songs were listed each week. When Price was in the southern Pennsylvania region—then as now a bastion of bluegrass involvement—his actions as a disc jockey and promoter reflected those audience tastes. His success as an effective deejay was rewarded in October 1955 when he was invited to be "Mr. Deejay USA" on the Grand Ole Opry—a weekly honor given to disc jockeys for their contributions to country music. And when, early in 1956, he moved to a 50,000-watt station, XERB at Rosarito Beach, Mexico, near San Diego, he began reporting local tastes in *that* region. It was Price who first reported to *Billboard* that a minor label's new artist, Buck Owens, had a hit that was "breaking big" in California with his first recording, "Down on the Corner of Love."[24] Audience responses were noted quickly by deejays like Price and record-store owners like Skinner because they were directly in touch with the consumers. Relaying new trends to the industry, they were important mediators in the country music marketing system.

Folk Music

This rising interest in bluegrass had another dimension to it as well, one in which people much less in touch with country music played an important role. These were the young people interested in "folk music," involved in what later became known as the folksong revival. In attendance at Sunset Park where Wild Bill Price was emceeing during the summer of 1955 were a group of young, urban, college-educated people, listening to bluegrass and old-time country music. One of them, New Jersey suburbanite Ralph Rinzler, recalled:

> There were a few of us from the city who were following Bill [Monroe]—
> Mike Seeger, myself, Willie Foshag, Jerry and Alice Foster. Mike and I
> would go to various parks sorting out who we liked—Bill, the Stanley
> Brothers, Grandpa Jones, Don Reno—but bluegrass had not got into the
> folk revival. But for me it was like going into another world. I was fasci-
> nated by the totally different life-style—dinner on the grounds, different
> speech patterns—a whole different way of life. The whole idea really
> astounded me—that this existed. That was in fifty-four and fifty-five.[25]

Although Rinzler recalls that bluegrass had not gotten into the folk revival, it would be more accurate to say that only part of bluegrass had gotten into the revival at this time, for there were revivalists playing five-string banjo in the style of Earl Scruggs prior to 1954–55.

But until Rinzler, Seeger *et al* began to attend live appearances, bluegrass and other kinds of country music had existed for them primarily on record. They were not country music fans; they were the young Turks of the folksong revival—a new group of listeners who perceived bluegrass as a separate and distinct musical art form. Educated in American folk music via Folkways and Library of Congress recordings which emphasized Appalachian folk music traditions, they quickly recognized the traditional elements in bluegrass performance practice and repertoire. And they discovered the five-string banjo was alive and well in bluegrass. At this time, virtually the only person outside country music using the instrument was Pete Seeger. He had a number of imitators within the folksong revival, but at this point in time—before the Kingston Trio—the folksong revival was still mainly a cult phenomenon.

The revival owed much to left-wing political ideas about American culture developed during the middle and late thirties. But by the fifties the openly political goals of its leaders—Woody Guthrie, the Almanac Singers, Pete Seeger, and the staff of *People's Songs* (predecessor of *Sing Out!*)—were of declining importance for many of the followers. It had become a social movement, a musical in-group similar to (though smaller than) those groups of middle-class youths who discovered jazz in the twenties and rhythm and blues in the fifties.

These folksong enthusiasts, most of whom lived in the New York City region, saw folk music as an appealing alternative to the insipid pop music and the difficult-to-follow jazz of the period. "Leadbelly" (Huddie Ledbetter) brought the twelve-string guitar to young New Yorkers; Pete Seeger brought the five-string banjo. By the late forties Pete Seeger had a number of musical disciples in Greenwich Village. One of the first, Roger Sprung, remembers being told about Earl Scruggs by another early disciple, Billy Faier, at a party in Greenwich Village in 1947 or 1948.

Seeger, who had published a five-string banjo instruction book in 1948, recalls first hearing of Scruggs around 1950. By 1954, when he revised the instruction book and prepared a record, *The Five-String Banjo Instructor* (Folkways FP 303) to accompany it, he included a short chapter on "three finger picking (Scruggs' style)."[26] Like Jimmie Skinner, Seeger recognized a market for this style of banjo and adjusted his "product" to take advantage of the interest in this music.

"Scruggs' Style" banjo was popular with the young folk enthusiasts who congregated every Sunday afternoon, from spring to fall, around the fountain at Washington Square in New York City's Greenwich Village to sing and play folk music. Folkways Records was aware of this when, early in 1957, they released *American Banjo Scruggs Style*. The first bluegrass LP, it brought the music into a revolutionary new recorded sound medium. Instead of six minutes worth of two songs, this record had close to an hour's worth of music, with thirty-one separate selections. Produced and recorded by Mike Seeger, the album included fifteen different banjo pickers. Among them were Earl Scruggs's older brother Junie and Snuffy Jenkins, both of whom demonstrated how the older three-finger styles sounded before Earl Scruggs came along. Also on the record were Joe Stuart, Bill Monroe's banjoist at the time of recording; Veronica Stoneman Cox, daughter of country music pioneer Ernest Stoneman and still active today as a comedienne and banjoist on "Hee Haw"; Larry Richardson, who had played with the Lonesome Pine Fiddlers and Bill Monroe; Don Bryant, a veteran from Mac Wiseman's band who had filled in for Earl Scruggs following his 1955 auto accident; Smiley Hobbs, a participant in one of Reno and Smiley's recording sessions in 1954; and Eric Weissberg, a young New Yorker who had studied banjo with Pete Seeger.

The album, which is still available from Folkways as this is written, was soon added to the mail-order ads of the Jimmie Skinner Music Center, gaining wide distribution through them. Several tunes from the disc became popular in bluegrass repertoires: Smiley Hobbs's arrangement of "Train 45" was used by several groups during the sixties, for example.

The album format created an important new dimension, by giving listeners photographs and written descriptions to accompany the music. Inside the jacket was a brochure with an introduction written by Ralph Rinzler. He described how, in 1945, "a well known mandolin picker and singer in Kentucky, Bill Monroe, organized a different type of band from those already in existence." A brief description of Scruggs and his banjo style followed, and then a bit more history: "Scruggs worked with Monroe for a short time before he and Lester Flatt, then Monroe's guitar picker, organized a band of their own. Before long this type of music was becoming popular in the South. The banjo along with many of the 'old-time' songs, had been revived and numerous 'bluegrass' bands, patterned on those of Scruggs and Monroe, were soon doing performances and making recordings for well-known companies."[27] Notice here how Rinzler echoes Wild Bill Price's description of the music as encompassing the banjo and old-time tunes. He adds, however, two key words, *revival* and *bluegrass*. As far as I have been able to determine, this is the first time that the word *bluegrass* was used in print to refer to this music.

Folkways' use of "Scruggs' style" in the album title reflected their knowledge of interest in this way of playing the banjo within the growing urban folk boom. But Rinzler's use of "bluegrass" called for an explanation. When this album was first released, many of the buyers were not country music followers, for few of them at this time owned long-play phonographs. The urban, middle-class, folk-music enthusiasts who first bought this album would not recognize the reference to Bill Monroe inherent in the term. Rinzler asserted (incorrectly) that "the term 'bluegrass' refers to that section of Kentucky where Bill Monroe originally lived" (Monroe is from further west in the "Pennyroyal" section of Kentucky) and that the music was most popular in this area at the outset (it wasn't, according to bluegrass fans in the Lexington area). With hindsight we may also question Rinzler's statement that "it was applied to this music by disc-jockeys . . . " although this is where Rinzler himself first heard the term used.

Rinzler's definition was the first to describe bluegrass in terms of instrumentation and repertoire: "[Bluegrass] is descriptive of a band usually consisting of a guitar and bass, used for backing, and one or two fiddles, a banjo and a mandolin used for lead or solo playing. The songs themselves, if not actually folk or "old-time" songs, generally are closer to that tradition than to the modern tradition of popular Tin Pan Alley or hillbilly songs."[28]

Emphasis is placed on instrumentation, the roles of instruments, and the closeness of the songs to folksong traditions. The fact that Monroe, Flatt, and Scruggs were Grand Ole Opry stars is not mentioned, and the songs are carefully differentiated from popular "hillbilly" songs. The message is: "This is a kind of modern folk music, defined largely by its instrumentation," Rinzler's interpretation of the meanings conveyed by the terms "old-time" and "featuring 5-string banjo."

This emphasis on instrumentation and repertoire was not shared by all of those who were using the word *bluegrass* in these years. Marvin Hedrick, of Brown County, Indiana, who, as noted above, recalled using the term from 1953 on, responded to my question of whether the music had to have the banjo to be qualified as bluegrass by saying, "Not necessarily the banjo. I'd say that it's the general beat and feel of the music rather than the instruments."[29] His viewpoint was that of one familiar with the historical and stylistic spectrum of country music through a life-long exposure to it via records, radio, and personal appearances.

By 1957 there were two ways of looking at the same kind of music—as a special kind of country music (i.e., Hedrick) and as a special kind of folk music (i.e., Rinzler). Debates about the definition of the term became possible once it spread beyond the oral traditions of those early die-hard fans who knew what the word meant when they heard it. By having a name, bluegrass was automatically defined as a special genre, even though there might be disagreements about what made it so.

The name appeared in print frequently during 1957. In the February 1957 issue of Charlton Publications' *Cowboy Songs* was an article on the Bluegrass Pardners, Curley Parker and Pee Wee Lambert, currently appearing on WJEL in Springfield, Ohio. They had been together since 1951, when they had first appeared as the Pine Ridge Boys on WHTN radio in Huntington, West Virginia. It is not surprising, given Lambert's reputation as an ardent follower of Monroe's music, that as the word *bluegrass* became a generic term he would be one of the first to adopt it for a band name.

The February issue of *Cowboy Songs* also carried an article on another band which used "bluegrass" in its name, the Blue Grass Champs. They were Champs on several counts. In 1956 they had won the band championship at the National Hillbilly (later, Country) Music Championships, held each year since 1951 by Washington promoter Connie B. Gay in nearby Warrenton, Virginia. Their fiddler, Scott Stoneman, had won a number of fiddle contests. In 1956 they began a long-running engagement at the Famous Restaurant, located next to the Trailways Bus Station on New York Street in Washington—a country music club that had previously hosted a young musician-singer named Roy Clark. The owner of the club, Sid Baumstein, wanted a name with more appeal than the one they'd been using, the Stone-man Family, and came up with Blue Grass Champs. Soon after that Baum-stein arranged for them to appear on the Arthur Godfrey talent show, where they became champs once more. The article called them the Stoveman [sic] Family, but in fact they were the children of Ernest V. Stoneman, one of the first and most prolific of the pioneer hillbilly recording artists of the twenties. The band consisted mainly of a number of his twenty-two offspring. Since the early forties they had been playing at dances and in bars around Washing-ton. *Cowboy Songs* did not mention that members of the family could be heard on a Folkways album edited by Ralph Rinzler (which emphasized the older styles of Stoneman and his wife rather than his children's bluegrass) or that Veronica Stoneman (Cox) was one of the pickers on Folkways' *American Banjo Scruggs Style.* Conversely, Rinzler's notes to these records do not men-tion that the Stoneman Family was calling itself the Blue Grass Champs. These differing perspectives on the same band indicate the distance between the country music and folk revival views at this time.

Both the Stoneman and the Parker-Lambert bands were local groups, known only within a small region and not having recording contracts with major companies. For such groups the use of a stylistic code word like *blue-grass* had promotional value, because it communicated integrity to country music fans dismayed by the way in which some country music performers were changing their music ("going modern") to get more airplay and teen sales. Both bands were located in regions which were hotbeds of interest in bluegrass—Parker and Lambert in southern Ohio and the Stonemans in the Washington–Baltimore–northern Virginia area.

These areas were (and still are) centers of interest in bluegrass because both regions contained substantial populations of recent immigrants from the southern highlands who were most likely to appreciate the music and pay to hear it on records and radio and in personal appearances.

Another center of immigration from the southern highlands was southern Michigan. Bluegrass bands were playing for Appalachian factory workers and their families on the radio stations and in the bars of Detroit as early as 1953, when the Lonesome Pine Fiddlers moved up from Bluefield, West Virginia. By 1957 there were several bands working in the area. One was that of singer-guitarist Jimmy Martin, who'd worked with Bill Monroe most of the time from 1950 to 1954. In the summer of 1954 he teamed up with Bob and Sonny Osborne. They worked out of Detroit together for a year. Their RCA Victor recording session of November 1954 yielded several influential per-formances, particularly the trio "20/20 Vision." After this talented but vola-tile group split up in August 1955, Martin formed his own band. In 1956 he began recording for Decca and soon developed a reputation which extended beyond Detroit. Thus he was a focus for local songwriters hoping for a hit. Martin's first Decca single included "Hit Parade of Love" written by Wade

Birchfield. Birchfield and his twin brother Wiley had come to Detroit from the mountains of North Carolina. They had been active in bluegrass music around Knoxville since the late forties, when banjoist Wiley had recorded with the Bailey Brothers and the Sauceman Brothers on Rich-R-Tone.

Both of the Birchfields were songwriters as well as musicians, and in 1957 they expanded their activities to include a record company, Wayside Records. Their first records—one by themselves and another by a young "mandolin virtuoso" named Frank Wakefield—were released in the spring of 1957. In May 1957 Wade Birchfield placed an ad for his two records in *Billboard*. Typical of the ads by small independents, it was a column an inch wide and an inch long; it listed the two records and their wholesale price, and gave Birchfield's Detroit home as the company's mailing address. At the top of the ad, right under the company name, was "(Music Blue Grass Style)."[30]

With Wayside's use of the term, the word had been taken a step further from its origins in fan requests. This new usage reflected a perception of economic value to be gained in identifying the music of Appalachian immigrants as a special style. That the first company to take advantage of this perception in their advertising was a native-run one is indicative of the origins of the word.

A larger company having national distribution and advertising, but still very much in touch with regional tastes, was next to catch on to the spreading popularity of the word. In the October 1957 issue of *Country Song Roundup* the regular Jimmie Skinner Music Center full-page ad contained a significant change in wording: the five-string banjo/old-time music record offer was now headed "Best Selling Blue Grass Type Records (featuring 5-string banjo, mandolin, etc.)."[31]

The appearance of the word elsewhere the following year certainly owes something to the influence of Skinner's ads, although the primary mode for the spread of the word was oral usage. Whatever their source, these new printings reflected growing country-music industry awareness of the word and the special music it described. Three examples from January 1958 demonstrate this.

In June 1957 a musician from Nova Scotia named Ron Scott, who described himself as "formerly [a] side man for Hank Snow" had written in to *Billboard* describing his first record release. He mentioned that this (the first Canadian bluegrass recording) was "done up in rank hillbilly fashion, using, besides Spanish [guitar] and bass, a fiddle, mandolin and five-string banjo."[32]

In January 1958 Scott wrote in again to plug his record and to indicate that he was doing a deejay show with another Canadian country singer: " 'Bobby Hill and I are running one of the two big country and western Saturday night deejay shows here in Canada's metropolis,' writes Ron Scott, of CFCF, Montreal. 'We devote about one night in four to Blue Grass music. The response to the latter has been terrific, considering this is Canada. Some of this 'rank' stuff is hard to get, though, as it's not released in Canada. We welcome promotion platters from Blue Grass bands across the South . . . ' "[33] Scott, whose program had an important role in the growth of interest in bluegrass music in Quebec, seems to have used, perhaps adapted, "rank" as another code word like "old-time" and "featuring 5-string banjo"; apparently sometime between June 1957 and January 1958 he began equating it with "Blue Grass".

Around the same time Louise Scruggs, wife of Earl and since 1956 manager and booking agent for Flatt and Scruggs, received a phone call from a disc jockey in the New Jersey-New York area who asked her to send some bluegrass. She asked him to repeat the request and he told her he didn't have any bluegrass records. She said she didn't understand what he was talking about, and they went back and forth until she got from him the fact that by bluegrass he meant the music of Flatt and Scruggs. This was her introduction to the word.

In January 1958 the Opry published an updated and revised edition of *WSM's Official Grand Ole Opry History-Picture Book*, edited by Red O'Donnell with Opry manager Dee Kilpatrick, Lester and Earl's old friend. In it was a brief description of the Flatt and Scruggs act which included the following: "A simple and solid presentation of grassroots entertainment, this pair is known in the trade as sincere salesmen of 'blue grass music.' "[34] The same book described Bill Monroe without using the words "blue grass music" even though it did mention the name of his band. Notice the phrase "in the trade" with reference to the use of the word *blue grass*. The editors of the book, which was designed for fans, saw *blue grass* as a term which would be new to fans and, anticipating questions about it, indicated that it was used by those involved with the business of marketing the music.

Moreover, this marked the association of "bluegrass" by people in the business with "name" rather than "local" groups, an important shift. With unknown groups like those on Wayside records, the words *bluegrass style* helped potential consumers identify the music. For Flatt and Scruggs, who recorded on a major label, appeared frequently on radio and television broadcasts, and toured extensively, such an identifying tag was hardly needed. In fact they lent their identity to the word more than the word lent its identity to them.

The spread of the word *bluegrass* continued in 1958, with more printings within the country music industry. The January 20 edition of *Billboard* described another band which, like Flatt and Scruggs, recorded for a major label: "Jimmy Martin and his Blue Grass band, heard on the Decca label . . . guested with 'Louisiana Hayride' (Shreveport), Saturday (18)."[35] Perhaps more significantly, the word was now being used in folksong revival publications and Japanese country music periodicals, indicating its spread into new social and cultural domains.

Bluegrass and Rock and Roll

Reviewing the spread of the word *bluegrass* from fans to the industry, let us return to my earlier point—that demand for the music grew during a period of uncertainty and stress for country music, the years in which rock and roll became entrenched as the new vital youth music. *Bluegrass* (the word), originating as a band name, became identified with the musical sound of Bill Monroe's group as it developed into a genre, surfacing first as a usage by fans to describe this genre. Disc jockeys and mail-order record shops in areas having a high proportion of immigrants from the southern highlands (where the music was initially popular, home of many of the musicians who first performed the music) were among the first to notice and cater to the demand for this genre. In the mid-fifties bluegrass was considered country music and existed totally within that milieu. The demand for it increased noticeably during the years 1955–57, the very years that Elvis Presley, Johnny Cash, Carl Perkins, Sonny James, Jerry Lee Lewis, the Everly Brothers, and similar teen-oriented acts were viewed as a threat to country music. What was happening?

First of all, remember that rock and roll, even in its beginnings, was not a monolithic musical style. It was a synthesis of pop, rhythm and blues, and country and western styles. A rhythmic dance music, it was defined more by its market than by particular musical characteristics: it sold to teenagers, a class of consumer that for the first time had disposable cash. In this fact, and in the stylistic confluence it represented, it was very much like early jazz or hillbilly music. The ways in which it affected country music were varied and contradictory. Its impact was substantial.

By 1956, country performers, especially those having contracts with major recording companies, were admittedly "changing styles to get air plays."[36] Some deejays and older fans reacted negatively to this disloyal behavior, but the record companies dismissed such reactions as an "anti-pop bias." They knew from their record sales that southern youths who had previously been country followers but had been exposed to rhythm and blues and rockabilly on television, would buy music of this type and listen to it on the radio.[37] Even though there were quite a few local country music shows, the networks had more programming time and aired rock and roll music more frequently, often during prime time. The younger segment of the southern/rural audience sought this music on the radio and on records. Record companies encouraged the marketing of such music because these younger fans bought more records than did the older, more conservative fans.

Not only that, rock and roll recordings sold well outside the South in markets where country music had not previously done well. So there were economic incentives as well as record company pressures on country musicians to change toward the teen market. A good case in point is that of Mac Wiseman. An early member of the Flatt and Scruggs band, he had spent most of 1949 as Bill Monroe's guitarist and lead singer. In 1950 he started his own group and the following year obtained a contract with Dot Records, a new independent located in Gallatin, Tennessee. In 1953 he joined the cast of the WRVA "Old Dominion Barn Dance" in Richmond, Virginia, where he remained until the end of 1956. During this period his records regularly made the territorial best-seller charts in *Billboard*. On record and in person Wiseman had a bluegrass band; one distinctive feature of his sound was the use of twin harmony fiddles, a country music sound not previously associated with bluegrass that was picked up and used by most of the best known bands of the period, including Monroe's. But Wiseman's instrumental sound was subordinated to his vocals. He never recorded an instrumental, and "I didn't record many duets, because I could see there would come a time where I would want to work a solo. And I always wanted to keep that solo identity." But by 1956 the music scene was beginning to change: "You could see the decline or lack of interest in country music, and rock music was coming on the scene. It was difficult to get exposure for a straight country product because the volume of the teen market was so big."[38]

Moreover, he was being booked on traveling package shows, where the promoters wanted only Mac Wiseman. They couldn't afford the cost of the full band, and felt that his name, not the sound of his band, drew the audiences. On the package tours just one set of sidemen was needed for the whole show; it was cheaper and more efficient. So Wiseman let his band go. When Dot Records moved to California and offered him a job running their country department, he accepted: "I didn't do any bluegrass while I was out there. I had the devil of a time erasing the nametag. . . . If they tab you with that, they feel that you're no good for anything else. I came out with [a version of rock and roller Smiley Lewis's] "I Hear You Knocking" . . . and sold records in northern markets that bluegrass hadn't sold in. But in the South, they broke them and threw them away!"[39]

Wiseman was lucky in comparison to some other bluegrass performers. Jim and Jesse McReynolds, who had recorded with Capitol from 1952 to 1955, were unable to obtain a recording contract until 1958 because they were not playing teen-oriented music. Jim Eanes, a singer-guitarist from Martinsville, Virginia, had recorded with Roy Hall in 1941, worked with Bill Monroe in 1948, and obtained a Decca recording contract in 1951 following his success with a Korean war song, "Missing in Action," on Blue Ridge, a small mountain company like Rich-R-Tone. Like Monroe, Eanes had to deal with Paul Cohen's eagerness to use Nashville studio musicians on his recordings. Because he was not a star like Monroe he had less leverage with the company, and most of his band was not used on his records, though he did do several bluegrass instrumentals (including "There's No Place Like Home," a cover of "Home Sweet Home") in 1954. In mixing bluegrass instrumentals with Nashville-style vocals, Eanes, who sings in a rich baritone voice not typical of bluegrass, was attempting to exploit two commercial trends at the same time.

But he too was unable to obtain a recording contract when his Decca pact ran out in 1955. Like Jim and Jesse, he blamed it on Elvis. Many other bluegrass and country performers had similar experiences at this time. Their records weren't selling briskly enough, and the company thought it was because they were no longer "commercial." They were dropped by the company or forced to change their style.

When a country music performer changed his style—and such changes were usually motivated by economic factors which reflected attempts to keep abreast with "progress," capture new listeners, and cash in on what seemed like an irreversible trend—the first instrument to go was the fiddle, which characterized the older country sound. As the fiddle became rare in most "modern" country recordings, those listeners who liked it began seeking recordings which maintained this sound. Many bluegrass bands had fiddlers, and thus part of the interest in it stemmed from the fact that it represented a sound otherwise unavailable to country music fans who liked the fiddle. In a more general way the high proportion of older songs, the shunning of electric instruments, and the general lack or understated use of drums on bluegrass recordings represented for many country music fans evidence that this musical genre was a bastion of purity within a sea of debasement and weak-kneed musical sellouts.

A similar process affected live country music performances. Ed Sullivan's censorship of Elvis Presley's lower torso on television is a well-known example of the reaction against the new rock and roll performance styles. Vic Mullen, a Canadian maritimes country music veteran of these years, describes what happened to country acts doing personal appearances then:

> They'd yell for "Blue Suede Shoes" and these other big rock songs, and if you happened to do one of those on the show, this group, wherever they were in the building, would, of course, get all carried away. And the girls would scream and the guys would stomp and clap their hands and they'd yell and all this. And the guy on stage would say, "hey, this is what I should be doing." Forgetting that the quiet country music crowd were sitting down there hoping that he'd get back to a country song, and probably there was three or four times as many of those in the room as there was the younger rock fans . . . and it fooled a lot of country entertainers into thinking that . . . country music was gone. . . . what it did was discourage the country fans from going to any country show that was advertised because they found out after they got there, most of the show was going to be rock.[40]

Bluegrass acts could derive some commercial benefit from billing their show in such a way to assure the fans who didn't like rock and roll that they would be playing only country music. While rock made inroads as a popular dance music at this time, concert-type shows still drew fans of the older style. Many bluegrass bands incorporated Elvis spoofs into their comedy routines, further testimony to their fans that they were on the right side of the rock and roll controversy. Thus in August 1956, when Reno and Smiley made their first recordings since becoming a full-time group, included was Don Reno's "Country Boy Rock and Roll," a tongue-in-cheek anthem to the joys of the music: "I guess to some folks I look foolish, Just let 'em make a fool out of me."[41] With full bluegrass instrumentation, including twin harmony fiddles, but featuring Reno's hot lead guitar in the foreground, this up-tempo piece was recorded "straight" but done as a burlesque at shows.

The burlesque of the Elvis parodies fit easily into the comedy routines of such groups as Reno and Smiley because these parodies were similar to the blackface acts which until recently had been part and parcel of such routines. During the early fifties the overt blackface acts had gone out of fashion. The older system of racial values and etiquette was being challenged and many in the country music business were nervous and uncertain about what was appropriate. In 1951 Jim Eanes had recorded "I Took Her by Her Little Brown Hand," a song popularized on record by Fiddling Arthur Smith in the thirties, for Rich-R-Tone. The first verse included the lines: "The prettiest little coon gal you ever did see, She's been my lady friend a year or more."[42] He did the song, which was one he sang regularly in public, for Decca in 1952, but Paul Cohen insisted on changing the lyrics to, "The prettiest little gal . . . "[43] Until then, "I just sung it like I got the words. It was real good for me. . . . I never had anybody question me at all about the song until I cut it for Decca."[44] Similarly, when Bill Monroe recorded his version of "John Henry" in January 1954, Decca executives decided not to release it because the first verse contained a description of John Henry as "a little colored boy."[45] Similar caution, born out of a fear of offending, led to the demise of blackface acts.

Rock and roll was a synthesis of black and white musics which took place as the courts were abolishing the separate but equal segregation doctrine. It is tempting to tie these two social events together. But musical integration has been a fact in country music since the very beginning: one has only to examine the content of the music of Jimmie Rodgers to see that. And the debts of bluegrass to Afro-American traditions in terms of instrumental techniques, musical vocabulary, and repertoire are extensive. But each new synthesis of white and black music has met some counter-reaction on the part of older listeners, and this was clearly the case with the music of Elvis Presley. The editor of *Billboard*, Paul Ackerman, recalled the resentment of Nashville executives when Elvis first hit the country charts: "He sings nigger music!"[46]

The racist reaction to the new music also played a part in the growth of bluegrass music. The relatively small black population in the southern highlands in comparison with other parts of the South made the shock of the move to the northern cities, with their large black enclaves, greater for Appalachian immigrants. The strength of their interest in bluegrass was doubtless heightened by the kinship of the new white rock music (some of it being played by their friends and children) with the music of black ghetto-dwellers with whom they were in not-always-harmonious contact and competition. As social identities were threatened, the identity offered by bluegrass with its familiar down-home sound became important.

Hence one white response to rockabilly, this new dilution of "our" country music, was to seek a "pure" country sound, even if in reality that sound was relatively new, as bluegrass was to many. The point was that it didn't sound like rock and roll. Ironically the same thing was happening with black audiences. As white culture has appropriated elements of black music, the response within black culture has been to synthesize a new black vernacular music which draws upon aspects of Afro-American musical tradition not yet appropriated by white pop musicians. The old down-home blues were losing favor with black listeners, who were turning to a mixture of secular and sacred styles as performed by musicians like Ray Charles—what would become known in a few years as "soul music." This too was new, like bluegrass, but with its familiar elements it had a certain Afro-American purity.

In this sense it would be a mistake to see the turning to bluegrass as a totally racist reaction to rock and roll. Rock and roll was not a black music; it was a new pop music aimed at a mass-culture teenage audience. Black musicians during this era also faced a loss of income and audience and were under pressures from the record industry to alter their music to fit the new youth demand. Bluegrass and soul music were, in this sense, similar phenomena in that they were the focus of audience reaction against rock and roll.

It is interesting that behind the scenes this opposition between bluegrass and rock and roll was not nearly so clear-cut. Among the musicians bluegrass played an important part in the process which created rock and roll, particularly that sector of the phenomenon called rockabilly. Elvis Presley's very first record for Sam Phillips's Sun Records was a classic statement of the synthesis which produced this new music. On one side was Elvis's version of Arthur ("Big Boy") Crudup's "That's All Right"; on the other the Mississippi rocker's arrangement of Bill Monroe's "Blue Moon of Kentucky." Monroe and Crudup represented the older, down-home, more conservative segments of their musical genres: Crudup was a black country bluesman, Monroe a Grand Ole Opry regular since 1939. The rockabillies were drawn to the rough-edged, rural-sounding performances in both black and white music, to the older styles closer to folk origins than to those of pop music—Bill Monroe, not Eddy Arnold; Big Boy Crudup, not Nat King Cole.

Elvis Presley did not just stumble onto "Blue Moon of Kentucky." Like Buddy Holly and the Everly Brothers, he grew up listening to the Opry. Elvis could sing a number of Monroe's songs, particularly those performed and recorded with Monroe by Lester Flatt and Earl Scruggs back in the mid-forties. This is documented by a studio recording made on December 4, 1956, in Memphis. Carl Perkins was recording for Sun when Elvis Presley and Jerry Lee Lewis dropped in. A jam session got under way, and the producer turned on the tape recorder. Presley and Lewis sang ten old hymns and then did four of Monroe's songs: "Little Cabin Home on the Hill," "Summertime Is Past and Gone," "I Hear a Sweet Voice Calling," and "Sweetheart You Done Me Wrong." All were from the Monroe-Flatt-Scruggs era repertoire, as was "Blue Moon of Kentucky," recorded by Monroe in 1946 as a follow-up to "Kentucky Waltz." Elvis's arrangement changed Monroe's waltz time to a rocking 4/4 boogie beat.

But was it Elvis's arrangement? Charlie Feathers, a little-known singer who worked in the Sun studios and recorded some now classic rockabilly sides for King Records in 1956, claims that he came up with the 4/4 arrangement of "Blue Moon of Kentucky." Like Elvis, he was from Mississippi and he was a Bill Monroe fan:

> Bill Monroe, he used to come through Hudsonville, set up tents and all, man I thought it was the greatest thing I ever heard. Well, you see, I loved bluegrass all my life, but I never did know how to play it. There wasn't nobody around who could play that type of music, only colored artists thumping on their guitars. . . . Sam [Phillips], he always said I was a blues singer, but I was really singing bluegrass and rapping on the guitar like I heard them colored artists do. Bluegrass rock, that's what it really was, Sam called it rhythm 'n' blues, some said it was country rock, but Bill Monroe music and colored artists' music is what caused rock 'n' roll.[47]

One man's view, of course, but a viewpoint which helps explain Monroe's response to the Presley recording. While the Nashville establishment was reacting in a negative way to this young man who "sings nigger music," Monroe's response was positive. Presley was a guest performer on the Grand Ole Opry shortly after his first Sun record was issued, and, according to Monroe, "he come around, apologized for the way that he'd changed 'Blue Moon of Kentucky' and I told him that if it would help him get his start and give him a different style, I was for him a hundred percent."[48]

On the last weekend of August 1954 the Stanley Brothers were in Nashville to record for Mercury. Their session was scheduled for Sunday, and Carter Stanley dined with Bill Monroe the night before, after the Opry. Monroe had Presley's Sun record with him, and after dinner he took Stanley up to the WSM studios where they found a record player. Carter recalled: "He said, 'I want you to hear something' and he had never said anything like that to me before. So, we went up and that's what we heard, 'Blue Moon of Kentucky,' by Elvis Presley. I believe that was his first number, his first record. I laughed a little bit and looked around and everybody else was laughing except Bill. He said, 'you better do that number tomorrow if you want to sell some records.' . . . he said 'I'm gonna do it the next Sunday.' He was scheduled to record the next week."[49]

Monroe came to the Stanley session the next day, bringing his banjoist, Charlie Cline. Cline, a talented musician who often fiddled with Monroe, occasionally played finger-picking-style lead guitar, and it was this kind of guitar which he played on the Stanley Brothers' duet version of the Presley 4/4 arrangement of "Blue Moon of Kentucky." Cline played riffs resembling those Clyde Moody used on his recording of "Six White Horses" with Monroe back in 1940 and did a Merle Travis-style break of a kind popular in early rockabilly music. This was the first time lead guitar was used on the Stanley Brothers' recordings (Cline also played on most of the other five songs recorded that day); soon it would become an essential ingredient in their sound.[50]

The following Saturday Monroe himself was in the recording studio, doing his version of the song. This arrangement started like his first one, in waltz time. After he'd sung a verse and chorus, three fiddles broke into the 4/4 version, after which he sang it again in the new rhythm. There was no banjo—the first Monroe secular song without a banjo since his early recordings—because Charlie Cline was helping out on the triple fiddles. Monroe's arrangement was not his first with the triple fiddles, for he had recorded three songs that way several months earlier. But this was his first song to be released with that sound. With its midstream shift from waltz to boogie, it was a striking arrangement, one which subsequently influenced other bluegrass groups. Thus while other country performers responded to the challenge of rock and roll by adopting some of its instrumental features ("changing styles to get airplay"), particularly drums, and by dropping the more blatantly "country" aspects of the backup such as the fiddle, Monroe's response through his and the Stanley Brothers' recordings was to emphasize instruments already in use by bluegrass musicians, in new roles and combinations, fitted to new concepts of rhythm and structural arrangement.

Two weekends later Bill was at his country music park, the Brown County Jamboree, in Bean Blossom, Indiana. The new recording of "Blue Moon of Kentucky" would not be released by Decca for another two weeks. But he was already doing it in his shows. Here's how he introduced it at the Sunday night show: "Friends we have a number now that'll be out on record for the second time, a new release on the 'Blue Moon of Kentucky.' A new arrangement, we'd like to do that for you here tonight. Charlie Cline joins in with another fiddle here and works along with Gordon Terry; and they's about three or four or five more groups throughout the country that has this number on record, and looks like it's gonna make a good comeback. We hope you enjoy 'Blue Moon of Kentucky.' "[51]

Monroe was promoting Presley's recording as the beginning of a phenomenon similar to the one that had taken place with "Kentucky Waltz," revived for a hit by Eddy Arnold in 1951. By encouraging Carter Stanley to record the song he was acting out of friendship as well as self-interest: he hoped it would sell well for the Stanleys. It would, of course, benefit composer Monroe if any of the recordings sold well. Monroe was not the only performer rushing to record covers of the rock and roll hits, but he was one of the few with the luxury of covering his own composition. His unpleasant experience in 1951, when Paul Cohen had talked him into covering "Kentucky Waltz" using Nashville studio musicians, no doubt strengthened his resolve to record his own arrangement with his own musicians for this cover. Monroe's amenability to rockabillies continued; in 1957 he employed young Cajun rocker Doug Kershaw as guitarist on a recording session at which he did one of Kershaw's songs.

While many bluegrass fans viewed rock and roll with contempt, some musicians, especially the younger ones, liked it. J. D. Crowe, a contemporary of Sonny Osborne, grew up near Lexington, Kentucky. He was thirteen when Flatt and Scruggs arrived in town and began playing at the "Kentucky Barn Dance." The banjo fascinated him; he attended every Saturday night to see Scruggs: "I'd always be the one on the front row, real close to the stage. And when they left, then I'd get up and leave too." Crowe played some with local bands and then spent a summer with Pee Wee Lambert and Curley Parker, doing construction during the day and music at night. By 1956 he was picking banjo in Detroit with Jimmy Martin. He was totally involved in bluegrass, particularly bluegrass banjo: "If it didn't have a banjo in it then I'd cut it off. . . . except, with the exception of rock and roll and blues. I've always liked it. I used to listen to blues, just all the *time* . . . B. B. King . . . and Fats Domino, Little Richard . . ."[52]

Crowe was performing as well as listening to this music. When Jimmy Martin played the country music park New River Ranch in Maryland, on April 27, 1957, J. D. sang the latest Little Richard number, "Slippin' and A-Slidin'," with the band to the accompaniment of his banjo. His solo would, of course, help Martin deal with requests of the kind described earlier by Vic Mullen. But the involvement of Crowe and others like him in the new music was to influence bluegrass in other ways. Crowe studied blues guitar, adopting aspects of it to his banjo work, and decades later, still plays such tunes as Fats Domino's "I'm Walking," while incorporating elements of country rock into his bluegrass sound.

Another young banjo picker from Kentucky who played bluegrass and rock and roll was Rusty York. Born in Harlan County in 1935, he was raised in nearby Breathitt County, where he first heard bluegrass: "I went to see Lester Flatt and Earl Scruggs first time up in Jackson Theater in about '53, I guess. And I just couldn't believe man, anybody could play a banjo like that, I just, Boy! I stayed for both shows, that night. . . . Boy, I mean it was just like heaven then, 'cause nobody, you couldn't never see it. There's so much of it now, you know. Everybody can play good now, you know. But then, it was only him."[53] Soon after this Rusty converted an old tenor banjo into a five-string, and by the time he moved to Cincinnati he had a regular five-string. One night at a bar near Cincinnati he met another boy from eastern Kentucky named Willard Hale. They teamed up and became a popular act at the bars and parks in the area. Occasionally Rusty played with singer–record-

store owner Jimmie Skinner, who helped him and Hale make several bluegrass records.

Then rock and roll came to town: "Willard and I used to just stand on the
stage, two of us, and play banjo and guitar and sing duets. Then Elvis came
along . . . and even country boys started liking Elvis, you know. And we had
to switch over to electric guitar . . . and switch over to bass, and we finally
had to add drums and then turned into modern country." In December 1957
they made their first rock and roll record, a cover of Buddy Holly's "Peggy
Sue" for King. But they continued to record bluegrass for Mercury and Starday in 1958. Then in the spring of 1959 they decided to wax a rock instrumental version of "She'll Be Coming Round the Mountain," which they
called "Red Rooster." On their way to the King Studios, which they had
rented for the session, they chose a Marty Robbins song, "Sugaree," for the
other side of the record. As happens so often in pop music, it was this, the
hastily selected "B" side, which was the hit. Says Rusty: "We tried to peddle
it to everybody—Mercury, and RCA—and nobody wanted it. So we put it
out ourselves on my (label), started Jewel. It got to be number two in
Cincinnati, and they said something must be happening, you know we
pressed ten thousand, sold them, pressed a few more and this guy, Pat Nelson,
negotiated with Chess Records and we leased it to them."[54] The song got
onto *Billboard*'s "Hot 100" chart, and York appeared on Dick Clark's "American Bandstand" and at a rock and roll show at the Hollywood Bowl. He cut
several other rock records but they "died." The following year he recorded a
six-song, extended-play record containing bluegrass renditions of such traditional songs as "Pretty Polly" and "Roving Gambler." It was sold through the
Jimmie Skinner Music Center and by deejay Wayne Raney (composer of "We
Need a Whole Lot More of Jesus and a Lot Less Rock and Roll") over
Cincinnati radio station WCKY. Although by then York had ceased to perform in public—he was already building his Jewel label into a successful
custom recording studio—the record sold over 200,000 copies by mail order
and radio offers alone.

That musicians like Monroe, Crowe, and York could in various ways mix
bluegrass and rock and roll was not unusual during the mid- to late fifties.
Among the many other examples of the rock-bluegrass connection are the
recordings made by Flatt and Scruggs during 1957–59. Such songs as "Don't
Let Your Deal Go Down," "Big Black Train" and "Foggy Mountain Rock"
featured a heavy drum beat and partook of Nashville studio-style rockabilly
sounds in other details while retaining most of their bluegrass features. In
particular the sound of Buck Graves's Dobro was used on such recordings to
approximate the sound of the blues slide guitar—an effect Graves was aware
of, being a long-time fan of country bluesmen like Blind Boy Fuller. Perhaps
Flatt and Scruggs's closest approach to the rockabilly spirit was in their
version of Clyde Moody's "Six White Horses," where Scruggs took Moody's

In this souvenir photo, on sale at the Opry during the war years, Monroe and the Blue Grass Boys can be seen in the middle row center with white shirts, ties, and Stetsons: Art Wooten, Cousin Wilbur, Clyde Moody, and Monroe. In the insert is a later band with Monroe, Howdy Forrester, Moody, Wilbur, and Stringbean (as he was known then). [Courtesy of Charles Wolfe]

Mainer's Mountaineers in the late thirties: Curley Shelton, blackface comedian "Greasy," J. E. Mainer, Wade Mainer, and Jack Shelton. [Courtesy
of the Country Music Foundation Library and Media Center, Nashville,
Tennessee]

The Monroe Brothers were dancing for the "WLS
Barn Dance" during the summer of 1933, when this
picture of a crowd waiting outside the Eighth Street
Theater was taken. [Courtesy of the Country Music
Foundation Library and Media Center, Nashville,
Tennessee]

Charlie and Bill Monroe, posing in the barnyard in their Sunday best; the photo is from the early thirties. [Courtesy of the Country Music Foundation Library and Media Center, Nashville, Tennessee]

Charlie and Bill Monroe in a publicity photo taken in the late thirties. Note Charlie's grin and Bill's serious demeanor, both characteristic. [Courtesy of the Country Music Foundation Library and Media Center, Nashville, Tennessee]

Wade Mainer's band at WPTF in Raleigh, North Carolina, in the late thirties, posing behind their mail. Rear: Jay Hugh Hall and Clyde Moody, the Happy-Go-Lucky Boys; front: Wade Mainer, Steve Ledford. [Courtesy of the Country Music Foundation Library and Media Center, Nashville, Tennessee]

A 1944 portrait of Tommy Magness published in Minnie Pearl's monthly, *The Grinders Switch Gazette*. [Courtesy of the Country Music Foundation Library and Media Center, Nashville, Tennessee]

Bill Monroe and the Blue Grass Boys of 1942, in their usual stage dress: Cousin Wilbur, Stringbean, Howdy Forrester, Monroe, and Clyde Moody. [Courtesy of the Country Music Foundation Library and Media Center, Nashville, Tennessee]

The Blue Grass Boys as a baseball team, circa 1944: "Cedric Rainwater" (Howard Watts), Chubby Wise, David "Stringbean" Akeman, Clyde Moody, Bill Monroe. [Courtesy of *Bluegrass Unlimited*]

Bill Monroe with his newly acquired 1923 Gibson F5 mandolin, 1945. [Personal collection of author]

Monroe's famous 1945–48 band in front of the Blue Grass Special: Birch Monroe, Chubby Wise, Bill Monroe, Lester Flatt, and Earl Scruggs. [Courtesy of the Country Music Foundation Library and Media Center, Nashville, Tennessee]

The cover of Monroe's second song folio, published in 1950, used the words *blue grass* in conjunction with the phrase "country songs," anticipating the more inclusive use of Monroe's band name to describe a musical genre. [Personal collection of author]

This tiny Wayside ad in a May 1957 *Billboard* was the first to describe records in print as "Music Blue Grass Style." [Author's personal collection]

The Jimmie Skinner Music Center first advertised "Blue Grass Type Records" in this *Country Song Roundup* ad of October 1957. [Courtesy of the Country Music Foundation Library and Media Center, Nashville, Tennessee]

Seventeen-year-old Sonny Osborne, already a five-year veteran with a string of records released under his own name, at the microphone of WJR in Detroit, 1955. [Courtesy of the Country Music Foundation Library and Media Center, Nashville, Tennessee]

Featuring the 5-String Banjo

"A BROTHER IN KOREA"

b/w "Sunny Mountain Chimes"
with **SONNY OSBORNE**
Gateway Record #3005

D. J.'s: If you haven't got your copy, let us know.

Order Direct or *Gateway* RECORDS

From Your Local Distributor

8930 Spring Grove Avenue
CINCINNATI 23, OHIO

This ad for one of Sonny Osborne's Gateway records appeared in a May 1953 issue of *Billboard.* [Author's personal collection]

Reno and Smiley in action at Sunset Park near Oxford, Pennsylvania, in the late fifties: Mac Magaha, Don Reno, John Palmer, and Red Smiley. [Courtesy of Eddie Stubbs]

The Flatt and Scruggs show has been a regular weekly feature on WDXI-TV Jackson, Tennessee; WJHL-TV in Johnson City, Tennessee; and WSAZ-TV in Huntington, West Virginia, for Martha White Foods.

Through their hundreds of cards and letters received each week from TV viewers, one of their most treasured compliments are the clean and decent shows they strive to bring you. This has been their No. 1 policy since organizing their own show. Lester and Earl often bring out the point of being proud to be working for a company that features fine quality, Martha White Foods. "Goodness Gracious They're All Good." As well as the finest people they have ever had the opportunity of being connected with. With these features combined, Lester and Earl always feel proud to take their show into any town or community.

The Flatt and Scruggs band in 1955: Scruggs, Paul Warren, "Cousin Jake" (E. P. Tullock, Jr.), Curly Seckler, Flatt. This photo and the accompanying caption appeared in their first WSM Grand Ole Opry songbook that year. [Author's personal collection]

April 1949: A publicity flyer for the Stanley Brothers' first release on Columbia. [Courtesy of the Country Music Foundation Library and Media Center, Nashville, Tennessee]

Except for the bass player, this is the Stanley Brothers Band that recorded "Blue Moon of Kentucky" in August 1954: "Cousin Winesap," Ralph Stanley, Joe Meadows, Carter Stanley, Bill Lowe. The photo appeared in the songbook they were selling from WCYB, Bristol, at the time. [Courtesy of the Country Music Foundation Library and Media Center, Nashville, Tennessee]

guitar riff and transposed it to the banjo, and Flatt took one of his very infrequent guitar breaks.

But while bluegrass musicians were in various ways responding to and appropriating from rock and roll—for both artistic and commercial reasons—their audiences tended to view examples of the process as minor aberrations. Rock and roll was the enemy against which bluegrass was taking a stand by remaining unamplified and firmly old-time. By 1958 the word *bluegrass* was being used by fans, disc jockeys, record companies, and critics to describe this musical genre because they were involved in a movement which sought to revitalize a music perceived as either "country" or "folk" music. The musicians themselves, particularly the full-time professionals, hesitated about becoming involved in this movement. Like Mac Wiseman, they were wary of being "tagged." The emergence of the word *bluegrass* into the lingua franca of the music business was the beginning of a split between fans and musicians which would widen during the sixties as bluegrass broke away from Nashville and was "discovered" by the folk music boom.

Notes

1. Johnny Sippel, "The Hillbilly Deejay," p. 61.
2. Johnny Sippel, "New Horizons for Country-Western Platter-Spinners," p. 58.
3. *Billboard*, Mar. 8, 1952, p. 43.
4. *Billboard*, June 30, 1951, p. 32.
5. *Billboard*, Dec. 20, 1952, p. 53.
6. Spoken onstage, New River Ranch, Rising Sun, Md., May 13, 1956.
7. Neil V. Rosenberg, *Bill Monroe and His Blue Grass Boys*, p. 47.
8. Carl Fleischhauer, "The Public Named Bluegrass Music," p. 5.
9. Lilly used this term while introducing his portion of a show at Rock Creek Park, Md., on June 10, 1979.
10. Marvin Hedrick, interview with author, Nashville, Ind., Dec. 10, 1965.
11. *Billboard*, July 7, 1951, p. 26.
12. Osborne also did his versions of songs from the repertoires of the Stanley Brothers, Jim Eanes, and Reno and Smiley.
13. *Billboard*, May 9, 1953, p. 37.
14. A 1952 Rich-R-Tone promotional flyer for seven new bluegrass singles guaranteed similarly: "Every record on this release features Fiddle and Banjo music with top notch vocals." Rounder, *Rich-R-Tone Story*, p. 12.
15. *Billboard*, Feb. 26, 1955, p. 86, Mar. 19, 1955, p. 47.
16. Bill Vernon, "The Don Reno Story, Part 3," p. 19. King Records files indicate that the recording was made Feb. 25, 1955.

17. *Billboard*, Apr. 16, 1955, p. 49.

18. Lambert, A *Biography of Lester Flatt*, p. 38.

19. Ibid., p. 117.

20. *Country and Western Jamboree* 1 (Dec. 1955): 8–9. The McCormick Brothers' Hickory singles juxtaposed bluegrass instrumentals with songs done in contemporary Nashville studio style.

21. *Country and Western Jamboree* 1 (Jan. 1956): 25.

22. *Country Song Roundup* 42 (Feb. 1956): back cover.

23. *Country and Western Jamboree* 2 (Mar. 1956): 23.

24. *Billboard*, Apr. 14, 1956, p. 61.

25. Jim Rooney, *Bossmen*, p. 77.

26. Pete Seeger, *The Five-String Banjo Instructor*, n.p.

27. Ralph Rinzler, brochure notes to *American Banjo Scruggs Style*, p. 1.

28. Ibid.

29. Hedrick interview.

30. *Billboard*, May 20, 1957, p. 148.

31. *Country Song Roundup* 52 (Oct. 1957): 29.

32. *Billboard*, June 24, 1957, p. 60.

33. *Billboard*, Jan. 6, 1958, p. 49.

34. Red O'Donnell with Dee Kilpatrick, *WSM's Official Grand Ole Opry History–Picture Book*, p. 20. Publication data is from *Billboard*, Jan. 13, 1958, p. 16.

35. *Billboard*, Jan. 20, 1958, p. 77.

36. "Rose Asks DJ Views on C&W," *Billboard*, Mar. 31, 1956, p. 18.

37. "No Foresight—Diskeries Score Anti-Pop Bias of Some DJs," *Billboard*, Mar. 3, 1956, p. 54.

38. Doug Green, "Mac Wiseman: Remembering," pp. 5–6.

39. Ibid., p. 6.

40. Vic Mullen, interview with author, St. John's, Newfoundland, June 15, 1972.

41. Don Reno, "Country Boy Rock and Roll," reissued on *Country Ballads*.

42. "I Took Her by Her Little Brown Hand," reissued on *Jim Eanes and the Shenandoah Valley Boys*.

43. "Little Brown Hand," reissued on *Jim Eanes*.

44. Pete Kuykendall, "Smilin' Jim Eanes," p. 10.

45. "New John Henry Blues," reissued on *Songs with the Blue Grass Boys*. The Decca single was not issued until 1963 and then only at the insistence of Ralph Rinzler. It was, however, issued in England in 1956, on Brunswick 45–05567.

46. Paul Ackerman, "What Has Happened to Popular Music," p. 37.

47. Peter Guralnick, *Lost Highway*, pp. 109–11.

48. As spoken to talk show host Dan Miller on "Miller's Place," WSM-TV, Nashville, Tenn., June 14, 1981.

49. Carter Stanley, interview with Mike Seeger, spring, 1966. For another version, see Ivan M. Tribe, "Joe Meadows," p. 31.

50. Also recorded that day but not issued (except in Japan) was their duet version of "Close By," the Monroe composition which Bill used for the flip side of his "Blue Moon of Kentucky" cover.

51. Bill Monroe, recorded onstage, Brown County Jamboree, Bean Blossom, Ind., Sept. 19, 1954.

52. J. D. Crowe, interview with author, Lexington, Ky., Aug. 14, 1972.

53. Rusty York, interview with author, Hamilton, Ohio, Aug. 15, 1972.

54. Ibid.

Bibliographical Notes

The history of country music parks is a fascinating topic worthy of further exploration. Two examples of their popularity in southern Pennsylvania during the thirties and forties have come to my attention: one is a passing mention by Canadian cowboy Wilf Carter (known in the U.S. as "Montana Slim") in *The Singing Cowboy*, p. 61. The other is a booklet published in the sixties to commemorate the anniversary of Sunset Park: Thurston Moore, *Sunset Park's Twenty-Fifth Anniversary Picture Album.*

Deejays have been written about in passing but few in-depth studies exist. Of interest is Bill Mack's *Spins and Needles*, the autobiography of a Texas deejay. My "Goodtime Charlie and the Bricklin" focuses upon a Canadian maritimes deejay who was also a songwriter and performer.

Examples of the use of "Blue Grass" with reference to music, show business, or both, abound. In 1911 the Bowman Brothers, a vaudeville comedy act, billed themselves as the Blue Grass Boys. See Edw. Le Roy Rice, *Monarchs of Minstrelsy*, second page of advertising in back. Charles Wolfe describes the 1925 Bluegrass Trio in *Kentucky Country*, p. 89. A 1931 Columbia Records catalog lists records by Lee Morse and Her Blue Grass Boys, a pop music outfit. In 1943 the Dixie Music Publishing Co. issued *Charlie and Mary—The Blue Grass Sweethearts Famous Folio of Songs to Remember, Book No. 1.* And a number of songs with "Blue Grass" in the title were recorded during the early years of hillbilly music, predating Monroe's recorded titles: "Blue Grass Rag" by the Fiddling Doc Roberts Trio and "Blue Grass Twist" by the South Georgia Highballers are two such tunes. There are passing references in *Billboard* to the Blue Grass Record label of Covington, Kentucky (Dec. 11, 1954, p. 44), and Blue Grass Music of New York (May 7, 1955, p. 44), neither having any connection with the genre. Nashville Grand Ole Opry pioneer Sid Harkreader has asserted that the Gallatin Blue Grass Serenaders, active on the Opry during the twenties, played bluegrass at that time: Walter D. Haden, ed., *Fiddlin' Sid's Memoirs*, pp. 32–33. But his claim is vague and has no support from other musicians of the period.

A useful history of early Nashville studios is John W. Rumble's "The Emergence of Nashville as a Recording Center." Paul Cohen's career is out-lined briefly in "Paul Cohen, Pioneer Disc Executive, Dies." An important Nashville studio fiddler who played on many bluegrass sessions during the fifties and sixties was the late Tommy Jackson. See Charles Wolfe, "From the Fiddling Archives (No. 32 in a Series)."

For a 1951 article on Flatt and Scruggs, see "Winning Combination," published in *Country Song Roundup*. In it Flatt's recordings with Monroe are mentioned, and several of those copyrighted in Monroe's name are identi-fied as Flatt compositions. Scruggs is described as "the most copied banjo picker around." For information on Flatt and Scruggs's recordings from this period, see Robert J. Ronald, "Lester Flatt and Earl Scruggs Discography," pp. 5–9. Sonny Osborne's recordings are listed in my "Osborne Brothers Discography," pp. 2–5.

For a portrait of a figure who, like Wild Bill Price, helped develop blue-grass listeners in the area around Baltimore, working as a deejay, an emcee at Sunset Park, and so forth, see George B. McCeney, "Don't Let Your Deal Go Down: The Bluegrass Career of Ray Davis."

Banjo historian Robert B. Winans indicates that "Home Sweet Home" was a standard banjo showpiece as early as 1880. See his "The Folk, the Stage and the Five-String Banjo in the Nineteenth Century," p. 429. Fur-ther details on the Hack Johnson recording of "Home Sweet Home" appear in Scott Hambly and Neil V. Rosenberg, "Allen Shelton," p. 10. Some additional material on Reno and Smiley's emergence as a full-time act ap-pears in Fred Bartenstein, Red Smiley Obituary, p. 1. See also Bill Vernon, "The Don Reno Story, Part 4," pp. 10–12, 21.

Music Center owner Skinner is profiled in Ivan M. Tribe, "Jimmie Skin-ner: Country Singer, Bluegrass Composer, Record Retailer."

The early years of the more political side of the folksong revival are chronicled in Serge Denisoff's *Great Day Coming*. Richard Reuss's "Ameri-can Folksongs and Left-Wing Politics: 1935–56" shows how politically mar-ginal the revival actually was within the radical left of that era. Also useful for gaining a perspective on the early years of the revival is Joe Klein's *Woody Guthrie: A Life*. A useful compilation which gives source materials on the folk boom of the late fifties and early sixties is David A. DeTurk and A. Poulin, Jr., *The American Folk Scene*. The best single piece on the early folksong revivalists' discovery of bluegrass during the fifties is Christopher Lehmann-Haupt, "Out of My Mind on Bluegrass."

Discoveries of esoteric musical forms by youth, like that of Lehmann-Haupt (whose brother was one of Ken Kesey's merry pranksters, out of his mind on another kind of discovery), can be seen in Mezz Mezzrow and Bernard Wolfe's *Really the Blues* for jazz, and Charles Gillett's *The Sound of the City*, pp. 1–27, for rhythm and blues. In the rock context, see the dis-cussion in R. Serge Denisoff, *Solid Gold*, pp. 1–43. A model useful in understanding the entire process is given by Richard A. Peterson, "A Process Model of the Folk, Pop and Fine Art Phases of Jazz." For documentation and discussion of black-white interactions in country music prior to the advent of rockabilly music, see Tony Russell, *Blacks, Whites and Blues.*

Connie B. Gay, founding member of the Country Music Association, began holding his annual contests in Warrenton, Virginia, in 1951. Many of the early winners were bluegrass musicians. See *Billboard,* Aug. 16, 1952, p. 37, and "Country Talent Contest," *Country Song Roundup* 28 (Jan. 1954): 14.

Early bluegrass activity in Detroit is detailed in Ivan Tribe, "The Goins Brothers: Melvin and Ray—Maintaining the Lonesome Pine Fiddler Tradition." For more on the Osborne Brothers–Jimmy Martin band, see my "The Osborne Brothers, Part One."

Canadian bluegrass pioneer Ron Scott is the subject of four articles published in Canadian magazines: David Tinkoff's "The Ronald D. Scott Story, Part One"; Scott's "The Life and Times of Ronald D. Scott"; his "Ron Scott Autobiography, Chapter Two"; and Martin Chapman, "Ron Scott, The Ghost of Canadian Bluegrass."

An early, perhaps the first, article on the genre in a folk revival publication was Roger Lass, "Bluegrass." Most of the people who wrote about the music at this time from a country music perspective called it *blue grass,* showing awareness of Monroe's relationship to the name. But Lass and other revivalists tended to use the single word form that subsequently became standard. A Japanese pop music periodical, *Music Life,* used the term "Blue Grass Type" in March 1958 as the subtitle of an article, "The Story of Mountain Music," published in their "Hillbilly's Corner." All of these terms (Blue Grass, Mountain Music, Hillbilly's) were translated into Japanese. I am indebted to Toru Mitsui for bringing these to my attention.

Information on Mac Wiseman (in addition to the articles cited in the notes to chapter 3) is found in Scott Hambly, "Mac Wiseman: A Discographic Enigma," and in two articles by Don Rhodes, both titled "Mac Wiseman."

The disappearance of the fiddle from much of country music during the late fifties, mentioned in this chapter, was one reason for the fiddle music revival of the sixties, discussed in chapter 8. See the notes to that chapter for further references.

Canadian bluegrass musician Vic Mullen is the subject of Kevin Berland's "Vic Mullen—Maritime Bluegrass Legend."

Additional information on Jim Eanes's career appears in Robert Ronald, "Jim Eanes—Biography" and "Jim Eanes—Discography." For information on Blue Ridge Records, see Walter V. Saunders and The Rounder Folks, liner notes to *The Church Brothers.*

Charles Keil discusses the black reactions to rock and roll in his *Urban Blues,* p. 78. See also John F. Szwed, "Musical Adaptation among Afro-

Americans," and Ray Charles and David Ritz, *Brother Ray*, pp. 148–52, 177–78.

In *Mystery Train*, pp. 191–94, rock music critic Greil Marcus discusses Presley's recording of "Blue Moon of Kentucky," showing how Elvis developed it into his own styling in the studio. Marcus's description is based on a bootleg recording of an early reject cut of the song that includes a conversation which took place during the recording session. In it Presley and Sun owner Sam Phillips discuss the arrangement. This raises questions about Feathers' claim to have originated the arrangement.

In "The Million Dollar Quartet" Peter Guralnick discusses the Dec. 4, 1956, Memphis recording session by Presley, Perkins, and Lewis. He does not mention the inclusion of Bill Monroe's songs in the repertoire performed. Other rockabilly singers who recorded Bill Monroe songs include Marty Robbins and Gene Vincent. See the following discographical notes for details.

Discographical Notes

Of Bill Monroe's instrumentals utilizing the name of his band, "Blue Grass Special" has been reissued on *The Classic Bluegrass Recordings*, vol. 1; "Blue Grass Stomp" on *The Classic Bluegrass Recordings*, vol. 2; and "Blue Grass Breakdown" on *The Original Bluegrass Band*. "Blue Grass Ramble" appeared only on a single, as did both the Eddy Arnold and the Bill Monroe Decca recordings of "Kentucky Waltz."

Flatt and Scruggs's version of "Pike County Breakdown" was later released on *Country Music* and *Original Sound*. Monroe's version was issued only on the single and an EP, *Bill Monroe and His Blue Grass Boys*. Sonny Osborne's "A Brother in Korea" and "Sunny Mountain Chimes" are available on *The Early Recordings of Sonny Osborne*, vols. 3 and 1, respectively.

Flatt and Scruggs's "Hall of Fame" instrumentals are reissued as follows: "Flint Hill Special" on *The Golden Era*; "Earl's Breakdown" on *The Golden Years*; "Foggy Mountain Chimes" on *Foggy Mountain Chimes*; and "Foggy Mountain Special" on *Don't Get Above Your Raisin'* and *Columbia Historic Edition*.

Hack Johnson's "Home Sweet Home" was reissued on *New Sounds Ramblin' from Coast to Coast*; Jim Eanes's "There's No Place Like Home" has not, to my knowledge, been reissued; and Wilma Lee and Stoney Cooper's "Home Sweet Home" appeared on their *The Big Wheel*.

Reno and Smiley's "I'm Using My Bible for a Road Map" was later released on their *Sacred Songs*. The sound of Flatt and Scruggs in 1955–57 is heard on their *Blue Ridge Cabin Home*. The McCormick Brothers' Hickory singles were anthologized in *Authentic Bluegrass Hits*. Curley Parker and Pee

Wee Lambert's Rich-R-Tone recordings of "Weary Hobo" and "Just a Memory" appear on *The Rich-R-Tone Story*. The Stoneman Family album which Rinzler helped to edit for Folkways is *The Stoneman Family: Old-Time Tunes of the South*.

Jimmy Martin and the Osborne Brothers' "20/20 Vision" was reissued on *Early Blue Grass*; Martin's "Hit Parade of Love" on his *Country Music*. Wade and Wiley Birchfield and Roger Johnson's "Flower Bloomin' in the Wildwood" and "I'm Goin' Down the Road Feeling Bad" on Wayside were not, to my knowledge, ever issued on LP. One side of the Marvin Cobb and Frank Wakefield Wayside single, "New Camptown Races," can be heard on *The Early Days of Bluegrass*, vol. 2, where it is incorrectly dated as a 1953 recording. The other side, "Tell Me Why (My Daddy Don't Come Home)," has not been reissued. The same is true for Ron Scott's "When the Bees Are in the Hive" and "The White Rose."

Mac Wiseman's "I Hear You Knocking" was released on his *Keep on the Sunny Side*. The Sun studio jam session with Elvis Presley, Carl Perkins, and Jerry Lee Lewis was issued on *Million Dollar Quartet*. Presley's "Little Cabin Home on the Hill" appeared on *Elvis Country*. His "That's All Right" and "Blue Moon of Kentucky" were reissued on *Sun Sessions*. The early version of "Blue Moon of Kentucky" by Presley which Marcus discusses was issued on *Good Rocking Tonight*. Other recordings of the song were issued in the fall of 1954 by country artists Phil Gulley and Cliffie Stone. In 1958 two other rockabillies recorded Bill Monroe tunes: Gene Vincent's "Rocky Road Blues" was released by Capitol that year; Marty Robbins's "Footprints in the Snow" for Columbia remained unissued until 1982, when it appeared on *Rockin' Rollin' Robbins*, an album by a German company, Bear Family. The Stanley Brothers' version of "Blue Moon of Kentucky" was reissued on their *Hard Times*, and Monroe's on *Country Music Hall of Fame* and *The Best of Bill Monroe*.

J. D. Crowe performs his version of "I'm Walking" on *The New South*. Rusty York's rockabilly recordings, "Peggy Sue," "Sugaree," and "Red Rooster," have not, to my knowledge, been reissued. The same is true for the two EPs he issued on the Bluegrass Special label, the first of which contained "Pretty Polly," "Rovin' Gambler," "Girl I Left in Sunny Tennessee," "Little Maggie," and "East Virginia Blues"; and the second, "Knoxville Girl," "Cindy," "Kentucky Mountain Chimes," "Short Life of Trouble," and "Over the Hills to the Poorhouse."

Of Flatt and Scruggs's rockabilly-flavored tunes mentioned in this chapter, "Six White Horses" and "Don't Let Your Deal Go Down" appeared on *Blue Ridge Cabin Home*; "Big Black Train" on *Songs to Cherish*; and "Foggy Mountain Rock" on *Breaking Out*.

Chapter 5

Bluegrass Breaks Away:
1957–60

Nineteen fifty-seven was a momentous year for the country music establishment in Nashville. After several years of confusion and shock it was responding to the "threat" of rock and roll music with the creation of the Country Music Association (CMA). The outgrowth of a Country Music Disc Jockeys' Association founded in 1954, it sought to represent to the business world the interests of performers, producers, and retailers and thereby to revitalize country music. The CMA's primary goal was to increase the number of radio stations playing country records. To do this it had to demonstrate that people who listened to country music on the radio would purchase the products advertised on such programs, allowing radio stations to charge more for the advertising, thus making country music radio a viable and attractive commercial venture. To ensure that more people would listen to country music on the radio, the CMA members who oversaw the production of records looked carefully at their own "product" to determine how they could attract most listeners. This led to the creation of the "Nashville sound" as a force not just in country music but in pop music as well.

In November 1957 a *Variety* report on the event known popularly as the Deejay Convention (actually the annual Grand Ole Opry Birthday Celebration), was titled "Where Does the 'Blue Grass' Grow?" Discussing the "pop move-in on the country field," the anonymous reporter began, "What's happened to real old country music or 'blue grass' as they call it, and where are its roots?" Columbia Records President Goddard Lieberson was quoted: "The line of demarcation between pop and country has been eliminated"; now there was just good music and bad music. Observing that the hillbillies were wearing Ivy League suits ("Roy Acuff . . . looked like he just came down from the Yale-Princeton game") instead of cowboy duds, the reporter talked of resentment toward "city slickers" and closed by saying that the final entertainment of the convention was provided by "a rock 'n' roll combo."[1]

The blurring of musical borderlines which rock and roll had caused had not gone unnoticed in Nashville. Previously such borders marked categories ("country and western," "rhythm and blues") which helped producers, retailers, and consumers identify a specific kind of music known to be preferred by a well-defined group of consumers. The major exception was "pop[ular] music" which by definition was supposed to appeal to everyone. In this sense "pop" was the most desirable label, because it meant greater sales potential. Now country music was seen as a potential kind of pop music by the "city slickers" from the heart of the old Tin Pan Alley industry and also by the new progressive hillbillies from Nashville. The latter perceived in their growing economic power an opportunity to shed the stereotypes of the past, which the *Variety* reporter labeled as "Blue Grass."

The more firmly established bluegrass bands maintained recording contracts during this period, but the music was generally treated with scorn by the businessmen who controlled things in Nashville. RCA, which had purchased Elvis's contract from Sun, dropped their last bluegrass act, a Cincinnati outfit called the Country Pardners, at the end of 1956. That year Decca signed on Jimmy Martin, but with him, as with Monroe, they issued an average of only two singles a year during the last half of the fifties. Even though some bands—Reno and Smiley, Flatt and Scruggs, Jim and Jesse— were doing well on local and regional television, record company people who had seen "gold in them thar hillbillies" during the postwar years were now seeking it elsewhere.

In the early fifties Hank Williams's songs had been "crossover" hits, moving from the country to the pop charts. Though these hits were performed by pop singers rather than by Williams himself, they showed the potential for country music within the larger pop market. By the mid-fifties successful crossover hits, like those of Elvis, Marty Robbins, and the Everly Brothers, were more profitable than a stream of hillbilly records with steady but unspectacular sales. And one pop hit would recoup the losses on the flops. As they adopted this high-risk, high-profit, pop-music business strategy, the Nashville record producers found they had an asset in their "Nashville sound." With a sizeable pool of talented musicians and singers available, and a relaxed approach in the studio which allowed for flexibility and innovation, they were able to countrify pop music or add pop to country.

While the Nashville sound didn't always involve the use of pop add-ons like choruses and string sections, it did place emphasis upon the use of certain instruments and musicians. Banjos, mandolins, fiddles, and Dobros were not, in the late fifties, part of the Nashville sound; drums, various types of electric guitars, and the piano were. The coterie of musicians called upon to produce the sound rarely included bluegrass musicians. Whether country singers and their producers sought cross-over hits or used only the basic string instruments and drums of the Nashville studio sound, emphasis was on the vocals. The tendency of bluegrass musicians to weave rich instrumental textures behind vocals was inappropriate in this context. Moreover, the leading producers identified bluegrass with the past and the rural. They worked (with much success) to make country music modern and palatable to urbanites.

Years later the most influential Nashville producers of this period would reflect on what they had done. In 1975 Chet Atkins re-evaluated his role in bringing pop music effects (horns, string sections, choruses) to country recordings: "I hate to see country going uptown because it's the wrong uptown . . . . We're about to lose our identity . . . . Of course, I had a lot to do with changing country, and I apologize."[2] Owen Bradley, who had produced many of Decca's Nashville-sound pop hits, observed to me in 1973 that the country singers who did best over the long run were those who didn't try to change too much during these difficult years. Hindsight, this; in 1957 it was hard to find an advocate of bluegrass in Nashville's music company offices and recording studios—with one important exception.

Don Pierce and Starday

In April 1957 an independent record company from the West called Starday set up offices in Madison, a Nashville suburb. In the next four years they would, through a combination of shrewd business sense and luck, play a leading role in recording new as well as older established bluegrass bands and in introducing bluegrass on long-playing albums to the country market. Established in 1953, when Jack and Neva Starnes of Beaumont, Texas, in partnership with Harold W. ("Pappy") Dailey of Houston, combined their last names to come up with the company name, Starday first specialized in Texas country and western music. In October 1953 Don Pierce, associated since 1947 with Four Star Records, a Los Angeles-based country independent, left that firm and bought a one-third interest in Starday. Four Star had had a number of substantial hits in the late forties and early fifties by such singers as T. Texas Tyler, Webb Pierce (no relation), Hank Locklin, and Jimmy Dean. Pierce utilized contacts he had developed in handling distribution for these and other Four Star country records to build up a network of national distribution for Starday out of Los Angeles.

Shortly after Pierce joined Starday the company had its first hit, "Y'All Come," written and sung by a Texas schoolteacher named Arlie Duff. Pierce was aware of the potential revenue to be made from publishing royalties because Four Star had owned the rights to crossover hits like "Don't Let the Stars Get in Your Eyes." Starday's publishing company, Starrite, owned "Y'All Come," and Pierce was able to place the song with Decca's Bing Crosby, who recorded a cover of it. (Bill Monroe also recorded a cover for Decca and adopted it as his theme song.) This was the first of many publishing-related deals which Pierce engineered for Starday.

In 1955, when the Starneses left the company, Pierce and Dailey became co-owners. Dailey, well known as an independent producer working out of the Gold Star Studios in Houston, handled the A&R side of the business while Pierce looked after distribution and publishing. Like Rich-R-Tone, Starday was a regional independent which took advantage of close contact with the local scene to sign on promising new artists who could sell a lot of records within the region and occasionally do well nationally. But while Rich-R-Tone's Hobe Stanton had a keen ear for the music, he was much less adept than Pierce at the business end of things.

Starday soon acquired George Jones, a locally popular singer who was gaining national recognition. His hits of 1955–56, like "Why Baby Why," were best-sellers, covered by other country singers. Similarly, Red Hayes's "A Satisfied Mind" was covered by Opry star Porter Wagoner. These and other hits brought Starday to the attention of Nashville. And because they were published by Starrite, they brought considerable income to Starday through covers by major label country singers like Wagoner.

At the same time, Starday benefited from the decision by the country music industry to begin releasing singles on 45-rpm plastic discs instead of 78-rpm shellac discs. This made it easy to ship records by mail, and Pierce immediately turned to developing mail-order sales for Starday. In particular he arranged with popular deejays like Randy Blake in Chicago to advertise Starday-produced "Hillbilly Hit Parade" and gospel music packages for sale by mail over the radio.

Starday's knack for finding promising singers with "strong material" and Pierce's innovative marketing ideas appealed to Mercury Records. In 1956 Dee Kilpatrick, who had been with Mercury since the forties and in charge of their Nashville office since 1953 left the company to take over Jim Denny's job as manager of the Grand Ole Opry. Mercury needed someone with experience and energy to operate and develop their operation in Nashville. Late in 1956 Starday signed a five-year contract with Mercury. The idea behind the pact, which was announced at the time as a merger with Mercury, was that Starday's contacts in the country music field would allow Mercury to expand its country and western catalogue. After March 1957 Starday would "continue to operate only as a regional label . . . ostensibly releasing 'test material' only, which if successful would then be transferred to Mercury-Starday and released nationally."[3] Under these terms Don Pierce left Los Angeles to open Starday's offices near Nashville.

While most Starday recordings continued to come from Dailey in Texas, some were done elsewhere. Among them were Starday's first Nashville bluegrass recordings, made in November 1956 by a singer named Bill Clifton. Clifton was, in background and training, quite unlike any other bluegrass musician. Born William August Marburg in 1931, he came from a prominent Baltimore family which had made a fortune in the tobacco trade during the nineteenth century. He was raised on a farm outside of Baltimore, where he discovered country music through radio and records. By the age of twelve he was singing and playing the guitar. Educated at private schools in New England and Florida, he entered the University of Virginia in Charlottesville in 1949. Here his interest in country music merged with a new-found love of folk music, a form he'd been introduced to by fellow students, New Englander Paul Clayton and New Yorker Dave Sadler, both folk enthusiasts.

By 1950 Clifton was performing professionally on small radio stations in central Virginia, often with Clayton. At this time he took the name Clifton to avoid embarrassment to his family, who did not share his deep love of the music. In 1952 with the help of Clayton and Sadler he made his first recordings, a curious mixture of old-time and bluegrass styles with folk revival repertoire. Through Sadler he then met Johnny Clark, a local farm boy who was a tenor singer and banjo player. They formed a band and played on a number of radio stations (including, briefly, WWVA) and recorded several records on Blue Ridge, the small North Carolina independent, during 1953–54. During this time he met and played music with such figures as A. P. Carter and the Stanley Brothers and corresponded with folk revival star Woody Guthrie. This broad range of contacts spanning old-time country, bluegrass, and folk music was at this time unusual, if not unique. Clifton's repertoire reflected these interests, including many traditional songs and older country songs, particularly those by the Carter Family. His singing style was more like that of a folk revivalist than a hillbilly, but his band's instrumental style was that of contemporary bluegrass. He was the first "citybilly" in bluegrass.

In 1956, following two years in the Marines, Clifton re-entered the music business. The Stanley Brothers, who had been with Mercury since 1953, introduced him to Dee Kilpatrick, Mercury's A&R man in Nashville, who invited him to record with Mercury. But by the time Clifton was ready to record, Kilpatrick had left Mercury to take over as WSM Artists' Service Bureau manager. He sent Clifton to Pierce, who expressed interest but said that Mercury-Starday would be unable to finance the recording. So Clifton, putting together his own studio band with the help of Ralph Stanley and two of the Clinch Mountain Boys who'd been in an earlier Clifton band, came to Nashville in November 1956 and cut four songs in the RCA studios at his own expense. He leased two songs from this session to Starday, which issued them on a trial basis early in 1957. The record, particularly the side with the old Carter Family song "Gathering Flowers from the Hillside," received considerable exposure by WWVA deejay Lee Sutton and sold well.

Starday acquired another bluegrass band in December 1956. That month, Jim Eanes, the smooth-voiced country singer from Martinsville, Virginia, who'd been recording with Decca since 1951 mainly using Nashville studio musicians, made his first recordings for Starday at the studios of WPTF in Raleigh, North Carolina. Like Clifton's, these were leased to Starday for trial release. For the first time since 1951 Eanes used his own band. Although it had bluegrass instrumentation, Eanes's sound, with his low-pitched, crooner-style vocals, the heavy, closed-chord "sock" rhythm of Arnell Terry's guitar, and banjoist Allen Shelton's specially rigged tuners which enabled him to change two strings at once to achieve shifting chords resembling contemporary pedal-steel guitar effects, was quite close to that of mainstream country music groups. Eanes's first Starday record, "Your Old Standby," was a minor hit which was covered by Opry star Ray Price.

The success of Clifton's and Eanes's first Starday releases led to their being moved to Mercury-Starday for their next sessions. Clifton's was again in Nashville, in April 1957, and Eanes again recorded at a radio station, this time in Martinsville, Virginia, during June. In the meantime, Dailey and Pierce had taken over management of Mercury's Nashville recording sessions. In late February they produced sessions for groups already under contract to Mercury for release on the Mercury-Starday label. Among those recorded at this time were the Stanley Brothers (with Pee Wee Lambert) and Carl Story and his Rambling Mountaineers.

Carl Story, born in 1916 in Lenoir, Caldwell County, North Carolina, on the eastern slope of the Appalachians, was the son of an old-time fiddler. Story began playing fiddle on radio while a teenager and had his own band by the time he was twenty. His pre-war group almost always included a five-string banjo played in three-finger style. In recent years this feature has been alluded to by some as an indication that Story's was one of the pioneer bluegrass bands, but in the late thirties and early forties such distinctions were not made. In 1942–43 Story played fiddle with Bill Monroe prior to wartime service in the Navy. After the war, he reorganized his band in Asheville and was one of the first country artists signed by Mercury, remaining with that label until 1953, when he moved briefly to the Columbia label. During these years he worked at several radio stations in the mountain region, most notably WNOX in Knoxville and WCYB in Bristol. His repertoire was a mixture of secular and religious songs, with emphasis on the latter; a number of his sacred-quartet recordings were best sellers. His instrumental sound, recorded and live, featured his guitar (he did not play fiddle after leaving Monroe), mandolin, Dobro, and bass—conservative but mainstream country instrumentation rather than that of bluegrass.

As of 1955, when Story returned to Mercury, he was not closely associated with bluegrass, even though during the late forties and early fifties the Rambling Mountaineers had dressed in the style of the Blue Grass Boys, in high boots, riding breeches, white shirts and ties, and narrow-brimmed Stetsons. But when he came to Nashville in February 1957 to record for Mercury-Starday, his band included the bluegrass instrumentation of fiddler Clarence ("Tater") Tate and the mandolin-banjo duo of the Brewster Brothers. At this session the band recorded two gospel quartets and Story's first two instrumentals, one of which, "Mocking Banjo," was destined to become a bluegrass standard. That Story's first recordings with bluegrass instrumentation coincided with his first session for Mercury-Starday is in part coincidental; he'd been working with Tate and the Brewsters for some months. But the inclusion of instrumentals at this session was Pierce's idea. He knew that instrumentals with five-string banjo were selling well at Jimmie Skinner's. Pierce told Story that if Mercury-Starday could issue singles with a gospel song on one side and an instrumental on the other, the instrumentals would help the single get radio play by deejays who would use them for openers and themes. They would also be picked up by juke box distributors, who rarely bought gospel discs but frequently took instrumentals. Story, accustomed to releasing his sacred and secular material on separate records, was talked into trying the gospel-instrumental mixture on one single, and subsequently three more were issued in the same configuration.

During the rest of 1957 Starday recorded or acquired bluegrass recordings by others not nearly as well known as Story, Eanes, or the Stanley Brothers. Among these were Hobo Jack Adkins, an eastern Kentucky performer who had recorded earlier for the small Kentucky independent label Acme and was now working out of Cincinnati; the Wright Brothers, a duo from Beech Mountain, North Carolina, living in Cleveland; Dave Woolum, another Kentuckian living in the Cincinnati area; Bill and Mary Reid, a pair who worked out of Lynchburg, Virginia, and had recorded earlier on Columbia; the Country Gentlemen, a new group from the Washington, D.C., area; the Flat Mountain Boys, an East Kentucky band; and Buzz Busby, a Louisiana native who had been working in the clubs around Washington, D.C., since the early fifties. As of the beginning of 1958, Starday had released at least one single by each.

During this first year and a half (approximately) of the Mercury-Starday association, several patterns emerged which would characterize Starday's activities for the next decade. First, the label issued recordings by a wide range of performers, from Opry stars like George Jones to little-known semi-professionals like the Wright Brothers. During 1957 and 1958 the bigger names would be on the Mercury-Starday label while the lesser ones were on Starday; later all would appear on Starday. Second, the company went against the grain by not consistently using the Nashville sound. They acquired recordings in many ways. Some were made in Nashville studios, like those of Clifton, Story, and the Stanley Brothers. Others were done at radio stations—those of Eanes, for example. Still others were done at independent recording studios, as was the case with the Country Gentlemen. And some of the recordings were acquired from small labels run by custom recording studios, like the Flat Mountain Boys disc, originally issued on the obscure Arrow label.

Pierce was able to acquire many of these recordings through contacts he'd developed over years of merchandising. Spreading the word that he was interested in bluegrass, he contacted people like Ben Adelman, an independent studio owner and producer in Washington, D.C., who had recorded some of the local country performers for Four Star, Decca, and Coral in previous years. Adelman learned of the Country Gentlemen. This new band, a spin-off from Buzz Busby's group, included singer-guitarist Charlie Waller, who had grown up in rural Louisiana; tenor-mandolinist John Duffey, the son of an opera singer who was from Bethesda, Maryland, an affluent Washington suburb; and banjoist Bill Emerson, also from Bethesda. Local deejay Don Owens, a performer himself and long a bluegrass enthusiast, had helped them obtain a morning show on WARL in Arlington, and soon after that Adelman recorded them at his Washington studio. He recouped his recording costs by having the group share the composer-copyright credits with him through his wife, Kay Adelman, who used the pseudonymn of "C. Davis." The recordings were leased by the Gentlemen to Starday, which, as usual, acquired the publishing rights. Adelman later recorded Buzz Busby, Bill Harrell, and other Washington-area bluegrass groups under similar arrangements.

Pierce was likewise in contact with Lou Epstein, manager of Jimmie Skinner's Music Center in Cincinnati, who kept him apprised of mail-order sales of bluegrass and gospel music and played a role in his acquisition of recordings by many lesser-known groups—like Dave Woolum, a familiar figure in the Cincinnati area. And the tie-in was strengthened by Jimmie Skinner's Mercury recording contract; he was recorded by Pierce and Dailey at about the same time (February 1957) as Story and the Stanley Brothers. Also recorded at this time were Rusty York and Willard Hale (who had recently done their first rockabilly record for King) doing a banjo instrumental, "Dixie Strut." Starday and Mercury-Starday recordings were prominently featured in Skinner's ads, so each benefited from the exchange of information and products.

Pierce was first and foremost an expert at merchandising; his work with distribution built the small Texas label to national stature. While other companies bemoaned the effect of rock and roll and attempted to create products for the teen/pop market, Pierce quickly saw and moved to exploit two alternatives to competing with hit singles. One was mail-order sales such as those of Skinner. The other was what he, in the business-world lingo which was becoming popular in Nashville, called "packaged goods"—better known as LPs or albums.

In August 1957 Pierce announced that Mercury-Starday was moving into the packaged-goods field with a series of LPs to be released on the Mercury label. A few country music albums had been appearing each year since the early fifties. But the "single"—a ten-inch, 78-rpm disc, supplanted slowly during the fifties by a seven-inch, 45-rpm disc, containing a song on each side—was the standard country music recording format. Folkways' Scruggs-style banjo album issued early in 1957 was the first LP on which bluegrass music could be heard. Next came a Flatt and Scruggs album, *Foggy Mountain Jamboree*, issued by Columbia at the end of the summer of 1957. This reflected Lester and Earl's popularity and high status as Opry performers, though they were by no means the first Columbia country artists to appear on LP. Conventional wisdom in Nashville was that the older country music consumers would buy singles; LPs were for only the very biggest groups or singers, those with crossover or pop sales potential. Hence Flatt and Scruggs were the exception, for bluegrass consumers were thought to constitute a singles market, and indeed many probably were at this time. Nevertheless there was more demand for bluegrass albums than anyone in Nashville realized. As had happened so often before in country music, the independents were moving more quickly than the majors; in December 1957 Syd Nathan's King label in Cincinnati released a Reno and Smiley album, *Sacred Songs,* and a second Reno and Smiley set, *Instrumentals,* followed soon after. But because Pierce was operating in Nashville, his activities attracted more attention. When Pierce left Starday in 1970, *Billboard's* country music editor noted that he was "the first really to push the album concept for country music. In doing so, he pioneered a trend for adult buyers."[4]

Pierce's Mercury albums were released in February 1958. They included LPs by Jimmie Skinner, Carl Story, Flatt and Scruggs, and the Stanley Brothers. Pierce's approach to merchandising can be seen in various aspects of the albums. One is that of repackaging. The best example of this is the Flatt and Scruggs album, which consisted entirely of material recorded in 1948–50. This was the first time these twelve songs, including "Foggy Mountain Breakdown," "Roll in My Sweet Baby's Arms," and "Old Salty Dog Blues"—some of their most popular—were on LP. So the album functioned as a collector's reissue, a dimension Pierce was to exploit further: eight of the twelve would reappear on a variety of Starday albums in the early sixties. The Stanley Brothers and Carl Story albums contained a mixture of newly recorded songs and previously issued singles, another practice which Pierce would follow in subsequent repackaging. This re-use of previously released material in new "packages" would eventually alienate bluegrass consumers when by the mid-sixties it seemed impossible to buy a new Starday album without getting songs already available on earlier LPs. But in 1958, the market was not flooded with such recordings, and albums like this, which mixed new and old in a variety format similar to that used by the artists on radio and at their shows, were appealing.

Another dimension of Pierce's merchandising savvy was the way in which he took advantage of the space provided on album covers to advertise directly to the consumer. This was done to some extent by all album manufacturers, but Pierce did it with a flamboyance which has seldom been matched. He treated the album title, the art work, and the written comments on the back of the album jacket (the liner notes) as a means of increasing the salability of the album, just as the box sells the soap. In this sense he was quite accurate in calling the albums "packaged goods."

Bold letters set forth the album titles on the cover, clearly and unequivocably identifying the performers with their type of music: *Country Music by Lester Flatt and Earl Scruggs and the Foggy Mountain Boys; The Stanley Brothers: Country Pickin' and Singin';* and *Gospel Favorites by Carl Story and the Rambling*

Mountaineers. The covers had brightly colored pictures of the band (Flatt and Scruggs, Story) or a country landscape (Stanley Brothers—a black and white shot of Carter and Ralph was on the back). And the liner notes gave histories of the groups and described the music in down-to-earth terms meant to make it quite clear that this was not rock and roll, rockabilly, or pop:

> . . . real, authentic, hill country pickin' and singin'. . . . You will notice that these artists use the traditional mountain ballads with harmony singing. Note how these songs tell a story, often sad, of actual things that happen. . . . Listen to the spirit and sincerity of the Stanley Brothers as they sing such beautiful hymns as . . . they really live and feel their music to the point where they do much more than just play it . . . sincerity and simplicity. . . . We, at Mercury, are extremely proud of the Stanleys, these hardy men of the hills, who are so true to their heritage.[5]

Also included in the same Stanley Brothers notes was the information that Carter maintained "a very fine pack of coon dogs" while Ralph bred Hereford cattle on the family farm. Similar phrases were used to describe Flatt and Scruggs, who

> play mountain music in the authentic style which was passed on by America's first settlers and which to the present day is the kind of pickin' and singin' that lovers of real country music like to hear. These are the old songs sung in the old mountain manner, without corruption by the many modern sounds that characterize some of the so called country music of today . . . they have a clean, down to earth variety show that all members of the family can enjoy. They seem to be equally at home with ballads, instrumentals, comedy songs, and songs of faith . . . so if you are one of those people who wants the real McCoy, who likes to hear the best traditional style country musicians in the business, playing the instruments that our forefathers played, and playing those instruments without electric amplification, just the way our forefathers played them before us, you are in for a treat when you listen to the greatest of the Flatt and Scruggs recordings which are contained in this package.[6]

These unsigned notes bear the stamp of Don Pierce's Starday rhetoric, with its homilies about the old mountain manner, the music of our forefathers, the hardy men of the hills. The same collection of images and ideas was to appear on hundreds of Starday albums and in their advertising copy for the next decade. The word *bluegrass* was not used; Bill Monroe was not mentioned; "hillbilly" was absent. Authenticity, realness, heritage, tradition, and association with the mountains were stressed. The goal was to sell records to people from the mountain regions who appreciated the old stuff by appealing to their sense of identity using positive stereotypes and avoiding the connotation of words like *hillbilly* or even *bluegrass* (already a pejorative term in Nashville). Behind this rhetoric lay Pierce's belief that a market for this material existed in people who didn't want compromise in their music.

By the time these albums edited by Pierce were released, Mercury and Starday were no longer associated. Early in 1958 Pierce and Dailey had divided up the extant Starday masters, and Dailey returned to Texas, where he founded his own label, D Records. Pierce took over Starday and, in his words, "reactivated it as an independent label specializing in country and gospel records with emphasis on blue grass and five string banjo music."[7] By his own account, having George Jones—one of the few mainstream country artists whose hit masters he retained—with the label gave Pierce credibility in Nashville: "He opened a lot of doors for us," in a city where small independents often came and went unnoticed.[8]

During 1958 Starday issued singles by a number of the performers previously on Mercury-Starday—Bill Clifton, Jim Eanes, Carl Story, the Stanley Brothers, and Rusty York and Willard Hale. Some of these recordings were left over from Mercury-Starday sessions, while others, like those of Carl Story and the Stanley Brothers, were from new sessions, some done in Nashville, some at radio stations. Starday also continued to release records by the more promising groups that they had already issued on the Starday label before the split like the Country Gentlemen and Buzz Busby. And they continued to lease recordings by bluegrass groups like Jim and Jesse and the Virginia Boys, who had not been on record since their Capitol contract expired in 1955, and the Kentucky Travelers.

Among the most interesting and significant of Starday's new groups was the Lewis Family of Lincolnton, Georgia. One of the first professional bluegrass bands in which female vocalists were regularly featured, they pioneered in a synthesis of modern gospel singing with bluegrass accompaniment. Pop Lewis had led a gospel quartet on WRDW, Augusta, in the early days of radio. His children grew up participating in family singing sessions, gathering around the piano to do old favorites and try songs from the new gospel songbooks, which Pop purchased regularly. By the late forties they were also trying songs from the new gospel records oldest son Wallace was buying. Little Roy Lewis, Wallace's petite younger brother, still recalls his excitement the day Wallace brought home Bill Monroe's first Columbia single to feature the Blue Grass Quartet, with "I'm Travelin' On and On" and "Shine Hallelujah Shine." Following the example of this and similar recordings, the family began incorporating bluegrass accompaniment, particularly Roy's five-string banjo.

Their professional career began modestly with singing for local church suppers. Next came appearances at regional singing conventions. Befriended by a leading professional gospel group, the Happy Goodman Family, they came to the attention of singer-gospel impresario Wally Fowler, who booked them at one of his famous all-night sings. With this step they had reached the big time in gospel music. By 1954 they had their own weekly television show on WJBD in Augusta, and late in 1957 they made their first Starday recordings. The Lewis Family's recordings were listed as "Songs of Faith with Banjo" in Starday ads.

By the fall of 1959 Pierce had assembled a catalog of recordings sufficient to enable him to once again enter "the package goods field"[9] with a line of EPs (seven-inch 45-rpm extended-play discs with four or six songs, in a jacket) and LPs. He continued to exploit his connections with national distributors but now placed greater emphasis on mail-order sales. He advertised in this way through Cincinnati deejay Wayne Raney, whose programs on WCKY were extremely popular, and through the various high-powered Mexican border radio stations like XERA in Del Rio, Texas. According to Pierce, however, Jimmie Skinner Music Center manager Lou Epstein "was a key man in our mail order sales."[10] Starday also encouraged direct mail-order sales. In an article published in 1960, the company invited "interested parties to write directly to Starday Records, Box 115, Madison, Tennessee for free listings of country and gospel records with special offer for mail order sales. This is done because Starday recognizes that many country music enthusiasts live in remote and rural areas and they do not have access to record dealers. To achieve distribution of country records, Starday recognizes that country and gospel records must be available by mail order as a supplement to sales through record retailers."[11] That some customers lived in "remote and rural areas" Pierce knew; mail-order record sales had been proven commercial with that market as far back as the thirties, when Montgomery Ward included hillbilly discs in their omnibus catalogs. But Pierce was not yet aware of a growing body of customers in a place remote to Nashville: Greenwich Village in lower Manhattan. During the late fifties, as informal music sessions there led to the development of bands, and New York folk music audiences responded enthusiastically to bluegrass performances at local concert sites (like Carnegie Hall) the awareness that some city folks appreciated bluegrass would gradually be brought home to Don Pierce and the other country music entrepreneurs who were marketing bluegrass. But this was a slow, gradual process.

Country Pickin' and Singin' in Washington Square

In the summer of 1945 (some accounts give 1947) a man named George Margolin began playing his guitar and leading songs like " 'Brown Eyes,' 'Midnight Special,' 'Cindy,' 'I Ride an Old Paint,' and a few spirituals and union songs from mimeographed song sheets" on Sunday afternoons in Greenwich Village's Washington Square.[12] By the early fifties summer Sundays in Washington Square were a focus of activity for folk music enthusiasts in the New York area.

These enthusiasts were part of the American folksong revival which blossomed in the post-war era, the confluence of a number of intellectual and social trends. The idea that folksong and music were the organic expression of cultural heritage came from nineteenth-century romantic nationalism. By the time of the First World War it had become part of the intellectual traditions of literary nationalism and regionalism in the United States. Since the twenties a growing number of academics and amateur enthusiasts had been collecting and publishing folksongs. Some of these people also brought such songs to the concert stage; others organized annual "folk festivals." Young middle-class people, particularly those of urban backgrounds with a college education and an interest in the arts, were the consumers of folksong books, concerts, and festivals. During the thirties the communist-supported popular front in New York embraced folksong as proletarian music. This influence remained strong in the literature and repertoire of folksong enthusiasts for the next decade, manifesting itself in repertoires like Margolin's, which mixed old traditional songs such as "Cindy" and "I Ride an Old Paint" with union songs, which were newly composed protest lyrics written in a folk style and meant to be sung on the picket line.

By the early forties "folksingers" were part of the urban entertainment scene. In New York there was a range of such individuals, from Burl Ives, a popular actor and singer who downplayed the political connections, to Woody Guthrie, the Oklahoma singer-songwriter who wrote regularly for the *Daily Worker.* A tangled web of mutual interests and social connections drew Ives, Guthrie, and many others in the New York scene together with figures like folksong collector John A. Lomax and his son Alan, both employed at the Library of Congress's Archive of American Folk Song since early New Deal days, and with musicologists Charles and Ruth Crawford Seeger, also working in Washington. Charles Seeger's son Pete was the moving force behind the Almanac Singers, a left-wing New York group that was the prototype for the Weavers (Seeger was with them, too) and other folk groups of the fifties like the Kingston Trio.

Pete Seeger had learned the five-string banjo in the late thirties, traveling in the rural South and visiting musicians like those who had been recorded by John and Alan Lomax for the Library of Congress. He popularized the instrument with folk enthusiasts through concerts and records. Within a few years of Margolin's first appearances in Washington Square young musicians began showing up there with five-string banjos. Among them were Tom Paley, a graduate of Bronx Science High School who was attending Yale and who had become a five-string banjo virtuoso; mandolinist Harry West, a native of Lee County in western Virginia; and Roger Sprung, son of a New York lawyer, who started learning Scruggs-style banjo in 1948. These young men brought old-time mountain-style country music—learned first-hand in West's case and from records (including reissues edited by Alan Lomax) in Paley's and Sprung's—to Washington Square. Arthur Jordan Field, who had been involved in the earliest sessions, reported that by 1953 "the Washington Square Sunday singing had degenerated into a free-for-all competition . . .

Paley and West had become the leaders of an important segment of the younger group which they carried en masse into country music and away from such English ballads . . . and political songs as were around before them. . . . By 1954 or so . . . there were so many performers of all kinds and qualities around that it would be impossible to catalogue the various cliques."[13]

Nineteen fifty-four was the year Pete Seeger added a section on Scruggs to his banjo instruction book, and by then there was a substantial number of folk enthusiasts studying the style. In the fall of that year Flatt and Scruggs were part of a short-running Broadway show, "Hayride," featuring the cast of the "Old Dominion Barn Dance" from WRVA in Richmond, Virginia. Of the groups in the show, Flatt and Scruggs received the greatest response, and Scruggs was met at the stage door after each show by young banjo pickers, part of the group who were coming regularly to Washington Square.

One of these youths, Eric Weissberg, was recorded by Mike Seeger for *American Banjo Scruggs Style* in 1956. At that time he was eighteen years old, a recent graduate of Music and Arts High School just starting his studies at the University of Wisconsin. At Washington Square he was usually seen in the company of fellow classmate and banjoist Marshall Brickman. Often they competed for audiences in the crowd with older pickers like Roger Sprung. From this competitive milieu came the first Yankee entrants in banjo contests held at old-time fiddling conventions in the South.

Fiddling Conventions: North Meets South

Fiddlers' contests or conventions have been held in the American South at least since the first half of the eighteenth century. By the end of the nineteenth century such events, often held annually, had become common in the South and were not unknown elsewhere. The core of such events was the contest, when fiddlers got up one by one and did their best in front of the audience. But what really animated these festive occasions were the social activities taking place before, during, and after the contest. Fiddlers and other musicians met, talked, and played music informally. Usually the formal portions of the contest were held on a stage, often covered or indoors. But much informal activity took place outside, in the warm southern sun. Acquaintances were renewed, tunes swapped, drinks taken (often clandestinely), and new musicians (often youngsters) initiated. Meals were shared, news exchanged, instruments swapped or sold, late hours kept; all were part of the offstage aspects of these events. It was such socializing that Ralph Rinzler encountered for the first time at country music parks, as described in the previous chapter.

These fiddlers' conventions, most of which were held during the warmer months of the year, were typically sponsored by communities or community-based groups like schools and fire departments, which used them for fund raising. The audience often included local people who attended out of loyalty to the fund raisers or curiosity about the event rather than an abiding interest in the music. Judging was often simply based on a poll of audience reaction; if there were judges they rarely were trained in the fine points of the music and based their decisions to a great extent on the audience's reponse. This depended upon personal loyalties to friends and neighbors as well as response to showmanship. None of it was taken too seriously; even the contest was just entertainment.

The Old Time Fiddlers Convention at Union Grove, North Carolina, was one such event. Established on an annual basis in the 1920s, its purpose was to raise money for the school board. It persisted and became a well-known regional event. At least part of its popularity was due to the practice of splitting the net proceeds between the school board and the musicians. In addition there was prize money for the contest winners. By the mid-fifties contestants were coming to Union Grove from all over North Carolina and from nearby Tennessee, Virginia, and West Virginia counties. From a fiddlers' contest it grew to include other instruments and a band contest, a response to changes in musical tastes and preferences in the region. Prizes were awarded to the best fiddlers, banjo pickers, and bands. A variety of musical styles could be heard even on a single instrument like the banjo. Banjo contestants in 1957 ranged from Bascom Lamar Lunsford, Asheville lawyer, folk festival founder, and pioneer recording artist who played in the old brushing style, to Larry Richardson, a Galax native who (with Bobby Osborne) had transformed the Lonesome Pine Fiddlers into a bluegrass band in 1949, worked with Monroe in 1954, and was included on the *American Banjo Scruggs Style* album in 1956. A similar stylistic range could be heard among the fiddlers.

For their 1957 event the organizers at Union Grove did make one significant change: they created two categories, old-time and modern, for the band contest. This reflected the arrival of local rock and roll bands during the previous year. For the next decade at Union Grove "modern" came to mean any band with an electric instrument in it; old-time included everything else.

Rock and roll, disseminated via the mass media, had caught on as a dance music and was taken up by local country musicians in North Carolina as elsewhere. There were enough of these musicians by 1957 to warrant the creation of a special category for them in the contest. That local musicians were playing this newest popular form is not surprising. Earlier contests had seen some, usually youngsters, playing jazz-influenced styles or Tin Pan Alley repertoire, competing against those with more conservative style and repertoires. What was different was that the contest committee now felt impelled to put them in a special category. Why? First, their very-much-louder instruments seemed to give them an unfair advantage over the unamplified bands.

Second, the way in which the youngsters in the crowd responded to their music with shouting and screaming might unduly influence the judging of crowd reaction in the contest, in the opinion of those running the festival, who preferred the old-time style. Thus, segregating those bands that came to the contest with electric instruments, ostensibly an attempt to be fair, was really a move to protect the older, preferred styles which they perceived to be threatened.

In 1958 the modern band contest was won by a group called the Rock-a-Billies. But there was another musical trend in evidence at this year's contest; for the first time entrants included musicians from outside the region—Mike Seeger from Washington, D.C., and the Greenbriar Boys from New York City.

Mike Seeger, younger half-brother of Pete, grew up listening to the Library of Congress field recordings which his parents were transcribing for John and Alan Lomax's book *Our Singing Country*. Exposed to a variety of traditional music in his youth, including the Seeger family's maid, black guitarist Elizabeth Cotten, Seeger began playing seriously in the early fifties when he flunked out of college while learning the banjo. During the Korean War Seeger, a conscientious objector, was assigned to work at Mount Wilson State Hospital in Baltimore. Here he met people of southern rural origins who got him interested in country music and in singing country style. He had already heard Scruggs-style banjo played by Roger Sprung; now he was introduced to live bluegrass: "In 1952 I first heard Lester and Earl out at the country music park not far from where I live now. Incredible! It was like a religious experience."[14]

Seeger became a key figure in linking the folk revival and bluegrass worlds. In the Washington-Baltimore area, where bluegrass could be heard on the radio, at parks, and in local bars, he met and played music with young bluegrass enthusiasts, most of whom were either from the mountains or from families of mountain descent. In conversation with one such young man, a deejay and banjo picker from Arlington, Virginia, named Pete Kuykendall, Seeger worked out the concept of the *American Banjo Scruggs Style* album. But the impetus to make the album first came directly from Folkways Records president Moses Asch: "Moe Asch dropped me a letter saying, 'Hey, how would you like to do an album for us on Scruggs-style music?' . . . it really changed my life—putting together an album of musicians that I knew were all around me, who couldn't be heard any other way."[15] Asch had written to Mike Seeger about Scruggs-style banjo because Folkways' best-selling artist was Pete Seeger, and Mike had been working with Pete on Scruggs-style banjo: "We would gather at my brother Pete's house and try to figure out what Earl Scruggs was doing. We'd share what we were able to figure out. One person might get very, very close to Earl during one of his appearances and try to learn that way. Then that information would be shared at the next

get-together."[16] It was through these gatherings that Eric Weissberg was included on the *Scruggs Style* album; not only was he known to Mike from
Washington Square, he had taken banjo lessons from Pete Seeger.

Another contact between the New York revival and the Washington-
Baltimore bluegrass scene was made when Mike Seeger met Ralph Rinzler.
Son of a New Jersey doctor, Rinzler was a student at Swarthmore College in
Pennsylvania. He met Seeger in 1953 when Mike came to the Swarthmore
Folk Festival. Rinzler recalls: "He said 'next year why don't you bring Ralph
Stanley to the festival?' I'd never heard of Ralph Stanley, and I said 'well,
that's an interesting idea, where could we hear him?' Well we went down to
New River Ranch to hear him and ah, it was there in, I guess, the spring of
fifty-three [sic] that we heard Ralph and Carter and later Bill Monroe . . ."[17]
Rinzler, who was learning mandolin, visited Washington Square the follow-
ing year, and when Seeger produced the *Scruggs Style* album Ralph helped
Mike back Eric Weissberg and, as we have seen, wrote the notes to the
album.

Hence Mike Seeger, a key figure in bringing Scruggs picking to New York
and linking the folk revival scene with the Washington bluegrass scene, was
in his way as important a figure at Union Grove as Lunsford or Richardson.
Nineteen fifty-eight was not the first time he had attended such a contest,
but it was the first time he appeared as an entrant at Union Grove.

The Greenbriar Boys represented a younger generation in Washington
Square bluegrass, the first full band to appear there. It originally consisted of
three young men from New York and New Jersey—guitarist John Herald,
who had been exposed to bluegrass by Weissberg and Brickman at the University of Wisconsin, banjoist Bob Yellin, and mandolinist Paul Prestopino.
Their appearance at Union Grove in 1958 came soon after the band was
formed; more would be heard of them at Union Grove in the early sixties, by
which time Prestopino had been replaced, first by Eric Weissberg, then by
Ralph Rinzler. This was the first band from the North to appear on the stage
at Union Grove.

That northern urban folk revivalists entered the contest in the old-time
category seemed proof of Charles Seeger's prediction that "citybillies" (his
coinage) would become more "hillbilly" in their musical style and repertoire
while the hillbillies were becoming more citybilly. There weren't as many
citybillies (folk revivalists) as rockabillies at Union Grove in 1958. But their
numbers would swell in the coming decade. Both rock and roll and the folk
revival were part of the same phenomenon—a breaking away from the popular music industry, dominated by New York-based publishers and record
companies. But while the rock and rollers seemed to threaten old-time music,
the folk revivalists appeared to affirm it, and they were welcomed at Union
Grove and similar events.

In the informal atmosphere away from the contests, it was relatively simple
for persons from outside the region to meet musicians, and hence the early

revival visitors to such festivals found them warm, exciting experiences. Certainly it was a surprise to North Carolinians that someone from New York or Washington was interested in their music; it was also flattering, and thus while such events served as an expression of local values they also became a meeting ground for people of diverse backgrounds and opinions.

Similar contacts occurred at country music parks. Virtually every park had at least one yearly talent contest. For example, beginning in 1951 Washington, D.C., country music entrepreneur Connie B. Gay sponsored an annual "National Hillbilly Music Contest" at a park in Warrenton, Virginia. Many local professional musicians participated in the banjo and fiddle contest at Warrenton; winners included fiddlers Chubby Wise, Scott Stoneman, and Buck Ryan, and banjoists Don Bryant, Pete Roberts (Kuykendall), and Roy Clark. By the mid fifties some revivalists were attending this event. But more popular and accessible was Sunset Park, located in southern Pennsylvania near the Maryland border. Its annual banjo contest drew musicians from a wide area. By 1959 contestants were coming from New York City.

At the end of 1958 Israel G. Young, the proprietor of the Greenwich Village Folklore Center, initiated a column called "Frets and Frails" in the small but influential New York folk music magazine, *Sing Out!* Young's center, established in 1957, was at this time an important meeting place for folk enthusiasts, and he was a regular spectator at nearby Washington Square, so it was significant when in the spring of 1959 he wrote in "Frets and Frails": "Sunset Park (on U.S. 1, between West Grove and Oxford, Pa.) features the best of Blue Grass Music with the Osborn [sic] Bros., The Louvin Bros., The Blue Grass Champs, etc. Admission is $1.00 and the show starts at 1:00 p.m. on Sundays. Mike Seeger is the most constant visitor . . . " In the next issue of *Sing Out!*, Young reported: "Mike Seeger, Eric Weissberg, and Roger Sprung were among the finalists at the annual banjo picking contest in Sunset Park, Pa., last July 4th. A local player, Gerald Flaherty, who just made the sixteen year age minimum, won the coveted Gibson Mastertone as first prize. . . . "[18]

Bluegrass Enters the Revival

The presence of a few interested folk revivalists as spectators or contestants at Union Grove or Sunset Park was significant because they represented the first of what was to become a flood. Such musical gatherings had their counterparts outside the South at college folk festivals. During the late fifties annual festivals gained popularity at colleges and universities in the Northeast, Midwest and West. The earliest seems to have been at Swarthmore, starting in the mid forties. Others began at Oberlin College in Ohio in 1957 and at the Berkeley campus of the University of California in 1958. These events were publicized locally and drew only a few people from outside the college community. They looked to the New York–centered folk revival scene for performers, and many of the college students who attended these festivals were themselves musicians. Though no bluegrass bands were booked as featured performers until the sixties, such music was present in the informal parts of the festivals, picking sessions like those at Union Grove, Washington Square, and the country music parks.

One aspect of these folk festivals not found at the parks and conventions was the "workshop." Like a school class or seminar, it was a session at which skills and methods were demonstrated and ideas discussed in ways which stressed practical applications. Its use at folk festivals is indicative of the academic intellectual traditions in which the folk revival was nurtured, the same mixture of education and entertainment which demanded that Folkways albums like *American Banjo Scruggs Style* include a brochure explaining the significance of the music. At folk festival workshops performers talked about and demonstrated their music, and were joined by folk music collectors and scholars. The audience was encouraged to join in the discussion. This type of informal performance-discussion had become a standard feature of most college and university folk festivals by the late fifties.

Although there were folk revivalists interested in bluegrass music, it had yet to appear on a festival stage in 1959. The main revival interest in the genre remained focused on "Scruggs picking," and all but a few young enthusiasts still viewed bluegrass as being outside the perimeters of folk music. This conception changed dramatically when, in 1959, Alan Lomax returned from eight years of self-imposed exile in Britain (he'd left during the years of McCarthyism and witchhunts). Already a well-known figure within the world of folk music studies through his work at the Library of Congress as well as his books, records, and radio broadcasts, Lomax was now deeply involved in the development of a theory which posited a direct and essential link between musical performance styles and culture. He at once began preaching this theory, which he eventually named "cantometrics," to the "folkniks."[19] Singing the words and melody is not enough, he said; one must perform songs in the style of their culture. Singing style, he asserted, conveyed the emotional content of the song, making it the authentic expression not just of an individual but of the group.

While urging the folk revival performers to be more authentic about style, he also set out to convince them not to be antiquarians; he wanted them to expand their definition of folk music to include contemporary forms. He did this in various ways, but his first substantial effort was a concert, "Folksong '59," held in Carnegie Hall on April 3, 1959. *New York Times* reviewer John S. Wilson quoted Lomax as saying he had returned to the country to find "war whoops coming out of juke boxes that I used to have to go down to Mississippi to record." Lomax told the Carnegie Hall audience that "the time has come for Americans not to be ashamed of what we go for, musically, from primitive ballads to rock 'n' roll songs."[20] The concert included Ozark country

folk singer Jimmy Driftwood (his "Battle of New Orleans" was a recent country hit), bluesmen Muddy Waters and Memphis Slim, the Selah Jubilee
Singers, the Drexel Quartet, Mike and Pete Seeger, Lomax himself, an un-
named (in all the publicity and reviews I have been able to find) rock and
roll band, and a bluegrass band, Earl Taylor and the Stoney Mountain Boys.

Lomax had been introduced to bluegrass by Mike Seeger and included it
in the concert because he perceived it as an updated form of the music he'd
heard in the southern mountains back in the thirties and forties. According
to Ralph Rinzler, who was present at the rehearsals of the concert, Lomax
first tried to get Bill Monroe: "He asked Bill Monroe to come to that and Bill
associated Alan with radical politics and told me later that he didn't accept
the invitation to play at that concert because he distrusted Alan's politics."[21]
According to Earl Taylor, Lomax then tried to get Flatt and Scruggs, but
because he called Lester Flatt, who did not handle booking, he was unable
to make arrangements. By the time their manager, Louise Scruggs, got in
touch with him he had booked Virginia singer Earl Taylor, whom Mike Seeger
had just recorded for a new Folkways album.

Reviewer Wilson compared "Folksong '59" to John Hammond's epochal
1938 "Spirituals to Swing" concert, also held in Carnegie Hall, but he was
skeptical of Lomax's concept. Wondering "what juke boxes Mr. Lomax has
been listening to," he questioned Lomax's suggestion that this music was
popular and familiar. What Lomax was presenting was not heard everywhere
on juke boxes, he thought, but was "the source material that juke boxes have
diluted and distorted."[22] Reviews by folk revival critics were even less sympathetic. Although the concept was debatable and the critical response
mixed, all agreed that of the various groups in the concert, Earl Taylor and
the Stoney Mountain Boys were the hit of the evening. Years later Taylor
recalled, "when we would end a number, I know that it would take five
minutes before we could go into another one—that was how much rarin' and
screamin' and hair-pullin' there was."[23]

Although electric blues, black gospel music, and even rock and roll would
eventually find their place on folk festival stages, the response which Taylor
received was a sign that among New York folk music fans bluegrass was ripe
for acceptance in 1959. Lomax sensed this and used it to advantage at a
workshop held at the second Berkeley Folk Festival at the University of
California that June. He started his lecture with examples of national musics
from various countries which he said were certain to evoke a response from a
native, such as bagpipe music for Scots and so forth. For the kind of music
to which Americans respond, his example was the Stanley Brothers' new
King single of "Train 45." The audience, which had been listening quietly,
responded with laughter and applause. Their reaction was a mixed one—
enthusiasm on the part of the small group of bluegrass fans present and
embarrassment on the part of those revivalists, like festival organizer Barry
Olivier, who felt bluegrass was beyond the pale.

Lomax's enthusiasm for bluegrass reflected not only his own theory-based reactions to it but the fact that it was the coming thing among the younger folk revivalists. A contemporary report from *Gardyloo,* a mimeographed folk magazine published in New York, communicates some of the excitement about bluegrass on the local scene: "Sunday June 14 [1959] saw an awsome [sic] assemblage of Bluegrassers in Wash. Sq.: Mike Seeger, Marshall Brickman, Ralph Rinzler, Eric Weissberg, and the Greenbriar Boys (Bob Yellin, Paul Prestopino, and John Herald) all in one group."[24]

A month later bluegrass made its first appearance on a folk festival stage at Newport, Rhode Island. Since 1954 promoter George Wein had held an annual jazz festival at Newport, and it had become the most important festival of its kind, receiving extensive notice in the press and drawing many thousands of spectators into staid Newport each July 4th weekend. In 1959 the growing popularity of folk music in the commercial marketplace led him to initiate a parallel folk festival, co-produced with folk music promoter Albert Grossman (later manager of folk stars Bob Dylan and Joan Baez). Among those appearing at the first festival were current favorites Odetta and the Kingston Trio. Also present were the Stanley Brothers and Earl Scruggs. Scruggs appeared with Hylo Brown and the Timberliners rather than with Flatt and the Foggy Mountain Boys because the festival organizers had invited only Scruggs to attend. Flatt, always sensitive about matters of billing and credit, refused to come under such circumstances. He was not missed by most in the audience, for at the time folk revivalists listened appreciatively only to Scruggs's banjo playing. (In a review of a Flatt and Scruggs appearance in New York that April, Winnie Winston, a young banjoist, called Flatt "as indistinct and mumbly as ever."[25]) But the very fact that Scruggs and the Stanleys were present at Newport was important for the future. Scruggs spent his time backstage getting to know a young singer who was a sensation in her brief guest appearance at the festival—Joan Baez.

Robert Shelton, describing the festival in the *New York Times,* spoke of the Stanley Brothers' "brilliant 'bluegrass' instrumental styles to which the unfortunate name 'hillbilly' still sticks" and described Earl Scruggs as "a banjoist rarely seen North of Nashville, Tenn. . . . who bears about the same relationship to the five-string banjo that Paganini does to the violin." He also said the Kingston Trio "caused the sort of stir that Valentino might have engendered visiting a spinster's home."[26] The festival producers had arranged the program so that Scruggs was slated to appear on the closing concert following the Kingston Trio. But the Trio was received with such enthusiasm that not until emcee Oscar Brand had promised they would encore after Scruggs played was it possible for Earl to come on and play. He was received politely. Israel G. Young described this difficult situation in his review for *Caravan,* another New York folk music magazine, and commented that Scruggs wasn't helped by Hylo Brown, whose "countrified presentation (was) phony and cheap. . . . Let us hope that next year Earl Scruggs returns with Lester Flatt or Bill Monroe, the people with whom he made his name."[27]

For most revival listeners Scruggs—with or without Flatt—was "too ethnic." Only the taste-makers, men like Lomax, Young, and Shelton, and the young pickers like Seeger, Rinzler, and the Greenbriar Boys, were really enthusiastic about bluegrass at this point. To the extent that the revival operated as a popular education movement, it was up to these members of the avant-garde to spread the word.

An important step in this process came with the new album produced by Mike Seeger, *Mountain Music Bluegrass Style,* released by Folkways at the beginning of the summer of 1959. Seeger's twelve-page brochure accompanying the album was a veritable ethnography of bluegrass music. Noting that " 'Bluegrass' became more a means of distinguishing any type of traditional music from the run of the mill performance by the steel guitars of the Nashville Philharmonic and later, hillbilly rock 'n' roll. Bands are now called Bluegrass that contain one element of the original style . . . ,"[28] he traced the history of the music and outlined the elements characteristic of the genre. This album, with its extensive notes, constituted the first detailed description of bluegrass published, one that still reads well over a quarter of a century later. The performances, which included songs by Earl Taylor and the Stoney Mountain Boys, B. Lilly and Don Stover, Eric Weissberg and Bob Yellin, and Tex Logan, were prefaced on the record by spoken introductions similar to those used by the musicians on stage and radio, giving an immediacy not found on other albums.

The album not only introduced the musical form, it set forth bluegrass ideology, starting with the history of the "original" Monroe band, the Stanley Brothers, Flatt and Scruggs, and so on. Pictures of posters and of cowboy-hatted bands in string ties posing seriously and proudly with instruments ushered in the visual world of bluegrass. A section on musical instruments made readers aware of in-group values: each instrument could be had in a variety of models, but there was a hierarchy. Bluegrass musicians didn't play just any mandolin, they played (or sought to play) the pre-war Gibson model F-5 as used by Monroe, just as banjo-pickers preferred the old Gibson Mastertone models, with the flat-head tone ring, as used by Scruggs and Reno. There were the words to and discographical information about each song, detailed biographies of the performers on the record, and brief histories of all the important bands. A list of lesser groups named the record labels on which they could be heard and gave mail-order record shops, including the Jimmie Skinner Music Center, where their records could be obtained. Four radio stations on which this music could be heard were listed along with their frequencies: WSM in Nashville, WCKY in Cincinnati, WWVA in Wheeling, and XERA in Del Rio, Texas. In many ways the brochure resembled the souvenir songbook-photo albums sold by bluegrass performers at their personal appearances and over the radio. This album with its notes served as a primer and guidebook for the young folk revivalists who were beginning to take notice of bluegrass and reinforced the idea that it was a separate and distinctive form.

In October 1959 Alan Lomax contributed to the process by bringing blue-grass to a mass readership with an article in *Esquire* magazine. He called bluegrass "folk music with overdrive."[29] Although the Kingston Trio was mentioned, the emphasis was on Flatt and Scruggs—subjects of a full-page illustration by Tom Allen—with the Stanley Brothers and the Osborne Brothers also receiving notice and illustrations. Allen won a prize for his illustrations, and the word *bluegrass* was now introduced to a world which stretched far beyond either the folk revivalists or Nashville.

Lomax, whose contacts in the record business rivaled those of Don Pierce, arranged for United Artists to record the band that had been the hit at his April concert. Released at about the same time as the *Esquire* article appeared, *Alan Lomax Presents Folk Songs from the Blue Grass—Earl Taylor and His Stoney Mountain Boys* had liner notes every bit as rhetorical and hard-sell as those on the Pierce Mercury packages: "Bluegrass music, the brightest and freshest sound in American popular music today, is a sort of Southern mountain Dixieland . . . bluegrass based itself firmly upon traditional mountain instrumental styles. . . . The bluegrassers have developed the first true orchestral form in five hundred years of Anglo-American music, and their silvery, pinging sound provides a suitable, yet modern and "hot," setting for the songs of the frontier with which America has recently fallen in love . . . [30] These notes were aimed not at the mountain people from which Taylor and his band came and for whom they played at Club 79 in Baltimore, but at the folk revivalists and sophisticated followers of the avant-garde musical arts. Lomax sought to sell by education, overcoming prejudices against hillbilly music by comparing it to jazz and other prestigious orchestral forms.

But the audience for bluegrass among urban sophisticates was still small. An appearance by Taylor and his band at New York's Village Gate nightclub was not a success. Israel G. Young described the audience as "blasé" and contrasted the working-class background of the band with the middle-class background of the Village Gate patrons: "Few in the audience realized that the steel strike, among other reasons, has cut their audiences in Baltimore. . . . "[31] It was not easy for the Stoney Mountain Boys to move from their rough-and-tumble Baltimore hillbilly bar, Club 79, where bass player–comedian Vernon ("Boatwhistle") McIntyre sang the bawdy "Nuts, Nuts, Red Hot Nuts" nightly, to a posh club like the Village Gate.

More willing to hear this new music were college folk music enthusiasts— the children of the kind of people who went to clubs like the Village Gate. A few months after Taylor's unsuccessful New York appearance there, the Osborne Brothers were booked for an appearance at Antioch College in

Yellow Springs, Ohio. A small liberal arts college located near Dayton, Antioch had a long history of interest in the arts and was a center of student interest in folk music. Among those on campus was Jeremy Foster, a friend and former classmate of Mike Seeger. Jeremy and his wife Alice Gerrard had organized a band, the Green County Stump Jumpers. Around this group, with the added attraction of the Fosters' collection of old-time and bluegrass recordings, instruments, posters, and songbooks, had coalesced a local college bluegrass scene which included a number of Antioch students and a similar group of students from Oberlin College in northern Ohio.

In late February 1960 Foster talked the student government into paying $300 for the Osborne Brothers to appear in the college auditorium on March 5. In planning the event, he decided the Osbornes would be most at ease in a context similar to those with which they were familiar. Like Seeger and Rinzler, he had been attending (and recording on tape) shows at Sunset Park and New River Ranch since the mid-fifties and knew that a typical bill of fare at a park included an afternoon and an evening show; that each show consisted of a performance by the "house band," then one or two local bands, and finally, following an intermission, the feature attraction or "headliner," the star band advertised for the day. Sunset Park at Antioch was the idea behind the structure of this first college bluegrass concert. The "house band" was the Green County Stump Jumpers; the visiting small-time or local group was the Plum Creek Boys from Oberlin College, and the Osbornes, living in Dayton but members of the cast of the World's Original Jamboree at WWVA in Wheeling, West Virginia, were the headliners.

After working in Detroit with Jimmy Martin during 1954–55, Bob and Sonny Osborne had moved to Wheeling, where they worked until Christmas with Charlie Bailey on WWVA. Back in Dayton at the beginning of 1956, they teamed up with Red Allen, another Kentuckian living in the Dayton area. Through the help of a local disc jockey they got a recording contract with MGM in spring 1956. Allen recalled: "Me and Bob Osborne were working at NCR (the National Cash Register Company) and playing the bars six nights a week. But when those first records came out, we got on the WWVA Jamboree in Wheeling and from there on, things started happening."[32] "Ruby" was their first record—Bob's version of singer/banjoist Cousin Emmy's old mountain song in which they featured the then novel arrangement of "twin banjos" played in harmony.

Their success with this record led to a series of follow-up recordings with twin banjos as well as some rockabilly-influenced songs, but by 1958 they had moved on to develop a specialty with which they are still identified, the "high lead" trio. In this vocal arrangement, the lead or melody voice is (with some temporary variations) the highest part, with the tenor harmony line (usually sung above the melody) placed an octave lower than usual, below the other harmony part (the baritone). Using this arrangement high-voiced Bob Osborne, who had been the conventional tenor singer in the band, could sing the melody and the highest part at the same time. This freed the Osborne Brothers from dependence upon a lead singer so that when Red Allen left the band in 1958 they became simply the Osborne Brothers. Maintaining bluegrass instrumentation, they began specializing in high lead arrangements of contemporary country songs. Their trios (the third singer was their guitarist, at the time of the Antioch concert, Jimmy Brown, Jr.) became complex, using ideas borrowed from the pedal steel guitar and ornate endings. Though Sonny's banjo recordings were still selling well from the Skinner Center, it was this style of singing that they were featuring when they arrived at Antioch.

Before the show the three bands met backstage in the dressing room. The local bands tuned and warmed up self-consciously in front of these stars. The etiquette of such backstage situations is well-defined: once the details of preparation (dressing, tuning, warmup) have been attended to, the performers "get acquainted." The guitar player with the Plum Creek Boys (myself) had a pint of corn whiskey and offered a drink to the Osbornes. Sonny, who was about the same age as the college boys, accepted. The ice was broken, and in the conversation that followed each questioned the other about their areas of special knowledge. One of the students asked Sonny how tight his banjo head should be. Sonny tapped the cinderblock wall, saying "like this." Bob Osborne, nervous about playing before college kids, asked if they should do some rock and roll. Definitely not, he was told; do bluegrass—tunes like "Ruby" and "Little Maggie." The two college bands played short sets—four or five songs. Although they were playing very elementary bluegrass, the audience whooped and screamed in approval after each number.

The Osbornes opened their set with "Ruby," which received a similar enthusiastic response. But the relaxed pace of Bob's introductory remarks, with jokes about each band member and several slightly coarse gags by Sonny—of a type common in country comedy routines—generated a different response. Someone in the audience shouted impatiently, "Play something!" Sonny replied: "We will. We'll get around to it. We have lots of time tonight. Ha ha ha ha ha."[33]

The audience laughed with him and the band began their program as they would have at Sunset Park, with their latest recordings, most of them relatively slow modern country songs. The audience applauded them politely but responded with shouts and whistles of approval to the faster tunes which featured the banjo. Bob noted this and brought Sonny up for an instrumental. The applause after the tune was long and loud, so he asked acoustic bass player Benny Birchfield to get out his banjo and do some twin banjos with Sonny. While they tuned, Bob talked:

I'd like to ask you a question, if any of you ever hear us up at Wheeling, West Virginia, on Saturday night. Any of you ever listen to the radio around? [Amused laughter.] Well, have any of you ever been up there to see the Jamboree? Anybody been up there to see it? [More amused laughter, a chorus of no's.] You been up to Wheeling? Well, we would like to . . . we're . . . it's not too far from here; you get right on Route 40 and it's only a couple a hundred miles and . . . [Another burst of laughter.] No, it isn't too far, I mean we're up there every Saturday night—except the Saturday nights that we're not, of course—but some time when you don't have anything to do on a weekend, why come up and see us. [Much uproarious laughter and shouting.] Well, I see right now you're pretty busy on the weekend here![34]

This formulaic invitation for the audience to visit them at WWVA was received differently than it would have been at Sunset Park. Most of these students did not listen to WWVA, and the idea of attending any kind of hillbilly music event at all was foreign to them; this, after all, was a folk music concert. To spend an entire weekend going to a radio jamboree (in the midst of the crowded college schedule) seemed so bizarre that it evoked laughter. The amused laughter contrasted with the serious and enthusiastic way in which the following twin banjo instrumentals were received. A few minutes later, another one of Bob's standard introductions met with an unexpected reaction: "You know, tonight is Saturday night and everything, but every place we go we try to please everybody, and by doing that, you know, why we try to do a little bit of every kind of a song that's a-going. And every place we go that we have a lot of requests for the religious songs, and we always set aside a little place in the program for some religious songs. In our kind of business why we try to please everybody and do everything."[35] Here there were a few hoots of laughter; Bob introduced the song, which was the only religious number they sang that night.

Those in the audience already committed to the music (principally the bands and their friends) were embarrassed by and annoyed at those in the audience who had not taken this portion of the show "seriously." Although this was the first real bluegrass show most of them had seen, they were prepared for the stock introductions, having heard them on Mike Seeger's *Mountain Music Bluegrass Style*, and for the mixing of slow country songs with instrumentals and religious songs, having encountered this on the Don Pierce–produced Stanley Brothers and Flatt and Scruggs albums. But even the Yankee bluegrass fans missed some of the jokes; for example at virtually every show during this period Bob Osborne would preface his introduction of Sonny's first banjo tune with the comment, "Down home, they say *banjer.*" Usually that was enough to provoke laughter from southerners who recognized the dialect usage, but at Antioch there was no response, so he continued with, "They don't say *banjo*, they say *banjer* down home . . ."[36] but still there was no response. For the rest of the evening he abandoned the ethnic in-joke and very carefully pronounced the word "*ban-jo*," with the accent on the second syllable.

The second half of their show reflected the impact of the first. Virtually all the songs performed were requests. Older uptempo Osborne Brothers songs like "Ho Honey Ho" and bluegrass standards like "Molly and Tenbrooks," "Jimmy Brown the Newsboy," "I Wonder How the Old Folks Are at Home," "Earl's Breakdown," "Little Maggie," "Salty Dog Blues," "Pretty Polly," "Cripple Creek," "Down in the Willow Garden," and "Wildwood Flower" predominated. The requests which they could not fill came similarly from southern Appalachian tradition: "Engine 143," "Shady Grove," "Columbus Stockade Blues," and "Bury Me beneath the Willow." They also did a few requests from the two college bands for the vocal trios which were their specialty, like "Once More" and "Under Your Spell Again," but most of the audience didn't appreciate the elegant vocal trio work on these slower and more commercial songs.

Other bluegrass bands would encounter similar problems when they presented country shows for college audiences who came to bluegrass perceiving it as folk music. The simple formulaic introductions, the pious and sincere references to religion, the down-home comedy routines, the clichés of contemporary country songs—all of this met with less than enthusiastic response. In contrast the fast instrumentals on the five-string banjo, thought of as a folk instrument, and the folksongs, with their archaic clichés, were received enthusiastically. All in all, the Osborne Brothers' appearance at Antioch was a success. Jeremy and Alice Foster had no trouble convincing the student government to support another concert by the Stanley Brothers just two months later.

In April 1960 the Greenbriar Boys returned to Union Grove. They had the polish of several years' experience, and their new mandolin player, Ralph Rinzler, had gotten them into serious rehearsals and provided new repertoire from his tape collection of old hillbilly records. They won first place in the old-time band contest, apparently because the judges were impressed that they'd come so far to enter. In July Flatt and Scruggs, along with the Foggy Mountain Boys, were at the second Newport Folk Festival. Thus by the middle of 1960 a number of the best-known bluegrass bands were appearing before folksong revival audiences, and at least one revival bluegrass band had appeared before a southern audience. Audiences and musicians from the country music–oriented bluegrass scene were exchanging ideas with their folk revival counterparts. The synthesis which these events implied was realized in the summer of 1960 when Folkways released *Country Songs, Old and New,* the first Country Gentlemen LP.

The Country Gentlemen had been recording for Starday since December 1957. During 1958 they began adding to their repertoire old country songs taken from sources which differed from those typically used by bluegrass bands. Like many country performers they included in their repertoire some old songs taken from oral traditions—folksongs—and songs learned from old, now obscure, hillbilly records. But the Country Gentlemen's folksongs came from recordings rather than directly from oral tradition. And their old hill-billy songs were not learned from records heard over the radio or purchased when new, but from records carefully preserved by record collectors as antiques. In both cases the songs and tunes were valued in part for the antique patina they preserved—old stories and attitudes, old melodies and styles of singing. This, as we will see in following chapters, resembled the way in which folk revivalists perceived the music they followed.

This approach to repertoire was facilitated by new technology—the LP and, most importantly, the tape recorder. In the mid-fifties, music buffs had begun to discover the advantages home recorders offered. Bluegrass followers had been taping shows at parks and radio broadcasts since 1953–54. By the late fifties they were swapping tape copies of such recordings and of old records. Members of the Country Gentlemen owned tape recorders, collected old records, and were also listening to new folk revival recordings on LP.

In 1958 the Gentlemen hired a new banjo player, Peter V. Kuykendall (he used the stage name of Pete Roberts), the deejay and record collector who had helped Mike Seeger plan his first Folkways album on Scruggs-style banjo. Like Seeger, he had performed on that recording and also on *Mountain Music Bluegrass Style*. The first bluegrass discographer, Kuykendall was at this time already working on lists of recordings by Flatt and Scruggs, Monroe, the Stanley Brothers, and Reno and Smiley which would appear in *Disc Collector*, the only serious country music research publication at that time. John Duffey, the group's tenor singer and mandolinist, was also finding texts and recordings of old songs through his research trips to the Archive of Folk Song at the Library of Congress. Kuykendall and Duffey both knew Mike Seeger and were aware of the growing interest in folk music. In the late summer of 1958, the Kingston Trio released "Tom Dooley," and it was number one on the pop charts by the end of that year. Pete Kuykendall and his wife wrote a new set of words for the Gentlemen's version of the Kingston Trio arrangement, and they recorded it as "Rolling Stone," released on a Starday single early in 1959.

Another important influence on the Country Gentlemen was the Stanley Brothers. Among the tape recordings collected by members of the Gentlemen were several informal and personal-appearance performances by the Stanley Brothers of older songs which they had not recorded commercially. Several of these became part of the Country Gentlemen's repertoire.

While developing their own repertoire, the Gentlemen also sought to achieve a distinctive sound by concentrating on singing, with particular emphasis on trios. As Duffey recalls, they were listening to the Osborne Brothers on WWVA the way the Stanley Brothers had been listening to Bill Monroe on WSM back in 1947–48: "It seems that Bob, Sonny and Red Allen were on the Wheeling Jamboree, and they were often on the late-night show. When I knew they were going to be on, I'd go find a place in the car where I knew the radio would come in good, and there I would park. . . . There were a few things, like those endings, that we "borrowed" from them. In those days, that was considered superior stuff, not that it still isn't."[37]

But the band's sound did not really jell until in the spring of 1959 they hired a young Virginian, Eddie Adcock, as banjoist. Adcock was a strong baritone singer and had a distinctive banjo style which included approaches borrowed from Travis- and Atkins-style electric guitar, as well as from the pedal steel guitar. He'd been working around the Washington area since the mid-fifties (except for a brief stint with Monroe) as a bluegrass banjoist and a rockabilly guitarist. Adcock's strong vocal parts and distinctive banjo, along with his crazy stage antics, gave the band a striking identity.

By the end of the year Duffey, who was their business manager, felt that they were ready to do an album. He was eager to do this because he saw that the more affluent consumers, the folk enthusiasts, were buying albums—rather than singles—of bands like the Stanley Brothers and Flatt and Scruggs. He tried to convince Don Pierce, who was just beginning to release Starday's "package goods," to issue a Starday Country Gentlemen album. But in 1959 Pierce was just getting started with LPs and was concentrating on anthologies and on albums by a few well-established groups like Carl Story and the Stanley Brothers. He was not ready to risk an album by a new local group.

So Duffey turned to another contact in the Washington area, Mike Seeger, whom he'd known since they had been at secondary school together in Bethesda, Maryland. Seeger, now working at a recording studio, Capitol Transcriptions, had the training and resources to produce the album. And with two successful bluegrass albums for Folkways under his belt, he was able to sell Moe Asch on the Country Gentlemen. The album (with a fashionably grainy black-and-white cover photo by New York professional photographer John Cohen, a musical partner of Seeger in the New Lost City Ramblers) sold well for Folkways, even though some reviewers considered it too slick and sophisticated. The brochure gave a history of the band, the words to and histories of the songs, and, at the end, a list of their Starday singles and the addresses of several mail-order houses, including Skinner's, where they could be obtained. Those who were beginning to collect bluegrass records recognized the Gentlemen from Starday anthology EPs and LPs which contained their earlier singles. These functioned to validate the Gentlemen: if they are on Starday, they must be authentic. And soon some of the Folkways album tracks were released on Starday singles.

As the song histories in the Folkways brochure demonstrated, a number of these old country songs, like "Ellen Smith" and "Jesse James," were versions of folksongs that had been recorded earlier by hillbilly singers and bluegrass bands. They were ballads—story songs that had been placed and kept in oral tradition by broadsides during the nineteenth century. Newer country songs on the album, like "The Story of the Lawson Family," represented a continuation of the broadside ballad tradition during the twenties on early hillbilly records. And one song on the album, "Long Black Veil," a 1959 hit single for Opry star Lefty Frizzell, was written in a style reminiscent of the old broadside ballads. It was picked from the Gentlemen's album and recorded by a number of folk revival singers, including the Kingston Trio and Joan Baez.

With their tradition-oriented repertoire and combination of Folkways albums and Starday singles, the Country Gentlemen were the first bluegrass band to successfully integrate the strands of country music and the folksong revival, tying Mike Seeger and Washington Square to Don Pierce and Nashville. And though they were hardly the first bluegrass outfit in the Washington, D.C.–Baltimore region, they were to bring that regional scene to national prominence and play an important role in moving bluegrass music to its own revival.

Notes

1. Where Does the 'Blue Grass' Grow?" p. 59.
2. William Ivey, "Chet Atkins," pp. 285–86.
3. Bernie Asbell and Joel Friedman, "Mercury to Absorb Starday Diskery."
4. Bill Williams, "Don Pierce Exits Starday."
5. [Don Pierce], unsigned liner notes to *Country Pickin' and Singing*.
6. [Don Pierce], unsigned liner notes to *Country Music*.
7. [Don Pierce], "Formation and Growth of a Record Company—Starday Records," p. 35.
8. "Days of Starday and Don Pierce," *The 1964 Country Music Who's Who*, p. 73.
9. [Pierce], "Formation and Growth," p. 35.
10. "Days of Starday," p. 73.
11. [Pierce], "Formation and Growth," p. 35.
12. Arthur Jordan Field, "Notes on the History of Folksinging in New York City," p. 11.
13. Ibid., pp. 14, 17.
14. Jim Hatlo, "Mike Seeger: Cherishing His Music and Its Traditions," p. 14.
15. Ibid.
16. Richard W. Brislin, "Mike Seeger," pp. 4–5.
17. Ralph Rinzler, interview with author, Pittsburgh, Pa., Oct. 18, 1980. It is probable that Rinzler first heard the Stanleys in the spring of 1954, for they were not active during the first half of 1953.
18. Israel G. Young, "Frets and Frails," *Sing Out!* 9 (Summer 1959): 26, and 9 (Fall 1959): 32.
19. Alan Lomax, "The 'Folkniks'—and the Songs They Sing," pp. 30–31.

20. John S. Wilson, "Program Given by Alan Lomax," p. 13.
21. Rinzler interview.
22. Wilson, "Program Given by Alan Lomax," p. 13.
23. Tom Ewing, "Earl Taylor," p. 12.
24. "New York Scene," p. 20.
25. Winnie Winston, "Scruggs and Flatt and the Wilburn Brothers,"
p. 15.
26. Robert Shelton, "Folk Joins Jazz at Newport."
27. Israel G. Young, "Newport Folk Festival," p. 27.
28. Mike Seeger, brochure notes to *Mountain Music Bluegrass Style*, p. 2.
29. Alan Lomax, "Bluegrass Background: Folk Music with Overdrive,"
p. 108.
30. Alan Lomax, liner notes to *Alan Lomax Presents Folk Songs from the Blue Grass*.
31. Israel G. Young, "Frets and Frails," *Sing Out!* 9 (Winter 1959–60): 34.
32. Tom Teepen, "Allen Grass: A Family Affair," p. 6.
33. Sonny Osborne, recorded onstage, Antioch College Auditorium, Mar. 5, 1960.
34. Bob Osborne, recorded onstage, Antioch College Auditorium, Mar. 5, 1960.
35. Ibid.
36. Ibid.
37. Bill Vernon, "The John Duffey Story," p. 6.

Bibliographical Notes

By 1957 the impact of rock and roll was less of a problem to Nashville; see Bill Sachs, "C&W Talent Booking, Discs Boom in Nashville." For a good historical analysis of the Nashville Sound, see William Ivey, "Commercialization and Tradition in the Nashville Sound."

Additional information on Starday can be found in John Boothroyd, "The Starday Catalogue"; William Henry Koon, "Grass Roots Commercialism"; Neil Rosenberg, "Don Pierce: The Rise and Fall of Starday and the Perplexing Patriot Problem"; and Pete Welding, "Starday, the Bluegrass Label."

The most important source of information on Bill Clifton is Richard K. Spottswood, "An Interview with Bill Clifton." See also Ron Petronko, "Bill Clifton Discography: June, 1971." References for Eanes appear in the notes to the preceding chapter.

Just before Pappy Dailey and Pierce parted company, they formed a rock 'n' roll label, Dixie. See *Billboard*, Jan. 27, 1958, p. 18.

For further information on Carl Story, see Ivan H. Tribe, "Carl Story:

Bluegrass Pioneer"; and Don Rhodes, "Carl Story." For Estil Stewart, Dave
Woolum, and the Wright Brothers, see Rounder Collective's brochure notes
to *The Early Days of Bluegrass,* Vol. 2, pp. 3–4, 5–6, and 8–9. Hobo Jack
Adkins is discussed in Rounder Collective's brochure notes to *The Early
Days of Bluegrass,* Vol. 1, p. 12.

For more on the Lewis Family, see Gary Henderson, "Lewis Family: The
First Family of Gospel Song"; Ed Davis, "The Lewis Family: Gospel Grass";
Ann Randolph, "Little Roy"; Don Rhodes's five articles, "1024 . . . The
Lewis Family," "Pop Lewis," "The Lewis Family," "On the Hallelujah Turn-
pike," and "Third Generation Lewis"; Bob Artis, "Entertainment Personi-
fied with the Lewis Family"; "Lewis Family Discography"; "Lewis Family
Women"; and Barbara Taylor, "Mom Lewis." See also the discussion of this
popular group in chapter 8, below.

The best history of the development of interest in folk song and music
during the twentieth century is D. K. Wilgus's *Anglo-American Folksong
Scholarship since 1898.*

Washington Square has been the topic of a number of articles. See Eric
Nagler's three articles, "An Unnecessarily Wordy and Frankly Inaccurate
History of the Development of Bluegrass in Washington Square Park and
the Surrounding Village from 1958 to 1967," "A History of Bluegrass Music
in New York City," and "New York Scene: Eric Nagler Tells it Like it Was";
and Barry Kornfeld, "Folksinging in Washington Square." The most recent
piece on the topic is Jay Feldman, "Sunday Afternoon at Washington
Square: A Nostalgic Event." For a biographical sketch of Eric Weissberg, see
Mark Greenberg, "Eric Weissberg"; for Roger Sprung, see Lionel Kilberg,
"Roger Sprung." Sprung, Kilberg, and Mike Cohen had a group called the
Shanty Boys, which predated the Greenbriar Boys and could in some ways
be considered a bluegrass band.

Space does not permit extensive citations on fiddlers' conventions and
contests; a good starting place is *The Devil's Box,* which has material on
both past and present events. See also the notes and text of chapter 8,
below. Burrison, cited in the notes to chapter 1, provides additional references for the many Atlanta contests. Most of my information on Union
Grove comes from Pat J. Ahrens, *Union Grove: The First Fifty Years,* but see
as well Mike Seeger, brochure notes to *The Thirty-Seventh Old Time Fiddler's
Convention at Union Grove, North Carolina;* Robert Shelton, "Old-Time Fiddlers"; Audrey A. Kaiman, "The Southern Fiddling Convention—A Study";
and David G. LeDoux, "Goings-On At Union Grove."

Additional information on Ralph Rinzler appears in Alice and Mike Seeger, "Bluegrass Unlimited Merit Award—Ralph Rinzler."

Charles Seeger articulated the idea of "citybilly" and related concepts in
an introduction to the *Journal of American Folklore*'s first record reviews, in
1948, "Reviews." Seeger's term was part of a schemata for evaluating performance—a forerunner, in a sense, of Lomax's system of cantometrics,

cited below. The book for which Charles Seeger and his wife Ruth Crawford Seeger were transcribing tunes when Mike Seeger was a youth was John
and Alan Lomax, *Our Singing Country*.

Workshops at a folk festival were first described, as far as I can find, in
Billy Faier's "Message from the West: A Weekend of Folkmusic," his description of what would later be called the first Berkeley Folk Festival.

Lomax's research on folksong performance evaluation and analysis culmi-
nated in his *Folksong Style and Culture*. Another (not very enthusiastic)
report on Lomax's Carnegie Hall Concert of April 1959 is given by Dick
Weissman in "Folksong '59."

The description of the Osborne Brothers show at Antioch is based on my
own experience and on a recording of the event. For another set of reminis-
cences based on the same occurrence, see Tom Teepen, " 'How Many Here
Like Baseball?': The Osborne Brothers at Antioch College, 1959 [sic]."
More details of the musical development of the Osbornes are given in my
liner notes to *The Osborne Brothers*. Though they popularized the "high
lead" trio, ultimately making it a part of their musical identity, the form
seems to have first appeared in a recorded bluegrass performance with the
Stanley Brothers' "A Voice from on High," made in 1953.

For more on the Greenbriar Boys, see Art Edelstein, "John Herald: New
Directions for an Ex-Greenbriar Boy"; and R. J. Kelly, "The John Herald
Band."

The extensive literature on the Country Gentlemen includes *The Country
Gentlemen 25th Anniversary 1957–1982*, a seventy-five-page book which includes a history, many photos, and a discography. Among the articles about
the group the following are most useful: Robert Kyle, "John Duffey"; "Interview: Eddie Adcock"; Tom Henderson, "On the Cuttin' Edge . . . with Eddie Adcock"; Don Rhodes, "Eddie and Martha Adcock: Finding Their Place
in Bluegrass Music"; Robert Kyle, "Bluegrass Bassist Tom Gray"; Jerry Dallman, "Tom Gray: Bluegrass Bassist"; Fred Bartenstein, "The Country
Gentlemen . . . Going Places!"; Tom Henderson, "Charlie Waller: The
Original Country Gentleman"; Doug Tuchman, "The Country Gentlemen";
and, finally, a series of excellent interviews with the three key members of
the group, Waller, Adcock, and Duffey: Bill Vernon, "The Sound That
Changed the Color of Blue Grass."

Discographical Notes

Arlie Duff's "Y'All Come" was reissued on an early Starday anthology, *Y'All
Come—Have A Country Christmas*. Monroe's version appears on *Bill Mon-
roe's Greatest Hits*. Two other early Starday hits, Red Hayes's "A Satisfied
Mind" and George Jones's "Why Baby Why," were reissued on *Hillbilly Hit
Parade*. Bill Clifton's "Gathering Flowers from the Hillside" was released on

his *Mountain Folk Songs;* Jim Eanes's "Your Old Standby" was reissued on *Hills and Home.*

Of the two instrumentals and two quartets recorded at Carl Story's first bluegrass session for Mercury-Starday, "Got A Lot To Tell Jesus" and "Mocking Banjo" were issued only on singles. "Light at the River" was released on his *Gospel Favorites,* and "Banjo on the Mountain" on the anthology *The Best of Bluegrass.*

Rusty York and Willard Hale recorded at least three pieces early in 1958 between rockabilly sessions. "Dixie Strut" appeared only on a Mercury single. Hale's name is not on the labels of these recordings but is included for "Banjo Breakdown" and "Don't Do It," which were released on a Starday anthology, *Banjo in the Hills.*

Flatt and Scruggs's first LP release was the Columbia album *Foggy Mountain Jamboree.*

Of the two Monroe quartets which caught the ear of Little Roy Lewis, "I'm Travelin' On and On" was reissued on *The Classic Bluegrass Recordings,* vol. 1, and "Shine Hallelujah Shine" on *The Classic Bluegrass Recordings,* vol. 2.

Roger Sprung's group, the Shanty Boys, had an album released on Elektra in 1957, *The Shanty Boys.* Earlier, in about 1953, Sprung had contributed the first bluegrass banjo on LP as part of the Folksay Trio's cut of "Tom Dooley" on *American Folksay: Ballads and Dances,* vol. 2.

Eric Weissberg was also recorded in 1957 for an album by Judson, a subsidiary label of Riverside Records, *Banjos, Banjos and More Banjos.*

Alan Lomax's Folksong '59 concert was recorded by United Artists; from this came an album, *Folksong Festival at Carnegie Hall,* which included three songs by Earl Taylor. The Stanley Brothers' "Train 45," which Lomax used as his lecture example, was from their first King single and was later released on *Stanley Brothers and the Clinch Mountain Boys.* Earl Scruggs's Newport appearance is preserved on *Folk Festival at Newport—1959,* vol. 3.

Of the Osborne Brothers' songs and tunes performed or requested by the audience at Antioch, four were from their MGM singles with Red Allen: "Ruby," "Ho Honey Ho," "Down in the Willow Garden," and "Once More." All were reissued on *The Osborne Brothers and Red Allen.* "Cripple Creek" was reissued on *The Early Recordings of Sonny Osborne, 1952-1953,* vol. 2.

The Country Gentlemen's "Rolling Stone" was reissued on a Starday anthology, *Banjo Jamboree Spectacular!* As with all Folkways albums, their *Country Songs, Old and New* remains in print today.

Chapter 6

In and Out with the Folk Revival: 1961-65

At the beginning of the sixties Bill Monroe was virtually unknown within the folk revival and, as a country music star, experiencing a decline in prosperity. By the middle of the decade his career had taken an upward turn, largely because of his "discovery" by the revivalists. During the first half of the sixties there was enough interest in bluegrass music within the folksong revival to sustain a few professional bands. Of these the Greenbriar Boys were the best known. Several others were not nurtured within the revival but played frequently for revival audiences—the Country Gentlemen and the Dillards (to be discussed later in this chapter). Both were influential—the former in the Northeast, the latter in the Southwest—but neither came close to the high profile Flatt and Scruggs had within the revival.

Louise Scruggs and the Foggy Mountain Folk Image

Although Lester and Earl missed being in Lomax's "Folksong '59" concert at Carnegie Hall and had been represented only by Earl at the first Newport Folk Festival, by the end of 1959 they had recognized the potential in the folk music boom and moved to take advantage of it. The key figure in this process was their manager, Louise Certain Scruggs.

Trained as a bookkeeper, Louise Scruggs married Earl in 1948, shortly after he and Lester formed the Foggy Mountain Boys. She became the band's booking and business manager in 1956. When she recognized the extent of folk revival interest in Flatt and Scruggs (particularly Scruggs), she took an active role in exploiting this interest and developing contacts with those involved in the revival. One of the first was with Manny Greenhill, the Boston booking agent, who added Flatt and Scruggs to the roster of artists he already represented—folk performers like Joan Baez, Pete Seeger, and Eric von Schmidt. Such contacts made sense from a business point of view, but there was more than business to it. Mrs. Scruggs was proud that the band had "received acclaim among people who never before showed any interest for southern mountain music" and endeavored to advance the group's prestige within the country music field by calling attention to their recognition as folk artists.[1]

The various ways in which Louise Scruggs exploited the revival interest in the band can be seen in the edition of the *Lester Flatt Earl Scruggs and the Foggy Mountain Boys Picture Album-Song Book* published at the beginning of 1961. This twelve-page 8½-x-11-inch booklet, which sold for fifty cents, was the latest version of an item which the band regularly hawked over the radio, on television, and at personal appearances. The cover picture was a still from their first appearance on national network television, a CBS special broadcast in June 1960 called "Spring Festival of Music—Folk Sound USA." On the inside cover was Earl's illustrated "Suggestions for Banjo Beginners," a standard feature in earlier Flatt and Scruggs songbooks but with one important difference in this edition. Instead of his previous offer to sell old Gibson Mastertone banjos, Scruggs advised "to those who might be interested in buying a Scruggs model-Vega banjo write me at Box 58, Nashville, Tenn."[2] Earl had just designed a new banjo for the Boston-based Vega company. This marked the first time any well-known bluegrass banjoist had played anything but a Gibson. Vega banjos were popular with folk revivalists. In 1958 the company had introduced their "Pete Seeger model"—distinguished by Seeger's invention, a longer-than-standard neck—and it was selling like hotcakes. As Scruggs became a familiar name in the revival, the Vega people saw an opportunity to exploit, and by 1961 Earl Scruggs model Vegas were being advertised not just by Scruggs but also in the pages of magazines like *Sing Out!*

Following Earl's "Suggestions" came a page which introduced and described the group. The seven-paragraph narrative, under the heading "Nationally Acclaimed Folk Music Favorites" in bold capital letters, was unsigned but was the work of Louise Scruggs. The first paragraph conveys impressionistically the points she would make at length elsewhere: "From the editorial desk of the *New York Times* to the mimeographed church bulletins of thousands of rural communities . . . from the pages of Compton's Encyclopedia to the Country and Western magazines on the news stands . . . from the sophisticated Newport Folk Festival and New York network television shows to the world-renowned WSM's Grand Ole Opry in Nashville . . . Flatt and Scruggs are coming into vogue!" One long paragraph was given over to quotes from Robert Shelton, the *New York Times* folk music critic who'd compared Scruggs with Paganini, and another to the *Esquire* magazine article in which "Alan Lomax eulogized Flatt and Scruggs . . . " with Tom Allen's award-winning "full-page oil painting of Lester and Earl."[3]

In the following six pages of pictures there was, in addition to the standard shots of the band and the band members with their families, an entire page devoted to the CBS special, which included John Jacob Niles, John Lee Hooker, Cisco Houston, and Joan Baez. Other pages contained pictures of the band in action elsewhere, with captions such as: "Lester Flatt sings a folk song to a big city audience New York" and from New River Ranch, "Earl Scruggs and Lester Flatt performing at Rising Sun, Maryland. The extra microphones were set up by fans who taped the show"; "Mike Seeger and Earl Scruggs are inspecting a banjo. Mike is a folk music enthusiast and a fine entertainer." Also included were shots of Earl with Japanese banjo picker Yoshio Ono, "considered the favorite entertainer in Japan . . . " and of Tom Allen with Earl holding the original of his *Esquire* painting.[4] The remainder of the booklet contained the words to thirty-two of their songs and, on the back page, a list of their records. On the back inside cover was an ad for Martha White Flour (with its new ingredient, Hot Rize) and Pet Milk, their two sponsors.

A few months later Tom Allen's painting appeared on the cover of their new instrumental album for Columbia, *Foggy Mountain Banjo*. The liner notes contained quotes from both the Lomax article and the *New York Times* review and pointed out that the group had "been headlined at folk music festivals throughout the country. . . . "[5] At about the same time as this album was released—March 1961—the *Tennessee Folklore Society Bulletin* published an article by Louise Scruggs, "History of the Five-String Banjo." This was a serious synthesis of available data on the instrument (though recent research has thrown into question some of her "facts" like the emphasis given to Joel Walker Sweeney in "inventing" the fifth string), as well as a (to use one of Mrs. Scruggs's favorite words) sophisticated kind of advertising, since it stressed Earl's role in rekindling interest in the instrument ("He is credited with creating a veritable banjo epidemic"). In praising the work of those record companies which were collecting "the pure authentic sound of the old mountain banjo" and preserving them "forever on long playing records" she cited as her example the Folkways *Scruggs Style* album. The article closed with a pat on the back to American folklorists, saying, "Knowledge of a nation's folklore is the knowledge of the creative workings of the minds of its folk. It is a key to a nation's value, a highway that leads into the heart of its people."[6]

With the songbooks, albums, and other advertising media available to her, Louise Scruggs developed a formula. She wove quotes from reviews and articles along with descriptions of prestigious (and sophisticated) places and publications into portraits of Flatt and Scruggs which stressed their artistry, authenticity, and universal appeal. Tom Allen's artwork became part of the Flatt and Scruggs public image, featured on all of their subsequent Columbia and most of their Harmony (the Columbia budget series) album covers.

During this period the band often seemed to have two different repertoires, with correspondingly different sounds. Their singles, which since the late

fifties had included drums and, often, five-part vocal harmonies on the chorus, were aimed at the traditional country music consumers who heard them
on the Opry and their Martha White broadcasts. These recordings were
successful: of sixteen singles issued between April 1959 and January 1965,
only three failed to make the *Billboard* country charts (one had both sides
charted). From August 1961 to June 1964 every single they released made
the charts.

At the same time their albums were mainly "concept" albums aimed at the
folk boom. The first and most successful (in terms of critical reception) was
Songs of the Famous Carter Family, which featured Mother Maybelle Carter.
The concept was Louise Scruggs's. It had come to her while Lester and Earl
were on a winter tour of the Midwest and Canada with Johnny Cash and she
was snowed in at their Madison home. She spent the time listening to a tape
of old Carter Family records which Pete Kuykendall had sent her and Earl,
and noted that there were a lot of good songs on it. A. P. Carter had recently
died, so a tribute album with Mother Maybelle, a fellow Opry member,
seemed like a good idea.

Louise Scruggs's signed liner notes graced their next album, *Folk Songs of
Our Land.* It included mainly older songs but also two compositions by the
dean of protest songmakers, Woody Guthrie—"This Land Is Your Land" and
"Philadelphia Lawyer." She quoted liberally from an article written by Peter
J. Welding in the *Saturday Review* about Lester and Earl; their next album
had liner notes written by Welding. In 1963 came albums illustrating their
urban and college appeal—live concerts at Carnegie Hall and Vanderbilt
University.

The Flatt and Scruggs sound on these records reflected the impact of the
folk boom not just in choice of repertoire (in which Louise Scruggs, who
stated in 1965 that her preference was for contemporary folk music, took an
active part) but also in arrangements. As they sought new listeners among
the fans of the Kingston Trio; Peter, Paul, and Mary; and the New Christy
Minstrels, tempos tended to be slower, background simpler. They were moving toward a folk revival sound, away from the classic bluegrass sound they
had done so much to establish and popularize. The mandolin was not audible
and few duets were sung; in 1962 tenor singer and mandolinist Curly Seckler
left the band. Just before he left, Ricky Skaggs, a seven-year-old mandolin
player from eastern Kentucky, appeared as a guest on Lester and Earl's television show. Admiring Curly's Gibson mandolin, Ricky asked, "Is that mandolin like Bill Monroe's?" Seckler looked at him sternly and said, "Well, I
hope not!"[7]

Bill Monroe, still well known to country audiences, was a distant figure to
folk music followers during the late fifties and early sixties. The Flatt and
Scruggs songbooks and record notes rarely mentioned him, and he had not
appeared at folk festivals or other events sponsored by the revivalists. Yet a
chain of events was occurring which would take Monroe into the folk revival

limelight and revive his lagging career. His very obscurity worked in Monroe's favor within the folk revival.

Bluegrass and the Folk Talent Scout System

In the early sixties the growing popularity of folk music among college youth created a boom in folk festivals, records, broadcasts, and concerts. To understand the part bluegrass music played in the boom it is necessary to look at the ways in which popular favorites developed in the revival. Booking talent in the folk revival differed from booking for jazz or classical music because, in theory, folk music was an egalitarian, nonprofessional art. Actually, most of the popular revival performers like the Kingston Trio, Joan Baez, and Pete Seeger were full-time professionals who had managers and worked through booking agencies. These people were mostly of urban, middle-class background; they gained popularity because they conveyed some essence or nuance of folk music that was perceived as "authentic" for the time, because they often sang topical message songs and because they were good entertainers. This was no less a commercial music than country music, and it had its recording, publishing, broadcasting, and other business dimensions. But in addition, folk music audiences expected some "real" or "authentic" or "ethnic" folk in concerts, on records, and at festivals, for part of the continuing appeal of the revival lay in the discovery of supposedly primitive (and proletarian) virtuosos in remote parts of the country.

The term *folk revival* has been called inaccurate and misleading, but in many ways it truly characterizes the movement. Those most interested and involved in it approached it with the missionary zeal of religious revivalists, motivated by a belief that folk music was meaningful and accessible in a way which other forms of music were not. Corollary to this belief was the idea that music is a transcendent language, a means of understanding and communication. By listening to and performing folk music one not only avoided the tasteless and wasteful commercialization of popular music and the arcane and inaccessible music theory and rigid conventions of classical music and modern jazz, one also could learn about and appreciate other classes and cultures, thus discovering alternative values. And by supporting the music of peoples whose artistic expressions they believed to be threatened by the homogenizing (and, therefore, deracinating) effects of mass culture, the revivalists hoped to rejuvenate—revive—such music, by giving the underprivileged and isolated a voice—a kind of artistic armchair activism.

While eschewing the excesses of popular, classical, and jazz musics, the folk music enthusiasts were at the same time seeking within folk music the qualities which they liked in those musics. Among people who performed music from their own oral traditions, the real folk, revivalists looked for virtuosi—often inarticulate and untutored but able to make artful performances. These were perennial favorites, valued as classical or jazz musicians were for their artistic abilities. Successful folk virtuosi became "hits" within the revival; their records sold well and they were sought after for concerts and festival appearances. In this way the revival was a microcosm of the popular music scene.

Only a fraction of the revivalists were seriously concerned with folksong ideology; most responded to folk music as a new pop form. Those who *were* seriously concerned tended to become talent scouts, seeking out new musicians who, through records (often field recordings) or personal appearances, might become popular. For these talent scouts the process was not one of conscious commercialism but rather of following one's own tastes and interests. Years later one reminisced, "Our motivation was a strange combination of ego, scholasticism, and power."[8]

In order to bring obscure new performers to festivals, coffeehouses, or record labels, it was necessary to raise capital and engage audiences by bringing in the sure sellers, the popular favorites, in the hope that those who came to see the big-name attractions would be captivated by (i.e., educated to the art of) the new performers. Thus the tastemakers used revival stars to support and introduce what they saw as the important, authentic, educational music. For example, the first Newport Festival starred Odetta, Theo Bikel, and the Kingston Trio—all very popular in 1959. They drew the audiences who paid enough to allow the promoters to book the less well-known acts that were "authentic" or of greater interest to the insiders in the revival, like Earl Scruggs and the Stanley Brothers.

Alan Lomax furnished a model for those interested in finding such performers. Young revivalists followed his path in making "field trips" into the mountains of the South and Afro-American communities (also mainly in the South). Such activities led them to events like Union Grove. One of the greatest outside influences on bluegrass music of the sixties and seventies, blind guitarist Doc Watson, was "discovered" as a result of Ralph Rinzler's chance meeting of old-time recording artist Tom ("Clarence") Ashley at Union Grove in 1960; Watson was his guitarist. Rinzler was at Union Grove partly as a member of the Greenbriar Boys (that was the year they won there) and partly because he was interested in meeting (i.e., discovering) and learning from old-time musicians.

These forays into the field were an important source of new talent for the revival. In this context revival musicians observed, recorded, learned from, and performed with "authentic" folk. The next best thing to bringing a new discovery to the coffeehouse, campus, record company, or festival was to perform something new and unique learned directly from a real folk musician. Hence those musicians who ventured into the field or to festivals and conventions in the South often returned with knowledge which helped their careers. This prompted other musicians to follow their example. The success of the Greenbriar Boys at Union Grove was mentioned in several of Robert

Shelton's influential *New York Times* articles on folk music, included in the notes of the album which Mike Seeger produced for Folkways at the 1961 Union Grove Convention, and advertised proudly by Vanguard Records when they released the first Greenbriar Boys LP. What better seal of approval for a group of city bluegrassers than a win at a famous southern contest? Each year in the sixties saw more and more bands from the North, Midwest, and West turning up at this and similar events.

Besides such activist fieldwork another important source of repertoire and personnel for the revival was old phonograph records. That record companies had been recording authentic folk performers for their hillbilly, "race," and ethnic series had been noted by folklore scholars as far back as the early thirties. In 1940 Alan Lomax had compiled a discography of folk music on commercial recordings in the Library of Congress. The following year John Lomax edited the first reissue of such music, RCA's *Smoky Mountain Ballads* set, which included recordings by the Carter Family, the Monroe Brothers, Uncle Dave Macon, and Mainer's Mountaineers. In 1947-48 Alan Lomax produced several reissue sets of hillbilly music for the Decca Records subsidiary, Brunswick. Reissues of significant early recordings in either authorized or unauthorized "pirate" recordings had begun with jazz in the thirties: performances originally marketed to blacks as popular dance music were repackaged and sold to collectors as influential art music. The hillbilly reissues were learned and performed by revival performers such as Pete Seeger, who credited his sources and suggested that people should copy them, not him.

In 1952 Folkways released the first long-playing reissues, a series of three two-record sets entitled *Anthology of American Folk Music*, compiled by Harry Smith from the hillbilly, race, and Cajun record series of the late twenties. More than any other single set of records, this provided folk revivalists with an entrée into the world of hillbilly music. Here was the Carter Family's "Engine 143," which Joan Baez sang on her first LP and also the recordings of "House Carpenter" and "The Cuckoo" that introduced Clarence Ashley to Ralph Rinzler.

During the early years of the revival, songs learned from reissues were only partially copied. Until the late fifties revival interests were eclectic, focusing on song texts and tunes rather than on performance style. Often the styles of singing and accompaniment were not copied because they were felt to be esthetically unsuitable or were beyond the abilities of the performers. Exceptions to this were the musicians interested in instrumental techniques like Gary Davis's guitar style or "Scruggs picking." Until Scruggs appeared at Newport, the only source of his music for most revivalists was Flatt and Scruggs's Columbia and Mercury recordings, which the revivalists perceived in a manner similar to the way in which they saw the Library of Congress albums and the reissues by Folkways and other companies—music made by an obscure and distant performer. Even those who saw him were disappointed because he shared the stage with other musicians in whom they were not interested—singers, fiddlers, comedians.

A major force in altering this perception was the New Lost City Ramblers, who burst upon the New York City folk scene in 1959. Mike Seeger, John Cohen, and Tom Paley were all known as instrumentalists and had learned extensively from old recordings. But in the NLCR they went a step further and set out to duplicate the old recordings in all dimensions, striving for the total sound. The Ramblers embodied and popularized Alan Lomax's emphasis upon the importance of performance style in folksong. In doing this they began calling their music by a term they had heard at Union Grove and elsewhere in the South—"old-timey music." They used it to refer to hillbilly recordings made in the golden era between 1925 and 1942, which they copied. In order to successfully duplicate this broad and stylistically diverse body of music the Ramblers were forced to carry a large number of instruments with them, and every song seemed to involve new combinations of voices and instruments, with pauses for retuning. So their shows were not always fast-paced, but the Ramblers treated this handicap with humor, and they were popular and successful at folk festivals during the sixties.

When the New Lost City Ramblers first appeared on the scene, *Sing Out!* called their music bluegrass. The magazine was quickly corrected by readers, but for a number of years their music was characterized as "pre-bluegrass." This folk revival term drew attention to the close relationship between their music and bluegrass while avoiding the use of the word *hillbilly.* But they eventually were best known by the label *old-time,* and more than any other group created an interest in southern rural string band music among urban listeners—an interest which paralleled and mingled with the similar interest in bluegrass.

Of the three New Lost City Ramblers, the one most involved with bluegrass was Mike Seeger. While working with the Ramblers he continued to produce bluegrass albums for Folkways, like the 1962 album by the Lilly Brothers, two West Virginians who'd been performing in Boston since 1952. Whenever the Ramblers appeared in concerts or festivals, folk enthusiasts interested in bluegrass converged upon Seeger, eager to talk with someone who could tell them about this obscure music. Seeger and the other members of the band were also available to play music informally with local musicians in after-concert sessions at which bluegrass often predominated.

John Cohen, most often the guitarist of the trio, contributed to the interest in bluegrass with his photography and through a short documentary film whose title has become closely associated with the music. In February 1963, when Cohen chose *The High Lonesome Sound* for his movie about Kentucky mountain music, he was seeking words to describe the high, intense quality of the singing which had impressed him during his research in the region and to convey also the expression *lonesome,* which Roscoe Holcomb, his principle performer in the movie, frequently used to describe the music. Cohen had heard the title of a song, "High Lonesome," an obscure early recording by the Country Gentlemen. Though there was no mountain or aural image in the song—composer John Duffey had used the word *high* as a synonym for a more common intensifier, *really*—the unusual combination of words appealed to Cohen. He gave the words their present meaning by combining them with *sound* in the film title. The film included footage of Bill Monroe and the Blue Grass Boys in a free concert at the 1962 Coal Carnival, on the courthouse steps in Hazard, Kentucky. It was the first documentary film to include bluegrass and marks the beginning of the association of Bill Monroe with the term *high lonesome sound.*

As the Ramblers became familiar figures on the folk festival and concert circuits, they were often in a position to suggest or recommend to organizers that they bring in performers representative of this music. In this way bluegrass groups such as the Lilly Brothers and the Stanley Brothers, both of whom had a strong commitment to old-time music, appeared at folk festivals in the early sixties. Writing to the president of a college folk club about its festival in 1961, Seeger advised: "In the future I would recommend the Stanley Bros. for you since they would have been glad to come . . . this year for $500 and would do so in the future if they could get another date nearby to pay expenses. The Lilly Bros. of Boston would also be a good bet."[9]

The Ramblers obtained their repertoire mainly from pre-war hillbilly recordings. Like reissue records, their performances had the effect of providing repertoire for other revivalists, as well as for bluegrass bands. In 1962 Flatt and Scruggs recorded "The Legend of the Johnson Boys," learned from a Ramblers album; in 1963 the Stanley Brothers included their version of "Pretty Fair Miss in the Garden" on a King album.

While the Ramblers played an important role as a point of contact between the revival and bluegrass, they were often preaching to the converted when they suggested that bluegrass be viewed as folk music. By 1961, two years after Scruggs's and the Stanleys' first appearance at Newport, there were many young enthusiasts at colleges and in the major urban areas where folk music was popular who wanted to hear more bluegrass.

The folk music boom of the early sixties attracted a wide variety of listeners but was most popular with young middle-class intellectuals. As British rock historian Peter Frame put it, "You have to understand that, in America, electric music was considered base and unworthy until the Beatles arrived in 1964. Up until then, folk was the only possible pursuit for a kid with brains."[10] Many of the young musicians who developed their musical skills within the revival had prior interests and training in other forms, from classical to rock and roll. Only a few were as totally and intensely committed to folk music as Mike Seeger and Ralph Rinzler.

Within the context of the folk boom, bluegrass's special appeal lay in ensemble interplay—it was like a small jazz combo or a classical string quartet—and its intensity and volume, about as close as one could get to rock and roll without electricity. Its impact upon revivalists who found it too hillbilly, mechanical, brash, and loud gave it the same sort of positive shock value for its young college-age proponents that rock and roll had for teen-agers: the controversy it engendered added to its excitement. By 1961 local bluegrass bands were playing at hootenannies and coffee houses all the way from Cambridge, Massachusetts, where a bunch of Harvard students had formed the Charles River Valley Boys, to San Diego, California, home of the Scottsville Squirrel Barkers.

These musicians, often college students, operated within the framework of their local folk revival scene, where they performed mainly for the fun of it, since they had neither the experience, time, nor contacts for a full-time professional career. Often they were involved in other, quite different, musi-cal pursuits at the same time. Three of the Plum Creek Boys, the Oberlin College band that appeared at the Osborne Brothers' Antioch concert, were working at the same time as guitarists in the rhythm section of Dick Sudhal-ter's Chicago-style jazz band at Oberlin concerts and recording sessions. Revival musicians brought new musical concepts and esthetics to bluegrass.

As they became more deeply involved in learning about bluegrass and developed their skill with it, they began to meet, through contacts in record shops, music stores, instrument repairmen, etc., older local musicians who had come to bluegrass through country rather than folk channels. Thus it was that in November 1961 the Redwood Canyon Ramblers, a band com-prised of University of California–Berkeley students, put together a joint concert at a local school with Vern and Ray and the Carroll County Country Boys, a group of Ozark natives living in nearby Stockton, California, who had recorded in 1959 for Starday an EP which included their "Bluegrass Style," one of the first songs extolling the virtues of bluegrass music. Members of the two bands had met through a mutual friend, a record collector, and had jammed informally during the previous year. When city and country bluegrass bands got together in this way publicly, each drew its own audiences to the shows, creating more contacts. Eventually these would lead to local bluegrass scenes which existed separate from both country music and the folk revival. These newly developing urban and college scenes showed that blue-grass was popular enough to make it worthwhile for festival organizers to include it in their plans.

Nineteen hundred sixty-one was a vintage year for bluegrass at folk festi-vals. In January the first University of Chicago Folk Festival was held. Com-ing at the semester break, it attracted students from all over the Midwest. The festival organizers stressed the presentation of new authentic talent, and among those on the first festival were the Stanley Brothers. This was their second festival and their second college appearance (having been at Newport in 1959 and Antioch in May 1960). They were relatively well-known but not as slick and commercial as Flatt and Scruggs—a perfect choice for Chicago. Israel G. Young, the epitome of the committed folk revival audience member, described their experience: "The Stanley Brothers after a night or two of misunderstandings with the audience as to what homespun humor was—stole the show on the last evening with songs and instrumentals that I'm sure even their audiences down south don't hear. They returned to the older traditional music under the wonderful influence of the Festival and everyone knew it and was happy."[11] Reminiscent of the reception which the Osbornes had at Antioch, the Stanleys' reception at Chicago, as described by Young, demonstrates the way in which revivalists tended to congratulate themselves for imposing their own esthetics upon the performers they discovered. Young believed that the festival had caused a conversion experience in the Stanley Brothers, leading them to find in themselves the authentic culture they'd been forced to abandon when they entered the mass-culture world of country music.

In the months following the Chicago Festival, a much smaller annual folk festival was being planned by the Oberlin Folksong Club. Aware of the Country Gentlemen because of their Folkways album, several club members had gone to hear them at the Crossroads Bar in Virginia near Washington. The students had liked the band's showmanship, and this, coupled with the fact that they were available for $375 while the Lilly Brothers and Jimmy Martin each were asking $400, overrode some reservations about their "modern" sound. Thus in May 1961 the Country Gentlemen made their first college and festival appearance as the featured group at the Oberlin Folk Festival, where they were enthusiastically received.

Because the band's comedy was an ad-libbed rather than the old-style vaudeville routine type and their repertoire chosen to appeal to folk revival tastes, they had few of the acculturation problems encountered by the Osbornes and the Stanleys. During the next five years the Gentlemen would play more college and coffeehouse engagements than any other bluegrass band in the East; in doing so they developed comedy routines (like their spoof of the Kingston Trio) tailored to these audiences.

They were popular with revival listeners, but their show was too commercial—too much like that of the Kingston Trio—for the serious revivalists. In September 1961 they shared the stage at *Sing Out!*'s annual Carnegie Hall Hootenanny with Hedy West, Alan Mills and Jean Carignan, Jack Elliot, Bessie Jones, and Pete Seeger. Duffey wrote to a friend: "We played Carnegie Hall last Sat. night and sold well to the people but not to the critics. The people at Folkways said we were just 'too slick' for them. They still want this music in the raw. From the looks of the other performers, (Pete Seeger included), we made a big mistake in dressing and shaving."[12]

In August, the first Mariposa Folk Festival was held in Orillia, Ontario, organized by Toronto folk music enthusiasts and promoters. Included on the bill were the York County Boys, a group from Ontario who had recently issued their first LP on Arc Records, a new Canadian-talent country label.

The reviewer of the festival for *Sing Out!* found them wanting: "The York County Boys with Al Cherny took over in the second half of the program, and this Canadian (?) Bluegrass group emitted a musical sound that pleased everyone in the audience except that small minority who look for invention between musicians, not repetition."[13] This is a sly way of saying that they were well received. Bluegrass would be regularly featured at Mariposa during the sixties and seventies, contributing to the popularity of the music in southern Ontario. But there had been bluegrass in the region since the early fifties, a natural outgrowth of contact with the country music scene in bordering U.S. states, particularly Michigan. The Canadian bluegrass musicians came mainly from the maritime provinces and rural Quebec and Ontario, though there were a few, like Ukrainian-Canadian fiddler Cherny, from the ethnic enclaves of the West. Hence groups like the York County Boys represented a strong regional interest within Canada, but because the music could not be identified as uniquely Canadian it did not assume the same importance within the revival there as it did in the U.S.

Having a bluegrass band at any North American folk festival in 1961 was a somewhat adventurous act on the part of the organizers because it met with mixed reactions; in general the audiences responded more positively than the critics, but for both the reaction depended upon the form of the band's presentation: they might be perceived as slick, corny, commercial, or authentic. In the next few years as bands and audiences became accustomed to each other, the inclusion of bluegrass became a sound commercial move for folk revival organizers. But for folk fans, bluegrass was just one kind of folk music and only some folk music fans were bluegrass enthusiasts. There was, however, one enthusiast who felt there was enough interest to devote an entire festival-like event to bluegrass in 1961—Bill Clifton. He was still recording for Starday and making occasional personal appearances in Virginia and the Washington-Baltimore area but, like many other bluegrass musicians, had a "day job." He had gotten his master's degree in business administration from the University of Virginia in 1959 and was working as a stockbroker and a sales broker, buying and selling radio and television stations.

Big Day at Luray

At the beginning of 1961 Clifton was hired as the producer for Oak Leaf Park at Luray, in northern Virginia not far from Washington, in partnership with a man who owned a string of radio stations in the Shenandoah Valley. That season, from May to September, they booked virtually every professionally active bluegrass band of the era, from the biggest names to those known mainly in the Washington area: the Stanley Brothers, Red Allen, Carl Story, Bill Harrell and Buzz Busby, and Flatt and Scruggs (with Mother Maybelle Carter)—each appeared on different Sundays. On July 4 what Israel G.

Young described as an "All Day Bluegrass Festival" was held there.[14] The groups appearing were the Country Gentlemen, Jim and Jesse, Mac Wiseman, the Stanley Brothers, Bill Monroe, and Bill Clifton.

The fourth of July show was unusual because the conventional wisdom held that one did not book two bands playing similar music at a country music park, just as one did not have two comedians or two female vocalists. The logic behind this was that a second bluegrass band would draw no more people than the first, whereas another kind of country music would attract its own (and different) audiences. There had been a few exceptions to this, as when, in 1956, Reno and Smiley shared the billing at New River Ranch with Flatt and Scruggs. But these were rare. Clifton's perception of the unity of bluegrass music and his awareness of the strong audience for it in the northern Virginia–Washington–Baltimore area led him to gamble on this unprecedented day of music. Ralph Rinzler recalls:

> Frequently you'd have Bill Monroe at one park and Carter and Ralph at another and they would come over to hear each other and talk but they'd never perform together. And I knew enough from having spent a lot of time dubbing tapes from Mike [Seeger] of records from the forties and fifties to know that all these people had learned from Bill, but no one ever thought they'd ever hear them perform together. And what I remember was that all of a sudden all of those people except Flatt and Scruggs were there and it seemed to me an astonishing feat for the son of a banker and insurance executive from a Baltimore social family to bring that together in that setting.[15]

The show was as interesting for what it did not achieve as for what did happen. The two most successful bluegrass bands of the period, Flatt and Scruggs and Reno and Smiley, were both absent because their managers could not come to terms with Clifton about details of the booking. But the reasons for each were quite different. Clifton had been able to talk all of the other groups into lowering their price for this event; even Jim and Jesse, who were coming all the way from southern Alabama, were willing to make this concession. But Reno and Smiley's manager, Carlton Haney, was unwilling to lower their usual fee of $500, even though they were living in nearby Roanoke and were not engaged for that date. Haney didn't agree with Clifton's concept; he felt there was no reason to have more than one bluegrass band. With Flatt and Scruggs, Clifton did not get as far as talking prices; Louise Scruggs told him at the outset that Lester and Earl would not appear on the same stage with Monroe. Clifton urged her to reconsider, but in a second conversation she indicated that there might be problems about appearing on the same stage with the Stanley Brothers. At this point Clifton decided bringing Flatt and Scruggs to the show was going to be too troublesome to arrange and made arrangements to book them separately later that summer.

One feature of the show, commented upon by all who reported on it, took place when Bill Monroe called former Blue Grass Boys working with other bands up to play with him. Monroe sometimes did this when there was a former sideman present at one of his shows. But here a number of them appeared at the same time, and the event was a kind of re-creation of some of Monroe's earlier bands. While this portion of the show celebrated the unity of the music by showing the common bonds which many of the musicians shared as Monroe's apprentices, it also revealed the conflicts which tempered these bonds.

These were articulated onstage at Luray during Monroe's portion of the show. Announcing that some former Blue Grass Boys would be playing with him, Monroe explained that whenever he was on the same show with Reno and Smiley or Mac Wiseman they would always come out and play a number with him. This brief comment was in fact a mild dig at Don Reno, who was present in the audience along with manager Carlton Haney. While not performing, he and Haney had come along to observe. Reno was not invited onstage to play with Bill this day. Monroe continued:

> It's a shame a lot of bluegrass people you know that thinks they are . . . they don't want to be on a show with you or something, if the folks will think you started them. Well it's the truth, so they shouldn't a-mind that and they should be glad that they got a start, they'd-a probably had to plowed a lot of furrows if they hadn't-a been in bluegrass music.

Following this abstract reference to Flatt and Scruggs he did a song and then Stanley came out to join him. After introducing the next song and exchanging pleasantries Carter said:

> I guess I'll just break into this kindly blunt like. I understand that they was a group that some of the folks asked to come in here today. They said no, they didn't want to play here because Bill Monroe and the Stanley Brothers was gonna be here. And that was Flatt and Scruggs. You know, we missed 'em a heck of a lot, ain't we? Huh? [Laughter, applause.] All right, it's your show, go on.

Monroe answered:

> Well, you're talking about Lester and Earl. Now I started the two boys on the Grand Ole Opry, and they shouldn't be ashamed to come on the show and work with us. [Laughter, applause.] And I am sure I wouldn't hurt either one of 'em.

That Stanley, who'd had a few drinks from Clifton's backstage spiked punch bowl and was "feeling no pain," was dwelling on past conflicts was shown clearly a few minutes later when Bill introduced "What Would You Give in Exchange for Your Soul." Monroe began, "We are gonna do a hymn

here that I recorded back in nineteen and thirty-five. It's entitled—"
Here Carter broke in, saying, "Who'd you record it with?" Monroe answered rapidly, "I-recorded-it-with-a-brother-of-mine-Charlie-Monroe, it's entitled—"[16] at which point he was drowned out by laughter from the audience.

These exchanges, which took only a few minutes in a day-long show and
were received with laughter, were nevertheless quite significant. They constituted the breaking of a taboo against speaking in public with Monroe about
two of the most traumatic incidents in his musical career, his split with
Charlie and the feud with Flatt and Scruggs. As Stanley's comments came at
a point in the concert at which former Blue Grass Boys were honoring their
mentor, it was taboo-breaking within a ritual. Hence the laughter from bluegrass fans in the audience, responding to the tension of the situation. That
this was a significant exchange is shown by the way in which it spread rapidly
and became a legend, part of oral tradition in the bluegrass world.

There was another detail which gave the story added significance. Louise
Scruggs was said to have obtained a tape recording of the exchange. For years
afterward there was recrimination and debate about who sent the copy of the
infamous tape to Louise Scruggs. At this show, as at most of the others in
the area, there were a number of fans down in front of the stage with tape
recorders. This was standard practice; only a few performers would not allow
it. So there were many suspects involved, among them Mike Seeger and
Ralph Rinzler. Later, Rinzler recalled: "Somehow that got on tape back to
Flatt and Scruggs. And Bill, because he had known Mike and myself for five
or six years then, seeing us recording at the stageside, although we'd never
talked to him, assumed that we'd done it."[17] Monroe knew about the tape
being sent to Flatt and Scruggs because, according to the legend, it was used
by Louise as a pretext for threats of lawsuit and attempts to have Monroe
removed from the Opry.

When queried recently about the Monroe-Stanley exchange at Luray, Mrs.
Scruggs told me she had never heard of it. She pointed out that everybody
knows Monroe was not speaking to Flatt and Scruggs and that they did not
have a working relationship with the Stanley Brothers. But, she said, after a
number of years such conflicts are forgotten and, she feels, should not receive
too much attention.

And in fact the attention which the exchange and its aftermath created in
the bluegrass world obscured another, more important, aspect of Clifton's
Bluegrass Day. Among the 2200 people at Luray that day, no one was more
observant than Carlton Haney. He recognized the extent to which bluegrass
fans would travel to see such an event. In 1965, he would initiate weekend
bluegrass festivals that incorporated features from Luray.

Clifton, who might have eventually solved some of the problems which
the Monroe–Stanley–Flatt and Scruggs conflict presented had he established
the Bluegrass Day as an annual event, did not continue with his arrangements at Oak Leaf Park. Early in 1962 he was asked to become a member

of the new Newport Folk Foundation, which was reorganizing the Newport Folk Festival (not held in 1961 and 1962) for 1963. He spent the rest
of 1962-63 involved with Newport. In September 1963 he moved to England.
Following his 1961 show there would be no festival-like activity within bluegrass music for another four years. But the show had been an eye-opener for
those folk revivalists who attended. Columnist Israel Young reported in *Sing
Out!*: "Lots of NYC kids went. . . . By the end of the day I wasn't yet sure of
a definition of Bluegrass Music but I realized, to my great satisfaction, that it
is a modern offshoot of traditional music and should not cause so many City
arguments. . . . "[18]

Ralph Rinzler and Bill Monroe

In the end the city bluegrass followers would play a central role in starting
the bluegrass festival movement. The key figure was Ralph Rinzler. He had
joined the Greenbriar Boys somewhat reluctantly; he was more comfortable
with the old-time music that the New Lost City Ramblers were playing.
During 1960, in addition to playing mandolin with the Greenbriar Boys, he
had organized the Friends of Old Time Music, a New York City club which
sponsored concerts by Clarence Ashley and other "rediscovered" recording
artists. When Vanguard Records approached the Greenbriar Boys to record,
Rinzler was not enthusiastic. *New York Times* folk music critic Robert Shelton
talked him into it: "He said if you record what you fellows do, the people
that you admire and learn from, that you're trying to encourage people to
listen to, will be heard by the people who are listening to you. But they won't
be heard if you don't pave the way, because you're an interpreter, you're a
middle road for city listeners. And the city listeners can go from digesting
your music to the more strident or deeper rural based material, but they won't
go to that if you don't serve as a transition group. . . . "[19]

Rinzler accepted Shelton's advice and used the liner notes of the first
Greenbriar Boys album to "explain why we were doing this preposterous
thing, because I thought it was preposterous for us to play (Monroe instrumental) 'Raw Hide' or any bluegrass on a recording and take it seriously."
Rinzler's essay focused on those from whom he had learned bluegrass and
emphasized Bill Monroe's role in the creation of the music because Rinzler
felt Monroe deserved more credit than he was receiving. In this way he used
the album as Shelton had suggested; but it had another ramification: "It
reached Joan Baez's ears and Joan became interested in doing something with
us and we recorded with her [she was also with Vanguard], and once we
recorded with her it gave us access to touring with her and to contacts which
I used to get Doc Watson and Clarence Ashley booked on the road."[20]

Thus it was that in April 1962 the Greenbriar Boys made a guest appearance on the Grand Ole Opry. Traveling as the warm-up act for Joan Baez,

they had appeared at Nashville's Vanderbilt University, in a concert that had been arranged for Baez by Louise Scruggs. "Louise arranged for us to be on the Opry, and Joan, I think, spent the night at the Scruggs's house. We stayed in a hotel. And we were on because they arranged it, and we were asked, I think, at that time, not to mention Bill Monroe's name."[21] Monroe was still a distant, silent figure to folk revivalists. Nothing of substance had been written about him, and he had yet to appear at a folk revival event. Shortly after the Greenbriar Boys were in Nashville, an article by Peter J. Welding, proclaiming Scruggs as "the master of bluegrass," appeared in *Sing Out!* Rinzler, who felt that the title overlooked Monroe's role, was angered and asked the editor for equal space to rebut it with an article on Monroe.

In June 1962 Rinzler approached Monroe at a country music park in Pennsylvania to request an interview for an article. Monroe, noting that he had seen him and Mike Seeger taping his shows, told him abruptly, "If you want to know about bluegrass music, ask Louise Scruggs."[22] Eventually, with the help of the Stanley Brothers, Rinzler got Monroe to agree to an interview in August. It appeared in the January 1963 issue of *Sing Out!*, just as Monroe made his first folk revival appearance (arranged with Rinzler's help) at the University of Chicago Folk Festival. Several days later Monroe played in New York for a Friends of Old Time Music concert, and soon after this Rinzler moved to Nashville to become Monroe's manager.

Immediately he was faced with a typical problem in this job: Bill had hired two banjo pickers, Del McCoury and Bill Keith, and one would have to go. Ralph's suggestion, which Monroe followed, was that McCoury be moved to the guitarist–lead singer role; even though he had formerly been only a banjo picker, McCoury soon developed into a strong lead singer. Bill Keith, whom Monroe called "Brad" (from Keith's middle name Bradford) so there would not be two Bills in the same band, quickly attracted attention of the sort Monroe's banjo players hadn't had since the late forties.

Keith was the best bluegrass banjo player to come out of the folk revival. A Bostonian, he was educated at Exeter Academy and Amherst College. Like most revival banjoists he'd first been exposed to the five-string through Pete Seeger, then records of Scruggs, and finally Washington Square pickers like Roger Sprung and Eric Weissberg. Unlike most revival banjo pickers he had previously studied tenor banjo, learning about chord construction, harmony, and other aspects of music theory. And in Boston he was in touch with a lively local bluegrass scene. Since 1952 the Lilly Brothers had been living and performing there with West Virginia banjoist Don Stover. Other bluegrass musicians had settled in the area, and by the late fifties the southern New England country music scene had developed its own bluegrass contingent, including migrants from Appalachia like fiddler Herb Hooven from Ashe County, North Carolina, as well as representatives of other ethnic and migrant groups—men like Bob French, of Nova Scotian and Newfoundland parents, and Joe Val, son of Italian immigrants. Keith got to know some of these musicians and took a few lessons from Don Stover. By 1962 he and his Amherst roommate Jim Rooney were in a band which was a mixture of folk revival and country bluegrass musicians, playing at such places as Cambridge's Club 47, the coffeehouse where Joan Baez had gotten her start.

What made Keith special was the banjo style he'd developed. He first came to the attention of listeners around Boston with his playing of fiddle tunes like "Devil's Dream" and "Sailor's Hornpipe" note-for-note as the fiddle played them, which involved going outside Scruggs-style technique to play parts of scales and other innovations. And his strong command of harmonic theory and a superb sense of rhythm enabled him to create his own grammar of banjo riffs and licks which, though based on those of Scruggs and Stover, tended to be more chordal, chromatic, and syncopated. It was a new and unique sound.

At the first annual Philadelphia Folk Festival in September 1962 he won the banjo contest, playing "Devil's Dream" and "Sailor's Hornpipe." A few months later he moved to Washington and began playing in the band of Red Allen and Frank Wakefield. Working in hillbilly bars and playing at WWVA with this band, called the Kentuckians, brought Keith to the attention of the Washington-Baltimore area bluegrass scene. Fred Geiger, a young college graduate from Baltimore who'd been playing in the local bars, recalls the impact: "One Saturday night, WWVA wasn't coming in very clearly and I was dozing off, half-consciously adjusting the dial, when the static briefly cleared during a 15-minute show featuring Red Allen and the Kentuckians. I caught the tail-end of the banjo break on 'Little Maggie.' Glory be! It was Bill Keith, Keith styling his way through the G and F scales. It was as though the banjo had been reinvented."[23]

That winter Flatt and Scruggs played a concert in Baltimore, and Boston folk music promoter Manny Greenhill took Keith backstage and introduced him to Scruggs. Keith, an extremely methodical and precise musician, had transcribed all of Scruggs's instrumentals into banjo tablature, in order to properly learn his style. He showed Scruggs his notebooks. Earl was impressed with them and invited Keith to visit him in Nashville and help him with a banjo instruction book he was beginning to write. Thus it was that one Saturday night early in 1963 Bill Keith arrived at the Opry with Scruggs. There, backstage, playing his showpiece "Devil's Dream," he was heard by Bill Monroe and his fiddler Kenny Baker. Later the same evening Baker approached Keith and told him Monroe was interested in hiring him. The upshot was that in March 1963 Keith became the first Yankee folksong revivalist to join the Blue Grass Boys.

Monroe was quick to exploit Keith's presence in the band. Within a few weeks Monroe had recorded six instrumentals featuring the banjo, including three which Keith had brought to Nashville with him—"Salt Creek," "Sailor's Hornpipe," and "Devil's Dream." Monroe's next single, released in September, featured "Devil's Dream." A few days after the record was released,

Keith played the tune during a show at Monroe's Brown County Jamboree. After he'd finished, Monroe made a brief speech, typical of the comments he made at least once every show about Keith's instrumental work:

> You can't beat that kind of banjo playing, I don't believe. That's one Yankee that's gonna make it hard on a lot of southern boys' banjo-pickin'. [Laughter and applause.] I always thought that these old-time fiddle numbers could be played on a banjo. I've told *all* the banjo-pickers from Stringbeans right on down through Earl Scruggs, Don Reno, and all of 'em that it could be played like Brad plays it, but they never had enough music in 'em to really learn to play the notes right, y'know. And I was in hopes that-a maybe somebody from the South would do that, but Brad Keith was the man come along.[24]

Keith's impact upon bluegrass was revolutionary. In the past other banjo pickers had vied with Scruggs for the reputation as the hottest or most innovative banjo picker in bluegrass—men like Reno, Sonny Osborne, Eddie Adcock, and J. D. Crowe. Each developed his own vocabulary but the basic syntax was that of Scruggs. Keith, with "Devil's Dream" in particular but also in the general complexities of his approach, suggested an alternative syntax, an approach which would eventually be called "chromatic," "melodic," "fiddle-picking," "Yankee-picking," or "Keith style." None of these names are completely adequate to describe the differences between this way of playing the banjo and that of Scruggs, but taken together they reflect the combination of social and musical dimensions which it represented.

Keith appeared at a crucial point in Monroe's career. Bill had fallen upon hard times, and his band was much less stable than it had been during the forties and early fifties. He was attracting few capable veterans, and those who did work for him—mainly fiddlers like Vassar Clements, who was with him in the fall of 1961, or Kenny Baker, for a few months in 1962-63—stayed only briefly. While Monroe worked hard to maintain a high quality of music in his often straggling band, bluegrass fans found his early-sixties bands compared badly with his earlier ones. The Keith-McCoury band (they had several fiddlers during their season with Monroe) reversed this trend. With the help of the Opry's wide coverage, it soon became evident that Monroe had some good musicians with him, and within a month or two of Keith's arrival banjo pickers all over the South (and North) were trying to figure out "Devil's Dream" and "Sailor's Hornpipe."

The combined impact of banjoist Keith and manager Rinzler upon Bill Monroe was considerable. Rinzler's article in *Sing Out!* along with his notes to the Greenbriar Boys' Vanguard album had convinced Monroe of Ralph's sincerity, and he began a series of in-depth interviews with Bill, gathering information for a biography. With his stimulus Monroe began for the first time to speak at length about the history of bluegrass music and his own past, expounding his musical philosophy to the audience.

In Monroe's account of how bluegrass started, Earl Scruggs was not the originator of bluegrass banjo; instead his banjo technique represented a step in an evolutionary process that began the moment Bill Monroe created the Blue Grass Boys. In this way Monroe placed himself at the center of a developmental process, and Flatt and Scruggs were seen as part of Bill Monroe's master plan, with Keith advancing bluegrass banjo further along lines suggested by Monroe. This change came at a time when Monroe, managed by Rinzler, was appearing for the first time before folk revival audiences, at folk festivals like those of Newport and UCLA. Because the folk revivalists were most interested in banjo and thus knew more about it, the elevation of Keith to a master on the level of Scruggs had a strong impact, of which Monroe took advantage. He had always made a point of advertising the home state of each Blue Grass Boy; now as he was beginning to appear before city audiences outside the South he had a Yankee city boy in his band.

These appearances brought Monroe into contact with the national network that had developed among folk revival bluegrass musicians outside the South. The result was that during the next four years he would have a number of "city boys" in his band—products of the Boston, New York, Washington, San Francisco, Los Angeles area scenes—and would come to know many other musicians from this previously isolated group. It was the beginning of a four-year process that would see the seriously involved urban/folk revival bluegrass followers move more fully into dimensions of bluegrass other than banjo—the emergence of singers like Peter Rowan, a young Boston protege of Keith and Rooney; mandolinists like David Grisman from New Jersey, introduced to that instrument by Rinzler; fiddlers like Richard Greene, weaned away from old-time fiddle in Los Angeles by Scott Stoneman and then given further training by Monroe.

Monroe's entry into the folk revival contrasts with that of Flatt and Scruggs. While Monroe developed contacts along a network of younger musicians upon whom he could draw as a pool of new talent, eventually raising the caliber of his band, Flatt and Scruggs developed their contacts among revival publicists like Shelton and Welding, among stars like Baez, and with booking agents like Greenhill. While this gave Flatt and Scruggs a commercial advantage during the early sixties when the revival was "into" unamplified old-time country music, this and the fact that they had gone so deeply into revival repertoire and style worked against them later. By 1965, Welding was concentrating on electric blues; Baez and the other revivalists were following Bob Dylan into folk-rock; and folk boom bookings at colleges, universities, and festivals began to tail off as bluegrass became "old hat." Monroe's contacts, while not so commercial, were on a strong emotional level among the hardcore urban bluegrass followers; with Rinzler's help he became a cult figure.

Rinzler and Keith lasted with Monroe in Nashville for only a short time. Rinzler made some sweeping changes in the six months he worked as Monroe's manager—such as replacing elder brother Birch Monroe as manager of the Jamboree at Bean Blossom with a twenty-four-year-old graduate student in folklore from nearby Indiana University and initiating a series of annotated reissue albums of Bill's best Decca recordings—but he found that life as Monroe's manager was not an easy one. Monroe has had a great many managers, few of whom have lasted for more than a season, for he prefers to keep most of the control of his business in his own hands or those of relatives. But he also tended to just let things go, for music definitely came first with him. As a result business suffered. For example, shortly after arriving in Nashville Rinzler went into Decca ready to negotiate a new contract for Bill only to discover that one had recently been signed. Monroe had forgotten about it. Moreover, in the early sixties Monroe was not in great demand on the country music circuit, and his folk festival, coffeehouse, and college concert bookings could not sustain a manager. By September Rinzler, having lost money, was back in New York City where he handled bookings for Monroe and Doc Watson while he kept the pot boiling by playing with the Greenbriar Boys. Keith too found life in Nashville difficult. With long hours on the road in Monroe's weary '58 Olds station wagon and rough hotel and motel accommodations, he found the romance of being a Blue Grass Boy wearing thin in a hurry. Monroe took to introducing Keith as "one of the best right now and if he stays with me a year there won't be a banjo player in the country that can touch him." The teacher's veiled warning was not enough to keep him in the band: just before Christmas of 1963, after eight months with Bill, Keith returned home.

At the beginning of 1964 the coming of a few revivalists to Nashville to work for Monroe seemed almost a fluke. The revitalization of Monroe's career (traced in the following chapters) grew out of the changes and connections generated during 1963, but the growth was gradual. Meanwhile, others in bluegrass music responded to the folk revival interest variously, ranging from those who sought to exploit the interest to those who took no heed whatsoever. Bluegrass albums produced during the first half of the sixties provide a convenient means for gaining a perspective on these responses and a clue to the fate of bluegrass in the folk revival.

Bluegrass Albums 1962-65

By 1962-63 bluegrass albums were no longer a novelty. All of the best-known groups had albums, often consisting of material previously issued on singles and frequently aimed at the urban folk music consumer. While country music followers of bluegrass generally heard the music first on radio or at personal appearances, the folk revivalists almost always heard it first on record, usually albums rather than singles. As we have seen, such albums were coming regularly from Flatt and Scruggs. Starday, already embarked upon their production of bluegrass and gospel "packages" (EPs and LPs), soon realized that there was a new market for this music. A few months after the Country Gentlemen were included in a hootenanny at Carnegie Hall, Starday finally issued their first and only Starday album, *Bluegrass at Carnegie Hall*. The title was misleading, for the album consisted of studio recordings and was not made at the actual Carnegie Hall appearance. But both the title and the liner notes showed that Don Pierce was courting the new consumers: "No longer is the sale of Bluegrass music confined to the mountain areas and country music field. Nowadays, the most sophisticated city dwellers in our biggest cities are hungry for more real down-to-earth Bluegrass pickin' and singin'. Folk music collector clubs are springing up all over America and it is in our colleges that the most profound students of folk songs, folk singing and folk music are to be found."[25]

Not long after this album appeared, Pete Welding brought Pierce's label to the attention of the readers of *Sing Out!* in an article entitled "Starday: The Bluegrass Label," reviewing its output and giving a brief history of the company. Starday did have some initial success in marketing their records to the urban bluegrass and old-time fans, but it was done without a clear idea of what these consumers preferred. As with their singles, most of their albums were the products of miscellaneous low-budget recording arrangements rather than of a coherent policy. When they opened their own studio and began producing records in Nashville, they concentrated on recording old main-stream country performers, seeking a market among people who would recall and appreciate the sound of old-timers like Lulu Belle and Scotty, the Blue Sky Boys, and Fiddling Arthur Smith. Analyzing their output between 1962 and 1965, William Henry Koon reported that they recorded "34 bluegrass LP's, 27 old-time LP's, 18 LP's of specialty and humor material, and 31 LP's of religious music—much of it bluegrass" in contrast to 64 C&W LP's.[26] But their best-known bluegrass bands had, by the end of 1962, all moved to other labels, and the new ones were not as well known (particularly to the folk revival) as those who had established Starday's reputation in the late fifties.

Other country-oriented labels, aware of the urban interest in bluegrass as folk music, made various attempts to take advantage of it. Chet Atkins produced an interesting album by Walter Forbes, a singer from Chattanooga who was working with guitarist and mandolinist Norman Blake and banjoist Bob Johnson, both active in that region's bluegrass scene. The Forbes LP sounded like the folk-revival music of the time rather than like bluegrass— quite unusual for the Nashville sound of 1961-62. But it was neither fish nor fowl and was commercially unsuccessful.

More successful were two albums produced in Nashville by Capitol's Ken Nelson in the spring of 1962. One featured a popular female country vocalist, Rose Maddox, an Alabama native who had been working with her brothers out of Southern California since the forties. On *Rose Maddox Sings Bluegrass* she was backed by Reno and Smiley and their band along with several other musicians including (on five cuts) Bill Monroe. One song included on this set was "Cotton Fields," a recent hit for the Highwaymen, a pop folk revival group; a few months earlier Monroe had recorded his version of this Huddie Ledbetter ("Leadbelly") composition. Issued at the same time as the Maddox album was *Bluegrass Favorites* by Mac Wiseman. The front cover described him as "Master Folk Singer," and the back liner notes were written by Ed Kahn, a graduate student in folklore and mythology at UCLA who was writing his Ph.D. dissertation on the Carter family. Also on the back liner was a laudatory quote from Robert Shelton's *New York Times* review of a Wiseman appearance at Carnegie Hall in May 1962. The songs on the album included "Cotton Fields" and several other folk revival favorites like "Freight Train." Also on the disc was a new song, Justin Tubb's "Bluegrass Fiesta," indicative of the commercial potential mainstream Nashville singer-songwriters like Tubb saw in the new interest in bluegrass.

More common than entire albums were token gestures to the folk revival market on liner notes or in titles of albums. The Osborne Brothers' second MGM album alluded in its liner notes to folk revival interest even though the contents consisted of singles from the late fifties not aimed at this market. One Stanley Brothers King album cover proudly labeled them as "Award Winners at the Folk Song Festival," a claim which had no specific factual basis.

While some groups and companies advertised in various ways that this music was now the darling of the folk set on campuses and at festivals and hootenannies, other groups—like Jim and Jesse on Epic and Reno and Smiley on King—did not. The folk revival record buyers who were already hooked on bluegrass didn't pay much attention to such advertising anyhow, and, more importantly, most of the country-oriented bands had neither the resources, the contacts, nor the motivation to move into this market as Flatt and Scruggs and the Country Gentlemen had done. Two of the most successful bands of the early sixties, Jim and Jesse and the Osborne Brothers, had seen their efforts rewarded in 1964 when they became members of the Grand Ole Opry cast. With their success in this arena of mainstream country music, they didn't need to shape their albums for the folk market; both bands regularly appeared at folk events like the Newport Folk Festival in any case.

On the other hand, record companies that previously had nothing whatsoever to do with country music were recording bluegrass for their folk music series. Folkways began with the Mike Seeger productions in 1956. These first records were essentially field recordings, a format unique to the folk music record industry. The technology of tape recording made it possible to preserve and document music hitherto inaccessible to the buying public. Folkways issued made-in-the-field recordings from every corner of the earth, including music from ceremonies and similar events which could not be duplicated in the studio. With each album came an extensive brochure which explained the cultural setting of the recording and gave the words to the songs. Their advertising emphasized the educational aspects of such albums, and their catalog included a number of spoken-word recordings developed for school use and musical instrument instruction records. With Folkways and other labels the field recording aura lingered with their folk series even when the recordings were produced in studios. The field recording functioned like the antique shoemaker's bench made into an end table or the authentic Navajo blanket hung on the wall like a painting; it was a musical conversation piece whose rough edges appealed to people for whom abstract expressionism was the latest thing in art. Alan Lomax sensed and utilized the commercial potential of field recordings in the forties with broadcasts and commercial pressings of his Library of Congress recordings; Asch's Folkways and other folk labels followed his path. In 1959 Lomax featured the Mountain Ramblers, a Galax, Virginia, bluegrass band, as part of his *Southern Folk Heritage Series,* a set of field recordings (seven albums, in stereo) which he produced for Atlantic Records. Another folk record producer who made his reputation in part with field recordings was Kenneth S. Goldstein who, since the early fifties, had produced hundreds of albums for various New York folk labels like Folkways, Riverside, and Stinson.

In 1960 Goldstein began a two-year association with Prestige Records, a New Jersey–based label which, like Atlantic, specialized in jazz. He coordinated a large number of releases for their Bluesville and International series, and in the latter included several bluegrass albums. One, recorded "in the field" by folklorist Harry Oster, was by a little-known Baton Rouge group called the Louisiana Honeydrippers, led by Jim Smoak, a South Carolina banjo picker who'd worked with Monroe, Flatt and Scruggs, and other Opry acts during the fifties. The other Prestige bluegrass album was produced by Goldstein and featured Harry and Jeanie West, a Virginia–North Carolina couple long resident in New York City and familiar to Washington Square audiences. These Prestige albums—like the Folkways ones, those produced by Lomax and Seeger, a Riverside album of the Lonesome River Boys, and the Greenbriar Boys' albums—were in one way or another products of the New York–centered folk scene. As the revival became a boom in 1962 other national centers began to play a role in the folk record business, and bluegrass was involved.

In 1962 Goldstein left Prestige, and Prestige owner Bob Weinstock went looking for other folk music producers. Manny Greenhill in Boston put him in touch with a young independent producer, Paul Rothchild. In Cambridge in the early sixties, Rothchild first worked in a record store then became a salesman for a record distributor, winning a prize for his sales of Elektra Records, the most commercial of the folk labels. Becoming interested in the local folk scene, he began checking out the coffeehouses. One night he and his wife went to Club 47, the best known of the Cambridge coffeehouses: "We got over there, walked in the door, and heard bluegrass for the first time in my entire life. The Charles River Valley Boys were on stage. At one point in my life, I had been a serious student of Bach, and now I heard bluegrass. It was country Bach! It had contrapuntal arrangements, all the fugal stuff. I just completely went insane. We both fell apart. We stayed the whole night."[27] At evening's end he approached a member of the band and asked if they had a record, explaining that he was a distributor and would like to help push it. Told they had no record, he returned the next night and offered to make one. Knowing nothing about production, he taught himself recording and editing techniques by trial and error. He marketed this first record himself and then began working on a second album by the other local revival bluegrass band, Keith and Rooney. He had just run out of money when Greenhill put him in touch with Weinstock, who bought the Charles River Valley Boys master. Rothchild went on to produce five other bluegrass albums for Prestige in 1963–64—the Keith and Rooney album, and two each by the Charles River Valley Boys and the Lilly Brothers. For Rothchild the bluegrass albums were the beginning of a career as a producer; soon he had placed the most popular young folk revivalists from the Boston-Cambridge scene on Prestige.

In 1963 Elektra followed Prestige into the bluegrass sector of the folk market. They began with a series of albums recorded in what seemed a most unlikely place for bluegrass, Los Angeles. Just as there was a single producer behind most of the bluegrass releases at Folkways and Prestige, so one individual, Jim Dickson, was behind Elektra's Los Angeles bluegrass albums.

A Los Angeles native, Dickson had grown up listening to country music on the radio, a private fan of the music until he joined the Army in 1946 and met others who liked it. In the early fifties an interest in jazz led him to the flourishing local coffeehouse scene, where that music often alternated with folk music. He liked the more country-sounding folk performers, those like Woody Guthrie and Jack Elliot, and preferred songs that told stories. Dickson became a record producer when hip comedian Lord Buckley, who also appeared at coffeehouses, "wanted to make a record . . . and more or less bullied me into bringing it about."[28] Like Rothchild, he was a self-taught producer. With the Buckley album, Dickson started his own label, Vaya. In 1962 Elektra's owner Jac Holzman opened a Los Angeles office, and Dickson sold the Buckley album (which was to remain in print for over twenty-five years), to Elektra and began producing for him.

Dickson produced a number of folk albums for Elektra, but he began with three bluegrass records. He recognized the folk as well as the country elements in bluegrass and particularly liked the high quality of musicianship which it required: "The folk guys were just sort of beating their guitars in those days. And having come out of jazz and having a little more critical ear, the other thing I really liked about bluegrass, that it was a—well, part formal and part improvisational breaks, the same kind of structure jazz had. You know, tight ensemble singing and then [a] break."[29]

His first Elektra bluegrass production was done in November 1962 by the

Greenbriar Boys and a Hollywood country singer, Dián James. Dickson had been working on an album of Dián for Elektra, but when he heard her do a guest set with the Greenbriars at the Ash Grove folk club, there was a change of plans: "We had approached The Greenbriar Boys to play some instrumentals behind her on three or four numbers, but the unique sound that emerged from that memorable evening deserved an entire album of its own."[30] Like Dickson, James was a fan of Rose Maddox, and a number of songs on the album came from the Maddox repertoire. But she was also branching out into the world of folk music (Dickson recalls she "wanted to be Mary Travers" of the popular folk trio Peter, Paul, and Mary[31]) and the album included songs from the repertoires of Leadbelly, Jean Ritchie, and other authentic folk as well as newer material from Los Angeles revivalists Travis Edmonson and Hoyt Axton.

While he was working on this album, another bluegrass band arrived in town: "The Greenbriar Boys were at the Ash Grove, [and] the Dillards showed up in town in a station wagon, set up in the lobby and started playing bluegrass and brought the audience into the lobby as well as Bobby Yellin who couldn't *believe* Douglas Dillard could possibly exist."[32] Everyone was impressed with the new group, which consisted of the two Dillard brothers, singer-guitarist Rodney and wizard banjoist Douglas, along with mandolinist Dean Webb and bassist Mitchell Jayne. They had come to California from Missouri, where the band had coalesced out of a bluegrass scene that had been active in the St. Louis area since the mid-fifties. Though the Dillard brothers were from Salem in the Missouri Ozarks, sons of an old-time fiddler, they were by no means unsophisticated country boys; Douglas, for example, had been a college student before embarking on his musical career. They had recorded several singles on the local K-Ark label while performing semi-professionally in the region. Jayne, the former deejay and schoolteacher who acted as the group's spokesman, understood the complexities of the music business and carefully shaped the image of the Dillards as real country boys to appeal to folk revival audiences. They had played their first concert at Washington University in the spring of 1962 and at that time decided to become full-time professionals. After a summer of saving money for the trip, they left in the fall for California. Stranded temporarily in Oklahoma City, they reached Los Angeles in November and went to the Ash Grove the very night they arrived. With the help of Ralph Rinzler, who convinced Elektra owner Jac Holzman that the Dillards were a good bluegrass group, they were signed to the label, with Dickson as producer. Douglas Dillard recounts: "Elektra printed a little blurb in *Variety Magazine* saying they had signed the Dillards, a bluegrass group from Missouri, and the people from the Andy Griffith Show saw that and asked us to come down and audition."[33] By the beginning of 1963 they were making regular network television appearances as musical members of the Darling family on the Griffith show, and their new album was issued by Elektra.

The Dillards were not folk revivalists themselves; they followed the lead of Flatt and Scruggs and the Country Gentlemen in pitching their product toward urban folk music consumers. Jayne's carefully crafted notes to their first album set forth revival thinking about bluegrass in romantic terms, linking it with folk music as the rural heritage of America and alluding to Bill Monroe as its creator. The album included a number of folksongs, including a dramatically arranged version of the old English broadside "Polly Vaughn." Musically competitive with the best new bands, they had a unique repertoire, tight harmony singing, and innovative banjo work by Douglas Dillard. The record sold well for Elektra and firmly established the Dillards as an influential group. On this first album were two original songs which have since become bluegrass standards, "The Old Home Place" and "Dooley," and their version of Carl Story's "Mocking Banjo," which they called "Duelin' Banjo."

A third Elektra bluegrass album made at this time in Los Angeles was *New Dimensions in Banjo and Bluegrass,* an instrumental record featuring Washington Square veterans Eric Weissberg and Marshall Brickman. These New York bluegrass pickers were recorded in Los Angeles because they were on the road with the commercial folk group, the Tarriers. Dickson co-produced this album with Holzman and added considerably to its musical value by bringing in two of the best bluegrass musicians in Los Angeles—fiddler Gordon Terry, a former Monroe sideman who had been working in the Los Angeles country music scene, and Clarence White, a seventeen-year-old guitarist playing with a band called the Country Boys.

White had come to Los Angeles in 1954 when his father had brought the family from their former home in Lewiston, Maine. Acadian French Canadian in background, they were originally LeBlancs from southeastern New Brunswick. Clarence and his older brothers Eric and Roland began appearing on Los Angeles country music television shows as "Three Little Country Boys." In 1958 they added a banjo picker, Ozarks native Billy Ray Latham, and changed the name of their group to the Country Boys. By 1963 they were appearing as The Kentucky Colonels with Clarence on guitar, Roland on mandolin, Roger Bush on bass, Billy Ray on banjo, and, for a time, Bobby Slone, an East Kentuckian, on fiddle. By then Clarence had experienced a turning point in his career: he'd seen blind guitarist Doc Watson in action at the Ash Grove.

Watson was at the Ash Grove as a rhythm guitarist in Clarence Ashley's old-time band. During his engagement there Ashley came down with laryngitis and Watson, called on to sing and take center stage, quickly showed himself to be a consummate entertainer. Particularly impressive was his lead work with the flat pick on the guitar. One of his most copied pieces was an arrangement of the old Leslie Keith–Curly Fox–Tommy Magness fiddle tune "Black Mountain Rag," and he did similar versions of other fiddle tunes. Fancy guitar runs laced the rhythm guitar work behind his vocals, too. Up to this point bluegrass lead guitar work, if heard at all, had generally been done with two guitars in the band, one taking the lead, the other providing rhythm. The two most frequently recorded lead guitarists of this type were Earl Scruggs, who used a finger-picking style, and Don Reno, whose flat pick work anticipated that of Watson. Occasionally rhythm guitarists took uncomplicated solo breaks—Bill Clifton, Charlie Waller of the Country Gentlemen, Edd Mayfield with Bill Monroe—but White, amazed by Watson at the Ash Grove, saw greater possibilities in Doc's combination of lead and rhythm functions in a single guitar. It gave White the impetus to further develop his own style—similar to Watson's but characterized by the unexpected placement of rhythmic accents—in the context of a bluegrass band. With Clarence White the Kentucky Colonels set a new fashion for bluegrass guitar in which a single guitarist did both lead and rhythm.

The Kentucky Colonels made several tours of the folk circuit in the East and Midwest, appearing at the 1964 Newport Folk Festival, where they shared the stage with the Osborne Brothers, the Greenbriar Boys, and the Stanley Brothers. Their album on World Pacific, *Appalachian Swing*, became an underground classic. But though influential and legendary, the Colonels did not have the kind of commercial success that the Dillards had.

Not only did the Dillards' first Elektra album sell well, but they received regular national televison exposure on the Andy Griffith shows. Working out of Los Angeles, they played major folk festivals at UCLA and Monterey during 1963. Their second Elektra album, issued in 1964, was recorded during a performance at the Los Angeles night club, The Mecca. Produced by Dickson, it showcased their highly polished act which was aimed at urban night club audiences and featured emcee Jayne's playful and urbane manipulation of hillbilly stereotypes and rural images. Included on the album, at the suggestion of Dickson, was the first Bob Dylan song released by a bluegrass band. Jayne introduced it in his usual style: "I don't know how many of you know who Bobby Dylan is, but he's probably done more for folk music, or had more influence on folk music than anybody. He has a voice very much like a dog with its leg caught in barbed wire. But that doesn't matter because what he does is *write* the songs. He wrote a song that we like real well and wanted to try to do it ourselves in a bluegrass style. This song is called 'Walking Down the Line.' "[34]

By recording a Dylan song on a bluegrass album for the folk market, the Dillards moved into a somewhat different sector of the folk revival. Revival repertoire was more or less divided between "folksongs" (old songs thought to be anonymous) and newly composed material in similar style but dealing with contemporary topics, often with social or political protest themes. Woody Guthrie's songs were the most influential models of the latter type; Flatt and Scruggs had included several Guthrie songs on their albums. Dylan began his songwriting career as a Guthrie disciple but by 1964 was moving into his own style in which the protest element was replaced by an often enigmatic personal iconography. Though based on old folk melodies and using lyric formulae drawn from folk texts, most of Dylan's songs were quite unlike the traditional songs that revival audiences expected from bluegrass bands, and they were also very different from the contemporary country songs that bluegrass bands did for their country audiences.

Dickson was suggesting Dylan songs to every group he recorded. He'd heard Dylan at the 1963 Monterey Folk Festival singing some of his new compositions and "was just overwhelmed because in folk music at that point we're already running out of songs." Seeking for ways to advance the groups he produced, Dickson was particularly aware of the importance of placing strong repertoire with them: "I wanted to take that bluegrass quality and get it into the folk field, you know, and get them to be able to play for the folk audience, and I really didn't give much care about whether or not it was a Flatt or Scruggs tune or not."[35] In 1963–64 he began working as an independent producer and did two best-selling albums of twelve-string guitar instrumentals for World Pacific featuring a young Los Angeles studio musician, Glen Campbell, along with the Dillards as "the Folkswingers." These albums too featured Dylan tunes.

In 1963–64, Dickson was also producing a southern California bluegrass band, the Hillmen. Known earlier as the Golden State Boys (the name would be used again by a slightly different aggregation), they included two local country singers, Vern and Rex Gosdin, who played guitar and bass; Kentucky-born banjo picker Don Parmley; and California mandolinist Chris Hillman, formerly with the Scottsville Squirrel Barkers. Following the success of his Folkswingers albums, Dickson had been given free access at night to the World Pacific studios, and he spent three months in 1963–64 "just going in there and using a three-track [recorder] and used tape, you know, the scrap tape, and doing everything and just collecting what was the best performances" by the Hillmen. From this he produced an album which he submitted to Elektra's Holzman, who had first refusal of all his work, but "by then he'd hired Paul Rothchild, and they turned it down, which . . . surprised me."[36] Eventually the album was issued in 1969, and in the notes to a 1981 reissue of that album Chris Hillman wrote: "We owe a great deal to our producer, Jim Dickson. Jim opened us up to the likes of Bob Dylan, Pete Seeger and Woody Guthrie. He also encouraged our own songwriting abilities."[37] They included two Dylan songs on the album.

A few months after recording the Hillmen album, Chris Hillman set aside his mandolin for the electric bass and began playing in a new rock band, the Byrds. The Byrds were formed after two folk revival performers, Jim (later Roger) McGuinn and Gene Clark, became interested in the Beatles by seeing *A Hard Day's Night,* the first Beatle movie. They began singing together and writing songs, and David Crosby, like them a folk revival singer active in Los Angeles, heard about them. Through Dickson, who was a mutual acquaintance, he approached McGuinn and Clark to team up with them.

Dickson began taping their rehearsals at the World Pacific Studios, just as he'd done with the Hillmen. Soon he added a drummer, Michael Clark, and then he brought in Chris Hillman to play electric bass. They utilized Crosby's expertise at arranging vocal parts to delve into Beatle music. Though folk revivalists were not supposed to be involved with rock music, McGuinn had been excited about the Beatles the moment he heard them. As he learned more about their music he understood why it appealed to him: "It became just electrified folk music to me. And the Beatles, whether they knew it or not, were doing what I'd always dug in music, but with electric instruments. They were into modal music, like mountain music and banjo picking, blue-grass harmonies, and things like that."[38]

With Hillman and drummer Michael Clarke in the group, the Byrds con-tinued rehearsing in the World Pacific studios with Dickson. He recorded everything and made suggestions about their sound and their repertoire. One of his suggestions was that they do Bob Dylan's "Mr. Tambourine Man." McGuinn, like more than a few revivalists at the time, didn't care for Dylan; the Byrds did the song only after "I shoved (it) down their throats. And they finally humored me and did it and got a number one."[39] It was their first Columbia record, issued early in 1965 and a hit by the beginning of that summer.

This synthesis of folk and rock music that would soon be called folk-rock brought together the music of the Beatles and Bob Dylan; the Byrds were in the vanguard of this movement, giving Dylan himself the impetus to move from acoustic to electric backing on his recordings, to the dismay of many of his folk revival fans. Producers like Dickson played an important role in the development of this music; he would continue to work with bluegrass and rock performers in the Los Angeles area and would be involved in the coun-try-rock synthesis of the late sixties. But in 1965 the focus of interest for such producers was shifting away from bluegrass. The urban folk music tastemakers were excited by Beatle music and were experimenting with electricity.

During the summer of 1965 Paul Rothchild produced a record by a Chicago group, the Paul Butterfield Band, an electric blues outfit. Was this folk music? It certainly was endorsed by all the right authorities. The liner notes to this Elektra album were by Peter J. Welding and included with them was a lau-datory quote from Bob Shelton's *New York Times* review of the band. When Dylan appeared on stage at Newport in July 1965 with his electric guitar, the Butterfield Band backed him.

In 1963–65 Newport had become the most important folk festival. By the summer of 1965, there was interest in a wide spectrum of "folk music" ranging from the old authentic folksingers to increasingly popular young figures like Dylan. All were represented at Newport. When Dylan did his electric guitar set with the Butterfield band, he was booed by half the audience and cheered by the other half.

To this point the revival had been dominated by those whose interest in meaningful music was fueled by their alienation from mainstream popular culture music. But for many new listeners folk music was merely another form of popular music. Often they had listened to Elvis Presley and Fats Domino before they heard the Kingston Trio, and for them the discovery of electric blues brought things full circle, leading to the revitalization of rock.

Some of the revival musicians, including a few of the bluegrass pickers, had now discovered marijuana, LSD, and the drug subculture that encouraged them to explore musical experiences previously off limits to revivalists. For them the "outlaw" sound of rock and roll had shock value, and, lo and behold, it was commercial, too. Dylan's recordings with rock instruments were selling well. And the Beatles and the Rolling Stones were changing the meaning of rock music. With *A Hard Day's Night* the Beatles won the urban intellectuals over with an image of these rockers as intelligent friendly young men with a sense of humor. The Stones too gained respect for their sincere homage to the Chicago blues roots of their repertoire. Suddenly, in 1965, rock music and folk music were no longer polarized, for at least some revivalists. In that sense Newport '65 was both a beginning and an end.

Up to 1965, the folk revival had been an underground movement, a network. Now, as the baby boom of the forties matured and an enormous audience of young people sought new musics, the underground mixed with the mainstream and popular music became more pluralistic. The revival network, which had been centralized in a few urban sites with outside colonies in colleges and universities, was no longer needed. Potential audiences were large enough to encourage people in the music business—record companies, media, and booking agencies—to experiment. Jug bands, carefully recreating black music of the twenties and thirties (in the spirit of the New Lost City Ramblers), and bluegrass bands suddenly became rock bands.

In 1965 the new electric folk music—whether it was the Butterfield band's recreation of city blues classics in the spirit of the New Lost City Ramblers or the Byrds' wedding of Dylan and Beatles—created the same kinds of response that bluegrass had engendered in 1960–61. The tastemakers endorsed it; the conservative critics decried it. This time, though, there would be no gradual assimilation of rock music into the revival; too much money was at stake, and the revival was split asunder. Producers who had been doing bluegrass in 1962–63 were by 1965 turning to rock music. Paul Rothchild would produce one more Charles River Valley Boys LP in 1966, an Elektra album recorded in Nashville called *Beatle Country* which featured Lennon and McCartney songs done bluegrass style. But by this time Elektra was involved with rock music in a big way, and Rothchild was producing a Los Angeles group, the Doors. Bluegrass bands would continue to appear regularly at the Newport Folk Festival, but the days of folk revival interest in the music had peaked. While it would retain a niche in the world of folk music— it is still heard at folk festivals in the eighties—it no longer had as strong an appeal to young folk enthusiasts. Many of the younger urban musicians who had been trying their hands at bluegrass, like Chris Hillman, moved into rock music; in 1965 Jerry Garcia of Palo Alto, who spent part of the spring of 1964 with Sandy Rothman, studying bluegrass with tape recorder and banjo at country parks and bars in the Midwest and upper South, recording groups like the Osbornes and Bill Monroe, was playing lead electric guitar as "Captain Trips" of the new San Francisco acid-rock group the Grateful Dead. The times, as Dylan sang, were a-changin'.

Notes

1. *Lester Flatt and Earl Scruggs Picture Album Songbook*, p. 1.
2. *Lester Flatt/Earl Scruggs and the Foggy Mountain Boys Picture Album–Song Book*, p. 1.
3. Ibid., p. 2.
4. Ibid., pp. 6–7.
5. (Louise Scruggs), unsigned liner notes to *Foggy Mountain Banjo*.
6. Louise Scruggs, "History of the Five-String Banjo," pp. 4, 5.
7. Jack Tottle, "Ricky Skaggs: Clinch Mountain to Boone Creek," pp. 8–9.
8. Eric von Schmidt and Jim Rooney, *Baby, Let Me Follow You Down*, p. 198.
9. Mike Seeger to the author, June 1, 1961.
10. Peter Frame, *Rock Family Trees*, p. 17.
11. Young, "Frets and Frails," *Sing Out!* 11(April-May, 1961): p. 47.
12. John Duffey to the author, Sept. 20, 1961.
13. Samuel Gesser, "In Canada: The Mariposa Folk Festival," p. 48.
14. Young, "Frets and Frails," *Sing Out!* 11(Oct.-Nov., 1961): p. 55.
15. Rinzler interview, Oct. 18, 1980.
16. Bill Monroe and Carter Stanley, recorded onstage, Oak Leaf Park, Luray, Va., July 4, 1961.
17. Rinzler interview.
18. Young, "Frets and Frails," *Sing Out!* 11(Oct.-Nov., 1961): p. 55.
19. Rinzler interview.
20. Ibid.
21. Ibid.
22. Ralph Rinzler, "Bill Monroe," p. 204.
23. Fred Geiger, "Where I Come From," p. 15.
24. Bill Monroe, recorded onstage, Brown County Jamboree, Bean Blossom, Ind., Sept. 22, 1963.
25. [Don Pierce,] liner notes to *Bluegrass at Carnegie Hall: The Country Gentlemen.*
26. William Henry Koon, "Grass Roots Commercialism," p. 7.
27. von Schmidt and Rooney, *Baby, Let Me Follow You Down*, p. 142.

28. Jim Dickson, interview with author, Hollywood, Calif., Jan. 18, 1983.

29. Ibid.

30. [Jim Dickson,] unsigned liner notes to *Dián and the Greenbriar Boys*.

31. Dickson interview, Jan. 18, 1983.

32. Ibid.

33. Bill Knopf, "Doug Dillard," p. 5.

34. Mitch Jayne, as spoken on *The Dillards—Live . . . Almost*.

35. Dickson interview, Jan. 18, 1983.

36. Ibid.

37. Chris Hillman, liner notes to *The Hillmen*.

38. Bud Scoppa, *The Byrds*, p. 16.

39. Dickson interview, Jan. 18, 1983.

Bibliographical Notes

Louise Scruggs's banjo history was reprinted twice, first as "A History of America's Favorite Folk Instrument," then as a chapter in *Earl Scruggs and the Five-String Banjo*, pp. 9–11. Each printing varied slightly from the others. Peter Welding's *Saturday Review* piece is cited in the notes to chapter 8. For a biographical sketch of Louise Scruggs, see Dixie Deen, "The 'Woman' behind the Man."

The mass media feedback ethic of the folk revival was articulated by Alan Lomax in *Folk Song Style and Culture*, pp. 4 and 9.

Clarence Ashley's story is told by Ambrose N. Manning and Minnie M. Miller, "Tom Ashley." A concise history of the "discovery" of Doc Watson is Ralph Rinzler, "Doc Watson." The Greenbriar Boys were touted by Robert Shelton in "Bluegrass, from Hills and City," and "City Folk Singers."

In 1936 Herbert Halpert published the first of a series of record reviews which pointed out the connections between commercial race and hillbilly discs and various types of folk music: "Some Recorded American Folk Song." See my "Herbert Halpert: A Biographical Sketch," pp. 3–4, and "The Works of Herbert Halpert," p. 28. Alan Lomax's 1940 discography, "List of American Folk Songs on Commercial Records," was reprinted in mimeograph form by the Archive of American Folk Song (now the Archive of Folk Culture) at the Library of Congress. John Lomax's *Smoky Mountain Ballads* is discussed, along with other albums in Victor's 1938–48 "P" series of folksongs for "serious music lovers" in Archie Green, "Commercial Music Graphics: Twenty-One." Norm Cohen's "Preface" to Willie Smyth's *Country Music Recorded Prior to 1943*, pp. 1–13, discusses the history and explains the significance of LP reissues of early country music—all of which are listed by Smyth.

Mike Seeger and John Cohen, *The New Lost City Ramblers Songbook*, presents a sampling of the repertoire of that group. It was the subject of articles by Doug Tuchman, Andrew Smith, and Mark Greenberg, all titled "The New Lost City Ramblers." The Lilly Brothers were the subject of several articles, of which the most substantial were James J. McDonald's "Principal Influences on the Music of the Lilly Brothers" and Ivan M. Tribe's response to it, "Pros Long before Boston: The Entire Career of the Lilly Brothers." See also Sam Charters, "The Lilly Brothers of Hillbilly Ranch."

For information on Vern and Ray, see Stephanie Davis, "The Vern Williams Band."

An unenthusiastic review of the Country Gentlemen's Carnegie Hall appearance is Robert Shelton's "Hootenanny Held at Carnegie Hall."

In addition to references given in the chapter 5 bibliographical notes for Bill Clifton, see Pete Kuykendall, liner notes to *Bill Clifton and the Dixie Mountain Boys.*

The article which motivated Rinzler to seek an interview with Monroe was Pete Welding, "Earl Scruggs—and the Sound of Bluegrass."

A good contemporary report on the Boston scene is Betsy Siggins, "Bluegrass Sprouts in Boston." Extensive retrospective material on the same era and musicians, particularly Bill Keith, appears in Eric von Schmidt and Jim Rooney, *Baby Let Me Follow You Down.* Bob French and Herb Hooven were later to be founding members in Joe Val's New England Bluegrass Boys. See Mike Greenstein, "Joe Val and the New England Blue Grass Boys."

The linguistic analogy I use to describe Keith's banjo work is a simplified metaphor for a complex process which has been explored at length in Thomas A. Adler's "The Acquisition of a Traditional Competence: Folk-Musical and Folk-Cultural Learning among Bluegrass Banjo Players." Additional information on Bill Keith appears in Roger H. Siminoff, "Bill Keith: Yesterday, Today and Tomorrow." The stylistic revolution which Keith spearheaded is reprised by his student Tony Trischka in *Melodic Banjo.* Red Allen and the Kentuckians are covered in Tom Teepen's "Allen Grass" and Vincent Sims's "The Red Allen Story"; for Frank Wakefield see Randall Colaizzi, "Frank Wakefield."

For Peter Rowan, see Alan Steiner, "Peter Rowan: Wandering Boy Returns to his Roots"; and V. F. Nadsady, "Peter Rowan, at the Crossroad Again: Part 1, Looking Back: Bluegrass to Om." Articles on Grisman, whose impact on mandolin in the late seventies resembles that of Keith on banjo in the sixties, include Dan Forte (with Dix Bruce), " 'Dawg': David Grisman"; Dan Forte, "David Grisman and Dawg Music"; Jon Sievert, "David Grisman"; and Pat Chappelle, "A Dawg's Life." For Richard Greene see Paul F. Wells, "Bluegrass Was Really My Center—An Interview with Richard Greene" and Marilyn Kochman, "Richard Greene."

The Ralph Rinzler liner notes which praised Bill Monroe appeared on *The Greenbriar Boys.* His later influential Bill Monroe album notes appeared on *Bluegrass Instrumentals; The High, Lonesome Sound of Bill Monroe; Bill*

Monroe and Charlie Monroe; A Voice from on High (written with Alice [Gerrard] Foster); *Kentucky Blue Grass;* and *Country Music Hall of Fame.*

Information on Kenneth S. Goldstein's work with Prestige came from my interview with him, Jan. 2, 1979.

Jim Smoak has been the subject of two articles: Douglas Green, "Jim Smoak," and Alex Shephert, "Interview: Jim Smoak."

A contemporary account of the Dillards' first days is Mitchell F. Jayne, "Cut of the Dillards." See also Douglas Dillard et al, *The Bluegrass Banjo Style of Douglas Flint Dillard.* The Ozark scene from which they emerged is described in the John Hartford articles cited in chapter 10 and in Don Ginnings, "Lonnie Hoppers."

Clarence White's guitar style is the subject of Russ Barenberg's *Clarence White Guitar,* and Jon Sievert's "Clarence White." For the Kentucky Colonels, sources include John Kaparakis, "1964 and the Kentucky Colonels," and Peter V. Kuykendall, "The Kentucky Colonels."

The best work on the Byrds is John Rogan, *Timeless Flight.* The story of the bluegrass Byrd, Chris Hillman, was presented by Mark Humphrey in "Chris Hillman."

Much of the information on Newport in 1965 comes from von Schmidt and Rooney. Contemporary bluegrass musicians reacted to Dylan much as did Byrd leader McGuinn. See my interview with Richard Greene and Peter Rowan in which they report about a Dylan session in Nashville: "Bob Dylan in Nashville." Jerry Garcia's role as "Captain Trips" is described by Tom Wolfe in *The Electric Kool-Aid Acid Test,* his bluegrass experience recounted in an interview with Ralph Gleason in *The Jefferson Airplane and the San Francisco Sound,* pp. 309–10.

Discographical Notes

Flatt and Scruggs's folk-oriented albums following *Foggy Mountain Banjo* were *Songs of the Famous Carter Family, Folk Songs of Our Land,* and *Hard Travelin'.* Their two "live" albums of 1962–63, *Flatt and Scruggs at Carnegie Hall* and *Flatt and Scruggs Recorded Live at Vanderbilt University,* were also aimed in part at the folk audience.

The Greenbriar Boys first appeared on a Vanguard sampler, *New Folks.* They next were heard on several cuts of *Joan Baez,* vol. 2. Their first album was *The Greenbriar Boys.*

After John Lomax's 1941 *Smoky Mountain Ballads,* the next hillbilly-as-folk reissue albums were done in 1947 by Alan Lomax: *Listen to Our Story* and *Mountain Frolic.* These were later issued on LP at about the same time Folkways released its *Anthology of American Folk Music.*

The first New Lost City Ramblers album is cited in the notes to chapter 9. In 1962 Mike Seeger produced *Folk Songs from the Southern Mountains* by the Lilly Brothers and Don Stover. One side had bluegrass; the other, brother duets with mandolin and guitar. The Country Gentlemen's 1958 Starday recording of "High Lonesome" was reissued in 1960 on *Banjo Jamboree Spectacular!* "The Legend of the Johnson Boys," which Flatt and Scruggs released as a single, appeared earlier on *The New Lost City Ramblers*, vol. 3, and was also included on Flatt and Scruggs's *Folk Songs of Our Land.* The New Lost City Ramblers' "Pretty Fair Miss" was issued on their *Gone to the Country* and recorded by the Stanley Brothers as "Pretty Little Miss in the Garden," on *Country Music Concert.*

Vern and Ray's EP was *Cabin on a Mountain;* the York County Boys' album, *Blue Grass Jamboree.*

Bill Keith's "Devil's Dream" arrangement was first recorded by Marshall Brickman and Eric Weissberg on the anthology *Folk Banjo Styles.* Keith's own version first appeared on *Philadelphia Folk Festival,* then on his album with Jim Rooney, *Bluegrass: Livin' on the Mountain.* Both of those performances combined "Devil's Dream" with "Sailor's Hornpipe." Monroe's recordings of "Devil's Dream" and "Salt Creek" on which Keith played were issued only on singles. "Sailor's Hornpipe" appeared on Monroe's *Bluegrass Instrumentals.*

Chet Atkins's production of Walter Forbes was issued as *Ballads and Bluegrass.* Rose Maddox, Mac Wiseman, and Bill Monroe all released versions of "Cotton Fields." Monroe's appeared on his *Bluegrass Ramble.* All three were recorded in Nashville, as was the Osborne Brothers' *Blue Grass Music,* which referred in its unsigned notes to the popularity of bluegrass on college campuses. The Stanley Brothers' King album which made a similar allusion in its title was *Award Winners at the . . . Folk Song Festival.*

Alan Lomax's 1959 recordings of the Mountain Ramblers of Galax, Virginia, were issued on four albums in the Southern Folk Heritage series which Lomax compiled for Atlantic Records: *Sounds of the South; Blue Ridge Mountain Music; White Spirituals;* and *American Folk Songs for Children.*

The two albums issued by Prestige under Goldstein's direction were the Louisiana Honeydrippers' *Louisiana Bluegrass* and Harry and Jeannie West's *Country Music in Blue Grass Style.* The Lonesome River Boys, a Washington-based group, was led by Dartmouth student Jack Tottle; the New York–based jazz and folk label Riverside released their *Raise a Ruckus* in 1961. The first and second Charles River Valley Boys Prestige albums were both titled *Bluegrass and Old Timey Music;* the third was *Bluegrass Get Together with Tex Logan.* The two Lilly Brothers Prestige albums, *Bluegrass Breakdown* and *Country Songs* (the latter featured brother duets with mandolin and guitar only), were subsequently reissued by Rounder.

Elektra reissued *The Best of Lord Buckley* on their subsidiary Crestview label. The Dillards' first album was *Back Porch Bluegrass;* it was released at about the same time as Marshall Brickman and Eric Weissberg's *New Dimensions in Banjo and Bluegrass.* Like the Kentucky Colonels' *Appalachian Swing,* these two Elektra albums are still in print today. The two Folkswingers albums, *Twelve-String Guitar*, vols. 1 and 2, are out of print. *The Hillmen* was reissued, with some differences in content, in 1981. The Byrds' hit single of "Mr. Tambourine Man" appeared later on an album of that name and was reissued on *The Byrds' Greatest Hits. The Paul Butterfield Blues Band* was released in the fall of 1965; the Charles River Valley Boys' *Beatle Country* appeared the following year.

In 1958 Bill Clifton compiled this songbook. It was sold by mail order from the Jimmie Skinner Record Center in Cincinnati. [Author's personal collection]

This 1958 Mercury album (produced under Don Pierce's direction) contained recordings from 1948–50, but pictured on the cover was a mid-fifties version of the Foggy Mountain Boys: Hylo Brown, Curly Seckler, Flatt, Paul Warren, Scruggs, "Uncle Josh" (Burkett "Buck" Graves), "Little Darlin' " (Kentucky Slim Elza). [Author's personal collection]

Carnegie Hall, April 3, 1959: Earl Taylor and the Stoney Mountain Boys at Alan Lomax's "Folksong '59" concert: Curtis Cody, Earl Taylor, Walter Hensley, Sam Hutchins, Vernon "Boatwhistle" McIntyre. [Photo by John Cohen]

Carnegie Hall, April 3, 1959: two generations of folksong ideologues who shaped American thinking about bluegrass: Pete Seeger, Alan Lomax, Ralph Rinzler, Mike Seeger. [Photo by John Cohen]

The prominence of Alan Lomax's name and the term "Folk Songs" on this 1959 album cover indicates the market United Artists hoped to reach with these recordings, made shortly after Earl Taylor's Carnegie Hall appearance. [Author's personal collection]

The Osborne Brothers at Antioch College, March 5,
1960: Bob, Sonny, and Jimmy singing a trio. [Photo
by Ann M. Rosenberg]

Charlie Waller, John Duffey
and
The Country Gentlemen
of
Starday Records.

This 1958 souvenir photo includes four of the most
influential figures in the Washington area bluegrass
scene: Pete Kuykendall, John Duffey, Charlie Waller,
Tom Morgan. [Author's personal collection]

The Country Gentleman—John Duffey, Eddie Adcock, and Charlie Waller—recording an instrumental for their first Folkways album. [Photo by John Cohen]

1960: recording the first Country Gentlemen LP: producer Mike Seeger (foreground), Charlie Waller (left), and the other band members and friends listen with critical concentration to the playback of a freshly taped performance. [Photo by John Cohen]

This portrait of the Scruggs family appeared in Flatt and Scruggs's 1961 *Picture Album–Song Book*: Steve, Earl, Randy, Louise, Gary. In 1965 Louise Scruggs described it as her favorite family photo. [Author's personal collection]

The cover of Flatt and Scruggs's 1961 souvenir booklet showed them in action on national network television, choreographing around a single microphone. [Author's personal collection]

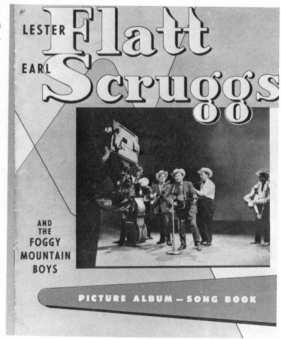

The New Lost City Ramblers (front to back: Tom Paley, Mike Seeger, John Cohen), 1959. [Photo by Robert Frank, courtesy of John Cohen]

A pioneer Washington area band—one of the first from that area to record for Starday—Buzz Busby and the Bayou Boys at the New River Ranch near Rising Sun, Maryland, May 20, 1956: Mike Hurney, Busby, Vance Truell, Charlie Waller, Teddy Miller. [Photo courtesy of Eddie Stubbs]

The Stanley Brothers at Luray, Virginia, July 4, 1961: Ralph Stanley, Bill Torbert, Carter Stanley, George Shuffler. [Photo by Phil Specht]

At the first Mariposa Folk Festival the York County Boys and Al Cherny were featured in a "Midnight Street Jamboree." It was repeated at the second festival, shown here on August 10, 1962, as Brian Barron, Mike Cameron, and Al Cherny provide music for the square dancers and caller. [Courtesy of the Mariposa Folk Foundation]

The Carroll County Boys (left, rear) and the Redwood Canyon Ramblers (right, front) at their Berkeley, California, concert of December 2, 1961: Vern Williams, Ray Park, Gerry Grove, Scott Hambly, Clyde Williamson, Pete Berg, Mayne Smith. [Photo by Campell Coe, courtesy of Scott Hambly]

Monroe's manager Ralph Rinzler on stage with the Blue Grass Boys in June 1963 at Mockingbird Hill Park near Anderson, Indiana: Bessie Lee Mauldin, Billy Sage, Rinzler, Bill Keith, Monroe, Del McCoury. [Photo by Jim Work]

A Dillards comedy routine from the mid-sixties: Dean Webb and Doug Dillard look on as straight man Mitchell Jayne talks to comic Rodney Dillard, who has partially ingested a harmonica. [Courtesy *Bluegrass Unlimited*]

The Kentucky Colonels in 1964: Roland White, Roger Bush, Clarence White, Bobby Slone, Billy Ray Latham. [Author's personal collection]

Chapter 7

The First Festival and Bluegrass Consumers: 1965–66

When Bob Dylan and the Butterfield Blues Band brought folk-rock to the Newport Folk Festival in the summer of 1965, Bill Monroe and the Blue Grass Boys were backstage witnesses. The times were changing for Monroe, too. He and his band—three citybillies and his son, James—were involved in plans afoot that summer for a bluegrass festival modeled in part on Newport. This, the first Roanoke Bluegrass Festival at Cantrell's Horse Farm in Fincastle, Virginia, was put together by Roanoke promoter Carlton Haney.

A thirty-seven-year-old native of Rockingham County in the North Carolina Piedmont, Haney had grown up immersed in, but not particularly liking, country music. A factory worker, he met Clyde Moody in Danville, Virginia, in 1953. Moody introduced him to Monroe, who, says Haney, somehow sensed in him an innate ability as a businessman. Accepting Monroe's invitation to book some local shows for him, Haney proved to have a knack for this kind of work and soon quit his factory job to become Monroe's manager. He lasted a long time with Monroe—a year and a half. Then he moved to Richmond, Virginia, where for several months he managed Hack Johnson's old band, the Farmhands. In December 1955 he became manager for another band working out of Richmond, Don Reno, Red Smiley and the Tennessee Cutups.

For Haney the primary attraction to the country music business was financial. While he liked Don Reno's banjo playing ("because he could play any song") and enjoyed the Reno and Smiley show, he didn't really appreciate bluegrass music until one night in 1957 when he witnessed a special jam session. Reno and Smiley were backstage at the Opry with Monroe and his band: "Don had the banjo and Bobby Hicks [Monroe's fiddler] was there and Charlie Cline; Chubby Wise was in that dressing room . . . and Jimmy Martin was there and I asked Jimmy Martin and Bill to sing a couple of duets like they used to, and Don was gonna play banjo and Red was there too with the guitar and they decided to do 'Live and Let Live.' Jimmy started it twice and Bill stopped both times and then Bill said 'let me start it,' and when he started it, it was in entirely different time than I'd ever heard music in and that must have been the first time that I really got interested in Blue Grass." For Haney the essence of Monroe was in the rhythm he created, a beat that would "make the hair stand up on your arm." As a promoter his thoughts quickly turned to the commercial value in his new interest: " . . . if I could get the ones who had sung with him—who *knew* it—they were the only ones who could *play* it. So I thought if I could get all of them, or some of 'em back together, and let people hear what I heard in the dressing room they'd buy tickets for it."[1]

Haney toyed with the idea for three years before he told Monroe. No doubt Haney took careful note of the subsequent success of Bill Clifton's July 4, 1961, Bluegrass Day at Luray, which he attended. But Haney does not mention this event in recounting the experiences which led him to organize the first festival. Instead he emphasizes an encounter which occurred in 1963, when Monroe introduced him to the man who would act as catalyst: "He brought Ralph Rinzler there and Rinzler started telling me things about the music that I would have never known, but even the average farmer in North Carolina or the South where they liked Blue Grass didn't know these facts, they just knew they liked it."[2] Rinzler, then Monroe's manager, found Haney a fascinating individual. "I realized he was really an intellectual, he was an historian and he was concerned with some interesting questions and we had a long and interesting talk."[3]

The following year Rinzler, now working for the Newport Folk Festival's newly created foundation, invited Haney to attend the festival. The foundation reflected a shift of emphasis by the festival directors; they were moving from a focus on stars to greater concern with the traditional, authentic, source performers and their cultures. There were fewer big concerts at the festival, more small simultaneous workshops. Rinzler was acting as a field researcher, seeking not just musicians but craftspeople, dancers, and storytellers; and he was helping to find and coordinate worthwhile folk cultural projects which the foundation could support with festival profits. Haney, Rinzler recalls, "wanted to do a real folk festival, . . . he wanted to intellectualize the approach to country and bluegrass presentations."[4] Rinzler supported and encouraged Haney by showing him Newport, particularly the workshops, which furnished a model for the history of bluegrass Haney hoped to stage.

With the festival concept in mind and Rinzler's support, Haney was close to realizing his 1957 inspiration. The final obstacle to it was removed in the spring of 1965 when Reno and Smiley split up. During their thirteen years of recording and nine years of performing together regularly, they had become one of the most influential bands in bluegrass. Of all the major bands they were the least prominent in the folk revival, never playing a festival or a coffeehouse and never the favorites of the educators and critics in the revival because of Reno's often flowery banjo style and their mainstream country music repertoire, which made them seem somewhat less "folk." Haney had not gone after the folk market, because they had plenty of business playing the country music circuits in their region. In the fall of 1964 Carlton had advertised that over 60 percent of 1965 and over 30 percent of 1966 were already booked for the band. When they split, although each formed groups which Haney continued to book, there was nevertheless more time left for festival planning.

The First Festival—September 1965

The festival was held on September 3–5, 1965. All the articles written about it call it the first bluegrass festival. Although Clifton's one-day event at Luray was also called a festival by some, Roanoke set the pattern. From it flowed first a trickle and then, in the early seventies, a torrent of bluegrass festivals. They stimulated a substantial growth of interest in bluegrass music during the early seventies and altered the music itself. Many aspects of the bluegrass festival movement grew out of the thinking of Carlton Haney.

Haney was not only an intellectual, he was a home-grown mystic who expressed his belief in the strength of Bill Monroe's music in terms of "vibrations." Seeing bluegrass as the effect of Monroe's genius and discipline upon a series of talented but unformed musicians from Clyde Moody to Peter Rowan, he set out to recreate the vibrations Monroe had caused.

As a promoter Haney knew that with relatively little advance notice he could book in most of the big names in bluegrass at the same time and place. Indeed he had been doing this since the mid-fifties within the Virginia–North Carolina region. For example, in September 1961 he booked the musical entertainment for the Surrey County Fair at Mount Airy, North Carolina. On the twenty-sixth, Bill Monroe and the Blue Grass Boys appeared; on the twenty-seventh, Jim Eanes and the Shenandoah Valley Boys; on the twenty-eighth, Don Reno and Red Smiley; on the twenty-ninth "girl singer" Barbara Allen; and on the twenty-ninth and thirtieth, the New Dominion Barn Dance Show. Bluegrass bands, all well-known in the region and certain to draw well, dominated the musical entertainment at the fair.

There are some important differences between booking a series of bluegrass shows at a county fair and bringing the same performers together for a bluegrass festival. For one thing, the county fair is attended by people who come for many reasons. It is a regular annual event which people plan to attend, to meet friends and neighbors and to view their produce and wares on display. Typically a variety of entertainment can be found—music, games, contests. In contrast the festival at Roanoke had no precedent and focused entirely upon one form of music. Haney was gambling that others shared his vision of Monroe's importance and would pay to hear little else but bluegrass for several days running.

His festival combined elements from Newport as well as from conventions like Union Grove and country music show parks like New River Ranch, Bean Blossom, and Sunset Park. During the days there were Newport-like workshops (conducted with Rinzler's aid) and Union Grove–type contests; at night, events resembled shows at country music parks and concerts at folk festivals. But it was more than a patchwork of tested elements, for it included two unique aspects, both on the final day of the festival. On Sunday morning there was a gospel concert. Religious music had always been an important part of bluegrass but rarely had any of the secular bands played an entire show devoted to this form, particularly on a Sunday morning. The religious feeling imparted in the camp-meeting setting of the festival, with its outdoor stage and open-air seating, was an appropriate preparation for the Sunday after-. noon show. This was the final event of the weekend, one which tied the festival together—an orchestrated concert which Haney titled "The Story of Bluegrass." During this, former members of Monroe's band appeared more or less in the order in which they had worked with Monroe. They recreated the songs they had recorded with Monroe and talked about his influence upon their own music. Haney acted as master of ceremonies.

Behind the scenes was Rinzler, with his knowledge about Monroe gained from interviews and research in Decca Records' Nashville files. He recalls that Haney "wanted me to emcee that and I said no way I would get up in front of an audience of country people and pontificate as an academic. I would give him the facts and, I had that discography, and tell him who played with whom, when, what songs and such; and depending upon who was available I would put together the combinations of people and he would introduce them and he'd, did a much better job than ever I could. I thought he was a brilliant emcee and that's how we put that together."[5] The "Story" (as Haney would come to call it) was in format much like the Newport workshops, but unlike those, which were held several at a time in front of relatively small groups, this was the main event, held on the main stage at a time when the largest crowd was present.

The festival was advertised in several ways. Carlton Haney Promotions mailed an 8½-by-14-inch flyer to individuals in various parts of the country that Haney had come to know through his activities as a promoter during the past decade. It began by announcing, "The nation's first All Blue Grass Music Festival will be stage [sic] Sept. 3, 4, 5 with the nation's greatest Blue Grass Musicians appearing." It promised that hundreds of great bluegrass musicians would be present, described the events, listed the bands and indi- vidual musicians appearing, and warned campers there would be limited water and cool nights. It also noted that "record companies will be recording Artist [sic] in Studio set up in Big Red Barn" all day Saturday—a planned aspect of the festival which apparently did not take place.[6] A full-page ad appeared in the September issue of *Sing Out!* It listed the bands appearing in the "First Annual Roanoke Blue Grass Festival" and mentioned in small print that there were both workshops and concerts. The tickets, which were $6.00 for the weekend, were available from Haney's Virginia address or could be purchased in New York City at The Fretted Instrument Shop, Israel Young's place on Sixth Avenue. Additional promotion appeared in the form of an announcement in *Billboard* magazine and an article by Rinzler in *Boston Broadside*, a magazine directed at folk revivalists in that region.

Among those who responded to the advertising was Mayne Smith, a 26-year-old Californian (he'd been with the Redwood Canyon Ramblers at the University of California) who had written a master's thesis, "Bluegrass Music and Musicians," for his degree in folklore at Indiana University the year before. Now enrolled in the folklore program at UCLA, he had just published a revision of his thesis—an article titled "An Introduction to Bluegrass"—in a special "hillbilly" issue of the *Journal of American Folklore*. He was sent to Haney's festival as an observer by the newly established John Edwards Memorial Foundation, an institution dedicated to the study of hillbilly and other recorded American folk music (to be discussed below).

On the day before the festival began, Smith overheard Carlton Haney explaining to a local musician that he didn't know exactly what "workshop" meant: "They have it up in New England at those festivals. It's just an instruction class." Afterwards Smith noted that Haney "had not anticipated traffic problems, and had made no plans for toilets and water supply to accommodate the numerous campers."[7] Numerous is a relative term, though. The 1965 Newport Festival attracted thousands; the blues workshop at which the Butterfield Blues Band made its debut had a crowd of over a thousand. By contrast the numbers at Roanoke were tiny. Rinzler reported afterward in *Billboard* that there had been 1,300. A report published in 1973 put it this way: "There were maybe 150 the first night and never more than 1,000."[8] The audience was characterized in various ways, but all descriptions shared the perception of the citybillies as a group apart. Rinzler reported: "Several hundred city-billy enthusiasts and musicians wearing the uniform (blue jeans, a few beards and sandals or tennis shoes) mixed with salt-of-the-earth farmers and factory workers from nearby Roanoke. It looked as though someone had grasped a handful of the Newport Folk Festival and dropped it in the midst of an informal Sunday country pickin' pickinic."[9] Mayne Smith called the citybillies "New York City Pickers" and noted that the New York Ramblers, who had won the band prize at Union Grove the year before, "impressed people during this afternoon's amateur concert." But he "noticed several evidences of resentment from local musicians at the expensive instruments and somewhat mechanical precision of city boys."[10]

While there was some polarization between the citybillies and the hillbillies in the small crowd, many of those present shared an enthusiasm for the music which transcended cultural differences. These were the people who worked hard to follow bluegrass, the dyed-in-the-wool followers. Searching local record shops for their favorite artists, they were often forced to order their records by mail from Jimmie Skinner or Starday. In order to hear bluegrass, they traveled to country parks, coffeehouses, hillbilly bars, and folk festivals. They tolerated other kinds of music they didn't like and audience members they found offensive in order to hear bluegrass. They eagerly read the few articles published about the music and gleaned what information they could from the down-home or folk revival rhetoric of bluegrass album liner notes. The bands that toured full time constituted a source of information about the music and were the links in a network of bluegrass followers. The enthusiasts attended the appearances of such bands not just to take in the show but also to tape it, buy the bands' latest records, and spend time backstage meeting or renewing acquaintances with the band members and other followers. Such enthusiasts were willing to make long pilgrimages to see a bluegrass show; often they made a point of going backstage to tell the band how far they had driven.

For every one person of this type around the country, there were four or five more friends, neighbors, co-workers, relatives, or schoolmates sharing an interest in the music. Often these people played bluegrass together at jam sessions or in local semi-professional bands. Their audiences and musical disciples formed an outer circle around the enthusiasts and their close friends and musical partners. Most of the people who showed up at Roanoke were at the center of such circles; they were the true believers, the leaders of the flock. And they returned home with reports of who was there and what it was like.

Not unexpectedly, a high proportion of those attending were musicians, and one of the things mentioned by almost everyone who attended was the high quality of the informal music sessions. Fred Bartenstein, later to be editor of one of the bluegrass monthlies, recalled that on the first day one of the first things he encountered as he walked toward the stage was "Fred Pike and Don Reno sitting on a picnic table playing guitars."[11] Similar stories were told of well-known figures, like Reno, seen in jam sessions with very capable but then little known regional favorites, like New Englander Pike.

Reports from Roanoke differed according to the perspective of the participants, but the consensus was that on stage "The Story of Bluegrass" was the centerpiece of the festival. It was the culmination of the process which had begun when Rinzler interviewed Monroe in 1962. Bluegrass fans knew that various important musicians had played with him. But on which recordings, and when? Not until June 1965 when Decca released the album *Bluegrass Instrumentals*—the first historically oriented collection of Monroe's recordings—was any such information publicly available. Rinzler's detailed notes explained the titles of and stories behind the tunes, sometimes using quotes from his interviews with Monroe, and who played what on each tune and when each was recorded. For most fans of Bill Monroe this album marked the first time his music had been explained.

In "The Story of Blue Grass Music" at Roanoke, Carlton Haney's mystic sense of the dramatic was added to Rinzler's research on the history of Monroe's music. This concert was supposed to show how Bill stood at the center of bluegrass music, interacting with various musicians who added their personal ingredients to it. The show began as Haney called for silence, so that Monroe and his band could open with "Mule Skinner Blues," the first song Monroe had performed on the Opry with the Blue Grass Boys in 1939 and, therefore, the first bluegrass song.

Stress was placed on the special rhythm of the music, rather than on the instrumentation, and emphasis was given to the fact that Clyde Moody (present on stage) was one of the first guitarists to play bluegrass guitar and Stringbean the first banjo picker. Haney passed quickly over Flatt and Scruggs: "Joining Bill Monroe then was two fellows that—one come from North Carolina and one came from Tennessee. We don't have 'em here with us today but we wished we could. Lester Flatt and Earl Scruggs. And they recorded many, many songs with Bill Monroe. And a . . . a lot of 'em are in your collections today."[12]

The day before the festival began, Monroe had read Mayne Smith's newly published "Introduction to Bluegrass" and, in Smith's words "was quite upset by it . . . felt I had overstressed Scruggs' importance and underrated his own by saying that bluegrass started in 1945." He challenged Smith to correct what he saw as "damn lies" about Scruggs's importance.[13] This behind-the-scenes bitterness was carefully kept down by Haney, although there were noticeable signs of tension when, following the brief mention of Flatt and Scruggs in "The Story," the Stanley Brothers were introduced.

In an enigmatic whispered aside to Monroe, Haney said, "I believe they gon' do a couple songs here while you all tune, Bill. I'm sorry. They'll be on this tape, but we'll cut it out." That the show was being taped revealed its importance to Monroe, who, with Haney and Rinzler, thought of it as a unique event which, like a ritual, had to be done properly and would be recorded as a document. Today the importance of that fact has been obscured by the repetition of "Story"-type rituals by Monroe at subsequent festivals. But there was no assurance in 1965 that this would ever happen again, and when the Stanleys came on stage, Monroe chose not to leave, sitting on the stage while they sang.

Later, after Bill had sung a duet with Carter Stanley, he made the statement, quoted earlier, about the Stanley Brothers being "the first group that I ever heard that was following in my footsteps. . . ." He was now able to discuss in public the copying that had so bothered him because it was part of the "Story," a ritual in his honor.

Having clearly established just who it was that started bluegrass and who followed whom in the history, Monroe welcomed his former sidemen, graciously accepting their adulation as teacher and boss. Don Reno told him:

"Bill, there's one thing that you've always tried to do and I respect you for it, to the highest, is try to help all these young folks that we can to learn this style of stuff to keep it going, 'cause it's something that we want folks a long time after we're gone to keep hearing it." Monroe replied, "Yes, sir." And Reno carried on, "I mean, that's how much, that's how much we love this sound." Monroe responded, "You do, right," and Reno continued, talking about how bluegrass "is just now getting ready to really go!" And Monroe replied, "Bluegrass music—a lot of music is died out but bluegrass music will never die, I don't believe." The audience began to applaud as Reno answered, "It'll never die out as long as folks like this here still like it. And it makes me feel good to see representatives from all over the United States."

This spontaneous exchange was the model for similar statements by Monroe in many subsequent festivals. It drew the audience into the music by calling for their support as believers. Like a true religion, it was worth sacrifice and hard work. Years later veterans of the first festival recalled sleeping in cars, the lack of food, the poor facilities. But, said one, "these were part of the dues that we paid to hear what was then an obscure music."[14]

In recalling the first festival, Ralph Rinzler points out that Monroe, who is now somewhat tired of being interviewed about his music, "still was thinking things through . . . enjoying the fact that he had never talked on the stage very much and all of a sudden he was becoming a valuable grandfather of bluegrass and everyone was acknowledging, because of what he was saying, the real role that he had played." In the "Story," he talked about the way he worked his men on the Opry: "I did work 'em hard, I'll own up to it. We worked six and seven days a week. I worked eleven years on the Grand Ole Opry, never missed a Saturday night. And I did work 'em hard, but it's made better men out of 'em." Jimmy Martin, who was standing next to him, broke in: "May I say something right now?" Monroe responded, "Take Jimmy Martin here, yes, sir." Martin began, "You said you worked us hard; I enjoyed it. . . . Did you ever hear me grumble?"

Monroe: "Never a bit."

Martin: "Get in the car and let's roll to another town, right?"

Monroe: "Always in there."

Martin: "Thank you, I appreciate that, I wanted to say that."

Monroe: "Yes, sir."

As the audience laughed and applauded in appreciation of this exchange, Monroe called Martin back to the mike. Martin said, "They always say, they always tell out, throughout the country, say Bill Monroe's hard on his boys. I say he ain't if you got what he wants and lay in there and work, you, he'll be good to you." "That's right, you're right," Monroe answered, and Martin continued, "I don't reckon I ever asked you for a dollar I didn't get." "You got every dollar, every penny," Monroe cracked, as the audience laughed again. He carried on with a long recital of how all the best Blue Grass Boys had worked hard. Later, Carter Stanley added his affirmation: " . . . what I've always said ever since I got acquainted with Bill Monroe. He wants you to do your job and be a man, ain't nothing wrong with that, are they?"

The parade of Monroe sidemen across the stage led up to the present band—citybillies Peter Rowan (from Boston), Lamar Grier (from Washington), and Gene Lowinger (the fiddler from Millburn, New Jersey, whom Monroe regularly introduced as "the only Jewish bluegrass cowboy in the country"),[15] along with his son James Monroe on bass. Afterwards festival-goers talked about how this relatively inexperienced band had risen to the occasion, giving a fitting climax to the afternoon's show.

Citybilly Rick Riman recalled in 1973: "I began to realize there was another side of Blue Grass different from Flatt and Scruggs and the Country Gentlemen . . . the intoxication of seeing Monroe with Reno, Benny Martin and Mac Wiseman, together for the first time since 1949, hearing Jimmy Martin and Bill Monroe sing 'Memories of Mother and Dad,' even the performances of the lesser known Clyde Moody, all really opened my head. It was more than a festival. It was, for me at least, the beginning of an education in Monroe and his music." Country boy Herschel Freeman saw it in somewhat different terms: "Looming above them all, larger than life, was the legend himself, Bill Monroe, satisfaction gleaming through his mute features at the return of all his prodigal sons. It was his festival and as he shed each set of noted sidemen in a glorious re-creation of his storied career, a feeling of awe and reverence rose in everyone. It was a scene of poignancy and power I shall never forget."[16]

The success of this show must be attributed in large measure to Haney. He was able to bring the diverse crowd together in part because of the way in which he presented his own experience with Monroe and bluegrass. He began by admitting that even when he was working as Monroe's manager he had not liked or understood Bill's music. The turning point at the backstage Opry jam session was described in such a way as to emphasize that he, like the citybillies, had only recently discovered Monroe and that even for country boys like him an appreciation of bluegrass music was an acquired taste, something one learned rather than took for granted. This discovery and learning, expressed in an affirmation of Monroe's central role in the music, was at the heart of the bluegrass festival movement.

The day after Roanoke ended, Mayne Smith interviewed Carlton Haney. Haney, speaking in mystical terms about Monroe's music and its effect on other musicians, told of Rudy Lyle, the Virginia banjo picker who had followed Don Reno in the Blue Grass Boys and had been on most of Monroe's recordings between 1949 and 1954: "There's a form of bluegrass that if a man reaches and plays it he'll never be able to play anything else again. And if he can't play that, he won't play nothing. . . . He'd rather quit than play anything else." Lyle had returned to Monroe's band after a stint in the Army and, according to Haney: "When he came back, his mind was at the same place as when he left but his hands couldn't do it. . . . If you can't play what your mind hears, . . . people won't pay to listen to it. The people know when you're transferring your mind—your thoughts—through your hands to them and that's when you're playing bluegrass. And that's when we did it yesterday—to thousands—which has been my dream; and that's why we had the festival. And I saw men crying. One time I had to leave the stage." Smith noted that "Haney's eyes—and mine— watered as he said this." It was, they agreed, a kind of religious experience, and even Lowinger, still somewhat of an apprentice fiddler, had played with inspiration during the "Story."[17]

As Rinzler, writing a few days later for *Billboard*, said, the atmosphere had become "more and more intense" and "the audience unified in response."[18] That Monroe could excite such emotion not just with his famous sidemen from his most creative years, but also with his current band, symbolized the blending of citybillies and country folk that attended the show. Those who were there talked about it to all their friends. It had never happened before, and who knew if it would happen again?

Bluegrass as Country Music: The Last Song

For a veteran pro like Jimmy Martin, the problems which bluegrass faced within the world of country music were underscored by the small crowds at Roanoke, for the music could only exist if fans supported it. During the Saturday night show, Martin performed "Widow Maker," his hit from the previous year, and talked to the audience about its success on the country charts: "It's real hard to get songs in the charts because other kinds of music is taking it over and so we got this one in there and got it up, about up number six. And we'd like to say thanks to you folks for asking us to do it. . . . " Then he introduced his newest recording: "Here's a song that we've got released on Decca. Just released, I don't know if you've heard it or not. If you like it, I'd like to ask you to write to all the disc jockeys and see if you can make it hit the top ten for me, 'cause I need the help. . . . I'll tell you true, somebody needs it. Somebody needs it, if we don't get no bigger crowds that this, how in the world we all gon' get paid?"[19] The song was called "The Last Song" and told of a country performer who was barely making ends meet but was caught up in his music and giving it "one more try."[20]

The blend of commercialism and altruistic devotion to the music which the song expressed, and to which Martin appealed in asking his audience to support the song, was typical of country music and bluegrass. Martin, more forthright on stage than most, put it bluntly: *if you like my kind of music, you will have to support it in the marketplace.* To him, as to most of his fellow professional bluegrass musicians, the emotional attachment to the music was intertwined with commercial pragmatism. "Other kinds of music" were "taking over," and only a concerted effort by fans would bring bluegrass back. Letters to disc jockeys, purchase of records, and support by attendance at personal appearances—these were the solution.

Martin's point of view reflected his training in the country music world of the early fifties. Like most pioneer bluegrass musicians, he thought of himself as a country musician. He believed that country musicians succeeded through the loyal support of fans, channeled through certain democratic communications institutions like the country deejay. But even during 1958–60, the period of Martin's first successes on his own as a country performer, when he moved from the bars of Detroit to the Louisiana Hayride and then to the World's Original Jamboree on WWVA, the role of the deejay as the arbiter of taste was changing.

Since the mid-fifties, when Presley and other rockabillies began to appear not just in the country charts but also in R&B and pop charts, the country deejays' programming decisions had grown complicated. These crossovers and others like them (pop records doing well in country, R&B in pop, etc.) led to good sales but made the market difficult to predict and follow. There was a trade-off, too, between high short-term sales and lower long-term sales; some performers had one massive hit and were never heard from again, others had long strings of lesser-volume successes. Which was more important? It was hard to tell. There were different constituencies involved; pleasing one might alienate another.

Many older listeners wanted what was being called, by 1958, the traditional sound. More younger listeners wanted the new pop-flavored sound. Some singers, like Rusty York, did well with both; others did not. But in general the so-called traditional singers were at a disadvantage because the pop-oriented singers got greater exposure in the media. As one analyst wrote in 1958, "Their continued appearances before the public in media more attractive to teen buyers in many cases surpasses the relative exposure of the traditional C&W artist."[21] To at least some disk jockeys, this seemed like unfair competition. *Billboard*'s country music diarist Bill Sachs described the result in a March 1958 article: "Most of the nation's top C&W deejays, particularly those in the more metropolitan areas, are going along with the country field's transition by placing the tunes requested by their listeners, whether they be so-called 'pure' country, rockabilly, or pop. A small percentage have dedicated themselves to keeping the C&W field cleansed of anything but the traditional or what they term 'pure' country music. In most instances this minority programs the type of music it feels its listeners should hear rather than the music the listener might prefer."[22]

Sachs was setting forth the standard perspective of the Nashville-dominated country music industry. "Progress" was highly valued. That country music should have a particular kind of sound, deal with certain topics, or take certain stances in its lyrics—these were restrictive ideas that impeded progress. That listener requests ought to govern programming had been a tenet of country music radio since the forties. But now the increasing divergence in audience tastes—between young and old, conservative and progressive—put the deejays on the spot. What *was* country music? Which were the more important constituencies?

Several months after Roanoke, early in 1966, novelist (*True Grit*) and country fan Charles Portis wrote in the *Saturday Evening Post* about the Nashville sound. He pointed out that "to ask serious questions about country music—apart from what it's doing in the charts—is to draw blank looks." An exception, he said, lay in Bill Monroe, "the father of bluegrass picking, and his proteges, Flatt and Scruggs." Like Chet Atkins, they took their work seriously. But "a good many of the singers, one gathers, would turn to pop music tomorrow morning if they could change their accents and get booked in Las Vegas. They yearn to see their records in the pop charts, where the money is. At the same time they must be careful not to alienate their country fans, who are a jealous lot." As Portis wryly noted, "the situation makes for curious ideas of loyalty." One example he gave was Buck Owens and his "Buck Owens Pledge to Country Music": " 'I shall sing no song that is not a country song,' it goes, and 'I shall make no record that is not a country record,' and so on. Fair enough, except that one of Buck's latest releases, a big seller, is an instrumental called 'Buckaroo' that you can do the Watusi to."[23]

Country music fans have always been more conservative than the performers, who must hew to a line between their own impulses to innovate and their conservative fans' pressures toward creative stagnation. The changes caused by rock and roll during the late fifties were disturbing to older fans, who were not used to and did not care for horns, echo chambers, drums, choruses, and string sections. These elements were components of the Nashville sound which made it palatable to people who didn't usually care for country music. Even when the obviously pop elements were not present, the Nashville-sound string ensemble rarely included the fiddle and steel guitar. They were "too corny." Under the impetus of the CMA initiative to make a product that would be more widely marketable, the country music of the late fifties and early sixties was moving "uptown" to resemble pop music. Some good solid country recordings were still being made, but they didn't seem to get a fair shake from the disc jockeys.

In the mid-fifties, when the charts listed no more than ten or fifteen songs each week, deejays had considerable control over what they played. In 1958 the *Billboard* charts began listing thirty songs, in 1964 the number went to fifty, and in October 1966 to seventy-five. As the numbers rose deejays tended more frequently to choose all of their songs from the charts. During the same period, there was extensive growth in country music radio as the cross-over phenomena enabled country music record programs to draw more listeners in metropolitan areas. Here advertisers and radio station owners became more interested in investing in country music.

Several factors made the new metropolitan country radio different from earlier country radio. The owners, advertisers, and deejays were rarely country music fans. They were involved with the music because it was a good *investment*. Since the deejays did not know much about the music, when they began doing their programs they turned to the charts for guidance. This tended to homogenize the music as regional favorites were neglected by deejays and radio stations that did not know they existed because they weren't in the charts. Moreover, these radio stations were not particularly interested in cultivating the older country music fans, since they had discovered that more new listeners could be attracted by the country music records closest in sound to pop music. Hence, the old ties between country music radio and other forms of country music performance tended to take on a somewhat different form. The deejays were more closely in touch with the national scene—they might even go to the annual deejay convention held each fall in conjunction with the Opry's birthday celebration—than with the local or regional scene. And because more often than not they were johnny-come-latelies to the music, they were not aware of its history.

The lack of awareness was not eased by the tendency of stations to turn to programming consultants when they adopted the country music format. In advising the urban country radio stations to play to urban tastes, they usually suggested avoiding the older "down-home" type music. And quite often the label they used for this was "bluegrass." No longer a fans' code word, the term was known widely in the music industry. By 1965 it had been used to associate this musical form both with country music and with folk music. For some this meant that it clearly did not belong on progressive country radio. Not only was it old-fashioned country music, it also was the music of the folkniks, long-haired beatniks, and protesters. So it was unacceptable on two counts.

Bluegrass was not completely absent from the post-1958 enlarged charts, which amalgamated data about juke box plays, retail sales, radio plays, and regional favorites. In fact it did better "on the charts" during the period between 1958 and 1963 than at any other time in its history. During this period an average of three bluegrass records appeared each year on the *Billboard* country top thirty. Flatt and Scruggs predominated, with half of all the chart songs during the period, but others were represented—Jimmy Martin, Bill Monroe, Reno and Smiley, and the Stanley Brothers. In 1964, when the charts were upped to fifty, there were seven bluegrass recordings—the highest for any single year—including four by Flatt and Scruggs.

There was (and is) no direct correlation between having a hit single and sales. In 1966, Portis reported that "a record can make the top five in the country charts and not sell more than 15,000 copies."[24] Most country singles went to juke boxes and radio stations; country performers made most of their

money from personal appearances and album sales. Hit singles helped promote appearances and sell albums because they gave much-needed media
exposure.

A song had to have some special selling point to do well on the charts. Of
the eighteen bluegrass songs on the charts between 1958 and 1963, most of
the eight which did better than the average of ten weeks on the chart,
reaching the number seventeen position or higher, were unusual in various
ways: they included a comedy routine (the Stanley Brothers' "How Far to
Little Rock"); "inspirational" songs ("Cabin on the Hill" and "Go Home" by
Flatt and Scruggs, Lonnie Irving's "Pinball Machine," a recitation); and
television-related items (Flatt and Scruggs's "The Ballad of Jed Clampett" and
"Pearl Pearl Pearl"). The plain old bluegrass country songs tended not to do
well on the charts. Bluegrass hits were, in one way or another, novelties.

In several ways, the sound of newer country music was beginning to diverge
from that of bluegrass. The basic beat of the honky-tonk sound of singers like
Ray Price dominated the country sound of the early sixties in the music of
Buck Owens, George Jones, and others like them. Held together by a steady
four-beat bass in generally slower tempos to a shuffle rhythm, it was not easy
to duplicate in bluegrass, which emphasizes the second and fourth beat.
Adding to the divergence was the fact that the volume and sustaining prop-
erties of electric instruments had become an integral part of mainstream
country. Occasionally an acoustic instrument was featured on a regular country hit—as in Cowboy Copas's "Alabam"—but in general the bluegrass sound
was beginning to seem anomalous.

Bluegrass recordings reached country music charts not on the basis of their
bluegrass-ness but because of novel or unique textual content. This is true,
in a way, for virtually all country hits; emphasis is on songs crafted with
striking punch lines called "hooks." The charts also show that once a band
had one good hit they were more likely to get on the charts with a second
one, and that records produced on major labels had a better chance of
appearing on the charts. The odd exception proved the rule: the Country
Gentlemen, recording for the small Washington, D.C., area label Rebel, had
"Bringing Mary Home" on the charts in 1965 for four weeks, reaching the
number forty-three position. Given the fact that the band was at that time
basically a regional favorite which played more colleges than country music
parks, its success was surprising and owed much to the popular appeal of the
"vanishing hitchhiker" legend it retold.

After 1964 the number of bluegrass singles on the charts dropped sharply.
Martin's "The Last Song" didn't make it in 1965, and in 1966 only one of
the four bluegrass songs to make the charts was on for more than four weeks
and got above number forty—the Osborne Brothers' "The Kind of Woman I
Got." And for some bluegrass fans, that was really not bluegrass; Sonny's
banjo sounded like an electric guitar. Things didn't look promising for bluegrass in the world of country music.

The Bluegrass Bulletin

The small group of committed musicians and fans at Roanoke hoped to revitalize bluegrass music. But doing this within the structure of the country music industry seemed a difficult, if not insurmountable, task. The leadership and structure would have to come from elsewhere. Just as the fans had named the music, they would now have to promote it and protect it. By the end of a year, at the beginning of the second Roanoke Festival, the beginnings of a bluegrass consumers' movement had appeared.

One sign of the beginnings of this bluegrass revival was the appearance of ads directed at bluegrass consumers in folksong revival publications. In the January 1965 issue of *Sing Out!*, a small ad appeared for a bluegrass banjo course from P.[eter] A. Richardson in Florida. By the November issue, Richardson was advertising as "The Bluegrass Bookshelf."[25] In the same month, he edited and published the first issue of the *Bluegrass Bulletin.* According to its masthead, it was "published by the American Bluegrass Society for the promotion and preservation of old time BLUEGRASS MUSIC." A major portion of the first three-page mimeographed number was devoted to Richardson's "The Bluegrass Band. . . . Article No. 1 in a LONG, LONG series on the subject." His first point was that "ALL INSTRUMENTS IN A BLUEGRASS BAND ARE NON-AMPLIFIED. . . . " By way of further explanation, he added: "Now, certainly you can play in the BLUEGRASS IDIOM or BLUE-GRASS STYLE with amplified instruments, but you cease to be a BLUEGRASS BAND when the amplifier is used. COUNTRY MUSIC means a million different things today, and the field is getting so broad that rock and roll and jazz are a regular part of it along with a heap of other rot. So, you can have (and call it) a COUNTRY BAND with all sorts of instruments, but it won't be a BLUE-GRASS BAND, not in the least."[26] He went on to list the mandatory instruments—guitar, string bass, mandolin, fiddle, Dobro, and five-string banjo.

Having drawn a clear, if opinionated, distinction between bluegrass and country music, Richardson proceeded in subsequent articles to expound on other definitions of the style. In the March 1966 issue he editorialized on "What Is and What Is Not 'Traditional Bluegrass' Anyhow?????" Here he dealt with the meaning, content, and lyrics of bluegrass music: "Bluegrass is charistically [sic] interested in interpreting the sounds of nature and material things of our human existence, say like trains, falling leaves, wagons hauling timber or cane, mules braying (the list went on) . . . and buddy, that is happiness and that is weariness like something else." But it was not folk music: "It doesn't concern itself with burning draft cards, that is for the pseudo-folknik who have had a hard day at the demonstrations, and all that democracy defeating junk. This thing called Bluegrass is interested in saying something about a human being, not a draft card—maybe the draft card holder, but not the draft card. . . . And it is indeed interested in long hair, but not the kind the Beatniks wear, but the kind a guy wears because he can't find the money and time for a decent haircut. He is the guy who needs a Banjo string more than a haircut."[27] To Richardson as to many outside the folk revival, folk music was "protest music" of beatniks—the sound of Dylan and Baez.

Richardson's editorials were shrill and feisty; the *Bulletin* often consisted mainly of his writing and ads for various services of the Bluegrass Bookshelf such as banjo and guitar courses, books, and instruments. In layout and writing style, the magazine was like many country music fan club publications—amateurish, enthusiastic. It was apparent that many of the contributors had never written for a magazine before, and there was little evidence of the editor's hand in matters of style. The very dimensions of the *Bulletin* changed from issue to issue, making it a librarian's nightmare. But it is unlikely that any library subscribed to it. The membership of the American Bluegrass Society appears to have reached no more than about 200, and the *Bulletin* was never widely circulated during its two years of existence. Nevertheless it attracted members and correspondents from many different places. For instance, Mike Hayes, a native of Bacchus Marsh, outside of Melbourne, Australia, wrote about his group, the Hayes Brothers. He told of their conversion to bluegrass and their use of Australian old-time music songs in that style: "We are able to play the country centres where there is not electricity for the twangy instruments of most country bands."[28]

Other readers described their musical experiences as participants or spectators. One regular contributor was Norman Carlson, a native of rural upstate New York, then a student at Purdue University in West Lafayette, Indiana. He began with reviews of shows he had attended at the Brown County Jamboree in Bean Blossom, eventually described the bluegrass scene at Purdue, and initiated a series of pieces on the history of bluegrass music. Carlson, like most of those writing for or to the *Bulletin*, felt frustrated by the lack of information; who, he wanted to know, was the fiddler on Monroe's early recordings? He speculated about such questions in his articles. As a fan he evaluated the performances he witnessed in subjective terms, praising highly the down-home sounds of the bands he liked in an articulate manner which reflected the well-thought-out intellectual position he took concerning the music he loved. Suspicious of city folk and eager to know more about the music he liked, Carlson wrote at length for virtually every issue of the *Bulletin*.

Features which appeared in this first bluegrass periodical that would be included in later magazines included banjo and guitar tablatures, record reviews, and articles about personal experiences with the music. One member wrote about growing up listening to the older country music and his discovery of bluegrass; a few issues later his wife contributed "Woes of a Bluegrass Wife." From time to time Richardson indicated that they would not print "argumentative or quarrelsome letters. . . . I receive a lot of this type of mail," he admitted.[29] As the publishers of later bluegrass magazines were to discover, enthusiastic and committed fans did not always agree about what was good or right about the music they loved.

There were many such problems inherent in promoting this commercial music. In one long editorial, Richardson dealt with a basic problem—the tendency of fan clubs to become personality cults. He began by expressing regret that country and western magazines and papers "spends [sic] so much time giving details about 'stars' life . . . and so little to the MUSIC per-se. . . . The whole thing seems to get turned around and upside down. We have fan clubs that are devoted to nothing else than getting the star popular and let the music per se be hanged. Earl Scruggs and Don Reno are great Banjo men, and I like them a heap, but I like them because they bring me good Bluegrass Banjo music. . . . I don't care about the string tie, pretty boots and all that junk." Like Carlson, Richardson wanted to know more about the music, wanted performers to discuss their performances. "Jazz singers and performers are much more ethical about this thing than our Bluegrass stars are—they will speak to the people about what they feel. . . . "[30]

The *Bluegrass Bulletin* reflected the ebullience of a group of people who, finding their voice in the media, had discovered interests which others shared. Tired of being manipulated as consumers of the music they liked, they wanted to learn, and they were ready to tell one another about their likes and dislikes. Like Richardson, they wanted the musicians they enjoyed to deal with their music as art, to talk seriously. It is this viewpoint which makes the *Bulletin*, as well as other early bluegrass periodicals, so interesting. They represent a combining of fan and critic as an intense love of the music was joined with a desire to know more about it and to understand why some performances were better than others. In addition, they projected a feeling that the music somehow existed in spite of, or transcended, the context in which they found it, namely the world of country music. In one way or another, the feeling was expressed that the paradox of this meaningful music in what was often a meaningless setting must be resolved and explained.

County Sales

This idea that the music deserved better than it was getting appeared in different forms at this time. Publications such as *Bluegrass Bulletin* represented one aspect; County Records and its mail-order outlet, County Sales, represented another. At the first Roanoke Festival, there was one individual present selling records—David Freeman, founder, owner, and manager of County Records of New York City. Freeman was an example of something rare in the business—a record company owner who truly loved and understood the music he marketed. A native New Yorker, Freeman had been collecting old-time hillbilly records since the fifties. Through operating his record auctions by mail and selling and buying records door to door in the

South he came to feel there was a potential market for reissues. Modeling his first albums on those produced by Origin Jazz, a blues reissue label, and using the expertise and facilities of his father, a printer, he got his own County label underway in 1963–64. The first four County albums (501–504) were anthologies of pre-war mountain region fiddle tunes, songs, and ballads. County's first brochure explained that the series "is intended to help preserve recordings of unusual quality and interest, and to make them available to the collector, student, and serious fan of Country & Old-Time Music."[31] He advertised that each record in the series was limited to an edition of 500, partially to avoid the attention of the various major labels that owned the rights to the reissued recordings but mainly to stimulate sales to collectors anxious not to miss out on each record. In 1964 County issued the first in its contemporary recording series, an album devoted to old-time clawhammer banjo.

By the time of the Roanoke Festival, Freeman's first bluegrass album (County 702), by Larry Richardson and Red Barker, was available. It was the first of a series of County bluegrass releases that would eventually have considerable impact on the market.

Freeman's early releases were not best-sellers. More important was his mail-order service, County Sales, which began in 1965. By 1966 he was publishing a newsletter advertising his own records and others which he kept in stock. Not only did he fill a void by providing a single source for purchasers of this music, he also furnished valuable and trustworthy information about the records he sold in brief reviews of new records in each newsletter. He advertised that County had "FASTEST SERVICE—BIGGEST SELECTION—DISCOUNTS—ALL POSTAGE PAID." "If you are looking for a COUNTRY, MOUNTAIN, OLD-TIME FOLK, or BLUEGRASS album, the chances are excellent that we can ship it the same day."[32]

Freeman's operation reflected changes taking place in the record business during the mid-sixties. Hit singles were selling in smaller numbers. Country music consumers, teenagers, and similar low-income groups that through the fifties and into the sixties had purchased singles were now buying albums. As this market grew, the demand for specialty albums of all kinds increased. At the same time, advances in electronics had brought the price of record making down. If performers made their own recordings on a "home recorder" (some of which were close to professional standard) or used local radio station facilities after hours, they could create a master tape at no cash cost other than that of the tape. Custom pressing plants sold package deals, offering 500 or 1000 albums with two-, three-, or four-color jackets at fixed rates. In this way a group could produce its own LP for a little more than a thousand dollars.

In such circumstances it was just as easy to make an LP as a single. Often the musicians would put up their own capital for such productions and divide the sales profits. One thousand copies of an album would cost $1.00 each and could be resold at three times that, so that the artist or band only had to sell 334 albums to break even. Performers sold these at personal appearances or through mail orders sent to their homes, and thus frequently the entire transaction was done without any tax being charged or collected. This was grass-roots capitalism of a kind only a step away from barter. Variations on this pattern were legion. A disc jockey might offer to produce and promote the record for a fixed price, with the band receiving so many records in return. Small local studios proliferated; many had come into being during the early years of rock and roll when "independent" singers were a good investment risk. Such studios did regional custom recordings—rock and country records, radio station jingles, custom albums of church choirs, high school bands, and barbershop quartets—and were in a position to handle whatever came their way, including bluegrass.

At the outset Freeman's own County label was an example of this type of operation. The reissues came not from the original record company masters but via tape copies of old 78s in the collections of Freeman and other country record collectors. Custom pressed, with jackets printed in an economical black and white, they represented a departure from the vertical integration of the big independents and the major companies. Other companies, like Piedmont and a host of other blues labels, were doing the same thing.

In *County Newsletter* no. 4 for June 1966 Freeman advertised a spectrum of records reflecting this and other trends in the bluegrass and old-time album business. There was a record "put out by Moose Lodge in Galax" of various old-time and bluegrass bands recorded at the 1965 Thirtieth Annual Galax (Virginia) Fiddlers Convention. "Poor recording quality," Freeman noted, "but collectors item."[33] His price: $3.50 (at this time major-label monaural records—remember them?—were selling for $3.98 and stereophonic for $4.98). Also on the list was a new album by Tom (Clarence) Ashley and Tex Isley. Decades earlier both of these Appalachian musicians had been hillbilly recording stars; now they were being marketed by Folkways, the oldest independent ethnic and "folk" label, as traditional performers. From the older country music independents there were reissues of bluegrass singles recorded in the fifties and early sixties—from Dot, an album of Mac Wiseman singles; from King, a Reno and Smiley retrospective. A new independent country label in southern California, Rural Rhythm, had one new record on Freeman's list, by an Ohio bluegrass band, Jim Greer and the Mac-O-Chee Valley Folks. Unlike Dot and King, Rural Rhythm did not have its own studio. The gossip among bluegrass musicians in Ohio and Indiana was that for a price this label would produce an album of twenty songs and guarantee to distribute it by mail order; all you had to do was send in the tape. The company, which had a mail-order business similar to Freeman's, flourished in the late sixties and early seventies.

This *County Newsletter* no. 4 included various other album types, such as a bluegrass gospel album "on odd Ala. label," Loyal, by the Sullivan Family, a little-known Mississippi outfit.[34] Also advertised were two reissues by a major label, Decca, of recordings by Bill Monroe and Uncle Dave Macon. These were the result of Ralph Rinzler's work as Monroe's manager, which led to contacts with Decca records. From time to time, such contacts resulted in significant reissues by major labels. Generally these companies seldom knew which among the many older recordings they owned were of marketable value. Although collectors clamored for reissues from the big companies, it was expensive for them to do the market research, find the masters, and produce the records. Only when someone like Rinzler, who had done the research and knew the market, was accessible to them, did such reissues appear. Typical of the lassitude of big companies like Decca with regard to reissues, these albums did not begin appearing until two years after Rinzler first went to Nashville. Finally, in addition to the reissues and small label recordings, County Sales listed a few new releases on major and independent labels of interest to serious collectors of bluegrass and old-time, like Jimmy Martin's new Decca LP, *Mr. Good 'N' Country Music*, with "The Last Song" on it, and Moore and Napier's King album, *More Truck Driver Songs*.

Though County was not selling just bluegrass, bluegrass dominated its sales lists. Most of the old-time recordings they marketed came from the Southeast, frequently from the mountain regions—music that some called "prebluegrass." Freeman sought his market not among the city consumers who had come to bluegrass and old-time through the revival, though his customers included some of those people, but among "serious collectors." Many of these were the same individuals who came to the first Roanoke Festival, so it was no accident that Freeman was there selling his records.

The John Edwards Memorial Foundation

The formation and growth of County Sales showed that in addition to the proliferation of specialty albums in old-time and bluegrass, there was new interest in the history of country music. Both reflected the activities of hillbilly record collectors. For at least a decade and a half, collectors like David Freeman had been buying and selling their used records via auction lists which were mailed out to other collectors who would then mail in their bids. Freeman, like some others who sold records in this way, offered to tape selections on the list for those who did not actually win the record they bid on. Through his participation in this country music record collectors' network, he came to know which records were most sought after. Individual collectors specialized in certain artists, seeking to obtain complete sets of these performers' recordings. They would pay dearly for obscure pressings, even if the performances on them were not very good. Often it was the poorly performed or badly recorded songs that had not sold well which became rare and sought after.

But not all collectors were speculators. Many were just trying to obtain records they had not been able to own when originally issued. As youths, these collectors had been introduced to hillbilly music by radio broadcasts and had become fans. They had not been able to afford records at that time. In some cases they lived on farms, many miles from stores that carried records. By the end of the fifties, country music mail-order stores like Skinner's were no longer carrying these out-of-print 78s, but they often put people in touch with collectors they knew about. In 1952 the first country music record-collector's publication, *Disc Collector,* appeared. It crowded auction lists, discographies, artist biographies, record reviews, and other disc-related items onto its mimeographed pages. From an interest in records came curiosity about the recording careers and lives of the performers and hence discographies and biographies of individuals. Just as antique collectors seek to authenticate the provenience of their old furniture to assure its value, record collectors found value in information pertaining to their old discs.

Serious interest in early country music was even rarer in the early fifties than in 1966, when Portis found little evidence of it in Nashville. There was some interest as a result of the Lomax and Folkways reissues, but few country music fans and record collectors knew of these, for such people rarely purchased albums. *Disc Collector* drew together people from many regions, representing a variety of perspectives and musical tastes. There weren't many record collectors seriously interested in hillbilly and folk music, so they found common cause in spite of their differences. Early issues dealt with everyone from Jimmie Rodgers to Burl Ives. Writing in the third issue of the magazine, for example, was "The Professor," D. K. Wilgus, the first scholar to work extensively with hillbilly recordings. Another early contributor was Australian record collector John Edwards. By 1959 Edwards, along with other record collector-scholars like Archie Green, a specialist in labor history and lore who had become interested in recorded coal miners' songs, was writing for folk music magazines like *Caravan.* Originally a mimeographed, fan-oriented publication, the New York–based *Caravan* had evolved by 1958 into a more serious journal. In it appeared the work of intellectuals who, through the folksong revival, had developed serious interests in studying various aspects of folk music such as the question of how folk and hillbilly music were related.

Edwards's untimely death in an auto accident in 1960 led to the creation of the first institution dedicated to the study of country music and related forms of recorded folk music, the John Edwards Memorial Foundation, or JEMF. Edwards's will had requested that his collection be kept intact and moved to the U.S. A group of collector friends (all contributors to *Disc Collector*) formed the JEMF in 1962, and through D. K. Wilgus, newly arrived at UCLA, Edwards's immense record and sheet music collection and the foundation were housed at the Folklore and Mythology Center on the UCLA campus. In September 1965 the JEMF helped support UCLA graduate student Mayne Smith's trip East as an observer to the Roanoke Festival; in

October the *JEMF Newsletter* began. Edited by Ed Kahn, this quarterly was the first scholarly journal devoted to country music. Only a few months before, scholarly interest in country music had been marked in another way by the appearance of a "Hillbilly Issue" of the *Journal of American Folklore,* edited by Wilgus. Smith's bluegrass article appeared in this publication; soon it and all of the other articles in that issue of the *Journal* were available separately in the *JEMF* Reprint Series.

Bluegrass Unlimited

In many ways the development of country music scholarship was an out-growth of record collecting. By the mid-sixties, an increasing number of individuals were involved in the serious study of hilllbilly music. Not all were professional scholars like Wilgus, Smith, Archie Green, and the others who wrote for the *Journal of American Folklore.* But together they constituted a community bound by a combination of esthetic involvement in the music and intellectual curiosity about its history and meaning. Members of this community studied, wrote about, and promoted country music in its various forms because they believed it to be a significant cultural expression. At the same time they wanted it to be successful in the marketplace.

In the spring of 1966, a one-page mimeographed questionnaire was distrib-uted in the Washington, D.C., area by Gary Henderson, a disc jockey at WDON in Wheaton, Maryland, and Dianne Sims, a Rockville, Maryland, housewife. "*ATTENTION ALL BLUEGRASS FANS:*" it announced, "We the undersigned would like to form a BLUEGRASS BOOSTERS CLUB and would like your opinion and views on how, why, and when and where this organi-zation should operate." The questionnaire asked for definitions of bluegrass music, whether it was "Country-Western" or "Folk," what the respondent's favorite bands were, and whether there was interest in supporting an organi-zation. Other questions asked about dues, meetings, and a newsletter.

The immediate result was a newsletter, *Bluegrass Unlimited,* volume 1, number 1 of which appeared in July 1966. On the masthead were the names of the group formed as a result of the questionnaire: Pete (Roberts) Kuyken-dall, chairman; Richard Spottswood, vice-chairman; Richard Freeland, vice-chairman; Gary Henderson, treasurer; and Dianne Sims, secretary. Following the list came a statement of purpose:

WE PROPOSE:
1. To support bluegrass music on record and in person by all groups, local, national and international and to encourage the furtherance of this music.
2. To provide an information service for new record releases on national labels and as many small labels as possible and use the purchasing

power of the group as an instrument of obtaining same. Discounts will
be made available when possible.

3. To publish a newsletter covering record releases, coming events, articles and information of interest.

dues———$3.00 per member annually[35]

That the first issue of *Bluegrass Unlimited* focused upon records is not
surprising considering the membership of its board. Henderson had become
one of the Washington area's better-known bluegrass deejays following the
death of Don Owens, the pioneer bluegrass supporter in the area, in 1963.
Richard Freeland was owner of Rebel Records, the company that had issued
the Country Gentlemen's "Bringing Mary Home" in 1965. Rebel had just
released a four-record set of LPs containing single recordings by various
groups—unavailable elsewhere—which had received favorable notice in the
Bluegrass Bulletin and was being advertised in *Sing Out!* as the "Bluegrass
Record Library." In the next decade Rebel would become one of the most
successful bluegrass independents. But at this time it was still a small local
company, growing under Freeland's energetic management.

By 1966 Richard Spottswood had been involved with records in various
ways. He started as a record collector and developed this into a scholarly
interest, cataloging the Library of Congress's 78-rpm recordings of blues,
hillbilly, spirituals, and early jazz for his master's thesis in library science at
Washington's Catholic University in 1962. With an interest in jazz, blues,
and old-time country as well as bluegrass, he owned or had been associated
with several record companies that specialized in reissues—Piedmont and
Melodeon. He had also been involved in the promotion of the career of
"rediscovered" bluesman Mississippi John Hurt. Spottswood thus had interests
in a variety of musics. He viewed bluegrass as he did jazz—as an art, to be
approached using a historically derived critical esthetic. His primary role at
Bluegrass Unlimited was as record reviewer.

Pete Kuykendall had worked with Spottswood in several recording ven-
tures, most recently helping in the production of a Melodeon reissue of the
Stanley Brothers' Rich-R-Tone recordings. His interests and background were
more squarely in bluegrass than those of Spottswood. A deejay in the mid-
fifties on WFCR (now WEEL) in Fairfax, Virginia, he had won the banjo
contest at Connie B. Gay's Country Music Championship in Warrenton,
Virginia, and had been active as a banjo and fiddle player (as "Pete Roberts")
in a number of local bands, including a one-year stint on banjo with the
Country Gentlemen in 1958. Since then he had worked with the Gentlemen
in a number of other ways. He had produced several of their albums, written
songs for them, and helped them find obscure old folksongs and country
songs in his record and tape collection as well as in the Library of Congress,
where for a short time he worked as a recording division technician. Like
Spottswood, he was a record collector, but his collection focused on more

recent music and included a large number of live recordings of bluegrass shows on tape. He was and is one of the most knowledgeable people in the country about bluegrass recordings. In the late fifties he published a series of bluegrass discographies and articles in *Disc Collector*, the first serious writing about the discographical aspects of the careers of Monroe, Reno and Smiley, Flatt and Scruggs, and the Stanley Brothers.

The first issue of *Bluegrass Unlimited*, mimeographed on 8½-by-14-inch paper, contained eight pages and an additional full-page ad for the one day "1st International Folk-Bluegrass Festival" sponsored by the Warrenton J.C.s and produced by WKCW in Warrenton at Whippoorwill Lake Park. From the beginning, editor (later managing editor) Dianne Sims produced a magazine which was laid out much more neatly and professionally than the *Bluegrass Bulletin*. The magazine led off with an article by Richard K.Spottswood (later editor) on County Records, which praised all of their issues but emphasized the bluegrass recordings, "Go out and buy a few of them," he urged; "some of the best old-time and bluegrass music today is to be found on small labels like this . . . they need all the support you can give them."[36] Most of the rest of this issue was devoted to record reviews, but in the back pages were informational features that would remain an important part of *Bluegrass Unlimited*—listings of bluegrass shows at local parks, bands playing in clubs, bluegrass radio shows, fan clubs, and publications. Emphasis was, naturally, on the active Washington-area scene, but the various well-organized listings created a format which the consumers of the music could turn to with confidence, and in future issues the listings would become more national in scope as the magazine's readership expanded. With the second issue began a four-part serial reprinting of Mayne Smith's *Journal of American Folklore* article, the same one now available as a JEMF reprint.

All these institutions that appeared during 1965 and 1966—the festival, periodicals, a mail-order record service—reflected the interests of bluegrass consumers. Each had antecedents in either the folk revival or the country music industry, but they were much more closely tailored to exclusive interests in bluegrass and related old-time music. Similar phenomena occurred with other musical forms at this time; old-time fiddling associations began to spring up in many places, as did publications devoted to the collection and study of blues music. Like the bluegrass consumer institutions, they included a mixture of alienated old-timers who felt their music was being unfairly ignored and excited newcomers, often urbanites from the revival, who had just fallen in love with this exotic and obscure music. Differences in esthetics between the two groups were not as important as the shared feeling that the music needed to be preserved and promoted.

In the world of bluegrass these people became the leaders in a consumer movement. Now all they needed were some followers. Therein lay a problem, for it was not easy to get the special sound of bluegrass before the public. Country deejays were not very helpful, and the folkies were going either psychedelic or "traditional" (as the new folk revival movement called the less commercial forms).

Bluegrass fell between these two streams—less commercial than rock, more commercial than the "purer" forms folk revivalists were turning toward. Yet the new bluegrass consumer movement itself took the music in a direction that attracted audiences through influences that were just as divergent. On the one hand, it would gain many new followers as a popular form through a most unexpected ally, the high-powered media world of network television and Hollywood movies (see chapter 9). It would also depend, as the next chapter shows, upon the support of those people who recognized in it a way of reviving, maintaining, and advancing the down-home forms they believed in, such as old-time fiddle music and gospel singing.

Notes

1. Fred Bartenstein, "The Carlton Haney Story," p. 9.

2. Ibid., p. 10.

3. Rinzler interview.

4. Ibid.

5. Ibid.

6. "1965 Roanoke, Va. Blue Grass Festival," flyer postmarked Aug. 24, 1965, Roanoke, Va.

7. Mayne Smith, "Notes and Interviews from the First Annual Bluegrass Festival at Roanoke, Virginia—1965," pp. 1, 21.

8. Mary Greenman Green with Tom Teepen, "The First Festival," p. 54.

9. Ralph Rinzler, "Blue Grass Fest a 'Pickinic'; Top Names Mark First Event," p. 8.

10. Smith, "Notes," pp. 11–12.

11. Green and Teepen, "The First Festival," p. 55.

12. Carlton Haney, recorded onstage, First Annual Roanoke Blue Grass Festival, Cantrell's Horse Farm, Fincastle, Va., Sept. 5, 1965. All subsequent quotes from participants in the first "Story" come from this recording.

13. Smith, "Notes," p. 2.

14. Green and Teepen, "The First Festival," p. 55.

15. Smith, "Notes," p. 11.

16. Green and Teepen, "The First Festival," p. 56.

17. Smith, "Notes," p. 23. This is, as Smith recalls, a paraphrase using key words from Haney's comments.

18. Rinzler, "Blue Grass Fest," p. 8.

19. Jimmy Martin, recorded onstage, First Annual Roanoke Blue Grass Festival, Fincastle, Va., Sept. 4, 1965.

20. Jimmy Martin, "The Last Song."

21. Howard Cook, "C&W Jocks Decide Top Sellers Spin," p. 30.

22. Bill Sachs, "Sin and Salvation: C&W Music Still Packs Vitality,"
p. 20.

23. Charles Portis, "That New Sound from Nashville," pp. 275, 276.

24. Ibid., p. 277.

25. *Sing Out!* 15 (Nov. 1965): outside back cover.

26. Peter A. Richardson, "The Bluegrass Band," p. 2.

27. Peter A. Richardson, "What Is and What Is Not 'Traditional Blue-grass' Anyhow????" p. 4.

28. Quoted in Peter A. Richardson, "Editorial Comment," p. 1.

29. Ibid., p. 3.

30. Peter A. Richardson, [untitled editorial], [p. 5].

31. *County Records—Publications*, 8-by-22-inch, quadruple-folded brochure (New York: David Freeman, [1965]).

32. David Freeman, *County Sales Newsletter* 4 (June 1966): [2].

33. Ibid.: [1].

34. Ibid.

35. Richard K. Spottswood, "County Records—Brief Summary," Ibid.: 2.

36. Ibid.

Bibliographical Notes

For more on Carlton Haney, see John Pugh, "Carlton Haney." Haney listed his 1965–66 Reno and Smiley booking statistics in an ad in Thurston Moore's *The Country Music Who's Who, 1965 Edition,* sec. 2, p. 28. An ad for Haney's Roanoke festival appeared in *Sing Out!* 15 (Sept. 1965): 76. Articles previewing it were printed in *Billboard* (Aug. 21, 1965, pp. 36, 38) and the Boston magazine *The Broadside* (Ralph Rinzler, "First Annual Blue Grass Festival Set").

Mayne Smith described his confrontation with Monroe in "Additions and Corrections." He also wrote an article "correcting" the statements Monroe objected to: "First Bluegrass Festival Honors Bill Monroe."

The most complete portrait of Jimmy Martin is Peter V. Kuykendall's "Jimmy Martin: Super King of Bluegrass." My analysis of mid-sixties country music views of bluegrass and its lack of country radio exposure draws upon Bill Vernon's "Bluegrass Stands the Test." The problem persisted into the seventies: see Paul W. Soelberg, "Modern Country Radio: Friend or Foe?" For the perspective of a bluegrass-conscious deejay during the sixties, see Doug Green, "John Hartford." In 1967 the association of bluegrass with beatniks, draft dodgers, homosexuals, and drug users was set forth by Starday's Don Pierce in a letter to *Bluegrass Unlimited.* It precipitated a flood of angry responses, including my own article on him, cited in the notes to chapter 5.

For a discussion of the honky tonk sound, see Bill C. Malone, "Honky

Tonk." Details of the vanishing hitchhiker legend are given in Jan Harold Brunvand, *The Vanishing Hitchhiker.*

The first *Bluegrass Bookshelf* ad appeared in *Sing Out!* 14 (Jan. 1965): back cover. Norm Carlson's *Bluegrass Bulletin* reports were published under the title "OnThe Scene" with the earliest appearing in December 1966. Sometimes his column was titled "The Bluegrass Scene." Carlson also published his own mimeographed *Bluegrass Handbook*, which went through four editions. The husband-and-wife articles to which I allude are Keith Tyler, "Keith Tyler Talks a Little Bluegrass—Loudly!" and Ilene Tyler, "Woes of a Bluegrass Wife."

County Records' story is told by Charles Wolfe in "Dave Freeman and County Records." A good sketch of early hillbilly record collectors is given in Bill C. Malone, *Country Music U.S.A.*, pp. 354–56. A number of articles by record collectors like John Edwards and scholars like Archie Green appeared in *Caravan*, which also published Fred Hoeptner's "Folk and Hillbilly Music." The "Hillbilly Issue" of the *Journal of American Folklore* was edited by D. K. Wilgus. Each article from that issue, including Mayne Smith's "Introduction," was made available by the JEMF separately in their reprint series. At the beginning of 1983 the JEMF was forced by financial stringencies to sell its collection. Now housed at the University of North Carolina as the John Edwards Memorial Collection, it is part of the Folk Music Archives at that school. At the same time the *JEMF Quarterly* changed its name to the *John Edwards Memorial Forum* (JEMF); it continues to be edited and published in Los Angeles.

Richard K. Spottswood's "A Catalog of American Folk Music on Commercial Recordings at the Library of Congress, 1923–1940" established his expertise in dealing with phonograph recordings. In recent years Spottswood has worked mainly with the ethnic material recorded commercially in the pre-war period. Peter V. Kuykendall's early discographies included the Stanley Brothers one cited in the notes to chapter 3; "Lester Flatt and Earl Scruggs and the Foggy Mountain Boys"; "Bill Monroe"; and "Don Reno and Red Smiley and the Tennessee Cutups."

Discographical Notes

Jimmy Martin's "Widow Maker" was released on an album of the same name. Buck Owens's "Buckaroo" appeared on his *Instrumental Hits.* The Stanley Brothers' "How Far to Little Rock," which is based on the old minstrel comedy routine of "The Arkansas Traveler" but uses a different melody, was included on the anthology *Country and Western Jamboree.* Flatt and Scruggs's "Cabin on the Hill" was issued on their *When The Saints Go Marching In;* "Go Home" on *Country and Western Classics.* Lonnie Irving's "Pinball Machine" was included on the anthology *Banjo Jamboree Spectacu-*

lar. Flatt and Scruggs's "The Ballad of Jed Clampett" was released on their *Hard Travelin'*; "Pearl Pearl Pearl" on *Flatt and Scruggs' Greatest Hits*. Cowboy Copas's "Alabam" was reissued on his *Unforgettable*. The Country Gentlemen's "Bringing Mary Home" was released on *The Country Gentlemen*. The Osborne Brothers' "The Kind of Woman I Got" was included on *Modern Sounds of Bluegrass Music*.

County's first non-reissue album was *Clawhammer Banjo*; their second, *Larry Richardson and Red Barker and the Blue Ridge Boys*. The records listed in County's *Newsletter No. 4* include *Seventeen Mountain Gems* (the Galax fiddle convention album); *Tom Ashley & Tex Isley*; *This is Mac Wiseman*; Reno and Smiley's *Variety Show*; Jim Greer and the Mac-O-Chee Valley Folks' *Memories in Song*; The Sullivan Family's *Bluegrass Gospel*; Monroe's *The High, Lonesome Sound*; Uncle Dave Macon's *First Featured Star of the Grand Ole Opry*; Jimmy Martin's *Mr. Good 'n' Country*; and Charlie Moore and Bill Napier's *More Truck Drivers' Songs*. The four-record Rebel anthology has recently been reissued as *Seventy-Song Original Bluegrass Collection*.

Chapter 8

The Old-Time Element:
Religion and Fiddle Music

During the late sixties and early seventies, festivals, magazines, and the other manifestations of the bluegrass consumer movement were altering the music in many ways. Bluegrass was being established as a form which existed more or less independently from those it previously had been closely associated with, particularly country music. Maintained and supported by "believers," it was coming to be considered a well-defined popular art form with strong folk "roots." Two such roots, embodying strongly held traditional values which strengthened the ties of bluegrass with older musical forms, were old-time fiddle music and gospel singing. As the consumer movement grew, both bluegrass fiddling and bluegrass gospel underwent changes in shape and meaning. In this chapter I will detail these changes, turning first to gospel music—its cultural connections, its role in Bill Monroe's show repertoire, and its evolution at bluegrass festivals.

Bluegrass gospel is a form of discourse about the sacred which occurs in a secular context. Religious music is found in the repertoires of most country music performers, but it has unusual prominence in the bluegrass repertoire. Religious songs constituted, on the average, 30 percent of the recorded and published (in songbooks) output of the most influential early bluegrass bands—Monroe, Flatt and Scruggs, the Stanley Brothers, and Reno and Smiley.

Jens Lund has suggested that the importance of religious songs in bluegrass reflects the music's close associations with Appalachian migrants in urban settings during its formative years.[1] Sociologists studying these immigrant communities reported that urban "hillbillies" rarely attended church, owing to their inferiority feelings, their distrust of liberal urban churches, and the inability of such churches to play a cohesive social role. Hence the music, marketed typically on singles and albums containing only gospel songs, filled needs not met by formal church services. The most common form of religion among Appalachian people, fundamentalist Protestantism, stresses that church attendance is not necessary for salvation, which may be achieved through daily faith and reference to the Bible as well as through such expressions of religious faith and thought as gospel music. In the city, fundamentalist Protestantism often becomes more "fundamental," so that the gospel repertoire may take on added significance and function in urban contexts.

But even in the rural and small-town context of Appalachia (as in other parts of the South), the religious dimension of bluegrass music was important. During the late forties and early fifties semi-professional family groups and gospel quartets had begun to assimilate bluegrass instrumental styles and vocal repertoire. When the Lewis Family became a full-time professional group in 1964, they, like the many all-gospel bluegrass groups which were to follow their example in the next decade, played most frequently in the mountain regions. And as the techniques and repertoire of bluegrass became familiar, the music was heard in the churches of those mountain sects which permitted or encouraged such musical expression by individuals in their congregations.

To the outsider, the profusion of mountain religious sects confirms the stereotype of mountaineers as a highly individualistic people given to feuding. One outsider, a minister named Jack Weller who lived in Appalachia for a number of years, observed in 1965 that the region had a high number of churches with a very low average membership. He noted also a widespread feeling that every person is his or her own preacher. In this context, he thought, the vague but powerful idea of "old-time religion," to which all subscribed, minimized conflict over the interpretation of the rules of organized religion. Weller also saw a connection between the widespread revivalism and the ease with which "backsliding" seemed to occur; individuals appeared to move through both phenomena in an endless cycle.[2] Weller, though, spoke as a representative of a mainstream American church. He appears to have confused some aspects of the local formal religions with aspects of folk religion, which—wherever it occurs—invariably includes idiosyncratic individual interpretations.

It is not always easy to untangle individual interpretations from those of small localized sects. Loyal Jones has shown that there is a wealth of such sects in Appalachia, each with its own history, theological doctrine, and social view. They share an approach to religion which Jones characterizes as "generally more emotional, [and] informal in preaching, singing and praying styles."[3] This informality and emotionalism, in conjunction with the large number of sects, may lead the outside observer to think that these are not really formal churches with a historical dimension. Adding to the confusion is the lack of stress on church attendance. In Appalachia, as in the urban immigrant communities, such official religious institutions create a place for essentially external but closely related folk institutions like bluegrass gospel music.

Five recurrent themes in bluegrass gospel repertoires, Howard Wight Marshall found, are "individual salvation, life's rocky road, the maternal hearth, grief for the deceased, and the good Christian's 'action orientation.' "[4] Songs on such topics speak to religion as a folk institution as well as to the church, particularly the fundamentalist Protestant variety, as an official institution. Weller points out that mountain people talk and think a great deal about religion, even when "they never go near the church."[5] Hence my description of bluegrass gospel music as discourse about the sacred within a secular context.

While bluegrass records and songbooks contained a high proportion of religious songs, a smaller proportion of such music was included in broadcasts and performances. From the very beginning of his Opry tenure, Bill Monroe rarely performed more than one gospel song a night. And in each live performance he has seldom done more than two gospel songs. Yet in spite of these small numbers, the religious segment in Monroe's show was almost never omitted, because it constituted an essential statement of values.

Hymn Time: Monroe's Bean Blossom Shows

Earlier I mentioned Bill Monroe's country music park, the Brown County Jamboree, in Bean Blossom, Indiana. The weekly shows held at Bean Blossom every Sunday from April to November, where, during the sixties, a crowd of 400 was considered quite large, have been overshadowed in recent years by Monroe's annual festival (established in 1967) which draws many thousands. But during the formative years of bluegrass, as for country music in general during the post-war era, weekly shows at country music parks like Bean Blossom were an important source of income and exposure. Two shows were held each Sunday at the Brown County Jamboree, one in the afternoon and one at night. Each show consisted of appearances by the house band, by visiting local or regional acts, and by the featured artist or name band.

At many parks the show was held outdoors with the performers on a raised, covered stage; but at the Jamboree there was a long, low barn with a stage at one end and food and soft-drink concessions at the other end. Folding chairs were set on a cement floor which doubled as a dance floor on Saturday nights. Outside, grassy parking areas with a few trees provided rest areas for performers and patrons who ate supper, visited, and played music between the shows. Most of those attending were families from rural and suburban southern Indiana. Some were migrants from Appalachia, others natives of the region. They were white, working-class, and, typically, Protestant fundamentalist. The Jamboree was a social center for this relatively homogeneous group.

The Brown County Jamboree was started in the mid-thirties by local businessmen. It operated for five or six years in a large tent; the present "barn" was built in 1941. The show format remained the same over the years, but until the end of World War II most of the performers appearing there were from Brown or neighboring counties. Occasionally radio singers from Indianapolis or from WLS in Chicago also appeared. During World War II, when many local people were working in Indianapolis, the local bus line had a Sunday special which left the county seat (Nashville, Indiana), stopped off at Bean Blossom for the show, and continued afterward to Indianapolis. A nearby army camp also contributed to wartime audiences, and by the late forties the Jamboree was drawing its patrons from all over the southern half of the state.

In 1951 Bill Monroe purchased the Jamboree. With his connections at the Grand Ole Opry he was able to book nationally known stars on a regular basis. In doing so he was following a general trend at country parks which saw stars taking over the headliner spots from local and regional acts. At Bean Blossom, as at other parks, there were radio broadcasts from the stage, and local music entrepreneurs—disc jockeys in particular—thus became involved in the Jamboree during the fifties.

Such changes reflected typical aspects of the Jamboree. Monroe's particular special interests were reflected in the ways in which he endeavored to maintain the local ties of the Jamboree. In this regard he was assisted by his older brother Birch, who moved to nearby Martinsville from Nashville, Tennessee, and became the manager of the Jamboree. Through Birch and through his visits to the Jamboree, Bill Monroe became acquainted with local singers and fiddlers. Many of these people were given free passes to the Jamboree and were regularly invited to appear on stage. They also participated in the backstage- and parking-area jam sessions which occurred regularly before and after the shows on Sunday. Some of them also played for the "big round and square dance" which Birch held Saturday nights in the Jamboree barn.

Besides these contacts, the simple fact that Monroe was the country music star who appeared at the Jamboree most frequently meant that the regular members of the audience got to know him well. By the early sixties, when audience numbers had dwindled to a group of die-hard fans, Monroe had taken to speaking of the place as "like home to me" and structuring his shows to include a large section of requests. In this sense the Jamboree was a special show context for Monroe. Yet many aspects of his shows, particularly the religious component, remained constant. Generally Monroe came on stage at the Jamboree after the house band and lesser-known local or visiting bands had performed. An intermission, before which the food concessions were advertised, followed these appearances and preceded Monroe's entrance on stage.

Once his show began it followed a fairly predictable structure which consisted of five segments: (1) the opening segment, (2) Monroe's solo portion, (3) the guest segment, (4) hymn time, and (5) the closing segment.

In the opening segment, as the band came on stage, the guitarist strode to the mike, playing three introductory bass notes. These were the cue for the fiddler, who played the opening theme, a fast instrumental chorus of "Watermelon Hanging on the Vine," which ended abruptly with a shave-and-a-haircut, two-bits. Monroe did most of the emcee work at his shows, in a laconic style that reflected his silent, reticent demeanor offstage. As with most of his stage announcements, his greeting was as formulaic as the music: "Howdy, howdy folks, glad to be back in Bean Blossom." The first complete tune played was often an instrumental, usually featuring the fiddle. Then Monroe introduced the members of the band, telling their home states. Almost always the next song was by the guitarist, who was expected to have one or two "solos"—usually recent hits of other country stars—in his repertoire. It is standard practice in country music shows for the sidemen to perform the hits of other stars, because the star generally does only his own songs. The sidemen field the inevitable requests for the hits of others, indicating to the audience the versatility of the group as popular entertainers. Next, often, was a brother-style duet performed by Monroe and the guitarist. Sometimes, however, a trio was done here. Often the final tune in this segment was an instrumental featuring the banjo player. This opening segment introduced the members of the band, showing their vocal and instrumental ability, and demonstrated Monroe's vocal and instrumental integration with the band through his mandolin breaks in the instrumentals and his harmony singing on the duet or trio.

Monroe's solo portion opened in typical formulaic fashion; Monroe stated modestly, "Now it's my turn to do a couple or three solos." This segment of the show was the most flexible, depending upon the audience and the amount of time available for the show. In a restricted performance (as at a package show or festival), where only twenty or thirty minutes were available for the full presentation ("set"), he would do only two or three songs here—his best-known hits, such as "Footprints in the Snow," "Blue Moon of Kentucky," "Uncle Pen," and "Mule Skinner Blues." However, at Bean Blossom during this segment he also called for requests. Depending upon the audience, he would play not only solos (although these were the most frequently requested) but also instrumentals, duets, trios, and even religious songs. This segment might include as many as eight songs. If there were too many requests to fill, he would string together four or five of his best-known songs in a medley which included one verse of each. It was characteristic of him to remember most of the requests, often in the order received.

The guest segment followed Monroe's solo portion. Occasionally (in 25 percent of the shows in my sample) a guest performer would be called onto the stage at this point in the show. It might be a well-known local musician, a former Blue Grass Boy, someone auditioning for a place in the band or at the Jamboree, or at Bean Blossom, his fiddle-playing brother, Birch. Generally the guest did two songs.

The hymn-time segment featured the vocal quartet; until the mid-sixties Monroe used only guitar and mandolin accompaniment on religious songs. When I first played banjo on a show with him at Bean Blossom, the senior member of the band (fiddler Vassar Clements) stepped back from front stage and told me to play the banjo more quietly, saying, "Bill doesn't like to have banjo on the hymns." I was not the only apprentice musician on stage that day who was unfamiliar with his gospel repertoire; a young man from Nashville, Tennessee, was auditioning for the guitarist/lead singer job. Monroe called upon him to help sing the first hymn of the day; when it was finished Monroe stated dryly "I do have that on record and it sounded better than we sung it right there." At the end of the hymn section, he remarked: "We didn't get to rehearse them here today, and it don't seem like we can do 'em just right."[6] Both comments reflect an attitude toward gospel quartet performance which is like that of ritual: to be effective, it must be properly executed. The vocal quartet is among the most demanding of bluegrass musical arrangements, involving the precise integration of four vocal harmony parts. So improper execution is much more noticeable, likely to make the quartet sound bad. Monroe rarely commented about the band's performance quality, with allusion to practice, in his secular repertoire, where individual members had more leeway and one man's mistake was not so damaging to the overall sound. Though extremely important to the show (and always included), the hymn segment rarely featured more than one or two songs.

In the closing segment two or three lively songs, usually including another fast instrumental number, provided contrast to the previous segment. If Monroe's most recent "single" was currently being promoted and played on the radio, it would be performed at this point. The closing of the show consisted of Monroe's formulaic "speaking for everybody, it's time we're saying, 'Y'All Come,'" after which a vocal and an instrumental chorus of this song, the closing theme, were played and the band left the stage. Encores were not expected; in fact the audience was already moving out of the Jamboree barn as "Y'All Come" was struck up. Some would be on the way to their cars, while others were gathering near the backstage door to ask for autographs or just say hello. In many ways audience activity following the show resembled the behavior of the congregation following church services.

Hymn time, with its emphasis upon quartet singing, contrasted with and balanced against the segments which preceded it. The contrast between these segments can be seen clearly in the differing roles played in them by Bill's brother Birch, who often participated in both. He was regularly invited to appear onstage during the guest segment to play one or two old-time fiddle tunes. Bill introduced these by urging the audience to attend the "round and square dance" held at the Jamboree on Saturday nights, at which Birch fiddled in his style. To show how danceable Birch's fiddling was, Bill often did a short buck-and-wing dance while Birch played. Afterward Birch stayed to help out as bass singer with the Blue Grass Quartet, usually doing several "bass lead" numbers such as "A Beautiful Life" or "Just a Little Talk with Jesus," or "The Boat of Love."

Birch Monroe fit as bass singer in the Blue Grass Quartet more easily than as a fiddler in the Blue Grass Boys because, while the secular and instrumental aspects of the music stress innovation, commercialism, and individual style, the religious aspects emphasize a traditional "right" way (more important than individual style) and family-like integration with the group, and Birch, some thirteen years older than Bill, was a confirmed traditionalist in his approach to music and singing. In a 1972 interview he spoke to me about his musical philosophy. He did not envy the modern fiddlers who "go through all them motions to sell." He felt that they sacrificed musical values for commercial ones, that there is a "right way" to play the fiddle tunes. Here he differed from Bill, who approached instrumental music from a more "progressive" and commercial perspective in which a "right" performance includes some room for individual innovation. Although an excellent square-dance fiddler, Birch suffered by comparison to the spectacular fiddlers in his brother's bands, and his scratchy, repetitive, short-bow fiddling was the butt of public and private joking by the Blue Grass Boys and other young musicians. Birch's approach to hymn singing was equally conservative, and his opinion of younger bass singers in bluegrass similar to that which he held about fiddlers: "Lots of them don't do it right."[7] He knew the right way, he said, because he'd learned it in a singing school. While Birch was kidded about his fiddling, his bass singing was respected, and Bill included him in several Blue Grass Quartet recording sessions.

Bill Monroe's attitude about religious music can be seen in the way he introduced it in shows. Rarely were the textual contents of the song mentioned in any way, in contrast to many of his secular songs such as "Uncle Pen," which was often prefaced or followed with a story about the wonderful old gentleman Bill learned from. Nor did he comment upon the musical aspects of the song, as when he described "Molly and Tenbrooks" as a good song for the banjo. He did not direct the attention of the audience to the skills of individual musicians as he sometimes did, particularly with fiddlers, when introducing an instrumental. All emphasis was placed on the total performance of the song in reverent and ritualistic way; this is the hymn, it's treated seriously, nothing more need be said.

An example from the experience of another musician shows that this distinction which separated hymn time from other parts of the performance was not limited to Monroe. The late Charlie Moore, a bluegrass guitarist and singer, began his career with Cousin Wilbur Wesbrooks, the comedian formerly with Monroe's Blue Grass Boys. In an interview with Washington, D.C., bluegrass deejay Gary Henderson, Moore described the shows he worked with Cousin Wilbur:

He did comedy. In fact he wore his comedy outfit every day for an hour on the show. And the only time he didn't wear it was, I believe we did some hymns, that he'd dress up on TV. . . . They used to be that you had comedy routines that you'd do that would run as much as twenty minutes, you know. Regular skits, like a play. Part of the show. And we used to do our country part of the show, then we'd do our comedy, and then take a short intermission and go back and do our hymns and close the show out. This is when we were doing television down in South Carolina, North Carolina, and Georgia and places like that. And just about everybody worked their shows like that.[8]

Notice that the hymns came at approximately the same place in Cousin Wilbur's show as they did in Monroe's. The match would be even closer if the sample on which I based the typical show structure had included performances from the forties and early fifties when Monroe still carried a comedian (like Cousin Wilbur) with his band. The juxtaposition of comedy and hymnody moved the performance from one extreme to the other—from the threatening anti-social (and therefore funny) behavior of the comedian to the affirmative, integrative, and serious behavior of the gospel performance. Appropriately, the only time Cousin Wilbur did not wear his comedy outfit was when he was singing hymns on television, where the medium demanded a serious visual image to set the religious music apart from the rest of the show.

In virtually every show, live or on radio, that I have seen or heard Bill Monroe present, this approach to the material has predominated. I think this represents his perception of his audience in most situations—that they are a mixed group who generally accept and believe in the ideas and sentiments expressed in the songs but do not want any particular brand of religion served up to them. This is consistent with the democratic and individualistic tenets of fundamentalist/revivalist Protestantism adhered to by many in the audience. And for those who do not accept or believe this particular religion, the performance does not demand a personal response, so they may enjoy it as "art."

Bluegrass Gospel at Festivals

Whether audience members viewed bluegrass gospel songs as statements relevant to their own values or as works of art (or both), this portion of the repertoire had an important place in the music as the festival movement grew during the second half of the sixties. In this new context, changes occurred in the way in which gospel music was presented.

The staging of Sunday morning all-gospel programs at festivals was accompanied in some cases by the introduction of sermons by fundamentalist preachers. This happened frequently at festivals Bill Monroe promoted. His behavior at these programs differed somewhat from his hymn time approach: he was more animated, expansive, preacher-like. He would stop playing the mandolin from time to time so that he could, by his hand-clapping, encourage the audience to get happy and feel the spirit of the music. The Sunday morning context was more overtly and completely religious; hence such behavior was more appropriate.

The Lewis Family, which had been appearing mainly at gospel-singing conventions and at schools and other community halls, played their first bluegrass festival in 1969. In contrast to the often sparse instrumental backing which characterized the Blue Grass Quartet and others, they brought to festival audiences a gospel sound set to full bluegrass instrumentation. While hymn time in secular shows was quiet, serious, and thus contrasted with the rest of the show, the Lewis Family's presentation differed because they presented an entire show consisting of sacred music. The fullness of their sound was a natural result of the need to present a complete "show" with dynamic variation. Since everything they did was sacred, they did not need to establish boundaries between sacred and secular as performers like Monroe did with hymn time. Hence they adapted the secular format of the full bluegrass (or country) show to their needs. For example, Little Roy Lewis performed instrumental versions of gospel songs on the banjo. In their repertoire, the Family followed the emphasis in gospel music of the time by choosing songs which stressed the happy, joyous side of religion. They developed a reputation for a highly polished and extremely entertaining show which included comedy and a good deal of musical variety.

The Lewis Family's show was typical of the professional gospel music performance style which burgeoned in the fifties and sixties. What made them special in the gospel circuit was their use of bluegrass instrumentation; they were special in bluegrass because of their happy approach to the music as embodied in their repertoire and show. Sometimes it was necessary for them to modify their show in order to accommodate festival audiences not conversant with bluegrass gospel. Little Roy Lewis tells of playing at a bluegrass festival for "a whole hippie crowd" in which they were successful because they kept the pace of the show moving quickly by playing up-tempo spiritual songs.[9]

While the Lewis Family and other all-gospel groups like the Easter Brothers were developing bluegrass gospel into a complete show form paralleling that of secular shows, the secular bands were turning to a type of gospel quartet which was even more sparse than earlier ones, the a cappella quartet. Introduced on record by Ralph Stanley in 1971, it quickly became fashionable. It served to heighten the contrast between secular and sacred which hymn time provided. The range of attitudes held about religion and sacred music is reflected in the way in which gospel music could move in several directions at the same time in the context of bluegrass festivals. The all-sacred groups adopted secular show features while the secular groups increased the sacred-secular distinction. The behavior of both at Sunday morning programs represented yet another way of altering the presentation of religious music. At about the same time this was happening, another down-home and old-time part of bluegrass—bluegrass fiddling—was also undergoing changes reflective of the varying uses of and attitudes toward the form.

Bluegrass Fiddle: Old and New

During the mid-sixties, the growth of interest in bluegrass was paralleled by a similar growth of interest in old-time fiddle music. It was impelled by similar feelings—that the music was being discriminated against by record companies, broadcasters, and others who controlled the media. Fiddle believers were like their bluegrass counterparts, too, in the religious intensity of their commitment. They felt the art of old-time fiddle music was being threatened and began forming local, state, and regional fiddling associations to counter this threat. In seeking ways to publicize and legitimize their art, these associations began to revitalize and reshape an old institution, the fiddlers' convention. It became a modern, festival-like, display event at which new (or, for some, the good old) high standards of fiddle performance were encouraged. As we have seen, fiddle contests had been held frequently in the Southeast for many years. But their often commercial nature and frequently uneven standards did not offer a particularly good model for promoting old-time fiddling as an art. For this reason the highly organized contests of Texas and neighboring southwestern states influenced the new contest fiddling styles which, after 1965, began to influence bluegrass fiddling.

From the very beginnings of Bill Monroe's Blue Grass Boys the fiddle had been given a prominent, even a leading, role. In spite of this prominence, though, emphasis in bluegrass fiddling had been upon the ability of the fiddler to provide settings and breaks for songs, rather than on the execution of traditional tunes. Tommy Magness's "Katy Hill," fast, furious, and clean, represented the early standards for old-time fiddle tune performance in bluegrass. But most bluegrass instrumentals on record were newly composed numbers in which the fiddle shared the lead with banjo and mandolin. Bill Monroe's recorded fiddle compositions of the fifties, though they used traditional forms and motifs, were carefully arranged showpieces which often featured two or three fiddles playing in harmony.

Traditional fiddle pieces were heard more frequently in radio, television, and show performances than on record. They were used to open and close shows and, as with Monroe, to punctuate segments of shows. When used in this way, they were often introduced with an allusion to traditional contexts.

Frequently Earl Scruggs and the fiddler for the Foggy Mountain Boys (after 1954, Paul Warren) would feature the fiddle and banjo alone, doing an old tune; Flatt would introduce it by saying that in the old days a dance band consisted of a fiddle and a banjo. In this way old-time fiddle tunes took on symbolic significance, becoming reminders of the traditions shared by the musicians and their audiences, and standing for the historical roots of the music.

Virtually all of the pioneer bluegrass fiddlers came from the rural Southeast. Their styles reflected their origins. Their playing emphasized speed and technical accuracy: Tommy Magness is a good example. Although bluegrass fiddlers like Howdy Forrester had been influenced by the Texas contest styles, this influence was more evident in the way they utilized techniques from these sources to enhance their accompaniments of and breaks in songs. An important aspect of the Texas contest style is the variation of the tune throughout the performance. The jazzy variation techniques had been assimilated into bluegrass accompaniment styles, but when bluegrass fiddlers played old-time tunes, they used far less variation and ornamentation than their southwestern counterparts. Then in 1963 a chance encounter brought the Texas contest style more firmly into bluegrass fiddling: one of the most commercial of the bluegrass bands, the Dillards, met a young southwestern contest fiddler named Byron Berline.

Pickin' and Fiddlin'

Byron Berline was born in 1944 in Caldwell, Kansas, and raised on a farm just over the border in Oklahoma. His was a musical family: his mother played the piano, and his father, Lue Berline, was an accomplished old-time fiddler. The fiddle music Lue Berline and his friends played in this region was dominated by the flourishing Texas fiddle contest tradition. Byron learned the fiddle in this setting through his family's visits with other fiddlers and their weekend trips, often many hundreds of miles, to contests throughout the southwest. Byron was playing the fiddle at five and won his first contest (beating his dad) when he was ten. He grew up listening to and learning from the great contest fiddlers in Texas and neighboring southwestern states, including men like Benny Thomasson, who had so impressed Howdy Forrester in Texas back in the forties, and Eck Robertson, one of the first old-time fiddlers on commercial records.

In addition to his prowess on the fiddle, Byron was a capable athlete; his successes in track, basketball, and football earned him an athletic scholarship to the University of Oklahoma, where he began his studies in 1963. At the Oklahoma campus in Norman, a suburb of Oklahoma City, Byron began playing music with three classmates who were folk revival fans. They called their band the Cleveland County Ramblers. It was at this time that he first heard and began trying to play bluegrass.

He had really learned only one bluegrass instrumental, "Hamilton County," when, on November 22, 1963, he heard the Dillards for the first time. They were playing in Oklahoma City at the Booteye Club, and the university booked them for a weekly campus program, the "Friday at Four Show," at which the Cleveland County Ramblers were also to appear. Berline stayed to listen to the Dillards: "I went out and sat down and watched their show. Man, when they came on I just forgot about everything. Man, those guys were really cooking! I was just sitting off the floor about that high. I just couldn't believe it! When they got through, they went back into the dressing room, and I finally found them just as they were leaving."[10] Doug Dillard asked Byron to play a tune with him there backstage, and he chose "Hamilton County." One tune led to another as they discovered that they shared a knowledge of old-time fiddle tunes, since their fathers were both fiddlers. Following a two-hour jam session, Berline ended up playing with the Dillards at the Booteye that night. He taped the show, and from this came the idea to make an album together.

The following summer Berline flew to Los Angeles for an Elektra session with the Dillards in the World Pacific Studios. As producer Jim Dickson recalls, the album was a labor of love for Rodney and Douglas Dillard. They did it in spite of Elektra owner Jac Holzman, who didn't agree with the concept: "After the beginning of the first session where Jac Holzman insisted that they have like a mandolin break or a banjo break, they went ahead and did the rest of the album the way they wanted to, to please their parents, all of them. It was an album that was designed entirely . . . to make their folks proud of 'em."[11]

That the Dillards pressed ahead with the concept showed how strongly they valued fiddle music, for this album was not as commercial as their first two Elektra albums had been, and, according to Dickson, Holzman was not happy with the way in which it featured the fiddle so prominently. The Dillards had been selling coffeehouse bluegrass to folk enthusiasts, most of whom did not appreciate fiddle music. Yet *Pickin' and Fiddlin'* was unlike any previous bluegrass album; it was an LP of old-time fiddle music played to bluegrass backing. Released in February 1965 the album had extensive scholarly notes by Ralph Rinzler, as if it were a set of field recordings. The record sold slowly. But it has never stopped selling and is still available today, described in County Sales' catalog as "(Classic fiddle LP)."

This was by no means the first fiddle album. Records of old-time fiddle music have been available since the early days of the phonograph. In 1922 Eck Robertson, one of the leading Texas contest fiddlers, had recorded a number of tunes for Victor. Fiddle music constituted an important segment of the material marketed as "hillbilly" or "old-time" music in the twenties. By the time LPs came along in the forties, such records were relatively common. Often they were not marketed to the hillbilly music consumer but aimed instead at the square dancers and other users and followers of fiddle music. This was a steady, if limited, market. The best-known fiddle albums of the fifties came from Nashville. Done by such studio regulars as Tommy Jackson, these did not have bluegrass backing. In style and repertoire they were representative of the southeastern fiddle tradition but were executed with a technique which owed much to commercial western swing fiddling.

Berline brought to his own album a style in which innovation and ornamentation were stressed to a much greater degree than in other fiddling styles. Texas fiddle contest rules require that traditional tunes be rendered so as to be recognizable, but fiddlers are judged on how well they decorate these standards and on how many different well-decorated variations they perform within the time limit set for each piece performed in the contest. Since it is played as a concert music rather than for dancing, this music is frequently somewhat slower in tempo than would be the case elsewhere (particularly the Southeast). This allows for more ornamentation. The traditional fiddling which Berline learned was considered an art by its practitioners; in it one had to follow a "right" form while also executing acceptable personal variations. This combination of traditional constraints with personal invention is typical of many folk art forms and is found to some extent in all fiddle traditions. But because of the contests, the personal invention side was emphasized to a greater degree here than elsewhere. Nowhere had so many techniques of variation and ornamentation been developed. In Berline's musical vocabulary were fancy double stops, triplets, third-position fingering, rhythmic intricacies, and jazz phrasing. The latter reflected the strong influence of western swing on Texas fiddling; at every Texas fiddle contest one encountered veterans from the bands of Bob Wills and other exponents of this form.

In his performances with the Dillards, Berline did not attempt to be commercial or, on the other hand, to be austerely or consciously "traditional." The repertoire which he brought to this album was, in its sources, typical of most fiddlers. Some tunes he had learned from his father or from friends, others at contests from famous regional fiddlers like Eck Robertson. Some Byron had just absorbed, and a few of these came directly or indirectly from fiddle records by men like Fiddling Arthur Smith and Tommy Jackson. Also included was one of his own compositions. Some of the tunes were contest favorites; others, showy pieces which, because of special tunings, "trick" techniques, or over-familiarity, had been banned at contests. This was a representative collection of tunes from the Southwest, played by an emergent master of that style. But because it combined this style with bluegrass accompaniment, it was a new synthesis. Though it took a while for its impact to be felt, Berline's was the first bluegrass fiddle album and introduced bluegrass musicians and fans to the Texas style and repertoire. It established Berline, then twenty-one, as a potent new fiddler.

Through Ralph Rinzler, Berline and his father were invited to appear at Newport in the summer of 1965, just a few months after the album with the Dillards was released. They arrived there only a few weeks after Byron had won the prestigious National Fiddle Championship contest at Weiser, Idaho. Though he was not playing with a bluegrass band at Newport, Berline quickly attracted the attention of fellow festival performer Bill Monroe, who offered him a job with the Blue Grass Boys. Berline still had two years of university left but promised to get in touch with Monroe when he was finished. Thus it was that in January 1967 Berline, with diploma in hand, went to Nashville to see Monroe. By March he was a member of the Blue Grass Boys, taking the place of city boy Richard Greene.

Berline represented a new type in the Blue Grass Boys. He was a country boy, but he was also a college graduate who had been introduced to bluegrass through the folk revival on campus. And while Monroe had previously hired some fiddlers who were familiar with the repertoire and techniques of the Southwest (Chubby Wise, Howdy Forrester, Kenny Baker), Berline was the first native of the region to fiddle in Monroe's band. He was in the band only from March to September 1967, and he recorded only three tunes with Monroe. But of those three, two became bluegrass classics: "The Gold Rush" and "Sally Goodin."

"The Gold Rush" was a Monroe composition which followed the form of traditional fiddle tunes. It was a simple but catchy tune, which Berline played with relatively little variation or ornamentation, in the style of Monroe's southeastern fiddlers. Released in the fall of 1968, it quickly became a standard piece in bluegrass fiddle repertoires.

"Sally Goodin" is an old and popular fiddle tune, known in both the Southeast and Southwest. But it has special significance in Texas, because Eck Robertson introduced a series of melodic variations into the tune which had in themselves become traditional. It was this tradition within a tradition which Berline, who had also learned variations from Benny Thomasson and invented some of his own, recorded with Monroe. By introducing the techniques of southwestern contest fiddling into a familiar bluegrass instrumental, Monroe's recording of "Sally Goodin" did for southwestern fiddle style what his "Devil's Dream" had done for Bill Keith's banjo approach: it gave a new old-time dimension to bluegrass music, adding new down-home territory to the genre.

Berline's fiddling represented a balance of personal innovation with regional traditions. For Monroe it was commercial because it was new to the Blue Grass Boys sound, but it was acceptable because Berline was playing the tunes the "right" way. Thus a single musician within the Blue Grass Boys could represent both the commercial and traditional dimensions of Monroe's music.

By the time Berline left Monroe to join the Army in the fall of 1967, he had not only brought more of the Texas style of fiddling into bluegrass through his work with the Dillards and Monroe, he was also introducing bluegrass to the world of contest fiddling. In August 1968, on leave from his Army billet in Louisiana, he entered a fiddle contest held in a shopping mall at Richland Hills, Texas, between Dallas and Fort Worth. This was an elaborately conducted event, typical of those held in Texas. Fiddlers were announced by number only; the judges listened in a closed room so that the fiddler's name and stage antics could not unduly influence judging. Only one accompanist per fiddler was allowed, so that no one would have an unfair advantage. Competing against some thirty fiddlers—including the best in Texas—Berline placed second.

Here, as at bluegrass festivals, significant musical events took place not only on stage but also in the parking lot, where contestants and their friends gathered to play informally. Most of this informal music was western swing oriented, but no jam session that day drew more spectators than the one which developed around Berline. It was the only bluegrass jam session at the contest and attracted so much attention that Berline and some of his friends were invited by the contest organizers to perform on stage between contestants. Among those picking with him in the parking lot were members of the Stone Mountain Boys, a Dallas band which had won the band contest at Monroe's Bean Blossom Festival the previous June. Also present were two young Kentuckians, guitarist Wayne Stewart and teenage mandolinist and fiddler Sam Bush. Bush had been fiddling since his early teens and by 1968 had won the Junior Championship at the Weiser contest twice. He would win it again in 1969, but by this time his interest was shifting to the mandolin. Also present at the jam session was a young banjo picker whom Berline had played with at the University of Oklahoma, Alan Munde.

Six months later Stewart, Bush, and Munde would record an instrumental album, *Poor Richard's Almanac*. It included a number of Texas fiddle contest standards, among them a five-minute version of "Sally Goodin." In a later chapter I will return to the influence of the jazzy Texas-style variation ideas on the "newgrass" music in which these young men were pioneers; here I note simply that what brought all of these bluegrass musicians together at this Texas fiddle contest was the presence of Byron Berline.

Berline finished his army service in 1969. He had hoped to return to Monroe, but with Kenny Baker firmly established in the Blue Grass Boys, Byron headed west. Within a few months he had recorded with the Rolling Stones and was on his way to a career as the most sought-after fiddler for recording session work in Los Angeles. He not only did records, he also played extensively on sound tracks.

As one of the most acclaimed fiddlers in bluegrass music, Berline showed how a single talented performer could move from success in the most tradition-oriented aspects of the music to work in the most commercial of settings. In a similar way, as the bluegrass consumer movement which stressed tradition was developing, the sound of bluegrass was, in an independent series of events, becoming an important facet of mass media through its use in movies and television.

Notes

1. Jens Lund, "Fundamentalism, Racism and Political Reaction in Country Music," p. 82. Lund draws from the work of Lewis M. Killian, especially his "The Adjustment of Southern White Migrants to Northern Urban Norms."
2. Jack E. Weller, *Yesterday's People,* discusses this in his chapter "The Mountaineer and the Church," pp. 121–33, noting that he is stressing those aspects which he finds characteristic of the region, what he calls "the 'purer' extremes" (p. 124).
3. Loyal Jones, "Studying Mountain Religion," p. 125.
4. Marshall, " 'Keep on the Sunny Side of Life,' " pp. 24–26.
5. Weller, *Yesterday's People,* p. 124.
6. As spoken onstage, Brown County Jamboree, Bean Blossom, Ind., Sunday, Oct. 22, 1961.
7. Birch Monroe, interview with author, Martinsville, Ind., Aug. 18, 1972.
8. Charlie Moore, interview with Gary Henderson, Washington, D.C., Feb., 1974.
9. Ann Randolph, "Little Roy," p. 21.
10. Bruce Powell, "Fiddlin' with Byron Berline," p. 12.
11. Jim Dickson, interview with author, Hollywood, Calif., May 7, 1983.

Bibliographical Notes

My statistics concerning religious songs in the repertoires of the four most influential bluegrass bands come from a number of sources. Most important are discographies. For Bill Monroe's 1939–74 recordings, I used my *Bill Monroe and His Blue Grass Boys.* For Flatt and Scruggs's 1948–66 recordings, I consulted R. J. Ronald, "Lester Flatt and Earl Scruggs Discography," and Earl Scruggs, "Discography." The Stanley Brothers information, covering the period 1947 to 1966, came from Pete Kuykendall, "The Stanley Brothers," with corrections and additional data from the Country Music Foundation's files and from Gary Reid. Reno and Smiley statistics came from the files of the Country Music Foundation. In addition to discography, I consulted my personal collection of songbooks of the type printed by local commercial printers for performers who sold and autographed them as "souvenir picture albums" at personal appearances. These pamphlets frequently include a special section of gospel songs, often at the back of the book.

In describing bluegrass gospel as a folk institution I am drawing upon the distinction between folk and formal religion set forth by Don Yoder in "Toward a Definition of Folk Religion." Further references to Appalachian culture studies—which include religion—are given in the bibliographical notes to the Introduction.

My sources for information about Bill Monroe's radio performance patterns with regard to gospel songs include my own listening experience, 1959–68, and a Grand Ole Opry fan's handwritten log from an earlier decade: Douglas B. Green, "The Grand Ole Opry, 1944–45." There was remarkably little difference in pattern between these two periods.

The history of the Brown County Jamboree comes largely from my interviews with Marvin Hedrick on Dec. 10, 1965, and Aug. 18, 1972. The description of Monroe's shows at Bean Blossom is based on the analysis of my collection of tape recordings of forty-eight such shows, as well as my experience as a spectator and musician at such shows. A selection of the recordings, covering the period 1954–64, is on deposit at the Indiana University Archives of Traditional Music under accession number 64-038-F. For more on Birch Monroe, manager of the Jamboree for most of the period between 1951 and 1980, see my "A Front Porch Visit with Birch Monroe."

References concerning the Lewis Family are given in the text, notes, and bibliographical notes to chapter 5. Ralph Stanley's a cappella quartets are discussed in the text and notes of chapter 11.

The definitive study of the growth of old-time fiddle music associations is Richard Blaustein's "Traditional Music and Social Change." The journal *The Devil's Box*, discussed in chapter 12, has published many articles pertaining to the various concerns of old-time fiddling association participants. A useful bibliography on fiddle music is Michael Mendelson's six-part "A Bibliography of Fiddling in North America."

Flatt's description of the fiddle and banjo as a full band is discussed in my brochure to *Country and Western Classics*, p. 25.

Articles on Byron Berline in addition to Powell's, cited in the notes to this chapter, include Roger H. Siminoff, "Byron Berline," and [Pat Chappelle], "Byron Berline (The Busy B.B.)." Also useful is Berline's monthly column in *Frets*.

Influential Texas fiddler Benny Thomasson has been the subject of a number of articles. See David Garelick, "An Interview with Benny Thomasson"; Michael Mendelson, "An Interview with Benny Thomasson"; Michael Mendelson, "Benny Thomasson and the Texas Fiddling Tradition"; and Charles Faurot, liner notes to *Benny Thomasson*.

A. C. (Eck) Robertson, a central figure in the development of modern Texas fiddling, has likewise been profiled by several researchers. See John

Cohen's "Fiddlin' Eck Robertson"; Stephen F. Davis's "A.C. (Eck) Robertson Discography"; Earl V. Spielman's "An Interview with Eck Robertson"; and Michael Bass's "Eck Robertson: Traditional Texas Fiddler."

The late Tommy Jackson, who dominated Nashville recordings of the fifties, received little attention from serious students of fiddle music. But Charles Wolfe's "From the Fiddling Archives (No. 32 in a Series)" and "A Preliminary Tommy Jackson Discography" have remedied this lack to some extent.

Texas fiddling has been described and analyzed by Earl V. Spielman in "The Fiddling Tradition of Cape Breton and Texas" and "The Texas Fiddling Style." The southwestern contest style, in and outside of Texas, is contrasted with bluegrass fiddling in Christopher Jack Goertzen, " 'Billy in the Low Ground,' " pp. 165–91. For an introduction to western swing, see Charles R. Townsend, *San Antonio Rose*, the definitive biography of Bob Wills. Although the term western swing was coined to describe the music of Spade Cooley, another influential fiddler who has received little scholarly attention, Wills is widely regarded as the central figure in the genre. Like Cooley, Wills was a fiddler; see Charles Wolfe's "From the Fiddling Archives (No. 33 in a Series)" which deals with Bob Wills as a fiddler.

For a description and history of the Weiser fiddle contest, see J. Barre Toelken, "Traditional Fiddling in Idaho." The description of the events at Richland Hills is based on my own observations and participation on the weekend of Aug. 17, 1968.

Discographical Notes

The closest thing to a recording of a Bill Monroe show is the album *Bean Blossom '79*, made at Monroe's festival that year. It includes "Watermelon Hanging on the Vine" (listed simply as "Theme"), "Y'All Come," and a "Molly and Tenbrooks Medley" which comprises parts of four requested songs. As well, Monroe's emcee work can be heard on this recording. Birch Monroe's fiddle playing, with the musical support of the Blue Grass Boys, is presented in an album produced by Bill Monroe: *Brother Birch Monroe*. Birch recorded as bass lead singer with the Blue Grass Quartet on "Boat of Love," reissued on Bill Monroe's album *A Voice from on High*, and on "Wicked Path of Sin," now available on Bill's album *The Original Bluegrass Band*. Both performances were originally on singles.

Ralph Stanley's first a cappella recordings were "Bright Morning Star" and "Sinner Man" on the album *Cry from the Cross*.

Tommy Magness's "Katy Hill," recorded with Monroe in 1940, is discussed in chapter 2. Byron Berline's first appearance on LP was on the Dillards' *Pickin' and Fiddlin'*. Of his influential 1967 recordings with Bill Monroe, "The Gold Rush" was first issued on a single, then on *Bill Monroe's*

Country Music Hall of Fame and later on *The Best of Bill Monroe.* "Sally Goodin" appeared only on *Kentucky Blue Grass.*

Eck Robertson's 1922 recording of "Sally Goodin" was reissued on *The Smithsonian Collection of Classic Country Music.* Poor Richard's Almanac was the name chosen by Sam Bush, Alan Munde, and Wayne Stewart for their band when they recorded the album *Poor Richard's Almanac.* Byron Berline recorded fiddle (on a Los Angeles sidewalk) with the Rolling Stones on their song "Country Honk," issued on the album *Let It Bleed.*

Chapter 9

Image and Stereotype:
Bluegrass Sound Tracks, 1961–72

In the early years of *Bluegrass Unlimited*, the guest articles, record reviews, and letters to the editor were written by representatives of virtually every viewpoint, including deejays, fans, musicians, and record company executives. From these believers in bluegrass came an outpouring of pent-up feelings about the music. A variety of ideas was expressed, but all agreed that their goal was to get more people listening to bluegrass. What then was the best way to do this? The assumption was if more people could hear good bluegrass, they would buy it. But the country deejays were blacklisting it, and the folkies were bored with it. Gone were the days when listening to the Kingston Trio or Pete Seeger was the beginning of a process leading through the Country Gentlemen, the Dillards, or Flatt and Scruggs to Bill Monroe. Wayne Raney wasn't hawking records on WCKY any more, and at Starday Don Pierce was busy deleting their bluegrass and old-time albums.

Yet even before *Bluegrass Unlimited* and the other manifestations of consumer involvement appeared, a more influential medium for spreading the sound of bluegrass had begun to make an impact—the movie and television sound track. Virtually everyone writing on the music has noted that its spread and popularity was partially the result of appearances in this audio-visual medium. And indeed the three best-known and highest-selling pieces in the bluegrass repertoire are sound track hits from successful productions—"The Ballad of Jed Clampett" from CBS-TV's "The Beverly Hillbillies" (1962), "Foggy Mountain Breakdown" from *Bonnie and Clyde* (1967), and "Dueling Banjos" from *Deliverance* (1972). The success of each reinforced and expanded the use of such music as a dramatic convention in the visual media, giving added cultural meaning to the bluegrass sound. The development of this convention, with its various connotations, began in the early sixties when bluegrass was relatively new to the folk revival.

In the summer of 1961 Joe Anderson, a film director in the Department of

Photography at Ohio State University in Columbus, put together a short movie consisting of time-lapse shots taken at Ohio State football games. In the time-lapse technique, a movie camera is run at a slow speed so that fewer frames per second are exposed. When the film is projected at standard speed the visual action appears rapid but jerky. Time has been compressed, motion fragmented. The technique is familiar to most of us from classroom biology films which show how seeds sprout and buds flower. During the early days of silent film, movies were shot at a smaller number of frames per second, and these, when played back on modern projectors, give a time-lapse effect to human motion which often seems strange, even funny. Anderson's football movie, *Football As It Is Played Today*, zipped through a day at the game, from the rolling back of the field tarp, the filling of the stadium, the frenetic scrimmage and half-time marching band show to the emptying of the parking lot after the game. It was about five minutes in length and was in color. This was an experimental art film which, like a cartoon, was meant to be humorous.

The film has a musical sound track by a Columbus bluegrass band, the Country Cutups, led by singer-guitarist Sid Campbell. It is an early and influential example, perhaps the first, of a bluegrass soundtrack used to accompany a visual image which does not consist of the musicians themselves. Prior to this, bluegrass bands had been shown on television and in a few country music films. In such visual/aural contexts the relationship between the image and the sound is concrete, essentially one-to-one. But with this film the visual image was not directly related to the aural signal; the relationship was abstract. Because the cinematic and video viewing situation engages the audience primarily with the visual sense, sound (particularly music) has been used from the beginning to reinforce or suggest nuances of meaning as part of the plot development in cinematic and video story telling.

Cartoon Sound Tracks: Jazz

The history of the use of music to accompany moving pictures is largely one of developing techniques for fitting music to edited film. With silent movies music was provided by musicians performing in the theater, using the symbolic conventions of western art and popular music to reinforce the formal aspects of the movie. Chase scenes involved music with fast tempi and many notes. Villains skulked about to minor keys, "bright" (high pitches, major keyed) music accompanied happiness and joy, and so forth.

With the advent of "talkies" in the late twenties the control of movie music moved from the theater to the studio. One of the earliest films to successfully exploit the integration of sound and image was a short cartoon produced by a new film company, Walt Disney Studios. Their *Steamboat Willie* introduced and starred Mickey Mouse. It was the first movie in which the film was edited so that visual motion corresponded precisely to musical meter. This technique has since become known among film-makers as "Mickey Mousing."

The importance of the musical sound tracks in the early Disney cartoons was underscored by the studio's series title for their products, "Silly Symphonies." In 1935, one such cartoon, *Music Land*, told a story in which the son of the king of the Isle of Jazz fell in love with the daughter of the queen of Symphony Land. Jazz was the raucous, upstart musical form of the time, railed against throughout the twenties by music critics and other guardians of art and culture as "noise" and degeneration; by contrast symphonic art music was the epitome of good taste and real music, supported by the financial and social elite.

The use of musical forms in conjunction with visual messages about class and culture can be clearly seen in this film. Although by the mid-thirties jazz was a familiar and widely popular form, it was still associated with (then called) Negro culture. In this cartoon, jazz with its racial, ethnic, and lower-class connotations, was literally wedded to classical music, with its contrasting mainstream and upper-class connotations. The film was a visual and aural parable about American society, specifically upward mobility and the melting pot ideal. Subsequently, jazz or music colored by it was often used in these short films, because it was, like other African-derived musics, a form which emphasized rhythm and percussion. Indeed, by the mid-forties the community of Hollywood studio musicians included a substantial number of jazzmen.

Avant-garde: From Jazz to Bluegrass in Sound Tracks

The sound track to *Football As It Is Played Today* came to the film because in 1961 people were beginning to perceive bluegrass as an avant-garde form of folk-derived music with similarities to jazz. By the fifties jazz was a kaleidoscopic mixture of personal, regional, and historical styles. Though still dominated by black musicians, it had become the avant-garde art music of young middle-class white intellectuals at colleges. At the same time, this group was becoming interested in other types of music, particularly jazz-related folk musics such as the blues.

In June 1961 Peter J. Welding (whose previous writings had been on blues and jazz) reviewed Flatt and Scruggs's *Foggy Mountain Banjo* album for the *Saturday Review*. Tying it historically to old-timey string band music and emphasizing its similarities to New Orleans jazz and differences from "the vapid banalities of most of the popular commercial offerings in the hillbilly vein," he praised the music of Flatt and Scruggs in terms dripping with meaning for the intellectual readership of the magazine: "Scruggs's brilliant, coruscating banjo lines and Flatt's equally facile guitar figures dart in and out of the dense polyphonic ensemble texture in one of the most exciting and fascinating experiences in all of American folk music."[1] (This flamboyant sentence, with its sophisticated terminology, was quoted on two Flatt and Scruggs album liner notes during the next two years.) A few weeks later, Welding reviewed the same record for the prestigious jazz monthly *Down Beat*, giving it five stars, the highest possible rating. For this readership he called it "another kind of soul music" and suggested that "if anything, it has even more passion, conviction, and drive than most soul jazz." He urged the readers to try the record, even though the "earthy, spontaneous, uncomplicated music rooted in U.S. folk-music tradition . . . played with driving intensity and fervor . . . might take some listening on your part to get accustomed to this approach."[2] Welding's perception of bluegrass as high-energy folk music echoed Lomax's description of it as "folk music with overdrive," and like Lomax, Welding sought to legitimize the music as art by likening it to jazz.

With *Football As It Is Played Today*, the jazz-bluegrass connection, already introduced to the avant-garde thinking of the time, was conveyed to a new medium, the experimental art film. Though the Ohio State University Department of Photography's film unit was, as part of a state-funded institution, involved in practical work, film unit directors could sometimes make experimental movies on their own. So it was that Joe Anderson made *Football* at the unit.

Like many film-makers, Anderson followed the world film scene avidly, utilizing ideas from experimental films in the practical movies he was making. He had co-authored a critical study of Japanese cinema and was involved in the Ohio State University Film Series, a group that brought to campus experimental, foreign, and historically significant works. At this time the idea of film as art was just gaining acceptance on American university campuses.

When Anderson began looking for a sound track, he showed a silent rough cut of the film to an anthropology graduate student named John Szwed. A native of Alabama, Szwed had grown up in a suburb of Philadelphia; he was an erstwhile jazz musician who was interested in film as art and worked on an occasional basis in the film unit. Anderson felt the film needed further shaping to make it more humorous and hoped that a sound track would achieve this. Szwed was aware of the use of jazz in movies, but jazz would not work for this sound track because the rhythm was not right. So he turned to a new interest of his, country music. Although Szwed remembers owning recordings by a wide range of country performers, from Jimmie Rodgers to Flatt and Scruggs, it was a folk revival group to which he turned in looking for a possible sound track for the movie: "I picked up the New Lost City Ramblers album with 'Dallas Rag' on it, it was playing at the time . . . and I was just playing and thinking about that film, and thought Jesus this is, you know, the right tempo first of all, so I suggested it to him. . . . It seemed to be strictly a matter of tempo. . . . We had talked about . . . how bizarre this is going to be, koto music for example, could be used, and I thought of it just in functional terms."[3] But when Anderson put the recording on along with the rough cut of the film, "everybody started laughing, and from then on it seemed to me that it was going to have to be of that genre at least."

The other young man involved in the making of the sound track for *Football* was Franklin Miller, a senior at Oberlin College, who arrived at the Ohio State Film Unit in mid-June of 1961. He became acquainted with Anderson because his father, a professor at Kenyon College, was working with Anderson as a consultant on a series of instructional films. Miller was soon introduced to the football film:

> I walked in and they were in a projection room, looking at this stuff. All these funny, you know, sped-up time-lapse stuff was going by. And they were dropping needles on records, listening to jazz, to see what jazz music would go with this stuff. And the guy who was doing this was named John Szwed . . . and I said you know there's some—why don't I bring in a bluegrass record, you know, what the hell, you should hear this. And they all sort of looked like, "What's bluegrass?" except that John Szwed seemed to know what bluegrass was but didn't own any records. And so I said no problem so I drag in a record, and I remember it was probably something like "Foggy Mountain Breakdown," . . . and they said, "that's great."[4]

Miller and Szwed remember, two decades later, that they both suggested a departure from jazz or some other avant-garde audio portion for this film. Each recalls initial experiments involving records from their personal collections. "Dallas Rag" and "Foggy Mountain Breakdown" are musically similar instrumental pieces involving a stream of sixteenth notes, a sequence of regularly spaced pulses at a brisk pace. In both, there is a strong and swift rhythmic background pattern with emphasis upon the off-beat. This music fit the rapid stream of images on the screen. Somewhat unexpectedly, it was also "funny." As Miller, who subsequently studied film-making with Anderson, remembers:

> We were fooling around trying to make a match between the time-lapse photography and something musical. And bluegrass struck us, for whatever reasons, as the correct match. We'd never seen that before. I don't think anybody had. But I think it had as much to do with the formal qualities of all those people moving around real fast—coruscating, what is that, coruscating arpeggios? Isn't that what the guy used to say? And we felt, we saw the formal connections in other words. And the problem was a lot of people saw the cultural thing. They thought we were poking fun at football because we were using hillbilly music, you see. Whereas we thought we were finding intricate little patterns and movements.

Human action seems strange and humorous in time-lapse photography because the effect draws attention to the mechanical workings of the movie.

Henri Bergson held that "the attitudes, gestures and movements of the human body are laughable in exact proportion as that body reminds us of a mere machine."[5] With time-lapse photography we perceive that the motion picture is an artifice, that it is imposing its order on reality, making human motion into jerky stick-figure cartoon-like action. When fluid motion is reduced to a series of quick, regular movements, it acquires its own artificial meter. Anderson wanted to find a music which paralleled this meter. The mandolin and banjo of "Dallas Rag" and the sound of bluegrass recordings like "Foggy Mountain Breakdown" both "worked." Records were not, however, used for the sound track.

Miller recalls Anderson suggesting, "Look, why don't you—it can cost nothing—why don't you try to assemble some musicians?" This led to a series of unsuccessful attempts to create the sound track in which Miller, who had been playing jazz, folk, old-time, and bluegrass music at college, participated with various local old-time and folk musicians.

The final version of the sound track began to take shape only after Anderson became aware of a bluegrass band playing at a hillbilly bar on North High Street, called Irv-Nell's. How did this happen? In August Miller and a friend met an instrument repairman at the Ohio State Fair who showed them a mandolin he had been working on for a local bluegrass musician, Sid Campbell. They visited Campbell, who took them to a jam session at the home of a young banjo picker named Johnny Hickman. There they learned of the regular bluegrass music at Irv-Nell's. Miller remembers: "As soon as I saw that group play at Irv-Nell's I knew that we had to scrap whatever was left of the track, whatever we had done."

Miller had played with the (Oberlin College) Plum Creek Boys at the Osbornes' 1960 Antioch concert. He had seen Jimmy Martin at the WWVA Jamboree and the Country Gentlemen at their first college appearance at Oberlin in 1961. He had worked or jammed with city/college bluegrass bands in New York, Ohio, and California. He recognized the quality of the music being made by Sid Campbell's band at Irv-Nell's because he had been trying to play such music and because he had been listening to records and tapes of personal appearances and radio shows of such music. He knew at once that this was the real thing.

Szwed, too, had been to Irv-Nell's. His perspective was somewhat different. He was not as aware of bluegrass as Miller. But as an anthropologist in training, he was fascinated by the cultural scene he found in the bar. He took Joe Anderson to see it:

> My idea was to sell him on this as a kind of urban ethnography thing
> although I had no idea about that at the time, but it was one of those
> nexes where it all comes together, where girls who would otherwise be at
> Sunday school picnics or things, are showing up here dressed as if they
> were at the damn picnics, and with the tension of all this going on, here

were drunks, you know, and all the rest of it, thugs and so on, and somehow it all hung together. There were old home songs and the honky tonk songs, and it was the first time, outside of the South, that I'd ever seen . . . this is the first time I had ever seen a place that looked like it belonged somewhere else. Had the feeling of all that. Of course that neighborhood was strictly country, you know.

The music too appealed to Szwed: "It had a really hot quality to it." And in Irv-Nell's it was presented dramatically on a small stage beneath a stairwell at the back of this store-front bar. Szwed recalled that "they were tightly organized visually and choreographed beautifully." Like Miller, Szwed felt that he had "stumbled" onto something. "On one hand you were discovering something new but it's well established and vital so that you can be both a discoverer and see a full blown art."

Both young men, the anthropologist-in-training and the budding film-maker, knew enough about the music to recognize the band's professional competence and skill. Miller's tentative efforts at making the sound track music himself were almost completely scrapped and the Country Cutups were brought from Irv-Nell's into the recording studio. Miller's name follows Anderson's in the credits ("A Film by Joseph L. Anderson/Music by Franklin Miller") as the second in a string of seventeen title boards which flash by at the end of the film, mickey moused to the standard bluegrass ending of two "shave-and a haircut, two bits" phrases. Miller plays mandolin on this final version of the sound track, but it is dominated by the regular members of the band: Sid Campbell, guitar; Ross Branham, banjo; Bill Moore, fiddle; Dan Milhon, Dobro; and Chuck Cordle, bass.

The use of a Columbus bluegrass band for this sound track involved a realization similar to that of Rinzler when he first went to Sunset Park and of Israel Young when he attended Clifton's Luray show in 1961. What had seemed an obscure recorded musical form was suddenly linked in vivid experience to a visual and social context; a network of performers and fans was revealed. It was the beginning of a process that brought revival bluegrassers like Miller together with local country bands like those of Campbell—the same sort of thing that was happening in Boston, Berkeley, and other urban areas. Within the next year local and national bluegrass bands would appear in concert on the Ohio State campus and for "gigs" at the local folk coffee-house, the Sacred Mushroom, Columbus' equivalent to Boston's Club 47 and the Ash Grove in Los Angeles.

But the film had a life of its own. In April 1962 the newly completed work was entered in a film festival which *New York Times* reporter Howard Thompson described as "the largest and most comprehensive non-theatrical film conclave in the world."[6] This was the fourth annual American Film Festival, sponsored by the Educational Film Library Association for 16-mm. documentary films. Held at the Biltmore Hotel in New York, it attracted some 600 entries. There were thirty-four different categories of film in which awards were given, and *Football As It Is Played Today* received the first prize in the "Film As Art" category.

The exposure which the prize-winning film received at the American Film Festival had several results. Anderson was approached by Columbia Pictures, who were interested in the rights for commercial distribution to movie houses in a 35-mm. format. But the film was considered an O.S.U. production, and the copyright was owned by the state rather than by Anderson, so the decision to allow distribution was not his to make. To his disappointment, the university decided the film would not be leased or sold for commercial distribution. Ohio State football coach Woody Hayes, in particular, was upset by the film, especially the music's negative connotation, and claimed "it made Ohio State look like a cow college."[7] He also tried to block CBS Sports' purchase of one-time television rights to use the film to introduce its special 1962 college football season preview. Hayes relented on the condition that the bluegrass track be dropped. CBS replaced the original track with speeded-up records of collegiate marches. They also cut from the film any closer shots where they thought people could be identified, to prevent lawsuits. It is ironic that Hayes later became a regular user of the original film, when he discovered how well it was received at the various fund-raising meetings to which he took it.

The American Film Festival drew "a surprising number of good movies . . . from university campuses," the *Times* reported, and was noteworthy also for a significant amount of participation by the television networks.[8] Apparently CBS News was impressed by the film, for within a few weeks of the festival, Anderson had received a contract from them to do a five-minute segment to be broadcast on a special summer edition of "CBS Reports" with Harry Reasoner. This "CBS Reports" was indeed special, for its approach was to cover its subject, "The American Housewife" (that was the title of the program) with humor. It was aired in a one-hour version at ten o'clock in the evening of July 12, 1962. Anderson's film opened the show, followed by various reports, essays, and discussions on the American housewife by Harry Reasoner, Mary Thicket, Vivian Vance, Bob and Ray, and Captain Kangaroo.

Anderson's five-minute segment had the working title of "How Swived." It dealt with a day in the life of an ordinary housewife. The film begins with a regular-speed sequence in which the husband is seen preparing to leave home; an instrumental version of a slow sentimental bluegrass song provides the proper setting for this introduction. As the front door closes and the husband leaves, the picture changes to a time-lapse effect and the music shifts to a fast instrumental as the wife rushes through her daily work— cleaning, laundry, shopping, etc. At the end the husband returns home and the tempo returns to the slow theme of the beginning. The sound track for this film was again made by Sid Campbell and the Country Cutups, with Miller on mandolin; Johnny Hickman replaced Ross Branham on banjo.

The impact of *Football* and "How Swived" on the media can be seen in the way in which their ideas were "borrowed." Within several months after the broadcast of "How Swived," Miller happened to see on television a thirty-second ad in which a Ford station wagon did a multitude of errands around town in time-lapse with a bluegrass sound track. Miller remembers wondering how they got that idea and being told that commercial production houses send people to film festivals to get new ideas for commercials. Several other commercials using these ideas also appeared around this time.

The fact that the time-lapse-photography/bluegrass-sound-track combination had been taken up by ad agencies influenced Anderson's thinking about the next network commission, which came as a result of *Football* and "How Swived." This was from an ABC show, "Update." Bo Goldman, who, with Andy Rooney, had been a writer for the "CBS Reports" show on the American housewife, was working as an independent producer for ABC on "Update." Remembering Anderson's earlier work, Goldman asked him to provide an opening number for a special edition of "Update." This was to be a brief humorous feature on high school cheerleaders; Anderson's working title for it was "Cheers."

Anderson and Miller, working again as independents, decided at the outset not to use either time-lapse photography or a bluegrass sound track. Filming at a few frames under standard camera speed ("undercranking") in order to slightly speed up the action, they followed the Worthington, Ohio, High School basketball cheerleaders through a season, amassing footage. For the sound track, they planned to mimic high school fight songs as played on a piano during a pre-game assembly. A jazz pianist from Columbus recorded the first part of the sound track. On New Year's Eve 1962 the edited footage with the piano track was shown to producer Goldman, who made a special trip from New York to check the production for the network. After viewing the print, he told Anderson and Miller that solo piano music doesn't work on television and that it was his understanding that the sound track would be bluegrass. They said no, they had planned from the start to do it with a piano. Since Goldman had sold the idea to ABC on the basis of its having a bluegrass sound track, he insisted that the film be completed with one.

Consequently, they were faced with a problem. They would have to re-edit the entire film in order to make it synch with another track. There was an element of time involved, as there usually is in such projects. Luckily the Country Gentlemen were booked to appear at the Sacred Mushroom on January 6. The Gentlemen were emerging into national stature among urban bluegrass followers, and Miller was glad to be able to hire them. The day after their concert they went into a small studio in Columbus, one used for making commercial jingles.

Although most movie sound tracks are recorded with the musicians playing along while a print of the movie is being screened, the Country Gentlemen found this distracting. Miller discovered that they were able to follow the timings needed closely enough so that it was not necessary to record in this manner. Moreover they considered the four microphones offered them unnecessary, preferring to work with one. The sound track was completed in a brief time, leaving Miller very impressed with the professionalism of the band. The "Update" special was shown later that year to good reviews.

"Cheers" depicts a high school basketball game from beginning to end but the action is not speeded up as in *Football* or "How Swived." It achieves its pace by the rapid editing and ellipsis between many events. The rhythm of both editing and the action synchronize closely with the Country Gentlemen's sound track.

In assessing the production of "Cheers" several aspects seem significant. ABC's insistence upon the bluegrass sound track reflected the fact that Anderson had developed a reputation within the television industry as the person to turn to for this sort of thing. In commissioning the brief humorous production with a bluegrass sound track, ABC was aware of CBS's use of similar material; the networks were engaged in fierce competition for the highest ratings, essential for advertising revenues. In a sense ABC commissioned the production because it was "trendy"; in another sense, the technique was a sure bet, having been used successfully by CBS.

The sound track for *Football* had been arrived at by experimentation, and the musicians discovered almost by accident in the summer of 1961. By January 1963 Miller was able to hire a nationally-known band because they were appearing at a Columbus coffeehouse. There was an element of luck here, but it was indicative of the way the Columbus bluegrass "scene" had grown from the Appalachian-dominated High Street network to the campus neighborhood coffeehouse.

The Beverly Hillbillies

In the fall of 1962 while Anderson and Miller were beginning work on "Cheers," CBS-TV premiered a new situation comedy series, "The Beverly Hillbillies." Its theme, "The Ballad of Jed Clampett," was performed by Flatt and Scruggs. Released (at Louise Scruggs's suggestion) as a single, the song was on the country and pop charts by the end of the year and early in 1963 became the first bluegrass recording to reach number one on the country charts, reflecting the success of the television show. No doubt its popularity was one of the factors which led Anderson and Miller to turn to other music for their "Cheers" sound track, just as it was probably an influencing factor in ABC's insistence in having bluegrass for "Cheers."

"The Beverly Hillbillies" used bluegrass music for the sound track in ways which differed from Anderson's. The weekly situation comedy demanded music more akin to that of full-length feature films than of cartoons. Hollywood feature-length movie music drew heavily upon the techniques of nineteenth-century opera, particularly those of Wagner, Strauss, Puccini, and Verdi. Like opera scores, film music was intended to be subordinate to dramatic action and dialogue. It was used to underscore or clarify points which were being made visually—from a fanfare when the producer's name was flashed on the screen to a swelling of lush strings when the female star appeared in ravishing soft focus. Music could also be used in more subtle ways—to build anticipation of coming or off-camera events, to convey conflict through asynchronous music, to communicate plot development through the variation of a musical theme or themes, to identify characters through leit-motiv, and so on. Successful techniques in the world of film are quickly borrowed, so the route from innovation to convention is short.

As Hollywood film composers ventured further afield from nineteenth-century popular and classical models, they began appropriating various popularly identifiable genres in order to convey theme through the use of cultural stereotypes. By the fifties this had become a convention. Elmer Bernstein used modern jazz-type music in *The Man with the Golden Arm,* a film about a jazz drummer who was a drug addict; Dmitri Tiomkin used cowboy singer Tex Ritter in the sound track for the first "intellectual western," *High Noon.* Bill Haley's "Rock around the Clock" introduced rock music as a thematic motif for *The Blackboard Jungle,* a film about high school violence. Although there were examples of entire musical genres being used this way, it was and is more common for movie music composers to borrow instruments, voicings, and themes from such forms as jazz, country, and rock as they seem appropriate. The film-makers' sense of the symbolic or affective dimensions of a particular musical form leads to a kind of stereotyping or typecasting of music. As Miller noted, some viewers reacted to the "hillbilly" aspects of the *Football* sound track, a response which was not sought by the film-makers. The creator of "The Beverly Hillbillies," in contrast, was looking for just such a connection.

At about the same time as *Football* was being completed, producer Paul Henning saw Flatt and Scruggs in one of their first folk music coffeehouse appearances, at the Ash Grove in Hollywood. Like Szwed and Miller at Irv-Nell's, he had stumbled upon a music form which fitted his needs—a theme and incidental music for his new series. Produced by Henning for Filmways, "The Beverly Hillbillies" ran on CBS from 1962 to 1971 and, in syndicated form, was rerun by many stations after that date. One of the most popular television situation comedies in history, it portrayed a stereotyped mountain family that had struck it rich and moved to Beverly Hills, where their bucolic innocence led to weekly adventures with money-grubbing city folks from which they emerged triumphant.

When Henning's music director, Perry Botkin, approached Louise Scruggs, she reacted strongly against being associated with a program about "hillbillies," for as Earl later recalled, "We had worked so hard to get away from what you might call the 'hillbilly' image." Only after they were shown a pilot film and convinced that it was "about hillbillies, but common-sense hill-billies," did they agree to participate in the venture.[9]

Flatt and Scruggs not only provided the successful theme and incidental music but also made yearly cameo appearances between 1962 and 1968, playing themselves as friends of the Clampetts, and composed and recorded at least one other song featured on the program, "Pearl Pearl Pearl." From this point on until the end of his career, Lester Flatt always danced his version of "Granny's Dance" from this show in his personal appearances. "The Ballad of Jed Clampett" brought Flatt and Scruggs to a new and far larger audience.

Unlike the Anderson films, in which bluegrass had been used because of its formal characteristics, "The Beverly Hillbillies" used bluegrass primarily because of its cultural connotations. This entailed not just instrumental music—although Scruggs's banjo was prominent and essential, particularly in the incidental passages (which, in later episodes, were played by Los Angeles banjoists Don Parmley and Doug Dillard)—but also involved Lester Flatt's singing of the theme lyrics which set the scene for the series. While Scruggs's banjo was archetypically "bluegrass," Flatt's vocalizing on the recording was low-pitched in style, closer to Johnny Cash than to the high lonesome sound of bluegrass singing. Flatt did not actually sing on the video sound track; this was done by Hollywood singer Jerry Scroggins.

Still, it was definitely country, and it carried an affective meaning which differed from the somewhat more abstract sound of instrumental music. It is significant that when Welding commended the music of Flatt and Scruggs to the readers of *Saturday Review* and *Down Beat* he did so in a review of an instrumental album. Most listeners who were not country music fans did not appreciate bluegrass lyrics and the vocal style in which they were delivered. In June 1961 just at the time Welding wrote his reviews, *Time* magazine reported on the success of Flatt and Scruggs in cynical tones, calling bluegrass "a particularly corny style of country music" and describing Flatt as "lift[ing] his nasal, sow-belly voice in an enduring country hit named 'Give Me Flowers While I'm Living.' "[10] Bluegrass, they reported, "is enjoying such a boom that it has now moved cheek by jowl with cool jazz into big city supper clubs." The *Time* article was a response to enthusiastic reports about bluegrass such as those of Welding and of Robert Shelton, whose comparison of Scruggs with Paganini was called "astigmatic" by *Time*. Avant-garde praise certainly did not insure acceptance by conservative highbrows; *Time* spoke to and for the conservative urban establishment in tying the music to rural images of pigs and corn.

For the producers of "The Beverly Hillbillies," these conflicting viewpoints enhanced the value of the music as a theme for the show by appealing to quite different audiences. The older country fans and the new avant-garde folk fans could respond to the music as something familiar and authentic, which they valued. And those for whom *Time*'s viewpoint seemed apt could recognize the music as the latest in country corn, commensurate with the stereotype of Jed Clampett and his kin as depicted on the program. As these "corny" characters triumphed over their sophisticated antagonists the program used the music in such a way as to provide comic synthesis of these opposing views of the music; the Clampetts' weekly triumphs were funnier because of their uncompromising corniness.

The new program was considered definitely low-brow by television critics. The *New York Times'* Jack Gould called it "perhaps the worst of the new season's entries, . . . steeped in enough twanging guitar, polkadot gingham, deliberative drawl, prolific cousins and rural no-think to make each half-hour seem as if it contained 60 minutes." It contained "every cliché in the book" and, Gould suggested, might persuade Perry Como, whose NBC show suffered in the ratings battle because of it, "to forget about the 'Kraft Music Hall' and just bring back 'Grand Ole Opry.' "[11]

Even Roy Acuff, who early in his career traded successfully on the hillbilly image, found the show a bit difficult to take: "I've shared the stage with performers who want to be country but overdo it, over-emphasize it. I accepted the Beverly Hillbillies show on television, for instance, because I enjoyed it and I knew a lot of those people who were on it, but we here in this part of the country would look at it and laugh. There's hardly anyone in our part of the world now who is as far backwoods as that is."[12]

The music for "The Beverly Hillbillies" quickly became another cliché, as much a part of the mountain stereotype as the dress, speech, and eating habits affected by the Clampetts. It is ironic that this happened with Flatt and Scruggs, for in appearing at the Ash Grove (and universities and folk festivals) they had cultivated a positive stereotype of the folk artist, not the derogatory stereotype of the mountain rube. But as Anderson, Miller, and Szwed found in their attempt to use the music for its exotic formal qualities, it generated response in terms of cultural stereotype. And if the creators of the Beverly Hillbillies characters meant them to stand for the transcendence of rural innocence, they were only partly successful, for the opinion of critics like Gould was that no serious, intelligent person could find anything meaningful in such a clichéd message. Thus, by the winter of 1962–63 bluegrass, outside its home grounds, was moving from an exotic art form known to hipsters and folkies to a type-cast sound, part of the imagery available to the visual mass media.

Flatt and Scruggs recorded theme songs from two other rural situation comedies produced by Paul Henning and Filmways for CBS, "Petticoat Junction" and "Green Acres." "Petticoat Junction" ran from 1963 to 1970 and according to one source "still had a sizeable audience when CBS cancelled it in 1970 in a general housecleaning to change the network's rural image."[13] "Green Acres" ran from 1965 to 1971; like "Petticoat Junction" it was set in a country village named Hooterville. It reversed the theme of "The Beverly Hillbillies," portraying a city couple's move to the country and their concomitant misfortunes. This couple occasionally made appearances on "Petticoat

Junction." By the fall of 1971, all three programs had been cut by CBS (as had a later CBS comedy show which utilized bluegrass, "Hee Haw") in their purge of rural shows. All were considered successful and they were seen long after 1971 in re-runs.

Bonnie and Clyde

The combination of the motion imagery projected by Anderson in *Football As It Is Played Today* (and the films and ads which followed it), and the cultural imagery projected by the themes of "The Beverly Hillbillies" and subsequent Henning-Filmways productions shaped the use of bluegrass in television. The first (or, at least, earliest known to me) bluegrass in a sound track was for a movie, and indeed the visual effect it accompanied was basically cinematic; video recording technology which creates the time-lapse effect is a recent invention. But following *Football* the uses of bluegrass sound tracks were predominately in television, even when they utilized time-lapse effects (as in the ads and "How Swived"). It was not until the music had been tried and accepted in television for some five years that bluegrass was utilized in a major motion picture sound track, that of *Bonnie and Clyde*.

In 1967 producer Warren Beatty, who was also playing the role of Clyde Barrow in the film, contacted Earl Scruggs, asking him to write the score. A few days later he called Scruggs again to let him know that he had gone through his record collection and chosen an instrumental they recorded in 1949, "Foggy Mountain Breakdown," for use in the film.

Beatty had been aware of bluegrass music for over a decade when he chose "Foggy Mountain Breakdown" for *Bonnie and Clyde*. During his senior year at Washington and Lee High School in Arlington, Virginia (1954–55), bluegrass was the subject of a civics presentation by Pete Kuykendall, one of several classmates who were playing bluegrass and collecting hillbilly records. After class Beatty stayed to talk with him, expressing strong interest in the music. Kuykendall (now editor of *Bluegrass Unlimited*), recalls this because it seemed "out of context for what I thought he liked." The musical interest of Kuykendall and his friends represented a kind of "counter culture" at the school, for such music definitely had a "hillbilly stigma." Because of this he was surprised at the positive response of Beatty, who was "a big man on campus and a jock"—class president and star center on the football team.[14] It is very likely that this incident planted the seed which led to Beatty's use of "Foggy Mountain Breakdown" in *Bonnie and Clyde*. Like other early middle-class "discoverers" of bluegrass (such as Miller and Szwed), Beatty was himself a musician; he supported his early acting career by playing piano in a New York cocktail bar.

Music was used, sparingly, several different ways in *Bonnie and Clyde*. Consonant with the careful attention to historical settings were recordings and film sound track music from the early thirties. A record of pop song "Deep in the Arms of Love" underlays the opening confrontation between Bonnie and Clyde; after their first bank robbery they are seen in a movie house watching a chorus line in *Gold Diggers of 1933* sing "We're in the Money." The lyrics of both songs mesh with and interpret the on-screen action. Later in the film, orchestral popular music recordings of the era are heard during scenes depicting the Barrow gang relaxing in various hide-outs. In its final such use the music is carried on behind a murderous gun battle.

Contrasting with music as part of the film's setting is that utilized in a more typical Hollywood fashion to underscore points being made by the film. For example, at several places conventional soft orchestral music can be heard—during a family reunion and following Bonnie and Clyde's only suc-cessful attempt at love making. But most of the music used to underscore in this fashion is, by the standards of the time, unconventional, for it is bluegrass.

"Foggy Mountain Breakdown," Flatt and Scruggs's first instrumental re-cording and generally considered the archetypal bluegrass banjo tune, is heard three times. The first comes early in the movie. Bonnie, who has just met Clyde and learned that he is an ex-con, fondles his pistol and challenges him: "You won't have the gumption to use it." Clyde responds by robbing a grocery store and as they careen off in a stolen car the music begins. It ends abruptly as Clyde stops the car and pushes Bonnie, who is frantically trying to make love with him, away: "I might as well tell you right off, I ain't much of a lover boy." This is but the first of Bonnie's attempts to seduce Clyde. The music serves, then, to heighten the exhilaration of the getaway, an exhilaration with sexual overtones. Its impact is great because it is the first music heard in the film which is not directly tied to the setting. Following this scene, we hear a different bluegrass theme (recorded for the film by Doug Dillard, Glen Campbell, Tommy Tedesco on tenor banjo, and a fiddler) at half a dozen other points where the exhilaration of the gang's outlawry and travel is emphasized. "Foggy Mountain Breakdown" appears again in the middle of the movie as they escape from their biggest bank robbery. This chase scene with its music is intercut with testimony from victims illustrating the growth of Bonnie and Clyde's self-perpetuated legend.

Finally Bonnie and Clyde, recovering from the wounds received in am-bush, are seen reading Bonnie's poem about them, published in a newspaper. Clyde tells Bonnie, "You made me somebody they gonna remember"; for the first and only time they make love. As this scene unfolds, "Foggy Mountain Breakdown" is heard and continues while the images on the screen cut back and forth from the lovers to scenes of their betrayal by the father of a gang member. These scenes precede and portend the fatal ambush which ends their lives and closes the film.

Bluegrass music in *Bonnie and Clyde* appears first as a structural complement to the chase scenes, which are very slightly undercranked to heighten the effect of motion without becoming mechanical. The music is connected to the exhilaration of lawlessness, escape, and travel, which from the outset have sexual connotations. In its final use it underlies a scene in which it ironically lends this exhilaration to love making and betrayal, so as to symbolize and portend death. Here the music is used symbolically by taking advantage of the effect created by its earlier formal and structural use. Like the setting-related music at the beginning of the film, it comments on the meaning of the movie. Thus was "Foggy Mountain Breakdown" used to create the movie's own aural iconography.

Though the movie was meant to depict the lives of southwestern outlaws, the mountaineer image somehow adhered to the film. Bosley Crowther, reviewing it in August 1967 called the film "a cheap piece of bald-faced slapstick comedy that treats the hideous depredations of that sleazy moronic pair as though they were as full of fun and frolic as the jazz-age cut-ups in 'Thoroughly Modern Millie' . . . striving mightily to be the 'Beverly Hillbillies' of next year."[15] Like "The Ballad of Jed Clampett," "Foggy Mountain Breakdown" was a best-seller but it did better in the popular than in the country music charts.

Film historians have marked *Bonnie and Clyde* as a turning point in American movies. Gerald Mast called it "perhaps the first full statement of the new [American] cinema's values," but, as Roy M. Prendergast points out: "with the influence this film exerted on American film values with its innovations also came merely a new set of conventions and cliches. Among these cliches is the use of music in as stereotyped a manner as its Strauss-symphonic counterpart of the 1930s and 1940s—only the Strauss is now replaced by the pop, and the symphonic by the Fender bass."[16]

As I noted earlier, it is typical of film music that successful innovations quickly become conventions, and this was certainly true of the use of bluegrass banjo in *Bonnie and Clyde*. It is significant that "Foggy Mountain Breakdown" was a pop music hit, for this reflected the fact that the people buying the record were not country music consumers. As with the "Beverly Hillbillies," Flatt and Scruggs were quick to exploit their success. Their *Bonnie and Clyde* album featured newly composed songs about the pair by up-and-coming Nashville songwriter Tom T. Hall and instrumentals with auto chase sound effects. On the cover, Flatt, Scruggs, and the Foggy Mountain Boys posed in an early thirties Packard Phaeton, togged out like gangsters of that period, carrying submachine guns.

The impact of *Bonnie and Clyde* extended beyond the Flatt and Scruggs band, as bluegrass performers utilized it in various ways to gain new markets. The Sawtooth Mountain Volunteers, a college band from Oregon, began appearing in double-breasted suits and two-tone shoes similar to those worn on the cover of the Flatt and Scruggs album. The Osborne Brothers, under the name of the Bluegrass Banjo Pickers, recorded a budget-priced album for RCA Camden entitled *Foggy Mountain Breakdown and Other Music from the Bonnie and Clyde Era.* These were just two examples out of many.

Following the introduction of bluegrass in a feature film sound track, there was a resurgence of its use in television ads. It even appeared in a political ad during the 1968 presidential primary race. From this point on, the music was used frequently in both feature movies and ads. And while the music by Flatt and Scruggs in *Bonnie and Clyde* had used a full bluegrass band, sound track composers tended to feature only the five-string banjo aspect of bluegrass, placing it in the context of an electric country band or a standard studio orchestra. This was typical of the adaptation of source musics (like jazz and cowboy song) into the conventional language of film usage.

Deliverance

Bluegrass was used in yet another way in the 1972 film *Deliverance*—as an on-screen musical element rather than just as sound to accompany action. The film, based on the 1970 novel of the same name by James Dickey, was a box-office success which had mixed reviews. One *New York Times* reviewer described it as "the experience of four Atlanta suburbanites . . . when they go on a weekend canoe trip that turns into a nightmare of the machismo mind," and called it "an action melodrama that doesn't trust its action to speak louder than words."[17] A few weeks later another critic on the same paper praised it, saying, "Along with deflating myths about nature and primitive life, the film is a devastating critique of machismo."[18]

The scene which involved bluegrass was, in the opinion of critic Arthur Knight of the *Saturday Review,* "perhaps the most extraordinary scene in American films of recent years." He described it:

> The cars pull up before an ancient shanty. The city men need drivers to deliver their cars to them downstream. They peek in the windows and see only a ravaged hag, and a child dying of malnutrition. Another child, almost catatonic, sits vacantly in a swing on a collapsing porch. While a simpleton gasses up their cars, one of the city men strikes a few notes on his guitar. The child on the porch responds on his banjo. A few more notes, another response. In no time the two are challenging each other with bits of music. It is a contest that the child—empty-eyed, toothlessly grinning—wins easily. And immediately he returns to his catatonic state.
>
>   It is a completely movie moment, emphasizing at once the connections between the city people and the mountain people but, more especially, the gulf that separates them.[19]

The scene was developed from a passage in Dickey's novel in which one of the city men, Drew, who "went in for all the really hard finger-picking stuff,

Reverend Gary Davis, Dave Van Ronk, Merle Travis, Doc Watson," is asked by the service station owner, who spots his guitar, to play a tune with a wall-eyed albino boy, Lonnie. Drew begins on "Wildwood Flower" and the boy (the service station owner says "Lonnie don't know nothin' but banjo-pickin' . . . he ain't never been to school") joins in gradually, by the end dominating the session and exciting Drew, who gets his name and address from the service station owner, hoping to return for more.[20]

In the movie the excitement that Drew feels for the chance encounter of a musical form is not emphasized; the brief rapprochement of the two musicians blending their versions of "Wildwood Flower" has been replaced by a musical piece which emphasizes conflict and confrontation, "Dueling Banjos."

"Dueling Banjos" derives ultimately from "Feuding Banjos," a recording made in 1955 by Don Reno and Arthur "Guitar Boogie" Smith. In it Reno played five-string and Smith tenor banjo. Two years later Carl Story, with the Brewster Brothers, recorded it for Mercury-Starday as "Mocking Banjo." This banjo-mandolin dialog (which the Brewsters copyrighted with Starday as publisher) was copied by many bluegrass bands in the late fifties and early sixties. In their 1963 version, "Duelin' Banjo," the Dillards claimed copyright as arrangers and adapters, with Elektra Records as publisher. Banjoist Eric Weissberg, along with guitarist Steve Mandell adapted it for the film score. Weissberg sent the Warner Brothers' producer his copy of the Arthur Smith recording, but the company copyrighted it in his name. Eventually Smith sued the company (and Weissberg), winning the rights to royalties from the tune as it was used in the film.

Mandell, like Weissberg, was a product of the New York bluegrass scene. Both Mandell and Weissberg had, at the time the movie was made, been working for years as sidemen and studio musicians out of New York and were not well known as bluegrass musicians. They stand in contrast to Flatt and Scruggs (who by 1972 had been disbanded for three years) in this aspect; by the time of *Deliverance* it was not necessary for film music arrangers to seek out big-name specialists in the style because studio musicians could do the job quite adequately. The *Deliverance* sound track album consisted of two 1972 tracks by Weissberg and Mandell along with all but two of the cuts made by Brickman and Weissberg in 1963 for their Elektra album, *New Dimensions in Banjo and Bluegrass*.

Owing to the success of the film and the recording, which, like "Foggy Mountain Breakdown," did well on the pop charts, many bluegrass bands recorded "Dueling Banjos." However, their arrangements tended to follow the older "Mocking Banjo" in form and in the use of the mandolin rather than guitar for the second instrument.

Through such performances, as well as through the popularity of the sound track recording, "Dueling Banjos" became frequently requested and often performed at bluegrass festivals. As we shall see in the following chapter, by the early seventies these festivals were being held in the Southeast, Midwest, Southwest, and (less frequently) in many other regions. Every summer weekend saw thousands of people traveling to parks and campgrounds for the concerts, workshops, and informal music making of these festivals. The bigger festivals brought together many of the best-known bluegrass stars and drew diverse audiences from wide geographical areas.

There is an interesting parallel between the kinds of country-city contacts which the festivals brought about and the confrontation depicted in *Deliverance*. A duel—formalized combat between two men of honor, which might be called a machismo confrontation ritual—was present in musical form both in the film and at the festivals. At the festivals the dueling took place in the informal picking in the campgrounds and parking lots when amateur and professional musicians (mostly men) mingled in small groups for impromptu jam sessions. Popular media reports of the festivals typically described such sessions with broadly painted images of rednecks and hippies meeting on neutral ground, drawn together by the powerful influence of the music. Depending upon the reporter's perspective and stance, tensions between the groups were depicted as resolved or expressed in the event.

The element of confrontation and contest certainly exists in the impromptu jam sessions of the bluegrass festival, but it is not always between representatives of city and country. Many possible polarities—age, geography, musical esthetics, etiquette, politics, religion, etc.—can emerge or be reflected in such sessions. And the element of contest or duel may be personal or psychological rather than deriving from group identity or ideology. Descriptions of cultural confrontation at the bluegrass festivals are like the duel in *Deliverance*—fictive, symbolic.

Sound track music, no matter what genre, must convey meaning if it is to work for the film-maker. With bluegrass there has been a tendency to move from emphasis upon the structural use of formal aspects of the music (as in *Football* and the beginning of *Bonnie and Clyde*) to the symbolic uses of the affective aspects (as in "The Beverly Hillbillies," the end of *Bonnie and Clyde*, and *Deliverance*). The two dimensions color each other, and the meanings generated by the successive uses of the music tend to persist in new uses, adding further levels of meaning. For example, the proliferation of bluegrass sound track ads following *Bonnie and Clyde* probably owed something to the sexual connotations the music had acquired, since this fits well with the subliminal use of sexual motifs, a conventional advertising technique.

The elements of bluegrass used in sound tracks were selected from among many aspects of the music; only those which met the special requirements of the medium were heard. Such selective borrowing has always been a feature of sound track music, which must be subordinate to the visual aspects of video and film. The images and ideas to which the bluegrass elements (particularly the banjo) were tied in movies and television were, in Anderson's work, abstract and comic; building upon this were the cultural stereotype reversal ideas of "The Beverly Hillbillies"; the linking of exhilarating lawlessness, escape, and sexual fulfillment with death in *Bonnie and Clyde*; and the formalization of rural-urban conflict in *Deliverance*. Each of these usages was so widely circulated that by the early seventies the bluegrass sound suggested, to people who knew nothing of the Bill Monroe story, vague images of comedy, exhilaration, sex, contest, and conflict—even death. While listener responses on this level were almost subliminal, they made the music somehow familiar and exciting to the substantial numbers of new listeners attending festivals in the late sixties and early seventies.

Notes

1. Peter J. Welding, "Music from the 'Bluegrass' Roots."
2. P[eter] W[elding], Review of *Foggy Mountain Banjo*.
3. John Szwed, interview with author, Pittsburgh, Pa. Oct. 17, 1980. All subsequent quotes of Szwed are from this interview.
4. Franklin Miller III, interview with Carl Fleischhauer, Iowa City, July 19, 1980. All subsequent quotes of Miller are from this interview.
5. Henri Bergson, *Le rire*, p. 79.
6. Howard Thompson, "The 16-mm. Circuit: National Movie Meet."
7. Joseph Anderson, interview with author, Boston, May 21, 1981.
8. Howard Thompson, "The 16-mm. Circuit: Top Films."
9. Earl Scruggs, "Workshop: Scruggs Style Banjo," p. 54.
10. "Pickin' Scruggs," p. 53.
11. Jack Gould, "TV: Beverly Hillbillies."
12. Roy Acuff, "Introduction," p. 11.
13. Les Brown, *The New York Times Encyclopedia of Television*, p. 332.
14. Peter V. Kuykendall, interview with author, Broad Run, Va., Mar. 1, 1982.
15. Bosley Crowther, review of *Bonnie and Clyde*.
16. Roy M. Prendergast, *A Neglected Art*, quotes Mast and makes the statement quoted here, p. 165.
17. Vincent Canby, review of *Deliverance*.
18. Steven Farber, " 'Deliverance'—How It Delivers."
19. Arthur Knight, " . . . And Deliver Us from Evil," p. 61.
20. James Dickey, *Deliverance*, pp. 11–12, 58–61.

Bibliographical Notes

An expanded version of this chapter appeared in *American Music* 1 (1983): 1–22. My sources for the history of movie music include Roy M. Prendergast, *A Neglected Art*, and Irving Bazelon, *Knowing The Score*. Information concerning the early work of the Disney studios comes from Christopher Finch, *The Art of Walt Disney*. The information upon which my account of Joseph Anderson's work is based comes in part from my interview with Carl Fleischhauer, June 9, 1978. According to Anderson, *Football* won prizes at several other festivals, including the Fifth Annual Vancouver International Film Festival in July 1962 and the International Sports Film Festival at Oberhausen, Germany, ca. 1964. The working title for the television film on housewives, "How Swived," was a pun based on the middle English verb "swive" (meaning to copulate) with which members of the Film Unit were familiar owing to its extensive use in the John Barth novel *The Sot-Weed Factor*. The producer who commissioned "Cheers," Bo (Robert) Goldman, won an Academy Award in 1981 for his screenplay, *Melvin and Howard*.

For Louise Scruggs's account of the events surrounding the *Beverly Hillbillies* theme, see Dixie Deen, "The 'Woman' behind the Man," p. 22. The success of "The Ballad of Jed Clampett" was, in the view of some recording industry observers, linked with the popularity of bluegrass in the folk revival. See for example "Bluegrass Style Is Moving Up in Folk-Pop Field." Additional information on the various Filmways-Henning productions appears in Les Brown, *New York Times Encyclopedia of Television*, pp. 40, 180, and 191. See also Vincent Terrace, *The Complete Encyclopedia of Television Programs, 1947–1979*, pp. 107–8, 397–98, 420, and 784–86.

Earl Scruggs tells how he was contacted by Warren Beatty concerning the music for *Bonnie and Clyde* in "The Earl Scruggs Revue: New Directions in Music." Information concerning Beatty is found in Charles Movitz, ed., *Current Biography Yearbook 1962*, p. 34. *Bonnie and Clyde* was nominated for nine academy awards and won two. In 1979 *Variety* ranked it as number 66 among the top 200 moneymaking films of all time. See Cobbet W. Steinberg, *Film Facts*, pp. 6, 241. The story of the Sawtooth Mountain Volunteers is told by their leader Steve Waller in "Sawtooth Mountain Volunteers." The post-*Bonnie and Clyde* proliferation of bluegrass-flavored television sound tracks was noted with approbation by the staff of and contributors to *Bluegrass Unlimited*. See "Editorial" 2 (Mar. 1968): 1 and Jeff Bay's "Send a Bluegrass Musician to Camp." These early reactions welcomed the "exposure" given bluegrass banjo in ad sound tracks. For a later and more cynical viewpoint see Bill Barkely, "The Subliminal Banjo." A political ad made by John Frankenheimer and Bill Wilson, utilizing *Bonnie and Clyde*-style sound, was used by the Robert Kennedy campaign in California in 1968. See Michael J. Arlen, "The Air: The State of the Art," p. 107.

For details on "Feuding Banjos" composer Arthur Smith, see Ed Davis, "Arthur Smith," and Don Rhodes, "Arthur Smith: A Wide and Varied Musical Career." The Country Gentlemen used "Mocking Banjo" as the basis for an elaborate comedy routine which they never recorded (it was too long and depended too much on visual effects to be worth putting on record) but which they included in virtually every performance during the mid-sixties.

Eric Weissberg's story concerning "Dueling Banjos" and the copyright suit which Smith brought against him and Warner Brothers is told in Mark Greenberg, "Eric Weissberg," p. 33. See also Arnie Berle, "New York's Session Men: Making a Career Out of Versatility," pp. 82, 84. *Deliverance* was listed by *Variety* in 1979 as number 69 among the top 200 moneymaking films of all time and was nominated for two Academy Awards. See Steinberg, *Film Facts*, pp. 6, 247.

Discographical Notes

"Dallas Rag" was on *The New Lost City Ramblers*, their first album, released in 1958.

Flatt and Scruggs's "The Ballad of Jed Clampett" first appeared on *Billboard's* country music charts on December 8, 1962, remaining there twenty weeks and reaching the number 1 position. It was soon issued on an album, *Hard Travelin'*. "Pearl Pearl Pearl" appeared on the charts on May 11, 1963, remaining for eleven weeks and reaching number 8. "Petticoat Junction" was on the charts for eleven weeks, reaching number 14. All three later appeared on *Flatt and Scruggs' Greatest Hits*. "Green Acres," which included the singing of June Carter, did not make the charts and was not included on an album.

The 1949 recording of "Foggy Mountain Breakdown" was released in 1968 on a single by Mercury. At about the same time a newly recorded version was issued by Columbia. They were both played on the radio and were listed together when they first appeared on *Billboard's* "Hot 100" pop charts on February 24, 1968, where they remained thirteen weeks, reaching number 55. They were on *Billboard's* country charts for six weeks beginning April 6, 1968, reaching the number 58 spot. The 1968 Columbia single appeared on Flatt and Scrugg's *The Story of Bonnie and Clyde*. At about the same time the 1949 recording of "Foggy Mountain Breakdown" was included along with other Flatt and Scruggs Mercury recordings on *Original Theme from Bonnie and Clyde*. Both albums sold well enough to make *Billboard's* country music LP charts briefly in May 1968. The Osbornes' *Bonnie and Clyde* album, released contemporaneously with the two above, was titled *Foggy Mountain Breakdown and Other Music from the Bonnie and Clyde Era*, and the musicians were called "The Bluegrass Banjo Pickers"; the name of the Osborne Brothers does not appear on the album.

Arthur Smith's "Feuding Banjos" was recorded in 1955. The Dillards' "Duelin' Banjo" was on their first album, *Back Porch Bluegrass*. Weissberg and Mandell's single appeared on an album titled *Dueling Banjos* and subtitled "from the original sound track of *Deliverance*/and additional material/ performed by Eric Weissberg and Steve Mandell."

Chapter 10

Festivals Get Big:
1966–73

Between 1965, when Carlton Haney's first three-day bluegrass festival was held, and 1973, when Haney put on his "first New Grass Music Festival," bluegrass festivals became a national, even international, phenomenon (New Zealand festivals began in 1967, Japanese in 1970, Canadian in 1971). The first festival was reported only in *Billboard* and *Sing Out!* By the early seventies *Newsweek, Playboy,* the *Wall Street Journal,* and *Atlantic Monthly* were among the publications with vast readerships representing diverse constituencies carrying stories about bluegrass festivals. In 1972 Piedmont Airlines was advertising, in *Time* and *Newsweek,* low-cost fares to various southern festival sites. In April 1973 *Mademoiselle* included bluegrass festivals in a list of ideas for fashionable vacations.

A combination of factors lay behind the growing awareness of and attendance at bluegrass festivals. Enthusiastic interest in camping and the marketing of recreational equipment, including fancy vehicles, had added to the resources of weekend campers. The interstate highway system, begun in 1956, had by the late sixties made it possible to travel long distances with relative ease on limited access highways, and fuel was cheap. This combination of recreational camping and its concomitant technology created a network of private and public recreational facilities catering to tourists on the road.

Travel has long been a metaphor for human growth, development, and experience. In western culture, it is a popular literary theme: Chaucer's use of the pilgrimage as a framework for the *Canterbury Tales* and the great popularity of Marco Polo's writings on his travels to China are but two examples. Americans bought many copies of Francis Parkman's 1848 guide to the Oregon Trail, and Jack Kerouac's *On the Road* was a best seller in 1957, the year after the interstate network was started. In 1968 Tom Wolfe chronicled the highway and acid trips of Ken Kesey in *The Electric Kool-Aid Acid Test.*

The word *trip* took on a new meaning in the late sixties, to describe the experience of drug-altered consciousness, a term which denoted an experiment which could be good or bad, in which one ascended, "got high" and descended, returning to the original "straight" condition. The trip, real or drug-induced, was like a rite of passage in which one was separated from one's surroundings, immersed in a new and special setting, and returned from the ritual to the old context as a changed person. For many the trips of the decade were the voyages made by astronauts, culminating in the first visit to the moon in the summer of 1969. Only three men took that trip, but millions followed it vicariously.

Tourism is a function of affluence. By the sixties, wealthy North Americans could vacation anywhere in the "free world." Air travel was relatively inexpensive, and the rate of exchange favored the dollar. Less wealthy North Americans did not take international vacations, but, like their more prosperous countrymen, they traveled farther and with more ease than ever before. For them as for any tourists part of their enjoyment came from the travel itself, as one moved from the familiar to the unfamiliar. But movement must have direction, and most tourists have an ostensible goal, a place of special interest to which they are traveling. The goal might be a reunion with relatives or friends; a visit to a shrine like the Louvre, Disneyland, Westminster Cathedral; or participation in a seasonal festival such as the Oktoberfest, the Rose Bowl, Mardi Gras, Easter vacation at Fort Lauderdale.

There is no more evocative description of the role of such directed escape in bluegrass music than Bob Artis's superb chapter, "An Endless Festival" in his book *Bluegrass*. He takes the reader along as he and his wife eagerly pack their camping gear, dream of past festivals while listening to their favorite bluegrass tapes en route in the car, and experience the rigors of the campout and the joys and frustrations of jam sessions, instrument selling, and the other experiences familiar to festival goers. But for non-goers, the nature of the event needs to be explained. How and why is this such a special experience? What made it so pivotal for bluegrass music in the early seventies?

Folk Festivals and Political Power

The emergence of bluegrass during the late sixties coincided with a general growth of similar events, including rock and folk festivals. When *Bluegrass Unlimited* and Carlton Haney's *Muleskinner News* (to be discussed later in this chapter) began publishing yearly festival editions, they listed folk festivals, fiddlers' conventions, and other musical events at which bluegrass was included, if not featured exclusively.

Among these were the yearly Festivals of American Folklife held by the Smithsonian Institution on the Mall in Washington, D.C., directed beginning in 1967 by Ralph Rinzler. He chose the term *folklife,* then newly fashionable in American folklore scholarship but long familiar in Europe, because it was broader, more inclusive. While "folklore" described specific oral traditions—songs, stories, beliefs, and so forth—folklife encompassed the entire spectrum of traditional culture, including not just oral traditions but artifacts, ceremonies, and patterns of daily life. The Smithsonian festivals differed from folk festivals like those at Newport in that they demonstrated many kinds of tradition—not just music—on their stage and represented a wide variety of regional and ethnic groups. The impact of these festivals, which employed trained researchers to seek out and stage folklife presentations, was extensive. It led to a growth of such festivals on the local and regional levels, and in these, as in the yearly events on the Mall, bluegrass bands were often included, for bluegrass fit the ideology which lay behind these events.

The Smithsonian festivals grew out of ideas first tested at Newport in the early sixties. These in turn reflected ideas developed within the American folksong revival. Particularly influential was Alan Lomax's belief that various forms of media and staged presentations could be used to give the folk a voice. He felt this was necessary because mass media were overwhelming vernacular culture, engulfing folk groups in a homogeneous culture which destroyed worthwhile local and regional traditions. And as we have seen in chapter 6, the revivalists believed that this "massification" and the cultural assimilation it promoted were demeaning, essentially racist in implication, and unnecessary.

Significantly, many who felt that folk and immigrant groups were being massified or assimilated out of existence came from the very classes and regions in which the massification and assimilation originated. They had the missionary's keen sense of noblesse oblige, honed on the whetstone of guilt. They perceived deterioration in the social fabric and sought to halt it. They were cultural conservationists, believing that greed and thoughtlessness on the part of the powerful had exploited and eroded the delicate patches of "small tradition" which gave the nation its strength. Corrective measures were needed, strategies and actions which (like contour plowing, reforestation, and the creation of parks) would restore pride in withered folk traditions. Among these measures were folk festivals.

The enshrinement of folk culture as embodied in language, song, and narrative was an important component of the romantic nationalism which emerged from Germany at the end of the eighteenth century and swept over Europe in the nineteenth. By this century it had become a tenet of nationalism; folk culture was national heritage, the living repository of the past. It could also be used by Marxist or populist ideologues demanding a voice for the dispossessed and disenfranchised. Whatever its use, political thinking about folklore and folklife shares the assumption that these unselfconscious aspects of culture can, when brought to consciousness, be a source of political power for democratic social and economic change.

The bluegrass festivals aimed more at economic than political ends; running through the literature of the bluegrass consumer/fan movement which began in the mid-sixties are dialogues concerning the best way to promote the music, to bring it to more people. Frequently the impact of the festivals was judged in such terms; enthusiasts asked if this feature or that format would attract or repel new listeners. In raising these questions they were, they believed, speaking in the best interests of the musicians. They thought that if bluegrass was properly presented it would attract a larger audience, which would give the music greater economic power and better access to the marketplace, particularly radio and records. Thus would festivals preserve the musical form which bluegrass consumer/fans loved.

As we will see, the festivals did have results of this kind. They altered the way in which the music was perceived in the two centers where bluegrass needed more political and economic clout—Nashville and Washington. These results were part of a gradual process which saw a number of changes in the music which the enthusiasts viewed with ambivalence, for the very nature of festivals is such that those who initiate them cannot always control what takes place in them.

How Festivals Work

The word *festival* is used to describe a variety of events. In its earliest usage the word was tied to periodical ("calendric") religious celebrations. Today, while the religious dimension is not always present, the word still conveys ideas of celebration and periodicity, along with performance, entertainment, and merrymaking. But while religious festivals generally bring together people who share cultural values (often from the same community), contemporary secular festivals attract diverse audiences. An analysis of such festivals by folklorist Roger D. Abrahams is useful in understanding the problems of crowd control and cultural conflict which beset the bluegrass festival movement during its period of greatest growth in the late sixties and early seventies. Abrahams shows that such problems are in fact part of the "festivity" these events require and promote. He suggests that festivals constitute "a successful model for cultural pluralism in operation" because they are held on what he calls "neutral ground." The contradictions which such events embody are an essential part of the structure: "If there are times during these events when the existing social structure is dramatized and reinforced, there are numerous other times when the festival feeling insists that such structure be ignored, or inverted, or flatly denied . . . there is often license for the calling out of neighborly names as a means simultaneously of projecting and breaking up social differentiations."[1] By "neighborly names," Abrahams means derogatory terms which may, in normal circumstances, lead to conflict; names like "gringo" and "greaser." At the bluegrass festivals, the most commonly encountered such neighborly names were "redneck" and "hippie."

Abrahams begins by examining folk festivals put on by immigrant and ethnic groups seeking to bolster their pride. He points out that in "going public" by displaying their folk culture in a festival context, they may continue to use separatist rhetoric, but they are in fact seeking to gain political power. They do this by staging performances which are as close as possible to the originals but are set in a framework which introduces them to non-members so that the performances can be understood and appreciated by outsiders.

In addition to ethnic and immigrant communities, many "interest groups . . . hobbyists and recreationists" also hold festivals. These individuals are deeply involved in a subject ("from birding to caving to owning different kinds of *gear*—vehicles, communication equipment, hunting and fishing devices, and so on").[2] Like the festivals of ethnic groups, those of special interest groups present the in-group or subculture by framing it in an appropriate setting which is accessible to outsiders. This is precisely what the first Roanoke bluegrass festivals did.

Abrahams suggests that any kind of festival is focused upon one of four types of occasion: (1) a performance or set of performances; (2) a game, contest, or sporting event; (3) a calendric festive gathering, occasioned by the time of year (harvest, mid-summer celebration) or a time of marked importance in a person's life; (4) a commemoration of an historical event. He also indicated that each type generates an intensity which tends to attract aspects of the other types to the events.

The first bluegrass festival embodied all four of Abrahams's types. The concerts on stage were the performance; the banjo contest furnished the gaming aspect; the setting of the festival on Labor Day weekend and its annual repetition constituted the calendric dimension; and the "Story of Blue Grass" commemorated historic events.

Each type of festival, says Abrahams, has its own special characteristics, all evident at the first bluegrass festival. The performance, which features concerts held on a raised stage with microphones in front of an audience, stresses audience/performer distinctions. In a similar way the contest stresses contestant/spectator distinctions. Most significant is the calendric dimension, which creates a situation where participants are equals in activities involving "a bombarding of the senses . . . drinking too much, an abundance of visual display through costume . . . all leading to a sense of surfeit and dizziness." In the first bluegrass festival this bombarding leading to a sense of surfeit took place most noticeably in the lengthy campground and parking-lot jam sessions. These marathons, which stretched on late into the night, were often described by festival goers in terms of surfeit. When festivals began to attract audience members who were not musicians, another kind of surfeit and dizziness, the result of drink or drugs, became a problem at bluegrass festivals. A natural consequence of the calendric festival setting, such excess is literally festive behavior and is, in the festival setting, always liable to get out of control. Finally, Abrahams points out that his fourth category, the historic commemoration, stresses status distinctions and resembles a ritual. This was true of Haney's "Story" at the first festival. Later other, similar, events such as popularity poll awards played a similar role at bluegrass festivals.

No matter what type or combination of types it includes, a festival's commercial dimension is downplayed: "The principal of not making profit except for charitable causes (another name for resource redistribution) holds firmly for most festive events, except those *produced* by showmen-entrepreneurs, people who are in the business of putting together 'good times.' "[3] Carlton Haney was one such producer, but he too played down his commercial motives, stressing cultural and artistic goals as well as the good times implied by his favorite terms—*vibrations* and *mind-blowing*.

All of the characteristics Abrahams describes for festivals can be identified in Haney's first bluegrass festival. But when festivals are viewed from a historical perspective additional dimensions emerge, for most festivals, because of their periodical (usually annual) nature, change over time. Everybody who participates in a festival more than once compares the two experiences. The repetitions are separated by enough time to allow participants to digest the experience and develop conscious opinions about it, creating expectations for the next one which may or may not be confirmed. The various characteristics seen by festival-watchers like Abrahams are "slots," cultural roles which are filled or played out by different individuals from year to year.

Because critical reactions to festivals are most often expressed by members of the subculture, who have attended more than once, such criticism contains the most meaningful (but also most biased) clues to the nature of the festival experience. The message which emerges most clearly is that festivals seem to have lives something like organisms—lives which develop from early vitality to later decline, with either demise or revival following. The decline begins when those initially enthusiastic subculture members lose interest, have a "bad" experience, or become involved in some other kind of recreational or tourist activity. Unless there are new recruits, the distance between the festival presenters and the festival goers grows beyond the point where the projecting and breaking up of social differentials referred to by Abrahams can take place. The history of bluegrass festivals in their formative years reflects this central problem of maintaining the essential experience, one of finding new converts within a pluralistic audience.

1966–1968

In the earliest years bluegrass festivals were occasions for trips, rites of passage, by people who had followed bluegrass music since before festivals began. In most cases these were musicians or long-standing fans of the music. All of these festivals focused upon Bill Monroe, affirming his status as the Father of Blue Grass Music. At the 1966 Roanoke Festival a banner covering the front of the stage urged the election of Monroe to the Country Music Association Hall of Fame. Carlton Haney's "Story" was a feature of each of his first six Labor Day weekend festivals, and for the knowledgeable fans who constituted most of the audience at the early festivals, to watch Monroe recreate his "hits" with the very musicians who recorded them was to witness a ritualistic reënactment of the history of the music. The musicians in the audience also related to and enjoyed the performance as an impromptu jam session—an opportunity to hear unique musical combinations of the kind encountered in the informal parking-lot and campground sessions "framed" on stage.

The glorified jam session structure also constituted the major appeal of workshops at the early Haney festivals. At a Roanoke workshop in 1966 David Grisman brought John Duffey, Ronnie Reno, Bob Osborne, and Bill Monroe together to play "Sally Goodin." The theory behind this was to show student mandolinists in the audience the different styles of these instrumentalists. But it also had the effect of a staged jam session, because these men were playing together, it seemed, for the first time, and, it appeared, reacting to one another almost as in a contest. This was exciting. Those who took part in the parking-lot and campsite jam sessions as a kind of festival activity in which all participants were equal could see the same kind of activity on stage in these workshops.

During its early years *Bluegrass Unlimited* regularly published festival reports. Like record reviews, these reports were evaluative and critical. Generally they focused on the events on stage and discussed them in terms of either the informed knowledge of a critic or the enthusiasm of a committed fan. The former tended to view Monroe as "true to his origins" and to evaluate others in comparison or contrast to this standard. Fan rhetoric required unquestioning loyalty, so that fan reports were generally not comparative but blandly or shrilly positive. Of the groups most likely to provoke comment, the Country Gentlemen were considered exciting, the Osbornes good but perhaps too commercial, and Ralph Stanley (carrying on bravely following brother Carter's death in December 1966) moving and soulful. Flatt and Scruggs were almost never mentioned in these reports for the simple reason that they were booked at very few festivals. They were still not appearing on the same stage with Bill Monroe, and because the festival movement in its early years was focused on Monroe, there was no place in it for Flatt and Scruggs.

Following the critical success of the first two Roanoke Labor Day festivals in 1965 and 1966 and the emergence of *Bluegrass Unlimited* and County Sales, the news of festivals began to spread. For 1967 Haney moved from Roanoke to Watermelon Park near Berryville, in northern Virginia. The site was within easy driving distance for the many bluegrass fans in the metropolitan Washington area. In June 1967 Bill Monroe held his first "Blue Grass

Celebration"—he didn't want to copy Haney by using the word *festival*, although the following year it was the Second Annual Blue Grass Festival— at Bean Blossom.

In *Bluegrass Unlimited* Norm Carlson noted the innovations at Monroe's 1968 Bean Blossom festival. There was a band contest on the first day, followed by a jam session open to all and, in the evening, a dance which was not successful because most of the audience wanted to listen to the band rather than dance. In spite of Monroe's "sincere but inadequate attempt to make this a real give-and-take" event, the workshops turned into concerts. The concerts, presented on a newly constructed outdoor stage, were marred by a poor sound system. Monroe had brought in two emcees, Grant Turner from the Grand Ole Opry and Ohio deejay Paul Mullins; both were voices familiar to many in the audience. Unfortunately, Carlson noted, few of the familiar local bluegrass bands were included in the event. After cataloging his complaints about the festival site's single water spigot, a "dark age restroom" and chigger bites, Carlson concluded that "the demands, complaints, and failings of the flesh were of small concern compared to the quantity and quality of the commodity offered."[4]

The rough and ready campground existence alluded to in Carlson's closing remarks contrasted with the on-stage organization of the festivals. At the close of the final show at Bean Blossom, Monroe brought all the featured performers on stage at once for a grand finale. Not only was this good show business, it had become a necessary part of the emerging bluegrass festival genre. That its importance resulted from the fact that it was a framed jam session does not seem to have been apparent to Carlton Haney, who saw such spectacular innovations in show business terms. Seeking further innovations of this kind, Haney included significant non-bluegrass acts on his Sunday afternoon shows between installments of "The Story" in subsequent years. Intended to make a spectacular event even more spectacular, the Chuck Wagon Gang (1967) and the Porter Wagoner Show with Dolly Parton (1968) were panned by bluegrass reviewers. At Haney's 1968 Berryville festival, six fiddlers were "massed" to provide backup for Bill Monroe's song "Close By" on "The Story of Blue Grass, Part IV." Even this was, to one reviewer, "contrived," in comparison with the recreation of historic bands like the Lonesome Pine Fiddlers and Reno and Smiley.[5] Clearly, the spectacular events on stage had to include elements of historical ritual and framed jam session in order to succeed.

Even though Haney's 1968 Sunday afternoon spectacular was not a complete critical success, it drew a big crowd: 9,000 were reported to be in attendance. Control of large crowds demanded organization, planning, and additional rules. As the festivals began to draw people from outside the subculture, the tendency toward the bombardment of the senses described by Abrahams was manifested not just in music-making but in other typical festival practices like drinking and drug use. Festival ads began stating that drinking was not permitted and that police would be present to enforce the rule.

Another dimension of the growth of Haney's festival was the addition of a "Blue Grass music camp" during the week preceding the festival. This was an attempt to make the workshop concept operate as planned—for education. Each day a professional band was present at the campground to hold workshops. In response to earlier criticism of on-stage workshops, these were held at picnic tables. By moving the workshops off the stage, Haney changed them from symbolic to real jam sessions. As in the camp and parking-lot sessions, people crowded around to listen and it was hard for more than a few to see what was going on. For most bluegrass musicians, learning of vocal or instrumental techniques had generally taken place in private, one-to-one situations. For the older musicians, style was a trade secret which did not translate well to a classroom demonstration situation. Still, these sessions were successful and edifying for many.

Even if details of staging and organization didn't always work out as planned, the extended length of this festival proved the popularity of the concept. Berryville 1968 was Haney's first financially successful festival. And already some long-time bluegrass supporters were worrying about the implications of success. In November 1968 Columbus bandleader Sid Campbell wrote to *Bluegrass Unlimited* complaining that there were too many festivals being held too close together in time and space. He foresaw saturation of the market and suggested that festival organizers needed to organize themselves.

1969

By the start of 1969 there were five festivals being planned—enough to warrant the publication of a list in the April issue of *Bluegrass Unlimited*. Others, not listed, would also be held during 1969. Not all these festivals were full weekend affairs, for since 1966 there had also been one-day events which brought together the big-name bands, or some of them, for marathon concerts. A one-day festival resembled a single day of a weekend festival, since many weekend festivals booked the most costly acts for only a single day, juggling the lineup over the weekend to create the impression in printed ads that all the stars would be present throughout the event.

While the one-day festivals did not have the campground participation and related features, they adopted bluegrass festival concert techniques. A festival organized in Louisiana by former Monroe sideman, fiddler Byron Berline, featured Monroe along with a number of other bands. The day ended with Monroe leading everyone on stage in a big jam session, followed by a sing-along on "Swing Low Sweet Chariot."

Other variations on the festival idea were emerging. A Florida enthusiast reported that a festival was held on March 14–16 at the Salt Springs Camp

Ground in the Ocala National Forest at which there was no charge; local bands and musicians got together and jammed for each other and had a wonderful time. It was like a big weekend festival without the stage concerts. The contrast between the one-day shows, which had the concerts without the camping, and this event, which had the camping without the concerts, demonstrates the mixed audiences festivals created. Some came to interact with other musicians at jam sessions ("parking-lot picking"), while others came to see the show.

The big weekend festivals needed both kinds of audience; generally they depended upon a base of weekend campers who would be present throughout, paying the full weekend fee and attending all the special events—workshops, gospel concerts, etc. But the success of the festivals also depended upon drawing daily crowds from the festival locality who would turn out for the Friday night, Saturday night, and Sunday afternoon concerts, the spectacular stage events.

The 1969 season began in June at Bean Blossom. Because Haney had prepared a new park at Reidsville, North Carolina, for the big Labor Day festival, his Berryville festival was moved to the Fourth of July weekend. An enthusiastic parking-lot picker, Dennis Cyporyn, wrote after Bean Blossom and Berryville of "Bluegrass Fever": "The force that made people drive through the night across the country, camp without water or ice, pick through the night, listen in the rain, and sit in front of a stage for three straight days! There must be a reason! To some it's a casual interest to most it's a burning obsession, an intense interest. . . . This thing called bluegrass is no longer an uneducated back-hill type of music. I talked with college students, grads and people who could intellectualize their wife's anger for playing 'just one more.' "[6] The growing festival crowds brought new kinds of audience members to the festivals. Anne Romaine, a folk festival organizer and performer, wrote enthusiastically of the first Lavonia, Georgia, festival in the Atlanta underground newspaper *The Great Speckled Bird*. Noting the all-white audience, she compared the event to a church supper. She contrasted it with fiddlers' conventions by describing the musicians on stage as "all professional" and commented that only one Georgia band participated. This was a common complaint of festival reviewers in the early years, but her next one was not: there were no women performers, singers like Hazel (Dickens) and Alice (Gerrard). Another complaint reflected her constituency; at four dollars a day, she said, the festival was costly. Still her report was positive, and she was writing for a substantial new group, the so-called "counterculture"—hippies or longhairs to some—who read the new underground newspapers and enjoyed outdoor happenings like bluegrass festivals.[7]

Another newcomer to festivals in 1969 was Bud Wendell, the new manager of the Grand Ole Opry. Interested in learning about bluegrass, he attended Monroe's festival and returned to Nashville impressed by what he'd seen. Wendell, a native of Akron, Ohio, with college training in economics, came to the Opry not from the country music business but out of the ranks of the insurance company that owned the Opry. As a salesman in West Virginia he had been aware of the popularity of country music but knew little about it. As the new Opry manager, he was impressed by the celebrities who were suddenly under his direction and found no one more interesting than Bill Monroe who, according to Opry chronicler Jack Hurst, "was so old-fashioned that he would not have a telephone in his house and so secretive that for a long time not even the Opry management knew where his house was. Opry officials had to call the patriarch's ex-wife to get in touch with him at all." Wendell returned from Bean Blossom impressed by the ambience of Monroe's festival: "Beanblossom kind of kindled a fire under me . . . I liked the people who picked bluegrass, and I wanted to help them if I could. I didn't think they were getting the kind of recognition and attention they deserved, and I didn't think there was anybody else who could help them as much as the Opry could."[8] It would be several years before Wendell's decision had its full impact, but it marked the beginning of a turnaround for bluegrass within the Nashville-centered world of country music.

Also significant for the future was the inclusion of Bill Monroe in the 1969 Smithsonian Festival of American Folklife on the Mall in Washington. The evening of Thursday, July 3, was devoted to "a tribute to the sons of James Buchanan Monroe," which brought together Bill, Charlie, and Birch Monroe for their first public performance in many years.[9] Also present were J. E. and Wade Mainer and the Morris Brothers. The Monroe family members were presented an award from the office of the governor of Kentucky "for their contribution to the world of music."[10] As director of the festival Ralph Rinzler played no small part in bringing the Monroes to the Mall. Like Bud Wendell, he was well placed. He helped to bring bluegrass, long popular in working-class bars and rural parks around Washington, into the more prestigious concert halls and similar venues of the national capital.

In 1969 as in 1968, the biggest bluegrass festival crowds were at Carlton Haney's Labor Day festival, held for the first time at his new Camp Springs park near Reidsville, North Carolina. *Bluegrass Unlimited* editor Dick Spottswood reported that "driving, eating, sleeping and rapping" kept him from seeing all "the music, but that it was good, particularly Part V of 'The Story' . . . "[11] But there was conflict to report, too. Haney and Jimmy Martin got into an argument about where Martin's bus was to be parked, and Martin packed up and left. Fiddler Benny Martin created another sort of problem by getting drunk and making a spectacle on stage. And there were other incidents which indicated that the event had become a handful, even for a conscientious promoter and organizer like Haney. Two festival-goers wrote to *Bluegrass Unlimited* complaining that they had been ejected from the park by Haney who, they said, used coarse language in informing them that their after-hours picking was disturbing others. So while the festival was a success, both the stage show and the campground aspects were marred by problems of control and management.

Yet such incidents seemed isolated. Just as Spottswood missed some of the on-stage events, so no one at this—or any other—festival could possibly participate in everything. Between the simultaneous jam sessions, concerts, and socializing between friends, it was easy to miss or avoid incidents of conflict between organizers, performers, and participants. The festivals continued to attract new audiences, and veteran festival goers remained enthusiastic about the experience. George McCeney wrote about his experience in a letter to *Bluegrass Unlimited*. He had driven to a festival in Shade Gap, Pennsylvania, with three friends. "About the only thing that we all had in common was an unswerving commitment to the music we all loved." Among the highlights he recalled were "the lady standing next to me in the soaking rain Saturday night saying, 'Great, isn't it?' " and "Doc Watson standing to applaud the banjo breaks of Bill Emerson and the singing of Del McCoury." McCeney's enthusiastic letter ended, "I remember sitting in the cold damp of Monday morning at 2:00 a.m. with a few hundred hangers-on hoping that it would never end, and as I looked around at faces I was more sure than ever that it would never end."[12]

In the early years of the bluegrass festivals letters like McCeney's were not uncommon. The testimony of festival goers to the camaraderie and good vibrations runs like a litany through these letters and shows up in articles about first-time experiences at festivals. Bluegrass on radio or record was one thing, but it meant much more in the live context of festivals. Physical discomfort did not diminish the quality of the experience; it brought audience members closer to one another—a common misery which heightened their appreciation of the music. Somehow this setting was right to this kind of music, the new converts felt, and they were sure others would like it. Through such descriptions of festival life and the process by which friends brought other friends, bluegrass festivals attracted ever larger crowds.

McCeney, a Maryland high school teacher, put this idea to the test in the fall of 1969 when he took eight of his students to the first annual Maryland Indian Summer Bluegrass Festival in Callaway, Maryland. He asked them to write about their reactions and from these he fashioned excerpts into an article which he titled "Remember the First Time?" Except for one who thought the music all seemed to sound the same, his students agreed that they liked bluegrass and came away with positive first impressions. That there were people who played music for the love of it was, for some, a pleasant surprise. This helped to explain the great popularity of parking-lot jam sessions and local bands for festival neophytes: the enthusiasm of such musicians contrasted with the cool professionalism of the big-name performers. Observers participated vicariously in the jam sessions and local band performances.

McCeney's students were amazed and pleased to see very young musicians, too; it was an impression that many of those reporting on festivals would mention in the next few years. Reactions to the bands on stage were mixed; the Bluegrass Alliance from Louisville, a band which included four long-haired young men, was most popular; some other bands seemed "too commercial."[13] One band, Bob Goff and his Bluegrass Buddies, elicited a negative reaction because of its racist humor. The students were surprised to see so many hippies, too. And several reported unpleasant experiences with obnoxious drunks.

Others at this same festival echoed the students' reactions. Two fans, reviewing it in *Bluegrass Unlimited,* agreed that the music of some of the newer groups—The Bluegrass Alliance, Emerson and Waldron—was excellent, and they commented with pleasure upon the performances of Bill Monroe and Doc Watson. The crowd was smaller than at some of the year's earlier festivals, but people came from states as far away as Michigan and North Carolina. Conflict backstage centered around Jimmy Martin, who once again was displeased with the location of the site for parking his bus. And the Country Gentlemen's part of the show was marred by two drunks doing "what might be called dancing" in front of the stage. The reviewers wrote, "We feel this display of exhibition shows ignorance on the part of a few individuals who seemed intent upon spoiling the quality of bluegrass music."[14] One festival-goer who had traveled to the festival from New York City wrote to complain about the racist humor of Goff's band, whom he dubbed "the Bluegrass Fascists." He noted "subtle hostility to Northerners" at the festival.[15] For everyone attending this particular festival—whether or not it was their first—it was a mixed experience.

It is tempting to interpret reports of hostility, obnoxious drunks, and racist humor as evidence of deterioration in the quality of the festivals. But much of this socially and culturally disruptive activity is in fact typical of festivals of all kinds, particularly of those aspects of festivals connected with calendric celebrations. Festival audiences had become more diverse, as the reports of good times at them attracted more and more casual and uncommitted individuals, people for whom the dizziness and bombarding of the senses involved not endless picking but endless drink, drugs, and dance. With respect to the racist humor, one *Bluegrass Unlimited* correspondent placed this in a cultural context by including some political "neighborly names" in a letter complaining about the criticism of Goff: "When the 'left-wingers' or Liberals criticize something or someone, it's free speech; when a Conservative or 'right-winger' does the same, it's racism, prejudice or suppression."[16] Many, he pointed out, enjoyed Goff's show. This was, after all, one of those much-requested (by reviewers) local bands. These groups were not used to playing for diverse audiences. The major bands had stopped doing racist comedy routines when they began playing the national folk festivals in the early sixties. The local groups, who played in ethnic bars or for local concerts, continued to tell in-group jokes denigrating to out-group members, along with other kinds of humor about rural life which didn't mean much to urban audience members at festivals.

Festival performances, Abrahams suggests, are meant to be as close as possible to the originals but are set in a framework which introduces them to outsiders. Framed on the festival concert stage, shows like Goff's took on new meaning as audiences and performers became aware of the their cultural differences. Responses to the new-found awareness varied from frequently enthusiastic approval to occasional disapproval as shown in the example of Goff. During the next few years bluegrass festivals would frame on their stages not only the old-fashioned racist humor of bands like Goff's but also the counterculture rhetoric of new groups like the Bluegrass Alliance. One could expect to find a combination of hostility and rapprochement as festivals drew bigger audiences.

1970

By the beginning of the 1970 bluegrass festival season, Carlton Haney was publishing his own magazine, *Muleskinner News*. The title was a pun on "Mule Skinner Blues," the Jimmie Rodgers composition said to be the very first song Monroe performed on the Grand Ole Opry and therefore used by Haney to open his "Story of Blue Grass." After its first irregular issues *Muleskinner* was edited for Haney by a young Harvard business student and amateur singer from North Carolina, Fred Bartenstein. Bartenstein brought intellectual energy and talent to his work, and it was reflected in the magazine's appearance and content. Unlike *Bluegrass Unlimited,* which was appearing in a booklet-like 7- × -8½-inch format, this was in standard magazine format, 8½- × -11-inches, with glossy paper. Like the "Story," it took a historical approach to bluegrass, with a strong emphasis upon the visual aspects through the use of rare old photographs. Haney's interests as a promoter were, at this point, closely linked with Bill Monroe's own perception of bluegrass music as synonymous with Monroe's career. The Haney festivals, particularly the Labor Day events, celebrated this vision through the ritualistic "Story." Hence Bartenstein not only featured bluegrass history in Haney's new magazine but also gave great emphasis to bluegrass festivals.

The third issue, dated May-June 1970, was a "Festival Edition," the first of a series that eventually became an annual special edition of *Muleskinner News,* sold separately as a yearly guide. In this edition was the program for Monroe's June Bean Blossom festival and a list of all the bluegrass festivals being held during the upcoming season. Compiled by Peggy Logan, its seventy-one entries included not just bluegrass festivals but also folk festivals, fiddlers' conventions, and similar events. *Bluegrass Unlimited* had published several festival lists in 1969 but not a complete schedule such as this one. They did publish a "1970 Festival Schedule" the month after *Muleskinner's* Festival Edition appeared.

Muleskinner News competed with *Bluegrass Unlimited* for the growing blue-grass readership market (created by festivals) by offering a contrasting alter-native. It avoided the provocative reviews and editorial comments which reflected the critical stance of *Bluegrass Unlimited's* Dick Spottswood. Its record reviewer was Bill Vernon, a New Yorker who had been researching and writing about bluegrass since the late fifties. His reviews were knowledgeable, fair, and balanced. No "badmouthing," just promotion and positive, useful features—this was the message *Muleskinner* conveyed through its contents. It took the position of the festival organizer and resembled a trade journal combined with a fan magazine, while *Bluegrass Unlimited* maintained its consumer-advocate stance. The contrast was epitomized by two lists of sug-gestions for improving festivals published within a month of each other.

The first, in *Muleskinner News'* Festival Edition, was Haney's list of things which would help to avoid creating hardships for festivals:

1. Please control the alcoholic beverages.
2. No firearms.
3. If the festival has a 2:00 curfew, please respect it. At our festivals we do this to keep order. You have too many trouble makers on the grounds without a curfew.
4. Please follow parking and camping rules.
5. Help keep grounds as clean as possible. The festival operators are busy putting on the best music and festival possible for you. We do not have but so much help and your cooperation will help tremendously.
6. Help keep rest rooms and showers clean as possible.
7. Conserve as much water as possible.
8. No fires outside without permission.
9. Put all food waste in the trash cans.
10. Leave the Festival in a good mood with plans to attend next year.[17]

The second list appeared a month later in *Bluegrass Unlimited*. Authors Dave Blood and Charlie Vaughn spoke enthusiastically of the festivals, par-ticularly the "giant bands with all the greats of bluegrass on the stage at the same time." But there were some things that could be improved. Their list included:

— lack of adequate sanitary facilities
— feeding facilities need improvement
— sound systems a sore point
— lack of amateur participation in festival talent contests, coupled with poor prizes and bad judging
— instrumental workshops should not be concerts but question and answer periods
— some groups fall into a set and predictable routine with the same com-edy routines and songs every time. More variation is needed
— more time should be devoted to gospel music

— more lesser known pros and local groups should be seen in concert
— more reunions for bands of the past[18]

Expectations about festival quality were emerging from the experiences of
both organizers and participants. Bluegrass festivals were becoming predictable and routine to both. They agreed that festivals were great, but they felt
that with a little tinkering they could be made better. Each abstracted and
focused upon those facets they wished to improve. Haney, looking from the
stage, saw the crowd creating bothersome and distracting problems. Blood
and Vaughn, facing the concert stage, with the exception of an expression of
concern about provisions for the most basic of human functions, demanded
more attention by the organizer to the content and quality of the concert
production.

The biggest problem for festivals was that as they became better known,
crowds grew more "festive" in a real sense, forcing organizers to devote ever
greater proportions of their attention to crowd control measures. Spectators,
on the other hand, were becoming tired of the ritual-like presentation of Bill
Monroe's music. Either they had heard a lot of it, or they came without the
preconceptions of the committed fan and, unwilling to participate in ritual,
wanted more variety in their musical experience.

To this new audience the mass media addressed their coverage of bluegrass
festivals. Even as these two lists were being published, reporters for a national
magazine were writing about Bill Monroe's fourth Bean Blossom festival.
Newsweek reported that 12,000 people, a "surprising" cross section of America from as far away as California and Canada, were expected at the festival.
While Haney stood on stage looking at the crowd, and Blood and Vaughn
stood in the crowd looking at the stage, the *Newsweek* reporters stood at the
edge of the crowd looking at both. They found the crowd more newsworthy
than the stage: "There was a good fellowship among leather-faced men in
western garb, teen-age groupies posturing around the musicians, long-haired
hippies with their no-bra chicks and red-neck farmers with their wives
sprawled in lawn chairs and print dresses."[19] The article called jam sessions
"impromptu groups" and described campers eating on the grounds. Alluding
briefly to the banjo and band contests, it mentioned that twenty-five big-
name bands, including that of Earl Scruggs (who had split up with Flatt the
year before) would be present. It spoke of bluegrass as a kind of chamber
music or jazz—a musician's music. Although the Country Gentlemen, said
to be "progressive," were mentioned, the focus was on Monroe, who spoke of
his hippie fans and college kids as his biggest audience. Conflict or disappointment stemming from differing expectations about the experience were
not discussed in this article. It portrayed bluegrass festivals as benign, democratic, pleasant experiences.

Similar reports were appearing in newspapers, too. In an article entitled
"No Generation Gap," a Florida newspaper reporter stressed the "informal

sings and get-togethers" (i.e., jam sessions) he saw, citing one participant's account of the pleasure he took in trading songs, showing off new instruments, swapping techniques, and gossiping about news concerning the cult heros. Like *Newsweek*, he celebrated the diversity of the crowd, particularly the musicians: "a youngster in fringed clothes and beads playing guitar with a bearded college student on banjo, a mechanic on bass, an optometrist on mandolin and a wizened, wrinkled Georgia clay farmer on fiddle."[20] These representatives of various age, social, and ethnic groups were described as sharing cigarettes, drink, and warm spots at fires in addition to the music shared in their marathon sessions. Also noted in the crowd were young people listening respectfully to older musicians, and even a black musician jamming with some whites. It was as if the generational and racial tensions of the times were, like social differences between jam-session participants, forgotten or neutralized at these festivals.

At his Labor Day festival in Camp Springs, Carlton Haney presented the sixth and last "Story of Blue Grass." In response to the pleas of festival-goers for more variety and new kinds of music, Haney also presented tributes to old-timers Charlie Poole and Roy Acuff, and "Stories" for the bands of Reno and Smiley and Jimmy Martin.

In 1970 there were more festivals than ever before. Some were now being held outside the Southeast, particularly in the Southwest, the Ozarks, and the upper Midwest. Not all were successful; reviewers and correspondents reported problems—small attendance, or good attendance but with no parking-lot jam sessions. With the proliferation of events not all the big name bands could be present at every event. Moreover, many festival organizers could not afford to pay the fees requested by these groups.

A number of successful festivals featuring local bands, sometimes adding one or two big-name bands, signaled the beginning of a new type of bluegrass festival. Large festivals in which all the big name groups were involved would remain an important part of the scene, but these smaller festivals appealed to the hard-core fans for whom the historical reenactments like the "Story" had begun to pall.

The spontaneity of the early Roanoke festivals remained an ideal for the fans. But for the musicians and others who made a living from bluegrass, the recent developments heralded a long awaited progress toward economic success for their music.

One sign of this came in the fall of 1970 when *Bluegrass Unlimited* changed from an informal part-time effort to a full-time operation. Within a month the new publishers, Pete and Marion Kuykendall, had altered its format to the same magazine size as that of *Muleskinner News*. Another sign came the same month when, at the annual deejay convention in Nashville, the Country Music Association announced that Bill Monroe had been elected to the Country Music Hall of Fame.

In that month's *Muleskinner News*, Carlton Haney published an editorial entitled "Blue Grass Music—It's Time To Organize" which spoke of the need for a bluegrass festival clearing office and gave a list of activities that such an office might provide:

1. Clear all festival dates and sanction all festivals.
2. Clear all artist bookings for 5% of the fee.
3. Provide a service to trade magazines wishing to verify ads.
4. Help festival promoters with pictures, mats, stories and write-ups.
5. Permit only one Festival in a state. If two can be run on the same weekend 400 miles or more apart, this is good, then all acts can work more.
6. See that prices are advertised correctly.
7. See that everybody is treated fairly in obtaining their money.
8. Obtain bookings on other shows, clubs, concerts, and college dates.
9. Help promote blue grass music parties, organizations, records, television shows, and trade magazines.
10. Fulfill our need for organization[21]

Haney offered his facilities for such an organization, which as he described it in the editorial would do little more than add a regulatory dimension to the activities in which he was already engaged. It would, with powers of sanction and percentages of the bookings, be a lucrative operation. But the time had passed for such an organization. Without sanctions and controls, there were already more successful festivals than failures. It appeared there was little to gain from grouping together under Haney. Besides, as his clash with Jimmy Martin and parking-lot pickers had shown, Haney could be headstrong and difficult at times. Many who knew him were willing to take the risk of operating without his advice and help, including Bill Monroe, now enshrined as a country music pioneer, busily planning his own festivals and creating his own organization.

Bill Monroe's election to the Country Music Association's prestigious Hall of Fame came as the success of bluegrass festivals was becoming apparent to the country music establishment in Nashville. Within a few years there would be Nashville agencies—including Monroe's own—devoted to bluegrass talent, and renewed interest in the music on the part of record companies there. Like Haney's list of proposed organizational goals, Monroe's new status seemed to promise much for the music. But in the fall of 1970 bluegrass promoters saw trouble from a new quarter—anti–rock festival legislation.

Only a year before, rock festivals had made international news, particularly the gentle, peace-love Woodstock festival in upstate New York and the paranoid, death-haunted Altamont festival in northern California. There were some successful rock festivals, but many had created problems for public officials—drugs, traffic jams, fraudulent ticket sales, lack of proper facilities, and conflicts between hippies and local citizens. The response in many localities where the festivals had been held or planned was to seek to legislate them out of existence.

In August 1970 Florida bluegrass promoter and enthusiast Don O'Neill wrote to *Bluegrass Unlimited* complaining that the state legislature was contemplating a law which would effectively outlaw all outdoor musical gatherings of more than 1,000 people. A few months later similar legislation was proposed in North Carolina; Nick Hancock wrote to *Bluegrass Unlimited* urging readers to write to the state representative in protest.

The problem was discussed in a letter to the magazine from Joseph Taylor, who commented on O'Neill's letter about the situation in Florida, saying that it would be a "mistake to equate bluegrass festivals with the rock variety." The excesses of rock festivals could very well lead to a need for public control, hence bluegrass festivals cannot afford Altamont-like happenings. Yet "some of these degenerate libertine creeps are beginning to show up at our festivals. There were drugs and gutless jerks who cannot face reality that use them at some of the festivals this past summer. . . . vulgar exhibitionists like the broad at Berryville who wore nothing but a wet tee shirt that was too small for her . . . . "[22] Not all long-hairs were this way, of course, but "we must prevent this selfish minority from spoiling our enjoyment of bluegrass as they did for the majority at rock festivals."

But how was this to be done? Bluegrass festivals were now attracting people who came not because they knew about the music but because they had heard good things about these events, outdoor musical festivals which resembled rock or folk festivals. The distinction between amplified instruments and acoustic ones meant relatively little to someone who was several hundred yards from a stage and not listening closely. There were differences in dress, the contents of song lyrics, and the very ethos of the festival, but in the final analysis they were not as important as the similarities.

These included an outdoor stage, the willing suspension of the need for modern amenities like the kitchen and the bathroom, the campers' good-natured acceptance of deprivation, and the sound of music through bad speakers. That both *Bluegrass Unlimited* and *Muleskinner News* listed other festivals—practically anything except rock and classical—reflected their perception that their readers did not limit their tastes to bluegrass and that the other festivals often included bluegrass along with other forms.

In the spring of 1970 *Rolling Stone* magazine published *Festival*, subtitled "The Book of American Music Celebrations," which presented photos from rock, pop, folk, country music, soul, blues, and bluegrass festivals. The running commentary was not closely related to the photos, reinforcing the book's thematic conclusion that in spite of musical and cultural differences all festivals of this kind had similar problems and rewards. The book was just one of many new publications selling counter-culture life style to middle-class youth, variations on the motif started by the *Whole Earth Catalogs*.

1971

With the 1971 season the center of attention for bluegrass festivals shifted. Haney's Camp Springs event was still quite important. But Monroe and Haney were no longer working together (in fact they were not on speaking terms). Allied with Monroe were a number of other bands which were appearing at various festivals with him and, en bloc, not appearing at Haney's festivals. Monroe was now expanding Haney's concepts to make his Bean Blossom festival a more spectacular attraction. The high point of his festival that June was the first reunion of Bill Monroe and Lester Flatt, who had not spoken to each other for decades. Flatt and Scruggs had parted company in 1969, with Flatt returning to the fifties bluegrass sound with his band while Earl moved into country rock. The reunion of members of the fabled "original" bluegrass band had long been hoped for; when Lester and Bill finally appeared together (the complete "original" band was never reunited) it made the cover of *Bluegrass Unlimited* and the pages of *Billboard*. But it was only one of the events that made this particular festival memorable. On Sunday morning there was a service, with bluegrass gospel music, by Monroe's cousin, the Reverend Wendell Rains, from the Hartford, Kentucky, Missionary Baptist church. Later, Monroe had his own "Story of Bluegrass," closing with *nine* fiddlers on stage together (in groups of three) playing "Sally Goodin."

Monroe brought other attractions on stage as well; he booked visiting foreign bands. Present was the Hamilton County Bluegrass Band, the only professional bluegrass group in New Zealand, where a bluegrass festival had been held in 1967. Also appearing were the Bluegrass 45, a group of young Japanese musicians who brought the audience to their feet with a version of "Arkansas Traveller" featuring comic dialogue in Japanese. Making his first festival appearance was John Hartford, nationally known as featured banjoist and singer on the Glen Campbell television show. Hartford was an old hand at bluegrass but had been working in other musical fields since the early sixties. With him at Bean Blossom was a band which included some other old hands: Tut Taylor on Dobro, Norman Blake on guitar, and Vassar Clements on fiddle. Also present at Bean Blossom were the "progressive" groups— like the new version of the Country Gentlemen with banjoist Bill Emerson and the Bluegrass Alliance, now hotter than ever. All the parking-lot pickers were doing their arrangement of "One Tin Soldier"; the band's oldest members, Ebo Walker and Lonnie Peerce, had been joined by banjoist Courtney Johnson, guitarist Tony Rice, and mandolinist Sam Bush. Like Charlie Finley's Oakland Athletics (the hot new team in American League baseball that year), they were surprisingly good even if they did have long hair and moustaches.

Those who attended the 1971 Bean Blossom festival considered it a milestone, confirming their faith in the power of the music. Bill Knowlton, who had been writing about and promoting bluegrass as a part-time disc jockey for over a decade, expressed his feelings in *Bluegrass Unlimited* in a brief piece written shortly after the festival in which he alluded to "the warm feeling to know that the music you love can unite hippies, the Establishment, kids, musicians, fans, old folk, collegians, farmers, professionals, fans, Easterners, Southerners, hawks and doves—all mankind, with love instead of conflict."[23]

The other big festival of the year was Haney's "Seventh Annual Labor Day Weekend Original Blue Grass Music Festival" at Camp Springs. It didn't have Monroe or Flatt, but Earl Scruggs was there with his Revue (a band centered around his sons), and there were special band reunion shows of famous (to knowledgeable fans) early bands—Jimmy Martin and the Osborne Brothers, Jimmy Martin and Paul Williams, and the Lilly Brothers with Don Stover and Tex Logan. For the first time, *Muleskinner News* held a Blue Grass Music Awards presentation, based on their readers' poll. This was to become an annual event at the festival, taking the place of the "Story." The band which won most of the awards that year was the Country Gentlemen; the most promising band was the Bluegrass Alliance. The emphasis in Haney's festivals was shifting from a celebration of the past through the recreation of Monroe's bands to a celebration of present and future through the awards ceremony. Haney (who continued to be active as a promoter of mainstream country shows) had no choice but to change in this way, since Monroe was now competing with him as a promoter.

In the year following his investiture into the Country Music Hall of Fame, Monroe began promoting his own festivals, working in cooperation with Ralph Stanley on several and laying plans for others with Lester Flatt. The on-stage reticence which had begun to fade following his association with Rinzler in 1963 had by 1971 disappeared almost completely. With regard to his music Monroe was now like a preacher and a proud inventor—a down-home mixture of Billy Sunday and Thomas Alva Edison.

He felt secure enough not only to make the music, but also to orchestrate the staging and marketing. During the seventies his interviews would acquire a certain sameness as he repeated the statements which had first been squeezed out with the help of Rinzler or Haney but now rolled forth with little prompting. Monroe's confidence seemed justified by the way in which Bud Wendell at WSM responded to his new stature. The Opry sponsored an "Early Bird Blue Grass Special" concert at the beginning of the annual deejay convention in Nashville which, for the first time, brought together the big names in bluegrass for a concert in that city. Monroe was at the center of this event, which embodied aspects of his festivals such as the massed fiddlers and the big jam session at the end. This was a special breakthrough for well-known bluegrass bands like Jimmy Martin and Ralph Stanley, that had never had much exposure to Opry audiences. Another Nashville breakthrough for bluegrass occurred at the end of the same convention when the Osborne Brothers were voted "Best Vocal Group" in the annual CMA awards.

Acceptance in Nashville was echoed by a growing awareness of the festival phenomenon on the part of national mass circulation magazines. It had become news.

1971: Media Views

In July 1971 *Playboy* magazine sent staff reporter David Standish to Carlton Haney's fifth Berryville Festival at Watermelon Park. His report appeared in the November issue. Standish wrote as an outsider, describing Flatt and Scruggs as being of Beverly Hillbillies theme fame, the "only bluegrass group that people who live in high-rises have ever heard of."[24] This music had limited appeal, said Standish; it would never fill Shea Stadium. When Ralph Stanley played for 8,000 people at Watermelon Park he had a sixth of his entire market in front of him. Standish contrasted the 300 people present for the Lewis Family's gospel set on the first afternoon—middle-aged men wearing drip-dry dacron shirts, women wearing cotton shifts, "diehards" absorbing it all with their cassette recorders—with the 8,000 at the Earl Scruggs Revue on Saturday night, when stoned hippies danced, cheered, and were resented by the others around them.

Most of what Standish described had been reported in the *Bluegrass Unlimited* festival reviews of previous years—the cultural mixture, the parking-lot jam sessions, the "bluegrass widows," and the importance of personal interaction as old friends met and talked in a relaxed setting. But he also included details not mentioned in other reports, like his description of Roy Lewis hawking Bibles from the stage and Ralph Stanley and his fiddler Curley Ray Cline giving the hard sell for their records. He observed a backstage conference between Charlie Waller of the Country Gentlemen and Carlton Haney, as Waller complained to Haney that Country Gentlemen records were being sold by a concessionaire for less than the band was selling them. Standish's outsider status led him to describe commercial aspects of the event which were never discussed in print by in-group members. As Abrahams points out, commercial exchange is never *supposed* to be an evident part of the festival; in discussing such matters Standish was breaking a rule of festival etiquette.

One vignette which stands out in his report is a description of a city woman taking a photo of a short-haired fan, which he called "instant folklore."[25] The stereotypes of the rural-urban dichotomy which this action suggested were then called into question when emcee Fred Bartenstein (editor of *Muleskinner News*) and fiddler Tex Logan were identified respectively as a Harvard Business School student and a Bell Laboratories Think Tank employee.

Bluegrass Unlimited responded to this article in an editorial calling it "uninformed," "cute" and "vivid": the magazine was not amused. In contrast, Robert Cantwell's "Believing in Bluegrass," published in the March 1972

Atlantic Monthly, was received enthusiastically by the bluegrass community. Cantwell had gone to Monroe's 1971 Bean Blossom Festival not as a staff reporter like Standish but as an obsessive believer in the music who had never before seen Bill Monroe. Cantwell's descriptions of the music and analysis of the lyrics reflected his involvement with the music and his explanation, in intellectual terms, of its emotional appeal. To Cantwell, Monroe was the first modern mountain man, the person who had found a voice for his people. He described several aspects of the festival not covered in other reports, such as Monroe's giant sunset jam session at the park entrance at which there were three microphones and 120 musicians, all under the direction of Monroe. Cantwell said it was "like an old-time camp meeting" and quoted Monroe, who proclaimed, "I call you all my children."[26]

Perhaps Cantwell's mystic and committed vision drew him mysteriously to this festival, where Monroe dominated the proceedings, rather than to the Berryville Festival at which Standish was able to remain aloof and objective. Yet it is probable that while Cantwell would not have found the same spirit at Berryville (Monroe wasn't there), Standish could have observed everything at Bean Blossom that he saw at Berryville. The two accounts come closest when describing the interpersonal relationships between representatives of different cultures in the field and, significantly, depicting the long-haired hippie bands on stage. The New Deal String Band at Berryville and the Bluegrass Alliance at Bean Blossom were both able to excite the admiration of a wide swath of the audience while at the same time incurring the displeasure of some of the conservatives, if not just by their looks then by comments on stage like Ebo Walker's joke, during a record pitch, that their records were "on the Oral Roberts label" and they'd "had some trouble with the holes healing up," or by songs like the Bob Dylan tune played by the New Deal String Band that brought some boos from the audience.

1972

The 1972 season saw more festivals than ever. At many, attendance was up. But the committed enthusiasts were beginning to question this success. At Union Grove, which was not a bluegrass festival but was still a meeting place for bluegrass musicians from all over the upper South and the Northeast, there were between forty and ninety thousand people in attendance. *Bluegrass Unlimited* said that fellowship and brotherhood encountered in earlier versions seemed to be fading and wondered if this mass appeal was really what we are after. Many at Union Grove seemed to have no appreciation of the music; it was just background for a happening. Tradition was so fragile, and these massive events seemed to threaten it. A letter writer agreed, saying that the first Roanoke festivals had been attended by bluegrass fans who played the music themselves, but now the festivals had grown and deteriorated. There are more people, but the scene is "crude" and "gross."[27] Had we, the writer wanted to know, made a pact with the devil? Did acceptance mean a loss of integrity? Those who wrote with enthusiasm these days were speaking of small festivals where the musicians could meet each other and there were good jam sessions.

That festivals had become as much a matter of business for those involved as an attempt to promote a music perceived as threatened can be seen in the editorial which appeared in the first issue of Bluegrass Unlimited edited by Pete Kuykendall. Noting that festivals were financially successful for the most part this season in spite of problems such as those with sanitary facilities, etc., it reported that the magazine was now receiving many letters concerning festivals and was no longer able to deal with them all. "We cannot function as a soapbox for personal grievances,"[28] the editorial said, advising readers to complain instead to those involved.

Like Bluegrass Unlimited, the Wall Street Journal recognized in 1972 that bluegrass festivals were a matter of business. In a front page story by Journal reporter Ralph E. Winter, datelined from a festival in Glasgow, Delaware, the Dow Jones publication gave the mandatory history of the music, an account of the rise of festivals, and the by now stereotyped descriptions of pluralistic audiences. Among those Winter spoke to was a dedicated parking-lot picker, the man who initiated the Washington Square sessions in New York back in 1945. He was still at it: " 'I don't go to the stage performances, I come to pick music,' says George D. Margolin, a corncob-pipe-smoking inventor from Manhattan. 'Usually I pick until about 4:30 in the morning, and by 8 a.m. we're picking again,' says the amateur mandolin player."[29]

Unlike most festival articles, this one provided some business statistics. Festivals, it reported, were boosting the incomes of bluegrass performers even though they were not getting rich overnight like rock stars: the best known bluegrass bands were being paid $750 to $1,500 a day as opposed to the $20,000 rock bands were getting. But that was better, said Winter, than 1965 when bluegrass bands were getting $250 to $450 per day. Actually the latter figures were somewhat low, at least for the top groups, for Flatt and Scruggs were asking between $800 and $1,200 during the early sixties, and Monroe around $700 in the mid-sixties. But there was no question that more money was now available for bluegrass; this could be seen in average incomes, now up to about $15,000 for "first-rate banjo pickers or fiddlers" who a dozen years earlier had made less than factory workers, and in the fact that there were more young people trying the music because of increased opportunities. Records too were selling better, though as before more money was to be made from hawking them in person than through royalties, as the records were still selling in the low thousands.

The Wall Street Journal also covered the matter of the festival promoters' financial viewpoint: bluegrass festivals were said to lose money during their first year but made it back as the festival became better known. Carlton

Haney was quoted on the mechanics of festival investment: "You shouldn't invest more than $10,000 the first year. . . . Even then you'll lose money, but if you spend the second year just what you took in the first year you'll make back your loss. After that you make money if you always invest just what you took in the previous year."[30] Winter pointed out that many festivals are sponsored by big-name performers, which "reduces cash outlays"; expenses are further reduced by volunteer help from members of sponsoring organizations. At the festival Winter attended Bill Monroe and Ralph Stanley hired performers and did national promotion; local nonprofit groups, the Delaware Association of Police and the Brandywine Valley Friends of Old Time Music, handled local arrangements and provided volunteer cleanup.

In the reporter's opinion the "folksy" atmosphere and the relatively small crowds (5,000 over three days was considered a success) contributed to the appeal of the event; it was possible for amateurs to jam with pros, and it was fun to watch Monroe's massed finale with thirty top musicians playing together on stage: "The working folk, middle-class professionals and informal youths get along smoothly, seemingly sharing an in-group feeling from belonging to a minority sneered at by more 'sophisticated' people."[31]

Carlton Haney spoke of an even more spectacular ending for his forthcoming Camp Springs festival—"a 52-man bluegrass orchestra" directed by Haney via "lights mounted at the bottom of the stage, flicking on red for fiddles, blue for mandolins, green for guitars. 'This is a whole new sound,' he says. 'It would blow your mind, man.' "[32]

Newgrass

Haney's enthusiasm for mind-blowing theatrics reflected his concern with maintaining features at his festivals which were novel and would attract larger crowds. One promoter who was thinking along similar lines was northern Virginian Jim Clark. In the fall of 1971 he successfully promoted a show at an Alexandria theater using most of his advertising in the Washington "underground media" to draw a young crowd to see a bill which included the Osborne Brothers, the Country Gentlemen, the Lewis Family, Jimmy Martin, Mac Wiseman—bluegrass acts all—along with the Earl Scruggs Revue and John Hartford.

Hartford, born in 1937, the son of a doctor, grew up in the St. Louis region. John was exposed from an early age to old-time fiddle music at square dances; the radio acquainted him with Stringbean's five-string banjo. In 1953 he first heard Flatt and Scruggs in person at a local country music park and became a bluegrass convert. He was part of the same regional scene from which the Dillards emerged, but after attending Washington University, Hartford embarked on a career as a songwriter and disc jockey which led him away from bluegrass. By 1965 he was in Nashville, where he joined the ranks of the young maverick singer-songwriters, of whom Kris Kristofferson became the most famous—the "New Breed." In 1967 he was the first of them to write and record a hit song, "Gentle on My Mind." Glen Campbell had a bigger hit with it, and in 1968 this brought John to Hollywood, where he worked with Campbell, first on the Smothers Brothers' television show and, beginning in the summer of 1968, on Campbell's shows.

Hartford's success gave him freedom to experiment with a mixture of old-time, country, rock, and bluegrass that represented his personal art. In California he put together a rock-influenced electric band which, with its banjo, anticipated the sound of the later Earl Scruggs Revue. Then in 1970, while in Nashville to appear in the Johnny Cash show's tribute to Bill Monroe, he met guitarist Norman Blake.

Like Hartford, Blake was a bluegrass veteran. Born in 1938 in Chattanooga, he'd worked in the early sixties with Hylo Brown on WWVA and recorded with Chattanooga folk-bluegrass musicians Bob Johnson and Walter Forbes. In 1963 he began recording with Johnny Cash, and by 1969 he was a Nashville sideman, appearing on Cash's network show, on Bob Dylan's *Nashville Skyline* album, and touring with Joan Baez and Kris Kristofferson. Hartford and Blake, meeting in 1970, both realized that they preferred acoustic to electric sounds and that they shared much in musical ideas.

By early 1971 Hartford had dissolved his California group and assembled a band which included Blake; Georgia Dobroist, sign painter, and instrument collector Tut Taylor; and fiddler Vassar Clements. Clements, from Florida, had first worked with Bill Monroe in 1950 while still in his teens. Later, between 1958 and 1961, he'd been with Jim and Jesse. Subsequent drinking problems had curtailed his career. He began his comeback as a fiddler with Faron Young in 1968.

This band was the one Hartford brought to bluegrass festivals in 1971. All were skilled bluegrass musicians. And though Hartford, with his wild beard and long, unkempt hair, looked like a hippie, he considered himself inspired by the creative traditions of bluegrass. He was, he felt, following his own muse just as Bill Monroe had done earlier. In 1973 he told musician/writer Doug Green: "Bill Monroe was probably a really big influence on me, and the way he was an influence was the fact that he was stubborn about what he does. . . . And Bill Monroe's the biggest hippie of all. He's always been a nonconformist, he's always had long hair and he's always been very dogmatic about what he does and he hasn't been ashamed to be."[33] Hartford appealed to a young middle-class audience, the same constituency the Scruggs Revue was courting. He appeared frequently at colleges and folk festivals. In featuring the Revue and Hartford, promoter Clark successfully combined country rock and folk country with various shades of bluegrass before an audience of young people who could dig what Hartford was getting at when he called Monroe a hippie.

In February 1972 *Muleskinner News* reported that four of the musicians in the Bluegrass Alliance had formed a new group which they called the New Grass Revival. The name had been chosen by Sam Bush, the group's mandolin and fiddle player. It would soon take on the connotations of a generic label—newgrass. Bluegrass musicians and fans had been referring informally to the music as "grass" since the early sixties. The Osborne Brothers' fourth and final MGM album, issued in 1963, had been titled *Cuttin' Grass*. When Bill Emerson and Cliff Waldron assembled a group that emphasized "contemporary" repertoire (particularly rock songs), they titled their first Rebel album *New Shades of Grass* (1968). The following year Rebel issued banjo picker Walter Hensley's album under the title *Pickin' on New Grass*. In 1970 the title of the Bluegrass Alliance's second album, *Newgrass*, came even closer to Bush's band name.

The New Grass Revival carried on musical trends established by the Dillards, the Country Gentlemen, Flatt and Scruggs, and other folk- and rock-influenced bluegrass bands during the late sixties. To this they added new ideas taken from rock music. One was the use of electric pickups for their acoustic instruments—a change which allowed them to move about on stage like rock musicians and to project their music with much greater volume. Of course it alienated those fans who defined bluegrass as acoustic music. But it heightened their appeal to rock fans.

A particularly striking aspect of their repertoire was the incorporation of lengthy improvisational instrumental passages within songs or tunes. Often these sections were set to simplified chord progressions, allowing greater freedom of improvisational expression. This technique, which in concert performances took on the character of an extended free-form jam session, had been borrowed from modern jazz and Indian raga music by the Butterfield Blues Band, which introduced it into the San Francisco rock scene in 1966. By the early seventies it was commonplace in rock music. Bush was adept within this form because he was able to bring to it the sense of variation he'd learned playing Texas-style contest fiddle. Hence in this as in other aspects of their music the New Grass Revival was breaking ground by resynthesizing the folk and popular elements of bluegrass.

As important as their music was the maverick counterculture image they cultivated. They joked defiantly about being hassled for their long hair and their affinity to rock music, and they, along with their name, became the symbol for groups which saw themselves as innovators who respected the old music of Monroe, Stanley, and others but had a new constituency. They were youth, outlaws, rebels—hippies, even.

A few months after the New Grass Revival formed, Jim Clark held his Bluegrass Folk Festival at the American Legion Country Music Park at Culpeper, Virginia. In addition to the acts he'd booked at Alexandria the previous fall, he included the Dillards, now playing country rock on electrified bluegrass instruments; Doc Watson and Son; the Stonemans; and two new groups started by former Country Gentlemen, II Generation and the Seldom

Scene. *Muleskinner News* reported that "Jim proved the success of Blue Grass Music's appeal to the youth audience; approximately 75 percent of the crowd was between the ages of eighteen and twenty-five."[34]

That September Clark, along with Otis Woody, helped promote the "Indian Summer Blue Grass Festival" at Timberlake Park in Fairfax County, Virginia. When posters advertising it as "three days of peace, love, blues and bluegrass" were seen by local residents, some became worried that their property would be overrun by hippies.[35] They complained to the county attorney, who went to court to ask that the festival be banned. In court the lawyer for the promoters argued that they did not need the county's permission, citing a recent Democratic Party rally held without a permit in the county. He also brought forward evidence that owners of property adjacent to the site had been consulted and had given permission for the event. But the judge banned the festival, and signs were posted at the site stating that it was cancelled by court order and that participants would be prosecuted. But in spite of this the event took place. *Muleskinner News* reported that "a large crowd, mostly young, saw the most varied 'Blue Grass' show ever put on, from the Country Gentlemen to [Cajun fiddler] Ambrose Thibodeaux, from Jimmy Martin to John Hartford, from the Osborne Brothers to [Jonathan Edwards's band] Orphan. A highlight was the small stage set up a mile away for quiet and intimate workshops. Richard Spottswood ran these. Other festival promoters should pick up on the idea."[36]

Bluegrass Unlimited was less enthusiastic about the event. In an editorial published the same month, they stated, "BU . . . had no connection with the festival or its promoters other than advertising for them. . . . " They concentrated on the complicated chain of events leading to and following the injunction, pointing out that "the local news media picked up on the preliminaries and gave the festival much coverage which did a lot to get the curious as well as the true fans to attend. While its appeal to the hardline bluegrass fan would be questionable it was a varied event, ranging from bluegrass through cajun music and beyond . . . Bluegrass festival was on everybody's mind whether they knew what bluegrass was or not . . . this type of problem is something that bluegrass music could easily do without."[37]

Muleskinner News's more positive stance toward such events reflected Haney's opinion that the audience for newgrass was an important group. In the spring of 1973, as the Nitty Gritty Dirt Band's *Will the Circle Be Unbroken* album (to be discussed in the next chapter) and Weissberg and Mandel's "Dueling Banjos" were climbing the best-seller charts, he promoted the "first New Grass Music Festival" at his Reidsville campsite. On the bill were the New Grass Revival, the Seldom Scene, the Country Gentlemen, and the II Generation. Though a successful event, it was somehow not as complete as the Clark festivals, for it stopped at newgrass and did not include the folk, folk-rock, and country-rock big names that shared much in repertoire, style, and audience with the newgrass favorites.

In June Jim Clark held a "Peace-Love-Blues and Blue Grass Festival" at Lake Whippoorwill Park in Warrenton, Virginia. Fred Bartenstein attended and reported the event enthusiastically in the following month's issue of *Muleskinner News*. He was impressed by the large crowd, mainly rock fans, attracted to the event. They came to see acts like Jerry Garcia (of the Grateful Dead), singer-songwriter Steve Goodman ("City of New Orleans"), and the Nitty Gritty Dirt Band. Bartenstein editorialized about this kind of festival: "Festivals in Hugo, Oklahoma, Spruce Pine, NC and McClure, Virginia, will not attract tremendous new audiences simply because they don't feature this kind of nationally prominent act. And this is good! There will be Festivals for the old-time Blue Grass Fan, just as there have been for the last eight years. But there will now be festivals for the new crowd, too. . . . " He reasoned that as long as such festivals included some real bluegrass bands like the Seldom Scene or James Monroe's Midnight Ramblers, then more people would be exposed to the music. What pleased him most was that on a second stage removed from the one where the big stars were holding forth, "Acts such as the Country Gentlemen, the Seldom Scene, Country Gazette, Osborne Brothers, Pete Rowan and David Grisman, the Allen Brothers and Breakfast Special played their hearts out . . . for the true Blue Grass music fan, this not only made the festival bearable, but a highlight of the summer schedule."[38]

There were problems with such festivals, though, for many merely used the word *bluegrass* in their title and included no groups which knowledgeable fans would agree were bluegrass. People wrote in to the bluegrass magazines complaining that such events were "little Woodstock(s)" with no parking-lot picking or similar attractions.[39] But behind this lay another problem; bands that had once been called bluegrass were playing strange music on electric instruments. Country rock seemed to be threatening the purity of bluegrass. Such accusations were not new by 1973-74, but as the success of festivals led to attempts to combine bluegrass with other forms in festivals in order to draw larger crowds, arguments about what was right and wrong about the music were complicated by the bewildering array of groups active under the label of bluegrass. To understand just what happened we must leave the fan/consumer—oriented world of festivals and look at bluegrass during the late sixties and early seventies from the viewpoint of the professional musician.

Notes

1. Roger D. Abrahams, "Shouting Match at the Border," p. 304.
2. Ibid., p. 313.
3. Ibid., p. 316.
4. Norman Carlson, "Bill Monroe's Bluegrass Festival," p. 4.
5. Carl Goldstein, "Berryville Bluegrass Festival," p. 5.

6. Dennis Cyporyn, "Bluegrass Fever," p. 2.

7. Anne Romaine, "Georgia Bluegrass Festival," p. 7.

8. Jack Hurst, *Nashville's Grand Ole Opry*, p. 318.

9. Alice [Gerrard] Foster, "Festival of American Folklife," p. 21.

10. Alice [Gerrard] and Mike Seeger, "Bluegrass Unlimited Merit Award—Ralph Rinzler," p. 5.

11. Richard K. Spottswood, "There Was Bluegrass at Camp Springs," p. 3.

12. George B. McCeney, "Festivals and Friends," p. 23.

13. George B. McCeney, "Remember the First Time?" p. 7.

14. Helen Lenard and Marsha Marders, "Maryland Indian Summer Bluegrass Festival," p. 9.

15. Bob Bovee, "To the Friends of Bluegrass Music."

16. Dave Blood, "Bob Goff."

17. Carlton Haney, "Sharps and Flats (or *The Lion Roars*)."

18. Dave Blood and Charlie Vaughn, "Festivals."

19. "Pickin' and Singin'."

20. M. P. Fleisher, "No Generation Gap at Folk Festival," p. 8.

21. Carlton Haney, "Blue Grass Music—It's Time to Organize."

22. Joseph Taylor, letter in *BU* 5 (Dec. 1970): 9.

23. Bill Knowlton, "Fresh Impressions of Bean Blossom," p. 6.

24. David Standish, "Shenandoah Breakdown," p. 190.

25. Ibid.

26. Robert Cantwell, "Believing in Bluegrass," p. 54.

27. David Morgan, "State of the Art."

28. [Peter V. Kuykendall,] editorial in *BU,* 7 (Aug. 1972): 4.

29. Ralph E. Winter, "Sentimental Songs: Awash with Nostalgia, 'Bluegrass Festivals.' "

30. Ibid.

31. Ibid.

32. Ibid.

33. Doug Green, "John Hartford," p. 32.

34. Maria Gajda, "Muleskinner Newsletter," *MN* 3 (July 1972): 4.

35. Rich Adams, "Timberlake Troubles Could be a Sign of the Times to Come," p. 16.

36. Gajda, "Muleskinner Newsletter," *MN* 3 (Oct. 1972): 17.

37. [Peter V. Kuykendall,] editorial in *BU* 7 (Oct. 1972): 4.

38. Fred Bartenstein, editorial in *MN* 4 (July 1973): 5.

39. Ben P. Robertson, letter in *MN* 5 (Oct. 1974): 7.

Bibliographical Notes

The first New Zealand bluegrass festival of 1967 is discussed, along with other aspects of the growth of interest in bluegrass in that country, by

Antony Hale in "A Comparison of Bluegrass Music Diffusion in the United States and New Zealand." The first Japanese festival (as reported in an American publication) was described by Takashi Shimbo in "All Japanese Bluegrass Festival." My own "The Hardwoodlands Festival" chronicles the Nova Scotia Bluegrass and Old Time Music Festival but mistakenly dates its first appearance as 1972 instead of 1971. A Piedmont Airlines ad featuring bluegrass festivals appeared in *Newsweek*, Nov. 20, 1972, p. 127A; the festival listing in *Mademoiselle* was published in their Apr. 1973 issue, p. 137.

Bob Artis's description of festivals is on pp. 121–40 of his *Bluegrass*. A useful study concerning the importance of travel and tourism in contemporary culture is Dean MacCannell's *The Tourist*. His "structure of tourist settings" (pp. 100–102) is a model with a number of applications to bluegrass festivals.

For more on Ralph Rinzler, see Richard D. Smith, "Ralph Rinzler: Preserving American Folk Arts." The Smithsonian Folklife Festival remains a yearly fixture on the Mall in Washington, and the impact of professional folkloric interest in such events has resulted in Joe Wilson and Lee Udall's *Folk Festivals: A Handbook for Organization and Management*. But many professional folklorists now question the advocacy of folk festivals as a means of preserving threatened folk cultures. See David Whisnant, ed., *Folk Festival Issues* and Charles Camp and Timothy Lloyd, "Six Reasons Not to Produce Folklife Festivals," for examples of this viewpoint. Recent thinking on the topic is given in Ormond H. Loomis, *Cultural Conservation*. This approach owes much to historical archeology. See also Alan Jabbour and Howard W. Marshall, "Folklife and Cultural Preservation."

There is an extensive literature on the many folk festivals which are seasonal and (often) religious events without conscious political or economic dimensions; a useful starting point is Robert J. Smith, *The Art of the Festival*.

Haney's second (1966) Roanoke festival was in some ways as important as the first, because it confirmed the calendric dimension of the phenomenon. See my "Reflections on Roanoke." The many festival reports and letters to the editors that appeared in *Bluegrass Unlimited* and other bluegrass periodicals during the first seven years of festivals form the basis for much of this chapter. Sid Campbell's letter about saturation appeared in *Bluegrass Unlimited* 3 (Nov. 1968): 18. Byron Berline reported on his Louisiana festival in "Fort Polk Bluegrass Special." The letter complaining about being ejected from Haney's festival appeared in *Bluegrass Unlimited* 4 (Nov. 1969): 16. The first issue of *Muleskinner News*, dated Aug. 26, 1969, was the program for Haney's Camp Springs Festival that year. An excellent survey and study of the spread of festivals is George O. Carney, "Bluegrass Grows All Around: The Spatial Dimensions of a Country Music Style." Cultural geographer Carney uses the methodology of his discipline to demonstrate the diffusion of bluegrass and the sense of place which it conveys. In 1969 Carlton Haney and Ralph Rinzler co-produced a version of the "Story of

Bluegrass" with Bill Monroe as part of the Newport Folk Festival. See Ruth
Tripp, "Mountain Music a Feature in Concert at Rogers High."

The *Rolling Stone* festival book is Jim Marshall, Baron Wolman, and Jerry
Hopkins, *Festival! The Book of American Music Celebrations*. A useful retrospective popular history on the same subject is Robert Santelli, *Aquarius
Rising: The Rock Festival Years*. The impact of rock festivals on bluegrass
festivals is reflected in Don O'Neill's letter to *Bluegrass Unlimited* 5 (Sept.
1970): 37, and in Nick Hancock's "A Threat to Festivals."

Carlton Haney's description of the way in which Monroe and others boy-
cotted his festivals is given in John Pugh, "Carlton Haney: True Great."

The first "Early Bird" concert was announced in "Fall Country Fete Sets
First Bluegrass Show." The changing perception of bluegrass in Nashville is
set forth in "Bluegrass Shakes Off It's [sic] Cobwebs and Emerges Healthy
and Vigorous."

Flatt's reunion with Monroe was noted in "Bill Monroe and Lester Flatt
Reunited at Hoosier Festival" and on the cover of *Bluegrass Unlimited* 6
(Aug. 1971). An editorial comment about the cover called this "a great
moment in the history of bluegrass" (4).

The first Japanese band to tour the U.S. festivals is described in Fred
Bartenstein, "Blue Grass 45: Gentlemen of Japan." The New Zealand group
was the subject of four articles in *Bluegrass Unlimited*: Dave Calder's three—
"Bluegrass in New Zealand?" "A Professional Bluegrass Band in New Zealand?" and "New Zealand Bluegrass Sequel"—and Mike Seeger's "Hamilton
County Bluegrass Band." See also Hale, cited above; Calder was a member
of the Hamilton County Bluegrass Band; Seeger toured New Zealand.

That much of the festival activity was male-dominated and oriented is
reflected in Cyporyn's allusion to the angry wife and Standish's comment
about bluegrass widows. For the female point of view see Connie Walker,
"The Plight of the Blue Grass Widow." Iline Tyler, "Woes of a Bluegrass
Wife," cited in the notes to chapter 7, makes it clear that the problems
(often the husband's intense involvement in the music and its trappings is
not shared by the wife, who finds it boring and alienating) preceded the
festival situation.

Haney's annual awards were documented in "First Annual Blue Grass
Awards." They continued annually to 1977; see "1977 Blue Grass Music
Award Winners."

A reprise of the 1972 festival season which articulates the unease of seasoned fans at the price of success is an untitled piece in *Rounder Review* by
Kathy Kaplan. She was particularly worried about the way various "mod-
grass" (her coinage) bands seemed to be forcing the traditionalists "underground again" (p. 5).

John Hartford's pioneering role is stressed in Frye Gaillard, *Watermelon
Wine*, a book that is a good source for the new Nashville of the late sixties
and early seventies. See also Bill C. Malone, "A Shower of Stars," pp. 432–

33, for information on the "new breed." Information on Hartford's 1971 all-star band members includes Mary Jane Bolle, "Norman Blake"; Art Coats, "Norman Blake"; and Art and Leota Coats, "Norman Blake, Ex-'Hot Licks Picker.' " For Tut Taylor, see Douglas B. Green, "Tut Taylor: Bluegrass Enigma." And for Vassar Clements, see Edgar Koshatka, "Vassar Clements"; Tex Logan, "Vassar Clements"; Doug Tuchman, "Vassar Clements," and Barry Silver, "Vassar Clements Out West."

The viewpoints and self-perceptions of the newgrass and progressive musicians of the early seventies are set forth in William Henry Koon, "Newgrass, Oldgrass, and Bluegrass." The New Grass Revival (particularly Sam Bush) has articulated a musical stance and a cultural image in a number of articles and interviews: Thomas A. Adler, "The Acquisition of a Traditional Competence," pp. 599–633; Fred Bartenstein, "A Conversation with the New Grass Revival"; Ronni Lundy, "The New Grass Revival"; and "Sam Bush: Electrifying Bluegrass"; Alanna Nash, "Sam Bush, New Grass Revival and Leon Russell"; John Sievert, "Sam Bush: 'Newgrass' Mover and Shaker"; Jon Sievert, "Sam Bush"; and Mel Smothers, "Between Sets with the New Grass Revival." Information concerning the extended-jam techniques in rock music comes from David Grisman, personal communication, and Rich Kienzle, "The Whiteface Connection," p. 32. Other bands mentioned in the newgrass section of this chapter are discussed in the next chapter.

The best way to get a feeling for the ambience of bluegrass festivals in the early seventies is to look closely at Nobuharu Komoriya's *Blue Ridge Mountains Friendly Shadows*, a collection of photographs taken during the 1974 season.

Discographical Notes

The Bluegrass Alliance's "One Tin Soldier" was issued on their *Newgrass*. John Hartford's "Gentle on My Mind" later appeared on *Earthwords and Music*. Hartford's 1971 band, along with Randy Scruggs on bass, can be heard on *Aereo-Plain*. The Butterfield Blues Band's second album, *East-West*, incorporated two lengthy cuts, "Work Song" and "East-West," which used the extended jam form. Both were produced by Paul Rothchild.

The Brown County Jamboree Barn at Bean Blossom, Indiana. The small extension at the right was the backstage area, a frequent site of jam sessions between shows. [Photo by Carl Fleischhauer]

Monroe called his first Bean Blossom festival in 1967 a "Big Blue Grass Celebration." [Photo by Carl Fleischhauer]

Birch Monroe singing with the Blue Grass Quartet at Bean Blossom, October 28, 1962: Bill Monroe, Roger Smith, Birch, Jim Maynard. [Photo by Jim Peva]

The Lewis Family Show at the Mountain State Bluegrass Festival in Webster Springs, West Virginia, July 5, 1974: Pop, Janice, Miggie, Polly, Roy, Talmadge. [Photo by Carl Fleischhauer]

Bill Monroe leads the entire festival cast and the audience with handclapping on a Sunday morning gospel session at his Kentucky Blue Grass Festival in Jackson, Kentucky, August 23, 1972. [Photos by Carl Fleischhauer]

Earl Scruggs, Irene Ryan ("Granny" in "The Beverly Hillbillies"), and Lester Flatt in 1968; Lester and Earl are in their *Bonnie and Clyde* outfits. [Courtesy of the Country Music Foundation Library and Media Center, Nashville, Tennessee]

This budget-line album of bluegrass instrumentals by a group of Nashville studio musicians (including the Osborne Brothers) was made by RCA to take advantage of the popularity of *Bonnie and Clyde*. [Author's personal collection]

The hit single from the sound track of *Deliverance* was issued in 1973 on this album along with recordings originally released by Eric Weissberg and Marshall Brickman in 1963. [Author's personal collection]

The 1949 Blue Grass Boys are recreated in the "Story of Bluegrass" at Carlton Haney's second Roanoke Bluegrass Festival, September 4, 1966: Bill Monroe, Don Reno, Carlton Haney, Mac Wiseman, James Monroe. [Photo by Ann M. Rosenberg]

Monroe Family Day at the 1969 Smithsonian Festival of American Folklife: Bill Monroe, Alice Gerrard, Birch Monroe, Charlie Monroe, Mike Seeger, Ralph Rinzler. [Courtesty of the Country Music Foundation Library and Media Center, Nashville, Tennessee]

Muleskinner News editor Fred Bartenstein selling the festival edition of his magazine at Jim Clark's Seventh Annual Culpeper Bluegrass Folk Festival, American Legion Country Music Park, Culpeper, Virginia, June 11, 1972. Behind him on stage is the Seldom Scene. [Photo by Carl Fleischhauer]

Parking lot picking—a jam session at the Bluegrass Camporee and Picker's Convention, August 27, 1977, at the Smithfield, Virginia, American Sportsman Family Campground. [Photo by Carl Fleischhauer]

John Hartford and Norman Blake at Jim Clark's Culpeper festival, June 10-11, 1972. [Photo by Carl Fleischhauer]

Festival promoter Jim Clark at his Culpeper
Bluegrass Folk Festival, June 10-11, 1972.
[Photo by Carl Fleischhauer]

The Bluegrass Alliance at the First Annual Bill Monroe Kentucky Blue Grass Festival, Ashland, Kentucky, August 14, 1971: Courtney Johnson, Lonnie Peerce, Sam Bush, Ebo Walker, Tony Rice. [Photo by Carl Fleischhauer]

At the Smithfield, Virginia, Pickers' Convention in 1977, a "Dance Hall" provided room for youths who combined boogie moves in a square dance framework to the music of the New Grass Revival. [Photo by Carl Fleischhauer]

The New Grass Revival's first LP put the hippie image on a Starday album cover: Curtis Burch, Courtney Johnson, Ebo Walker, Sam Bush. [Author's personal collection]

Bill Monroe and his Blue Grass Boys (Kenny Baker, Dwight Dillman, Monroe, Randy Davis, Ralph Lewis) in action at Bill Monroe and Ralph Stanley's First Annual Old-Time West Virginia Bluegrass Festival at Aunt Minnie's Farm, Stumptown, West Virginia, on Sunday, August 18, 1974. [Photo by Carl Fleischhauer]

Lester Flatt and Bill Monroe lead the massed bands in a typical festival finale at Bill Monroe's Second Annual Kentucky Blue Grass Festival, Jackson, Kentucky, August 23, 1972. [Photo by Carl Fleischhauer]

Chapter 11

But Is It Bluegrass? The Bands:
1967–74

It is ironic that during the late sixties and early seventies when the bluegrass consumer and festival movements brought national attention to the music increased its audiences, a number of the most influential bands broke up or moved away from the stylistic center of bluegrass toward other musical forms—Nashville-sound country, country-rock, folk-rock. Haney's "Story" had reinforced the concept of bluegrass as a musical genre with an evolutionary, linear history. The fans and amateur historians who wrote for the consumer magazines offered evidence for the same viewpoint. But the musicians, particularly those who were full-time professionals recording on major labels, had always faced pressures forcing them away from "pure" bluegrass. While festivals began to catch on in the late sixties, the phenomenon was not large enough to support very many bands on a full-time basis. And major record companies and radio stations still did not see much value in bluegrass as a commercial music.

The ways in which musicians dealt with these problems had important and long-lasting effects on the music. Many younger (and a few older) musicians followed the youth music trends of the time, combining bluegrass with rock, folk, and the various hyphenated fusion musics of the period (country-rock, folk-rock, etc.). They did so in part because they were caught up in the spirit of creative innovation associated with the fusion process, which at the time was widely viewed as symbolizing the new, integrative, social consciousness of the counterculture. This was the spirit in which newgrass emerged. These musicians hoped that through their new music they might reach the larger urban audiences and achieve crossover hit sales. The older, more established musicians, who were the first to enjoy the benefits of the festivals, sought to revive bluegrass audiences by appealing to the sense of tradition created by festivals. Heeding the often strident appeals for purity from diehard fans, they maintained and re-emphasized the elements of "old-time" music in their art and spoke out in opposition to the changes being made by the cross-over bands. Here again age was not an absolute factor, for some younger musicians followed the lead of these traditionalists.

It should come as no surprise that the professional musicians perceived things differently than did their listeners and fans. As we have seen, during the fifties most musicians had responded in some way to the biggest threat of the time, rock and roll. In the early sixties they responded to the folk boom. In both cases the responses were in terms of style, repertoire, and marketing. There was no single threat or boom, however, during the last half of the sixties and the first part of the seventies. Instead a new musical pluralism presented bluegrass musicians with a myriad of problems, challenges, and opportunities. While the festival and consumer movements were expanding bluegrass audiences, the genre became more viable than ever before in urban and college markets, where musical eclecticism was the order of the day for a generation that believed in "doing your own thing." And there were more opportunities for musicians with bluegrass training in mainstream country, rock and roll, and the folk scene. Their responses to all of this varied greatly. In Nashville each of the four Grand Ole Opry bluegrass bands made some changes. Characteristically, Bill Monroe's was the smallest.

Bill Monroe

Monroe's revitalization following his season with Ralph Rinzler had led in the mid-sixties to a series of "city boy" bands, culminating in the 1966-67 aggregation of guitarist Peter Rowan, fiddler Richard Greene, banjoist Lamar Grier, and bassist James Monroe. By 1968 both Rowan and Greene had moved to folk-rock bands. No longer drawing new musicians from the city-billy ranks, Monroe fell back on an earlier pattern, that of carrying a strong southern fiddler as the backbone of his band. That man was Kenny Baker, a coal miner from the east Kentucky community of Jenkins.

Son of an old-time fiddler, Baker had not been encouraged by his father to play the fiddle; his early years as a musician were spent as a guitarist. He appreciated the work of one local fiddler, Marion Sumner. But he was not an old-time fiddle music enthusiast; he was much more a fan of Tommy Dorsey and Glenn Miller. His liking for jazz finally motivated him to take up the fiddle. Stationed in New Guinea during World War II, Baker heard there for the first time the smooth sound of Bob Wills's western swing fiddling and the hot jazz fiddle of Stephane Grappelli with Django Reinhardt. Soon after this he began playing in country bands and worked around his home in eastern Kentucky as a semiprofessional during the postwar years. By the early fifties he was working for country singer Don Gibson and began listening with interest to Monroe's recordings, particularly the fiddle instrumentals. Baker worked (and recorded) with Bill in 1957–58 and 1962–63. But he was unable to remain with Monroe because he had a family to raise and could make more money as a coal miner than as a fiddler.

Baker rejoined Monroe early in 1968. His family was now grown, and he felt free to play music. But he could not have stayed with Monroe had it not been for County Records. In the spring of 1969 County released Baker's first fiddle instrumental album, *Portrait of a Bluegrass Fiddler*. Backed by members of the Blue Grass Boys past and present, he performed his own compositions and several older pieces on an album that became County's best selling album to date. The success of this and his subsequent County albums made Baker one of the best known bluegrass fiddlers. And because he sold albums at personal appearances, which contributed to his income, he was able to continue working with Monroe during these still somewhat lean years.

Bill took to introducing Baker as the best fiddler in bluegrass. He had a distinctive sound, reflecting Monroe's tutelage as well as his grounding in western swing and jazz. Baker's tone was somewhat sweeter and fuller than that of most other bluegrass fiddlers and his harmonies, too, tended to be sweet. But rhythmically and melodically the jazz influence was evident. It was his opinion that "bluegrass music is nothing but a hillbilly version of jazz."[1] Laconic, wry, he exuded a sense of humor as well as an intensity about his music. With Baker the fiddle regained a prominence in the sound of the Blue Grass Boys that had been overshadowed somewhat by the banjo during the early sixties. In 1969 Monroe began working with Baker on a project he'd been planning for years, an album of Uncle Pen Vandiver's fiddle tunes. Baker recalls being told of this idea in 1957: "After I got to playing his stuff a little bit, he told me about these old numbers of his Uncle Pen's. He said he was saving them back for the right fiddler, the man he thought could play them and do them right."[2] Recordings for the album were made carefully and assembled over a three-year period. Issued in 1972 as *Bill Monroe's Uncle Pen*, it was well received and remains one of Monroe's best albums. Kenny Baker's role in Monroe's sound continued to grow throughout the seventies, with Monroe eventually reciprocating by appearing with him on one of his County albums. Baker, still a Blue Grass Boy as this is written, has been with Monroe longer than any other musician.

Another major change in Monroe's band came in 1969 when his son James moved from bass to guitar and became lead singer, replacing Roland White who had been hired away by Lester Flatt. James sang with Bill until 1972, and they eventually recorded two albums together. James then formed his own band, the Midnight Ramblers. While his career was emotionally important for Monroe, it had relatively little impact on the rest of bluegrass music.

From this point on Monroe's role was largely defined by his historical stature as a Hall of Fame member. As the Father of Bluegrass, he was expected to represent and recreate the music of his past. Promoters who decided to try bluegrass were now most likely to turn to him. In 1971, when the Armadillo World Headquarters, an Austin, Texas, rock palace, set out to expand its musical fare to effect a country-rock fusion—a move that eventually brought Willie Nelson to Austin—Monroe's was one of the first country acts booked. Another group which appeared there at that time was the Flying Burrito Brothers, a Los Angeles country-rock band that included a bluegrass set in their shows. They represented the newest bluegrass mutation, while Monroe upheld what was more and more frequently called the "traditional" side of bluegrass.

Flatt and Scruggs

In contrast with Monroe's, Flatt and Scruggs's music seemed to many listeners to deteriorate during the late sixties, and they split in 1969. As with any breakup of this sort, there were many causes. At the center of their problems lay disagreements about repertoire and style which in turn reflected differences of opinion about markets and audiences.

The extent to which Flatt and Scruggs had tied their sound and repertoire to the folk revival created problems for them when, in the mid-sixties, the nature of the revival changed radically. With the emergence of folk-rock, the predominately young urban folk-revival market began to merge with the much larger rock market. Instead of a polarity perceived between mindless rock on the one hand and meaningful folk on the other, there now existed a perception of a musical spectrum ranging from the electrified commercial music of the Beatles and Bob Dylan to the acoustic or unaccompanied non-commercial music of ethnic or traditional performers. Being acoustic rather than electric was no longer so important to urban audiences. All kinds of music appealed to the catholic tastes of audiences now very much under the influence of what came to be called, variously, the counterculture, the underground, consciousness III, or the youth market. Drug-culture values became part of the commercial and social rhetoric of the music industry, with visions of new universes and "mindblowing" recombinations being used to market and merchandise the product. This was the age of the "hype."

Previously Flatt and Scruggs had managed to shape their repertoire and sound so that much of it appealed to both the country music and the folk music followers among their audiences. This became more difficult now as there were such varied tastes to cater to. The bluegrass purists were already unhappy with their sound: they'd dropped the mandolin in 1962 when Curly Seckler left, and it was not heard on any of their records after 1964. While they continued to use acoustic instruments, they followed contemporary Nashville practice when, beginning in 1965, they began using the harmonica and guitar of studio musicians Charlie McCoy and Grady Martin on their records to achieve a fuller sound. Banjo and fiddle were less prominent. Essentially this was a compromise—neither hardline bluegrass nor mainstream Nashville.

Performed in this compromise sound was an increasingly diffuse repertoire. On the six albums released between 1965 and the summer of 1967, they began doing songs by the new more sophisticated Nashville songwriters like Billy Edd Wheeler and Tom T. Hall. A number of older style songs came from Flatt's friends (later, biographers) Jake Lambert and Olan Bassham. Songs by Johnny Cash and the Carter Family also appeared. With the exception of *Strictly Instrumental*, recorded with Doc Watson in 1966, they moved away from the folksong orientation in their albums, though a few older country and traditional numbers were included on each one.

Now their singles were "covers" of contemporary folk songwriters' hits, like Donovan's "Colours," [sic] and Peter, Paul, and Mary's version of the Gordon Lightfoot song "For Loving Me." They also did singles of rock tunes by the Monkees and the Lovin' Spoonful. But these records did not sell as well as their singles of a few years before: none reached the charts for most of 1965 and 1966. In the summer of 1967, during a period when both men were having health problems—Earl hospitalized for surgery stemming from injuries sustained in a 1955 auto accident, Lester suffering his first heart attack— Columbia announced that their records would no longer be handled by Don Law, their producer of many years. Columbia had a hot new producer in Nashville, Bob Johnston, who was attracting attention with the Bob Dylan records he'd done. According to Louise Scruggs, Johnston, knowing Columbia was concerned about Flatt and Scruggs's declining sales, offered to help by becoming their producer. Seeking an explanation for their records' recent lack of success, he called around town to get the opinions of others in the business and came back with the suggestion that Flatt and Scruggs add heavier rhythm to their recorded sound by using extra rhythm guitars and drums. Johnston also had ideas about material. He instituted a new procedure in repertoire selection, in which he provided Lester and Earl with a sampling of songs (many coming from other Columbia artists he was producing); from these they chose and developed the songs they would record.

This summer brought another development that would have future significance for Flatt and Scruggs—the emergence of Earl's sons as professional musicians. For some time Randy, the Scruggs's second son, had been appearing occasionally with Lester and Earl on television and at concerts in Nashville, playing the autoharp. Now Louise Scruggs announced that her oldest son, Gary, was embarking on a musical career, and she would be handling his bookings. Although at this stage his career had been confined to performing in a combo with some high school friends, Gary was signed to Columbia Records in 1967, and he too was produced by Johnston.

The fruits of Flatt and Scruggs's association with Johnston were three albums and three singles, as well as two singles by Gary Scruggs. Two albums, *Changin' Times* and *Nashville Airplane*, featured "contemporary" material, including a large number of Bob Dylan songs. The third album, which came between these two, was the *Bonnie and Clyde* album mentioned previously.

In terms of sound, all three reflected Johnston's penchant for using a large number of Nashville studio musicians to produce a kind of down-home version of the then popular "wall of sound" approach. Included on the *Bonnie and Clyde* album was Earl's second son Randy; both Randy and Gary appeared on the final album.

The liner notes of the albums carried the hype of the times: "With their smash appearance at the Avalon Ballroom (a West Coast temple of rock and light-shows) when they turned on the whole of San Francisco, there are no new worlds left for Flatt and Scruggs to conquer. Flatt and Scruggs are for everyone,"[3] said *Changin' Times*, an album title which played on the title of a Dylan song, and on *Nashville Airplane*, an allusion to the Jefferson Airplane, a San Francisco rock group, Louise Scruggs wrote coyly, "We hope your 'trip' will be pleasant one. . . ."[4]

These albums sold well but were very poorly received by bluegrass fans; reviews in *Bluegrass Unlimited* and the County Sales *Newsletter* were extremely negative. Moreover, even though they were enthusiastically received during their March 1968 tour of Japan, knowledgeable observers of the band's performances were unenthusiastic, as Clarence Green's report on their appearance at a folk festival in Johnson City, Tennessee, in October 1968 indicates: "They were billed as 'bluegrass'—so, happily, the current crop of commercialized junk heard on their recent recordings was . . . omitted. . . . Earl's banjo picking was more or less as usual—jerky, with a few discords thrown in for good measure. . . . All in all they presented a good, if brief, performance, although anyone who was there to hear top-notch bluegrass entertainment went away disappointed. . . . It seems that the ability is still there, but the incentive is not."[5]

Behind the scenes, Lester Flatt was very dissatisfied with their material; he didn't like singing Bob Dylan and was disgusted by the long-haired hippies and their drugs. He refused to perform the new songs, and this became a source of contention between him and the Scruggses.

On the other hand Earl was bored with playing bluegrass; he wanted to work more with his sons and try other kinds of music; he was caught up in their enthusiasm for contemporary music. Acceptance or rejection by bluegrass fans was not very important to Earl at this point. He felt his position was justified by the sales of their Johnston-produced albums. Lester, in contrast, was more concerned by the response of their fans: "When we were doing Flatt and Scruggs music as what I call it . . . it's something that we helped to build, we could go fifteen or twenty miles out of Nashville and just stack the place. After we switched and did some of the other stuff, even though you jump to 100,000 on your albums, you could see the difference in the spirit of the country people, the people that made you. It was very easy to see it."[6] Had *Bonnie and Clyde* not come along in 1968, it is doubtful that they would have remained together as long as they did. As it was Flatt and Scruggs split up in March 1969. They could not resolve the differences about repertoire which, to bluegrass enthusiasts, had been apparent in their recent records and personal appearances.

The Osborne Brothers

The Osbornes presented similar problems for bluegrass enthusiasts in that they, like Flatt and Scruggs, seemed too "commercial." The fans objected not so much to their repertoire as to their sound, because they included so many of the trappings of the Nashville sound on their recordings. Yet no one denied that Bobby was one of the best singers, Sonny one of the best banjoists, and their vocal trio one of the best in bluegrass. They had, by the late sixties, become one of the most popular and imitated bluegrass bands in spite of their impure sound.

The Osbornes, on the cast of the WWVA Jamboree since 1956, joined the Grand Ole Opry in 1964. This move coincided with changes in record company (MGM to Decca) and publisher; all three were accomplished under the patronage of the Opry stars, the Wilburn Brothers. During the decade between 1965 and 1975, they mixed aspects of bluegrass with the Nashville sound, striving to create their own sound, one which would retain their bluegrass following while attracting additional listeners from the considerably larger arena of mainstream country music.

They had been using drums on their records since 1957 and had acquired a reputation for experimenting in the studio; occasional recordings between 1958 and 1964 had included the tiple, electric guitar, pedal steel guitar, female chorus, and twelve-string guitar. But there was little consistency or long-range planning behind these early experiments. The real change began in 1965 when Sonny started experimenting with a top-tension Vega banjo in a special tuning which gave a distinctive bassy sound like that of an electric instrument. In 1966 this was teamed with a piano for their biggest hit to date, "Up This Hill and Down." In 1966–67, they added an electric bass, which first appeared on their next hit, "The Kind of Woman I Got." With the success of that record, they added an electric bass player to their road band—much to the consternation of conservative bluegrass fans. In 1968 came another addition to their recorded sound, the pedal steel guitar, and with it an even bigger hit, "Rocky Top." Their strategy of mixing Nashville and bluegrass seemed to be paying off. But it came in for heavy criticism by some bluegrass fans—a subject of intense controversy in the pages of *Bluegrass Unlimited.* Essentially the debate was over strategies to bring more listeners to bluegrass so as to improve its economic prospects. How, some asked, could you do this with music that wasn't really proper bluegrass?

At the time of "Rocky Top" the Osbornes put on record their response to this criticism with an album entitled *Yesterday, Today and the Osborne Brothers.* On the first side were six songs taken from the 1945–48 Monroe band and the early recordings of Flatt and Scruggs. Every detail of each performance was as close to the original as possible—the instrumental breaks, the harmony parts, even the phrasing of Bobby Osborne's voice as he sang the parts of Bill Monroe, Lester Flatt, and Curly Seckler. Sensitive to the insinuations by critics that they, like Flatt and Scruggs, had lost their skill and appreciation of hard-line bluegrass, the Osbornes wanted it understood that they could play in the style of the bluegrass pioneers just as well today as yesterday. Their own music of today, they felt, did not reflect a loss of skill or ignorance of the early music; it was the logical outcome of their decision to strike out on their own. As the second side of the album showed, they were moving in new directions. The pedal steel seemed a natural part of their music, as did new recording techniques like double-tracking voices (to be discussed later). This music had a contemporary sound. For those not closely involved with early bluegrass, it was this side of the record which sounded best on the stereo.

In 1969 the Osbornes took their most daring step by "going electric," adding pickups to their acoustic instruments. At the time, Sonny told *Bluegrass Unlimited* interviewers, "It's the same damn thing as a good PA system."[7] They didn't intend to alter their sound using the special effects associated with electricity. Their purpose was to raise the volume level, which they had to do if they were to compete with their electrified Opry colleagues, with whom they often appeared in big package shows. The audiences at these events were so overwhelmed by the volume of the amplified groups that they could, it seemed, barely even hear the Osbornes' unamplified instruments. And although the voices came across satisfactorily through the public address system, technological changes had altered microphones so that they no longer picked up instruments as well as they once had.

During the forties and fifties it was rare to see more than one or two microphones used on stage for a public performance or in the studio for a radio broadcast. These microphones were omnidirectional—picking up sounds from any direction—and sensitive to sounds from a considerable distance. Photos of bluegrass bands performing during the early fifties show that featured singers or instrumentalists rarely came closer than half a foot from the microphone. Bluegrass performance technique therefore included the ability to "work the mike," properly sensing one's distance from the microphone and thereby manipulating the balance of sound coming through the public address system or over the radio. Indeed, with a large band, it was part of the show: many observers commented on the "choreography" of Flatt and Scruggs during the late fifties and early sixties as they worked the mikes, as Buck Graves recalled:

We had to learn that when you hit the microphone you play wide-open, and when somebody's singing you soften up. They used to call us a football team at the Opry. Earl was the quarterback, and I was the running back. Earl would hand it off to me, and I'd cut through that hole. One time we had this boy come in—he'd worked with us before—and he'd forgotten the patterns that we'd run. That poor boy, I remember, I caught him on the back of the head with my Dobro neck. Liked to plumb knock him off the stage. Flatt told him, "You better learn these patterns; you're gonna get killed." It all looked pretty from the audience.[8]

By the beginning of the sixties the technology was undergoing rapid change. The introduction of solid-state electronics made it possible to build much larger amplifiers for electric instruments, because the transistors were smaller and lighter than tubes. As the amplifiers became larger they also became louder. Consequently, the public address (PA) systems used by singers and for acoustic instruments required more volume. As the PA systems became larger and louder, the possibility of feedback increased. Feedback occurs when an amplified sound is picked up and recycled (fed back) through the system which produces it, resulting in an unpleasant ringing or squealing noise. The most common way of cutting down on this was to shift from omnidirectional microphones to ones which were unidirectional and sensitive only to sounds which came from very near them. With such microphones, feedback risk was reduced, but it became very difficult to "work the mike" with acoustic instruments. Hence, by 1969, when the Osborne Brothers went electric, they argued that by putting the equivalents of small microphones (pickups) in their instruments there were merely trying to preserve the kind of sound they had been able to obtain in earlier times.

But to the bluegrass aficionados, this was an act of treason, for bluegrass was defined as a music played on acoustic instruments. That the use of microphones was just as much a part of bluegrass as acoustic instruments mattered little to those who opposed "electrification"; they argued that pickups destroyed the natural sound qualities of the instruments and that musicians playing electrified instruments played their music too loud. The Osbornes received more critical reviews because of this change and lost bookings because some festivals were beginning to advertise that electric instruments were not allowed—a response to the conservative fans who had been put off by rock festivals advertised as bluegrass events.

But their first recording with electric instruments, "Tennessee Hound Dog," was the Osbornes' biggest hit to date. And the younger fans who had discovered bluegrass at festivals were not so hung up about electric bluegrass, for chances were they'd first heard bluegrass through the Byrds, Flying Burrito Brothers, Nitty Gritty Dirt Band, or other country-rock groups that were beginning to mix electric and acoustic musics. By 1970, when Sonny introduced his new six-string banjo (it had an additional bass string), the bluegrass record reviewers were tiring of this conflict and routinely described the Osbornes' music as "experimental" or alluded to their unique combination of Nashville and bluegrass. In 1971, when the CMA voted them the "Best

Vocal Group," they moved a step further toward Nashville, releasing "Georgia Pineywoods," their first recording with an overdubbed string section.

For a while, in 1971, they added a drummer for their tours—one of Bobby's sons. But a change in personnel led to his being switched to bass, and drums were subsequently not included in the traveling group. By 1974 the Osbornes decided to discontinue their electric instruments. They were no longer playing so many package shows. In their own concerts they had more control over the sound. Like most bluegrass bands during the seventies, they no longer worked one or two mikes; now a microphone for each instrument and voice was regularly provided at most festivals, concerts, and broadcasts.

In spite of all the fuss about electrification and the Nashville sound aspects of their recordings, the Osbornes were able to retain their following in the bluegrass world because their own vocal and instrumental work retained its appeal and because they had an attractive repertoire, songs which were mainly newly composed Nashville tunes juxtaposed with older songs of Monroe, Ernest Tubb, and similar performers. They particularly benefited from association with songwriters Felice and Boudleaux Bryant, who had first made a reputation with compositions for the Everly Brothers. The Osbornes' big hits of the late sixties and early seventies, all Bryant compositions, gave them the freedom to direct their own musical career and preserve their bluegrass sound, as Monroe's hits of 1946–47 had done for him.

Jim and Jesse

Starting in the mid-fifties, the McReynolds Brothers had been working in the deep South, with television and radio programs in Alabama, Georgia, and north Florida. During 1959 Martha White Mills began co-sponsoring some of these broadcasts, and Jim and Jesse became the number two Martha White unit behind Flatt and Scruggs. In 1960 they left Starday to sign with Columbia Records, and the following year, with the release of their first Columbia single, they began appearing regularly as guests on the Grand Ole Opry. In 1962 Columbia moved them to the subsidiary label Epic, where they had a series of albums and singles which were popular but never quite made it to the charts. Well received by folk revival audiences, they appeared at Newport in 1963. In March 1964 they became members of the Grand Ole Opry.

Lead singer Jesse (whose banjo-like "cross-picked" mandolin style was a distinctive and much imitated feature of their music) and tenor singer Jim did light-textured, high-pitched duets in the style of the Blue Sky Boys and the Louvin Brothers, carrying on the old "brother duet" sound. Like Flatt and Scruggs, they put on a full show, following the old-time country approach to entertainment. From 1960 to 1964, their band was considered one of the best in bluegrass. It included fiddler Jim Buchanan, banjoist Allen Shelton, and comedian-bassist Dave Sutherland ("Joe Binglehead"). Their repertoire mixed newly composed songs with country classics from the late forties and early fifties, issued on six Epic albums between 1962 and 1966.

Along with these albums came a number of singles; the best-received, "Cotton Mill Man," appeared to be developing as a hit in 1963, but it lost valuable exposure when radio stations in several southern mill towns refused to air it because of its protest-type lyrics. In 1964–65 a song from their humor album, *Better Times A-Comin'*, appeared on the *Billboard* charts; later in 1965 "Memphis" from an album of Chuck Berry songs bluegrass style appeared to be taking off when Flatt and Scruggs's version, released at the same time, drew some sales from it; neither made the charts.

Popular on the Opry, and, by 1966, having a string of near-misses at hit songs, Jim and Jesse were under pressure from Epic to move their sound from bluegrass to mainstream country so as to gain a wider audience. At this time they began doing a series of syndicated television shows out of Springfield, Missouri, in which they used lead electric and steel guitars instead of banjo and fiddle. The following year, under the direction of their producer Billy Sherrill, they made their first Nashville-sound recording, a humorous truckers' song, "Diesel on My Tail," which was their first big hit; the album including it also did well. In its wake the trade publication *Record World* voted them the most promising vocal duo for 1967. As with Flatt and Scruggs and the Osborne Brothers, they were subjected to criticism by record and concert reviewers writing for *Bluegrass Unlimited*. But it appeared that the move to a mainstream country sound had been a wise one; during the late sixties and into the early seventies they had several other hits and continued to produce and market syndicated television shows.

Moving from Epic to Capitol in 1971, Jim and Jesse had one album touted as "modern bluegrass" with electric instruments. Following this they returned to their former acoustic sound on record. In actuality they had never completely abandoned the bluegrass sound, picking up musicians to provide the proper banjo and fiddle sound when they played festivals. By 1972, when they began producing their own albums, their appearances on the festival and concert circuit were frequent enough to require a full-time bluegrass band once again; having survived the changes of the sixties, they were now regularly enumerated as one of the pioneer bluegrass bands.

Nashville Skyline

The four Grand Ole Opry bluegrass acts of the sixties—Monroe, Flatt and Scruggs, the Osborne Brothers, and Jim and Jesse—each followed its own pathway through what was a difficult period for bluegrass. But in Nashville bluegrass was slowly gaining acceptance. This happened in several interrelated ways. The earliest was reflected by Flatt and Scruggs's partial and strife-torn move into folk rock.

In 1968 the Byrds, the Los Angeles folk-rock band, came to Nashville to record a country album. *Sweetheart of the Rodeo*, the result, was largely the inspiration of Gram Parsons, a new member of the Byrds; it included some Bob Dylan songs, several new McGuinn and Parsons compositions, and a number of older country songs, among them Woody Guthrie's "Pretty Boy Floyd" done bluegrass style with John Hartford playing banjo. Also participating on the album was former Kentucky Colonels guitarist Clarence White, who would soon join the Byrds as a regular member. While in Nashville, the Byrds made an appearance on the Grand Ole Opry. Said Roger McGuinn, "we were the first rock group ever to do so. Columbia had to pull strings to get us on the bill."[9] During that stay, members of the band also visited the Scruggses and jammed with Earl's sons.

Though there was a certain air of unreality about the Byrds' Opry appearance and Nashville recordings in 1968, other folk-rockers were also recording in Nashville. Dylan had been doing so since 1966, and in 1969 his *Nashville Skyline* with his duet with Johnny Cash underscored the fact that the folk-rock performers were sympathetic to country music. Unlike most in the Nashville music industry, these musicians perceived bluegrass as an important dimension of country music, a viewpoint reflecting their education within the folk revival.

Another indication of the growing interest in bluegrass came in October 1968 when Earl Scruggs's banjo instruction book was published; it went into a second printing within a year. Reviewing it in March 1969 *Billboard's* executive editor Paul Ackerman quoted publisher Peer-Southern's manager Roy Horton, who explained the demand for the book in both national and international markets: "Factors in this . . . have been [Flatt and Scruggs's] success on the college circuit, on the Beverly Hillbillies Show and the film 'Bonnie & Clyde.' Horton added that he envisioned increasing use of bluegrass material by contemporary records acts. 'Up-coming artists and underground groups are interested in this musical category.' "[10]

A few months later Scruggs himself joined the up-coming and underground when he formed a new group with his sons, the Earl Scruggs Revue. A June press release by Louise Scruggs stated that the group would do "contemporary as well as country music."[11] The following year Randy and Gary Scruggs issued their own album on Vanguard, the label Doc Watson and Joan Baez were recording for, and the Revue was booked into a round of colleges, festivals, and other events where their youth-oriented contemporary sound was well received. Scruggs continued on the Opry, appearing with his sons; their folk-rock sound, not so different from that of the Byrds, was now more familiar. In July 1970 Earl's first Columbia solo album appeared; it was titled *Nashville's Rock*. In August 1970 John Hartford, now well-known because of his television appearances with Glen Campbell, returned to Nashville to appear on the Opry for the first time. The new sounds were slowly gaining acceptance.

The following summer the Nitty Gritty Dirt Band came to town to make an album in tribute to the country musicians who had influenced them. The Dirt Band had begun in southern California during the mid-sixties as an acoustic folk revival jug band. By the end of the decade they were in Colorado and had evolved into an electric folk- and country-rock group. In 1971 their version of the Jerry Jeff Walker song "Mr. Bojangles" became a pop hit. John McEuen, their banjo picker, was a bluegrass enthusiast who had studied with Douglas Dillard and was largely responsible for the inclusion of bluegrass segments in Dirt Band shows. The idea for the Nashville album began when, following an Earl Scruggs Revue concert in Denver, McEuen met Scruggs and asked him if he would be interested in doing an album with them. Earl said he would, and from this John McEuen, along with his brother William, the group's manager, developed the concept of the album, which William produced.

The album featured pioneer country performers Mother Maybelle Carter, Roy Acuff, and Merle Travis. Also included were Jimmy Martin, Earl Scruggs, and Doc Watson. Each of the six did four or five numbers associated with them, like Earl's "Flint Hill Special" and Roy's "The Precious Jewel." Participating in the session as sidemen were two members of John Hartford's band, Vassar Clements and Norman Blake; Randy and Gary Scruggs from the Earl Scruggs Revue were also present, as was Roy Acuff's Dobro player and tenor singer Pete "Oswald" Kirby. In addition to their backup work, Clements, Kirby, and Randy Scruggs were each featured doing instrumentals. Veteran bluegrass and Nashville studio musician Roy "Junior" Huskey did most of the bass work. Members of the Nitty Gritty Dirt Band played on most cuts and furnished the lead vocal and instrumental work on several.

McEuen aimed at spontaneity in the recording studio, and everyone involved fell into the spirit of the event, which became a musical "happening." Clements was particularly impressive; his work on this album helped build his reputation as a hot, versatile fiddler. But it was the closing and title song, "Will the Circle Be Unbroken," in which all present (including wives, children, and reporters) sang along, which symbolized the character of this communal event. The album's subtitle, "Music Forms a New Circle," accurately described the concept. At its center, and heard on nearly half of the album's thirty-seven cuts, was Earl Scruggs. He was also largely responsible for gathering together the guest musicians, some of whom (particularly Acuff) were suspicious of the long-haired rock musicians. Some tracks on the resulting three-record set were pure bluegrass; others old-time country. Released at the end of 1972, *Will the Circle Be Unbroken* was a popular and critical success, bringing the sound of these musicians to a large new urban youth audience. In 1973 it climbed the country and pop charts at exactly the same time as did the sound track recording of "Dueling Banjos" from *Deliverance*. These were the crossover hits bluegrass enthusiasts had hoped for, it seemed.

Articles from *Rolling Stone* and the Nashville newspapers describing the recording sessions for the album were reprinted as part of the liner notes for the lavishly packaged Nitty Gritty Dirt Band set. They portrayed the sessions as the site of rapprochement between the young western longhairs and the older conservative Nashville musicians and placed emphasis on the musical respect each had for the other.

In the early seventies the contrast between youth and age was often stated first in terms of their hair length. This contrast suggested others, like those between drug use and drinking, or between dove and hawk positions on Vietnam. That everyone could be separated into two groups was of course unrealistic, and for that reason both sides were often surprised and encouraged by unexpected behavior on the part of representatives from the "other side." The Nitty Gritty Dirt Band, like the Bluegrass Alliance, were longhairs *but* they liked "our" music. Nashville greeted them with open arms, for the most part. However, the rumor circulated that one Nashville pioneer, Bill Monroe, had turned down the Nitty Gritty Dirt Band's invitation to participate in the *Will the Circle Be Unbroken* sessions. In a recent interview Monroe confirmed this, saying he was "stickin' straight to bluegrass" at the time, didn't care for the name of the group (nitty connoted "lice" to him), and felt "they could do better with people like Earl Scruggs."[12] The Dirt Band sessions were made only a few months after Monroe had made his celebrated reconciliation with Flatt. Flatt was still estranged from Scruggs, and Monroe's sense of loyalty to Flatt probably also played a part in his decision not to participate in the project.

Nowhere was the hair-length contrast (and all it symbolized) more striking than between former partners Flatt and Scruggs. Earl championed the long-haired country-rock synthesis in Nashville. His 1970 NET special "Earl Scruggs: His Family and Friends"—later issued as a soundtrack album by Columbia—included Earl with the Byrds, Bob Dylan, a Moog Synthesizer, Joan Baez, Doc Watson, and his sons, as well as footage from their appearance at the 1969 Vietnam Moratorium demonstration in Washington. The title of his third solo album, *I Saw the Light with Some Help from My Friends* (1972), telegraphed the punch with its melding of Hank Williams and Beatles song titles. Included on it were the Nitty Gritty Dirt Band, Linda Ronstadt, Arlo Guthrie, and Tracy Nelson. Produced by Don Law, its liner notes described eclectic jam sessions at the Scruggs home and asserted that "Earl Scruggs is far more than a bluegrass banjo picker."

Flatt moved quickly in very different directions following the breakup; within a few weeks he had hired Vic Jordan (banjo) and Roland White (mandolin) from the Blue Grass Boys. By mutual agreement between the former partners, Lester's band could no longer be called the Foggy Mountain Boys, but they sounded very much like the Flatt and Scruggs bands of the early fifties. Still under the sponsorship of Martha White, Flatt carried on much as before. He continued to record with Columbia, but by June 1970 he had publicly expressed his dissatisfaction with them, leaving them in August and signing with RCA Victor. In a contest sponsored by Martha White, a new name was chosen for his band: The Nashville Grass. Although "Grass" had obvious connotations of hippies and drugs, and Flatt would play on the double entendre in jokes at personal appearances ("Keep on supportin' that grass"), the name was clearly meant to allude to bluegrass. Personally, Flatt was opposed to both long hair and marijuana. He told friends that he was sure Scruggs and his sons were smoking dope, and his feelings about long hair were expressed publicly in his first single for Victor, "I Can't Tell the Boys from the Girls," released in January 1971.

During 1971, while Scruggs developed his Revue and participated in the Nitty Gritty Dirt Band sessions, Flatt's first Victor album publicized his return to the classic sound of their older bands, and he recorded the first of three reunion albums with Mac Wiseman, who was also with Victor at that time. Then in June came the much publicized reunion with Monroe at Bean Blossom, the beginning of an association between the two which included partnerships in festival promotion and, in 1973 and 1974, appearances on each other's live albums.

As Monroe's Bean Blossom Festival continued to grow, he expanded his entrepreneurial activities, starting a booking agency in Nashville and working to promote his son James's band. The decision not to participate in the Nitty Gritty Dirt Band sessions typified Monroe's response to newgrass, country rock, and related forms. Unlike Carlton Haney, with whom he was now competing as a festival promoter, Monroe viewed them as being outside the boundaries of bluegrass. Certain groups were, for various reasons, not acceptable at his festivals. For example, Monroe went on record with the bluegrass community as being opposed to the electric sound of the Osbornes, inviting them to Bean Blossom but refusing to allow them to bring their amps, whereupon they turned down his invitation. In 1972 he also told the New Grass Revival and other long-haired performers that he would not allow them to appear unless they cut their hair, so they too were absent from the festival.

By 1972–73 Monroe was promoting festivals in a number of states, working closely with the groups of his son, Flatt, Jim and Jesse, Don Reno and Bill Harrell, and Ralph Stanley. The latter two bands were carrying on traditions of earlier groups: Reno had paired up with Harrell in 1968 and would remain with him for a decade, working out of the Washington, D.C., area. They maintained much of the sound and repertoire of the old Reno and Smiley band, and Smiley also frequently performed with them during the years between his retirement in 1969 and his death in 1972.

Ralph Stanley had worked in the shadow of his brother Carter throughout their association together. At their shows, Carter did most of the emcee work and the lead singing. Banjoist Ralph only occasionally took vocal solos, usually doing old mountain folksongs like "Pretty Polly," "Little Maggie," or "Man of Constant Sorrow." When Carter died of a liver ailment in 1966 at the age of 41, Ralph was thrust into the position of bandleader. Since the early sixties the "band" consisted mainly of lead guitarist and baritone singer George Shuffler, who had worked with them off and on since the early fifties. Once in a while a fiddler, comedian-bassist, or mandolinist was added. Their repertoire reflected Carter's continuing attempts to find songs which would make successful country hits; both he and Ralph were wary of being labeled "bluegrass."

Within a few months of Carter's death Ralph Stanley had reorganized the band. Gone was Shuffler. In his place was a young man from southern Ohio, Larry Sparks, who had a lead vocal style remarkably similar to Carter's and played both lead and rhythm guitar. Stanley also hired fiddler Curley Ray Cline, brother of long-time Monroe sideman Charlie Cline and a former member of the West Virginia bluegrass band the Lonesome Pine Fiddlers. Another veteran of that band, Melvin Goins, also joined Stanley, moving from his former speciality of lead singer-guitarist to the bass player–comedian role, as "Big Wilbur." Their sound in some ways resembled that of the old Stanley Brothers but was more consciously old-time and down-home in both texture and content. Ralph sang lead much more frequently, did the most-requested Stanley Brothers duets with Sparks, and gave Cline a featured role in the band similar to that of Kenny Baker with Monroe.

By 1971 Sparks had been replaced by east Kentuckian Roy Lee Centers; Jack Cooke, a familiar figure in the Baltimore area bluegrass scene who'd worked with Monroe in the late fifties, was on bass. And also appearing with Stanley were two teenagers, Keith Whitley and Ricky Skaggs, both from eastern Kentucky. Stanley had discovered them substituting for him at a concert he was delayed in reaching. Whitley and Skaggs sang all the old Stanley Brothers duets and almost sounded more like Carter and Ralph than Carter and Ralph themselves. They spent the festival seasons of 1970, 1971, and 1972 with Stanley and made albums with the same companies Stanley was recording for, Jalyn and Rebel. They also appeared on Stanley's albums.

At the same time, Stanley was developing a new dimension in his musical presentations which was to become fashionable in bluegrass during the seventies—the a capella gospel quartet. Like other aspects of Stanley's music, it was an exaggeration of older elements in his musical background—an almost mannerist version of the old-time way. He told interviewers that they did not sing unaccompanied quartets like this in the church where he grew up. The sound might have come from unaccompanied black gospel quartets in the Carolinas, popular on records and radio since the thirties. But more recently in southwestern Virginia, Stanley's home territory, unaccompanied white gospel quartets like the Chestnut Grove Quartet had become local favorites. They sang a cappella because instruments were not allowed in some of the fundamentalist churches at which they performed. By bringing this form into bluegrass, Stanley added to the genre an element which *sounded* traditional, old-time, and authentic, even if it was an innovation. It contrasted strikingly with most bluegrass song performances, in which the instrumental accompaniment attracted as much or more of the listener's attention as did the voices. Some of the hymns which Stanley did in this style were traditional, others newly composed.

In May 1971 Stanley initiated an annual festival on his farm near McClure, Virginia. It quickly acquired a reputation similar to that of his music; hard to find, it was very down-home and guaranteed to be authentic. At it Stanley gave an annual "Carter Stanley Memorial Award," which in 1972 went to the Grand Ole Opry's Bud Wendell in recognition of his support for bluegrass music.

The award to Wendell reflected the extent to which bluegrass, from traditional to newgrass, was being accepted in Nashville. Although there had long been bluegrass bands in town, never before had an infrastructure existed. In 1970 this started to change when GTR, Inc., an instrument sales and repair shop specializing in the old acoustic instruments sought by bluegrass musicians, was opened by dealer George Gruhn, collector-musician Tut Taylor, and repairman Randy Wood. At about the same time nightclubs specializing in bluegrass were opening. The Station Inn and Exit Inn with their full-time bluegrass, were new phenomena in Nashville. They were followed in July 1972 by the Old Time Pickin' Parlor, owned by Randy Wood, who with Tut Taylor had left GTR. Wood ran the Parlor, which combined his instrument shop with a nightclub, in collaboration with Taylor and Grant Boatwright, a member of Red White and Blue (Grass), a newgrass band active in the early seventies. Also involved in the venture was singer, songwriter, and instrumentalist Norman Blake, who had played bluegrass in Chattanooga during the fifties and sixties before coming to Nashville to work as a studio musician.

The ambience of the Old Time Pickin' Parlor resembled that of other new bluegrass clubs opening in the early seventies. Unlike the rough and tumble bars that had been the primary locale for bluegrass bands in earlier times, these places were consciously, even self-consciously, countrified in decor. Like the Storefront Congregation in Louisville and the Picking Parlor Restaurant in New Haven, Connecticut, Nashville's Pickin' Parlor had gingham tablecloths, potbellied stoves, and other folksy fittings in its decor. It became a meeting place for local and visiting bluegrass and old-time musicians, and presented at one time or another on its stage virtually every active bluegrass group.

Another significant change came in 1971 when the Country Music Foundation, a research institution associated with the Country Music Association's Hall of Fame, hired William Ivey as its director. A native of Michigan who had become a folk enthusiast while an undergraduate at the University of Michigan and subsequently did graduate work in folklore at Indiana University, Ivey was knowledgeable about and sympathetic toward bluegrass. Within a short time he had hired a former Michigan classmate, Douglas B. Green, as the foundation's editor and oral historian. Green, who had been in Nashville since 1969 doing graduate work in English at Vanderbilt, had worked in the bands of Bill Monroe and Jimmy Martin before starting his own band in the early seventies. With Ivey and Green at the CMF, bluegrass was more strongly represented within the country music establishment. During the seventies the foundation would expand and grow, overshadowing the JEMF because of its location, access to resources, and funding.

Other signs of the growing awareness of bluegrass within the establishment came in 1972 when the Don Light Agency, one of the leading gospel music booking agencies, began booking bluegrass acts like Mac Wiseman and Lester Flatt. Light promoted a "festival" at Vanderbilt that year. Also in October 1972 Starday Records, which had gone bankrupt the previous year and changed hands, became active in bluegrass for the first time since the mid-sixties. Don Pierce had left the company in 1970, following a series of moves which had begun in 1967 with its acquisition of King Records of Cincinnati. By the beginning of 1973 they were recording a group of performers representative of the range of styles and repertoire active at bluegrass festivals. In the works was an album by Charlie Monroe, whom Carlton Haney had lured out of retirement to work at his 1972 festivals in a move calculated to counter Bill Monroe's absence. Also being recorded was Larry Sparks, who maintained much of the soulful Stanley sound in a band described as hard driving and traditional, and the band of Don Reno and Bill Harrell, who were carrying on the old Reno and Smiley sound.

Early in 1973 Starday signed the band of J. D. Crowe and the New South. Banjoist Crowe, who had worked with Jimmy Martin during the late fifties and early sixties, had been playing and recording out of his home town of Lexington, Kentucky, since leaving Martin. Three records on the Lemco label, under the name of J. D. Crowe and the Kentucky Mountain Boys, had featured a traditional sound and a repertoire similar to that of the Country Gentlemen in its mixing of old bluegrass songs with modern country and rock. In 1971 his mandolinist (sometimes guitarist) Doyle Lawson moved to the Country Gentlemen and was replaced by Tony Rice of the Bluegrass Alliance. Rice, whose brother Larry had been playing mandolin with Crowe for some time, was a Californian of Appalachian background who patterned his guitar work after that of Clarence White. By the time Rice joined the band, Crowe had decided to follow the Osborne Brothers' example, going electric. His 1973 Starday recordings were his first with electric backup but they were not released until 1977.

On the other hand, Rice's former partners, who'd left the Bluegrass Alliance to form the New Grass Revival, did have their Starday album issued in 1973. It featured their versions of Leon Russell's "Prince of Peace" and Jerry Lee Lewis's "Great Balls of Fire" and a seven-minute rock-style jam of Vassar

Clements's "Lonesome Fiddle Blues." Unlike Crowe's group, they did it with acoustic instruments (except for the bass) but the liner notes of the album established a no less radical stance, in a poem by Radio John of Topanga Canyon:

> . . . more traditional folks have ask for removal
> Of excess locks of hair
> But the New Grass Revival they don't care, cause their heads and
>   hands are not there
> They are off somewhere all pickin' fast
> And you bet your ass
> They play that grass
> And do alot of things to it also not recommended by the chief.[13]

Also released by Starday at this time was a retrospective album of Reno and Smiley King recordings as a tribute to Red Smiley, dead the previous year.

By the beginning of 1973 bluegrass seemed to be really taking off commercially: "Dueling Banjos" and the Nitty Gritty Dirt Band record set were climbing the charts. Decca (soon to be MCA) sent a mobile crew to Bean Blossom that June to record a two-record album of Monroe's festival which featured Monroe but also included Jimmy Martin, James Monroe, Jim and Jesse, Lester Flatt, and twelve fiddlers who gathered on stage the final day to play "Down Yonder," "Soldier's Joy," and "Grey Eagle" and to back Monroe as he led an audience singalong of "Swing Low Sweet Chariot." At about the same time, Bill and James Monroe set up their own talent agency. College bookings had grown for most of the groups, particularly Flatt's, and Don Light even promoted a "festival" at the University of Illinois. National recognition seemed assured when the Osborne Brothers along with Merle Haggard, performed for President Nixon, at the White House. In the works was a series of new RCA *Bluegrass Celebration* albums which would be issued in 1974, promoted with ads urging consumers to "have a bluegrass festival in your home this summer."[14]

Nashville's response to the growth of bluegrass during the early seventies was typical of the way the country music industry moved to exploit new trends. Emphasis was on image as much as substance, with efforts made to exploit the phenomenon as quickly as possible. During these years the bluegrass publications spoke positively of the recognition the music was getting in Nashville; in their opinion it was belated. Yet while there was much bluegrass activity in Nashville, it did not become the center of the music at this time.

Capitol Bluegrass

In March 1974 a lengthy *Washington Post* article was headlined "D.C. Is Also Nation's Bluegrass Capitol." Author Barbara Bright-Sagnier described the capitol as "the nation's bluegrass mecca," site of a "$1.5 to $2 million indus-try."[15] The capitol and its hinterlands—northern Virginia, southern Mary-land—along with nearby Baltimore and its hinterlands—northern Maryland, Delaware, and southeastern Pennsylvania—had for several decades seen much bluegrass activity. The entire region had long been a center for mi-grants from the eastern side of the southern Appalachians. By the 1950s the children of Appalachian migrants were joining their parents in playing music once called old-time or hillbilly and now labeled by some as bluegrass.

The Stonemans, described earlier, were one such family. During the sixties their career took them outside of the region. Their rise to national promi-nence began when they signed with Starday in 1962. By 1966 they were doing their own syndicated television show, produced in Nashville. In the early seventies they were in California, playing at hippie ballrooms and col-leges with a repertoire which mixed contemporary songs of love, peace, and freedom with their parents' old-time sentimental songs. Their recordings of the late sixties and early seventies for MGM and RCA used a mixture of bluegrass and Nashville sounds. Also from the Washington scene was Roy Clark. He'd won local banjo contests in the early fifties, before becoming a country vocalist, instrumentalist, and humorist on Washington radio and TV. Moving to Las Vegas in 1960, he'd become a familiar figure in television when, in 1969, he began co-hosting the CBS show "Hee Haw." After moving from the network to syndication in 1971, "Hee Haw" went on to become one of the most widely seen country music shows of all time. Clark still includes some bluegrass banjo in his performances. But like the Stoneman Family, he was not typical of the Washington scene from which he'd emerged. Both had built their careers outside the region, and both had moved away from the pure bluegrass sound that remained popular there.

During the fifties and sixties bluegrass was popular in the region with working-class people, many of them first or second generation southern mi-grants. It also became popular with young middle-class people, exposed to it in a variety of ways. For example, important personal contacts occurred at high schools in suburbs like Arlington and Bethesda where youths from a variety of classes and regions mingled. Among them, during the fifties, blue-grass was a sort of underground favorite along with rhythm and blues, a form similarly popular in other suburban areas. However it might be acquired, an interest in bluegrass was soon reinforced by local and regional institutions. In small bars at urban and suburban locations there were always several local bluegrass bands. One of the first was that of Louisiana mandolinist Buzz Busby, with whom many of the bluegrass musicians who later became well-known in the region got their start. On weekends, big-name bluegrass bands like Monroe, the Stanleys, Flatt and Scruggs, and Reno and Smiley were often featured at the country music parks that were located out in the country to the south and north of the towns. Radio too carried bluegrass, sometimes in live shows but most often on record. Country deejays like Ray Davis in

Baltimore and Don Owens in Washington promoted bluegrass over the air. Owens, who died in an auto accident in 1963, was particularly knowledgeable about bluegrass. At a time when the music was getting less and less air time he consistently played both old and new recordings and spoke in a charismatic way about the music and the musicians.

Country music in general was a profitable business in Washington and environs because since the late forties it had been vigorously promoted by Connie B. Gay. Gay, who owned radio and television stations, promoted shows, and put together various kinds of country music tours, was a pioneer in developing urban country music markets. He had coined the term *Town and Country* to describe his activities in this domain. A founding father of the Country Music Association, he was strongly committed to promoting the Nashville sound as a means of expanding country music's urban appeal. Nevertheless Gay occasionally included some bluegrass acts on his television and radio stations, and at some of his package shows.

Though bluegrass flourished more on the grassroots level than in Gay's big-time productions, his presence, like those of the other institutions—bars, parks, radio stations—provided a broad base of support in the region for bluegrass. But what really made Washington the bluegrass capitol was the way in which the music developed its own character and quality. Here to a greater degree than elsewhere were musicians and followers committed to bluegrass in particular rather than to country music as a whole. Here developed early on a sense of tradition within bluegrass. Most influential in this process were the Country Gentlemen. While they frequently appeared at colleges and coffeehouses during the sixties when they were on the road, they were also working regularly at a Washington bar, the Shamrock. Between 1962 and 1969 they were there almost every Thursday night. Though it was not a fancy nightclub—Mitch Jayne of the Dillards called it "a dump" and said its lack of class was epitomized by a sign over the stage reading "Yes, we have Cold Duck!"[16]—the Shamrock became known as a bluegrass showplace, an underground success; it was a working-class establishment that began attracting young middle-class listeners. During the mid-sixties the Gentlemen built a strong local following here.

At the same time, they continued to make records. In December 1962 they did a Christmas song 45 for Rebel, a small local label. In 1963, at the crest of the folk boom, they appeared on albums for three different labels. First came *Hootenanny: A Blue Grass Special*, recorded for Design, a dime-store label. Widely distributed, it sold for ninety-nine cents, giving them exposure if not income. In September Folkways released *The Country Gentlemen on the Road*, their third album on that label. It consisted of live performances from concerts at Antioch College and the Sacred Mushroom coffeehouse in Columbus, Ohio. This was followed in November by their first major-label album, *Folk Scene Inside*, on Mercury. Also released in 1963 was their final Starday record, a single featuring "Copper Kettle," a folk revival song done in an arrangement which mixed bluegrass with Kingston Trio. As the folk boom began to subside, the Gentlemen's Mercury ties were severed; a second album was recorded in 1964 but never released. By 1965 they were recording exclusively with Rebel.

Started in the early sixties in suburban Maryland by Charles R. ("Dick") Freeland, Rebel began with singles by various local groups. In 1965 Freeland put these together with other, unissued, recordings in his vaults for a series of four anthologies which were sold on a mail-order basis. The same year Rebel's first hit record, the Gentlemen's "Bringing Mary Home," made the *Billboard* charts for a few weeks. This was followed in early 1966 by the Gentlemen's first Rebel album, which included that hit as well as a Bob Dylan song, "Girl of the North Country," and several other songs aimed at the emerging audience for contemporary singer-songwriter lyrics of the kind pioneered by Dylan. Their blend of bluegrass and contemporary songs performed in tight vocal and instrumental arrangements featuring innovative trio harmonies were, at this time, labeled "progressive" bluegrass; in the early seventies the younger newgrass musicians would acknowledge them as an influence.

In spite of their popularity with folk revival audiences, the Country Gentlemen never appeared at the Newport Folk Festival. For the tastemakers who controlled the choices of talent at that event, they were too "folkie"— that is, clearly betraying their debt to slick commercial revival groups like the Kingston Trio—and also too "uptown"—brash, jazzy, sophisticated. Even though their first Folkways album had been produced by Mike Seeger, the Gentlemen blamed him, along with Ralph Rinzler, for not allowing them the exposure at Newport they felt they deserved. Dick Freeland alluded to this feeling in his notes to their first Rebel album: "Although basically they are considered a bluegrass band 'THE COUNTRY GENTLEMEN' have a distinctive progressive style that can be classified only as their own! This particular style of playing is condemned by certain influential people and thus explains their absence at such places as the Newport Folk Festival and lack of their mention in articles pertaining to this type of music."[17]

If they had been slighted by Newport, they could not be overlooked at bluegrass festivals, and when they appeared at their first one, Haney's second Roanoke Festival in September 1966, they were enthusiastically received. During the next three years they were favorites on the festival circuit, and Rebel continued to release new albums by them each year.

Early in 1969, at about the same time that Flatt and Scruggs split, John Duffey left the Gentlemen. Factors contributing to this were his dislike of work on the road and a feeling of disillusionment with the music business, reflecting the many struggles that the band had had—not only their rejection at Newport but the inability to place what they considered to be their most commercial singles (like the 1963 "Copper Kettle") on a major label. Duffey retired from music to concentrate on instrument building and repair, playing only informally and participating in a few recording sessions for Rebel. He joined a considerable body of semi-professional musicians, maintaining "day jobs" and keeping music as an avocation, generally playing in bars. Many bluegrass groups everywhere operated in this manner, but nowhere were there so many part-time performers of high caliber as in Washington. Unlike Nashville, which was filled with musicians who had gambled everything on professional success and were willing to compromise in order to gain a foothold in the business, the Washington musicians had lower professional expectations and felt more secure in sticking to their esthetic values.

One band Duffey recorded with at this time was the newly formed outfit of Bill Emerson, Cliff Waldron, and the New Shades of Grass. This group, which made three albums for Rebel between 1969 and 1970, had much of the flavor of the Country Gentlemen in both their musical sound and, more importantly, their approach to repertoire, drawing heavily from contemporary rock (Creedence Clearwater Revival), soul (Al Wilson), and country (Merle Haggard). Their most successful song was a version of British rocker Manfred Mann's single "Fox on the Run." Today this song is performed and recorded so frequently that it has lost the impact it and similar songs had in 1969 when one festival reviewer praised Emerson and Waldron for choosing "songs whose emotional dimensions are somewhat wider than those which explain that it's sad to have no mother or dad."[18] Instrumentally the band was characterized by Bill Emerson's precise, driving banjo work and by the spare and lilting Dobro of Mike Auldridge. Emerson, from middle-class Bethesda, had been one of the original Country Gentlemen in 1957. During the sixties he took J. D. Crowe's place with Jimmy Martin, who, as Martin was wont to do with banjo players, straightened out and cleaned up his picking. Commercial artist Auldridge was representative of a large number of Washington area musicians who played only at parties and jam sessions. Before working with Emerson and Waldron he had performed only informally. Yet within a year of joining them he was on his way to becoming the most influential Dobroist in bluegrass since Buck Graves introduced that instrument to the music with Flatt and Scruggs's band in 1955.

While the Washington scene's musical development came about in bands that worked mainly in bars, often on a semiprofessional basis, the proliferation of festivals brought these bands to wider audiences than before. Emerson and Waldron's was one of the first new bands to benefit from festival exposure. Another factor in their success was the availability of their music on the Rebel label which was getting increasingly wider distribution because of the Gentlemen's popularity.

The Country Gentlemen carried on under the leadership of Duffey's former partner Charlie Waller. Duffey was replaced by Jimmy Gaudreau, a Rhode Island Yankee whose earliest musical experience had been in rock and folk music. His mandolin and vocal styles demonstrated the extent to which Duffey had influenced younger musicians. In 1970 the Gentlemen changed again when banjoist Eddie Adcock left; his place was taken by Bill Emerson. Waldron soon reformed his group with banjoist Ben Eldridge, another informal picker, taking Emerson's place. Later in 1971 Gaudreau left the Gentlemen to form a band with Adcock, the II Generation, and he was replaced by Doyle Lawson from J. D. Crowe's band. This aggregation of Country Gentlemen—Waller, Emerson, Lawson, and bass player Bill Yates—brought the Gentlemen the acclaim they had sought in the sixties. In 1972 and 1973 they swept Carlton Haney's *Muleskinner News* polls, winning the "Best Band" along with various individual awards. And they were once again signed to a major label, Vanguard. In 1972 they toured Japan, the first bluegrass band from the Washington area to do so.

During the late sixties another influential group working in the Washington-Baltimore area was Don Reno and Bill Harrell. Reno, who'd left Red Smiley in 1964, had led a series of short-lived bands in the next two years. At the end of 1966 he went into partnership with Harrell, a thirty-two-year-old southwest Virginia native who had discovered bluegrass while a student at the University of Maryland. Harrell played in a series of Washington area bands in 1955-57, recording for a number of small labels. Following Army service and a long convalescence after an auto accident, he emerged in the early sixties as leader of the Virginians, a Washington band that recorded for Starday and United Artists.

At first Reno and Harrell had in their band George Shuffler, who'd come from the Stanley Brothers following Carter's death, and Don's son Ronnie on mandolin. When Ronnie left in 1968 to join the Osborne Brothers (he later went with Merle Haggard), fiddler Buck Ryan joined the group.

They first recorded a spate of minor-label albums in which they did remakes of other groups' best-known songs. In 1968 they released the first of three King albums which featured newly composed songs, most of which were in the mold of the old Reno and Smiley repertoire. In 1969-70 they had a popular weekly television show on a local channel. When Red Smiley retired in 1969 (his band continued on as the Shenandoah Cutups), he subsequently joined Reno and Harrell, touring and recording with them until his death in January 1972.

During this period particularly, but in a general way throughout their history (1966–1978), Reno and Harrell did not break new ground so much as carry on the repertoire and sound of the old Reno and Smiley outfit. Reno, secure in his status as a bluegrass banjo pioneer, remained the major attraction in this group, despite Harrell's considerable talent as a lead singer. They toured more extensively than any other group in the Washington area with the possible exception of the Country Gentlemen, but they were really not a part of the region's "progressive" band scene.

In 1971 further changes in the Washington bar scene were bringing a new progressive band into existence. As the popularity of Cliff Waldron's Rebel recordings, festival dates, and Washington area appearances led to an increase in his bookings, Dobroist Auldridge and banjoist Eldridge were forced to quit in order to keep their day jobs. Still interested in playing semiprofessionally, they joined forces with John Duffey, bassist Tom Gray (another former Country Gentleman), and John Starling, a U. S. Army surgeon at a local hospital. All had day jobs. Unlike most such groups, this one did not hide its semi-professional approach but incorporated it into their name, the Seldom Scene, given in jest by a friend who averred that if those musicians were working together, they would certainly be seldom seen. In January 1972 they began appearing at the Red Fox Inn in Bethesda, where Waldron had been playing. Owner Walter Broderick told *Post* reporter Bright-Sagnier that Waldron " 'brought in a nice crowd' " that "had more money, behaved more seriously, and covered a broader age range" than his previous rock audiences. After a month of the Seldom Scene at the Red Fox, said Broderick, "the popularity spread and we were in the business full time."[19] The Seldom Scene quickly became favorites in the Washington area. Appearances at festivals during the summer months brought them to bluegrass fans in the southern and eastern states, and by 1974 they had crowded the Country Gentlemen out of first place in the *Muleskinner News* awards.

Waldron, still recording for Rebel, maintained the sound his band had developed with Emerson and Auldridge, drawing on a pool of younger musicians who played in the styles established by men like Duffey, Auldridge, and Emerson. By 1974 the "progressive" Washington sound as established by the Gentlemen, the Seldom Scene, and Waldron was one of the most popular in bluegrass. These bands treated bluegrass instrumentation and performance style as a kind of methodology. Unlike their Nashville counterparts they rarely used non-bluegrass instruments, and they did not follow the electrification trend. Instead, they applied bluegrass methodology to a repertoire which drew heavily from contemporary (often rock) sources, mixing these with older standard bluegrass repertoire. Hence the music sounded youth-oriented as well as traditional. By the early seventies it was being followed in the Washington region by both working-class and middle-class listeners.

In addition to these bands and the other lesser-known local groups following their example, institutions within the Washington area helped to support the music. One was *Bluegrass Unlimited* which, though national and international in its coverage, was edited in the Washington region and often reflected local tastes and preferences in its contents. Another was Rebel Records, which by the early seventies was, with the Country Gentlemen, the Seldom Scene, Ralph Stanley, Cliff Waldron, and many lesser known groups, one of the strongest of the handful of independent companies specializing in bluegrass. Perhaps most important was the amount of bluegrass that could be found in the area on a regular basis at bars and nearby show parks.

In the early seventies the number of concerts increased. Some were sponsored by cultural institutions like the Smithsonian, which supported local interest in bluegrass as part of a campaign to bring recognition to the folk arts through the establishment of a national Folklife Center. By 1974 there was an extensive youth audience in Washington for progressive bluegrass, newgrass, and related music. One theater assembled a concert schedule aimed at this audience; it was reported by *Muleskinner News* in June 1974: "The American Theater in Washington, D.C. is sponsoring a 6-week Kaleidoscope of Music at the L'Enfant Plaza. Featured in the first week, May 21 to 26, were Country Gazette, Emmylou Harris & the Angel Band, John Hartford, Grass Menagerie, Osborne Bros., Cliff Waldron, Vassar Clements, Seldom Scene, Red White & Blue (Grass), Norman Blake, New Grass Revival and the Star Spangled Washboard Band. Tickets ranged from $3 to $6. At press time we have no word on attendance, but this may be the most ambitious indoor promotion ever! A good audience response may open the door for other concert bookings."[20] This lineup represented a large proportion of the best-known modern, progressive, newgrass, and similar groups active at the time. Most were from Washington, Nashville, or elsewhere in the South, with two important exceptions. Both had connections to the Los Angeles country-rock group The Flying Burrito Brothers. The Country Gazette was a spinoff of a bluegrass segment in the Burrito Brothers' tour shows, and Emmylou Harris had been the singing partner of Burrito founding member Gram Parsons during the period between his leaving that group and his death in 1973. The bluegrass connections with country rock were extensive in Los Angeles and followed patterns unique to the area.

Sin City

In contrast to Washington, where a raft of institutions provided intellectual focus and entertainment forums for bluegrass, Los Angeles presented a picture as diffuse and decentralized as its own geography and demography might suggest. While there was no single strong focus for bluegrass there, the music did play a role in many activities. Because Los Angeles was a production center for television and films, studio work was available for a few talented musicians like Byron Berline, the championship fiddler who'd recorded with the Dillards, appeared at Newport, and worked with Bill Monroe; and Alan Munde, his banjo-picking protegé from Oklahoma who had worked for several years with Jimmy Martin in the late sixties and recorded an influential instrumental album, *Poor Richard's Almanac*, with mandolinist Sam Bush. They rubbed elbows with a host of other talented musicians who played some bluegrass in the LA area.

Another factor was the thriving club scene in the region. Establishments like the Ash Grove, the Troubadour, and the Ice Houses (in Pasadena and Burbank) presented a range of musics which sometimes included bluegrass or bluegrass-influenced acts. Many aspiring musical performers (as well as established acts) worked in the area, and a considerable musical industry—recording studios, booking agencies, record companies—reflected the fact that by the end of the sixties Los Angeles was one of the international pop music industry's centers.

Because the music industry was so well developed there, almost any local trend immediately took on a national dimension as promising new acts were snapped up by major record companies, talent agencies, and the media. One example of this was the process whereby folk-rock metamorphosed, with considerable record company hype, into country-rock. From the start some bluegrass musicians were involved, and ultimately the bluegrass sound of the area was affected by it.

We have already touched on the role of the Byrds, with their epochal *Sweetheart of the Rodeo* album. At about the time this was being recorded in Nashville in 1968, the Dillards returned to the studio in Los Angeles to make their first album since 1965. For the first time they included a pedal steel, electric bass, and drums. And banjoist Doug Dillard had been replaced by Herb Pedersen, a young Berkeley, California, native who had been working with Vern and Ray. While in Nashville with them in 1967 he substituted for Earl Scruggs in the Foggy Mountain Boys while Earl was in the hospital. Pedersen brought new dimensions to the Dillards—ability as a songwriter, a clear high tenor voice, and a knack for harmony work. The new Dillards sound was much closer to that of the Byrds—particularly in vocals—than to contemporary bluegrass bands. Pedersen recalls, "We were one of the first groups to ever double vocals . . . which was different and gave a more celestial sound. . . . "[21] Former Dillards producer Jim Dickson recalls: "I'd gone in with the Dillards . . . after we'd done the Byrds and I cut three sides before, while Douglas was still in the group, before Herb, with doubling of voices, right? That stuff didn't get released but Rodney and Herb were able to hear that and then Herb went in and polished the idea of doubling the voices in bluegrass and did the *Wheatstraw Suite* which I think is . . . a magnificent piece of work . . . it was evolutionary in the music process, . . . it precedes . . . Crosby Stills and Nash and other things that we all did later."[22]

The process involves the use of multiple track recording technology to add duplicate versions of the harmony parts two or three times so that vocal sound is smoother sounding and, as Pedersen called it, "more celestial." It also allows the level of the instruments to be higher on the recording, giving a fuller sound. Although the technique was used by many groups, including the Beatles and, on several recordings in the late sixties, the Osborne Brothers, it was used most extensively by the Los Angeles-based groups and became known during the seventies as the "West Coast Sound." Some aspects of *Wheatstraw Suite* kept it from gaining much acceptance from bluegrass listeners at this time; the added orchestral arrangements—"sweetening"—made it seem too pop, and the use of pedal steel, Nashville-style high-string rhythm guitar,[23] and drums made it seem too much like mainstream country. The suite concept also put off bluegrass fans. Like many albums made at this time, it reflected the influence of the Beatles' *Sgt. Pepper*. Instead of being a collection of separate tracks, one for each song, it included several in which stereo collage effects were used and others which overlapped the end of one song with the beginning of another. This was too avant-garde for those who expected something like the Dillards' previous album, *Pickin' and Fiddlin'*.

At the same time *Wheatstraw Suite* was being recorded, Doug Dillard, who had been playing occasionally with the Byrds, was forming a new band with Gene Clark and Bernie Leadon. Leadon, a Minneapolis native who moved to San Diego in 1957, had been the banjo picker with the Scottsville Squirrel Barkers. Following the demise of that group in 1962 he spent several years in Florida and then became a member of a group called Hearts and Flowers. This folk-rock group played only in California but, because of their proximity to the pop industry, had two albums on Capitol. After Hearts and Flowers broke up, Leadon and Dillard began picking together and were heard by ex-Byrd Gene Clark. The result was the Dillard and Clark Expedition, which, like Hearts and Flowers, played mainly in California and had two albums on a major label, A&M, in 1968 and 1969. Resembling the Byrds and the Dillards in sound, the band carried on in various forms through the end of 1970; by this time, however, both Leadon and Clark had left, replaced by Byron Berline, Roger Bush, and Billy Ray Latham. Bush and Latham were former Kentucky Colonels (the other Colonels, Roland and Clarence White, were playing with Lester Flatt and the Byrds, respectively). This lineup, which performed as Doug Dillard and the Expedition, played much more bluegrass than the earlier version of the Expedition but, like the other LA groups mentioned, melded rock, country, folk, and bluegrass elements in various ways which foreshadowed the synthesis that emerged in the first album of the Flying Burrito Brothers in March 1969.

At the outset members of the Flying Burrito Brothers included former Byrds Gram Parsons and Chris Hillman. Their first album, *The Gilded Palace of Sin*, received critical acclaim and is now regarded as a classic, but the group achieved only limited commercial success in the high-powered world of rock music. Later in 1969 Bernie Leadon joined that group and remained with them into the middle of 1971. Unlike most of the others mentioned here, the Burritos toured extensively, bringing the sound of country rock to places like the Armadillo World Headquarters in Austin, Texas, and the Philadelphia Folk Festival. They were particularly popular in England and Holland.

Following the departure of Gram Parsons from the Burritos, they began incorporating a bluegrass segment in their shows. During the early months of 1971 they toured in this manner using three members of Doug Dillard's Expedition—Byron Berline, Roger Bush, and Kenny Wertz (another former

Scottsville Squirrel Barker) as a bluegrass band that played the separate segment in the middle. Jim Dickson, who had become their producer, recalls:

> The bluegrass would always get 'em on their feet. You couldn't have gone there and played it to thousands of people with a bluegrass show, they wouldn't even have come. But once you got 'em there with the name rock and roll group and then you put 'em on, it's like putting a dixieland band in the middle of something for three . . . or five songs; . . . somehow the change just turns people on. And we could put Byron Berline on there and have him play "Orange Blossom Special," it'll sound like they made the touchdown in the last three seconds. So we were exposing them, exposing bluegrass through the vehicle of the Burrito Brothers.[24]

Dickson produced a live recording album in the fall of 1971, *Last of the Red Hot Burritos,* which included examples from the bluegrass segment of a Burritos concert. Following this the group embarked upon a European tour, for which banjoist Alan Munde was added. By this time Chris Hillman had left for Steven Stills' band Manassas. At the end of the tour, early in 1972, the Burritos broke up.

Bernie Leadon had moved on to playing occasionally with a band formed to back a newly popular singer, Linda Ronstadt. An Arizonan, she had first recorded with a folk-rock outfit called the Stone Poneys and had then branched out on her own in 1969. By 1971 she was touring nationally. Following her 1971 tour the backup unit stayed together, and with several changes in personnel—Leadon became a regular member—it emerged in 1972 as the Eagles, the most successful of the LA country-rock bands.

In 1972 the bluegrass segment from the Burritos show made a similar decision to stay together and, as the Country Gazette, obtained a contract with United Artists. Their first album, produced by Jim Dickson, appeared in October 1972. Berline, Wertz, Bush, and Munde were joined on various tracks by Herb Pedersen. Their repertoire combined older country and bluegrass with new country-rock compositions, a combination characteristic of LA country rock, as was the vocal texture, with its double-tracked harmonies. Following a summer of playing at Disneyland, contacts through friends in the LA country-rock world led to bookings with Crosby and Nash, Don McLean, Steve Miller, and other popular rock acts. The goal, says Dickson, was to "try and sell 'em to the urban audience and make records that were not so obscure, use songs that would have more appeal to the general audience, you know, we, everybody has that dream of breaking bluegrass out some way or another. I know we had it for years, all of us."[25]

In 1973 Dickson did another United Artists album for the Gazette, and a second LA bluegrass band appeared when Roland and Clarence White reunited for an East Coast and European tour. But that effort was cut short when

Clarence White was killed by a drunken driver in a nightclub parking lot in July 1973. Roland White subsequently carried on within the Gazette. He and Munde became the supporting members of the group following Berline's departure in 1974.

Until the appearance of the Country Gazette, most of the bluegrass-related changes in the LA rock scene (and I have touched only on the most important) went unnoticed by the bluegrass "establishment." The Dillards and Dillard and Clark Expedition albums were not reviewed by *Bluegrass Unlimited* or *Muleskinner News*, and the County Sales *Newsletter* did not list them. The Burritos, Gram Parsons, and Linda Ronstadt were "pop"—not of interest to bluegrass fans.

Only when this music touched directly on established figures did it receive much notice, as when in 1973 Gene Parsons, former Byrds drummer, flew Ralph Stanley in to sing on one cut of his solo album for Warner Brothers. Parsons's album, like most of those done by country-rock groups in these years, probably sold three or four times as many copies as any of Ralph Stanley's albums. But it was in print and available only a short time, for unlike Stanley's it had been very costly to produce and market and therefore had to sell a lot of records just to break even.

Such factors required that rock records be produced with an eye to quick impact for high sales. If the record caught on, the band or artist got together the resources for a tour to exploit it. This was just the opposite of the procedure followed by most bluegrass groups, which followed the older practice of using records to publicize and exploit the group's popularity which had been developed through personal appearances. Developments in the LA scene foreshadowed what was beginning to happen with bluegrass during the early seventies. Gradually elements of this rock approach to recording and exploitation of artists were being incorporated. This change came about because those who produced bluegrass were becoming more adept at defining and developing their markets, and because in these markets, which had been in flux during the late sixties and early seventies, there were now discernible patterns.

Notes

1. Jim Rooney, *Bossmen*, p. 69.
2. Doug Green, liner notes to *Kenny Baker Plays Bill Monroe*.
3. [Louise Scruggs], unsigned liner notes to *Changin' Times*.
4. Louise Scruggs, liner notes to *Nashville Airplane*.
5. Clarence H. Green, "Third Annual Tennessee State—ETSU Folk Festival," p. 12.
6. Pete Kuykendall, "Lester Flatt and the Nashville Grass," p. 3.
7. [Sonny Osborne], "Sonny Tells It Like It Is," p. 8.

8. Bob Krueger, "Josh Graves: Thirty-Five Years of Dobro," p. 29.
9. Bud Scoppa, *The Byrds*, p. 80.
10. Paul Ackerman, " 'Scruggs and Five-String Banjo.' "
11. "Nashville Scene," *Billboard*, June 28, 1969, p. 48.
12. Pat Chappelle, "Gunning for Bluegrass," p. 28.
13. Radio John, liner notes to *New Grass Revival*.
14. [RCA Victor ad], *BU* 8, (June 1974): 8.
15. Barbara Bright-Sagnier, "D.C. Is Also Nation's Bluegrass Capitol."
16. Mitch Jayne, "Observations: The Dillards, Music and Blue Grass," p. 13.
17. Charles R. Freeland, liner notes to *The Country Gentlemen*.
18. Fred Geiger, "Bluegrass Day at Culpeper," p. 2.
19. Bright-Sagnier, "D. C. Bluegrass Capitol."
20. Maria Gajda, "Muleskinner Newsletter," *MN* 5, (June 1974): 4.
21. Mark Humphrey, "Herb Pedersen," p. 25.
22. Jim Dickson interview, Jan. 18, 1983.
23. High-string guitars, developed for use in Nashville recording sessions, are regular steel-string guitars on which the bottom three strings have been replaced with strings tuned an octave higher than standard.
24. Dickson interview.
25. Ibid.

Bibliographical Notes

For further information on Kenny Baker, see Alice [Gerrard] Foster, "Kenny Baker"; Maria Gajda, "Kenny Baker: Jazz Fiddler"; Kathleen Stanton, "The Bluegrass Fiddlers: Kenny Baker"; and Roger H. Siminoff, "Kenny Baker." For James Monroe see Pete Kuykendall, "James Monroe," and Bill Vernon, "James Monroe: The Sun Also Rises." The appearances of Monroe and the Burrito Brothers at World Armadillo Headquarters were reported in Frye Gaillard, *Watermelon Wine*, p. 137.

Flatt and Scruggs's visit to Japan was reported in *Newsweek* ("Bluegrass in Nippon") and *Bluegrass Unlimited* (Naoki Hirose, "F&S in Japan" [letter]). Much of the information upon which this chapter's account of Flatt and Scruggs is based comes from Jake Lambert's *Biography of Lester Flatt*.

Contemporary works about the youth culture of the late sixties and early seventies convey the feeling of the times, particularly the optimistic Charles Reich, *The Greening of America*; see also Theodore Rozak, *The Making of a Counter Culture*. For a historical perspective, consult Godfrey Hodgson's *America in Our Time*.

Aspects of the Osborne Brothers' career during the sixties and seventies are detailed in Bill Emerson, "Electric Bluegrass"; Pete Kuykendall, "The

Osborne Brothers"; and Neil V. Rosenberg's liner notes to *The Osborne
Brothers* and "The Osborne Brothers, Part Two." Wayne W. Daniel has writ-
ten about the Bryants in " 'Rocky Top'—The Song and the Man and
Woman Who Wrote It."

A detailed and accurate biographical sketch of Jim and Jesse is provided
by Scott Hambly in his liner notes to *The Jim and Jesse Story.*

The Nitty Gritty Dirt Band–Earl Scruggs liaison is described in Gaillard,
pp. 163–70, and in Jim Hatlo, "John McEuen."

Flatt's dissatisfaction with Columbia was reported in *Billboard*'s "Nashville
Scene" for June 20, 1970, p. 38; his leaving that company in "Flatt Leaves
Col; Starts Negotiations for New Deal."

Monroe's 1972 stand against long hair was documented in "Bluegrass
Summer '72," p. 3.

Of the many articles about Ralph Stanley I have found the following
most substantial: Fred Bartenstein, "The Ralph Stanley Story"; John
Cohen, "Ralph Stanley's Old Time Mountain Bluegrass"; Tom Henderson,
"Ralph Stanley Interview"; Nobuharu Komoriya, "Ralph Stanley Goes to
Japan"; Douglas Gordon, "Ralph Stanley: Traditional Banjo Stylist"; Ralph
Rinzler, "Ralph Stanley"; and Jack Tottle, "Ralph Stanley."

The first ad for GTR appeared in *Bluegrass Unlimited* 5 (Oct. 1970): 6.
See also Maria Gajda, "The Old Time Picking Parlor"; and Douglas B.
Green, "Randy Wood's Old Time Pickin' Parlor." In 1976 Steve Buckingham
wrote about "Randy Wood: The Nashville Craftsman," but by the end of
1978 Wood had decided not enough support for bluegrass existed in that
city and had moved: Don Rhodes, "*Frets* Visits . . . Savannah, Georgia—
Randy Wood."

The Country Music Foundation is the research arm of the Country Music
Association's Country Music Hall of Fame. Foundation historian Douglas B.
Green wrote a number of articles about the Hall of Fame and the founda-
tion in the mid-seventies, as well as a popular book on country music,
Country Roots. He is now the lead singer for Riders in the Sky, a Grand Ole
Opry band which has revived the sound of cowboy groups like the Sons of
the Pioneers.

A brief untitled piece on Don Light Talent's move into bluegrass booking
appeared in *Bluegrass Unlimited* 8 (Sept. 1973): 29.

Charlie Monroe's emergence from retirement in the early seventies is cov-
ered in two articles published shortly after his death in September 1975:
Ivan Tribe, "Charlie Monroe," and Bill Vernon, "Last Respects to the Giant
Charlie Monroe." Among the pieces on Larry Sparks are Thomas Cook,
"Larry Sparks: I'm Givin' It All I've Got"; Doug Green, "Larry Sparks";
Terry Lickona, "Going to the Top . . . with Larry Sparks"; and Tom Teepen,
"Larry Sparks . . . on the Road." For J. D. Crowe, see Fred Bartenstein,
"J. D. Crowe and the New South"; Mary Jane Bolle, "Happy Medium—

J. D. Crowe and the New South"; and Marty Godbey, "A Conversation with J. D. Crowe."

With the exception of Robert Kyle's "Bluegrass in Washington," documentation on the Washington scene has come to me largely through newspaper articles: John Carmody, "Bluegrass Group Joins March to Urbanization"; Bruce Cook, "In Washington, Bluegrass is Capitol"; Phil Gailey, "Welcome to the Capitol . . . of the Nation's Bluegrass"; Stephanie Mansfield, "Birchmere's Bluegrass: 'The Ultimate' " and "Nothin' But Bluegrass, All Day Long"; and William C. Woods, "Country Music—Little-Noticed Nightlife for Hundreds."

The best history of the Stonemans is Ivan H. Tribe's "The Return of Donna Stoneman: First Lady of the Mandolin." For Roy Clark's retrospective on his Washington years, see Jon Sievert, "Roy Clark," and Roger H. Siminoff, "Roy Clark." Buzz Busby is profiled briefly in the Rounder Collective's liner notes to *Honkytonk Bluegrass*. A biography of Country Music Hall of Fame member Connie B. Gay is included in Chet Hagan's *Country Music Legends in the Hall of Fame*, pp. 229–34.

The Country Gentlemen's band of the seventies is the subject of Bill Evans, "Good Music, Good Friends: The Country Gentlemen"; Michio Higashi, "Japan Welcomes the Gentlemen"; and Bill Vernon, "The Country Gentlemen—On Tour in Japan."

For more on Rebel Records, see Jerry Dallman, "Introducing Dick Freeland (of Rebel Records)." The Emerson and Waldron band lasted only a short time. Subsequently there were three articles on Waldron, all titled "Cliff Waldron and the New Shades of Grass," by Ann Randolph, Bill Vernon, and Lloyd "Stretch" Whittaker. Waldron now performs only gospel music. For the II Generation see Pete Kuykendall, "II Generation" and Fred Bartenstein, "The IInd Generation." In addition to the Don Reno citations given earlier, see, for Reno and Harrell, Roger Siminoff, "Inside Reno-Harrell."

The Seldom Scene were first profiled in Bill Vernon, "Part-Time Professionals: The Seldom Scene"; subsequent articles were Bob Cantwell's "Is the 'Scene' Grass?" Pat Mahoney's "The Scene as Heard," and Don Rhodes's "The Stability and Versatility of the Seldom Scene."

Much of my information on the developments in the Los Angeles scene comes from two charts in Pete Frame's *Rock Family Trees*: "Byrds of a Feather: 1," p. 8 and "Poco and the Eagles," p. 18. Also useful is Judith Sims, "The Eagles Take It Easy and Soar." The complicated tale of the early days of the Country Gazette is told in John Delgatto's "The Country Gazette." For a slightly different account, see Todd Everett's liner notes to *Country Gazette Live*. Also useful is Jack Tottle, "The Country Gazette: Keep On Pushing." The Gene Parsons-Ralph Stanley story was printed in *Muleskinner News* 3 (Dec. 1972): 17.

Discographical Notes

Bill Monroe appeared on Kenny Baker's County album *Kenny Baker Plays Bill Monroe*. Bill and his son James did two albums together: *Father and Son and Together Again*.

The six Flatt and Scruggs albums released between the beginning of 1965 and summer 1967 were *The Versatile . . . , Town and Country, When the Saints Go Marching In, Greatest Hits, Strictly Instrumental with Doc Watson*, and *Hear The Whistles Blow*. The Lovin' Spoonful song they recorded was "Nashville Cats"; the Monkees piece was "Last Train to Clarksville." Neither appear on an album. Flatt and Scruggs recorded one album after they had officially separated, in order to fulfill contractual obligations with Columbia: *Final Fling (One Last Time)*.

Jim and Jesse's "Better Times A-Coming" was released on their *Y'All Come: Bluegrass Humor*. Their "Memphis" was included on *Berry Pickin' in the Country*, an album consisting entirely of Chuck Berry compositions. (Flatt and Scruggs's "Memphis" appeared on their *Town and Country*). Jim and Jesse's "Diesel on My Tail" was on the album of the same name. Their 1971 Capitol album was *Freight Train*.

Randy and Gary Scruggs's first album was *All the Way Home*. The Nitty Gritty Dirt Band's "Mr. Bojangles" appeared on *Uncle Charlie and His Dog Teddy*. Portions of the sound track from Earl Scruggs's NET special became an album, *Earl Scruggs: His Family and Friends*.

Lester Flatt's first Victor album was *Flatt on Victor*; his first album with Mac Wiseman, *Lester 'n' Mac*.

Although Ralph Stanley is usually credited with introducing a cappella gospel singing to bluegrass record audiences, the Dillards' rendition of "I'll Fly Away" on *Wheatstraw Suite* is an a cappella performance by a bluegrass band that predates Stanley's by three years.

The Starday albums of 1973 included Charlie Monroe's *Tally Ho!*, Larry Sparks's *Ramblin' Bluegrass*, Reno and Harrell's *Bluegrass on My Mind*, the New Grass Revival, and Reno and Smiley's *Last Time Together*. J. D. Crowe and the New South did not appear until 1977.

RCA Victor's 1974 "Bluegrass Celebration" releases were Danny Davis's Nashville Brass, *Bluegrass Country*; *Bluegrass for Collectors*, an anthology; *The Best of Lester Flatt*; *Bluegrass at Its Peak* by the McPeak Brothers, and Lester Flatt's *Live! Bluegrass Festival*, which included an appearance by Bill Monroe. Monroe's festival album (on which Flatt appeared) was *Bean Blossom*.

The Country Gentlemen's first Rebel single paired "Christmas Time Back Home" with "Heavenward Bound." Their album from Haney's second festival was titled *Roanoke Bluegrass Festival*. Emerson and Waldron's "Fox on the Run" appeared on their second Rebel album, *Bluegrass Country*. Bill Harrell's album with the Virginians was *The Wonderful World of Bluegrass Music*; his first with Reno on King, *All the Way to Reno*.

The two Dillard and Clark albums were *The Fantastic Expedition of . . .* and *Through the Morning, Through the Night*. The first Country Gazette album was *A Traitor in Our Midst*; the second, *Don't Give Up Your Day Job*. Gene Parsons sang "Drunkard's Dream" with Ralph Stanley; it was issued on Parsons's *Kindling*.

Chapter 12

Books, Records, Believers: Bluegrass Today

Following the rapid expansion and stylistic proliferation of the late sixties and early seventies, bluegrass experienced a period of steady growth, stability, and consolidation. Acceptance of it as a historical part of country music by Nashville was reflected in Monroe's status and the continuation of the Early Bird bluegrass concerts at the annual Opry Birthday Celebrations and Fan Fairs, even though its followers felt that it was still stigmatized by the country music recording and radio industry in terms of both production and exposure. Acceptance as a significant national folk art in Washington was symbolized by the praise for the area's most popular bluegrass deejay, Gary Henderson, read into the Congressional Record by former Senate majority leader Robert Byrd, whose County fiddle album was made with the assistance of members of the Country Gentlemen and by the presence of Bill Monroe and Doc Watson at President Carter's barbecue on the south lawn of the White House in August 1980. Today most Americans know at least vaguely that bluegrass is a kind of country folk music and many have read about or heard of Bill Monroe.

In recent years performers who had earlier mixed bluegrass with other styles have dealt with fan angst about stylistic impurity by shaping separate albums and concerts for differing audience tastes. Traditional, progressive, newgrass, and styles related to but distinct from bluegrass are in vogue; fusion and mixing are no longer as fashionable as they once were. Several new consumer magazines have appeared, and those that have survived have grown in size and circulation, staking out their own markets.

A flood of self-instruction books for bluegrass instruments echoes this growth, as do many new songbooks. Several major houses have published serious popular histories of the music and musicians. By the late seventies most of the important bands were recording for independent record companies that specialized in bluegrass and related forms. These companies now are more successful in competition with the major labels for the enlarged bluegrass market because they know the bluegrass scene so much better; understanding patterns of demand and consumption, they anticipate fashion.

As the musicians and those who market their music became better organized, so too did the followers of the music. In spite of rising travel costs and economic malaise, the number of festivals continued to grow through the seventies, producing a new generation of bluegrass enthusiasts. During this period came also a growth of "area committees"—clubs which sponsored festivals, concerts, and regular local jam sessions. Many publish newsletters or magazines.

Bluegrass magazines now appear in Japan, Canada, and the British Isles, and festivals have been held in all three, with enough interest in the genre in these countries as well as in western Europe, Australia, and New Zealand to support occasional local bands and tours by American groups. But the center of the music continues to be in the areas of early interest and activity; in 1979 the largest numbers of festivals were held in Ohio, Virginia, and North Carolina, with Georgia, Alabama, and Missouri close behind.

Another indication of the growth of serious interest in the music can be seen in the proliferation of instrument craftsmen, repairmen, manufacturers, and sales outlets. There is now an international trade in bluegrass instruments, old and new.

Bluegrass is now an independent musical form with its own business infrastructure. Festivals and clubs make it possible for more professional musicians to perform it regularly than ever before. Still, for many bluegrass is a hobby, a musical pastime similar to barbershop quartet singing, dixieland jazz, chamber music, and other well-defined forms that involve musical skills requiring practice and experience but that have limited commercial viability. Such forms attract a large proportion of musicians in relation to the size of the audience and are likely to be called (like bluegrass) "a musician's music." For many others (particularly in rural areas and in the Southeast) it is a much less self-conscious musical expression, a kind of music that has extended and altered, while growing from, older traditions—in short, contemporary folk music.

All of the phenomena outlined above are tangled together, as is typical in the ecology of human culture; at one festival or within a single area committee it is possible to find individuals with widely varying tastes and involvements, all united by commitment to bluegrass. As Mitch Jayne, the former Dillards bassist and emcee, put it, "Bluegrass doesn't make fans, it makes believers . . . "[1] By the beginning of the eighties, the tenets of faith had been codified.

Bluegrass Books and Magazines

The first scholarly study of the history of country music, Bill C. Malone's *Country Music, U.S.A.*, was published in 1968 by the University of Texas

Press for the American Folklore Society. Originally written as a Ph.D. dissertation in history at the University of Texas, Malone's book closed with a chapter titled "Bluegrass and the Urban Folk Revival." His detailed approach focused on the music's folk revival connections because these were, at the time he was writing, most apparent. His treatment of bluegrass in a separate chapter, removed from the mainstream of country music, was in some ways logical and convenient; yet it foreshadowed the standard approach to bluegrass in virtually all subsequent country music popular histories, in which the music was sequestered from the rest of country music and the important parallels and connections between the forms neglected. But this is as many bluegrass followers would have it, and most of the books on bluegrass have devoted relatively little space to contemporaneous bluegrass-country music connections, focusing instead upon its historical development from older country music forms.

The first book to give more than a chapter to bluegrass music was James Rooney's *Bossmen: Bill Monroe and Muddy Waters*, published by New York's Dial Press in 1971. Rooney, successor to Ralph Rinzler as a director of the Newport Folk Festival and an occasional picking partner of Bill Keith, hypothesized that Monroe and Chicago blues pioneer Waters had played similar roles in the development of seminal musical styles based on down-home music during the post-war years. Both had acted as teachers to a series of sidemen-apprentices who perpetuated the bossman's music and philosophy, making his sound into a genre. Rooney devoted the first half of the book, about eighty photo-illustrated pages, to Monroe. He made extensive use of interviews with Monroe as well as with present and former Blue Grass Boys. More than any other single source, this volume documents Monroe's own theories and beliefs about bluegrass music. Rooney captured Monroe at a time when he was still relatively fresh in expressing such ideas, and the book remains useful and enlightening, even though by its very theme it somewhat overstates Monroe's importance. Dwelling on his role as a teacher-bandleader, the book did not deal with the tensions between him and progressive/newgrass musicians. Rather it served to portray Monroe succinctly though in more depth than any previous writing about him. And it came at a time when his canonization by the Country Music Hall of Fame had made many people interested in knowing about him.

The following year Collier Books published Dennis Cyporyn's *The Bluegrass Songbook*, the first of its kind from a major press. Cyporyn, a bluegrass enthusiast and banjoist from Detroit who was a dedicated Ralph Stanley follower, included brief historical comments on leading bluegrass figures and several pages of basic bluegrass guitar and banjo methodology. Out of print for some time following its publication because of copyright problems, it was, in its combination of words, music, history, and methodology, the forerunner of a flood of similar books already in the works.

In 1974 Oak Books, a New York press originally connected with *Sing Out!*

magazine, published the first four of their many bluegrass instruction books—
Bluegrass Banjo by Peter Wernick, *Bluegrass Fiddle* by Gene Lowinger, *Bluegrass Mandolin* by Jack Tottle, and *Bluegrass Guitar* by Happy Traum. Lavishly illustrated with photos, each contained music, tablature ("tabs"), and, in addition to the graduated self-instruction format, varying amounts of historical and philosophical discussion designed to acquaint students with the music's social context. All except Lowinger's included a flexidisc record containing musical examples. All four authors had learned bluegrass during the late fifties and early sixties folk boom, and were city-boy musicians—Tottle from Washington, the others from New York.

Like Cyporyn's book, these were practical volumes intended for the growing numbers of people, exposed to bluegrass through festivals, records, and broadcast media, who wished to play it but were not in close enough contact with it on a regular basis to find teachers. In 1974 *Muleskinner News* editor Fred Bartenstein, introducing a reader survey, pointed out that "devotees are spread quite thinly over a large area, forming a statistical rather than a geographic community."[2] This, he said, led to festivals and a specialized press. The instruction books, with their historical and philosophical focus, were in this sense an extension of the consumer movement. They were quite successful; Wernick's banjo book sold over one hundred thousand copies within a few years, even though it was competing with Scruggs's best-selling volume.

These books reflected and fueled a revolution in the learning and communication of bluegrass performance skills. What previously had been learned aurally by listening to and watching musicians and copying records now became a matter of musical literacy. In the seventies this had the effect of considerably raising and broadening the base of bluegrass competency. Even though many who purchased the books never actually progressed very far, these volumes nevertheless created a new generation of pickers who had learned from tablature and could communicate and teach with it. "Tabs" appeared not just in books, for starting in the fall of 1972, *Muleskinner News* had begun carrying Wayne Shrubsall's monthly column, which spotlighted a well-known bluegrass banjo picker and gave tabs for one of his tunes. In 1973 the *Banjo Newsletter,* a monthly publication containing tabs, appeared. Similar publications for mandolinists, *Mandolin World News* and *Mandolin Notebook,* would appear in 1976 and 1977. By 1975 all bluegrass periodicals published some tablature at least occasionally, and some instrumental stars published tabs to complement their albums.

The self-instruction books focused on instrumental techniques. Not until 1976, when Oak published Peter Wernick's *Bluegrass Songbook,* was there anything in print on vocal techniques, and that aspect of the music remains the least explored of all topics in the literature. In part this is because of a belief that vocalizing is much more a matter of personal style than is instrumental technique: one is supposed to sing bluegrass "from the heart." It is also because the people who are attracted to bluegrass as a discrete form—urban middle-class youth and young adults, generally—are initially more interested in learning how to play the instruments than in singing.

Appearing at the same time as the first Oak instruction books was another work dealing with practical matters in a somewhat different realm, my *Bill Monroe and His Blue Grass Boys: An Illustrated Discography*, published in Nashville in 1974 by the Country Music Foundation. Though by no means the first bluegrass discography published—Kuykendall had pioneered them in *Disc Collector* in the late fifties and *Bluegrass Unlimited* had published a number during its early years—this was the first full book devoted to the topic. Covering Monroe's recording career from 1939 to 1973, it carried Rooney's perspective of Monroe as a bossman further by identifying the men who had performed on Monroe's recordings, discussing their roles in his music. It also functioned as a guide for record collectors by dating discs and identifying unpublished performances. During the sixties Rinzler had produced a series of reissues featuring Monroe's best Decca recordings. Now, in the wake of the discography, reissues of the more obscure Monroe cuts became available on authorized Japanese MCA reissues and other unauthorized albums, showing that the record collector market had grown, too.

The historical interest which Rooney's *Bossmen* and the Monroe discography addressed, also reflected in the inclusion of historical sections in song and instrumental instruction books, was noted within the publishing industry. The result was the appearance in 1975 of two general history-introductions to bluegrass for a popular readership—Steven D. Price's *Old as the Hills* and Bob Artis's *Bluegrass*. Price was a relative newcomer to the music; his slim volume was uneven, sometimes inaccurate. Artis, on the other hand, was an experienced musician, a Los Angeles native of Appalachian descent who had been working in the band of Pittsburgh bluegrass singing veteran Mac Martin. Artis's book was accurate, informative, and well written. Both books included appendices listing recordings and publications. Artis's also gave lists of radio stations and organizations. Like the other books, these were intended to make this previously obscure music more accessible.

An important part of this access was provided by magazines. By 1975 there were three nationally distributed monthlies. The oldest, *Bluegrass Unlimited*, had acquired a more polished look but maintained the features it had carried from the start. Spurred on by the popularity of *Muleskinner News'* historical pieces on groups and individuals, it was including more such features, notably those of historian Ivan Tribe. In addition to his work with bluegrass pioneers, Tribe wrote about the older country musicians from the mountain regions who had influenced and shared radio and concert venues with the early bluegrass musicians in the 1930-60 era. In this emphasis *Bluegrass Unlimited* differed somewhat from *Muleskinner News*. But in both, festival reviews were less frequent, and both strove to cope with the ever increasing number of new records. In addition to articles on historical figures both featured the up and coming new bands and the established favorites. Articles on instrumental technique and the care and repair of instruments continued; photo essays and fiction began to appear.

While these two remained the principal bluegrass magazines during the early seventies, other publications appeared which regularly dealt with bluegrass topics even though they were not exclusively devoted to the genre. One was *The Devil's Box*, published since 1968 by the Tennessee Valley Old Time Fiddlers' Association. A quarterly, it reviewed fiddle contests and records, presented historical and biographical articles on fiddlers and fiddling, and printed tunes and tabs. By the end of the seventies it had become the most important fiddle music periodical and gave bluegrass fiddling regular coverage. Another was *Old Time Music*, published beginning in 1971 in London, England, by Tony Russell. Focusing on histories and discographies of the music produced in hillbilly, old-time, Cajun, western swing, and similar genres during the period from the twenties to the fifties, Russell's magazine occasionally had bluegrass-related articles and regularly reviewed bluegrass albums. Like *The Devil's Box*, it showed that many of its readers shared their interest in the magazine's primary topic with an interest in bluegrass.

A third bluegrass monthly, *Pickin'*, was established in February 1974 by its editor Douglas Tuchman, a New Yorker who had been actively promoting bluegrass concerts in the New York area through his New York Bluegrass Club. *Pickin'*, "The Magazine of Bluegrass and Old Time Country Music," resembled *Muleskinner News* and *Bluegrass Unlimited*, but it was designed for the newsstand instead of the subscriber-fan. With full-color covers, heavy slick paper, and color photos inside, it carried in the center of each early issue a folded 16-x-20-inch color poster, bluegrass equivalents of the *Playboy* centerfold. Most popular were shots of the sought-after old instruments, the ones with fancy inlay and carving. *Pickin'* marketed the posters separately, along with logo T-shirts and reprints of pre-war instrument catalogs. Ultimately the emphasis upon instruments differentiated *Pickin'* from the other two magazines. This was an indication of its northern, urban, and youth-focused constituency.

Much of the impetus behind this came from the magazine's technical editor, Roger Siminoff, who stayed with *Pickin'* through changes of editor and publisher. Neophyte musicians' preoccupation with instruments had been growing since the early sixties, coinciding with the growth of urban folk revival interest in bluegrass. More responsive to the instrumental aspects of bluegrass than the vocal, young northern musicians believed it was very important to have the right instrument. And generally they were better fixed to obtain one, since many came from middle-class backgrounds and had college educations so that they had more disposable cash than the working-class men who'd been the first bluegrass followers during the fifties.

Because only a limited number of old pre-war Martin guitars and Gibson banjos and mandolins of the kind considered best for this music still existed, prices for them began going up quickly at the beginning of the seventies as the number of new bluegrass musicians seeking old instruments increased. In 1972 a magazine devoted to instruments, *Mugwumps*, appeared. Although it published histories of instruments and their makers, its main purpose was stated on its cover logo: "The Classified Market-Place of Folk Instruments for Sale." By the end of the seventies Gibson F5 mandolins (like Monroe's) that had sold for $250 new in 1924 and $500 used in 1964 were regularly going for $7,000.

During the same period demand grew for skilled craftsmen, who could repair and make copies of the old instruments. Their trade stimulated the creation of instrument parts supply and manufacturing businesses. Most successful was Stewart-MacDonald, a southern Ohio firm which capitalized on the home-building and custom markets with their banjo and mandolin parts and kits. By the mid-seventies they were producing and marketing on both the wholesale and retail levels. Siminoff and others in *Pickin'* contributed to the process by publishing information on building and repairing instruments. In 1977 Siminoff published his *Constructing a Bluegrass Mandolin*, a step-by-step instruction book which included 130 photos and a complete set of plans for building a copy of the Gibson F-5 mandolin.

While the small (often one-man) custom shops and do-it-yourself suppliers were developing, established companies moved into the market. In the late sixties Fender and Baldwin, never before involved in the bluegrass trade, brought out high-quality competitors to the Gibson Mastertone banjo. Threatened by the new competition, Gibson sent representatives to Bean Blossom and other festivals in the early seventies. The result was that they redesigned their banjos and mandolins to make them as close to the pre-war versions as possible. Martin too responded to consumer demand by putting discontinued guitar models and styles back into production so that by the mid-seventies it was possible to buy from these companies, still recognized as the established leaders for bluegrass, copies of their old pre-war style instruments.

In competition with these firms were new American and Canadian banjo, mandolin, and guitar builders who'd gone from custom building into production-line manufacture—companies like Stelling, Ruby, Mossman, Unicorn, Tennessee, and others. Some survived and prospered—most notably Stelling, which successfully gained a significant share of the banjo market with its new design—while others did not. One problem for the North American companies, new and old alike, was the competition from Japan. By 1974 fairly good cheap copies of the most desirable old Gibson and Martin bluegrass instruments were being exported from Japan.

Able to undercut North American prices, the Japanese built on their cultural tradition of learning from one's predecessors, working hard to emulate them, and then applying these lessons. Their market research was made easier because of the strong Japanese bluegrass movement from which they could quickly learn about consumer preferences. Manufacturers like Ibanez improved the quality of their instruments during the seventies, especially on the medium-price level. By the end of the decade American firms like Washburn and Gold Star were having instruments built to their specifications in Japan. Now a wide range of instruments is available to bluegrass pickers, reflecting the market which *Pickin'* cultivated.

During 1974–75, there were three monthly bluegrass magazines. *Pickin's* focus on instruments made it an attractive alternative to the other two, and its wide distribution gave it a healthy circulation. *Muleskinner News,* on the other hand, was losing vitality and readers. After 1975, when editor Fred Bartenstein left, it no longer appeared on a monthly basis. Changed to a newspaper format, it soldiered on into 1978 as *Music Country.* The decline of *Muleskinner News* coincided with a decline in Carlton Haney's activity as a festival organizer; by the end of the seventies he was no longer promoting any festivals.

Pickin' prospered during the mid-seventies, but the pressure for newsstand success led to its sale, at the end of 1977, to a larger publishing house, which set out to appeal to a broader readership, changing the cover logo description to "The leading magazine for people into Grass Roots Music."[3]

Although it carried on for two more years, *Pickin'* was eclipsed by *Frets,* a magazine which began operation in March 1979. Published by *Guitar Player* publications, it was "For All Acoustic Stringed Instrument Players." Its editor was Roger Siminoff, and it maintained his focus on instruments while adding *Guitar Player's* successful format of interview-articles with star performers along with regular columns on technique by instrumental specialists like Earl Scruggs, Byron Berline, Alan Munde, and David Grisman. *Frets* did not offer as many bluegrass-oriented reader services as *Pickin', Muleskinner News,* or *Bluegrass Unlimited.* News of local bands, radio shows, and clubs was not as detailed; there were fewer and briefer record reviews.

In December 1979 *Frets* absorbed *Pickin'* and its 35,000 subscribers when that magazine folded. Because it was considerably better supported by its publishers, who were more knowledgeable about the markets for music magazines through their other publications, it soon gained a large readership. It was also different enough from *Bluegrass Unlimited* to create its own niche in the marketplace. An informal reader survey conducted in 1979 by Jim Crockett, publisher of *Frets,* revealed that 80 percent of their readers were males between twenty and forty, with 45 percent currently in college. The readers who responded to his request for information told Crockett that they owned an average of 3½ instruments each; over 70 percent read musical tablature and 60 percent read regular musical notation. Most interesting was the expression of preferences for musical styles: "Bluegrass is the most popular style among *Frets* readers (38%), with 34% into folk, 31% playing predominantly country, and blues and classical tied at about 25%. Naturally, many players are into more than one style, so the totals exceed 100%. While jazz ranked below all these as the style most often played, it placed number one (22%) as the musical form that most readers are interested in learning."[4] Hence while bluegrass is well represented in every issue, *Frets* does not presume to be a bluegrass magazine. *Frets'* approach—covering an eclectic mixture of acoustic musics in which bluegrass is an important element—resembles that taken by many of the record companies specializing in acoustic and folk music.

Record Companies

In 1976 the John Edwards Memorial Foundation's *JEMF Quarterly* published Robert Carlin's "The Small Specialty Record Company in the United States." Carlin examined those companies issuing what he broadly categorized as "folk music." In contrast to less than a dozen companies during the fifties, said Carlin, as of 1975 there were 134 companies issuing American folk music. He found an extremely diverse group of businesses (he described several in detail), but all shared a business philosophy at variance with that of the major labels. The owner often acted as producer, and artists were given a substantial role in production. This contrasted with major labels' assembly line approach to recording. Promotion was limited to ads in specialty magazines; no one was "hyping" the product to deejays and reviewers. Distribution was through a few specialized distributors and mail-order houses rather than through nationwide distributors with links to the big retail chains. Advance payments to artists were rarely made and a relatively small number of records were pressed. However, those records were allowed to stay in print as long as the company was in business, because low production, promotion, and distribution costs meant that records did not have to sell a large number quickly to recoup costs. This approach was, said Carlin, "concurrent (with the) movement by many started in the 1960s toward decentralization, toward smallness, toward humanizing business and life."[5]

He organized his statistical findings into a series of tables, two of which comment on the significance of bluegrass within the overall picture. One chart categorized forty-nine companies recording only one type of music. More of these companies (thirteen) released bluegrass than any of the nine other types he listed (blues, traditional, women's music, old-time, American Indian, contemporary folk, gospel, Irish). But since the larger companies, which usually have better distribution, typically market more than one type of music, the other chart, which listed the types of music recorded by all labels, was the more significant of the two. It too had bluegrass at the top of the list with some forty-six companies including bluegrass in their catalogs; the next closest categories were old-time (forty-three), traditional (thirty-seven), blues (twenty-eight), and contemporary folk (twenty-eight). Briefly

put, the companies that were marketing folk music records found blueg...
an attractive product.

The reason for this can be found in Bartenstein's 1974 *Muleskinner News*
reader survey. His respondents reported owning an average of 157 bluegrass
albums, purchasing an average of sixteen albums a year at local record stores
(40 percent), from mail-order services (22 percent), at festivals (15 percent),
from artists at local appearances (6 percent), or a combination of these
sources (17 percent). Bartenstein characterized this rate of consumption as
"high" and explained it by alluding to the fact that bluegrass listeners are
"often isolated from live performances."[6] Relatively low radio exposure was
another contributing factor. Although Bartenstein did find some differences
in the amount of record consumption according to income, age, and region
(older, less-educated non-southerners had the largest collections), the patterns seemed, by 1973–74, to be evening out. Just as there was a diversity of
bluegrass performances to choose from on record, so there was a diversity of
consumers and, as the seventies wore on, of independent companies staking
out their claims to a share in this market.

During the late sixties the two big country independents, Starday and
King, virtually dropped out of the picture as far as new bluegrass releases were
concerned. By 1970 Rebel had emerged as the leading bluegrass independent.
County had also begun to grow; it released more old-time music, both newly
recorded and reissues of pre-war hillbilly records, than did Rebel. Fiddle
music played an important part in County's catalog; vocal music was more
significant with Rebel. In 1970 they were joined by Rounder, the company
that would within five years have the largest catalog of all those studied by
Carlin.

Rounder was one of the first post-festival independents to move into bluegrass in strength. Like *Rolling Stone* magazine and the many enterprises described in the *Whole Earth Catalog,* Rounder was a form of counterculture
capitalism. Their quarterly newsletter, *The Rounder Review,* described the
basis of the company in 1972: "Rounder is a collective, with all members
pooling all resources. There is no real division of labor . . . no bosses, no
hierarchy, and we workers own the whole thing collectively."[7] Located in
the Boston suburb of Somerville, the collective included Ken Irwin, Bill
Nowlin, and Marion Leighton, along with various other less permanent
members. In the early days of the collective, all held "day jobs" in order to
help keep the company afloat, and they operated a mail-order service which
provided capital for new records.

Rounder proclaimed a "policy of allowing artistic control to the artists
. . ."[8] and, operating on shoestring budgets, produced many of their early
albums as field recordings. Like County they initially issued old-time music,
with their first bluegrass album appearing in 1971. Unlike County they
produced albums containing many kinds of folk music, quickly building a
catalog rivaling Folkways' in its diversity. But bluegrass and related forms

remained at the center of their activities. In 1972 they made their first three Nashville-recorded albums. Two were by former members of John Hartford's band—Tut Taylor and Norman Blake. Inspired by Hartford's songwriting, Blake had, with his album, embarked upon his career as a featured singer and instrumentalist. The third album was by an instrumentalist who, like Blake, had been on the Nitty Gritty Dirt Band album—Roy Acuff's Dobroist Pete "Oswald" Kirby. At about the same time as the Nashville albums appeared, Rounder released their first re-issue of pre-war hillbilly music. By 1973 they had divested themselves of the mail-order service, which became Round-house (later Roundup) Records, in order to devote full attention to their new recording projects. These included productions of avant-garde, bluegrass-trained instrumentalists like Vassar Clements, who'd gone from Hartford to the Earl Scruggs Revue in October 1971 and was, by the time his record appeared, putting together his own solo act, and Tony Trischka, a banjoist who'd first recorded for Rounder with Country Cooking, a Syracuse University band which also included banjo and songbook author Peter Wernick. A disciple of Bill Keith, Trischka, like Clements, sought to take his art toward jazz, beyond the instrumental and formal confines of bluegrass.

In 1972 the Rounders received a grant from the National Endowment for the Humanities to prepare a series of records on the history of bluegrass. The first fruits of this appeared with three volumes of their Early Days of Bluegrass reissue series in 1975. These albums documented the first growth of bluegrass during the late forties and early fifties by presenting recordings of little-known local and regional performers. Though somewhat flawed by idiosyncratic choice of contents and lack of hard information about some of the more obscure recordings, these albums, with their detailed booklets, were well received, reflecting the development of a growing interest in bluegrass history.

Also in 1975 Rounder established itself as a label with outstanding contemporary bluegrass when it released *J. D. Crowe and the New South*, one of the most influential bluegrass albums of the decade. Crowe, who had not released a new album since 1972, came to Rounder with a hot band. It included guitarist Tony Rice, who had developed into a polished lead singer and was pushing his guitar techniques in directions suggested by the work of the recently killed Clarence White. Playing mandolin and singing tenor (and acting as emcee in shows) was Ricky Skaggs, who had left Ralph Stanley, retired briefly, joined the Country Gentlemen for a short stint as fiddler in 1973–74, and then joined the New South. In Crowe's band Skaggs began building his reputation as a spectacular singer and entertainer as well as an instrumentalist. Also with Crowe was Jerry Douglas, a young Dobro player from Ohio. Like Skaggs, he had worked with the Country Gentlemen. His style contrasted with those of Auldridge and Graves, and placed him in the front ranks of the interpreters of that instrument. The New South's repertoire was similar to that of the Seldom Scene and the Country Gentlemen in its mixture of old bluegrass and new contemporary songs; their sound too fell into the "progressive" camp—acoustic, sophisticated. Today this edition of the Crowe band (which also included bassist-fiddler Bobby Slone), is called the *original* New South, just as Monroe's 1945–48 band is called the original Blue Grass band.

With the Early Days of Bluegrass series and the Crowe album, Rounder solidified their position as a major bluegrass independent. While they were recording a number of established bands they also took a leading role in producing a different kind of bluegrass record, the "studio-star" album. The concept was not unique to bluegrass; it represented ideas in programming which had come to records from television and cinema. Like a television entertainer's "special," this album concept focused on a single star who brought into the studio for this particular occasion a number of other stars as "guests," as if they were friends, just helping out. Although these guests might be better known than the host as "stars," they were given subordinate "cameo" roles. Vassar Clements's Rounder album, for example, included guitarist-singer David Bromberg, a Columbia recording star well-known for his work with Bob Dylan. Aside from the additional exposure this gave Bromberg, whose name was prominent on the album jacket, it also helped Rounder sell copies of Clements's album. An early example of the studio-star album by a bluegrass picker was *Earl Scruggs: His Family and Friends,* discussed in the previous chapter. Based on a television soundtrack, it included Baez, Dylan, and the Byrds. Scruggs subsequently did a number of similar albums during the seventies. These, like the Clements album, only touch the bluegrass sound peripherally. Basically this was folk and country rock. And in fact the studio-star albums resembled contemporary rock productions which centered around a single star performer, often the member of a well-known group, who assembled his own recording musicians, often other stars, and handled the production himself. One of the earliest bluegrass examples of this was a pair of albums made by Seldom Scene Dobroist Mike Auldridge for Takoma Records in 1972 and 1974, which included many well-known musicians from within and outside the bluegrass world—John Duffey, Linda Ronstadt, David Bromberg, Vassar Clements, Ricky Skaggs. Rounder's Clements and Trischka albums followed soon after. Another example of this was David Grisman's Rounder album of 1976 which included Tony Rice, Ricky Skaggs, Bill Keith, and Jerry Douglas. The music was, in this case, mainly older bluegrass done in "progressive" style, mixed with some of Grisman's "dawg" style (about which, more later) instrumentals. Some of the same musicians appeared on Tony Rice's Rebel instrumental album, recorded at about the same time. Often reciprocity was an important part of this process; thus the Seldom Scene appeared on a Linda Ronstadt album at about the same time as she appeared on one of their albums. And with the studio-star concept, geographical and cultural boundaries were regularly crossed. Parts of albums were recorded at different studios on the east or west coast or in Nashville

and mixed together musicians associated with traditional or progressive bluegrass or with rock.

Other new independents were making similar records. Bruce Kaplan, a
former member of the Rounder Collective, founded Flying Fish in 1974. This
Chicago-based label resembled Rounder but placed more emphasis on jazz-
and newgrass-related musics. Still it, too, covered the field broadly: in 1974
Lester Flatt left RCA; he appeared on Flying Fish in 1975. At this time
Flying Fish also issued albums by the New Grass Revival and John Hartford.

A few of the new independent labels were owned by bands, who produced
and issued their own music. Jim and Jesse began releasing albums on their
Old Dominion label in 1973. Country Life was initiated in the early seventies
by the McLain Family of Berea, Kentucky, a band consisting of musicologist
Raymond McLain and his son and daughters. In addition to their festival
appearances the McLains began in the mid-seventies to perform for the State
Department in concerts which took them all over the world as "musical
ambassadors." Their annual festival was devoted to groups, which, like themselves, were built around a nuclear family; they represented a growing phenomenon on the local and regional level in this respect. Their records were
sold mainly at their personal appearances.

As the new labels proliferated, County Records grew apace. In June 1974
they moved from New York City to the little community of Floyd in southwestern Virginia. County owner David Freeman told Robert Carlin his markets were changing: "When my first re-issues were on the market, most of my
sales were to the folk-oriented college age groups, selling primarily through
stores in the larger cities. However, in the past couple of years, this market
has fallen off almost entirely, so that I sell very few LPs in the big cities
anymore. Fortunately, this drop-off has been more than made up for by a
large number of scattered rural customers throughout the country who have
learned of County in one way or another."[9] In addition to his company and
County Sales, the mail-order business, Freeman opened Record Depot, a
company which distributed in the Southeast some thirty-five different labels
specializing in bluegrass and old-time.

Although historical reissues such as the Rounder Early Days of Bluegrass
series were attracting some attention, clearly at this time the majority of new
bluegrass consumers were most interested in progressive, contemporary, or
newgrass styles. This was the market that offered the greatest opportunities
for the new independents; County on the other hand catered to an older,
established rural market.

In the fall of 1974 Freeman wrote in his newsletter about the state of the
music, saying that he guessed from his orders that "at least 60% of our
customers prefer the hard, traditional type of Bluegrass over the modern." He
assured his readers that he too preferred such music and was certain that "a
straight bluegrass band, playing with the polish and sublety of say Flatt &
Scruggs in the early 50s, or with the drive of the Stanley Bros. of the same

era, would 'turn on' just as many people as the modern groups do." But, he said, "most of today's better records—those that are produced with thought & care—happen to be in the modern category." The "bigger established names," Freeman opined, are "just going through the motions . . . producing little of real interest—no wonder that kids & people just getting interested in Bluegrass turn to the SELDOM SCENE, COUNTRY GENTLEMEN, etc. for inspiration—their music does show the time & interest put into it."[10] These "better records" were, by this point, on independent labels.

By 1976–77 Nashville's role in bluegrass recordings had diminished considerably. RCA had dropped their bluegrass artists in 1974. In 1976 MCA (formerly Decca) dropped Jimmy Martin and the Osborne Brothers from their roster, leaving Bill Monroe the only major bluegrass performer still appearing on a major label. At about the same time the bankrupt Starday-King was purchased by Gusto Records, which began reissuing older recordings from their massive catalog. But though they would eventually issue some of the material recorded in 1972–73, Gusto remained a reissue label, with the exception of Jimmy Martin, who began doing new albums with them in 1978. The new independents were filling the void left by the major labels: in 1976–77 Flying Fish released albums featuring the New Grass Revival, the Dillards, Mike Auldridge, Vassar Clements, and the Country Gazette. And in 1976 another new independent, CMH, appeared on the scene.

Established in June 1976 in Los Angeles, CMH was created by Martin Haerle, a West German immigrant who had worked at Starday during the early sixties and subsequently worked in country radio. From 1968 on he'd been the general manager of United Artists Records manufacturing division. He brought to CMH a wealth of knowledge about production, distribution, and marketing; his partner in CMH was Arthur ("Guitar Boogie") Smith, the South Carolina country band leader who composed "Feuding Banjos." CMH geared up to release some twenty-five albums in its first year of operation, many by bluegrass musicians. Among those signed on were Mac Wiseman, Lester Flatt, Don Reno and Bill Harrell, Carl Story, Benny Martin, the Osborne Brothers, the II Generation and the Stonemans. Haerle and Smith's decision to enter the field was based on their perception of its continuing growth. Said Haerle: "The college educated consumer has been the largest contributing factor in the marked rise in sales of bluegrass product. I attribute this to the attempt of young people today to shed their urban surroundings and get back to their more traditional roots."[11] CMH's records, which included a number of annotated double albums, were marketed from Los Angeles but mainly produced by Smith in South Carolina. Some CMH artists produced their own albums in Nashville.

By 1977, in addition to Rebel, County, Rounder, Flying Fish, and CMH, a number of smaller companies specialized in bluegrass. Often they combined one or two nationally prominent acts with lesser known regional or local artists. Atteiram in Marietta, Georgia, had the Pinnacle Boys (a popular

Knoxville group) and James Monroe. Revonah of Hanover, New York, issued discs by Del McCoury and by Red Smiley's old group, the Shenandoah Cutups. In Texas, Ridge Runner put out Country Gazette albums. Jalyn, owned by Jack Lynch of Dayton, Ohio, issued several Ralph Stanley albums. Most of these companies were virtually one-man operations, working with low overhead and taking advantage of festival and artist sales and the distribution offered by County Sales, Roundhouse, and similar mail-order companies.

Several of the new independents were operated by entrepreneurs long involved with bluegrass in other ways. Vetco, in Cincinnati, was owned by Lou Ukelson of the Jimmie Skinner Music Center. It issued albums by many of the locally popular southern Ohio groups, including the Hotmud Family, which combined old-time and bluegrass, and Earl Taylor. It also produced reissues of old-time music like those of County and Rounder. Old Homestead, based in Michigan, was run by John Morris, a native of Tennessee who worked as a pharmacist during the week but was known to thousands in southern Michigan and northern Ohio as a knowledgeable disc jockey who played the best in authentic old-time and bluegrass. Morris began his label with recordings of hillbilly veteran Wade Mainer and continued to issue performances by Mainer and similar older Appalachian artists as well as albums by contemporary bluegrass groups like that of Larry Sparks. Old Homestead also did reissues. Both Vetco and Old Homestead were located in the midst of heavy Appalachian migrant settlement, where bluegrass had been popular for decades; their products represented responses to the interests of local record buyers (Vetco) and radio listeners (Old Homestead).

While country music stations continued to exclude most bluegrass recordings from their programs, there was by the middle seventies a substantial number of weekly bluegrass radio shows. The monthlies regularly listed the times and call letters of these shows, many of which were hosted by musicians or long-time followers of the music, often on FM stations.

In the Washington area where the density of the bluegrass listening audience was greater than elsewhere, a number of bluegrass FM shows—like those of Katie Daley, Tom Cat Reeder, and Red Shipley—were heard regularly. One local disc jockey emerged in the mid-seventies who was at once a typical and an exceptional example of this trend. Gary Henderson began working as a country music deejay in the mid-sixties at WDON in Wheaton, Maryland. In 1966 he was one of the founders of *Bluegrass Unlimited.* In July 1967 he began engineering Dick Spottswood's *Bluegrass Unlimited* show on WAMU, the FM station at American University in Georgetown, a National Public Radio outlet. Henderson subsequently took over this half-hour show, broadcast Wednesday nights at 11:00. In September 1973 he began broadcasting four hours every Saturday morning over WAMU, which increased its power to 50,000 watts that fall. Later a similar Sunday morning show—"Stained Glass Bluegrass," devoted to religious music—was added. Because of Henderson's informed and relaxed approach and his extensive record collection, this quickly became one of the most listened-to radio shows in its time slot.

A native of the area, Henderson grew up in Silver Spring, Maryland, where as a child he listened to country music on the radio. Among the deejays he heard was Don Owens, on WARL in Arlington: "Don Owens was my inspiration for a knowledgeable country music disc jockey . . . country music was his life literally. . . . He knew the roots of the music . . . I try to . . . duplicate his show, putting out bits of information on the background of the artist, some humorous or original anecdotes that may have occurred in the recording studio that he would know from talking to the artist, but he wouldn't go on a long dissertation, he'd just make a few sentences and then play the record. It was just so tasteful the way he did it—he just had a knack for timing."[12]

Henderson took advantage of the new audiences created by the Seldom Scene and the Country Gentlemen to develop listener interest in the pioneering bluegrass groups as well as in older country music. His shows mixed newer progressive bluegrass with early bluegrass, forties and fifties southeastern string band country music, and mountain gospel singing. Emphasis was on the music: three or four cuts would be played without interruption between each of his comments. On any weekend one might find musicians and cognoscenti visiting at the station; Henderson might speak briefly with them on the air or broadcast a telephone interview with a local star.

Programs like those of Henderson and John Morris helped to stimulate consumer interest in the older bluegrass recordings. A majority of those now listening to bluegrass had first heard it during the seventies and had not heard the 78s and the early albums on major labels, long out of print, which had been models for bluegrass repertoire and style in the fifties. Since the beginning of the decade the number of pirate or bootleg reissues of these old recordings had grown, particularly on the mysterious Collectors Classics label, operated by someone who had access to the best bluegrass recordings and, judging from packaging and selection, knew a lot about their history. Also popular were bootleg albums of personal appearances and radio broadcasts, the kind of material that many bluegrass followers had been collecting on tape since the fifties. All of this, along with the activities of historically-minded deejays, led to the move which both County and Rounder made in 1977 when they began issuing authorized historical reissues using leased major-label recordings. Rounder opened with the Lilly Brothers Prestige albums of 1963 and 1964, but two early fifties Flatt and Scruggs collections licensed through Columbia's Special Products Division—one on County, the other on Rounder—really got things rolling. During the next five years similar reissues in County's CS and Rounder's SS series brought clean, extensively annotated collections of the most popular early performers (Monroe, Flatt and Scruggs, Stanley Brothers, Osborne Brothers) to the market. At the same time Gusto expanded its reissue activities, so that by the beginning of the eighties the amount of early bluegrass available on LP was greater than at any time in the past.

In June 1977, following the release of County's first Flatt and Scruggs reissue, David Freeman wrote that it had sold more copies than any other album he had carried. At the same time he felt compelled to reply to critics of his policy of not reviewing albums by the New Grass Revival and similar groups. He explained that he now carried such albums (customers wanted them) but that because the volume of new albums had risen ("we now get more LPs to review in *one month* than we had in our entire stock the first year we operated") a choice had to be made: "I think the music revolution we have gone through since the advent of the Beatles has had many positive side effects, perhaps the greatest of which has been a breaking down of barriers and an opening up of peoples [sic] minds to different forms & types of music. I think it is admirable that many or most of today's younger generation music fans are tolerant of, and will accept and at least give a listen to most any type of music that exists." But, he added, as County Sales set out in 1965 "to preserve and promote authentic rural American music, mainly old-time, Bluegrass and fiddle music," he had to limit his review coverage, felt unqualified to fairly judge the New Grass Revival and similar groups, and also believed that priority should be given to "real country music—which is actually fast disappearing in the forms that we knew 20 years and more ago."[13]

Ironically Freeman expressed his concern at a time when, as the success of his own Flatt and Scruggs reissues showed, the balance of interest was tending away from the progressive and newgrass styles. Bill Monroe, whose music was by the early eighties frequently described as "traditional bluegrass," continued to work regularly on the road, much in demand and carrying on in spite of a bout with cancer in 1981. Other established groups moved in a "traditional" direction: the Osborne Brothers recorded two double-disc albums of bluegrass standards, one with Mac Wiseman, for CMH in 1978 and 1979. By 1983, for the first time since the mid-fifties, a fiddle was a regular part of their band. Regionally popular groups like Joe Val and the New England Bluegrass Boys (Rounder) and Larry Sparks and the Lonesome Ramblers (Rebel) developed strong followings by the early eighties on the basis of their records and festival appearances featuring repertoires and arrangements that were variously described as mainstream, hardcore, or traditional bluegrass.

The most popular new bands in the period between 1977 and 1984 reflected similarly this shift of taste; even the progressive groups included more of the older material in their repertoires. The Bluegrass Cardinals, formed in Los Angeles by Don Parmley, the Monticello, Kentucky, native who had been banjoist for the Golden State Boys and the Hillmen back in the sixties, migrated to the Washington area, where they were praised for their skillful mixture of traditional and progressive strains. They recorded one album with Rounder before moving on to CMH. Boone Creek, formed in 1977 by Ricky Skaggs and Jerry Douglas, was a bit more on the progressive side of the balance. After a promising debut with Rounder and Sugar Hill albums, they disbanded when Skaggs joined Emmylou Harris's Electric Hot Band. Another disbanding, that of Reno and Harrell, led to the appearance in 1978 of a new version of Bill Harrell and the Virginians (he'd used the same name in the sixties before joining Reno), and his popular albums on the Rebel and Leather labels featured a sound more mainstream than progressive. Firmly traditional or hardcore was the music of southern Ohio banjoist Dave Evans, whose intense Ralph Stanley–style singing Dave Freeman described as "raw power . . . it might actually scare a few folks."[14] His first album appeared on Vetco in 1979, and he now records for Rebel. Another group, based in southern Ohio, which began to receive recognition at about the same time was Dry Branch Fire Squad, fronted by mandolinist Ron Thomason. Thomason's wry humor as the group's emcee reaffirmed the traditional values associated with bluegrass music while at the same time gently poking fun at them. *"Lonesome,"* he said in the introduction to his pamphlet *Lonesome is a Car up on Blocks,* "is to bluegrass music what *blue* is to the blues. It is a word which encompasses feelings, beliefs, and concepts that cannot be readily defined in the usual manner" (p. [ii]). His introductions and comments in the band's shows, like his book, reflected the perspective of a sophisticated native offering numerous observations based on affection for a culture which he (like many of his listeners) felt with the ambivalence of the migrant. Humor played an important part in the performances of another group, the Colorado band Hot Rize, whose progressive bluegrass sound was replaced for a portion of each performance by their burlesque of fifties country music, Red Knuckles and the Trail Blazers. Hot Rize made an impressive debut album for Flying Fish in 1979. Jimmy Gaudreau and Glen Lawson left J. D. Crowe the same year to form the short-lived Spectrum with New York banjoist Bela Fleck, and Doyle Lawson left the Country Gentlemen at about the same time to form his group, Quicksilver. The former recorded for Rounder, the latter for Sugar Hill. Both reflected the progressive heritage of the Country Gentlemen in their sound, but Quicksilver, with its more conservative repertoire, was the more successful of the two groups, particularly because of its highly acclaimed gospel singing. By 1983 Spectrum was no more; Bela Fleck was working with the New Grass Revival, and Gaudreau had returned to Washington to rejoin the Country Gentlemen. Interestingly, in the Washington area the most talked-about band of the early eighties was not in the progressive mold but was neotraditional in repertoire and performance style—the Johnson Mountain Boys. Recording for Rounder, they became one of the most popular groups on the festival circuit. Like Thomason, they both believed in and kidded about the lonesome and sentimental side of the old-style bluegrass songs that made up the bulk of their repertoire.

These new bands were quickly signed for albums on the various independents. In 1978 a new label, Sugar Hill, was formed in North Carolina by Barry Poss. A Toronto native who'd become involved in the old-time music scene at the University of North Carolina while working on a graduate degree in sociology, Poss entered the record business in 1974 as an employee of County Records. By 1977 he was producing for Freeman, including the best-selling album of fiddle tunes by Senate majority leader Robert Byrd with bluegrass accompaniment, mentioned earlier. Sugar Hill's first release was a Boone Creek album. Handling the progressive acts that Freeman did not consider appropriate for County, Poss explained to *Billboard* that his company was established "to provide a format for musicians who are doing contemporary and significant music in more traditional settings."[15] The two labels worked together on projects, sharing resources in various ways. And when in 1979 County bought out Rebel, both the Seldom Scene and the Country Gentlemen moved from Rebel to Sugar Hill.

Like the other independents, Sugar Hill offered the benefits of artistic control. And by the beginning of the eighties it and the other larger companies like Rounder and Flying Fish were being distributed as widely as some of the major labels and were competitive not just in contents but also in packaging. With their low overhead and lack of bureaucratic and top-heavy management they could move quickly to exploit new trends and allow artists to play a significant role in the creation of records. Increasingly the best selling and most influential were of the studio-star variety. Among the most popular were Ricky Skaggs's Rebel (1975) and Sugar Hill (1979) efforts; a series by Tony Rice on several labels; three separate Rounder albums by Byron Berline, guitarist Dan Crary, and banjoist John Hickman, who had their own production company and played concerts together; and a Doyle Lawson mandolin album produced by Poss for County.

Such albums had become easier to create now because of the recording technology. Recorded on sixteen- or twenty-four-track machines (studios with such facilities were increasingly common by the end of the seventies), they could be mixed by the artist and producer with relative ease because the multiple tracks, recorded in isolation from each other, allowed total control over the final sound. Often these studio-star albums were recorded on a piecemeal basis so that the star could bring in the appropriate musicians for each cut. By the early eighties studio-star albums on the bluegrass independents often featured combinations of a small coterie of musicians—guitarists like Tony Rice or Dan Crary; banjoists like Alan Munde, Bill Keith, or Bela Fleck; mandolinists like Sam Bush, Doyle Lawson, or David Grisman; fiddlers like Kenny Baker, Mark O'Connor, Blaine Sprouse, or Bobby Hicks; and other well-known musicians like Jerry "Flux" Douglas, Mike Auldridge, and Ricky Skaggs. While they worked in or led bands that did various types of music, they shared a bluegrass background. Appearing on one another's albums (they were always identified in the liner notes, as with jazz albums) was a form of reciprocity which was mutually beneficial because it had the effect of creating an all-star album, giving exposure and enhancing saleability. Some of the same musicians were also appearing as studio sidemen on the records of lesser-known bluegrass groups, as well as those of popular singers like Emmylou Harris and Jesse Winchester.

In their role as studio musicians these stars could no longer be easily categorized as belonging to one particular stylistic camp: they moved easily from traditional to progressive bluegrass and beyond to modern country, jazz, folk revival. During the late sixties and early seventies, emphasis had been on fusion. Now the trend was toward the presentation of music in discrete, easily identifiable styles. Three examples of this process can be seen in the careers of Tony Rice, Ricky Skaggs, and J. D. Crowe, the core and vocal trio of Crowe's original New South of 1974–75.

When Tony Rice left Crowe he moved to the San Francisco Bay Area to join the David Grisman Quintet. Grisman, who'd played everything from bluegrass to rock and roll and also worked as a producer in the years since 1966, when he'd left New York, developed in the Quintet a musical format which he labeled "dawg" music (Dawg was his nickname). This was sophisticated acoustic instrumental music performed on mandolin (and mandolin family instruments), violin, guitar, and bass, deliberately excluding banjo. Grisman considered it a kind of classical music, but it was most often described by others as jazz. Its bluegrass antecedents were clear, though. With his distinctive ornate solo guitar style, now very much his own even though its roots in Clarence White's work would still be heard, Rice set the pattern for that instrument in this new form and by 1980 had formed his Tony Rice Unit, calling his music "spacegrass." By the early eighties this music was selling very well: Grisman had moved to a major label and achieved national media coverage. Rice is now considered one of the pioneers in the emergent "new acoustic music," as dawg/spacegrass is frequently labeled.

Ricky Skaggs, upon leaving Crowe, had first formed Boone Creek and then moved on to join Emmylou Harris's Hot Band. Harris, born in 1949 in Alabama, had grown up in northern Virginia near Washington. A folk revivalist in the sixties, her professional career began at the end of that decade in New York and Nashville. By 1971 she was appearing in Washington clubs doing a mixture of contemporary folk, country, and rock. "Discovered" by the Flying Burrito Brothers just as that group broke up, she spent 1972–73 recording and touring as a singer with Gram Parsons, who greatly influenced her music, directing her toward a country sound. Following Parsons's death in 1973 she returned to Washington and formed a country band. She appeared at the Red Fox, a club that was booking the Seldom Scene, Cliff Waldron, and the Country Gentlemen. She asked Skaggs to join her at this time, but, planning to form his own group, he declined. In 1975 she signed with Warner Brothers and moved to Los Angeles. Her best-selling and award-winning albums regularly included duets of the kind she'd first done with Parsons, and her band included bluegrass-trained sidemen like Herb Pedersen.

When rhythm guitarist and duet partner Rodney Crowell left Harris's band in 1978, Skaggs took his place. With Skaggs, she recorded *Roses in the Snow*, a bluegrass-flavored album which included studio-star performances by Tony Rice and Jerry Douglas as well as Willie Nelson, Dolly Parton, and Linda Ronstadt. At about the same time Skaggs did his solo album for Sugar Hill (Harris was a guest singer on it) which alternated bluegrass with country tracks. One of the latter, a version of Carter Stanley's "I'll Take the Blame," received considerable air play as a Sugar Hill single, and this led to a contract with Epic. Skaggs then left Harris to put together his own mainstream country band.

Although bluegrass followers found some evidence of bluegrass instrumentation and vocal style in Skaggs's country recordings, his major debt to the music came in the form of repertoire. The two hits from his first Epic album (1981) were Flatt and Scruggs songs from the fifties—"Don't Get above Your Raisin' " and "Crying My Heart Out over You." Also included on that album were songs from the forties and fifties repertoires of the Stanley Brothers, Hylo Brown, Roy Acuff, Webb Pierce, and Merle Travis. Skaggs's second Epic album (1982) also included a measure of old songs, like Roy Hall's "Don't Let Your Sweet Love Die," Monroe's "Can't You Hear Me Callin'," and Jim Eanes's "I Wouldn't Change You If I Could."

Skaggs demonstrated that the basic bluegrass repertoire differed little from that of mainstream country music from the forties and fifties. His hits testified not only to the new life which Skaggs's singing, arrangements, and production infused into them but also to the fact that these relatively simple songs were as well crafted as those of the more sophisticated Nashville songwriters who had attracted so much attention during the seventies. And the songs were new and fresh to younger listeners while appealing to the older audience as traditional and nostalgic. Skaggs had rapid and spectacular success as a mainstream country music performer: within two years he had become a member of the Grand Ole Opry and received the Country Music Association's prestigious Singer of the Year award.

In spite of their early association with J. D. Crowe, Ricky Skaggs and Tony Rice were now apparently headed in quite different directions. But in 1980 they got together and recorded an album of old Monroe, Flatt and Scruggs, Stanley Brothers, and similar groups' duets sung in brother style with only the traditional guitar and mandolin accompaniment. The album, which they produced together for Sugar Hill, was both a commercial and critical success.

Since 1975, J. D. Crowe had been moving the sound of his music in a direction which created controversy within bluegrass circles because of its combination of elements of country rock (drums, electrification) with bluegrass. Those critical of this trend in Crowe's music were pleased when, in 1981, he joined Rice, Doyle Lawson, fiddler Bobby Hicks (now a member of Skaggs's country band), and bassist Todd Phillips (from the Rice and Grisman bands) to do an album for Rounder titled simply *The Bluegrass Album*. Like the Skaggs and Rice duet album, it was a critical success and popular enough to bring the group together for special festival and club appearances and the production of sequel albums. These LPs were just what David Freeman had called for in 1974—a band playing fifties-style bluegrass with polish and drive, doing songs from the repertoires of the influential early bands. A similar album by Here Today, a group assembled by David Grisman and Herb Pedersen, was reviewed as follows in *Frets*: "As a genre, bluegrass has yet to hit the half-century mark, and already we've had 'newgrass,' 'jazzgrass' and a spate of other offshoots. If . . . Here Today (is) any indication, the '80s will find us setting aside yet another shelf—for 'supergrass.' "[16] A reception like this epitomizes the way in which it is possible for musicians trained in bluegrass but playing regularly in other forms to retain their reputation and following within the bluegrass community. It also shows the extent to which bluegrass enthusiasts of the early eighties had become more interested in performances which maintained and refined the repertoire, techniques, and esthetics of earlier models than in performances which sought to expand the boundaries of the genre.

Such albums, designed to sell to those preferring the pure old bluegrass, reflect a growth in the market for such music stimulated by the County, Rounder, and Gusto reissues. They mark a graduation to a more sophisticated approach to marketing, as the most popular artists now shape their products for specific audiences. Controlled by independents, the bluegrass record market is treated as an entity separate from live performance markets. Spacegrass is Tony Rice's bread and butter, and mainstream country Ricky Skaggs's, but there is still considerable benefit to recording music aimed at the smaller group of bluegrass followers. This is a more sensible way of dealing with appeals for stylistic purity than the earlier attempts to move, mold, and shape bluegrass followers as part of the larger audiences for commercial consumption; such attempts, like those of Flatt and Scruggs and others in the late sixties, generally alienated rather than converted the bluegrass enthusiasts. The professional musicians and independent labels have accepted the existence of the bluegrass consumer movement and recognized that though it is a relatively small group, it has effective power because it is organized and vocal, has access to media, and is the arbiter of a music form now viewed as an art, the jazz of country music. The believers to which Jayne and Cantwell referred have, in this sense, gotten their way.

Believers

Bluegrass, like all forms of show business, has had its share of fan clubs. Generally they have been headed by women and focused on the personalities of the performers, enthusiastically promoting all of their products. The Jim & Jesse Fan Club, whose president, Jean S. Osborn, has held that position since the fifties, stuck with Jim and Jesse throughout their stylistic changes of the late sixties, loyally defending them in the pages of *Bluegrass Unlimited* on several occasions. Fay McGinnis of the Stanley Brothers International Fan Club played an important part in helping to launch and promote Ralph Stanley following Carter's death.

But the bluegrass believers are cut from a somewhat different cloth. Their loyalty is not to the musicians but to a musical concept, an ideal against which they measure every bluegrass performance. The realization that such believers, their ranks swelled by new recruits from the festivals and the consumer movement, constitute an important part of the market for record sales, helped create the albums just described. Records play an important role in making the music accessible to isolated listeners, for, as *Muleskinner News'* Bartenstein found in 1974, bluegrass followers are everywhere a minority. Yet they are a larger minority in some places than in others.

The regions in which most bluegrass activity and interest can be found today are, not surprisingly, those in which the music was nurtured. If one draws 400-mile radius circles around four of the radio stations most active in the programming of bluegrass during the forties and fifties—WSM Nashville, WCYB Bristol, WCKY Cincinnati, and WWVA Wheeling—they encompass a territory which includes much of the eastern United States and a part of Canada. In the center is the upper South—Tennessee, North Carolina, Kentucky, West Virginia, Maryland, Delaware—plus the tier of states running east from Illinois—Indiana, Ohio, Pennsylvania, and New Jersey. To the south, portions of Mississippi, Alabama, Georgia, and Florida are touched; to the west parts of Louisiana, Arkansas, Missouri, and Iowa; to the north Wisconsin, Michigan, Ontario, and New York. Of 343 bluegrass festivals advertised for the 1979 season (in *Bluegrass Unlimited*), over half were held in eight states within this region—Ohio (34), North Carolina (28), Virginia (25), Georgia (22), Missouri (22), Alabama (21), Florida (17), and Kentucky (17). Bluegrass followers in these states could attend a festival virtually every weekend during the summer months.

With so many festivals taking place, demand is great for the best-known groups. In 1984 nationally popular acts like the Lewis Family, Doyle Lawson and Quicksilver, the Johnson Mountain Boys, the Osborne Brothers, Bill Monroe, Bill Harrell and the Virginians, the Country Gentlemen, Ralph Stanley, and Jim and Jesse can be found each weekend as headliners at festivals somewhere. Rarely do all of them appear at one festival; they usually share billing with somewhat lesser known groups or individuals with strong regional followings or historical reputations, such as Curly Seckler and the Nashville Grass (carrying on the legacy of Lester Flatt since his death in 1979), the Goins Brothers, Bob Paisley, Del McCoury, the Boys from Indiana, Raymond Fairchild and the Crowe Brothers, or Joe Stuart and Josh Graves. Also encountered are performers who straddle the lines between bluegrass and other forms. The close connections between country and bluegrass are reflected in festival appearances by former bluegrass artists, like

Ricky Skaggs and the Whites, who began their rise to prominence as Buck White and the Down Home Folks at bluegrass festivals in the sixties. Similarly, a number of groups once known as mainstream country performers now use bluegrass instrumentation; among them are Grand Ole Opry veterans Wilma Lee, and Lonzo and Oscar. Other overlapping areas are represented by performers such as Vassar Clements, Tony Trischka and Skyline, Peter Rowan, and the New Grass Revival, all of whom include bluegrass as part of musical performances shaped for the followers of folk, new acoustic, or rock music. Other festival drawing cards may be bands relatively new on the scene, like the Blanchard Valley Boys, winners of an important band contest at the Kentucky Fried Chicken Festival in Louisville in 1983 and booked at 1984 festivals on this basis; or veteran local groups moving to a national market, like Joe Val and the New England Bluegrass Boys out of Boston or High Country out of San Francisco.

Many festivals now share their headline performers with other events: Bill Monroe or the Osborne Brothers may appear one day at one festival and the next day at another in a neighboring state. A substantial number of the smaller festivals, however, book just one "name" group or none at all, depending instead upon regional and local bands, often semi-professionals, to fill out the bill. There are many more such groups now than ever before. The small festivals are sometimes organized by local promoters, sometimes by bands. During the late sixties and early seventies another important mechanism for festival organization emerged—the area committee or club.

One of the first of these was the Toronto Area Bluegrass Committee, formed in September 1968 by Doug Benson, a Quebec native who had been following bluegrass for over a decade at the time. He had attended the first bluegrass festivals and in 1967 initiated his own Canadian bluegrass journal, *Bluegrass Breakdown*. The southern Ontario region, of which Toronto is the metropolitan center, lay within the scope of the radio coverage mentioned earlier, and bluegrass bands from the U.S., particularly that of Bill Monroe, had occasionally played in the region. Local country musicians were playing bluegrass by the mid-fifties, and one of the first Canadian record companies to market albums of Canadian country music, Arc, included an album by a Toronto-based group, the York County Boys, among their first releases in 1959. As we have seen in chapter 6, bluegrass was included at the Mariposa Folk Festival near Toronto just as it was during the sixties at similar U.S. festivals.

In addition, the fifties and sixties had seen massive migrations of rural working-class people to the Toronto area from the maritime provinces of Nova Scotia, New Brunswick, and Prince Edward Island. Country music had long been popular in that region (home of Hank Snow and Wilf Carter, Canada's best-known country singers), and bluegrass groups toured and broadcast regularly there. During the fifties Jimmy Martin, Mac Wiseman, and Charlie Bailey had appeared in the maritimes, as had local bluegrass bands like Ray

Phillips and the River Valley Boys and Vic Mullen's Birch Mountain Boys. Hence bluegrass in Toronto was partly the music of rural migrants, just as it was in Detroit, Cincinnati, Pittsburgh, and the Washington, D.C., area.

During the sixties bluegrass was a component of folk revival interests among urban Toronto-area youth, and at the end of the decade a substantial number of younger Americans arrived in the city, having left the U.S. to avoid the draft. Among this group were some bluegrass followers. Hence when in 1968 Benson started the TABC he was aware of a potential community of bluegrass supporters. His goal was to organize them to help promote and develop the music locally.

An organizational meeting of twelve individuals led to the establishment of the TABC. A four-person executive group functioned on a pragmatic level (without a constitution at the outset) to manage the various events which the committee promoted. TABC was constituted as a non-profit organization. "You'd be surprised at the number of doors that are opened to a non-profit committee whose aim is the advancement of cultural activity," said Benson in an article on how to form an area bluegrass committee, in *Bluegrass Unlimited.*[17] The committee sponsored concerts, first by Canadian professionals like the York County Boys with Ron Scott, and the Southern Ramblers; then one by Ralph Stanley. In organizing these concerts, the members of the TABC acted as a collective, voting to cover losses out of their own pockets. They also had regular meetings to deal with committee business and to pick. The regular jam sessions reflected the central interest of the group—bringing together interested amateurs and semi-professionals to make music.

In subsequent years TABC would publish a newsletter, organize and direct bluegrass workshops at the Mariposa Folk Festivals, operate monthly jam sessions at various local taverns and coffeehouses, and continue to sponsor concerts. The committee lasted through the seventies, during which period the Ontario region experienced a mushrooming of festivals, including the large Bluegrass Canada events which began at Carlisle, Ontario, in 1972 and in which, during the early years, TABC played an organizing role in assisting promoter Jim Clark. During the same period changes in federal legislation concerning Canadian content in broadcasting helped subsidize the Canadian recording industry so that by the end of the decade a number of full-time professional bluegrass bands were working out of Ontario and recording on nationally distributed labels. By then the focus of bluegrass activity in the region had moved outside of Toronto to a number of smaller communities. In one such community, Waterdown, a national bluegrass magazine, *Canadian Bluegrass Review,* began publishing in 1978 on a semi-monthly basis. This, along with a number of new clubs in smaller communities, took over some of the functions of the TABC in Ontario bluegrass activities; the TABC published their last newsletter in 1980. That the club lasted as long as it did is remarkable, for it was basically a small operation which depended upon a few individuals to maintain it, and it died when deprived of their interest and energy.

Between the mid-seventies and the early eighties bluegrass area committees, clubs, and similar organizations existed in at least twenty-seven states and three Canadian provinces. Among these were several large urban clubs, like the Boston Area Friends of Bluegrass and Old-Time Country Music, established in 1969, which presented concerts, sold records and books to members at discounts, and held jam sessions. The moving force behind this group was Nancy Talbott, who in 1976 began the much acclaimed Berkshire Mountains Festival. In its early and most active years the BAF included members of the Rounder Collective and *Muleskinner News* editor Fred Bartenstein. Another urban organization active in the early seventies was Douglas Tuchman's New York Bluegrass Club, which put on concerts, a festival, and informal musical get-togethers. Record and magazine connections existed here as in Boston: Tuchman's work with the club led to his editorship at *Pickin'* and County's David Freeman was an active member of the club until his move to Virginia in 1974.

These urban organizations were unusual in their size, concentration, and access to media resources. Much more common were groups headquartered in small towns and rural locales. A number of states have or had more than one club; at various times there have been five active in Texas and five in New York state; four each in Florida, Missouri, and Oklahoma; three each in Indiana and California. These statistics indicate that the kind of interest needed to sustain clubs is most often encountered in the peripheral areas, in locales where there has been some exposure to bluegrass over a long period but which are not saturated with festivals and bands. Larry McPeak, one of the McPeak Brothers, a progressive band from Virginia with albums on RCA and County, speaks of the difference from a performance perspective: "In the mid South, the Virginias, the Carolinas and in Georgia, they hear *so much* bluegrass that they get worked up but they don't really get into it like the people do, say in Florida. Those people down there—they flat let you know in a hurry if they like you. That's some of the finest bluegrass people in the world because they don't have that many good bluegrass groups *in* Florida."[18]

Although some of the clubs publish newsletters, promote festivals, and arrange concerts, *all* are involved in arranging situations for members to play music regularly—picking or jam sessions. This is the primary purpose of most of the smaller rural associations, which are often little more than formal versions of a widespread North American folk tradition, the jam session.

The kernel of this tradition is a regular meeting—weekly or monthly—at which all musicians are encouraged to participate. The session may be held in a private home, a garage, a barn, a closed gas station or barbershop, a school, or a hall. Shaped by the musical tastes of the participants, jam session repertoires usually include the folk dance repertoire, performed on fiddles, along with folk- and country-music-derived songs performed to guitar accompaniment. Other musical streams—popular, rock, jazz, ethnic—may also be represented depending upon region. Emphasis is upon egalitarian music-making: younger musicians who are just learning are encouraged to attend and participate. At such sessions, audiences are not generally expected or catered to although a few friends of the musicians may drop in occasionally. Some jam sessions have developed into regular, though informal, concerts or dances.

This format lends itself well to bluegrass, and by the end of the seventies, many such jam sessions, whether organized by clubs or run by individuals, had incorporated bluegrass repertoire and technique. This was possible because bluegrass, once a form accessible only to a few skilled professionals, was now easily learned. Songbooks perpetuated the repertoire, and there were now many instruction books and tape courses, as well as a growing number of musicians able to teach the methodology. The musicians who played in jam sessions like these and in the campground and parking-lot sessions at festivals were frequently also involved in semi-professional or amateur bands. Many such groups produced albums; reviews by bluegrass magazines were seldom very positive about them, for these musicians were recording the same old songs and arrangements, and there was little innovation. The record would appeal to the friends and fans of the band but presented nothing new for the collectors of bluegrass records.

That the sound and repertoire of many of these groups playing bluegrass on an amateur or semi-professional basis was often derivative and predictable shows the success of the festival and consumer movements in preserving and promoting the music. Today bluegrass is in many ways more of a traditional art than it was when the folk revivalists discovered it. Like most traditional art forms, its persistence is best guaranteed if the practitioners agree to certain conservative restraints. But these tend to limit its commercial viability, for commercial art is supposed to be innovative, attracting new consumers with its changes. By the beginning of the eighties those involved with the marketing of the music had become more sophisticated about this conflict, accepting the fact that full-time professionals had to vary their music in order to achieve commercial viability.

In the meantime bluegrass repertoire and technique had diffused to a variety of places sometimes far removed from the music's origins. For example, a folklorist studying Finnish-American musical traditions in northern Wisconsin and Michigan's Upper Peninsula noted that the fiddlers, who had some classical training, played pop-jazz tunes, Finnish dance music, and, most recently, "bluegrass music which they learned from books and records."[19] Bluegrass clubs, festivals, and jam sessions afforded "umbrellas" for other forms of music with limited commercial viability. Under their auspices came other forms of music which were predominantly acoustic, viewed by their followers as art forms—jazz, folk revival, older country music, regional and ethnic folk musics, and fiddle music. While the festivals and clubs have tended to take a relatively purist approach to bluegrass, like that of *Bluegrass Unlimited*, around them has clustered a larger group representative of the readership of *Frets, Old Time Music,* and *The Devil's Box.*

As we have seen, many of the best-known full-time professionals have increasingly turned to the strategy of separating their bluegrass performances from activities in other more lucrative genres. Amateurs, on the other hand, have tended to mix bluegrass with other musics. Esthetics and taste shape such eclecticism on the part of amateurs. Their mixing and the separate performances of the pros have made bluegrass an important force in the North American music scene: it underlies, subsumes, or colors portions of a number of commercial and folk musics, acting as a channel between them in terms of technique and repertoire. There are many more musicians and singers who do *some* bluegrass than ones who do nothing but bluegrass. In fact it is probably best to view intensive involvement in bluegrass as an exceptional activity more typical of the neophyte musician than of the experienced one.

Today the community of bluegrass musicians is much more diverse than in the fifties and sixties. Local and regional scenes in all parts of North America and beyond have contributed instrumentalists and singers. One example is Akira Otsuka, who came in the early seventies to the U.S. with the Bluegrass 45 from Japan (they made two Rebel albums) and remained to play brilliant mandolin in a series of Washington-area bands, including that of Cliff Waldron. Another is singer-songwriter Phil Rosenthal, a Connecticut native who took John Starling's place in the Seldom Scene in 1977, having already contributed songs to their repertoire. It seems good pickers and singers can start their bluegrass careers almost anywhere. At the same time, there is little doubt that in the upper and middle Southeast there is more activity on the local level in bluegrass today than ever before or in any other regions. There, the large number of festivals and bands has led to a situation in which more youngsters are exposed to the skills of the music at an early age. There also is a growing number of bands comprised of family units, and in this context one most frequently encounters women, who were practically unknown as bluegrass musicians prior to the beginning of the festival movement.

Bluegrass has moved from being a minor sub-genre within country music to an officially recognized art form. Bluegrass musicians and bands now perform in various state and regional school programs, presenting the music in a historical setting to students who are thus introduced to it as a legitimate art form with folk and popular connections. Several colleges have included bluegrass in the curriculum, not just in extension programs (of which there are many) but also as part of professional musical training, as at South Plains State College in Plains, Texas. Another sign of recognition and legitimization can be seen in appearances which two bluegrass bands, the Osborne Brothers and the McLain Family, now regularly make with symphony orchestras. Concern about preserving and presenting the music's historical aspects in an educational format is reflected in several museums: the Bill Monroe Bluegrass Hall of Fame and Museum, which opened in Nashville in April 1984, and the Kentucky Bluegrass Music Center, under development in Louisville. Public broadcasting has also had an important part through radio and television in presenting bluegrass within an educational matrix as a national art form. In this sense again, the consumer movement and the festivals have done what they set out to do—preserve and promote. While bluegrass may never have the total national success and big hits that most of its ardent supporters have hoped for, it seems assured of a future for the very reason that the hits will be difficult to achieve: it has become openly articulated and defined as a traditional art form which cannot tolerate too much deviation. While some innovation is now accepted as part of bluegrass, anything likely to gain mass success would probably be considered not really bluegrass. As long as there are believers around, this paradox will sustain their hopes.

Notes

1. Mitch Jayne, "Observations: The Dillards, Music and Blue Grass," p. 13.
2. Fred Bartenstein, "The Audience for Bluegrass," p. 74.
3. [masthead], *Pickin'* 4 (Dec. 1977): 2.
4. Jim Crockett, "From the Publisher," p. 3.
5. Robert Carlin, "The Small Specialty Record Company in the United States," p. 68.
6. Bartenstein, "The Audience," p. 88.
7. Editorial in the *Rounder Review* 4 (Oct. 1972): 2.
8. Review in the *Rounder Review* 2 (Feb. 1972): 1.
9. Carlin, "The Small Specialty Record Company," p. 67.
10. David Freeman, editorial in *County Sales Newsletter* 68 (Sept. 1974): 1.
11. [Eddie Birt,] "CMH Records," p. 18.
12. Gary Henderson interview, Apr. 10, 1977.
13. David Freeman, editorial in *County Sales Newsletter* 88 (June-July 1977): 2.
14. David Freeman, review in *County Sales Newsletter* 103 (June-July 1979): 7.
15. Kip Kirby, "Hot Catalog a Sugar Hill Asset."
16. Jim Hatlo, "On Record," 59.
17. Doug Benson, "How to Form an Area Bluegrass Committee," p. 6.
18. Rhonda Strickland, "The McPeak Brothers," p. 15.
19. Matthew Gallmann, "Matti Pelto: Finnish-American Button Accordion Player," p. 43.

Bibliographical Notes

Senator Robert C. Byrd's remarks in the Senate on February 6, 1978, in which he praised Gary Henderson and mentioned his forthcoming County album, appeared in the *Congressional Record,* March 15, 1978, S3722-23. President Carter's barbecue at which Rinzler served as emcee for Watson and Monroe was reported in Carla Hall, "Friendly Feast: The Carters Find Support in Their Own Backyard."

June Apple is the best known of the Japanese bluegrass magazines. *Canadian Bluegrass Review* has appeared six times a year since 1978. *The British Bluegrass and Old Time Music Journal* began in 1979; by 1982 it had become *British Bluegrass News.* Also from Britain is *'Grass Scene,* which first appeared in 1983.

There are now many instruction books on the market. In 1978–79 Oak Publications issued a Bluegrass Masters series, including five titles—Tony Trischka and Bill Keith, *Bill Keith Banjo;* Russ Barenberg, *Clarence White Guitar;* David Brody, *Kenny Baker Fiddle;* Andy Statman, *Jesse McReynolds Mandolin;* and Matt Glasser, *Vassar Clements Fiddle.*

The very first book on bluegrass music appeared in Japan—Toru Mitsui's *Burugurasu Ongaku* [*Bluegrass Music*] of 1967. A revised and enlarged second edition was issued in 1975 by a Tokyo publisher. For descriptions of the contents of these books, see my reviews of both editions in the *JEMF Quarterly.* A more recent popular history is Fred Hill, *Grass Roots,* subtitled "An Illustrated History of Bluegrass and Mountain Music."

The chronicle of the company which produced the standard bluegrass guitar is Mike Longworth's *Martin Guitars, A History.* It was published, as was Siminoff's *Constructing a Bluegrass Mandolin,* by the press which put out *Pickin'.* The standard banjos and mandolins came from Gibson; see Tom Morgan, "Gibson Banjo Information" and three pieces by Roger Siminoff— "Gibson: The Early Years," "Gibson (Part II)," and "The Gibson Banjos, Twenty Golden Years." These are the most substantial surveys; the various bluegrass periodicals are filled with shorter surveys, as well as articles dealing with specific models.

During the seventies the interest in collecting the older bluegrass instruments created demand which helped create and sustain a number of instrument dealers. One was Mandolin Brothers in the New York area. See Steve Arkin, "An Interview with the Mandolin Brothers," and Marc Horowitz, "Mandolin Bros." George Gruhn, of Nashville's GTR, later developed his own business and has written interestingly in several magazines about the old instruments. An early example is his "A Brief Guide to Blue Grass Instruments."

The pioneer in the building of reproductions of the old bluegrass instruments, particularly banjos and mandolins, was Tom Morgan. See Tom

Foote, "Interview: Tom Morgan"; Gary Henderson, "Tom Morgan"; and Richard McFalls, "Tom Morgan: Patriarch of Bluegrass Luthiers." Morgan tells his own story in "Love Affair with a Taterbug (A Chronology)." For similar figures see Kathryn Fanning, "Gary Price: Banjo Man," and Ray Alden, "Craftsmen and Creativity."

The processes underlying the adaptation of the mandolin into country and bluegrass music were examined in Scott Hambly, "Mandolins in the United States: An Industrial and Sociological History since 1880."

The appearance of new banjos competing with Gibson's in the late sixties was the catalyst for Bill Emerson's three-part series, "A Comparative Analysis of Current Banjos." Stelling Banjos is the topic of Jim Hatlo, "*Frets* Visits . . . Spring Valley, CA., Stelling Banjo Works"; George Martin, "Stelling Banjo Works" and "Stelling Mandolins—A New Direction"; and Hub Nitchie, "Interview: Geoff Stelling." Stelling's difficulties in dealing with a batch of defective paint from a major manufacturer—-it nearly put Stelling out of business—are described in Ed Schilling, "Lutherie's Day in Court." For other new manufacturers see John Southern, "Old-Fashioned Craftsmanship: Mossman Guitars"; Robert Gruene, "Unicorn Mandolins"; and Rolfe Gerhardt, "The Blue Grass Mandolin." Yairi of Alvarez-Yairi is described, and some information on the Japanese instrument business given, in Mark Andrews, "A Look at a Japanese Guitar Maker." For a joint Japanese-American venture see Jody B. Larson, "Building the J. D. Crowe Model Gold Star Banjo."

A more recent survey of the *Frets* readership confirms the leading position of bluegrass among the interests of that group. See Jim Crockett, "From the Publisher: Who Are You."

Robert Carlin's article on folk record companies was reprinted with an updated conclusion in *Pickin'* during 1977. Thomas A. Adler's "Bluegrass Recordings" reviews trends in the late seventies and early eighties. Comparing the perspectives of full-time professionals with those of parking-lot pickers, Adler describes bluegrass as "a vernacular musical system."

Among the articles on Ricky Skaggs, the most important from a bluegrass perspective are Jim Hatlo, "Ricky Skaggs: Bluegrass Prodigy Comes of Age"; Robert K. Oermann, "Ricky Skaggs Remembers the Stanley Brothers"; Steve Price, "Ricky Skaggs—Portrait of a Young Bluegrass Musician"; and Jack Tottle, "Ricky Skaggs: Clinch Mountain to Boone Creek." For Dobroist Douglas, Skaggs's contemporary and partner in several groups, see Jan Campbell, "Jerry Douglas: They Call Him Flux"; and Jim Hatlo, "Jerry Douglas, Dobro Dynamo." Seldom Scene Dobroist Mike Auldridge is the subject of Ed Davis's "Auldridge: Tops with Dobro"; Byron Merritt and Keith Fields's "If You Can't Pick, Bring Spoons!" and Roger H. Siminoff, "Mike Auldridge." The McLain Family of Kentucky has been described in Chandler Davis, "Bluegrass Family—Family Bluegrass"; Marty Godbey, "The McLain Family Band"; Marilyn Kochman, "The McLain Family Band"; and

Stephanie P. Ledgin, "On the Road and Off." Del McCoury's career has been outlined in articles by Eugenia Snyder, Gwen Taylor, and Bill Vernon; all were titled, "Del McCoury."

An excellent study of John Morris that explains his importance as a dee-jay is Atelia Clarkson and W. Lynwood Montell, "Letters to a Bluegrass DJ." Also about Morris are Barbara Zill, "John Morris Talks about Old Home-stead Records"; and Eric Zorn, "A 'Homestead' for Using Talent."

A useful discussion of the processes whereby older recordings have been republished is Scott Hambly's "Flatt and Scruggs Releases, Re-Releases, and Reissues."

In addition to the citation in the bibliographical notes to chapter 6, see Nancy and Dick Kimmel, "Joe Val and the New England Bluegrass Boys." On the Bluegrass Cardinals, see Frank Godbey, "Who in the World Are the Bluegrass Cardinals?" Richard D. Smith, "The Bluegrass Cardinals on the Wing"; Vicki Westover and Kathy Plunkett, "The Traditionalist Bluegrass Cardinals Prepare to Join Washington's Select List"; and Brett F. Devan, "The Bluegrass Cardinals." For Bill Harrell's post-Reno band, see Don Rhodes, "Bill Harrell." For information on Dave Evans, see Herschel Free-man, "Dave Evans: The Voice of Traditional Bluegrass." "The Dry Branch Fire Squad" by Sharon Wright introduces the members of that group and mentions Thomason's emcee work. On Hot Rize, see Dick Kimmel, "Hot Rize: Pete Wernick's Secret Ingredient"; for Spectrum, Marty Godbey, "Spectrum"; and William E. Lightfoot, "Playing Outside: Spectrum." Quick-silver has been covered by Jack Tottle, "Doyle Lawson and Quicksilver"; the Johnson Mountain Boys in Don Rhodes's "Band on the Run."

The growth of Sugar Hill is described by Wayne Erbsen, "Barry Poss and Sugar Hill Records." Contemporary record making frequently involves an independent production which is then sold to an established label. In many ways this differs from the way small local productions are done only in terms of the scale of the costs. For a discussion of record making geared to this lower-level activity, see Dave Samuelson's two-part "Making a Record."

Also in two parts is Jack Tottle's description of "Berline, Crary and Hick-man." Articles on Tony Rice include Pat Chappelle, "Twice as Rice"; Mark Hunter, "Tony Rice"; Jon Sievert, "Tony Rice"; and Jack Tottle, "Tony Rice."

The February 1984 issue of *Frets* was substantially devoted to "New Acoustic Music," with four articles on the topic as well as a number of regular columns by contributors ("workshops") dealing with aspects of this musical genre.

Information on Emmylou Harris comes from Jas Obrecht, "Emmylou Har-ris: A Pro Replies," and Richard Harrington, "Emmylou Harris."

From the middle sixties until the middle seventies Fay McGinnis headed the Stanley Brothers (later Ralph Stanley) International Fan Club, editing its publication, *The Stanley Standard*. Norm Carlson frequently contributed to this irregular and miscellaneous mimeographed journal. In 1967 he published "The Fan Club and the Folk Scholar" in it. He discussed the differences between these two points of view indicating his commitment to the fan club perspective. There he pledged to work for the preservation of bluegrass, a stance which took him beyond the typical fan club orientation toward personality. Carlson was an uncommon fan in many ways, but his viewpoint was echoed by other fans of specific bluegrass bands who, at this time, tended to move beyond fanship to become believers in bluegrass.

An early piece by fan club president Jean S. Osborn, "Jim and Jesse— 'The Virginia Boys'," appeared in *Disc Collector.*

The festival statistics given in this chapter are based on listings and advertisements in *Bluegrass Unlimited* during 1979. I have not included one-day events or festivals which had bluegrass along with other types of music (as, for example, folk festivals) or as part of a non-musical presentation (like a craft fair). Hence the figures I use are conservative. The 1983 festival listings in the March issue of *Bluegrass Unlimited* total 490 events. I have encountered claims of over 700 bluegrass festivals a year.

In my discussion of bands performing at festivals in 1984, I have mentioned those groups which appear most frequently in advertisements and listings in the May 1984 issue of *Bluegrass Unlimited.* Most have been discussed elsewhere in this book; several have not. Longtime Flatt and Scruggs sideman Curly Seckler took over Flatt's band on his death; see Barry Silver, "Curly Seckler." Kentuckians the Goins Brothers, cited in the bibliographical notes to chapter 4 for their role in the Lonesome Pine Fiddlers, have been active since the early seventies on their own: see Marty Godbey, "The Goins Brothers." Singer and guitarist Bob Paisley worked for years with banjoist Ted Lundy, recording for Rounder; see Lucy Hunsicker, "Ted Lundy, Bob Paisley and the Southern Mountain Boys." In 1979 Paisley formed his own band, as related in Alan J. Steiner, "Bob Paisley and the Southern Grass." Also active through the seventies and into the eighties were the Boys from Indiana. See Judith A. Feller and Marty Godbey's articles "The Boys from Indiana" as well as Ivan Tribe's "Old Actors in a New Play: The Boys from Indiana." Eccentric banjoist Raymond Fairchild has been profiled in Wayne Erbsen, "Raymond Fairchild: Making His Own Way"; Frank Fletcher, "Raymond Fairchild: The Young-Old Man of the Mountains"; and Ivan M. Tribe, "Someone Really Different: Raymond Fairchild." Joe Stuart, who played with Bill Monroe at various times from the mid-fifties to the mid-seventies, is the subject of Judy Paris's "Joe Stuart, On. . . . " In 1984 he was appearing at festivals with former Flatt and Scruggs sideman Josh Graves. In addition to the citation for Graves in chapter 11, see Wayne W. Daniel, "Josh Graves"; and George Martin, "Josh Graves." The Whites are discussed below in connection with family bands; for other articles on the group see Douglas Green, "Buck White and the Down Homers," and Boris Weintraub, "Buck White and the Down-Home Folks." Wilma Lee's recent career is the subject of Wayne W. Daniel's "Wilma Lee Cooper: America's Most Authentic Mountain Singer." Opry members since the forties, comedians Lonzo and Oscar only recently became associated with bluegrass as Doug Green shows in "Lonzo and Oscar Join the World of Bluegrass." New acoustic banjoist Tony Trischka and his band are the subject of Richard D. Smith, "The Skyline's No Limit." Active since the early seventies, High Country was the subject of an article near the start of its career by George Martin, "High Country."

Statistics on clubs and committees are imprecise. I synthesized my figures from a series of monthly columns published in *Pickin'* during the mid-seventies, supplementing these from the monthly "Now Appearing: Bluegrass Music" column in *Bluegrass Unlimited*. A list published by the Library of Congress was useful: Kathryn W. Hickerson and Kathleen Condon, comps., *Folklore and Ethnomusicology Societies in North America.*

For additional information on the TABC, see Doug Benson, "TABC Part One: The Ontario Bluegrass Scene: Then and Now," and Chuck Crawford, "TABC Part Two: Toronto Area Bluegrass Committee, Years—1973 to 1978." Nancy Cardwell, "Missouri Area Bluegrass Committee: Success Story," tells of a group similar in age and history to the TABC. An early report on the Boston activities is Nancy Talbott, "The Boston Blue Grass Scene." Doug Tuchman is described in John Rockwell, "Bluegrass Hitting High Note Tonight."

Observations on jam sessions are based on my own field research in Indiana and eastern Canada. The only studies I know of on such events are Bert Feintuch, "Sointula: A Finnish Community in British Columbia," and Philip Nusbaum, "Traditionalizing the Session: Ongoing Activities, Behavior, Music and Friendship Relations." A study of a local weekly show, The Lucy Opry, which has important jam session dimensions, is Tony Hale's "Grassroots Bluegrass in Memphis."

The spread of bluegrass beyond its earliest geographical and cultural contexts is discussed in theoretical terms by Thomas Adler, "The Concept of Nidality and its Potential Application to Folklore." A number of studies and reports offer quite varied illustrations of this process. Bob Doyle reports on a study of the fiddle traditions in a region adjacent to the southern Appalachians, showing how bluegrass coexists with various older fiddle traditions: "The Traditional Music of Central Pennsylvania." In "Bluegrass Music in the Great Plains," Michael D. Patrick considers the meaning of southern references in bluegrass lyrics for the urban descendants of rural southerners who migrated to the Great Plains region. Two who have looked at the northern California Bay Area region and found great cultural differences are Toni Brown and Scott Hambly. Brown's brief and impressionistic "Can Blue Grass Grow in City Streets?" of 1964 is in a sense answered by Hambly's detailed and scholarly "San Francisco Bay Area Bluegrass and Bluegrass Musicians: A Study in Regional Characteristics" of 1980.

Among the descriptions of bluegrass outside North America are Antony
Hale's "A Comparison of Bluegrass Diffusion in the United States and New
Zealand," Hedley Charles and Bob McCarthy's "A Brief Look at Bluegrass in
Australia," and John E. Hopkins, "The British Bluegrass Scene."

For Japanese mandolinist Otsuka, see the articles about The Blue Grass
45 cited in the bibliographical notes to chapter 10. Information on Phil
Rosenthal comes from Jim Hatlo, "Phil Rosenthal."

The most successful family band doing secular music in which women
have a central role is the Whites. The group, which consists of White and
his two daughters, has in recent years achieved more success in country
music than in bluegrass. Earlier they encountered some reluctance on the
part of bluegrass fans to accept women as bluegrass musicians. See Sharon
White's comments in Doug Tuchman, "Buck White and the Down-Home
Folks," p. 10. For other statements on the same topic see Patty Hall, "The
Writing on the Wall . . . Women and Bluegrass"; and Mia Boynton, "Sugar
in the Gourd," *BU* 12 (Oct. 1977): 6.

South Plains College's curriculum is described by Dianne Whisenand
Lawson, "South Plains Bluegrass." The dean of college relations at South
Plains, Eddie Trice, collaborated with Opry star Tom T. Hall to produce a
bluegrass program at the 1979 Early Bird concert in Nashville. See Bonnie
Smith, "Bluegrass Spectacular: A Television First." Another example of
bluegrass on educational television is given in Marty Godbey, "Bluegrass,
Bluegrass . . . A Television Series." National Public Radio has also publicized bluegrass in special programs such as the series "A Bluegrass Hornbook," broadcast in 1976. See Michael Weiss, "A Bluegrass Hornbook";
Leon Smith, "Talking with the Stars"; and "Summer Bluegrass from National Public Radio."

The ambivalence with which bluegrass fans view success or its possibility
can be seen in many articles. Pete Kuykendall's " 'Starvin' to Death' " argued that many of the influential early bluegrass performances—those
which inspired others to help create the genre—were made by musicians
who were economically, if not literally, starving. My "Bluegrass and Serendipity" stressed the preference for encountering the music in obscurity rather
than being deluged with it. In "Pick a Peck of Parking Lot Pickers," Judy
Paris documented the feelings of bluegrass musicians (including some well-
known professionals) about their preference for informal jam sessions over
formal concerts. See also Richard Blaustein, "Will Success Spoil Old Time
Fiddling and Bluegrass?" and Hub Nitchie, "Can Bluegrass Survive
Popularity?"

Discographical Notes

Senator Byrd's album was titled *Mountain Fiddler*. The three-disc Japanese
set which appeared following publication of the Bill Monroe discography

(its notes presented much of the discography in tabular form) was *Bill Monroe and His Blue Grass Boys, vol. 2, 1950–1972.*

Rounder's first three Nashville albums were Tut Taylor's *Friar Tut,* Norman Blake's *Back Home in Sulphur Springs,* and Pete Kirby's *Brother Oswald.* During the next two years came Vassar Clements's *Crossing the Catskills* and Tony Trischka's *Bluegrass Light.*

Mike Auldridge's two albums for Takoma were *Dobro* and *Blues and Blue Grass.* David Grisman's first solo album was the *Rounder Album;* Rice's (for Rebel), *Tony Rice.*

Flatt's Flying Fish album was *Lester Raymond Flatt;* the New Grass Revival's first, *Fly through the Country.* Hartford's debut on the label was *Mark Twang.*

Jim and Jesse's first on their own label was *Superior Sounds of Bluegrass;* the McLain Family began on their own label with *The McLain Family Band.* Jimmy Martin's first on Gusto was *Me 'n' Old Pete.*

Flying Fish's 1977 releases included the New Grass Revival's *When the Storm is Over,* the Dillards' *The Dillards vs. the Incredible L. A. Time Machine,* Mike Auldridge's *Mike Auldridge,* Vassar Clements's *The Bluegrass Sessions* and the Country Gazette's *Out to Lunch.*

Debut albums by bluegrass groups on CMH included *The Mac Wiseman Story,* Lester Flatt's *A Living Legend,* Reno and Harrell's *The Don Reno Story,* Carl Story's *Bluegrass Gospel Collection,* Benny Martin's *The Fiddle Collection,* The Osborne Brothers' *Number One,* II Generation's *State of Mind,* and the Stonemans' *Cuttin' the Grass.*

The Pinnacle Boys, *Take a Look and Listen to . . . ,* and James Monroe, *Midnight Blues,* were the first albums by each on Atteiram. Early Revonah albums included *Del McCoury and the Dixie Pals* and the Shenandoah Cutups' *Bluegrass Autumn.* The Country Gazette's *What a Way to Make a Living* was their first for Ridge Runner. Ralph Stanley did *The Bluegrass Sound* for Jalyn. The Hot Mud Family's *Till We Meet Here Again . . .* was their first on Vetco; *The Bluegrass Touch,* Earl Taylor's first on that label. Old Homestead's Wade Mainer album *Sacred Songs of Mother and Home* was a reissue of some of his late thirties and early forties Bluebird recordings. Newly recorded was their Larry Sparks album, *Bluegrass Old and New.*

Rounder's leased reissues of the Lilly Brothers' *Bluegrass Breakdown* and *Country Songs* were followed in 1977 by the two authorized Flatt and Scruggs reissues: County's *The Golden Years* and Rounder's *The Golden Era.*

The two albums featuring older bluegrass repertoire which the Osborne Brothers made for CMH were *The Osborne Brothers' Bluegrass Collection* and *The Essential Bluegrass Album* (with Mac Wiseman). Joe Val's fourth for Rounder, *Bound to Ride,* was released in 1979; Sparks recorded for many labels during the seventies; his first for Rebel was *John Deere Tractor* in 1980. The Bluegrass Cardinals' Rounder album was *Welcome to Virginia;* their next, on CMH, *Livin' in the Good Ole Days.* Boone Creek too started on Rounder, with *Boone Creek*, and then was featured on Sugar Hill's first album, *One Way Track*. Harrell's Rebel album was *I Can Hear Virginia Calling Me*; his *The L&N Don't Stop Here Anymore* was one of his most popular for Leather. Dave Evans's Vetco opener was *Highway 52*. The Dry Branch Fire Squad's first Rounder album, issued in 1979, was *Born to Be Lonesome*. Hot Rize's first album was titled *Hot Rize*; the band name comes from an ingredient in Martha White Flour, named in Flatt and Scruggs's singing ads of the fifties and sixties. Spectrum's debut album for Rounder was titled *Opening Roll*; Doyle Lawson's band on Sugar Hill, *Quicksilver*. Released at about the same time by Rounder was *The Johnson Mountain Boys*. Ricky Skaggs's first solo album was *That's It! Sweet Temptation*, from which the single of "I'll Take the Blame" was taken, was his Sugar Hill album.

Berline, Crary, and Hickman's Rounder albums, issued simultaneously, were *Dad's Favorites, Lady's Fancy,* and *Don't Mean Maybe*. Doyle Lawson's County instrumental album was titled *Tennessee Dream*. David Grisman's first album totally in his own style was *The David Grisman Quintet*; his next was the major-label *Hot Dawg*. Rice's somewhat similar new acoustic sound was heard first on *Mar West*.

Ricky Skaggs's first Epic album was *Waitin' for the Sun to Shine*; his second, *Highways and Heartaches*. Late in 1983 a third album appeared; *Don't Cheat in Our Hometown* was recorded shortly after *Sweet Temptation* and bore the Sugar Hill logo as well as that of Epic. In content, it was even more blue-grass-oriented than the first two Epics, with no less than half its songs from the Stanley Brothers. The Skaggs and Rice duet album was titled *Skaggs and Rice*.

Crowe et al's *The Bluegrass Album* has had two sequels—the first called volume 2; the second, volume 3, subtitled *California Connection*.

Kenny Baker at Ralph Stanley's Third Annual Memorial Bluegrass Festival, McClure, Virginia, May 24-27, 1973. [Photo by Carl Fleischhauer]

RALPH STANLEY & HIS CLINCH MOUNTAIN BOYS

Curley Ray Cline   Melvin Goins   Larry Sparks   Ralph Stanley

A 1968 souvenir picture: Larry Sparks is proudly holding the late Carter Stanley's guitar, now in the Country Music Hall of Fame Museum in Nashville. [Author's personal collection]

Ricky Skaggs, Ralph Stanley, and Keith Whitley at Carter Stanley Memorial Bluegrass Festival, McClure, Virginia, May 24-27, 1972. [Photo by Carl Fleischhauer]

January 20, 1969: Flatt and Scruggs and the Oxon Hill Cloggers representing the Opry on the state of Tennessee's float at the inaugural parade of Richard M. Nixon. A few months later Scruggs was in Washington again, playing with his sons at a Vietnam moratorium rally. [Courtesy of the Country Music Foundation Library and Media Center, Nashville, Tennessee]

The Earl Scruggs Revue at Monroe's Bean Blossom Festival, June 1970: Randy, Earl, and Gary Scruggs. [Photo by Carl Fleischhauer]

Jim and Jesse fan club president Jean Osborne is flanked by Jesse (l.) and Jim (r.) McReynolds in an informal snapshot from 1965. [Courtesy of the Country Music Foundation Library and Media Center, Nashville, Tennessee]

During the summer of 1972 the TABC presented a jam session along with a concert by a local band, the Bluegrass Revival, at the Yonge Street Festival's pedestrian mall in the center of downtown Toronto. Bob Forrest of the Bluegrass Revival, banjo, jams with Jim Hale, guitar. [Photo by Doug Benson]

Nashville, 1971: a scene from the Nitty Gritty Dirt Band recording sessions at the Woodland Sound Studios—producer Bill McEwen with Roy Acuff and Earl Scruggs. [Courtesy of the Country Music Foundation Library and Media Center, Nashville, Tennessee]

John Hartford, Gram Parsons, Chris Hillman, and Roger McGuinn at Columbia's Nashville studio during the recording of the Byrds' *Sweetheart of the Rodeo* album. [Courtesy of John Hartford]

The Country Gazette at the Kerrville Bluegrass and Country Music Festival, Kerrville, Texas, September 2, 1974: Alan Munde, Byron Berline, Roger Bush, Roland White. [Photo by Rick Gardner, courtesy of Byron Berline]

Rebel Records founder Dick Freeland at the *Bluegrass Unlimited* Second Annual Indian Springs Bluegrass Festival, Indian Springs, Maryland, June 1-3, 1973. [Photo by Carl Fleischhauer]

Los Angeles bluegrass producer Jim Dickson (r.) with his partner, Ed Tickner, at the Palomino Club in North Hollywood, California, October 22, 1979. [Photo by Carl Fleischhauer]

Gary Henderson doing his "Stained Glass Bluegrass" show at WAMU-FM in Georgetown, Sunday, March 27, 1977. [Photo by Carl Fleischhauer]

John Kaparakis, Akira Otsuka, Tony Trischka, and Gary Henderson in a round-table discussion at WAMU-FM, April 10, 1977. [Photo by Carl Fleischhauer]

David Grisman and Tony Rice playing with the David Grisman Quintet, Great American Music Hall, December 31, 1978. [Photo by Jon Sievert]

Tony Rice and Ricky Skaggs during the recording session for Rice's album *Manzanita*, January 1978. [Photo by Jon Sievert]

The Rounder Collective in their first office in Somerville, Massachusetts, in 1971: Ken Irwin, Marion Leighton, Bill Nowlin. Behind them on the wall are the covers of the first five Rounder albums. [Photo by Carl Fleischhauer]

Sugar Hill founder Barry Poss with Doyle Lawson and engineer Bill McElroy at Bias Recording Studio, Springfield, Virginia, during the recording of Lawson and Quicksilver's gospel album, *Rock My Soul*, November 20, 1980. [Photo by Carl Fleischhauer]

Bibliography

The following bibliography contains all the substantive pieces cited in this book's text, chapter notes, and bibliographical notes. As such it reflects the problems encountered in studying a relatively new vernacular musical form and the strategies developed to deal with those problems.

As the word *bluegrass* did not appear in print to describe this music until 1957, and an extensive literature about the music did not develop until the 1970s, most of the early works cited are more or less ephemeral documents—trade or fan publications. There are also a few scholarly items—folksong collections, sociological studies, etc.—from earlier dates. But the bulk of the material cited comes from books, journals, record album notes, and, most substantially, magazines of the past two decades. It represents the work of journalists, enthusiasts, professional musicians, promoters, and others involved in the music business; to these can be added the work of a few professional scholars, mainly from the fields of folklore, history, and cultural geography.

The most frequently cited magazines are *Bluegrass Unlimited, Frets, Muleskinner News,* and *Pickin'*. These and others like them contain a variety of materials, of which the most useful for this work have been the historically oriented biographical articles. Usually presented as interviews, these constitute a popular version of that form of historical narrative known today as oral history. Created with the aid of tape-recorded interviews which are then edited, usually topically or chonologically, they present an anecdotal biography. (For a useful discussion of the distinctions between oral biography, autobiography, and history, see Jeff Todd Titon's "The Life Story.")

At their best, these articles present detailed portraits of individuals and convey a strong impression of the texture of social and musical experience. Whether sketchy or detailed, however, as documents they have certain biases and limitations. For example, many tend to telescope, reorganize, or warp the chronological framework. More importantly, they represent the testimony of people who have a stake in making the historical record come out in their favor. I have sought to minimize these problems in several ways. First, I have compared different versions of biographical interviews of the same individual in competing magazines. Through a single individual's retellings a kind of consensus appears: different interviews focus on special kinds of detail, and performers change their stories more or less from one telling to the next. Still, professional performers are interviewed frequently and thus tend to organize their memories into a colorful personal mythology for the media. This is useful in itself as long as it is understood for what it is, a document of belief and self-image. But often it is not possible to make such accounts of a significant event by different participants quite tally. This is to be expected when studying events in which there are conflicting personalities and motives. By examining different narrators' versions of the same event a certain level of consensus can be developed. In such cases it is helpful if one can consult accounts offering circumstantial evidence by commenting on matters peripheral to the interviewee's experience—verification, as it were, in passing comments. An example of this is the testimony of Mac Wiseman concerning the early relations between Bill Monroe and the Stanley Brothers; Wiseman was there, but it wasn't *his* fight, so his comments are relatively disinterested and thus more useful and less subjective than those of the participants.

The reader will notice that some authors appear more than once. Douglas B. Green, Ivan M. Tribe, Frank and Marty Godbey, Wayne Erbsen, Bill Vernon, Peter V. Kuykendall, Charles K. Wolfe, and others have contributed extensively to the literature. Through their experience in researching and writing about the genre they have developed appropriate, informed critical approaches. Though they perforce write in a style designed for fans, they work with posterity in mind, providing substantial information about individuals and events otherwise not well documented. Like many of the other authors in this bibliography, they have an esthetic commitment to the music. Indeed a high proportion of those who have written about bluegrass are or were musicians. One example, Bill Emerson, mentioned in several chapters for his role in the Country Gentlemen and his band with Cliff Waldron, appears in the bibliography as the author of articles on the Osborne Brothers and on banjos.

Another important research source represented in this bibliography is record album notes. Frequently these are the only sources for details concerning biography, song history, and the music business. A prime example is the work of Ralph Rinzler on Bill Monroe. The notes to historical reissues often draw upon oral history–type interviews and sometimes use rare documents in the possession of the interviewees for illustrations. In the introduction to the discography which follows the bibliography I discuss the ways in which such record albums can be obtained.

Most of the magazines and journals cited in this bibliography are not kept at public libraries; only a few can be found in typical college or university research libraries. Consequently I have relied to a great extent upon my personal library to provide the reference material needed for my research. I have been aided in this by friends and colleagues who have sent me clippings and references to out-of-the-way items I would otherwise have missed. (As this book goes to press, many of the *Frets* articles cited in this bibliography have been reprinted, along with instrument instruction columns, in Marilyn Kochman's *The Big Book of Bluegrass*.)

For the past decade I have maintained my own bibliography of bluegrass (on 5-by-8-inch cards), excerpting all material which came to my attention. I have found this file indispensable for the research on this book. A copy of it was made in 1979 for Scott Hambly, then working under the auspices of the JEMF toward the compilation of an extensive and definitive bluegrass bibliography. Such a bibliography would, if available, be similar to the various jazz compilations, such as Alan P. Merriam and Robert J. Benford's *A Bibliography of Jazz*, published by the American Folklore Society in 1954. Unfortunately, Hambly was unable to procede to publication with his bibliography, and presently no such work is available. In this context I must emphasize that this bibliography is in no way meant to be definitive. It is selective in at least two ways. First, I have not had access to all the possible published sources concerning bluegrass music. In recent years local and regional newsletters and magazines have proliferated. I do not have the resources to keep track of all (or even more than a few) of these. Because they are so difficult to find, I have generally not quoted such publications even when I have them; therefore they are under-represented here. Even with the larger magazines discussed earlier there is a degree of selectivity: I cite but a fraction of the contents of such publications, those which bear directly on points or topics discussed in the book. Yet the very size of the bibliography points to the wealth of materials available to future researchers wishing to specialize in aspects of the study of bluegrass or to re-examine questions raised in this work.

Abbreviations

BB	*Bluegrass Breakdown*(Toronto)
BBU	*Bluegrass Bulletin*
BN	*Banjo Newsletter*
BU	*Bluegrass Unlimited*
CBR	*Canadian Bluegrass Review*
CD	*Country Directory*
DB	*The Devil's Box*
DC	*Disc Collector*
JAF	*Journal of American Folklore*
JCM	*Journal of Country Music*
JEMFQ	*John Edwards Memorial Foundation Quarterly*
MN	*Muleskinner News*
OTM	*Old Time Music*
SO	*Sing Out!*

Bibliography

Abrahams, Roger D. "Shouting Match at the Border: The Folklore of Display Events." In *"And Other Neighborly Names" Social Process and Cultural Image in Texas Folklore*, 303–21. Austin: University of Texas Press, 1981.

Ackerman, Paul. " 'Scruggs and Five-String Banjo' Gets Picked in U.S., Abroad." *Billboard*, Mar. 1, 1969, 8.

———. "What Has Happened to Popular Music." *High Fidelity* 8 (June 1958): 34–37, 107–8.

Acuff, Roy. "Introduction." In *Nashville's Grand Ole Opry*, by Jack Hurst, pp. 9–12. New York: Harry N. Abrams, Inc., 1975.

Adams, Rich. "Timberlake Troubles Could Be a Sign of the Times to Come." *BU* 7 (Nov. 1972): 16.

Adler, Thomas A. "Bluegrass Recordings." *JAF* 97 (1984): 367–77.

———. "The Acquisition of a Traditional Competence: Folk-Musical and Folk-Cultural Learning among Bluegrass Banjo Players." Ph.D. diss., Indiana University, 1980.

———. "The Concept of Nidality and Its Potential Application to Folklore." In *Conceptual Problems in Contemporary Folklore Study*, ed. Gerald Cashion, pp. 1–5. Bloomington, Ind.: Folklore Forum Bibliographical and Special Series, no. 12, 1974.

Ahrens, Pat J. *A History of the Musical Careers of Dewitt "Snuffy" Jenkins, Banjoist, and Homer "Pappy" Sherrill, Fiddler*. Columbia, S.C.: The Author, 1970.

———. "The Role of the Crazy Water Crystals Company in Promoting Hillbilly Music." *JEMFQ* 6 (Autumn 1970): 107–9.

———. *Union Grove: The First Fifty Years*. Columbia, S.C.: The Author, 1975.

Alden, Ray. "Craftsmen and Creativity." *Pickin'* 5 (Mar. 1978): 32–39.

Andrews, Mark. "A Look at a Japanese Guitar Maker." *Pickin'* 5 (June 1978): 16, 18, 20.

Arkin, Steve. "An Interview with the Mandolin Brothers." *Pickin'* 1 (June 1974): 4–10.

Arlen, Michael J. "The Air: The State of the Art." *New Yorker*, Feb. 18, 1980, 107–8, 111–17.

Artis, Bob. *Bluegrass*. New York: Hawthorne Books, 1975.

———. "Entertainment Personified with the Lewis Family." *Pickin'* 4 (Apr. 1977): 6, 8, 10, 12.

Asbell, Bernie, and Joel Friedman. "Mercury to Absorb Starday Diskery." *Billboard*, Dec. 15, 1956, 31.

Ashby, Clifford. "Folk Theater in a Tent." *Natural History*, Mar. 1983, 6, 8, 12, 14, 16, 20.

Ashby, Clifford, and Suzanne DePauw May. *Trouping through Texas: Harley Sadler and His Tent Show*. Bowling Green, Ohio: Bowling Green University Popular Press, 1982.

Atkins, John, ed. *The Carter Family*. London: Old Time Music, 1973.

Barenberg, Russ. *Clarence White Guitar*. New York: Oak Publications Bluegrass Masters Series, 1978.

Barkely, Bill. "The Subliminal Banjo." *MN* 7 (1976): 19; *Pickin'* 3 (Jan. 1977): 30.

Barker, Pamela J. "Nashville Fun Fair." *Country Music News* 3 (Aug. 1982): 15.

Bartenstein, Fred. "The Audience for Bluegrass: *Muleskinner News* Reader Survey." *JCM* 4 (Fall 1973): 74–105.

———. "Blue Grass 45: Gentlemen of Japan." *MN* 3 (Aug. 1972): 8–11.

———. "The Carlton Haney Story." *MN* 2 (Sept.-Oct. 1971): 8–10, 18–21.

———. "A Conversation with the New Grass Revival." *MN* 3 (Dec. 1972): 4–8, 17, 22.

———. "The Country Gentlemen . . . Going Places!" *MN* 1 (Sept.-Oct., 1970): 2–4.

———. Editorial in *MN* 4 (July 1973): 5.

———. "J. D. Crowe and the New South." *MN* 6 (July 1975): 9–14.

———. "The Ralph Stanley Story—An Interview with Fred Bartenstein." *MN* 3 (Mar. 1972): 6–18.

———. Red Smiley Obituary. *Muleskinner Newsletter* 7 (Feb. 1972): 1.

———. "The IInd Generation." *MN* 3 (Sept. 1972): 6–8.

Barth, John. *The Sot-Weed Factor*. Garden City, N. Y.: Doubleday, 1960.

Bass, Michael. "Eck Robertson: Traditional Texas Fiddler." In *Country Music Who's Who, 1970*, p. 7, edited by Thurston Moore, 8–9. Denver: Heather Publications, 1969.

Bassham, Olan. *Lester Flatt, Baron of Bluegrass: Cragrock to Carnagie [sic] Hall*. Manchester, Tenn.: The Author, 1980.

Bay, Jeff. "Send a Bluegrass Musician to Camp." *BU* 2 (May 1968): 12–13.

Bazelon, Irving. *Knowing the Score: Notes on Film Music*. New York: Van Nostrand Reinhold, 1975.

Benson, Doug. "How to Form an Area Bluegrass Committee." *BU* 4 (July 1969): 6–10.

———. "TABC Part One: The Ontario Bluegrass Scene: Then and Now." *CBR* 1 (Sept. 1978): 6–7.

Bergson, Henri. *Le rire* (1900), translated as "Laughter." In *Comedy*, edited by Wylie Sypher, 61–190. Garden City, N. Y.: Doubleday Anchor, 1956.

Berland, Kevin. "Vic Mullen—Maritime Bluegrass Legend." *CBR* 2 (June-July 1979): 22–26.

Berle, Arnie. "New York's Session Men: Making a Career Out of Versatility." *Guitar Player* 11 (Dec. 1977): 33, 64, 66, 68, 72, 74, 76, 80, 82, 84.

Berline, Byron. "Fort Polk Bluegrass Special." *BU* 3 (Feb. 1969): 3–5.

"Bill Monroe and Lester Flatt Reunited at Hoosier Festival." *Billboard*, July 17, 1971, 34.

Bill Monroe's Blue Grass Country Songs. New York: Hill and Range Songs, 1950.

[Birt, Eddie.] "CMH Records—Creating a Market for Bluegrass." *Country and Western Spotlight* n.s. no. 9 (Dec. 1976): 17–18.

Blaustein, Richard J. "Traditional Music and Social Change: The Old Time Fiddlers Association Movement in the United States." Ph.D. diss., Indiana University, 1975.

———. "Will Success Spoil Old Time Fiddling and Bluegrass?" *DB* 17 (June 1972): 21–24.

Blood, Dave. "Bob Goff." *BU* 4 (July 1970): 21.

Blood, Dave, and Charlie Vaughn. "Festivals." *BU* 5 (July 1970): 6.

"Bluegrass in Nippon." *Newsweek*, Mar. 25, 1968, 98.

"Bluegrass Shakes Off It's [sic] Cobwebs and Emerges Healthy and Vigorous." *Billboard*, Oct. 16, 1971, sec. 2, 34.

"Bluegrass Style Is Moving Up in Folk-Pop Field." *Cash Box*, Dec. 1, 1962, 7.

"Bluegrass Summer '72." *Rounder Review* 4 (Oct. 1972): 3.

Bolick, Bill. " ' I Always Liked the Type of Music That I Play': An Autobiography of the Blue Sky Boys." In brochure notes to *Presenting the Blue Sky Boys*, JEMF-104, edited by Paul F. Wells, pp. 3–6.

Bolle, Mary Jane. "Happy Medium—J. D. Crowe and the New South." *BU* 8 (Feb. 1974): 7–9.

———. "Norman Blake." *BU* 8 (Oct. 1973): 9–12.

Boothroyd, John. "The Starday Catalogue." *Country and Western Spotlight* n.s. no. 7 (June 1976): 18–25.

Bovee, Bob. "To the Friends of Bluegrass Music." *BU* 4 (Jan. 1970): 8.

Bright-Sagnier, Barbara. "D.C. Is Also Nation's Bluegrass Capitol." *Washington Post*, Mar. 11, 1974, A1, A4.

Brislin, Richard W. "Mike Seeger." *BN* 7 (Feb. 1980): 4–6.

Brody, David. *Kenny Baker Fiddle*. New York: Oak Publications Bluegrass Masters Series, 1979.

Brown, James S., and George A. Hillery, Jr. "The Great Migration, 1940–1960." In *The Southern Appalachian Region, A Survey*, edited by Thomas R. Ford, 54–78. Lexington: University of Kentucky Press, 1962.

Brown, Les. *The New York Times Encyclopedia of Television*. New York: New York Times Books, 1977.

Brown, Toni. "Can Blue Grass Grow in City Streets?" *American Folk Music Occasional* 1 (1964): 97–99.

Bruce, Dix. "An Interview with Bill Monroe: 'Bluegrass—There's Not a Prettier Name in the World' " *Frets* 1 (May 1979): 20–24.

Brunvand, Jan Harold. *The Vanishing Hitchhiker*. New York: W. W. Norton, 1981.

Buckingham, Steve. "Randy Wood: The Nashville Craftsman." *Pickin'* 3 (June 1976): 18, 20–21.

Burrison, John A. "Fiddlers in the Alley: Atlanta as an Early Country Music Center." *Atlanta Historical Bulletin* 21 (Summer 1977): 59–87.

Byrd, Senator Robert F. [Praises Gary Henderson]. *Congressional Record*. Washington, D. C. Mar. 15, 1978, S3722-23.

Calder, Dave. "Bluegrass in New Zealand? You Must Be Joking!" *BU* 4 (Aug. 1969): 6–8.

———. "New Zealand Bluegrass Sequel." *BU* 4 (Dec. 1969): 15.

———. "A Professional Bluegrass Band in New Zealand? . . . You're Out of Your Mind!" *BU* 4 (Sept. 1969): 3–4.

Calloway, Cab, and Bryant Rollins. *Of Minnie the Moocher and Me*. New York: Thomas Y. Crowell Co., 1976.

Camp, Charles, and Timothy Lloyd. "Six Reasons Not to Produce Folklife Festivals." *Kentucky Folklore Record* 26 (1980): 67–74.

Campbell, Jan. "Jerry Douglas: They Call Him Flux." *BU* 16 (Nov. 1981): 31–32.

Canby, Vincent. Review of *Deliverance*. *New York Times*, July 31, 1972.

Cantwell, Robert. "Believing in Bluegrass." *Atlantic Monthly* 229 (Mar. 1972): 52–54, 58–60.

———. *Bluegrass Breakdown: The Making of the Old Southern Sound*. Urbana: University of Illinois Press. 1984.

———. "Is the 'Scene' Grass?" *BU* 8 (Apr. 1974): 32–33.

Cardwell, Nancy. "Missouri Area Bluegrass Committee: Success Story." *BU* 17 (Mar. 1983): 26–27.

Carlin, Robert. "The Small Specialty Record Company in the United States." *JEMFQ* 12 (Summer 1976): 63–73; *Pickin'* 4 (Aug. 1977): 16, 18–26.

Carlson, Norman. "Bill Monroe's Bluegrass Festival." *BU* 3 (Aug. 1968): 4–7.

———. *Bluegrass Handbook*. 4th ed. West Lafayette, Ind.: The Author, 1969.

———. "The Fan Club and the Folk Scholar." *The Stanley Standard* 2 (May 1967): 51–53.

———. "On the Scene." *BBU* 2 (Dec. 1966): 3.

Carmody, John. "Bluegrass Group Joins March to Urbanization." *Louisville Courier-Journal/Times*, Feb. 25, 1968.

Carney, George O. "Bluegrass Grows All Around: The Spatial Dimensions of a Country Music Style." *Journal of Geography* 73 (1974): 34–55.

Carpenter, Mike, and Don Kissil. "Chubby Wise . . . Sweet Fiddler from Florida."
    Pickin' 4 (Oct. 1977): 6–7, 10, 12, 14, 16–17.
Carter, Wilf. *The Singing Cowboy.* Toronto: Ryerson, 1961.
Chapman, Martin. "Ron Scott, The Ghost of Canadian Bluegrass." *CBR* 6 (Dec./
    Jan. 1984): 7–11.
Chappelle, Pat. "Byron Berline (The Busy B.B.)." *'Grass Scene* 1 (1983): 6–11.
———. "A Dawg's Life." *'Grass Scene* 1 (1983): 12–18, 40.
———. "Gunning for Bluegrass." *British Bluegrass News* 7 (May 1983): 22–23.
———. "Twice As Rice." *'Grass Scene* 1 (1983): 20–25.
Charles, Hedley, and Rob McCarthy. "A Brief Look at Bluegrass in Australia."
    Country and Western Spotlight n.s. no. 4 (Sept. 1975): 15–19.
Charles, Ray, and David Ritz. *Brother Ray.* New York: Dial Press, 1978.
Charlie and Mary—The Blue Grass Sweethearts Famous Folio of Songs to Remember,
    Book No. 1. New York: Dixie Music Publishing, 1943.
Charters, Sam. "The Lilly Brothers of Hillbilly Ranch." *SO* 15 (July 1965): 19–22.
Clarkson, Atelia, and W. Lynwood Montell. "Letters to a Bluegrass DJ: Social
    Documents of Southern White Migrants in Southeastern Michigan, 1964-
    1974." *Southern Folklore Quarterly* 39 (1975): 219–32.
Coats, Art. "Norman Blake." *Frets* 1 (Apr. 1979): 22–26.
Coats, Art and Leota. "Norman Blake, Ex-'Hot Licks Picker.' " *Pickin'* 5 (Apr.
    1978): 6–8, 10–11, 78–80.
Cogswell, Robert. " 'We Made Our Name in the Days of Radio': A Look at the
    Career of Wilma Lee and Stoney Cooper." *JEMFQ* 9 (Summer, 1975): 67–79.
Cohen, Anne and Norm. "Folk and Hillbilly Music: Further Thoughts on Their
    Relation." *JEMFQ* 13 (Summer 1977): 49–57.
Cohen, John. "Fiddlin' Eck Robertson." *SO* 14 (Apr.-May 1964): 55–59; *DB* 11
    (Jan. 1970): 7–11, 17 (June 1972): 14–17.
———. "Ralph Stanley's Old Time Mountain Bluegrass." *SO* 23 (Dec. 1975): 2–8.
Cohen, Norm. *Long Steel Rail.* Urbana: University of Illinois Press, 1981.
———. Preface to *Country Music Recorded Prior to 1943: A Discography of LP*
    Releases. Compiled by Willie Smyth. Los Angeles: JEMF Special Series no. 14,
    1984.
———. "Record Reviews." *JEMFQ* 14 (1978): 159.
Colaizzi, Randall. "Frank Wakefield: The Bluegrass Adventurer." *Frets* 3 (Apr.
    1981): 18, 20–22.
Coltman, Bob. "Across the Chasm: How the Depression Changed Country Music."
    OTM 23 (Winter 1976/77): 6–12.
Cook, Bruce. "In Washington, Bluegrass is Capital." *New York Times,* Apr. 14, 1975.
Cook, Howard. "C&W Jocks Decide Top Sellers Spin." *Billboard,* Mar. 24, 1958, 30.
Cook, Thomas. "Larry Sparks: I'm Givin' It All I've Got." *BU* 12 (Aug. 1977):
    14–18.
The Country Gentlemen Twenty-fifth Anniversary 1957–1982. Warrenton, Va.: Lendel
    Agency, 1982.
"Country Talent Contest." *Country Song Roundup* 28 (Jan. 1954): 14.
Crawford, Chuck. "TABC Part Two: Toronto Area Bluegrass Committee, Years—
    1973 to 1978." *CBR* 1 (Sept. 1978): 8–9.
Crockett, Jim. "From the Publisher." *Frets* 1 (Nov. 1979): 3, 66.
———. "From the Publisher: Who Are You." *Frets* 5 (Nov. 1983): 6.

Crowther, Bosley. Review of Bonnie and Clyde. New York Times, Aug. 14, 1967.

Cyporyn, Dennis. "Bluegrass Fever." BU 4 (Aug. 1969): 2–5.

Dallman, Jerry. "Introducing Dick Freeland (of Rebel Records)." Pickin' 2 (Mar. 1975): 19–20.

———. "Tom Gray: Bluegrass Bassist." BU 11 (Feb. 1977): 32–40.

Daniel, Wayne W. "From Barn Dance Emcee to Recording Company Executive—The Story of Cotton Carrier." JEMFQ 15 (Winter 1979): 230–36.

———. "Josh Graves: Dobro Virtuoso." BU 17 (July 1982) 44–48.

———. " 'Rocky Top'—The Song and the Man and Woman Who Wrote It." BU 16 (Apr. 1982): 20–23.

———. " 'We Had to be Different to Survive'—Billy Carrier Remembers the Swanee River Boys (with a Preliminary Numerical Record Listing)." JEMFQ 18 (Spring/Summer 1982): 59–83.

———. "Wilma Lee Cooper: America's Most Authentic Mountain Singer." BU 16 (Feb. 1982): 12–17.

Davis, Chandler. "Bluegrass Family—Family Bluegrass." BU 7 (Oct. 1972): 5–8.

Davis, Ed. "Arthur Smith." MN 6 (Feb. 1975): 9–11.

———. "Auldridge: Tops with Dobro." MN 6 (Feb. 1975): 16–17.

———. "The Lewis Family: Gospel Grass." MN 3 (Nov. 1972): 4–7.

Davis, Stephanie. "The Vern Williams Band." BU 17 (Dec. 1982): 16–19.

Davis, Stephen F. "A. C. (Eck) Robertson Discography." DB 17 (June 1972): 17–19.

———. "Jilson Setters: The Man of Many Names." DB 12 (Mar. 1978): 42–45.

"Days of Starday and Don Pierce." The Country Music Who's Who, edited by Thurston Moore, 73. Denver: Heather Publications, 1963.

Deen, Dixie. "The 'Woman' behind the Man." Music City News 3 (Nov. 1965): 17, 22–23.

Delgatto, John. "The Country Gazette." BU 7 (Nov. 1972): 5–7.

Delmore, Alton. Truth Is Stranger than Publicity. Nashville: Country Music Foundation Press, 1977.

Denisoff, R. Serge. Great Day Coming. Urbana: University of Illinois Press, 1971.

———. Solid Gold. New Brunswick, N.J.: Transaction Books, 1975.

DeTurk, David A., and A. Poulin, Jr. The American Folk Scene: Dimensions of the Folksong Revival. New York: Dell Publishing, 1967.

Devan, Brett F. "The Bluegrass Cardinals." BU 15 (June 1981): 20–28.

Dickey, James. Deliverance. Boston: Houghton Mifflin, 1970.

[Dickson, Jim.] Unsigned liner notes to Dián and the Greenbriar Boys. Elektra EKL233, 1963.

Dillard, Douglas, Kathryn Gleason Dillard, and Bill Knopf. The Bluegrass Banjo Style of Douglas Flint Dillard. Hollywood: Alamo Publications, 1980.

Dixon, Robert, and John Godrich. Recording the Blues. New York: Stein and Day, 1970.

Dorson, Richard M. "Fakelore." Zeitschrift für Volkskunde 65 (1969): 56–64.

———. "Folklore and Fake Lore," American Mercury 70 (Mar. 1950): 335–43.

———. "A Southern Indiana Field Station." Midwest Folklore 11 (1961): 133–38.

Douglas, Curtis. "The Murphy Brothers—One of North Carolina's Originals." BU 18 (July 1983): 24–28.

Doyle, Bob. "The Traditional Music of Central Pennsylvania." Pickin' 4 (Mar. 1977): 32–35.

Dudley, Gene. Introduction to *Bill Monroe's Grand Ole Opry WSM Song Folio No. 2,* 4. New York: Peer International, 1953.

"The Earl Scruggs Revue: New Directions in Music." *American Sound* 1 (Feb. 1973): 38–41.

Edelstein, Art. "John Herald: New Directions for an Ex-Greenbriar Boy." *Frets* 1 (Dec. 1979): 22–25.

Emerson, Bill. "A Comparative Analysis of Current Banjos." *BU* 3 (Sept. 1968): 2–4.

———. "A Comparative Analysis of Current Banjos. Part II." *BU* 3 (Nov. 1968): 9–10.

———. "A Comparative Analysis of Current Banjos. Part III." *BU* 3 (Feb. 1969): 11–13.

———. "Electric Bluegrass." *BU* 3 (Mar. 1969): 3–5.

———. "The Osborne Brothers: Getting Started." *MN* 2 (July-Aug. 1971): 2–11.

Erbsen, Wayne. "Barry Poss and Sugar Hill Records." *BU* 17 (Oct. 1982): 28–33.

———. "Cleo Davis—The Original Blue Grass Boy." *BU* 16 (Feb. 1982): 28–30.

———. "Cleo Davis—The Original Blue Grass Boy—Conclusion." *BU* 16 (Mar. 1982): 59–64.

———. "Jim Shumate—Bluegrass Fiddler Supreme." *BU* 13 (Apr. 1979): 14–23.

———. "Lester Woodie: Coming up the Hard Road." *BU* 14 (Mar. 1980): 41–48.

———. "Raymond Fairchild: Making his Own Way." *BU* 16 (Mar. 1982): 14–17.

———. "Wiley and Zeke—The Morris Brothers." *BU* 15 (Aug. 1980): 40–50.

Evans, Bill. "Good Music, Good Friends: The Country Gentlemen." *BU* 12 (June 1978): 18–25.

Evans, James F. *Prairie Farmer and WLS.* Urbana: University of Illinois Press, 1969.

Everett, Todd. Liner notes to *Country Gazette Live.* Antilles AN-7014. 1976.

Ewing, Tom. "Earl Taylor: One of the Bluegrass Greats." *BU* 11 (Sept. 1976): 10–14.

Faier, Billy. "Message from the West: 'A Weekend of Folkmusic.' " *Caravan* 12 (Aug.-Sept. 1958): 11–17.

"Fall Country Fete Sets First Bluegrass Show." *Billboard,* July 31, 1971, 36.

Fanning, Kathryn. "Gary Price: Banjo Man." *BU* 15 (June 1981): 37–42.

Farber, Steven. " 'Deliverance'—How it Delivers." *New York Times,* Aug. 20, 1972.

Faurot, Charles. Liner notes to *Benny Thomasson: Country Fiddling from the Big State,* County 724.

Feintuch, Bert. "Sointula: A Finnish Community in British Columbia." *Canadian Folk Music Journal* 1 (1973): 24–30.

Feldman, Jay. "Sunday Afternoon at Washington Square: A Nostalgic Event." *BU* 17 (Mar. 1983): 20–25.

Feller, Judith A. "The Boys from Indiana." *BU* 17 (Aug. 1982): 14–20.

Field, Arthur Jordan. "Notes on the History of Folksinging in New York City." *Caravan* 17 (June-July, 1959): 7–14, 17.

Finch, Christopher. *The Art of Walt Disney.* New York: Harry N. Abrahams, 1973.

"First Annual Blue Grass Awards." *MN* 5 (Oct. 1971): 5–8.

Fisher, Stephen L., J. W. Williamson, and Juanita Lewis. "A Guide to Appalachian Studies." Special issue of *Appalachian Journal* 5 (1977): 1–192.

"Flatt Leaves Col; Starts Negotiations For New Deal." *Billboard,* Aug. 22, 1970, 3.

Fleischhauer, Carl. "The Public Named Bluegrass Music." *OTM* 21 (Summer 1976): 4–7.

Fleisher, M. P. "No Generation Gap at Folk Festival." *BU* 5 (Oct. 1970): 7–8.

Fletcher, Frank. "Raymond Fairchild: The Young-Old Man of the Mountains."
      Pickin' 2 (Nov. 1975): 20–22.

Foggy Mountain Boys Number Two Edition of Radio Favorites. N. p., n.d.

Foote, Tom. "Interview: Tom Morgan." *BN* 5 (Jan. 1978): 10–13.

Forrester, Howdy. "Howdy Forrester Recalls Grand Old Days of Country Fiddling."
      Billboard, Oct. 30, 1965, sec. 2, 58–62.

Forte, Dan. "David Grisman and Dawg Music." *Musician Player and Listener* 30 (Feb.
      1981): 72–76, 106–7.

Forte, Dan, with Dix Bruce, " 'Dawg': David Grisman: Taking the Mandolin beyond
      Tradition." *Frets* 1 (Mar. 1979): 30, 32–36.

Foster, Alice [Gerrard]. "Festival of American Folklife." *BU* 3 (June 1969): 21–22.

———. "Kenny Baker." *BU* 3 (Dec. 1968): 8–11.

Foster, George M. "Treasure Tales, and the Image of the Static Economy in a
      Mexican Peasant Community." *JAF* 77 (1964): 39–44.

Frame, Peter. *Rock Family Trees.* New York: Quick Fox, 1979.

Freeland, Charles R. Liner notes to *The Country Gentlemen.* Rebel RLP-1478, 1966.

Freeman, David. Liner notes to *Charlie Monroe on the Noonday Jamboree—1944.*
      County 538, 1974.

Freeman, Herschel. "Dave Evans: The Voice of Traditional Bluegrass." *BU* 15 (Jan.
      1981): 10–14.

Gailey, Phil. "Welcome to the Capitol . . . of the Nation's Bluegrass." *New York
      Times*, Mar. 3, 1982.

Gaillard, Frye. *Watermelon Wine.* New York: St. Martin's Press, 1978.

Gajda, Maria. "Kenny Baker: Country Jazz Fiddler." *MN* 3 (Oct. 1972): 4–6.

———. "The Old Time Picking Parlor." *MN* 3 (Dec. 1972): 11.

Gallmann, Matthew. "Matti Pelto: Finnish-American Button Accordion Player."
      Midwestern Journal of Language and Folklore 8 (Spring 1982): 43–47.

Garelick, Burney, and Don Ridgway. "The Sun Also Rises on California Bluegrass:
      Dick Tyner and the Golden West Bluegrass Festival." *BU* 13 (Sept. 1978):
      38–43.

Garelick, David. "An Interview with Benny Thomasson." *DB* 24 (Mar. 1974):
      19–26.

Geiger, Fred. "Bluegrass Day at Culpeper." *BU* 4 (July 1969): 2.

———. "Where I Come From." *BN* 9 (Oct. 1982): 15.

Gentry, Linnell. *A History and Encyclopedia of Country, Western, and Gospel Music.*
      2nd rev. ed. Nashville: Clairmont Corp., 1969.

Gerhardt, Rolfe. "The Blue Grass Mandolin." *MN* 6 (Jan. 1976): 8–10.

Gesser, Samuel. "In Canada: The Mariposa Folk Festival." *SO* 11 (Dec.–Jan. 1961–
      62): 48–49.

Gillett, Charlie. *The Sound of the City.* New York: Outerbridge & Dienstfrey, 1970.

Ginnings, Don. "Lonnie Hoppers." *BU* 17 (Mar. 1983): 31–35.

Glasser, Matt. *Vassar Clements Fiddle.* New York: Oak Publications Bluegrass Masters
      Series, 1978.

Gleason, Ralph J. *The Jefferson Airplane and the San Francisco Sound.* New York:
      Ballantine, 1969.

Godbey, Frank. "Pee Wee Lambert." *BU* 13 (Jan. 1979): 12–20.

———. "Who in the World Are the Bluegrass Cardinals?" *BU* 10 (May 1976): 12–17.

Godbey, Marty. "Bluegrass, Bluegrass . . . A Television Series." *BU* 12 (Nov. 1977): 9–11.

———. "The Boys from Indiana with Paul Mullins and Noah Crase." *BU* 11 (Nov. 1976): 7–11.

———. "A Conversation with J. D. Crowe." *BU* 16 (July 1981): 14–21.

———. "The Goins Brothers." *BU* 18 (Aug. 1983): 16–23.

———. "The Lost Fiddler: Art Stamper." *BU* 17 (Nov. 1982): 24–27.

———. "The McLain Family Band." *BU* 15 (Feb. 1981): 12–16.

———. "Spectrum." *BU* 15 (Dec. 1980): 14–21.

Goertzen, Christopher Jack. " 'Billy in the Low Ground': History of an American Instrumental Folk Tune." Ph.D. diss., University of Illinois at Champaign-Urbana, 1983.

Goldstein, Carl. "Berryville Bluegrass Festival." *BU* 3 (Oct. 1968): 5–11.

Gordon, Douglas. "Ralph Stanley: Traditional Banjo Stylist." *Frets* 1 (Nov. 1979): 14, 16, 18, 20–21.

Gould, Jack. "TV: Beverly Hillbillies." *New York Times*, Nov. 2, 1962.

Green, Archie. "Commercial Music Graphics: Twenty-One." *JEMFQ* 8 (Summer 1972): 77–89.

———. "Hillbilly Music: Source and Symbol." *JAF* 78 (1965): 204–28.

———. *Only a Miner.* Urbana: University of Illinois Press, 1972.

Green, Douglas B. "Bill Ivey—Country Music Hall of Fame." *BU* 8 (Jan. 1974): 7–9.

———. "Bluegrass and Old Time Music at the Country Music Hall of Fame." *Pickin'* 3 (Oct. 1976): 6–8, 10, 12.

———. "Buck White and the Down-Homers." *BU* 7 (May 1973): 7–10.

———. "The Charlie Monroe Story, Part II: The Monroe Brothers." *MN* 4 (Feb. 1973): 8–11, 18.

———. "The Country Music Hall of Fame: Remodeled and Expanded." *BU* 11 (June 1977): 26–27.

———. *Country Roots.* New York: Hawthorne Books, 1976.

———. "The Grand Ole Opry, 1944–45: A Radio Log Kept by Dick Hall, of Tecumseh, Nebraska." *JCM* 5 (1974): 91–122.

———. "Jim Smoak." *BU* 8 (Feb. 1974): 12–14.

———. "John Hartford: 'I Haven't Been Right Since.' " *MN* 4 (Aug. 1973): 12–17, 32–34.

———. "Larry Sparks." *BU* 7 (Dec. 1972): 7–8.

———. Liner notes to Bill Monroe and His Blue Grass Boys, *The Classic Bluegrass Recordings.* Vol. 1. County CCS104, 1980.

———. Liner notes to *Kenny Baker Plays Bill Monroe.* County 761, 1976.

———. "Lonzo and Oscar Join the World of Bluegrass." *BU* 14 (Apr. 1980): 14–19.

———. "Mac Wiseman: Remembering." *MN* 3 (July 1972): 2–8.

———. "Pete Pyle: Bluegrass Pioneer." *BU* 12 (Mar. 1978): 22–25.

———. "Randy Wood's Old Time Pickin' Parlor." *Pickin'* 3 (Feb. 1976): 18–21.

———. "Tut Taylor: Bluegrass Enigma." *BU* 12 (Sept. 1977): 10–12.

Green, Mary Greenman, with Tom Teepen. "The First Festival." *MN* 4 (Apr. 1973): 54–57.

Greenberg, Mark. "Eric Weissberg, Ten Years afters [sic] 'Dueling Banjos.' " *Frets* 5 (Nov. 1983): 32–34.

———. "New Lost City Ramblers: Energetic Traditionalists." *Frets* 1 (Oct. 1979): 19–23.

Greene, Clarence H. "Pee Wee Davis: His Own Story." *BU* 6 (Feb. 1972): 12–14.

———. "Third Annual Tennessee State—ETSU Folk Festival." *BU* 3 (Dec. 1968): 12–13.

Greenstein, Mike. "Joe Val and the New England Bluegrass Boys." *BU* 12 (July 1977): 14–16.

Grendysa, Peter A. Liner notes to *The Golden Gate Quartet.* RCA CL42111, 1977.

Gruene, Robert. "Unicorn Mandolins." *BU* 11 (Mar. 1977): 14–16.

Gruhn, George. "A Brief Guide to Blue Grass Instruments." *MN* 2 (May–June 1971): 40–47.

Guralnick, Peter. *Lost Highway.* Boston: David R. Godine, 1979.

———. "The Million Dollar Quartet." *New York Times Magazine,* Mar. 25, 1979, 28–30, 41, 43, 45.

Haden, Walter D., ed. *Fiddlin' Sid's Memoirs: The Autobiography of Sidney J. Harkreader.* Los Angeles: JEMF Special Series, no. 9, 1976.

Hagan, Chet. *Country Music Legends in the Hall of Fame.* Nashville: Thomas Nelson, Inc., 1982.

Haglund, Urban, and Lillies Ohlsson. *A Listing of Bluegrass LPs.* Västerås, Sweden: Kountry Korral Productions, 1971.

Hale, Antony. "A Comparison of Bluegrass Music Diffusion in the United States and New Zealand." Master's thesis, Memphis State University, 1983.

———. "Grassroots Bluegrass in Memphis: The Lucy Opry." *Tennessee Folklore Society Bulletin* 49 (1983): 51–64.

Hall, Carla. "Friendly Feast: The Carters Find Support in Their Own Back Yard." *Washington Post,* Aug. 8, 1980, C1, C9.

Hall, Patty. "The Writing on the Wall: No Female I Ever Knowed Could Quite Get Them Harmonies Right: Women and Bluegrass." *Folk Scene* 3 (July/Aug. 1975): 7–10.

Halpert, Herbert. "Some Recorded American Folk Song." *American Music Lover* 2 (Nov. 1936): 196–200.

Hambly, Scott. "Flatt and Scruggs Releases, Re-Releases, and Reissues: Preeminent, Then as Now." *JEMFQ* 19 (1983): 112–21.

———. "Jim and Jesse, A Review Essay on Fan Historiography." *JEMFQ* 13 (Summer 1977): 96–99.

———. Liner notes to *The Jim and Jesse Story.* CMH-9022, 1980.

———. "Mac Wiseman: A Discographic Enigma." *JEMFQ* 7 (Summer 1972): 53–58.

———. "Mandolins in the United States: An Industrial and Sociological History since 1880." Ph.D. diss., University of Pennsylvania, 1977.

———. "San Francisco Bay Area Bluegrass and Bluegrass Musicians: A Study in Regional Characteristics." *JEMFQ* 16 (Fall 1980): 110–20.

Hambly, Scott, and Neil V. Rosenberg. "Allen Shelton." *BN* 4 (Mar. 1977): 6–13.

Hancock, Nick. "A Threat to Festivals." *BU* 5 (May 1971): 7.

Haney, Carlton. "Blue Grass Music—It's Time to Organize." *MN* 1 (Sept.–Oct. 1970): inside front cover.

————. "Sharps and Flats (or *The Lion Roars*)." *MN* 1 (May–June 1970): 12.

Harrington, Richard. "Emmylou Harris—Return of the Electric Cowgirl." *Washington Post*, July 6, 1980.

Harris, Perry F., and Howard G. Roberts. "Howard 'Big Howdy' Forrester." *DB* 25 (June 1974): 7–14.

Hatlo, Jim. "*Frets* Visits . . . Spring Valley, CA., Stelling Banjo Works." *Frets* 1 (Oct. 1979): 12, 14.

————. "Jerry Douglas, Dobro Dynamo." *Frets* 2 (Nov. 1980): 20–23.

————. "John McEuen." *Frets* 3 (Nov. 1981): 26–33.

————. "Mike Seeger: Cherishing His Music and Its Traditions." *Frets* 1 (Mar. 1979): 12, 14–15.

————. "On Record." *Frets* 5 (Feb. 1983): 59.

————. "Phil Rosenthal, The Seldom Scene's Multi-Faceted Flatpicker." *Frets* 4 (Feb. 1982): 40–42.

————. "Ricky Skaggs: Bluegrass Prodigy Comes of Age." *Frets* 2 (Aug. 1980): 16, 18, 20–21.

Hay, George D. *A Story of the Grand Ole Opry.* Nashville: n.p., 1953.

Healey, Bob. "The Prairie Ramblers." *CD* 3 (1962): 4–14.

Heilbut, Tony. *The Gospel Sound.* Garden City, N.Y.: Anchor Books, 1975.

Henderson, Gary A. "Lewis Family: The First Family of Gospel Song." *BU* 4 (June 1970): 2–5.

————. "Tom Morgan." *BU* 7 (Feb. 1973): 14–15.

Henderson, Gary A., and Walter V. Saunders. "The Bailey Brothers." *BU* 5 (July 1970): 3–5, 5 (Feb. 1971): 3–8.

Henderson, Tom. "Charlie Moore: 'It's an Honest Music.' " *MN* 4 (July 1973): 10–12.

————. "Charlie Waller: The Original Country Gentleman." *MN* 4 (Dec. 1973): 6–9, 18.

————. "Mac Wiseman." *Pickin'* 2 (Aug. 1975): 4–6, 8, 10–12, 14.

————. "On the Cuttin' Edge . . . with Eddie Adcock." *Pickin'* 2 (Oct. 1975): 4–6, 8, 10–12.

————. "Ralph Stanley Interview." *MN* 7 (Aug. 1976): 8–11.

Hickerson, Kathryn W., and Kathleen Condon, comps. *Folklife and Ethnomusicology Societies in North America.* Washington, D.C.: Archive of Folk Culture, Library of Congress, 1982.

Higashi, Michio. "Japan Welcomes the Gentlemen." *BU* 6 (Feb. 1972): 4.

Hill, Fred. *Grass Roots.* Rutland, Vt.: Academy Books, 1980.

"Hillbilly's Corner." *Music Life* 3 (Mar. 1958): 30.

Hillman, Chris. Liner notes to *The Hillmen.* Sugar Hill SH 3719, 1981.

Hirose, Naoki. "F&S in Japan." *BU* 2 (Apr. 1968): 14.

Hodgson, Godfrey. *America in Our Time.* New York: Vintage, 1976.

Hoeptner, Fred. "Folk and Hillbilly Music: The Background of Their Relation(ship)." *Caravan* 16 (April–May 1959): 8, 16–17, 42, 17 (June–July 1959): 20–23, 26–28.

Hoeptner, Fred, and Bob Pinson. "Clayton McMichen Talking." *OTM* 1 (Summer 1971): 8–10, 2 (Autumn 1971): 13–15, 3 (Winter 1971/2): 14–15, 19, 4 (Spring 1972): 19–20, 30.

Hopkins, John E. "The British Bluegrass Scene." *BU* 15 (Nov. 1980): 24–26.

Horowitz, Marc. "Mandolin Bros." *MN* 7 (1977): 2–3.

Humphrey, Mark. "Chris Hillman." *Frets* 5 (Oct. 1983): 20–22, 25.

———. "Herb Pedersen: Picking His Way from the Dillards to Denver." *Frets* 4 (Feb. 1982): 24–27.

———. "Interview: Merle Travis, Part 2: Drifting Pioneers, Brown's Ferry Four, and Off to California." *OTM* 37 (Autumn 1981–Spring 1981): 20–24.

Hunsicker, Lucy. "Ted Lundy, Bob Paisley and the Southern Mountain Boys." *BU* 13 (July 1978): 16–19.

Hunter, Mark. "Tony Rice." *Frets* 2 (Apr. 1980): 26–30.

Hurst, Jack. *Nashville's Grand Ole Opry.* New York: Harry N. Abrams, 1975.

"Interview: Eddie Adcock." *BN* 5 (Dec. 1977): 6–8.

Ivey, William. "Commercialization and Tradition in the Nashville Sound." In *Folk Music and Modern Sound,* edited by William Ferris and Mary L. Hart, 129–38. Jackson: University Press of Mississippi, 1982.

———. "Chet Atkins." In *Stars of Country Music,* edited by Bill C. Malone and Judith McCulloh, 274–88. Urbana: University of Illinois Press, 1975.

"J. E. and Wade Mainer—Bluegrass Roots." *Country and Western Spotlight* n.s. no. 11 (June 1977): 10–11.

Jabbour, Alan, and Howard W. Marshall. "Folklife and Cultural Preservation." In *New Directions in Rural Preservation,* edited by Robert E. Stipe, 43–49. Washington, D.C.: U.S. Department of the Interior, Heritage Conservation and Recreation Service, 1980.

Jayne, Mitchell F. "Cut of the Dillards." *Hootenanny* 1 (Dec. 1963): 56–57, 66.

———. "Observations: The Dillards, Music, and Blue Grass." *MN* 4 (June 1973): 12–17, 28, 36.

Jones, Loyal. "Studying Mountain Religion." *Appalachian Journal* 5 (1977): 125–30.

Kahn, David. "I Play Because This Is My Life—Music." *Hoot* 3 (Feb.–Mar. 1967): 27.

Kaiman, Audrey A. "The Southern Fiddling Convention—A Study." *Tennessee Folklore Society Bulletin* 31 (1965): 7–16.

Kaparakis, John. "1964 and the Kentucky Colonels." *BU* 3 (Apr. 1969): 5–7.

Kaplan, Kathy. [untitled.] *Rounder Review* 4 (Oct. 1972): 4–5.

Keil, Charles. *Urban Blues.* Chicago: University of Chicago Press, 1966.

Kelly, R. J. "The John Herald Band." *BU* 17 (Feb. 1983): 10–15.

Kienzle, Rich. "The Whiteface Connection." *Guitar World* 3 (Mar. 1982): 29, 31–33, 76.

Kilberg, Lionel. "Roger Sprung." *BU* 3 (Jan. 1968): 14.

Killian, Lewis M. "The Adjustment of Southern White Migrants to Northern Urban Norms." *Social Forces* 32 (1953): 66–69.

Kimmel, Dick. "Hot Rize: Pete Wernick's Secret Ingredient." *BU* 13 (Mar. 1979): 13–18.

Kimmel, Nancy and Dick. "Joe Val and the New England Bluegrass Boys: One of the Best Kept Secrets in Bluegrass." *BU* 17 (May 1983): 18–23.

Kirby, Kip. "Hot Catalog a Sugar Hill Asset." *Billboard,* July 26, 1980, 70.

Klein, Joe. *Woody Guthrie: A Life.* New York: Alfred A. Knopf, 1980.

Knight, Arthur. ". . . And Deliver Us from Evil." *Saturday Review,* Aug. 5, 1972, 61.

Knopf, Bill. "Doug Dillard." *BN* 8 (June 1981): 4–7.

Knowlton, Bill. "Fresh Impressions of Bean Blossom." *BU* 6 (Aug. 1971): 5–7.

Kochman, Marilyn. *The Big Book of Bluegrass.* New York: Quill/A Frets Book, 1984.

———. "The McLain Family Band," *Frets* 2 (Apr. 1980): 34–36, 38–40.

———. "Richard Greene: Classical Violin's Newgrass Renegade." *Frets* 3 (Jan. 1981): 14, 16, 18, 20–21.

Komoriya, Nobuharu. *Blue Ridge Mountains, Friendly Shadows.* Tokyo: Kodan-sha Press Service Center, Ltd., 1974.

———. "Ralph Stanley Goes to Japan." *MN* 2 (July–Aug. 1971): 18–19.

Koon, William Henry. "Grass Roots Commercialism." *JEMFQ* 7 (Spring 1971): 5–11.

———. "Newgrass, Oldgrass, and Bluegrass." *JEMFQ* 10 (Spring 1974): 15–18.

Kornfeld, Barry. "Folksinging in Washington Square." *Caravan* 18 (Aug.–Sept. 1959): 6–12.

Koshatka, Edgar. "Vassar Clements Is Learnin' without Labels." *Concert* 4 (Aug. 1975): 18–19.

Krueger, Bob. "Josh Graves: Thirty-Five Years of Dobro." *Guitar Player* 11 (Apr. 1977): 28–29, 68, 72, 76.

Kuykendall, Peter V. "Bill Monroe." *DC* 15 (1961): 29–33.

———. "Don Reno and Red Smiley and the Tennessee Cutups." *DC* 17 (1961): 18–20.

———. "Don Reno, Red Smiley, Bill Harrell and the Tennessee Cutups, Part 2: Don Reno." *BU* 6 (July 1971): 11–17.

———. "James Monroe." *BU* 8 (July 1973): 9–12.

———. "Jimmy Martin: Super King of Bluegrass. Bluegrass Music Is His Life." *BU* 14 (Sept. 1979): 10–17.

———. "The Kentucky Colonels." *BU* 3 (Apr. 1969): 3–4.

———. "Lester Flatt and Earl Scruggs and the Foggy Mountain Boys." *DC* 14 (1960): 37–44.

———. "Lester Flatt and the Nashville Grass." *BU* 5 (Jan. 1971): 3–6.

———. Liner notes to *Bill Clifton and the Dixie Mountain Boys: Blue Ridge Mountain Blues.* County 740, 1973.

———. "The Osborne Brothers." *BU* 12 (Dec. 1977): 10–16.

———. "II Generation." *BU* 9 (Mar. 1975): 10–15.

———. "Smilin' Jim Eanes." *BU* 7 (Feb. 1973): 7–11.

———. "The Stanley Brothers." *DC* 16 (1961): 21–27.

———. " 'Starvin' to Death.' " *BU* 1 (Feb. 1967): 4–5.

Kyle, Robert. "Bluegrass Bassist Tom Gray." *Frets* 1 (July 1979): 32, 33–36.

———. "Bluegrass in Washington." *Pickin'* 6 (May 1979): 31–33.

———. "John Duffey." *Frets* 2 (May 1980): 24–26, 28–29.

Lamb, Charles. Liner notes to *Knee Deep in Blue Grass—Bill Monroe and His Blue Grass Boys.* Decca DL8731, 1958.

Lambert, Jake, with Curly Sechler. *A Biography of Lester Flatt: "The Good Things Outweigh the Bad."* Hendersonville, Tenn.: Jay-Lyn Publications, 1982.

Larson, Jody Bytheway. "Building the J. D. Crowe Model Gold Star Banjo." *BN* 9 (Oct. 1982): 6–7.

Lass, Roger. "Bluegrass." *Caravan* 12 (Aug.–Sept. 1958): 20–23.

Lawrence, Keith. "Arnold Shultz: The Greatest? Guitar Picker's Life Ended before Promise Realized." *JEMFQ* 17 (Spring 1981): 3–8.

Lawson, Dianne Whisenand. "South Plains Bluegrass: A Unique College Program."
     BU 14 (Jan. 1980): 42–44.
Ledgin, Stephanie P. "On the Road and Off—Talking with the McLain Family
     Band." *Pickin'* 4 (July 1977): 6–8, 10, 12, 14, 16, 18–19.
LeDoux, David G. "Goings-On at Union Grove." *North Carolina Folklore* 15 (1967):
     18–20.
Lehmann-Haupt, Christopher. "Out of My Mind on Bluegrass." *New York Times
     Magazine*, Sept. 13, 1970.
Lenard, Helen, and Marsha Marders. "Maryland Indian Summer Bluegrass Festival."
     BU 4 (Nov. 1969): 8–9.
Lester Flatt and Earl Scruggs Picture Album Songbook. Nashville: privately printed,
     1962.
Lester Flatt/Earl Scruggs and the Foggy Mountain Boys Picture Album–Songbook.
     Nashville: privately printed, 1961.
"Lewis Family Discography." *Pickin'* 4 (May 1977): 44–45.
"Lewis Family Women." *MN* 6 (Aug. 1975): 7–11.
Lickona, Terry. "Going to the Top . . . with Larry Sparks." *Pickin'* 4 (May 1977):
     4–6, 8–9.
Lightfoot, William E. "Playing Outside: Spectrum." *Appalachian Journal* 10 (1983):
     194–198.
Logan, Tex. "A Conversation with Chubby Wise." *MN* 3 (Sept. 1972): 2–4.
———. "Big Howdy! Howdy Forrester, Fiddler." *MN* 4 (Sept. 1973): 12–19.
———. "Vassar Clements—A Musician's Musician." *MN* 4 (May 1973): 10–15.
Lomax, Alan. "Bluegrass Underground: Folk Music with Overdrive." *Esquire* 52
     (Oct. 1959): 108.
———. "The 'Folkniks'—and the Songs They Sing." *SO* 9 (Summer 1959): 30–31.
———. *Folk Song Style and Culture.* Washington, D.C.: American Association for
     the Advancement of Science, 1968.
———. Liner notes to *Alan Lomax Presents Folk Songs from the Blue Grass—Earl
     Taylor and His Stoney Mountain Boys.* United Artists UAL 3049, 1959.
———. "List of American Folk Songs on Commercial Records." In *Report of the
     Committee of the Conference on Inter-American Relations in the Field of Music,*
     William Berrien, Chairman, 126–46. Washington, D.C.: Department of State,
     1940.
Lomax, John and Alan. *Our Singing Country.* New York: Macmillan, 1941.
Longworth, Mike. *Martin Guitars, A History.* Cedar Knolls, N.J.: Colonial Press,
     1975.
Loomis, Ormond H., coordinator. *Cultural Conservation.* Washington, D.C.: Library
     of Congress, 1983.
Lowinger, Gene. *Bluegrass Fiddle.* New York: Oak Publications, 1974.
Lund, Jens. "Fundamentalism, Racism and Political Reaction in Country Music." In
     The Sounds of Social Change: Studies in Popular Culture, edited by R. Serge
     Denisoff and Richard A. Peterson, 79–91. Chicago: Rand McNally, 1972.
Lundy, Ronni. "The New Grass Revival." *BU* 13 (Nov. 1978): 10–15.
———. "Sam Bush: Electrifying Bluegrass." *Esquire* 98 (Dec. 1982): 124–127.
MacCannell, Dean. *The Tourist.* New York: Schocken Books, 1976.
McCeney, George B. "Don't Let Your Deal Go Down: The Bluegrass Career of Ray
     Davis." *BU* 9 (June 1975): 28–35.

———. "Festivals and Friends." *BU* 4 (Oct. 1969): 23.

———. "Remember the First Time?" *BU* 4 (Nov. 1969): 4–7.

McCuen, Brad. "Mainer's Discography." *CD* 4 (1962): n.p.

———. "Monroe Brothers on Records." *CD* 2 (Apr. 1961): 14–16.

McDaniel, William R., and Harold Seligman. *Grand Ole Opry.* New York: Greenberg, 1952.

McDonald, James J. "Principal Influences on the Music of the Lilly Brothers of Clear Creek, West Virginia." *JAF* 86 (1973): 331–44.

McFalls, Richard. "Tom Morgan: Patriarch of Bluegrass Luthiers." *Frets* 5 (1983): 36–38.

Mack, Bill. *Spins and Needles.* Fort Worth, Tex.: Bill Mack Enterprises, 1971.

Mahoney, Pat. "The Seldom Scene as Heard." *BU* 8 (June 1974): 12–21.

Malone, Bill C. *Country Music U.S.A.* Austin: University of Texas Press, 1968.

———. "Honky Tonk: The Music of the Southern Working Class." In *Folk Music and Modern Sound,* edited by William Ferris and Mary L. Hart, 119–28. Jackson: University Press of Mississippi, 1982.

———. "A Shower of Stars: Country Music since World War II." In *Stars of Country Music,* edited by Bill C. Malone and Judith McCulloh, 397–445. Urbana: University of Illinois Press, 1968.

———. *Southern Music American Music.* Lexington: University of Kentucky Press, 1979.

Manning, Ambrose N., and Minnie M. Miller. "Tom Ashley." In *Tom Ashley, Sam McGee, Bukka White, Tennessee Traditional Singers,* edited by Thomas G. Burton, 9–59. Knoxville: University of Tennessee Press, 1981.

Mansfield, Stephanie. "Birchmere's Bluegrass: 'The Ultimate.' " *Washington Post,* Aug. 3, 1978.

———. "Nothin' But Bluegrass, All Day Long." *Washington Post,* Nov. 11, 1977.

Marcus, Greil. *Mystery Train.* New York: E. P. Dutton & Co., 1976.

Marshall, Howard Wight. " 'Keep on the Sunny Side of Life': Pattern and Religious Expression in Bluegrass Gospel Music." *New York Folklore Quarterly* 30 (1974): 3–43.

Marshall, Jim, Baron Wolman, and Jerry Hopkins. *Festival! The Book of American Music Celebrations.* New York: Collier Books, 1970.

Martin, George. "High Country." *BU* 6 (June 1972): 10–13.

———. "Josh Graves." *BU* 7 (Dec. 1972): 18–19.

———. "Stelling Banjo Works." *BU* 10 (Mar. 1976): 24–31.

———. "Stelling Mandolins—A New Direction." *BU* 14 (June 1980): 28–33.

Mendelson, Michael. "Benny Thomasson and the Texas Fiddling Tradition." *JEMFQ* 10 (1974): 116–21.

———. "A Bibliography of Fiddling in North America." *JEMFQ* 11 (1975): 104–11, 153–60, 201–4; 12 (1976): 9–14, 158–65; 13 (1977): 88–95.

———. "An Interview with Benny Thomasson." *JEMFQ* 10 (1974): 122–32.

Merriam, Alan P. *The Anthropology of Music.* Evanston: Northwestern University Press, 1964.

Merritt, Byron, and Keith Fields. "If You Can't Pick, Bring Spoons! A Chat with Mike Auldridge." *Pickin'* 3 (July 1976): 8–10, 12, 14–15.

Metheny, Arlie. "Lonnie Glosson and Wayne Raney: The Harmonica Duet—Are Back." *BU* 17 (Feb. 1983): 38–39.

Mezzrow, Mezz, and Bernard Wolfe. *Really the Blues.* New York: Random House, 1946.

Mitsui, Toru. *Burugurasu Ongaku [Bluegrass Music].* Toyohashi, Japan: Traditional-Song Society, Aichi University, 1967.

———. *Burugurasu Ongaku [Bluegrass Music].* Rev. 2nd ed. Tokyo: Bronze-Sha, 1975.

Moore, Thurston, ed. *The Country Music Who's Who, 1965 Edition.* Denver: Heather Publications, 1964.

———. *Sunset Park's Twenty-Fifth Anniversary Picture Album.* Denver: Heather Publications, 1965.

Morgan, David. "State of the Art." *BU* 6 (May 1972): 16.

Morgan, Tom. "Gibson Banjo Information." *BU* 5 (Jan. 1971): 11–16.

———. "Love Affair with a Taterbug (A Chronology)." *BU* 9 (July 1974): 26–27.

Movitz, Charles, ed. *Current Biography Yearbook 1962.* New York: H. W. Wilson Co., 1962.

Nadsady, V. F. "Peter Rowan, at the Crossroad Again: Part 1, Looking Back: Bluegrass to Om." *Folk Scene* 3 (Nov. 1975): 14–19, 25.

Nagler, Eric. "A History of Bluegrass Music in New York City." *BB* 1 (Aug.–Sept., 1968): 7–9.

———. "New York Scene: Eric Nagler Tells It Like It Was." *BB* 1 (Mar. 1969): 4–5.

———. "An Unnecessarily Wordy and Frankly Inaccurate History of the Development of Bluegrass in Washington Square Park and the Surrounding Village from 1958 to 1967." *BB* 1 (Mar. 1968): 56.

Nash, Alanna. "Sam Bush, New Grass Revival and Leon Russell." *BU* 8 (Oct. 1973): 22–23.

"New York Scene." *Gardyloo* 4 (July 1959): 20.

"1977 Blue Grass Music Award Winners." *Music Country* 8 (Apr. 1978): 12–13.

Nitchie, Hub. "Can Bluegrass Survive Popularity?" *BU* 8 (Apr. 1974): 40–41.

———. "Interview: Geoff Stelling." *BN* 5 (Nov. 1977): 5–7.

Nusbaum, Philip. "Traditionalizing the Session: Ongoing Activities, Behavior, Music and Friendship Relations." Typescript, 1982.

Obrecht, Jas. "Emmylou Harris: A Pro Replies." *Guitar Player* 12 (Nov. 1978): 8, 152, 154, 158–59.

O'Donnell, Red, with Dee Kilpatrick. *WSM's Official Grand Ole Opry History–Picture Book.* Rev. 2nd ed. Nashville: WSM, Inc., 1957.

Oermann, Robert K. "Ricky Skaggs Remembers the Stanley Brothers." *BU* 15 (May 1981): 26–29.

Osborn, Jean S. "Jim and Jesse—'The Virginia Boys.'" *DC* 17 (May 1981): 16–17.

[Osborne, Sonny.] "Sonny Tells It Like It Is." *BU* 3 (June 1969): 7–15.

Paris, Judy. "Joe Stuart, "On . . ."" *Pickin'* 4 (Feb. 1977): 30–32.

———. "Pick a Peck of Parking Lot Pickers." *Pickin'* 3 (Nov. 1976): 31–33.

Patrick, Michael D. "Bluegrass Music in the Great Plains." *Mississippi Folklore Register* 12 (Spring 1978): 58–64.

"Paul Cohen, Pioneer Disc Executive, Dies." *Billboard*, Apr. 11, 1970, 3.

Peterson, Richard A. "A Process Model of the Folk, Pop and Fine Art Phases of Jazz." In *American Music: From Storyville to Woodstock*, edited by Charles Nanry, 135–51. New Brunswick, N.J.: Transaction Books, 1972.

Petronko, Ron. "Bill Clifton Discography: June, 1971." *BU* 6 (Oct. 1971): 13–15.

Phillips, Stacy, and Kenny Kosek. *Bluegrass Fiddle Styles.* New York: Oak Publications, 1978.

"Pickin' and Singin'." *Newsweek,* June 29, 1970, 85.

"Pickin' Scruggs." *Time,* June 30, 1961, 53.

[Pierce, Don.] "Formation and Growth of a Record Company—Starday Records." *DC* 14 (May 1960): 34–36.

———. letter to *BU* 1 (Mar. 1967): 8–9.

———. Liner notes to *Bluegrass at Carnegie Hall: The Country Gentlemen.* Starday SLP 174, 1962.

———. Unsigned liner notes. *Country Music—Lester Flatt and Earl Scruggs.* Mercury MG 20358, 1958.

———. Unsigned liner notes. *Country Pickin' and Singing—The Stanley Brothers.* Mercury MG 20349, 1958.

Porterfield, Nolan. *Jimmie Rodgers.* Urbana: University of Illinois Press, 1979.

Portis, Charles. "That New Sound from Nashville." In *A History and Encyclopedia of Country Western and Gospel Music,* edited by Linnell Gentry, 269–282. Rev. 2d ed. Nashville: Clairmont Corp., 1969. (Reprinted from *Saturday Evening Post,* Feb. 12, 1966.)

Powell, Bruce. "Fiddlin' with Byron Berline." *Pickin'* 3 (Feb. 1976): 12–16.

Prendergast, Roy M. *A Neglected Art: A Critical Study of Music in Films.* New York: New York University Press, 1977.

Price, Steven D. *Old as the Hills.* New York: Viking, 1975.

———. "Ricky Skaggs—Portrait of a Young Bluegrass Musician." *Pickin'* 1 (Feb. 1974): 18–19.

Pugh, John. "Carlton Haney: True Great." *BU* 18 (Sept. 1983): 22–25.

Radio John. Liner notes to *New Grass Revival.* Starday SLP 482–498, 1973.

Randolph, Ann. "Cliff Waldron and the New Shades of Grass." *BU* 8 (May 1974): 33–34.

———. "Little Roy." *MN* 4 (Nov. 1973): 10–13, 21.

Reich, Charles. *The Greening of America.* New York: Random House, 1970.

Reno, Don. *The Musical History of Don Reno: His Life . . . His Songs.* Hyattsville, Md.: The Author, 1975.

Reuss, Richard. "American Folksongs and Left-Wing Politics: 1935–56." *Journal of the Folklore Institute* 12 (1975): 89–112.

Rhodes, Don. "Arthur Smith: A Wide and Varied Musical Career." *BU* 12 (July 1977): 20–23.

———. "Band on the Run—The Johnson Mountain Boys." *BU* 16 (Dec. 1981): 12–17.

———. "Bill Harrell: The New Direction." *BU* 14 (May 1980): 16–21.

———. "Carl Story." *Pickin'* 4 (Jan. 1978): 6–8, 10, 12–13.

———. "Eddie and Martha Adcock: Finding Their Place in Bluegrass Music." *BU* 16 (Apr. 1982): 34–38.

———. "Frets Visits . . . Savannah, Georgia—Randy Wood." *Frets* 1 (Nov. 1979): 12–13.

———. "The Lewis Family." *Pickin'* 2 (Apr. 1975): 22–27.

———. "Mac Wiseman." *BU* 10 (July 1975): 14–18.

———. "Mac Wiseman." *BU* 16 (Aug. 1981): 16–22.

———. "On the Hallelujah Turnpike with the Lewis Family." *BU* 14 (June 1980): 18–24.

———. "Pop Lewis." *BU* 9 (Dec. 1974): 11–12.

———. "The Stability and Versatility of the Seldom Scene." *BU* 15 (July 1980): 14–19.

———. "1024 . . . The Lewis Family." *BU* 8 (Apr. 1974), 13–16.

———. "Third Generation Lewis." *BU* 11 (July 1976): 16–22.

Rice, Edw. LeRoy. *Monarchs of Minstrelsy, From 'Daddy' Rice to Date.* New York: Kenny Publishing Co., 1911.

Richardson, Peter A. "The Bluegrass Band." *BBU* 1 (Nov. 1965): 1–2.

———. "Editorial Comment." *BBU* 2 (July 1967): 1–2.

———. "[Untitled editorial.] *BBU* 2 (Dec. 1966): [5].

———. "What Is and What Is Not 'Traditional Bluegrass' Anyhow????" *BBU* 1 (Mar. 1966): 4.

Rinzler, Ralph. "Bill Monroe." In *Stars of Country Music,* edited by Bill C. Malone and Judith McCulloh, 202–21. Urbana: University of Illinois Press, 1975.

———. "Bill Monroe—'The Daddy of Blue Grass Music.'" *SO* 13 (Feb.–Mar. 1963): 5–8.

———. "Blue Grass Fest a 'Picknic'; Top Names Mark 1st Event." *Billboard,* Sept. 18, 1965, 8.

———. Brochure notes to *American Banjo Scruggs Style.* Folkways FA 2314, 1957.

———. "Doc Watson." In *The Songs of Doc Watson,* 8–11. New York: Oak Publications, 1971.

———. "First Annual Blue Grass Festival Set for September 3–5." *Broadside* 4 (Aug. 18, 1965): 22.

———. Liner notes to *Bill and Charlie Monroe.* Decca DL75066, 1969.

———. Liner notes to *Bill Monroe's Country Music Hall of Fame.* Decca DL75281, 1971.

———. Liner notes to *Bluegrass Instrumentals.* Decca DL4601, 1965.

———. Liner notes to *The Greenbriar Boys.* Vanguard VRS 9104, 1962.

———. Liner notes to *The High Lonesome Sound of Bill Monroe and His Blue Grass Boys.* Decca DL4780, 1966.

———. Liner notes to *Kentucky Blue Grass.* Decca DL75213, 1970.

———. "Ralph Stanley: The Tradition from the Mountains." *BU* 8 (Mar. 1974): 7–11.

Rinzler, Ralph, and Alice [Gerrard] Foster. Liner notes to *Bill Monroe and His Blue Grass Boys: A Voice from on High.* Decca DL75135, 1969.

Rockwell, John. "Bluegrass Hitting High Note Tonight." *New York Times,* July 18, 1973.

Rogan, John. *Timeless Flight: Definitive Biography of the Byrds.* London: Scorpion Publications, 1980.

Romaine, Anne. "Georgia Bluegrass Festival." *BU* 4 (Sept. 1969): 5–8. Reprinted from *Great Speckled Bird* (Atlanta), Aug. 4, 1969.

Ronald, Robert J. "Jim Eanes—Biography." *Country Western Express* 29 (1972): 3–10.

———. "Jim Eanes—Discography." *Country Western Express* 29 (1972): 11–20.

———. "Lester Flatt and Earl Scruggs Discography." *BU* 2 (Jan. 1968): 2–4, 2 (Feb. 1968): 5–9.

Rooney, James. *Bossmen: Bill Monroe and Muddy Waters.* New York: Dial Press, 1971.

Rorrer, Kinney. *Rambling Blues, The Life and Songs of Charlie Poole.* London: Old Time Music, 1982.

Rosenberg, Neil V. "Big Fish, Small Pond: Country Musicians and Their Markets." In *Media Sense: Folklore and Popular Culture,* edited by Martin Laba and Peter Narváez. Bowling Green: Popular Culture Press, forthcoming. [scheduled for 1985]

————. *Bill Monroe and His Blue Grass Boys: An Illustrated Discography.* Nashville: Country Music Foundation, 1974.

————. "Bluegrass." In *Encyclopedia of Southern Culture,* edited by William Ferris and Charles R. Wilson. Chapel Hill: University of North Carolina Press, forthcoming. [scheduled for 1986]

————. "Bluegrass and Serendipity." *BU* 2 (Nov. 1967): 2–3.

————. "Bluegrass Music." In *The New Grove Dictionary of Music and Musicians,* edited by Stanley Sadie, 2:812. London: Macmillan Publishers, 1980.

————. "Bob Dylan in Nashville." *JCM* 7 (Dec. 1978): 54–66.

————. "A Brief Survey of Bluegrass Haberdashery." *BU* 2 (Mar. 1968): 6.

————. Brochure to *Country and Western Classics: Flatt and Scruggs.* Time-Life Records, TLCW-04, 1982.

————. "Don Pierce: The Rise and Fall of Starday and the Perplexing Patriot Problem." *BU* 1 (May 1967): 4–5.

————. "The Folklorist and the Phonograph Record: An Introduction to Analytic Discography." *Canadian Folklore Canadien* 3 (1981): 127–35.

————. "From Sound to Style: The Emergence of Bluegrass." *JAF* 80 (1967): 143–50.

————. "A Front Porch Visit with Birch Monroe." *BU* 17 (Sept. 1982): 58–63.

————. "Goodtime Charlie and the Bricklin: A Satirical Song in Context." *Journal of the Canadian Oral History Association* 3 (1978): 27–46.

————. "The Hardwoodlands Festival." *TABC News,* April 1975, 1–2.

————. "Herbert Halpert: A Biographical Sketch." In *Folklore Studies in Honour of Herbert Halpert,* edited by Kenneth S. Goldstein and Neil V. Rosenberg, 1–13. St. John's: Memorial University of Newfoundland, 1980.

————. "Into Bluegrass: The History of a Word." *MN* 5 (Aug. 1974): 7–9, 31–33.

————. Liner notes to *Early Bluegrass.* RCA Victor LPV-569, 1969.

————. Liner notes to *Hills and Home: Thirty Years of Bluegrass.* New World Records NW225, 1976.

————. Liner notes to *The Osborne Brothers.* Rounder SS04, 1978.

————. "Osborne Brothers Discography." *BU* 1 (July 1967): 2–5.

————. "The Osborne Brothers, Part One: Family and Apprenticeship." *BU* 6 (Sept. 1971): 5–10.

————. "The Osborne Brothers, Part Two: Getting Off." *BU* 6 (Feb. 1972): 5–8.

————. "Reflections on Roanoke." *BU* 1 (Jan. 1967): 3–4.

————. "Regional Stereotype and Folklore—Appalachia and Atlantic Canada." *Appalachian Journal* 7 (Autumn–Winter 1979–80): 46–50.

————. Review of Toru Mitsui, *Bluegrass Music,* 1st ed. *JEMFQ* 5 (Spring 1969): 31–33.

————. Review of Toru Mitsui, *Bluegrass Music,* 2nd ed. *JEMFQ* 12 (Spring 1976): 46–47.

———. "The Works of Herbert Halpert." In *Folklore Studies in Honour of Herbert Halpert,* 15–30.

Roszak, Theodore. *The Making of a Counter Culture.* Garden City, N.Y.: Anchor Books, 1969.

Rounder Collective [Ken Irwin, Marian Leighton, Bill Nowlin]. Brochure notes to *The Early Days of Bluegrass.* Vol. 1. Rounder 1013, 1975.

———. Brochure notes to *The Early Days of Bluegrass.* Vol. 2. Rounder 1014, 1975.

———. Brochure notes to *How Can a Poor Man Stand Such Times and Live? . . . The Songs of Blind Alfred Reed.* Rounder 1001, 1972.

———. Brochure notes to *The Rich-R-Tone Story. Early Days of Bluegrass.* Vol. 5. Rounder 1017, 1975.

———. Liner notes to *Honkytonk Bluegrass.* Rounder 0031, 1974.

Rumble, John Woodruff. "The Emergence of Nashville as a Recording Center: Logbooks from the Castle Studio, 1952–53." *JCM* 7 (Dec. 1978): 22–41.

———. "Traditionalism and Commercialism in American Bluegrass Music: A Survey of Stylistic Change in Its Institutionalized and Cultural Context, 1965–1975." Master's thesis, Vanderbilt University, 1976.

Russell, Tony. *Blacks, Whites and Blues.* New York: Stein and Day, 1970.

Sachs, Bill. "C&W Talent Booking, Discs Boom in Nashville." *Billboard,* Apr. 27, 1957, 21.

———. "Sin and Salvation: C&W Music Still Packs Vitality." *Billboard,* Mar. 24, 1958, 20.

Samuelson, Dave. "Making a Record—Part 1—Should You Do It?" *BU* 16 (Dec. 1981): 39–41.

———. "Making a Record—Part 2—Preparing to Record." *BU* 16 (Jan. 1982): 16–22.

Santelli, Robert. *Aquarius Rising: The Rock Festival Years.* New York: Delta, 1980.

Saunders, Walter V. "Johnny Whisnant Musical History." *BU* 4 (June 1968): 8–14, 5 (July 1968): 7–11, 5 (Aug. 1968): 17–22.

Saunders, Walter V., and the Rounder Folks. Liner notes to *The Church Brothers.* Vol. 8, *The Early Days of Bluegrass.* Rounder 1020, 1981.

Sayers, Bob. "Leslie Keith: Black Mountain Odyssey." *BU* 11 (Dec. 1976): 13–17.

Schilling, Ed. "Lutherie's Day in Court." *Frets* 4 (Dec. 1982): 20.

Schlappi, Elizabeth. "Roy Acuff." In *Stars of Country Music,* edited by Bill C. Malone and Judith McCulloh, 179–201. Urbana: University of Illinois Press, 1975.

Scoppa, Bud. *The Byrds.* New York: Scholastic Book Services, 1971.

Scott, Ronald D. "The Life and Times of Ronald D. Scott." *BB* 1 (May 1968): 2–3.

———. "Ron Scott Autobiography, Chapter Two." *BB* 1 (Mar.–June 1969): 6–8.

Scruggs, Earl. "Discography." In *Earl Scruggs and the Five-String Banjo.* New York: Peer International Corporation, 1968.

———. *Earl Scruggs and the Five-String Banjo.* New York: Peer International, 1968.

———. "Workshop: Scruggs Style Banjo." *Frets* 3 (Aug. 1981): 54.

Scruggs, Louise. "The History and Development of America's Favorite Folk Instrument." In *Earl Scruggs and the Five-String Banjo,* by Earl Scruggs, 9–11. New York: Peer International, 1968.

———. "A History of America's Favorite Folk Instrument." *SO* 13 (Dec.–Jan. 1963–64): 26–29.

———. "History of the Five-String Banjo." *Tennessee Folklore Society Bulletin* 27 (Mar. 1961): 1–5.

———. Liner notes to *Nashville Airplane*. Columbia CS9741, 1968.

———. Unsigned liner notes to *Changin' Times*. Columbia CS9596, 1967.

———. Unsigned liner notes to *Foggy Mountain Banjo*. Columbia CL1564, 1961.

Sears, Nelson. *Jim and Jesse: Appalachia to the Grand Ole Opry*. Lancaster, Pa.: The Author, 1976.

Seeger, Alice [Gerrard] and Mike. "Bluegrass Unlimited Merit Award—Ralph Rinzler." *BU* 7 (Dec. 1972): 5.

Seeger, Charles. "Reviews." *JAF* 61 (1948): 215–218.

Seeger, Mike. Brochure notes to *Mountain Music Bluegrass Style*. Folkways FA2318, 1959.

———. Brochure notes to *The Thirty-Seventh Old Time Fiddlers' Convention at Union Grove, North Carolina*. Folkways FA2434, 1961.

———. "Hamilton County Bluegrass Band." *BU* 5 (June 1971): 19–20.

———. "Mountain Music Bluegrass Style." *SO* 11 (Feb.–Mar. 1961): 10–12.

Seeger, Mike, and John Cohen. *The New Lost City Ramblers Songbook*. New York: Oak Publications, 1964.

Seeger, Pete. *The Five-String Banjo Instructor*. Rev. 2nd ed. New York: Oak Publications, 1954.

Shapiro, Henry. *Appalachia on Our Mind*. Chapel Hill: University of North Carolina Press, 1978.

Shelton, Robert. "Bluegrass, From Hills and City." *New York Times*, Sept. 30, 1962.

———. "City Folk Singers." *New York Times*, Apr. 8, 1962.

———. "Folk Joins Jazz at Newport." *New York Times*, July 19, 1959.

———. "Hootenanny Held at Carnegie Hall." *New York Times*, Sept. 18, 1961.

———. "Old-Time Fiddlers." *New York Times*, Apr. 9, 1961.

Shephert, Alex. "Interview: Jim Smoak." *BN* 5 (May 1978): 4–8.

Shimbo, Takashi. "All Japanese Bluegrass Festival." *BU* 5 (Dec. 1970): 11.

Sievert, Jon. "Clarence White: Legendary Flatpicking Stylist." *Frets* 1 (Sept. 1979): 18–20, 22.

———. "David Grisman." *Frets* 3 (Feb. 1981): 20–22, 24–25.

———. "Roy Clark." *Guitar Player* 12 (Nov. 1978): 54–56, 120, 124, 126, 128, 130, 132–33, 136.

———. "Sam Bush." *Frets* 4 (Aug. 1982), 22–26.

———. "Sam Bush: 'Newgrass' Mover and Shaker." *Frets* 1 (July 1979): 18–20, 22–33.

———. "Tony Rice: Bluegrass-Jazz Innovator." *Guitar Player* 11 (Dec. 1977): 26, 130, 132–34, 136–37.

Siggins, Betsy. "Bluegrass Sprouts in Boston." *Hootenanny* 1 (Nov. 1964): 28–29, 74.

Silver, Barry. "Curly Seckler: From Foggy Mountain to Nashville Grass." *BU* 14 (Nov. 1979): 10–16.

———. "Vassar Clements Out West." *BU* 12 (May 1978): 18–23.

Siminoff, Roger H. "Bill Keith: Yesterday, Today and Tomorrow." *Pickin'* 4 (Dec. 1977) 4–6, 8, 10, 12, 14, 16–17.

———. "Byron Berline." *Frets* 4 (Mar. 1982): 26–31.

———. *Constructing a Bluegrass Mandolin*. Denville, N.J.: Colonial Press, 1977.

———. "Earl Scruggs." *Frets* 3 (July 1981): 24–26, 28–30, 32, 34–35.

———. "Gibson: The Early Years." *Pickin'* 2 (June 1975): 4–6, 8–10, 12–25.

———. "The Gibson Banjos, 20 Golden Years." *Frets* 3 (Jan. 1981): 24–29.

———. "Gibson (Part II)." *Pickin'* 2 (July 1975): 20, 22–25.

———. "Inside Reno-Harrell." *Pickin'* 2 (Jan. 1976): 4–6, 8–9.

———. "Kenny Baker." *Frets* 4 (July 1982): 24–26, 28.

———. "Mike Auldridge." *Frets* 3 (May 1981): 26–31.

———. "Roy Clark," *Frets* 1 (Dec. 1979): 26–30, 32.

Sims, Judith. "The Eagles Take It Easy and Soar." *Rolling Stone* 115 (Aug. 17, 1972): 12.

Sims, Vincent. "The Red Allen Story." *BU* 2 (Aug. 1967): 2–3.

Sippel, Johnny. "The Hillbilly Deejay Prime Asset to Country & Western Music." *Billboard*, Sept. 15, 1951, 61.

———. "New Horizons for Country-Western Platter-Spinners." *Billboard*, Feb. 28, 1953, 58.

Smith, Andrew. "The New Lost City Ramblers." *Country and Western Spotlight* n.s. no. 15 (June 1978): 6–8.

Smith, Bonnie. "Bluegrass Spectacular: A Television First." *BU* 14 (Jan. 1980): 16–19.

Smith, Leon. "Talking with the Stars: Two Interviews from 'A Bluegrass Hornbook.'" *BU* 11 (Sept. 1976): 22–25.

Smith, Mayne. "Additions and Corrections." *BU* 1 (Jan. 1967): 4–6.

———. "Bluegrass as a Musical Style." *Autoharp* 3 (Feb. 1963): A–F.

———. "Bluegrass Music and Musicians." Master's thesis, Indiana University, 1964.

———. "First Bluegrass Festival Honors Bill Monroe." *SO* 15 (Jan. 1966): 65, 67, 69.

———. "An Introduction to Bluegrass." *JAF* 78 (1965): 245–56.

———. "Notes and Interviews from the First Annual Bluegrass Festival at Roanoke, Virginia—1965." Typescript, Dec. 1965.

Smith, Richard D. "The Bluegrass Cardinals on the Wing." *Pickin'* 4 (July 1977): 40, 42.

———. "Ralph Rinzler: Preserving American Folk Arts." *Pickin'* 6 (Nov. 1979): 11–14.

———. "The Skyline's No Limit." *BU* 18 (Oct. 1983): 11–13.

Smith, Robert J. *The Art of the Festival.* Lawrence, Kans.: University of Kansas Publication in Anthropology, no. 6, 1975.

Smothers, Mel. "Between Sets with the New Grass Revival." *Pickin'* 4 (Apr. 1977): 14–16, 18, 20–21.

Smyth, Willie. *Country Music Recorded Prior to 1943: A Discography of LP Reissues.* Los Angeles: JEMF Special Series no. 14, 1984.

Snyder, Eugenia. "Del McCoury: Low-Key but Powerful." *BU* 16 (May 1982): 17–24.

Soelberg, Paul W. "Modern Country Radio: Friend or Foe?" *Billboard*, Oct. 17, 1970, sec. 2, 44, 46.

Southern, John. "Old-Fashioned Craftsmanship: Mossman Guitars." *Pickin'* 2 (Oct. 1975): 14–17.

Spielman, Earl V. "The Fiddling Traditions of Cape Breton and Texas: A Study in Parallels and Contrasts." *Anuario* 8 (1972): 39–48.

———. "An Interview with Eck Robertson." *JEMFQ* 8 (1972): 179–87.

———. "The Texas Fiddling Style." *DB* 14 (Sept. 1980): 24–32.

Spottswood, Richard K. "Carl Sauceman: The Odyssey of a Bluegrass Pioneer." *BU* 11 (Aug. 1976): 10–17.

———. "A Catalog of American Folk Music on Commercial Recordings at the Library of Congress, 1923–1940." Master's thesis, Catholic University, 1962.

———. "County Records—Brief Summary." *BU* 1 (July 1966): 1–2.

———. "An Interview with Bill Clifton." *BU* 2 (Mar. 1968): 3–5, 2 (Apr. 1968): 9–12, 2 (May 1968): 7–11.

———. "There Was Bluegrass at Camp Springs." *BU* 4 (Oct. 1969): 3–7.

Standish, David. "Shenandoah Breakdown." *Playboy* 18 (Nov. 1971): 188–90, 193–94.

Stanley, Linda. "The Lost and Found." *BU* 12 (Mar. 1978): 12–16.

Stanton, Kathleen. "The Bluegrass Fiddlers: Kenny Baker." *Pickin'* 1 (Dec. 1974): 18–21.

Statman, Andry. *Jesse McReynolds Mandolin.* New York: Oak Publications Bluegrass Masters Series, 1979.

Steinberg, Cobbet W. *Film Facts.* New York: Facts on File, 1980.

Steiner, Alan J. "Bob Paisley and the Southern Grass." *BU* 18 (Nov. 1983): 10–14.

———. "Peter Rowan: Wandering Boy Returns to His Roots." *BU* 13 (Feb. 1979): 12–13.

Strickland, Rhonda. "The McPeak Brothers." *BU* 17 (Jan. 1983): 10–16.

"Summer Bluegrass from National Public Radio." *MN* 7 (Oct. 1976): 11.

Szwed, John F. "Musical Adaptation among Afro-Americans." *JAF* 82 (1969): 112–21.

Talbott, Nancy. "The Boston Blue Grass Scene." *MN* 2 (Mar.-Apr. 1971): 14–15.

Taylor, Barbara. "Mom Lewis." *BU* 9 (Dec. 1974): 10.

Taylor, Gwen. "Del McCoury." *BU* 7 (June 1973): 17–19.

Teepen, Tom. "Allen Grass: A Family Affair." *MN* 4 (Feb. 1973): 4–7.

———. " 'How Many Here Like Baseball?': The Osborne Brothers at Antioch College, 1959 [sic]." *MN* 4 (July 1973): 19, 39.

———. "Larry Sparks . . . on the Road." *MN* 3 (Nov. 1972): 8–12.

Terrace, Vincent. *The Complete Encyclopedia of Television Programs, 1947–1979.* rev. 2nd ed. South Brunswick and New York: A. S. Barnes, 1979.

Thomas, Jean. *The Singin' Fiddler of Lost Hope Holler.* New York: E. P. Dutton, 1938.

Thomason, Ron. *Lonesome Is a Car up on Blocks.* Springfield, Ohio: The Author, 1979.

Thompson, Howard. "The 16-mm. Circuit: National Movie Meet, Superior New Fare." *New York Times*, Apr. 15, 1962.

———. "The 16-mm Circuit: Top Films, New Sources Seen at Assembly." *New York Times*, June 3, 1962.

Thurston, Anne, comp. *Bluegrass Discography, 1980.* Menlo Park, Calif.: The Author, 1980. (n.p., hand bound, reduced photocopy of typescript).

Tinkoff, David. "The Ronald D. Scott Story, Part One." *BB* 1 (Mar. 1968): 7–8.

Titon, Jeff. *Early Downhome Blues.* Urbana: University of Illinois Press, 1977.

———. "The Life Story." *JAF* 93 (1980): 276–92.

Toelken, J. Barre. "Traditional Fiddling in Idaho." *Western Folklore* 24 (1965): 259–62.

Tottle, Jack. "Berline, Crary and Hickman—Part 1." *BU* 15 (Sept. 1980): 12–19.

————. "Berline, Crary and Hickman—Conclusion." *BU* 15 (Oct. 1980): 34–39.

————. *Bluegrass Mandolin.* New York: Oak Publications, 1974.

————. "The Country Gazette: Keep On Pushing." *MN* 5 (July 1974): 6–11, 16.

————. "Doyle Lawson and Quicksilver." *BU* 15 (Nov. 1980): 16–22.

————. "Ralph Stanley: The Stanley Sound." *BU* 15 (May 1981): 14–21.

————. "Ricky Skaggs: Clinch Mountain to Boone Creek." *BU* 11 (Jan. 1977): 8–16.

————. "Tony Rice: East Meets West." *BU* 12 (Oct. 1977): 10–16.

Townsend, Charles R. *San Antonio Rose.* Urbana: University of Illinois Press, 1976.

Traum, Happy. *Bluegrass Guitar.* New York: Oak Publications, 1974.

Tribe, Ivan M. Brochure to *Roy Hall and His Blue Ridge Entertainers.* County 406, 1980.

————. "Carl Story: Bluegrass Pioneer." *BU* 9 (Jan. 1975): 8–14.

————. "Charlie Monroe." *BU* 10 (Oct. 1975): 12–19.

————. "Chubby Wise: One of the Original Bluegrass Fiddlers." *BU* 11 (Feb. 1977): 10–12.

————. "Curly Fox: Old Time and Novelty Fiddler Extraordinary." *DB* 27 (Dec. 1974): 8–21.

————. "The Goins Brothers: Melvin and Ray—Maintaining the Lonesome Pine Fiddler Tradition." *BU* 8 (May 1974): 11–18.

————. "Jimmie Skinner, Bluegrass Composer, Record Retailer." *BU* 11 (Mar. 1977): 34–37.

————. "Joe Meadows, Mountain State Fiddler." *BU* 13 (Oct. 1978): 30–35.

————. "Old Actors in a New Play: The Boys from Indiana." *Pickin'* 5 (Mar. 1978): 10, 12, 43.

————. "Pros Long Before Boston: The Entire Career of the Lilly Brothers." *BU* 9 (July 1974): 8–17.

————. "The Return of Donna Stoneman: First Lady of the Mandolin." *BU* 17 (June 1983): 16–26.

————. "Someone Really Different: Raymond Fairchild." *BU* 9 (Oct. 1974): 24–25.

Tribe, Ivan M., and John W. Morris. "Clyde Moody: Old-Time, Bluegrass and Country Musician." *BU* 10 (Nov. 1975): 12–21.

————. "J. E. and Wade Mainer." *BU* 10 (Nov. 1975): 12–21.

Tripp, Ruth. "Mountain Music a Feature in Concert at Rogers High." *Providence* (R.I.) *Journal,* July 20, 1969.

Trischka, Tony. *Melodic Banjo.* New York: Oak Publications, 1976.

Trischka, Tony, and Bill Keith. *Bill Keith Banjo.* New York: Oak Publications Bluegrass Masters Series, 1978.

Tuchman, Doug. "Buck White and the Down Home Folks." *Pickin'* 2 (July 1975): 4–8, 10–12.

————. "The Country Gentlemen." *Pickin'* 1 (Mar. 1974): 4–12.

————. "The New Lost City Ramblers." *Pickin'* 2 (Mar. 1975): 4–6, 8–10, 12–13.

————. "Vassar Clements." *Pickin'* 1 (Jan. 1975): 4–9.

Tyler, Ilene. "Woes of a Bluegrass Wife." *BBU* 2 (June 1967): 4–5.

Tyler, Keith. "Keith Tyler Talks a Little Bluegrass—Loudly!" *BBU* 2 (Feb. 1967): 3–4.

van Gameren, Henk, comp. *A Listing of Bluegrass Albums.* Poortugaal, Holland: The Author, 1977.

Vernon, Bill. "Bluegrass Stands the Test." *Billboard*, Oct. 28, 1967, sec. 2, 84–86.

―――. "Cliff Waldron and the New Shades of Grass." *MN* 2 (Jan.-Feb. 1971): 8–9.

―――. "A Conversation with Lester Flatt." *MN* 3 (Aug. 1972): 2–6.

―――. "The Country Gentlemen—On Tour in Japan." *MN* 3 (June 1972): 2–5.

―――. "Del McCoury and the Dixie Pals." *MN* 2 (Nov. 1971): 2–6.

―――. "The Don Reno Story, Part 1: Early Years." *MN* 4 (June 1983): 8–11.

―――. "The Don Reno Story, Part 2: Bill Monroe and Beyond." *MN* 4 (Aug. 1973): 8–11.

―――. "The Don Reno Story, Part 3: Birth of the Tennessee Cutups." *MN* 4 (Sept. 1973): 8–11, 19.

―――. "The Don Reno Story, Part 4: The Glory Years." *MN* 4 (Dec. 1973): 10–12, 21.

―――. "James Monroe: The Sun Also Rises." *MN* 7 (Sept. 1976): 6–9.

―――. "The John Duffey Story: The Sound That Changed the Color of Bluegrass." *MN* 7 (May 1977): 4–9.

―――. "Last Respects to the Giant Charlie Monroe." *Pickin'* 2 (Jan. 1976): 14–17.

―――. Liner notes to *The Songs of Charlie Monroe and The Kentucky Pardners*. County 539, 1974.

―――. "Part-Time Professionals: The Seldom Scene." *MN* 4 (Mar. 1973): 6–8.

―――. "The Sound That Changed the Color of Blue Grass." *MN* 7: 6 (1976): 6–9, 7:7 (1976): 7–9.

von Schmidt, Eric, and Jim Rooney. *Baby Let Me Follow You Down*. Garden City, N.Y.: Anchor Books, 1979.

Walker, Connie. "The Plight of the Blue Grass Widow." *MN* 3 (May 1972): 60–61.

Waller, Steve. "Sawtooth Mountain Volunteers." *BU* 2 (May 1968): 2.

Weintraub, Boris. "Buck White and the Down Home Folks." *BU* 16 (Nov. 1981): 9–13.

Weiss, Michael. "A Bluegrass Hornbook." *Pickin'* 3 (July 1976): 38.

Weissman, Dick. "Folksong '59." *Caravan* 17 (June-July 1959): 30–31.

Welding, Peter J. "Earl Scruggs—and the Sound of Bluegrass." *SO* 12 (Apr.-May 1962): 4–7.

―――. "Music from the 'Bluegrass' Roots." *Saturday Review*, June 10, 1961, 48.

―――. Review of *Foggy Mountain Banjo*. *Down Beat*, July 20, 1961, 50–51.

―――. "Starday, the Bluegrass Label." *SO* 12 (Summer 1962): 63, 65.

Weller, Jack E. *Yesterday's People*. Lexington: University of Kentucky Press, 1965.

Wells, Paul F. "Bluegrass Was Really My Center—An Interview with Richard Greene." *Pickin'* 2 (Nov. 1975): 10–12, 15–18.

―――, ed. Brochure to *Presenting the Blue Sky Boys*. JEMF LP104, 1976.

Wernick, Peter. *Bluegrass Banjo*. New York: Oak Publications, 1974.

―――. *Bluegrass Songbook*. New York: Oak Publications, 1976.

[Wesbrooks], Cousin Wilbur, with Barbara M. McLean and Sandra S. Grafton. *Everybody's Cousin*. New York: Manor Books, 1979.

Weston, Frank, and Silvia Pitcher. " 'We Got a Few Old Songs That We Do.' " *OTM* 38 (Summer-Autumn 1982): 5–10.

Westover, Vicki, and Kathy Plunket. "The Traditionalist Bluegrass Cardinals Prepare to Join Washington's Select List." *Music Country* 8 (May 1978): 9.

"Where Does the 'Blue Grass' Grow?" *Variety*, Nov. 20, 1957, 59.

Whisnant, David, ed. *Folk Festival Issues: Report from a Seminar*. Los Angeles: JEMF
    Special Series no. 12, 1979.
Whittaker, H. Lloyd ("Stretch"). "Cliff Waldron and the New Shades of Grass." *BU*
    5 (Apr. 1971): 5.
Wilgus, D. K. *Anglo-American Folksong Scholarship since 1898*. New Brunswick, N.J.:
    Rutgers University Press, 1959.
———. "Country Western Music and the Urban Hillbilly." In *The Urban Experience
    and Folk Tradition*, edited by Americo Paredes and Ellen J. Stekert, 137–64.
    Austin: University of Texas Press, 1971.
———. " 'Ten Broeck and Mollie': A Race and a Ballad." *Kentucky Folklore Record* 2
    (1956): 77–89.
———. ed. "Hillbilly Issue." *JAF* 78 (1965): 195–288.
Williams, Bill. "Don Pierce Exits Starday." *Billboard*, Aug. 8, 1970, 8.
Wilson, Joe. "Bristol's WCYB: Early Bluegrass Turf." *MN* 3 (Oct. 1972): 8–12.
Wilson, Joe, and Lee Udall. *Folk Festivals: A Handbook for Organization and
    Management*. Knoxville: University of Tennessee Press, 1982.
Wilson, John S. "Program Given by Alan Lomax: Folklorist Offers Impressive Array
    of American Artists in Carnegie Hall Concert." *New York Times*, Apr. 4, 1959,
    13.
Winans, Robert B. "The Folk, the Stage, and the Five-String Banjo in the
    Nineteenth Century." *JAF* 89 (1976): 407–37.
Winkelman, Donald M. "The Brown County Project." *Midwest Folklore* 11 (1961):
    15–23.
"Winning Combination." *CSR* 13 (Aug. 1951): 18.
Winston, Winnie. "Scruggs and Flatt and the Wilburn Brothers." *Gardyloo* 4 (July
    1959): 14–15.
Winter, Ralph E. "Sentimental Songs: Awash with Nostalgia, 'Bluegrass Festivals'
    Revive Old-Time Music." *Wall Street Journal*, Oct. 20, 1972.
Wolfe, Charles K. "Bluegrass Touches: An Interview with Bill Monroe." *OTM* 16
    (1975): 6–12.
———. "Dave Freeman and County Records." *BU* 15 (Dec. 1980): 50–55.
———. "Fiddler's Dream: The Legend of Arthur Smith." *DB* 11 (Dec. 1977): 26–
    64.
———. "From the Fiddling Archives: McMichen in Kentucky—The Sunset Years."
    DB 11 (Mar. 1977): 10–18.
———. "From the Fiddling Archives (No. 32 in a Series): The Tommy Jackson
    Story." *DB* 16 (Mar. 1982): 26–37.
———. "From the Fiddling Archives (No. 33 in a Series): Bob Wills, Fiddler." *DB*
    16 (June 1982): 16–22.
———. *The Grand Ole Opry: The Early Years, 1925–35*. London: Old Time Music,
    1975.
———. *Kentucky Country*. Lexington: University of Kentucky Press, 1983.
———. "Man of Constant Sorrow: Richard Burnett's Story." *OTM* 9 (Summer
    1973): 6–9, 10 (Autumn 1973): 5–11.
———. "The Mystery of 'The Black Mountain Rag.' " *DB* 16 (Dec. 1982): 3–12.
———. "A Preliminary Tommy Jackson Discography." *DB* 16 (Mar. 1982): 45–46.
———. "String." *BU* 16 (June 1982): 45–51.
———. *Tennessee Strings*. Knoxville: University of Tennessee Press, 1977.

————. "What Ever Happened to Karl and Harty?" *BU* 18 (Oct. 1983): 26–29.

Wolfe, Tom. *The Electric Kool-Aid Acid Test.* New York: Farrar, Straus and Giroux, 1968.

Woods, William C. "Country Music—Little-Noticed Nightlife for Hundreds." *Washington Post*, Aug. 30, 1970.

Wright, Sharon. "The Dry Branch Fire Squad." *BU* 14 (Jan. 1980): 12–15.

Young, Israel G. "Newport Folk Festival." *Caravan* 18 (Aug.-Sept. 1959): 25–27.

Yoder, Don. "Toward a Definition of Folk Religion." *Western Folklore* 33 (1974): 2–15.

Zill, Barbara. "John Morris Talks about Old Homestead Records." *Pickin'* 3 (Nov. 1976): 22–24.

Zorn, Eric. "A 'Homestead' for Using Talent." *BU* 14 (Dec. 1979): 24–26.

Discography

The following list of records includes all of the *singles* (7-inch 45 and 10-inch 78-rpm discs with a single song on each side) and *albums* (10-inch or 12-inch 33 ⅓-rpm discs, also called LPs, and collections of three to five 78-rpm discs issued together in a single album) mentioned in the text, cited in the chapter notes, or listed in the discographical notes. An individual song, one side of a single, is listed here only if it was originally issued on a single and was therefore discussed in that form somewhere in the book. Other individual songs, which appeared on albums only, can be found in the index. The albums on which they were included are given in the text, notes, or discographical notes and therefore appear in the following discography. Where singles have been reissued on albums, both the original single and the album are listed; but the connection between the two is given only in the discographical notes to the chapter in which the original single is discussed. EPs (Extended Play)—7-inch discs, usually 45- but sometimes 33 ⅓-rpm, with more than one song on a side—are treated as albums.

To an extent even greater than is the case with the materials in the bibliography, the records listed below are difficult to find. Many of them are out of print. Few libraries have collections of bluegrass phonograph recordings substantial enough for purposes of research. Like most who study this music I have had to depend to a large extent upon my own collection and those of fellow scholars, record collectors, musicians, and fans.

As with bluegrass bibliography, there is no inclusive general bluegrass discography available presently. Evanston, Illinois, collector Don Hoos has been working with Northwestern University music librarian Bruce Miller on a computer-based discography of this scope for some time. It is hoped that eventually a publication will result. Fortunately, in print are several less comprehensive bluegrass discographies in which record numbers and titles for unobtainable items can sometimes be found. Anne Thurston's *Bluegrass Discography 1980*, a small, hand-produced booklet which lists songs on albums, is useful in tracking down variant performances. Henk van Gameren's *A Listing of Bluegrass Albums*, a 1977 compilation produced in a manner similar to Thurston's, is up-to-date for the mid-seventies. Urban Haglund and Lillies Ohlsson's *A Listing of Bluegrass LPs*, published in 1971 by the Swedish magazine *Kountry Korral*, is the most useful of the three because of its completeness: it includes material from the fifties and sixties not covered in other listings. For dating of albums, I have relied upon *County Sales Newsletter* and on the record reviews in *Bluegrass Unlimited*. For the latter I was aided considerably by Frank Godbey's privately printed computer list of album titles and review dates. Dating singles was not always so easy; for this information I have depended upon record company information and reviews or release notices in *Billboard*. My final recourse for hard-to-get information was the Country Music Foundation's master discographer, Bob Pinson.

All dates given refer to the time at which the record was released (technically, "published"). It is sometimes possible to ascertain recording dates, but generally speaking these dates are not as important for the purposes of this study as are the dates when the records came on the market. For this reason I do not include in the following entries master (also called matrix) numbers, the symbols assigned to records at the time of recording by companies in order to identify them in their files. Master/ matrix numbers enable one to group together all recordings made at a single time and to identify them as coming from a single, dated recording session. Such information is contained in the analytic discographies cited in the bibliography (such as my Bill Monroe one, and those by Kuykendall of Flatt and Scruggs and the Stanley Brothers) but to present it here makes little sense as it would, in this setting, be incomplete. For an extended discussion of the art of discography (along with relevant bibliography), see my "The Folklorist and the Phonograph Record."

For those who wish to obtain their own copies of the records listed here, the quickest way is via the various speciality outlets such as County Sales. These advertise regularly in publications like *Bluegrass Unlimited* and *Frets*. There are more old bluegrass recordings in print today than ever before. It appears that if one waits long enough versions of significant old songs or albums become available in new forms. But this means that to build a record collection one must follow the new reissues rather closely, as many are not in print for long.

It is also possible to obtain older singles and albums through record auction sales conducted through the mails by collectors. Many of these private collectors, who buy and sell old albums and singles in this way, are interested in first or original editions and will pay, therefore, large sums for records which may be available as reissues or new repressings. Unless you share this interest, don't buy from an auction list without first checking for in-print new copies. Some auction list sellers will make tape copies of items in their collection for researchers—for a fee.

For those who lack the resources or interest to build a private collection, publicly accessible research collections which contain a significant proportion of bluegrass recordings include the John Edwards Memorial Collection, now housed in the Folk Music Archives at the University of North Carolina at Chapel Hill, North Carolina, 27514, and the Country Music Foundation at the Hall of Fame and Museum, 4 Music Square East, Nashville, Tennessee, 37203. Be advised, however: owing to copyright regulations, it is not possible to build a private tape collection using the resources of these institutions. For a fee, the CMF will supply researchers with tape copies of out-of-print recordings. They allow listening on the premises for research purposes. But no public collection has the resources or the legal right to let their collection be used for entertainment. Bluegrass musicians were among the first to complain about the way taping cut into record sales. If you want bluegrass recordings for your personal entertainment, you should pay for them.

American Banjo Scruggs Style. Folkways FA 2314, 1957.

American Folk Songs for Children. Atlantic 1350, 1960.

Anthology of American Folk Music. Folkways FA2951-2953, 1952.

Arnold, Eddy. "Kentucky Waltz." RCA Victor 21-0444, 1951.

Ashley, Tom, and Tex Isley. *Tom Ashley and Tex Isley.* Folkways FA-2350, 1966.

Auldridge, Mike. *Blues and Blue Grass.* Takoma D-1041, 1974.

———. *Dobro.* Takoma/Devi D-1033, 1973.

———. *Mike Auldridge.* Flying Fish FF-029, 1977.

Baez, Joan. *Joan Baez.* Vol. 2. Vanguard VRS-9094/VSD-2097, 1962.

Bailey Brothers, The, and the Happy Valley Boys. "Happy Valley Special." Rich-R-Tone 421.

———. *Have You Forgotten?* Vol. 6, *The Early Days of Bluegrass.* Rounder 1018, 1974.

———. "John Henry." Rich-R-Tone 446.

———. "Rattlesnake Daddy Blues." Rich-R-Tone 421.

Baker, Kenny. *Kenny Baker Plays Bill Monroe.* County 761, 1976.

———. *Portrait of a Bluegrass Fiddler.* County 719, 1969.

Banjo in the Hills. Starday SLP 104, 1959.

Banjo Jamboree Spectacular! Starday SLP 136, 1960.

Banjos, Banjos and More Banjos. Judson J3017, 1957.

Berline, Byron. *Dad's Favorites.* Rounder 0100, 1977.

The Best of Bluegrass. Mercury Wing MGW12267, 1964.

Birchfield, Wade and Wiley, and Roger Johnson. "Flower Bloomin' in the Wildwood." Wayside 0-100, 1957.

———. "I'm Goin' Down the Road Feelin' Bad." Wayside 0-100, 1957.

Blake, Norman. *Back Home in Sulphur Springs.* Rounder 0012, 1972.

Blue Ridge Mountain Music. Atlantic 1347, 1960.

Blue Sky Boys, The. *"The Sunny Side of Life."* Rounder 1006, 1973.

Bluegrass Alliance, The. *Newgrass.* American Heritage AH 10-305, 1970.

The Bluegrass Banjo Pickers (Osborne Brothers). *Foggy Mountain Breakdown and Other Music from the Bonnie and Clyde Era.* Camden CAS-2243, 1968.

Bluegrass Cardinals, The. *Livin' in the Good Ole Days.* CMH 6229, 1979.

———. *Welcome to Virginia.* Rounder 0097, 1978.

Bluegrass for Collectors. RCA APL1-0568, 1974.

Boone Creek. *Boone Creek.* Rounder 0081, 1978.

———. *One Way Track.* Sugar Hill SH-3701, 1979.

Brickman, Marshall, and Eric Weissberg. *New Dimensions in Banjo and Bluegrass.* Elektra EKL238/EKS7238, 1963.

Butterfield Blues Band, The. *East-West.* Elektra EKS7315, 1966.

———. *The Paul Butterfield Blues Band.* Elektra EKL294/EKS7294, 1965.

Byrd, Senator Robert. *Mountain Fiddler.* County 769, 1978.

Byrds, The. "Mr. Tamborine Man." Columbia 42371, 1965.

———. *Mr. Tambourine Man.* Columbia CL2372/CS9172, 1965.

———. *Sweetheart of the Rodeo.* Columbia CS9670, 1968.

———. *The Byrds' Greatest Hits.* Columbia WKCS9516, 1967.

Carson, Fiddlin' John. *"The Old Hen Cackled and the Rooster's Going to Crow."* Rounder 1003, 1972.

Charles River Valley Boys, The. *Beatle Country.* Elektra EKL4006/EKS74006, 1966.

———. *Bluegrass and Old Timey Music.* Prestige International 13074, 1961.

———. *Bluegrass and Old Timey Music.* Prestige Folklore 14017, 1963.

———. *Bluegrass Get Together with Tex Logan.* Prestige Folklore 14024, 1964.

Church Brothers. "A Sweeter Love than Yours I'll Never Know." Blue Ridge 202.

———. *The Church Brothers.* Vol. 8, *The Early Days of Bluegrass.* Rounder 1020, 1981.

Clawhammer Banjo. County 701, 1966.

Clements, Vassar. *Crossing the Catskills.* Rounder 0016, 1973.

———. *The Bluegrass Sessions.* Flying Fish FF-038, 1977.

Clifton, Bill, and the Dixie Mountain Boys. "Gathering Flowers from the Hillside." Starday 290, 1956.

———. *Mountain Folk Songs.* Starday SLP111, 1959.

Cobb, Marvin, and Frank Wakefield and the Chain Mountain Boys. "New Camptown Races." Wayside 105, 1957.

———. "Tell Me Why (My Daddy Don't Come Home)." Wayside 105, 1957.

Copas, Cowboy. "Alabam." Starday 501, 1960.

———. "Kentucky Waltz." King 598, Queen 2270, 1947.

———. *Unforgettable.* Starday 234.

Country and Western Jamboree. King 697.

Country Gazette, The. *Don't Give Up Your Day Job.* United Artists UA-LA090-F, 1973.

———. *Out to Lunch.* Flying Fish FF-027, 1977.

———. *A Traitor in Our Midst.* United Artists UAS-5596, 1972.

———. *What a Way to Make a Living.* Ridge Runner RRR-008, 1977.

Country Gentlemen, The. "Bringing Mary Home." Rebel 250, 1965.

———. "Christmas Time Back Home." Rebel F-236, 1962.

———. "Copper Kettle." Starday 628, 1963.

———. *Country Songs, Old and New.* Folkways FA2409, 1960.

———. *Folk Session Inside.* Mercury MG20858, 1963.

———. "Heavenward Bound." Rebel F-236, 1962.

———. "High Lonesome." Starday 367, 1958.

———. *Hootenanny—A Blue Grass Special.* Design DLP-613, 1963.

———. *Roanoke Bluegrass Festival.* Zap 101, 1967.

———. "Rolling Stone." Starday 415, 1958.

———. *The Country Gentlemen.* Rebel RLP1478, 1965.

———. *The Country Gentlemen on the Road.* Folkways FA-2411, 1963.

Crary, Dan. *Lady's Fancy.* Rounder 0099, 1977.

Crowe, J. D., and the New South. *The New South.* Rounder 0044, 1975.

———. *J. D. Crowe and the New South.* Starday SLP489-498, 1977.

Crowe, J. D., Tony Rice, Doyle Lawson, Bobby Hicks, and Todd Phillips. *The Bluegrass Album.* Rounder 0140, 1981.

———. *The Bluegrass Album.* Vol. 2. Rounder 0164, 1982.

———. *California Connection.* Vol. 3, *The Bluegrass Album.* Rounder 0180, 1983.

Danny Davis's Nashville Brass. *Bluegrass Country.* RCA Victor APL1-0565, 1974.

Day, J. "Kentucky Waltz." Flint 1786, 1948.

Dean, Eddie. "Kentucky Waltz." Majestic 11004, 1947.

Delmore Brothers, The. *Brown's Ferry Blues, 1933–41 Recordings.* County 402, 1971.

Dexter, Al. "Pistol Packin' Mama." Okeh 6708, 1942.

Dillard and Clark. *The Fantastic Expedition of. . . .* A&M SP4158, 1968.

———. *Through the Morning, Through the Night.* A&M SP4203, 1969.

Dillards, The. *Back Porch Bluegrass.* Elektra EKL232/EKS7232, 1963.

———. *Copperfields.* Elektra EKS74054, 1969.

———. *The Dillards—Live . . . Almost.* Elektra EKS7265, 1964.

———. *The Dillards vs. the Incredible L. A. Time Machine.* Flying Fish FF-040, 1977.

———. *Wheatstraw Suite.* Elektra EKS74035, 1968.

Dillards, The, with Byron Berline. *Pickin' and Fiddlin'.* Elektra EKS7285, 1965.

Driftwood, Jimmy. "Battle of New Orleans." RCA Victor 47-7534, 1959.

Dry Branch Fire Squad. *Born to Be Lonesome.* Rounder 0119, 1979.

Duff, Arlie. "Y'All Come." Starday 104, 1953.

Dylan, Bob. *Nashville Skyline.* Columbia KCS-9825, 1969.

Eanes, Jim, and the Shenandoah Valley Boys. "A Sweeter Love than Yours I'll Never Know." Blue Ridge 301, 1952.

———. "I Took Her by Her Little Brown Hand." Rich-R-Tone 1046, 1951.

———. *Jim Eanes.* Bluegrass Special 2.

———. *Jim Eanes and the Shenandoah Valley Boys.* Vol. 4, *The Early Days of Bluegrass.* Rounder 1016, 1978.

———. "Little Brown Hand." Decca 28522, 1952.

———. "There's No Place Like Home." Decca 29536, 1955.

———. "Your Old Standby." Starday 297, 1956.

Early Blue Grass. RCA Victor LPV569, 1969.

The Early Days of Bluegrass. Vol. 1. Rounder 1013, 1975.

The Early Days of Bluegrass. Vol. 2. Rounder 1014, 1975.

Early Rural String Bands. RCA Victor LPV552, 1968.

Emerson and Waldron. *Bluegrass Country.* Rebel SLP1489, 1969.

———. *New Shades of Grass.* Rebel SLP1485, 1968.

Evans, Dave. *Highway 52.* Vetco 3033, 1979.

Flatt, Lester, and the Nashville Grass. *The Best of Lester Flatt.* RCA APL1-0578, 1974.

———. *Country Boy.* RCA APL1-0131, 1973.

———. *Flatt on Victor.* RCA Victor LSP-4495, 1971.

———. "I Can't Tell the Boys from the Girls." RCA Victor 47-9953.

———. *Lester Raymond Flatt.* Flying Fish FF-015, 1975.

———. *Live! Bluegrass Festival.* RCA APL1-0588, 1974.

———. *A Living Legend.* CMH 9002, 1976.

Flatt, Lester, and Mac Wiseman. *Lester 'n' Mac.* RCA Victor LSP-4547, 1971.

Flatt, Lester, Earl Scruggs, and the Foggy Mountain Boys. "Baby Blue Eyes." Mercury 6200, 1949.

———. "The Ballad of Jed Clampett." Columbia 42606, 1962.

———. "Big Black Train." Columbia 41125, 1958.

———. *Blue Ridge Cabin Home.* County CCS102, 1978.

———. "Bouquet in Heaven." Mercury 6200, 1949.

———. *Breaking Out.* Columbia C30347, 1971.

———. "Cabin on the Hill." Columbia 41389, 1959.

———. *Changin' Times.* Columbia CL2796/CS9596.

———. "Colours." Columbia 43627, 1966.

———. *Columbia Historic Edition.* Columbia FC37469, 1982.

————. *Country and Western Classics.* Time-Life Records TLCW-04, 1982.

————. *County Music.* Mercury MG20359, 1958.

————. *Don't Get Above Your Raisin'.* Rounder SS08, 1979.

————. "Don't Let Your Deal Go Down." Columbia 40990, 1957.

————. "Down the Road." Mercury 6211, 1949

————. "Earl's Breakdown." Columbia 52010, 1954.

————. *Final Fling (One Last Time).* Columbia CS9945, 1970.

————. *Flatt and Scruggs.* Mercury MG20542, 1960.

————. *Flatt and Scruggs at Carnegie Hall.* Columbia CL2045/CS8845, 1963.

————. *Flatt and Scruggs' Greatest Hits.* Columbia CL2570/CS9370, 1966.

————. *Flatt and Scruggs Recorded Live at Vanderbilt University.* Columbia CL2134/CS8934.

————. "Flint Hill Special." Columbia 52010, 1954.

————. *Foggy Mountain Banjo.* Columbia CL1564, 1961.

————. "Foggy Mountain Breakdown." Columbia 44380, 1968.

————. "Foggy Mountain Breakdown." Mercury 72739, 1968.

————. "Foggy Mountain Breakdown." Mercury 6230, 1950.

————. "Foggy Mountain Chimes." Columbia 52025, 1954.

————. *Foggy Mountain Chimes.* Harmony HS11401.

————. *Foggy Mountain Jamboree.* Columbia CL1019, 1958.

————. "Foggy Mountain Rock." Columbia 41518, 1959.

————. "Foggy Mountain Special." Columbia 52025, 1954.

————. *Folk Songs of Our Land.* Columbia CL1830/CS8630, 1962.

————. "God Loves His Children." Mercury 6161, 1949.

————. "Go Home." Columbia 42141, 1961.

————. *The Golden Era.* Rounder SS05, 1977.

————. *The Golden Years.* County CCS101, 1977.

————. "Green Acres." Columbia 43497, 1966.

————. *Hard Travelin'.* Columbia CL1951/CS8751, 1963.

————. *Hear the Whistles Blow.* Columbia CS9486/CL2686, 1967.

————. "I'm Going to Make Heaven My Home." Mercury 6161, 1949.

————. "Last Train to Clarksville." Columbia 44194, 1967.

————. "Legend of the Johnson Boys." Columbia 42413, 1962.

————. "Memphis." Columbia 43412, 1965.

————. "My Cabin in Caroline." Mercury 6181, 1949.

————. *Nashville Airplane.* Columbia CS9741, 1968.

————. "Nashville Cats." Columbia 44040, 1967.

————. *Original Sound.* Mercury MG20773, 1963.

————. *Original Theme from Bonnie and Clyde.* Mercury SR61162, 1968.

————. "Pearl Pearl Pearl." Columbia 42755, 1963.

————. "Petticoat Junction." Columbia 42982, 1964.

————. "Pike County Breakdown." Mercury 6396, 1952.

————. "Six White Horses." Columbia 40853, 1957.

————. *Songs of the Famous Carter Family.* Columbia CL1664/CS8464, 1961.

————. *Songs to Cherish.* Harmony HL7465, 1968.

————. *The Story of Bonnie and Clyde.* Columbia CS9649, 1968.

————. *Town and Country.* Columbia CL2443/CS9243, 1966.

————. *The Versatile . . . .* Columbia CL2354/CS9154, 1965.

———. "We'll Meet Again, Sweetheart." Mercury 6181, 1949.

———. *When the Saints Go Marching In.* Columbia CL2513/CS9313, 1966.

———. "Why Don't You Tell Me So." Mercury 6211, 1949.

———, with Doc Watson. *Strictly Instrumental.* Columbia CL2643/CS9443, 1967.

Flying Burrito Brothers, The. *The Gilded Palace of Sin.* A&M SP4175, 1969.

———. *Last of the Red Hot Burritos.* A&M SP4343, 1971.

Folk Banjo Styles. Elektra EKL217, 1961.

Folk Festival at Newport—1959. Vol. 3. Vanguard VRS-9064, 1959.

Folksay Trio, The. "Tom Dooley." On *American Folksay: Ballads and Dances.* Vol. 2. Stinson SLP6, 1953.

Folksong Festival at Carnegie Hall. United Artists UAL3050, 1959.

Folkswingers, The. *Twelve-String Guitar.* Vol. 1. World Pacific WP1812, 1963.

———. *Twelve-String Guitar.* Vol. 2. World Pacific WP1814, 1964.

Forbes, Walter. *Ballads and Bluegrass.* RCA Victor LPM/LSP 2472, 1962.

Fox, Curley. "Black Mountain Rag." King 710, 1948.

Galax Fiddlers' Convention. *Seventeen Mountain Gems.* MG-17, 1966.

Greenbriar Boys, The. *The Greenbriar Boys.* Vanguard VRS-9104, 1962.

Greenbriar Boys, The, and Dián. *Dián and the Greenbriar Boys.* Elektra EKL233, 1963.

Greer, Jim, and the Mac-O-Chee Valley Folks. *Memories in Song.* Rural Rhythm RR-152, 1966.

Grisman, David. *Hot Dawg.* Horizon SP731, 1979.

———. *The David Grisman Quintet.* Kaleidoscope F-5, 1977.

———. *Rounder Album.* Rounder 0069, 1976.

Gulley, Phil. "Blue Moon of Kentucky." Decca 29288, 1954.

Hall, Roy. "Don't Let Your Sweet Love Die." Bluebird B-8656.

———. "Loving You Too Well." Bluebird B-8676.

———. *Roy Hall and His Blue Ridge Entertainers.* County 406, 1979.

Harrell, Bill, and the Virginians. *I Can Hear Virginia Calling Me.* Rebel 1592, 1980.

———. *The L&N Don't Stop Here Anymore.* Leather 8101, 1981.

———. *The Wonderful World of Bluegrass Music.* United Artists UAL3293/ UAS6293, 1964.

Harris, Emmylou. *Roses in the Snow.* Warner Brothers QBS3422, 1980.

Hartford, John. *Aereo-Plain.* Warner Brothers WS 1916, 1971.

———. *Earthwords and Music.* RCA Victor LPM/LSP 3796, 1967.

———. "Gentle on my Mind." RCA Victor 47-9175, 1967.

———. *Mark Twang.* Flying Fish FF-020, 1976.

Hayes, Red. "A Satisfied Mind." Starday 164, 1954.

Hensley, Walter. *Pickin' on New Grass.* Rebel SLP1488, 1969.

Here Today. *Here Today.* Rounder 0169, 1982.

Hickman, John. *Don't Mean Maybe.* Rounder 0101, 1977.

Highwaymen, The. "Cotton Fields." United Artists, 370, 1961.

Hillbilly Hit Parade. Starday SLP102, 1959.

Hillmen, The. *The Hillmen.* Together ST-T-1012, 1969. Reissued on Sugar Hill SH3719, 1981.

Hills and Home. New World NW225, 1976.

Hinchee, Jimmy, and the Mississippi Valley Boys. "Kentucky Waltz." Continental C8031, 1947.

Hot Mud Family, The. *Till We Meet Here Again. . . .* Vetco LP501, 1974.

Hot Rize. *Hot Rize.* Flying Fish FF206, 1980.

Irving, Lonnie. "Pinball Machine." Starday 486, 1960.

Jim and Jesse and the Virginia Boys. *Berry Pickin' in the Country.* Epic LN24144, 1965.

———. "Better Times A-Coming." Epic 5-9729, 1964.

———. "Cotton Mill Man." Epic 5-9676, 1963.

———. "Diesel on My Tail." Epic 10138, 1967.

———. *Diesel on My Tail.* Epic LN24314, 1967.

———. *Freight Train.* Capitol ST-770, 1971.

———. "Memphis." Epic 5-9851, 1965.

———. *Superior Sounds of Bluegrass.* Old Dominion 498-05, 1974.

———. *Y'All Come: Bluegrass Humor.* Epic LN24144, 1964.

Johnson, Hack, and His Tennesseeans. "Home Sweet Home." Colonial CR401, 1955.

Johnson Mountain Boys. *The Johnson Mountain Boys.* Rounder 0135, 1981.

Jones, George. "Why Baby Why." Starday 202, 1956.

Keith, Bill, and Jim Rooney. *Bluegrass: Livin' on the Mountain.* Prestige Folklore 14002, 1963.

Kentucky Colonels, The. *Appalachian Swing.* World Pacific WP1821/31821, 1964.

Kincaid, Bradley. "Footprints in the Snow." Majestic 6011, 1947; Mercury 6169, 1949.

King, Pee Wee. "Kentucky Waltz." RCA Victor 20-2263, 1947.

———. "Tennessee Waltz." RCA Victor 20-2680, 1948.

Kingston Trio, The. "Tom Dooley." Capital 4049, 1958.

Kirby, Pete. *Brother Oswald.* Rounder 0013, 1972.

Lawson, Doyle. *Tennessee Dream.* County 766, 1977.

Lawson, Doyle, and Quicksilver. *Quicksilver.* Sugar Hill SH-3708, 1980.

Lee, Wilma, and Stoney Cooper. *The Big Wheel.* Hickory LP100, 1960.

———. "Wicked Path of Sin." Rich-R-Tone 417, 1948.

Lilly Brothers, The. *Bluegrass Breakdown.* Prestige Folklore 14010, 1963. Reissued on Rounder SS01, 1977.

———. *Country Songs.* Prestige Folklore 14035, 1964. Reissued on Rounder SS02, 1977.

Lilly Brothers, The, and Don Stover. *Folk Songs from the Southern Mountains.* Folkways FA2433, 1962.

Listen to Our Story: A Panorama of American Balladry. Brunswick B-1024, 1947.

Little Richard. "Slippin' and A-Slidin'." Specialty 572-B, 1956.

Lonesome River Boys. *Raise a Ruckus.* Riverside RLP7535.

Lord Buckley. *The Best of Lord Buckley.* Crestview CRV-801/CRS-7801, 1963.

Louisiana Honeydrippers, The. *Louisiana Bluegrass.* Prestige International 13035, 1960.

Macon, Uncle Dave. *First Featured Star of the Grand Ole Opry.* Decca DL4760, 1966.

Maddox, Rose. *Rose Maddox Sings Bluegrass.* Capitol T1799, 1962.

Mainer, J. E., and Mainer's Mountaineers. "Mother's Only Sleeping." King 534, 1946.

Mainer, Wade. *Sacred Songs of Mother and Home.* Old Homestead 90001, 1971.

Mainer's Mountaineers. *Mainer's Crazy Mountaineers*. Vols. 1 and 2. Old Timey
    LP-106, 1962; LP-107, 1963.
————. "Maple on the Hill." Bluebird B6065, 1935.
Martin, Benny. *The Fiddle Collection*. CMH9006, 1976.
Martin, Jimmy, and the Sunny Mountain Boys. *Country Music Time*. Decca
    DL4285, 1962.
————. "Hit Parade of Love." Decca 30118, 1956.
————. "The Last Song." Decca 31846, 1965.
————. *Me 'n' Ole Pete*. Gusto GD-5024X, 1978.
————. *Mr. Good 'n' Country*. Decca DL4769, 1966.
————. "Widow Maker." Decca 31558, 1964.
————. *Widow Maker*. Decca DL4536, 1964.
Martin, Jimmy, and the Osborne Brothers. "20-20 Vision." RCA Victor 5958, 1955.
McCormick Brothers, The. *Authentic Bluegrass Hits*. Hickory LM108, 1962.
McCoury, Del. *Del McCoury and the Dixie Pals*. Revonah RS916, 1976.
McLain Family, The. *The McLain Family Band*. Country Life 2, 1973.
McMichen, Clayton. *McMichen: The Traditional Years*. Davis Unlimited DU-33032,
    1977.
McPeak Brothers, The. *Bluegrass at Its Peak*. RCA Victor APL1-0587, 1974.
Mel and Stan. "Mother's Not Dead." Majestic 11030, 1947.
Monroe, Bill, and His Blue Grass Boys. "Back Up and Push." RCA Victor 20-3295,
    1948.
————. *Bean Blossom*. MCA2-8002, 1973.
————. *Bean Blossom '79*. MCA-3209, 1980.
————. *The Best of Bill Monroe*. MCA 2-4090, 1975.
————. *Bill Monroe and His Blue Grass Boys*. Decca ED2353, ca. 1956.
————. *Bill Monroe and His Blue Grass Boys*. Vol. 2, 1950–1972. MCA-9269-9271,
    ca. 1976.
————. *Bill Monroe with Lester Flatt and Earl Scruggs, "The Original Bluegrass Band."*
    Rounder SS06, 1978.
————. *Bill Monroe's Country Music Hall of Fame*. Decca DL75281, 1971.
————. *Bill Monroe's Greatest Hits*. Decca DL75010, 1968.
————. *Bill Monroe's Uncle Pen*. Decca DL75348, 1972.
————. "Blue Grass Breakdown." Columbia 20552, 1949.
————. *Bluegrass Classics: Radio Shows 1946–1948*. BGC80, ca. 1980.
————. *Bluegrass Instrumentals*. Decca DL4601, 1965.
————. "Blue Grass Ramble." Decca 46266, 1950.
————. *Bluegrass Ramble*. Decca DL4266, 1962.
————. "Blue Grass Special." Columbia 37960, 20381, 1947.
————. "Blue Grass Stomp." Columbia 20648, 1949.
————. "Blue Moon of Kentucky." Columbia 37888, 1947.
————. "Blue Moon of Kentucky." Decca 29289, 1954.
————. "Blue Yodel No. 7." Bluebird B886I, 1941.
————. "Blue Yodel No. 7." RCA Victor 20-3163, 1948.
————. "Boat of Love." Decca 46254, 1950.
————. *The Classic Bluegrass Recordings*. Vols. 1 and 2. County CCS-104, CCS-
    105, 1980.
————. "Close By." Decca 29289, 1954.

———. "The Coupon Song." Bluebird B8893, 1941.

———. "Devil's Dream." Decca 31540, 1963.

———. "Dog House Blues." Bluebird B8692, 1940.

———. *The Father of Bluegrass Music.* RCA Camden CAL719, 1962.

———. "Footprints in the Snow." Columbia 37151, 20080, 1945.

———. "The Gold Rush." Decca 32404, 1968.

———. *The High, Lonesome Sound.* Decca DL4780, 1966.

———. "I Hear a Sweet Voice Calling." Columbia 20459, 1948.

———. "I'm Travelin' On and On." Columbia 38078, 1948.

———. "In the Pines." Bluebird B8861, 1941.

———. "It's Mighty Dark to Travel." Columbia 20526, 1948.

———. "Katy Hill." Bluebird B8692, 1940.

———. "Katy Hill." RCA Victor 20-3295, 1948.

———. *Kentucky Blue Grass.* Decca DL 75213, 1970.

———. "Kentucky Waltz." Columbia 36907, 20013, 1946.

———. "Kentucky Waltz." Decca 46314, 1951.

———. "Little Community Church." Columbia 20488, 1948.

———. "Molly and Tenbrooks." Columbia 20612, 1949.

———. "Mother's Only Sleeping." Columbia 37294, 1947.

———. "Mule Skinner Blues." Bluebird B8568, 1940.

———. "Mule Skinner Blues." RCA Victor 20-3163, 1948.

———. "New John Henry Blues." Decca 31540, 1963.

———. "New Mule Skinner Blues." Decca 46222, 1950.

———. "No Letter in the Mail." Bluebird B8611, 1940.

———. "Orange Blossom Special." Bluebird B8893, 1941.

———. "Pike County Breakdown." Decca 28356, 1952.

———. "Rocky Road Blues." Columbia 36907, 20013, 1945.

———. "Salt Creek." Decca 31596, 1964.

———. "Shine Hallelujah Shine." Columbia 38078, 1948.

———. *Sixteen All-Time Greatest Hits.* Columbia CS1065, 1970.

———. "Six White Horses." Bluebird B8568, 1940.

———. *Songs with the Blue Grass Boys.* Vocalion VL3702, 1964.

———. "Tennessee Blues." Bluebird B8813, 1940.

———. "Toy Heart." Columbia 20552, 1949.

———. "True Life Blues." Columbia 37151, 20080, 1945.

———. "Uncle Pen." Decca 46283, 1950.

———. *A Voice from on High.* Decca DL 75135, 1969.

———. "Walking in Jerusalem." Decca 28608, 1953.

———. "When You Are Lonely." Columbia 20526, 1948.

———. "Wicked Path of Sin." Columbia 20503, 1948.

———. "Will You Be Loving Another Man?" Columbia 37565, 1947.

———. "Y'All Come." Decca 29021, 1954.

Monroe, Bill and James. *Father and Son.* MCA-310, 1973.

———. *Together Again.* MCA-2367, 1978.

Monroe, Birch. *Brother Birch Monroe Plays Old Time Fiddle Favorites.* Atteiram API-L-1516, 1975.

Monroe Brothers, The. "All the Good Times Are Passed and Gone." Bluebird 7191, 1937.

————. *Feast Here Tonight.* RCA Bluebird AMX2-5510, 1975.

————. "He Will Set Your Fields on Fire." Bluebird 7145, 1937.

————. "My Long Journey Home." Bluebird 6422, 1936.

————. "New River Train." Bluebird 6645, 1936.

————. "Nine Pound Hammer Is Too Heavy." Bluebird 6422, 1936.

————. "Roll in My Sweet Baby's Arms." Bluebird 6773, 1937.

————. "This World Is Not My Home." Bluebird 6309, 1936.

————. "What Would You Give in Exchange?" Bluebird 6309, 1936.

Monroe, Charlie. *Charlie Monroe's Boys: The Early Years.* Old Homestead OHCS-133, 1982.

————. "Mother's Not Dead, She's Only Sleeping." RCA Victor 20-2055, 1946.

————. *Tally Ho!* Starday SLP484-498, 1975(?)

Monroe, James. *Midnight Blues.* Atteiram API-L-1524, 1976.

Moody, Clyde. "Shenandoah Waltz." King 619, 1947.

Moore, Charlie, and Bill Napier. *More Truck Drivers' Songs.* King 936, 1966.

Mountain Frolic: The Tale of a Tennessee Frontier Dance in 1840. Brunswick B-1025, 1947.

Mountain Music Bluegrass Style. Folkways FA2318, 1959.

New Folks. Vanguard VRS-9096, 1961.

New Grass Revival, The. *Fly through the Country.* Flying Fish FF-016, 1975.

————. *New Grass Revival.* Starday 482-498, 1973.

————. *When the Storm Is Over.* Flying Fish FF-032, 1977.

New Lost City Ramblers, The. *Gone to the Country.* Folkways FA2491, 1963.

————. *The New Lost City Ramblers.* Folkways FA23961, 1958.

————. *The New Lost City Ramblers,* vol. 3. Folkways FA2398, 1961.

New Sounds Ramblin' from Coast to Coast. Vol. 3, *The Early Days of Bluegrass.* Rounder 1015, 1983.

Nitty Gritty Dirt Band, The. "Mr. Bojangles." Liberty 56197, 1970.

————. *Uncle Charlie and His Dog Teddy.* Liberty LST7642, 1970.

————. *Will the Circle Be Unbroken.* United Artists UAS 9801, 1972.

Osborne Brothers, The. *Blue Grass Music.* MGM E4018, 1961.

————. *Cuttin' Grass.* MGM E4149, 1963.

————. "Georgia Pineywoods." Decca 32794, 1971.

————. "The Kind of Woman I Got." Decca 32052, 1967.

————. *Modern Sounds of Bluegrass Music.* Decca DL74903, 1967.

————. *Number One.* CMH6206, 1976.

————. *The Osborne Brothers' Bluegrass Collection.* CMH 9011, 1978.

————. "Rocky Top." Decca 32242, 1968.

————. "Tennessee Hound Dog." Decca 32516, 1969.

————. "Up This Hill and Down." Decca 31886, 1966.

————. *Yesterday, Today and the Osborne Brothers.* Decca DL74993, 1968.

Osborne Brothers, The, and Mac Wiseman. *The Essential Bluegrass Album.* CMH 9016, 1979.

Osborne Brothers and Red Allen. "Down in the Willow Garden." MGM K12420, 1957.

————. "Ho Honey Ho." MGM K12420, 1957.

————. "Once More." MGM K12583, 1957.

————. *The Osborne Brothers and Red Allen.* Rounder SS03, 1977.

―――. "Ruby." MGM K12308, 1956.

Osborne, Sonny. "A Brother in Korea." Gateway 3005, 1953.

―――. "Cripple Creek." Gateway 3009, 1954.

―――. *The Early Recordings of Sonny Osborne, 1952–3.* Vols. 1, 3. Gateway [no number], 1979.

―――. *The Early Recordings of Sonny Osborne, 1952–53.* Vol. 2. Gateway [no number], 1979.

―――. "Sunny Mountain Chimes." Gateway 3005, 1953.

Owens, Buck. "Buckaroo." Capitol 5517, 1965.

―――. "Down on the Corner of Love." Pep 105, 1956.

―――. *Instrumental Hits.* Capitol T-2367, 1965.

Parker, Byron, and the Mountaineers. "Married Life Blues." Bluebird B8708, 1940.

―――. "Peanut Special." Bluebird B8673, 1940.

―――. "Up Jumped the Devil." Bluebird B8432, 1940.

Parker, Curley, and Pee Wee Lambert. "Just a Memory." Rich-R-Tone 1054, 1952.

―――. "Weary Hobo." Rich-R-Tone 1054, 1952.

Parsons, Gene. *Kindling.* Warner Brothers BS2687, 1973.

Philadelphia Folk Festival. Prestige International 13072, 1962.

Pinnacle Boys, The. *Take a Look and Listen to . . . .* Atteiram API-L-1510, 1974.

Poole, Charlie. *Charlie Poole and the North Carolina Ramblers,* vols. 1–4. County 505, 509, 516, 540, 1965–71.

Poor Richard's Almanac. *Poor Richard's Almanac.* American Heritage AHLP401-255, 1970. Reissued, with some changes in programming, on Ridge Runner 0002, 1976.

Prairie Ramblers, The. *Tex's Dance.* Cattle LP32, 1982.

Presley, Elvis. "Blue Moon of Kentucky." Sun 209, 1954.

―――. *Elvis Country.* RCA LSP4460, 1971.

―――. *Good Rocking Tonight.* Bopcat 100, n.d.

―――. *Sun Sessions.* RCA APM1-1675, 1976.

―――. "That's All Right." Sun 209, 1954.

―――. Carl Perkins, and Jerry Lee Lewis. *Million Dollar Quartet.* OMD-001, 1981.

The Railroad in Folksong. RCA Victor LPV532, 1966.

Reno, Don, Bill Harrell, and the Tennessee Cutups. *All the Way to Reno.* King 1033, 1968.

―――. *Bluegrass on My Mind.* Starday 481-498, 1973.

―――. *The Don Reno Story.* CMH9003, 1976.

Reno, Don, Red Smiley, and the Tennessee Cutups. *Country Ballads.* King 621.

―――. "Country Boy Rock and Roll." King 5002, 1956.

―――. "I'm Using My Bible for a Roadmap." King 1045, 1951.

―――. *Instrumentals.* King LP552, 1958.

―――. *Last Time Together.* Starday SLP485-498, 1973.

―――. *Sacred Songs.* King LP550, 1957.

―――. *Variety Show.* King 932, 1966.

Rice, Tony. *Mar West.* Rounder 0125, 1980.

―――. *Tony Rice.* Rebel 1549, 1975.

Richardson, Larry, and Red Barker. *Larry Richardson and Red Barker and the Blue Ridge Boys.* County 702, 1966.

The Rich-R-Tone Story. Vol. 5, *The Early Days of Bluegrass.* Rounder 1017, 1975.

Robbins, Marty. *Rockin' Rollin' Robbins*. Bear Family BFX 15045, 1982.

Roberts, Fiddling Doc, Trio. "Blue Grass Rag." Perfect 13073, Romeo 13073, 1934.

Robertson, A. C. ("Eck"). "Sally Gooden." Victor 18956, 1922.

Rodgers, Jimmie. "Blue Yodel No. 8 (Mule Skinner Blues)." Victor 23518, 1931.

Rolling Stones, The. *Let It Bleed*. London 4, 1969.

Sauceman Brothers, The. "Please Don't Make Me Cry." Mercury 6130, 1948.

———. *The Sauceman Brothers*. Vol. 7, *The Early Days of Bluegrass*. Rounder 1019, 1976.

———. "Your Trouble Ways Keep Us Apart." Mercury 6130, 1948.

Scott, Ron, with Bobby Hill and His Rank Band. "When the Bees Are in the Hive." Sparton 447R, 1957.

———. "The White Rose." Sparton 447R, 1957.

Scruggs, Earl. *Earl Scruggs: His Family and Friends*. Columbia C30584, 1971.

———. *I Saw the Light with Some Help from My Friends*. Columbia KC31354, 1972.

———. *Nashville's Rock*. Columbia CS1007, 1970.

Scruggs, Gary and Randy. *All the Way Home*. Vanguard VSD6538, 1971.

II Generation. *State of Mind*. CMH6208, 1976.

Seventy-Song Original Bluegrass Collection. Rebel RLP1473-76, 1965.

Shanty Boys, The. *The Shanty Boys*. Elektra EKL142, 1957.

Shenandoah Cutups, The. *Bluegrass Autumn*. Revonah RS904, 1972.

Skaggs, Ricky. *Don't Cheat in Our Hometown*. Sugar Hill/Epic FE38954, 1983.

———. *Highways and Heartaches*. Epic FE37996, 1982.

———. "I'll Take the Blame." Sugar Hill SH45-3706, 1980.

———. *Sweet Temptation*. Sugar Hill SH-3706, 1979.

———. *That's It!* Rebel 1550, 1975.

———. *Waitin' for the Sun to Shine*. Epic FE37193, 1981.

———, and Tony Rice. *Skaggs and Rice*. Sugar Hill SH-3711, 1980.

Skillet Lickers, The. *The Skillet Lickers*. Vols. 1 and 2. County 506, 526.

Smith, Arthur ("Fiddlin' "). *Fiddlin' Arthur Smith and His Dixieliners*. Vols. 1 and 2. County 546, 547, 1978.

Smith, Arthur ("Guitar Boogie"). "Feuding Banjos." MGM 12006, 1955.

The Smithsonian Collection of Classic Country Music. The Smithsonian Collection P8 15640, 1981.

Smoky Mountain Ballads. RCA Victor P-79, 1941.

Sounds of the South. Atlantic 1346, 1960.

South Georgia Highballers. "Blue Grass Twist." Okeh 45155, 1927.

Sparks, Larry. *Bluegrass Old and New*. Old Homestead 90004, 1972.

———. *Ramblin' Bluegrass*. Starday 480-498, 1973.

———, and the Lonesome Ramblers. *John Deere Tractor*. Rebel 1588, 1980.

Spectrum. *Opening Roll*. Rounder 0136, 1981.

Stanley Brothers, The, and the Clinch Mountain Boys. *Award Winners at the . . . Folk Song Festival*. King 791, 1962.

———. "Blue Moon of Kentucky." Mercury 70453, 1954.

———. *The Columbia Sessions, 1949–50*. Rounder SS-09, 1981.

———. *Country Music Concert*. King 864, 1964.

———. "Death Is Only a Dream." Rich-R-Tone 466, 1950.

———. "The Girl behind the Bar." Rich-R-Tone 420, 1947.

———. *Hard Times*. Mercury MG20884, 1963.

————. "How Far to Little Rock." King 5306, 1960.

————. "I Can Tell You the Time." Rich-R-Tone 466, 1950.

————. "Let Me Be Your Friend." Columbia 20590, 1949.

————. "The Little Glass of Wine." Rich-R-Tone 423, 1948.

————. "Little Maggie." Rich-R-Tone 423, 1948.

————. "Molly and Tenbrooks." Rich-R-Tone 418, 1948.

————. "Mother No Longer Awaits Me at Home." Rich-R-Tone 420, 1947.

————. *Stanley Brothers and the Clinch Mountain Boys.* King 615, 1960.

————. *The Stanley Brothers, Their Original Recordings.* Melodean MLP7322, 1965.

————. "Train 45." King 5155, 1958.

————. "A Voice from on High." Mercury 70340, 1954.

Stanley, Ralph, and the Clinch Mountain Boys. *The Bluegrass Sound.* Jalyn JLP-120, 1968.

————. *Cry from the Cross.* Rebel SLP 1499, 1971.

Stone, Cliffie. "Blue Moon of Kentucky." Capitol 2910, 1954.

Stoneman Family. *The Stoneman Family: Old-Time Tunes of the South (Sutphin, Foreacre and Dickens).* Folkways FA2315, 1957.

Stonemans, The. *Cuttin' the Grass.* CMH6210, 1976

Story, Carl, and the Rambling Mountaineers. "Banjo on the Mountain." Mercury 71143, 1957.

————. *Bluegrass Gospel Collection.* CMH9005, 1976.

————. *Carl Story and the Original Rambling Mountaineers, 1939.* Puritan 1001, 1973.

————. *Gospel Favorites.* Mercury MG20323, 1958.

————. "Got a Lot to Tell Jesus." Mercury 71143, 1957.

————. "Light at the River." Mercury 71088, 1957.

————. "Mocking Banjo." Mercury 71088, 1957.

Sullivan Family, The. *Bluegrass Gospel.* Loyal 168, 1966.

Taylor, Earl, and His Stoney Mountain Boys. *Alan Lomax Presents Folk Songs from the Blue Grass—Earl Taylor and His Stoney Mountain Boys.* United Artists UAL3049, 1959.

————. *The Bluegrass Touch.* Vetco LP3017, 1974.

Taylor, Tut. *Friar Tut.* Rounder 0011, 1972.

Trischka, Tony. *Bluegrass Light.* Rounder 0048, 1974.

Val, Joe, and the New England Bluegrass Boys. *Bound to Ride.* Rounder 0109, 1979.

Vern [Williams], and Ray [Park]. *Cabin on a Mountain.* Starday SEP-175, 1959.

Vincent, Gene. *Greatest.* Capitol/Fame FA 3017.

————. "Rocky Road Blues." Capitol 4010, 1958.

Weissberg, Eric, and Steve Mandell. "Dueling Banjos." Warner Brothers, 7659, 1973.

————. *Dueling Banjos.* Warner Brothers BS2683, 1973.

West, Harry and Jeannie. *Country Music in Blue Grass Style.* Prestige International 13049, 1960.

White Spirituals. Atlantic 1349, 1960.

Whitey and Hogan. "Jesse James." Cowboy CR-1301-B, 1948.

Wiseman, Mac. *Bluegrass Favorites.* Capitol T1800, 1962.

————. "I Hear You Knocking." Dot 1273, 1955.

————. *Keep on the Sunny Side.* Dot DL3336, 1960.

———. *The Mac Wiseman Story*. CMH-9001, 1976.

———. *This Is Mac Wiseman*. Dot 3697, 1966.

York County Boys, The. *Blue Grass Jamboree*. Arc 502, 1959.

York, Rusty. "Dixie Strut." Mercury 71285, 1958.

———. "Peggy Sue." King 5103, 1957.

———. "Red Rooster." Chess 1730, 1959.

———. "Sugaree." Chess 1730, 1959.

York, Rusty, and the Kentucky Mountain Boys. [no title]. Bluegrass Special EP-600, 1960.

———. [no title]. Bluegrass Special 824 EP-603, 1961.

Y'All Come—Have A Country Christmas. Starday SLP123, 1959.

Aural History

The seventies saw a tremendous growth of interest in the technique (some might say discipline) of oral history. In Canada those concerned with it fought to a standoff over whether to call it oral or aural history (the problem being that "aural" cannot be translated directly into French). But much of what I have utilized in the research for this book is in fact aural history—not spoken accounts but recordings of the aural portions of events in which bluegrass music took a central role—recording sessions, concerts, shows, and broadcasts.

In the introduction to the preceding section I alluded to analytic discographies. Such discographies serve to document recording sessions. Other aural history documents are not so easily discovered. I mentioned at several points in the text that bluegrass fans have been taping performances by their favorites since the first half of the fifties. And before that a few technological adventurers had made home disc recordings of radio broadcasts (apparently not of shows). This taping of live performances reached a zenith between the late fifties and the late sixties. At least two show parks that I know of, both of which frequently booked bluegrass, were so popular for taping that they installed systems which allowed private tape-recorder owners to tap the main sound system—Sunset Park and the Brown County Jamboree at Bean Blossom. Carlton Haney's festival sites at Fincastle and Berryville, Virginia, were similarly equipped. There were probably others. And pictures of bluegrass bands on stage in the late fifties and sixties show clusters of private microphones on extra stands or taped to the public address (p.a.) system stand.

In the seventies this kind of taping began to diminish and is now rather infrequent. There are two reasons for this. First is that (as discussed in chapter 10) by the end of the sixties bluegrass was changing from the single omnidirectional microphone to multiple unidirectional microphones. It was no longer possible to set up a single microphone and record the total sound as the band "worked" the p.a. mike. So recording the sound meant either plugging into the p.a. system (as described above) or miking the sound as it came out over the speakers (a difficult and not very satisfactory practice). Second, at the same time as this was happening, tape-recorder technology was changing from reel-to-reel to cassette machines. The new cassette recorders (particularly the small portable ones) frequently had only a built-in mike and thus could not be used to tape directly on stage. Often these machines had no provision for the line input needed to tape from the p.a. system. They were and are now used to record the p.a. sound from the audience, producing recordings of a quality inferior to that of the earlier reel-to-reel ones. Occasionally one still sees someone taping a show from the sound system using a high quality portable cassette deck. And at a festival I attended recently one of the musicians was taping his favorites with a home video recorder.

The result of all this activity is a pool of tape recordings which document various aspects of bluegrass—radio broadcasts as far back as 1946, park shows from at least 1954, college and university concerts from 1960, and festivals from 1965—in varying degrees of fidelity. Typically performers knew about and permitted the taping of shows (but not broadcasts). Several did not allow taping, fearing the recordings might be made into unauthorized phonograph recordings ("pirates") or new and unique repertoire taken and used by other performers. But most performers treated such activity as they treated photograph taking by fans: this was the creation of personal souvenirs for home use. And certainly very few people either performing or making the tapes thought of them as "documents."

Consequently such recordings are found only rarely in scholarly research collections. One exception is the collection of Monroe shows which I deposited in the Indiana University Archives of Traditional Music, cited in chapter 8. But these tapes can be found in private collections. The largest such collection of which I am aware contains over 2,000 tapes; my own is over 300. In each case, only a fraction of the collection was recorded by the owner. Many tapes are copies one or more generations removed from the original. In contemplating this kind of collection one is reminded of the holdings of ancient manuscripts in medieval monastery libraries. They are highly valued, but their documentary worth is not always fully understood. Frequently the name of the recordist, the specific dates of recording, and other supplementary data have been lost. Sometimes portions of the show were edited during the process of recording in order to save tape, eliminating spoken introductions, commercial pitches (for songbooks and records), and comedy routines.

Such tapes constitute a substantial element of my research materials but are quoted directly infrequently. What follows is a brief list of those cited in the text. Most of these recordings I made myself; others came to me through trades with collectors (this is how most such collections are built). I do not always know who made the original recording.

Aural History

Antioch College Auditorium, Yellow Springs, Ohio, Mar. 5, 1960.
Brown County Jamboree, Bean Blossom, Ind. Sept. 19, 1954.
———, Oct. 22, 1961.
———, Sept. 22, 1963.
First Annual Roanoke Bluegrass Festival, Fincastle, Va., Sept. 4, 5, 1965.
"Miller's Place," WSM-TV, Nashville, Tenn., June 14, 1981.
New River Ranch, Rising Sun, Md., May 13, 1956.
Oak Leaf Park, Luray, Va., July 4, 1961.

Interviews

Interviews created as historical documents are often called oral history. In the introduction to the bibliography I have discussed the problems that treating such material as actual historical documents can create. Nevertheless I have utilized such material in preparing this work, and in the following list are all those from which I have quoted. Most are my own; a few are by others. With one exception, all are tape recordings; for all but one of these I have both tape and transcript in my possession. I should add that to this list could be appended a much longer list of informal interviews—backstage conversations, telephone calls, and other informal exchanges—which have contributed substantially to my understanding of the topic.

Interviews

Anderson, Joseph. Interview with author. Boston, May 21, 1981.

Crowe, J. D. Interview with author. Lexington, Ky., Aug. 14, 1972.

Dickson, Jim. Interviews with author. Hollywood, Calif., Jan. 18, 1983, May 7, 1983.

Fleischhauer, Carl. Interview with author. Washington, D.C., June 6, 1978.

Goldstein, Kenneth S. Interview with author. St. John's, Newfoundland, Jan. 2, 1979.

Hedrick, Marvin. Interviews with author. Nashville, Ind., Dec. 10, 1965, Aug. 18, 1972.

Henderson, Gary. Interview with Carl Fleischhauer. Washington, D.C., Apr. 10, 1977.

Kuykendall, Peter V. Interview with author. Broad Run, Va., Mar. 1, 1982 (Not recorded).

McReynolds, Jesse. Interview with author and Scott Hambly. Chicago, Ill., Feb. 5, 1966.

McReynolds, Jim. Interview with author and Scott Hambly. Chicago, Ill., Feb. 5, 1966.

Monroe, Birch. Interview with author. Martinsville, Ind., Aug. 18, 1972.

Moore, Charlie. Interview with Gary Henderson. Washington, D.C., Feb., 1974.

Mullen, Vic. Interview with author. St. John's, Newfoundland, June 15, 1972.

Miller, Franklin. Interview with Carl Fleischhauer. Iowa City, July 19, 1980.
Osborne, Bob. Interview with author. Bean Blossom, Ind., Sept. 26, 1965.
Rinzler, Ralph. Interview with author. Pittsburgh, Pa., Oct. 18, 1980.
Stanley, Carter. Interview with Mike Seeger. Northern Europe, Spring, 1966
     (Transcript only).
Szwed, John. Interview with author. Pittsburgh, Pa., Oct. 17, 1980.
York, Rusty. Interview with author. Hamilton, Ohio, Aug. 15, 1972.

Index

Song Title Index

Following some song titles are parentheses which contain either a combination of a capital letter and a number, or simply a number. The former refer the reader to the parallel syllabi of G. Malcolm Laws, Jr., *American Balladry from British Broadsides* (Philadelphia: American Folklore Society, 1957) and *Native American Balladry* (Philadelphia: American Folklore Society, 1964). The single number refers to the numbering scheme in Francis J. Child's *English and Scottish Popular Ballads*, North American versions of which are referenced in Tristram Potter Coffin and Roger deV. Renwick, *The British Traditional Ballad in North America* (Austin: University of Texas Press, 1977).

Books in the Series Music in American Life

Bibliographical Handbook of American Music
D. W. Krummel

Goin' to Kansas City
Nathan W. Pearson, Jr.

"Susanna," "Jeanie," and "The Old Folks at Home": The Songs of
Stephen C. Foster from His Time to Ours
Second Edition
William W. Austin

Songprints: The Musical Experience of Five Shoshone Women
Judith Vander

"Happy in the Service of the Lord": Afro-American Gospel
Quartets in Memphis
Kip Lornell

Paul Hindemith in the United States
Luther Noss

"My Song Is My Weapon": People's Songs, American Communism,
and the Politics of Culture
Robbie Lieberman

Chosen Voices: The Story of the American Cantorate
Mark Slobin

Theodore Thomas: America's Conductor and Builder
of Orchestras, 1835–1905
Ezra Schabas

"The Whorehouse Bells Were Ringing" and
Other Songs Cowboys Sing
Guy Logsdon

Crazeology: The Autobiography of a Chicago Jazzman
Bud Freeman, as Told to Robert Wolf

Discoursing Sweet Music: Brass Bands and Community Life
in Turn-of-the-Century Pennsylvania
Kenneth Kreitner

Mormonism and Music: A History
Michael Hicks

Voices of the Jazz Age: Profiles of Eight Vintage Jazzmen
Chip Deffaa

Pickin' on Peachtree: A History of Country Music in Atlanta, Georgia
Wayne W. Daniel